MW01618683

ENCYCLOPEDIA
science
supplement
A Modern Science Anthology for the Family

75

A Modern Science Anthology for the Family

ISBN 0-7172-1506-7
Library of Congress Catalog Card Number: 64-7603

contents

WALLACE S. MURRAY
Vice-President and Editorial Director, Grolier Incorporated

LOWELL A. MARTIN
Editorial Consultant

EDITORIAL	**HERBERT KONDO**	Editor in Chief
	BARBARA TCHABOVSKY	Senior Editor
	PATRICIA ELLSWORTH	Associate Editor
	WILLIAM E. KENNEDY	Associate Editor
	STEVEN MOLL	Associate Editor
	PATRICIA M. GODFREY	Proofreader
	J. MICHAEL RAIKES	Proofreader
	VITRUDE DeSPAIN	Indexer
	JITKA M. SALAQUARDA	Administrative Assistant
ART	**FRANK H. SENYK**	Art Director
	NATALIE GOLDSTEIN	Photo Researcher
MANUFACTURING	**RAYMOND H. LABOTT**	Director
	WALTER SCHENONE	Assistant Director

contributors

TOM ALEXANDER, Associate Editor, *Fortune*
THE COMPUTER RIP-OFF

LAWRENCE K. ALTMAN, M.D., Medical reporter, *The New York Times*
REVIEW OF THE YEAR—HEALTH AND DISEASE

ALAN ANDERSON, JR., Free-lance writer; author, *Drifting Continents*
WINDOW ON EARTH'S CORE

ANN W. APPELBAUM, M.D., Staff Psychiatrist, The Menninger Foundation
Coauthor, SHOPLIFTING

ERWIN A. BAUER, Free-lance writer
THE RACE IS ON FOR ANTARCTICA

J. KELLY BEATTY, Staff member, *Sky and Telescope*
A LOOK AT MERCURY

GREGORY BENFORD, Member, Department of Physics, University of California, Irvine
TITAN

JERRY BERGER, Staff Engineer, Vehicle Emissions, Research and Development, Shell Oil Company
ALTERNATIVE AUTOMOTIVE FUELS

GEORGE A. W. BOEHM, Free-lance science writer; author, *The New World of Math*
Coauthor, REVIEW OF THE YEAR—COMPUTERS AND MATHEMATICS

ROBIN BURTON, Free-lance writer and broadcaster
INSTANT ISLANDS

JEAN BUTLER, Free-lance writer
FALSE TEETH

ALAN P. CARR, Member, Institute of Oceanographic Sciences, England
THE EVER-CHANGING SEA LEVEL

PETER CHEW, Staff writer, *The National Observer*
BEHAVIOR MODIFICATION

MICHAEL CUSACK, Associate Editor, *Science World*
"HANGING IN" AT L–5
PEAT—THE FORGOTTEN FUEL

W. L. DACK, Free-lance writer; Senior Editor, *Financial Post,* MacLean-Hunter Limited, Toronto
ATHABASCA TAR SANDS

G. EDWARD DAMON, Retired consumer writer, Bureau of Foods, U.S. Food and Drug Administration
A PRIMER ON VITAMINS

PHILIP J. DAVIS, Professor of Applied Mathematics, Brown University; coauthor, *3.1416 and All That*
THE BAND-AID PRINCIPLE

TERENCE DICKINSON, Editor, *Astronomy*
NEW JOVIAN VISTAS

THOMAS FLEMING, Author, *The Man Who Dared the Lightning*
BENJAMIN FRANKLIN: SCIENTIST

M. A. FREIBERG, Member, Museo Argentino de Ciencias Naturales, Buenos Aires, Argentina
Coauthor, ANIMAL BEHAVIOR

LES GAPAS, Washington staff reporter, *The Wall Street Journal*
OFFSHORE OIL

ROBERT GILLETTE, Staff writer, *Science*
OIL AND GAS: HOW MUCH IS THERE?

DANIEL GROTTA-KURSKA, Free-lance writer
VEGETARIANISM

GEORGE HABER, Contributing writer, *The Sciences*
AEROSOLS AND THE OZONE LAYER

KATHERINE HARAMUNDANIS, Research Associate, Smithsonian Astrophysical Observatory; coauthor, *Introduction to Astronomy*
REVIEW OF THE YEAR—ASTRONOMY

JAMES HASSETT, Lecturer, Psychology Department, Boston University; coauthor, *A Primer of Psychophysiology* (in preparation)
REVIEW OF THE YEAR—BEHAVIORAL SCIENCES

HUGH F. HENRY, Head, Department of Physics, DePauw University
Coauthor, REVIEW OF THE YEAR—PHYSICAL SCIENCES

EUGENIA KELLER, Managing Editor, *Chemistry*
HOW SAFE IS OUR DRINKING WATER?

WILLIAM E. KENNEDY, Associate Editor, *Encyclopedia Science Supplement* and *Encyclopedia International*
EARTHCARE
REVIEW OF THE YEAR—MAN AND HIS WORLD

IRENE CUMMING KLEEBURG, Author, *Bicycle Repair*
BICYCLES: CARE AND MAINTENANCE

HERBERT KLEMMER, M.D., Staff Psychiatrist, The Menninger Foundation
Coauthor, SHOPLIFTING

FRANK W. KNIGHT, JR., Director, Environmental Resources, Stockton State College, New Jersey
REVIEW OF THE YEAR—ENVIRONMENTAL SCIENCES

BARRY KRAMER, Staff reporter, *The Wall Street Journal*
VINYL CHLORIDE

HENRY LANSFORD, Information Officer, National Center for Atmospheric Research
PROJECT GATE

JOEL LEGUNN, Free-lance writer
NATURAL GAS

LAWRENCE LESSING, Board of Editors, *Fortune*
LASER FUSION: TOMORROW'S ENERGY?

ALAN LINN, Naturalist and free-lance writer
EUROPE'S CESSPOOL

SUZANNE LOBEL, Science Editor, The Arthritis Foundation
ARTHRITIS

B. D. LONCAREVIC, Director, Atlantic Geoscience Centre, Dartmouth, Nova Scotia, Canada
MINING THE SEAS

TOM MAHONEY, Free-lance writer
HOW TO READ A CAN

JEAN MAYER, Professor of Nutrition, Harvard University School of Public Health
FAMINE

WILLIAM D. METZ, Staff writer, *Science*
DISCOVERY OF TWO NEW PARTICLES

STEVEN MOLL, Associate Editor, *Encyclopedia Science Supplement* and *The Book of Popular Science*
THE BERMUDA TRIANGLE
THE 1974 NOBEL PRIZES IN PHYSICS AND CHEMISTRY
Coauthor, REVIEW OF THE YEAR—COMPUTERS AND MATHEMATICS

WILLIAM MULLOY, Professor of Anthropology, University of Wyoming
CONTEMPLATE THE NAVEL OF THE WORLD

NORMAN MYERS, Roving Editor, *International Wildlife;* a wildlife biologist
HERE COMES THE TRANSAFRICAN HIGHWAY

IAN C. T. NISBET, Associate Director of the Scientific Staff of the Massachusetts Audubon Society
ACID RAIN

FREDERICK I. ORDWAY, Coauthor, *History of Rocketry and Space Travel* and *International Missile and Spacecraft Guide*
Coauthor, SPACE STATIONS

MICHAEL W. OVENDEN, Professor, Department of Geophysics and Astronomy, University of British Columbia; Author, *Life in the Universe*
THE LOST PLANET

JAMES K. PAGE, JR., Board of Editors, *Smithsonian* magazine
Coauthor, CUTTING YOUR HOME ENERGY BUDGET

RICHARD M. PEARL, Professor of Geology, Colorado College; author, *Cleaning and Preserving Minerals, Handbook for Prospectors*
REVIEW OF THE YEAR—EARTH SCIENCES

JOHN PETERSON, Staff writer, *The National Observer*
INSOMNIA

ROBERT REINHOLD, Science reporter, *The New York Times*
THE REPORTER'S NEW TOOL: THE COMPUTER

NICHOLAS ROSA, Marine naturalist; author, *What's Ecology;* contributing editor, *Oceans*
WHALES

J. A. ROZÉ, Research Associate, Herpetology Department, The Museum of Natural History, New York
Coauthor, ANIMAL BEHAVIOR

JANE SAMZ, Assistant Editor, *Science World*
IS GRAVITY GETTING WEAKER?

GEORGE SARTON, Author of *Six Wings: Men of Science in the Renaissance*
LEONARDO DA VINCI

JOAN SCHUMAN, Free-lance magazine, television, and radio science writer
PARAPSYCHOLOGY
REVIEW OF THE YEAR—BIOLOGY
SUGAR

F. G. WALTON SMITH, Editor, *Sea Frontiers*
HURRICANES

KURT H. STEHLING, Science and Technology Adviser, Manned Undersea Activities, Office of Coastal Environment
Coauthor, THE HELIUM HORSE

LILLIAN STROHM, Free-lance garden editor and writer
GARDENS UNDER GLASS

WALTER SULLIVAN, Science Editor, *The New York Times*
A NEW FORM OF MATHEMATICS

BARBARA TCHABOVSKY, Senior editor, *Encyclopedia Science Supplement* and *The Book of Popular Science*
THE 1974 NOBEL PRIZE IN PHYSIOLOGY OR MEDICINE
IN MEMORIAM

JENNY ELIZABETH TESAR, Editor, *Columbia Today;* free-lance science writer
FLOWERS
REVIEW OF THE YEAR—ENERGY
SOYBEANS

J. GORDON VAETH, Director, Office of System Engineering, National Environmental Satellite Service
Coauthor, THE HELIUM HORSE

MARGUERITE VILLECCO, Senior Editor, *Architecture Plus*
SOLAR ENERGY

WERNER VON BRAUN, Vice President, Engineering and Development, Fairchild Industries
Coauthor, SPACE STATIONS

NICHOLAS WADE, Staff writer, *Science*
THE NEW ALCHEMY INSTITUTE

NORMAN J. WARD, Director, Public Affairs, National Association of Rocketry
ROCKETS AS A HOBBY

RAYMOND N. WATTS, JR., Special Assistant to the Director, Smithsonian Astrophysical Observatory
APOLLO-SOYUZ TEST PROJECT

JOHN P. WILEY, JR., Associate Editor, *Smithsonian* magazine
Coauthor, CUTTING YOUR HOME ENERGY BUDGET

JOHN NOBLE WILFORD, Science reporter, *The New York Times*
REVIEW OF THE YEAR—SPACE EXPLORATION

BOB WILSON, Associate Director, Duke University News Service
FINDING THE IRONCLAD MONITOR

JAY A. YOUNG, Hudson Professor of Chemistry, Auburn University; coauthor, *Keys to Chemistry*
Coauthor, REVIEW OF THE YEAR—PHYSICAL SCIENCES

The cover shows a photomicrograph of the crystalline structure of vitamin B_{12}, or cyanocobalamin. Vitamin B_{12} is necessary for the normal development of red blood cells and for the functioning of all cells. It has also been shown to be responsible for much of the activity of the "animal protein factor." The existence of this factor was first postulated to explain the nutritional deficiency observed in chickens and turkeys on an all-vegetable diet. Since then it has been found that vegans, people who eat absolutely no animal products, develop the B_{12} deficiency disease pernicious anemia unless they take some form of vitamin B_{12} supplement. For a roundup discussion of all the vitamins, see "A Primer on Vitamins" on page 241. For a discussion of the health aspects of a non-meat diet, see the article "Vegetarianism" on page 251.

astronomy

Wyoming's famous Big Horn Medicine Wheel could have been a prehistoric observatory, according to astronomer John A. Eddy of the National Center for Atmospheric Research. The unusual arrangement of stones could have served as sighting points for solar observation.

review of the year

astronomy

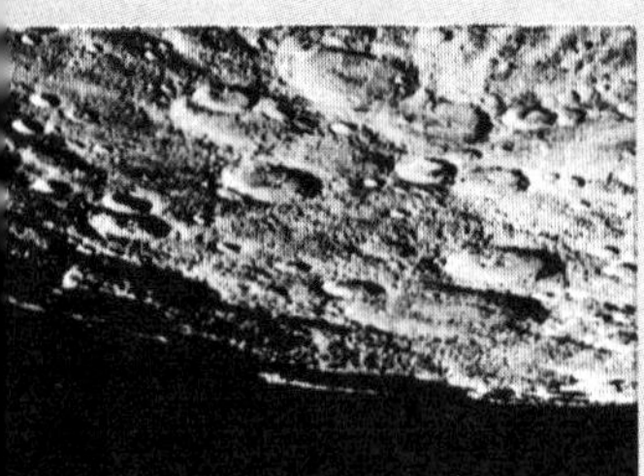

View of the south pole of Mercury taken by Mariner 10 cameras during the second flyby of the planet in September 1974.

Southern hemisphere heavens can now be carefully studied thanks to the new 4-m (13-ft) telescope at Cerro Tololo Observatory in Chile. The first photo taken using this telescope shows 47 Tucanae, the brightest globular star cluster known to man.

Mercury. Mercury, the planet closest to the sun, was approached by the U.S. Mariner 10 spacecraft in March 1974 and again in September. The probe revealed that the planet is heavily cratered, like the moon, and that the craters seem to be covered with a fine dust or fragmented material. Some of the surface features are unique. The most striking are the enormous scarps, or cliffs, some of which are up to 5 km (3 mi) high and 80 km (50 mi) long. There are also huge basins up to 2,080 km (1,300 mi) wide. Mercury's features do not appear to have been modified by the wide temperature variations experienced there—from about −130° C (−200° F) to 430° C (800° F) in the course of one rotation. Unlike the moon, Mercury has a very slight trace of an atmosphere, made up primarily of the gas helium, and a weak magnetic field. The field is strong enough to produce a magnetosphere, which extends outward from the planet as a "tail." This tail is opposite the direction of the solar wind—the particles flowing outward from the sun. The tail does not close but rather has particles constantly streaming out from it.

These observations pose many new questions. Mercury's features differ so much from those of the earth and the moon that it seems that Mercury may have formed under unique conditions. For example, Mercury has a smoother side and a more cratered side, as does the moon. In the moon's case, this has been thought of as a result of the moon's gravitational "lock" on the earth, with the smoother side always turned toward us. Such an explanation cannot suffice for Mercury, which does not keep one face turned toward the sun or in any other preferred direction.

Venus. While heading toward Mercury, Mariner 10 took several ultraviolet pictures of Venus. The photos revealed the circulation patterns of that planet's upper atmosphere. Enhanced by computer techniques, the photographs clearly show spectacular cloud vortices, or whirlpools, that travel around Venus and spiral poleward. There seems to be little vertical mixing of the atmosphere. The upper atmosphere moves at speeds of up to 320 km (200 mi) per hour, but nearer the planet's surface the atmosphere is probably slow-moving and densely packed. An enormous, long-enduring "storm," somewhat like Jupiter's Great Red Spot, was observed in the atmosphere. This Venusian "Eye" is roughly as large as the United States. Other data revealed that Venus has an ionosphere but does not appear to have a magnetosphere. Radio observations as Mariner 10 passed behind Venus indicated that Venus is much more spherical than is our pear-shaped earth.

The Soviet Union has published the final findings of its Venus probe, Venera 7, which landed on the planet's surface in 1970. The highest temperature it measured there was 468° C (874° F). The atmospheric pressure was 93 kg/cm² (1,320 lb/in²), which is about 90 times the sea-level air pressure on earth. The amount of light that reaches the surface of Venus is only about 1 per cent of that striking the topmost clouds. It is thought that this will be bright enough to allow pictures of the Venusian surface to be taken.

Jupiter. The major achievements of the U.S. Jupiter probes, Pioneer 10 and Pioneer 11, are discussed in the article "New Jovian Vistas." A new model of the giant planet is being constructed from the wealth of new data. It is now thought that the hottest temperatures in the solar system, outside of the sun, are to be found deep within Jupiter's layers of gases. Close-up photographs revealed many smaller "red spots" besides Jupiter's well-known Great Red Spot. The spots are thought to be the vortices of long-lasting "storms." In the equatorial zone of Jupiter are many bright white spots, some of which appear to be cloud plumes. The thirteenth moon of Jupiter has been discovered. Currently simply called "J-XIII," it was found in September 1974 by Charles Kowal of Hale Observatories through the use of the 122-cm (48-in) Schmidt telescope on Mount Palomar. Kowal calculates that this thirteenth moon cannot be much larger than 5 to 8 km (3 to 5 mi) in diameter.

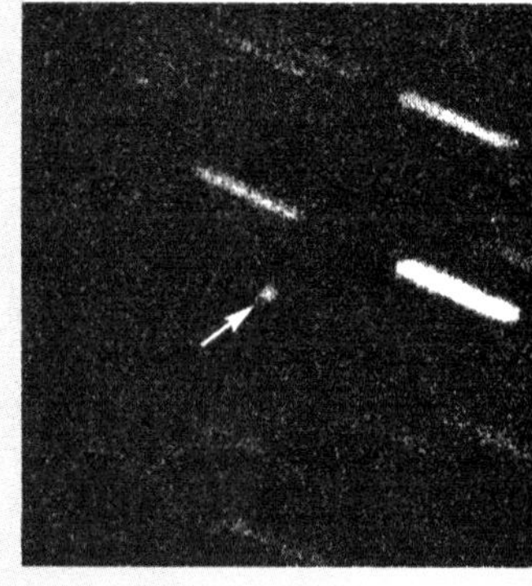

J-XIII, the thirteenth moon of Jupiter, was discovered in 1974. It is thought to be the smallest natural satellite of any planet in the solar system.

Other solar system news. The oldest known moon rock has now been established. It is dated at 4,600,000,000 years. The oldest known earth rock is less than 4,000,000,000 years old. ■ From a study of particles in the solar wind, Michael Papagiannis of Boston University suggests that the solar wind may have enough force to move the earth's magnetic poles. This concept may be a step toward the solution of the problem of why the earth's magnetic poles wander and occasionally reverse polarity. ■ Canadian astronomers, through visual observations of Saturn, have detected a thin gas envelope that may extend 130 km (80 mi) beyond the planet's rings.

Molecules in space. Analyses of two meteorites have revealed the presence of fatty acids—which, like the amino acids found earlier in meteorites, are among the building blocks of life as we know it. This suggests that complex organic compounds might have "seeded" the earth hundreds of millions of years ago and contributed to the development of life. ■ Studies of molecules between the stars have indicated the presence of the organic molecules dimethyl ether and methylamine. ■ Radio observations of clouds at the center of our galaxy have revealed the presence of carbon monoxide. Some also contain carbon dioxide. Temperature changes occur in waves within these clouds, which are hottest at the center. One possibility is that these clouds are collapsing gravitationally and will eventually form stars.

Large radio objects. Radio astronomers at Leiden University have detected the largest known objects in the universe. These enormous radio sources are complex objects with compact bright spots. The largest, 3C-236, is almost 19 million light-years wide. Our galaxy, in comparison, has a diameter of 100,000 light-years. (A light year is a unit of length used in astronomy. It is equal to the distance that light travels in one year, or 5,878,000,000,000 miles.)

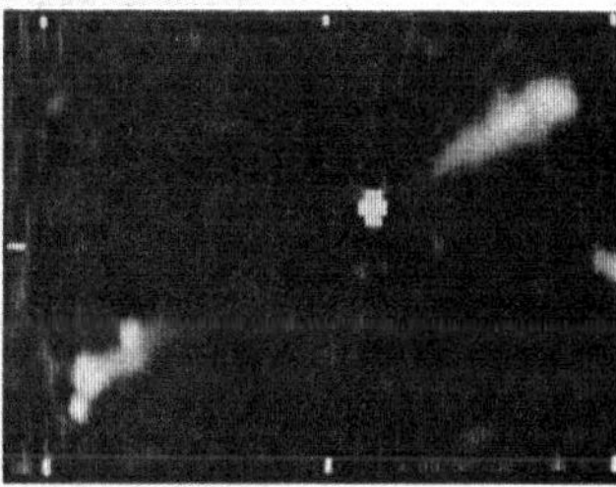

Largest known "object" in the universe shown in photograph produced from its radio emissions. Thought to have been produced by huge explosions, this "object" is 18.6 million light years wide.

Cosmology. One of the most difficult and important issues in astronomy is the debate over whether the universe is closed or open. A closed universe would ultimately stop expanding and begin to contract, whereas an open universe would expand indefinitely. One way to try to resolve this issue is to measure the density of the universe. Observations made with the 1972 U.S. satellite, Copernicus, seem to indicate a density so low that a closed universe, gravitationally bound, would not be possible. Radio observations of a distant cluster of galaxies have also had negative results. However, a study made by Jeremiah Ostriker of Princeton University suggests the contrary. Ostriker thinks that the way galaxies rotate indicates that they contain 20 per cent more mass—in the form of invisible halos surrounding them—than can be observed optically. This would be enough density to imply that the universe is closed.

Katherine Haramundanis

New Jovian Vistas

by Terence Dickinson

WINDS of 500 kilometers per hour (300 mph) whip up storms that could swallow a continent the size of Asia. Lightning bolts capable of vaporizing a city the size of New York rip open the sky. A surging, volcanolike hurricane larger than the planet earth, already raging for centuries, shows no sign of abating. And above these scenes of chaotic activity hangs a blanket of deadly radiation.

This is Jupiter, a planet that might have become a star—a bizarre giant that dwarfs every standard of comparison familiar to earthlings.

THE MEASURE OF A GIANT

Jupiter, the fifth major planet out from the sun, is the fourth brightest object in the sky after the sun, the moon, and the planet Venus. Jupiter is five times as distant from the sun as our earth is—that is, it is about 770,000,000 km (480,000,000 mi) from the sun. The giant planet makes its way around the sun once every 12 years. It drags along with it 13 known moons, two of which are larger than the planet Mercury.

The size of Jupiter is mind boggling. Its diameter is more than ten times that of the earth, or some 142,800 km (88,730 mi). The king of planets would span more than one third of the distance that separates the earth from the moon. In volume, Jupiter exceeds 1,000 earths. Its visible surface represents an area of nearly 62,000,000,000 km² (24,000,000,000 mi²). If the earth were peeled like an orange, its "skin" would not quite cover Jupiter's Great Red Spot.

Yet for all its size, Jupiter manages to complete one rotation on its axis, or one day, in only ten hours. This is the shortest day of any of the nine planets. It means that a point on Jupiter's equator races along at about 35,000 kph (22,000 mph). A point similarly located on the earth's equator moves at a speed of only 1,600 kph (1,000 mph). Because Jupiter rotates with such great speed and because of its physical nature, the planet bulges greatly at the equator. In fact, the diameter of Jupiter from pole to pole is seven per cent less than the diameter of the planet at its equator.

Physically, Jupiter is very much like a liquid. It is made of material that is of extremely low density. The mass of the planet is only 318 times that of the earth, in spite of the much greater difference in volume. Thus Jupiter's average density is only one fourth that of the earth and only one and a third times that of water. The reason is that the giant planet is made up of a mixture of elements similar to that found in the sun—primarily the very light elements, hydrogen and helium. Together they make up 98 per cent of the planet. It is thought that the same mixture of elements existed in the gas cloud from which the solar system formed billions of years ago.

STUDYING A DISTANT NEIGHBOR

Because Jupiter is the major entry in the sun's family of planets, scientists have long been interested in studying its many mysteries. What is the meaning of its beautiful bands of color? What is the explanation for the Great Red Spot? Why does Jupiter radiate more heat than it receives from the sun? What causes it to emit, or give out, strong radio signals? Might some form of life be able to exist deep within the planet's atmosphere? These are only some of the questions that are being asked about our giant neighbor.

Astronomers have studied Jupiter for many years, and with the opening of the space age they even began to think of traveling there. But Jupiter is a violent and dangerous world. It is almost inconceivable that human beings will ever be able to protect themselves well enough to visit even the outermost layers of the planet. Jupiter is dangerous even for the unmanned spacecraft that approach it.

The Great Red Spot, the vortex of a violent storm, is Jupiter's foremost feature. Pioneer 11 took this photo on Dec. 2, 1974, at 1,100,000 km (660,000 mi).

The first such spacecraft to make the long journey, Pioneer 10, flew past Jupiter in December 1973. It met levels of radiation that almost disabled its instruments. But it survived the ordeal and managed to return a wealth of new data. In an even more spectacularly successful mission, Pioneer 11 passed within 42,800 km (26,600 mi) of the tops of the Jovian cloud cover on Dec. 3, 1974. Pioneer 11 was subjected to intense radiation for a short period of time. The rain of radioactive particles affected the spacecraft's electronic equipment for a while, but eventually all systems returned to normal and the craft was put on course for Saturn.

This article looks back at the findings of Pioneer 10, findings that scientists in

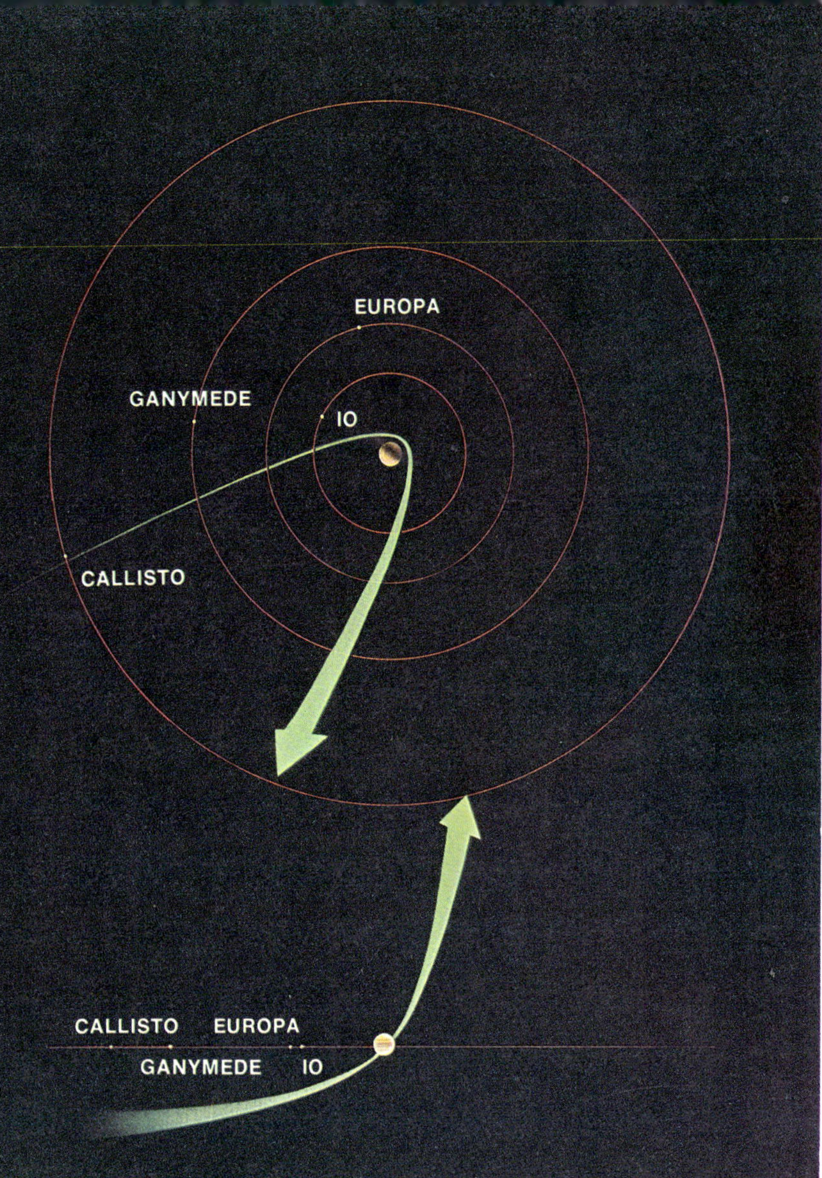

Pioneer 11 passed by Jupiter on Dec. 3, 1974, coming within 42,800 km (26,600 mi) of its cloud tops. These two views show the craft's path as seen from Jupiter's north pole and from the plane of its equator. The edge-on (equatorial) view of Jupiter and its four largest moons is about the way the system looks from earth.

many different fields have had some time to analyze and piece together. The picture of Jupiter so far revealed confirms some earlier ideas about the planet but shatters others. The information seems to support the theory that Jupiter is primarily a spinning ball of liquid hydrogen and that it lacks any detectable solid surface. In many respects, Jupiter seems more like a star than a planet. At best, it has only a small rocky core thousands of kilometers, or miles, below the heavily clouded atmosphere. The structure of the planet is much more accurately known now than at any time in the past because of the Pioneer findings.

DESCENT INTO THE CLOUDS

Let's suppose we are high above the ocean of clouds that blankets the visible surface of Jupiter. When viewed from this point the turbulence of the atmosphere is obvious. Everywhere the clouds are billowing and surging as if they are being stoked by some furnace far below.

Descending to within 160 km (100 mi) of the cloud tops we pass through thin haze layers of ethane and acetylene. Ethane and acetylene are both colorless gases. A further descent through the atmosphere, which is made up of hydrogen and helium with some ammonia and methane mixed in, would plunge us into streaming white clouds. These clouds are similar in appearance to earthly cirrus clouds. These are the brilliant white ammonia-ice clouds that amateur astronomers see in their telescopes as wide white "zones" on the planet.

The most prominent white zone, the home of the Great Red Spot, is called the south tropical zone. The atmospheric pressure at the top of the ammonia clouds is about 70 per cent of the atmospheric pressure at the surface of earth. Thus a probe suspended by a balloon inflated with heated hydrogen could hover here indefinitely. Such a probe, filled with instruments to study the planet, is, in fact, being planned for the 1990's. The temperature at this level is −120° C (−184° F), whereas the temperature about 13 km (8 mi) above the cloud tops, at 30 per cent the earth's atmospheric pressure, is −146° C (−230° F).

Continuing our descent into the clouds, we come to a point 20 km (12 mi) below the tops of the white ammonia-ice cloud decks. Here we find brownish-orange belts of ammonium hydrosulfide crystals. These belts alternate with the higher level zones and make up the two main features of the planet's clouds as seen from earth. The tops of the dark belts are 8° C (15° F) warmer on the average than the upper reaches of the bright zones of ammonia clouds. It is believed that we can see about 200 km (125 mi) into these cloud decks with our telescopes.

WHY JUPITER IS BANDED

Perhaps the best-known features of Jupiter are its relatively permanent belts and zones. We will pause in our descent to observe activities in this region. The belts and zones appear to be comparable to the continent-spanning cyclones and anticyclones that produce most of the weather in earth's temperate zones. On both Jupiter and the earth, cyclones and anticyclones are huge regions of rising or falling atmosphere powered by the sun. In Jupiter's case they are also powered by the planet's internal heat source.

There are important differences, however. On earth, huge masses of warm, light gas rise to high altitudes, cool off, get heavier, and then roll down the sides of new, rising columns of gas. The general direction of this atmospheric heat flow on earth is from the tropics toward the poles. Coriolis forces, produced by the planet's rotation, cause the descending gas, which would normally move north or south, to flow around the planet west to east. Unstable flow then converts this west-east motion into the enormous spirals known as cyclones and anticyclones. These systems in turn generally move from west to east.

Because of Jupiter's instabilities it might seem that the weather flow there should be in even more violent spirals than it is on earth. However, several factors appear to have a "calming effect," so that Jupiter's weather motion is mostly linear—that is, in straight lines—instead. These factors include Jupiter's internal heat source and heat circulation, its lack of a solid surface, and the general liquid character of the huge planet. The combination of convection due to the sun's heat plus internal heat, and coriolis due to

Never before photographed: this Pioneer 11 view shows Jupiter's north pole, roughly on the line of the terminator, or boundary between the sunlit and dark portions of the planet, at top.

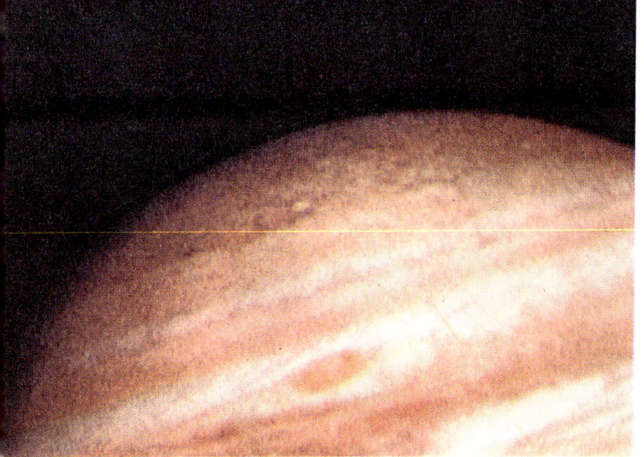

Jupiter's Little Red Spot, in the northern hemisphere, is thought to be a storm area.

Jupiter's 35,400 km per hour (22,000 mph) rotation, stretches the planet's large permanent weather features completely around the planet. The resulting features are the familiar belts and zones. Another "calming effect" in Jupiter's weather is that heat radiated from Jupiter's center reaches all parts of the planet's surface in equal amounts. In contrast, earth's heat from the sun is received mostly in the tropics and circulates toward the icy poles.

HIGH-SPEED JET STREAMS

The gray-white zones of Jupiter are warm, upward rising "stretched" weather cells, whose tops are high clouds of ammonia crystals. The lower red-brown areas are descending weather cells, believed to be clouds of mainly ammonium hydrosulfide crystals.

The tops of the bands of lightweight, upward rising white clouds flow from the center to the edges of the bands. Cloud material in the heavier dark belts funnels downward from the edges to the center of the belts. Because of the tremendous forces of planetary rotation each belt or zone tends to have its own speed. This means that Jupiter's various bands are jet streams of atmosphere whose speeds of flow can differ by as much as 580 km per hour (360 mph). Continent-sized eddies, or whirlpools, are created when one stream has a high speed relative to another. These eddies are clearly visible in the detailed Pioneer pictures of the planet. In general, these atmosphere streams flow most rapidly near the equator.

THE STORMY RED SPOTS

Jupiter's most famous feature, the Great Red Spot, appears to be a centuries old vortex of a violent storm. This idea was first proposed by the late Dutch-American astronomer Gerard P. Kuiper. The spot, according to calculations, rises some 8 km (5 mi) above the surrounding cloud deck. This was determined by the fact that the clouds at the top of the spot have less atmosphere above them and are cooler and hence higher than surrounding clouds.

Jupiter's liquid character, plus the fact that the spot was not "seen" by Pioneer 10's gravity-sensing experiment, which should have detected even small variations in density, seem to eliminate most previous theories on the nature of the mystery. Pioneer pictures show that the spot's internal structure appears to be a vortex like a pinwheel. A rapid circulation pattern in the vortex makes it rigid enough to displace the clouds of the south tropical zone. Somehow the spot seems to be continually "fed" from far below.

A second Red Spot, about one third the size of the Great Red Spot, is located in the northern counterpart of the southern hemispheric zone containing the larger Spot. The Little Red Spot also is cooler than its surrounding clouds and is believed to rise as high as the Great Red Spot. This second Spot lends support to the idea that the Red Spots are occasional meteorological events on Jupiter, to be found in the middle of the planet's bright zones where the atmosphere is rising.

GETTING WARMER

All of the savage weather visible at the cloud tops and taking place within the belts and zones of the giant planet is part of the atmosphere of Jupiter. Below the bright zones and belts, the exact structure of Jupiter's atmosphere is less clearly known. Pioneer 10 data have shown that the region defined as the atmosphere of Jupiter is about 1,000 km (600 mi) thick. As we continue our descent into the clouds the temperature continues to rise because of the internal heat of the planet and because of the "greenhouse effect." By the "greenhouse effect" we mean the retention, or holding in, of the sun's heat by the atmospheric gases.

Not far below the upper cloud decks the temperature is high enough so that ammonia is no longer frozen. Water ice—perhaps in the form of snowflakes—is drifting around in the weather circulation along with ammonia droplets. Continuing farther down, we find that temperature and atmospheric pressure increase more rapidly. Water is abundant in the form of droplets that contain ammonia in solution. It is on this region that speculation about the possibility of life on Jupiter has been focused. Pioneer data have neither confirmed nor denied the existence of some form of airborne life that might float in the atmosphere at this level. Just what the weather is in these lower cloud layers is unknown—aside from the up-down circulation of the atmosphere in general. There may be lightning and violent storm activity, but the conditions here are still largely a mystery.

About 1,000 km (600 mi) from the topmost levels of the atmosphere, a strange change takes place. The atmospheric pressure increases rapidly and the sky becomes totally dark. Pressures here produce such densities that the helium and hydrogen gases are compressed to what we would consider a liquid. Temperatures of about 2,000° C (3,600° F) make this a bizarre environment.

A FAILED STAR?

Going still deeper, at 2,900 km (1,800 mi) down we find the temperature is about 5,500° C (10,000° F) and the pressure is 90,000 times the atmospheric pressure on the surface of earth. At this point the weight of the Jovian atmosphere has gradually compressed the hydrogen into the form of a liquid that is about one fourth as dense as water. At 24,000 km (15,000 mi) down—about one third of

The general circulation of Jupiter's atmosphere is east to west. At the same time, there is a vast welling up and sinking of atmospheric gases. Jupiter's rapid spinning and internal heat stabilize the circulation patterns.

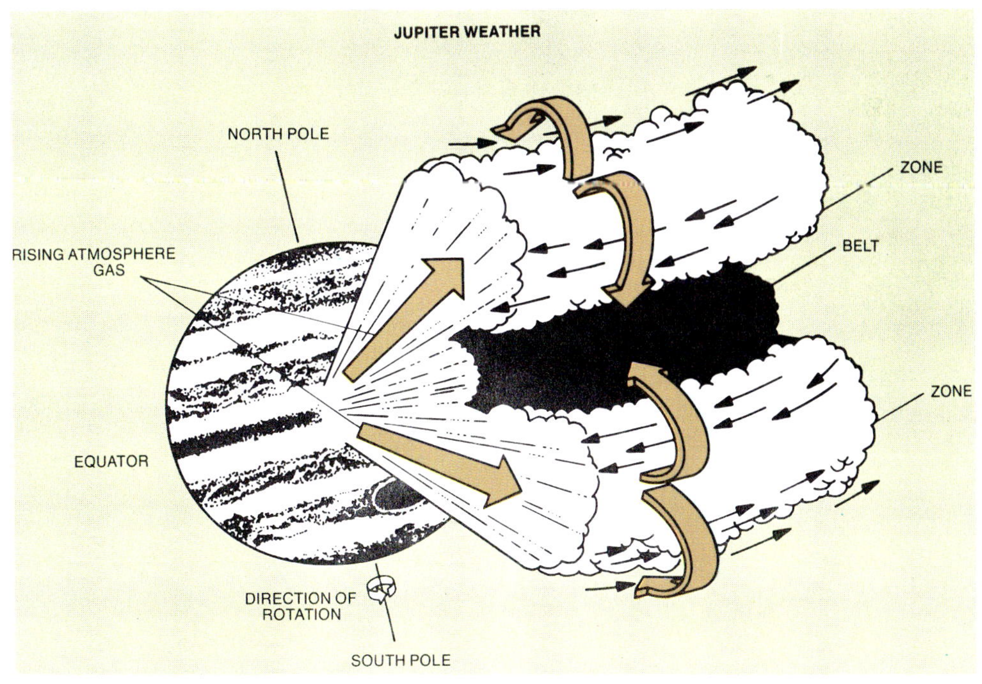

the way to the core—the temperature reaches 11,000° C (20,000° F) and the pressure is 3,000,000 atmospheres. At this level, liquid hydrogen turns to liquid metallic hydrogen.

This new portrait of Jupiter reveals the big planet as truly a strange body, totally unlike earth. Indeed, in some ways it is more like a star than a planet.

Deep inside Jupiter, near the core, unbelievably high pressures are concentrated on a region where the temperature is 30,000° C (54,000° F)—six times hotter than the surface of the sun. Yet this is still a long way from the several million degrees required to ignite the nuclear "fires" that power stars. Jupiter then may be a star that has failed. It may simply have been too small to produce the needed temperatures.

HEAT FLOW IN JUPITER

As we have seen, the temperature of Jupiter decreases steadily from the center outward to the very cold cloud tops at the "surface." Jupiter's hot interior is believed to seethe as currents circle and whirl, carrying the heat to the surface. It is estimated that hydrogen moving up from Jupiter's center covers the 71,000 km (44,000 mi) from the center of the planet to the top of the atmosphere in 10 to 100 years. Interior currents may move as fast as 2,400 km (1,500 mi) per year. The rapid transfer of heat is reflected in the constant rise and fall of the atmosphere.

Jupiter's moon Io is seen above and to the right of the planet's north pole.

This is shown by a number of prominent, semipermanent features seen in the planet's clouds. Among such features are striking white ovals of rising atmosphere surrounded by darker borders of descending atmosphere.

The best explanation for Jupiter's tremendous internal heat is that it is heat left over from the planet's formation at the time the solar system was formed. The central temperature could have been kept to the present by a slow shrinkage of the planet amounting to only 1 mm (0.04 in) per year. The high heat of formation is confirmed by Pioneer measurements of the closest large moons of Jupiter, Io and Europa. These two moons are rocky, but Jupiter's other moons, lying farther out, are "ice" moons. One possible reason for the rocky nature of Io and Europa is that Jupiter when first formed radiated enough heat to prevent water vapor from condensing into ice during the formation of Io and Europa. An alternative explanation for part of Jupiter's internal heat is that it is energy released by the breaking up of hydrogen and helium. This is a process believed to be currently underway somewhere near the center of the planet.

A WOBBLING MAGNETIC FIELD

Pioneer 10 found that the strength of Jupiter's magnetic field at the planet's cloud tops is more than ten times the strength of earth's field at earth's surface. The total energy in the Jovian magnetic field is 400,000,000 times that of earth's. Jupiter's inner magnetic field extends into space in a doughnut shaped ring. The ring reaches about 1,300,000 km (800,000 mi) from the planet's cloud tops. The outer field extends in a flatter ring to a minimum distance of 3,400,000 km (2,100,000 mi) from Jupiter's cloud tops, and it sometimes reaches out three times as far. The poles of Jupiter's magnetic field are the reverse of earth's.

Jupiter's inner field is tilted about 10 degrees to the planet's axis of rotation, and the center of the field lies about 2,120 km (1,320 mi) north of the center of the planet and 7,790 (4,840 mi) outward from

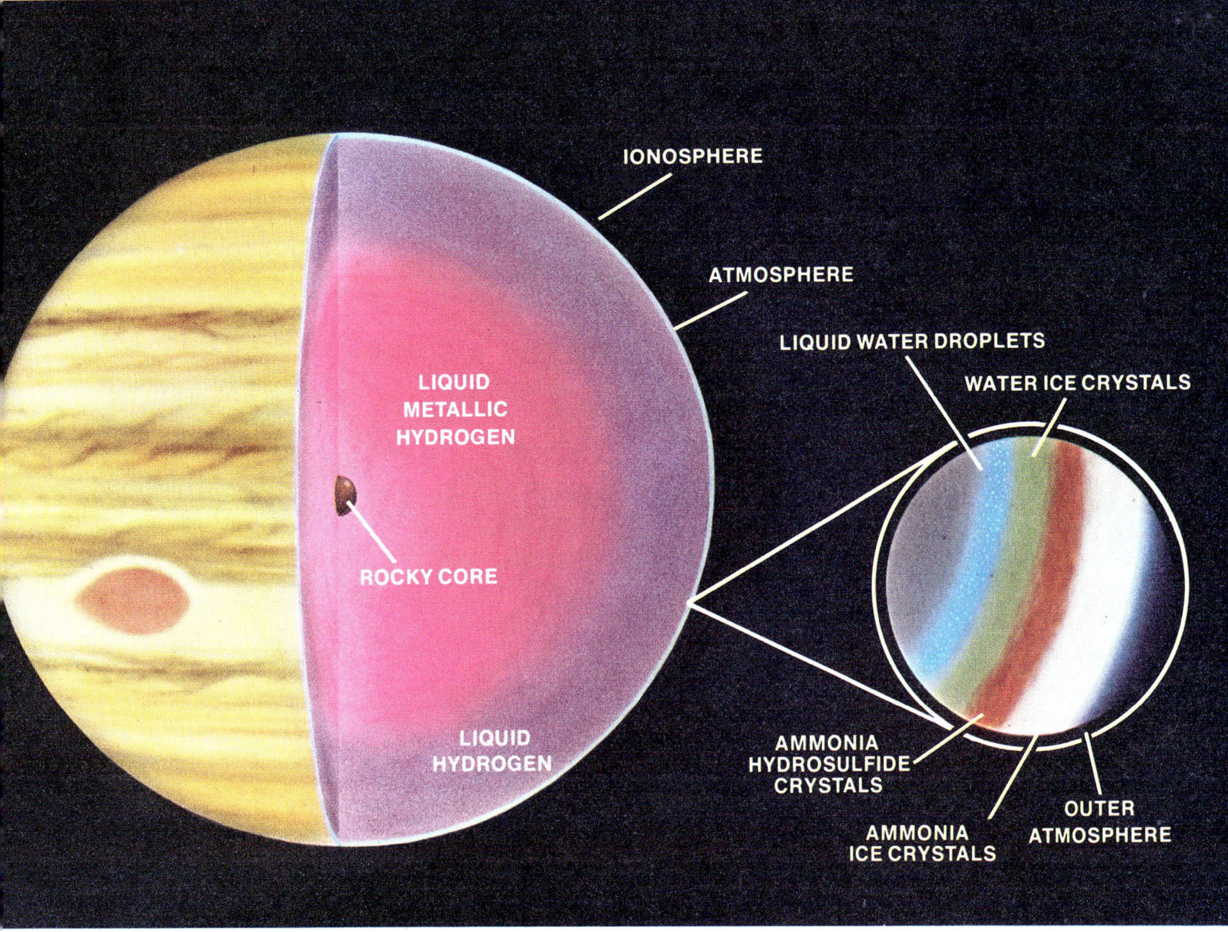

This model of Jupiter's interior shows Jupiter as primarily a ball of liquid hydrogen, perhaps with a small rocky core. The atmosphere, about 965 km (600 mi) deep, consists of several layers as shown in the small closeup.

the rotational axis in a direction parallel with the equator. Because the center of the magnetic field is not in the center of the planet, the strength of the field as it emerges from the cloud tops varies over the clouds' surface. Magnetic induction is measured in a unit known as a gauss. A comparison of measurements of earth's field and of Jupiter's gives an idea of how strong the magnetic field of Jupiter is. To illustrate—earth's field at the surface is 0.35 gauss. At a point 130,000 km (81,000 mi) above Jupiter's cloud cover, Pioneer 10 recorded a magnetic field strength of 0.2 gauss.

Because Jupiter's magnetic field is tilted, the inner field—as seen from space—wobbles up and down through an arc of 20 degrees once during each Jupiter day.

The displacement of the center of Jupiter's magnetic field and the tilt of the field, further confirm the idea that Jupiter is a huge, flattened, fast-spinning ball of liquid hydrogen. Jupiter's magnetic field, like earth's, is thought to result from a "dynamo effect" within the planet. That is, circular currents within the liquid interior are thought to produce electric currents, and hence magnetic fields. Only a planet with a tremendously active interior, scientists believe, could produce a magnetic field as far offset from its center as Jupiter's.

DANGEROUS RADIATION BELTS

As on earth, the high energy particles that form Jupiter's inner radiation belt are trapped within the planet's inner magnetic field. In the weak outer magnetic field, particles bounce around but eventually make their way to the field's outer edge. There they are spun off into space by the high-speed rotation of the planet and by the radiation belts themselves.

Jupiter's radiation belts have the highest intensity ever observed by space measurements, according to James Van Allen of the University of Iowa. The maximum radiation measured by Pioneer 10 was about 100 times the lethal dose for humans, and was near the limit of radiation tolerance for spacecraft systems. The belts' intense particle radiation poses the greatest threat to spacecraft flying close to Jupiter, or orbiting the planet. Three of the four planet-sized moons lie within the intense inner radiation belt. Hence a manned landing on one of them would be impossible without very advanced technology to protect the men. The fourth big moon, Callisto, lies outside the region of intense radiation, and would be somewhat more suitable for a manned landing.

In general, the most dangerous part of Jupiter's radiation zone is in the planet's equatorial plane. Even though Pioneer 11 zoomed in three times closer than its predecessor on Dec. 3, 1974, it didn't stay long in the equatorial region. The spacecraft's path was a looping trajectory that swung from the south polar region through the equatorial zone, and back out over the north pole on its way to a rendezvous with Saturn in 1979. Information gathered from Pioneer 11's visit to Jupiter is already adding to the legacy of the first flight to Jupiter. Complete analysis of the data may reveal new and startling information about a strange and alien world that probably will long hold many mysteries□

"Jupiter." *Astronomy*, April 1974.

Jupiter, The Largest Planet by Isaac Asimov. Lothrop, 1973.

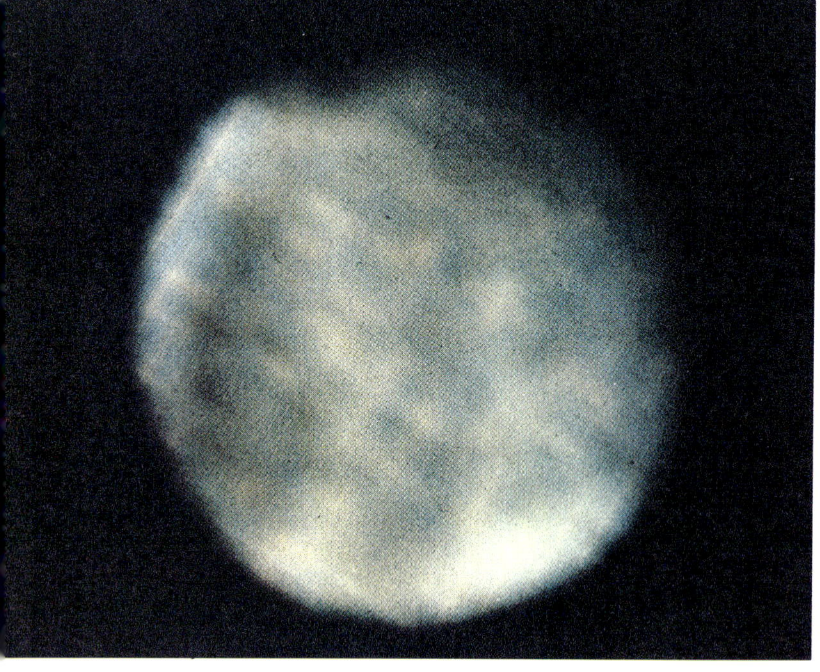

Taken by Pioneer 10, this photo is the best ever taken of Ganymede, Jupiter's largest satellite. Ganymede's north pole is near the dark region in the upper left.

Asteroids are tiny planetary bodies that orbit the sun—perhaps the remains of a lost planet. In this three-hour exposed photograph, the trail, or part of the orbital path, of one asteroid is shown against a field of stars.

The Lost Planet

by Michael W. Ovenden

ABOUT 1770, Johann Daniel Titius, a professor at the University of Wittenberg, was translating into German a popular French book on astronomy. He decided to include, in a footnote to his translation, a curious little formula that he had found. Working out the formula led to the numerical series 4, 7, 10, 16, 28, 52, 100. Titius noticed that these numbers, with the exception of 28, were each very close to 10 times the distances of the then known planets from the sun in units of earth's distance. The skipped number 28 corresponds to the gap between the planets Mars and Jupiter. Titius didn't take his numbers game very seriously. He died in 1776 without having had any reason to change his mind.

Then in 1781, William Herschel accidentally discovered the planet Uranus. When the orbit of Uranus was calculated shortly after, German astronomer Johann Elert Bode pointed out that its distance from the sun exactly fitted the next number—196—in the sequence. It is not clear whether Bode discovered the series independently, or whether he just drew attention to Titius' earlier work, but from then on, the sequence was known as Bode's law. At this point everyone became very excited, and began looking for the "missing" planet between Mars and Jupiter at position number 28. A society was formed in Germany just for this purpose.

DISCOVERY OF CERES

After nearly 20 years of searching, nothing turned up. Enthusiasm for the project began to wane. Then on Jan. 1, 1801, Italian astronomer Giuseppe Piazzi (not a member of the society) accidentally found a small planetary body known as an asteroid, minor planet, or planetoid. He actually discovered the largest of the asteroids, now called Ceres. Ceres is only 965 km (600 mi) across, but it does fall at the predicted distance—number 28 in the sequence. Since 1801, several thousand asteroids have been discovered. Most of them are very small—less than 2 km (1.2 mi) in diameter. Presumably there are many others, undiscovered because they are too small for us to pick up even in a large telescope.

Patient watchers of the skies had expected a planet between Mars and Jupiter. Instead they found a pile of interplanetary dust. So right from the start, it was suggested that asteroids were debris from the planet that they had hoped to find, which had exploded at some time in the past. However, the combined mass of the known asteroids adds up to less than 1/100 the mass of earth—not much of a planet. Still, who knows how much solid material could be even more widely dispersed or how much of the original planet could have been gaseous, leaving no debris after the explosion?

Bode: his law started a hunt for a planet

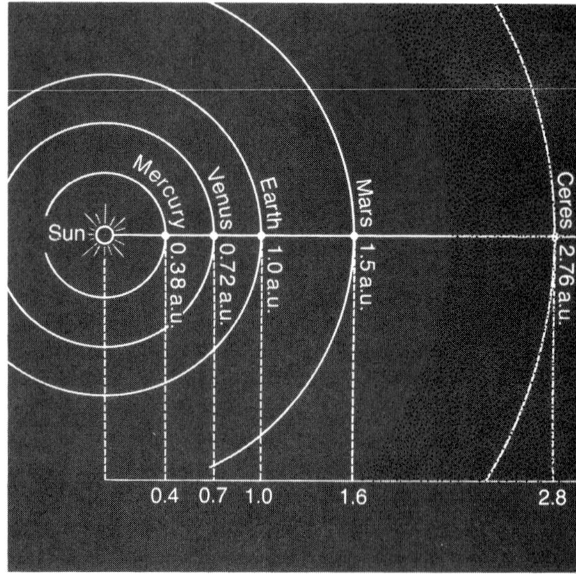

ASTEROID FORMATION

Two facts discovered later lent some support to the idea that the asteroids came from a lost planet. First, accurate measurements have shown that many asteroids vary in brightness in a manner to be expected of light that is reflected from rotating, irregular, fractured chunks of rock. For example, the asteroid Eros seems to be in the form of a long cylinder, 32 km (20 mi) long and only 12.8 km (8 mi) across, rotating once every few hours.

The second fact concerns meteorites. Meteorites are chunks of space debris that survive the fiery plunge through the atmosphere. Knowledge of the orbits meteorites had before they hit earth tells us that most of them come from the asteroid belt between Mars and Jupiter. Meteorites are, in fact, just stray asteroids that happen to collide with earth. The interiors of some meteorites show a complicated crystalline structure that could have been formed only if the material of the meteorite had once been hot, and then cooled very slowly—perhaps by only a degree in a million years. The rate at which a hot body can radiate away its internal heat, or cool down, is proportional to the area of

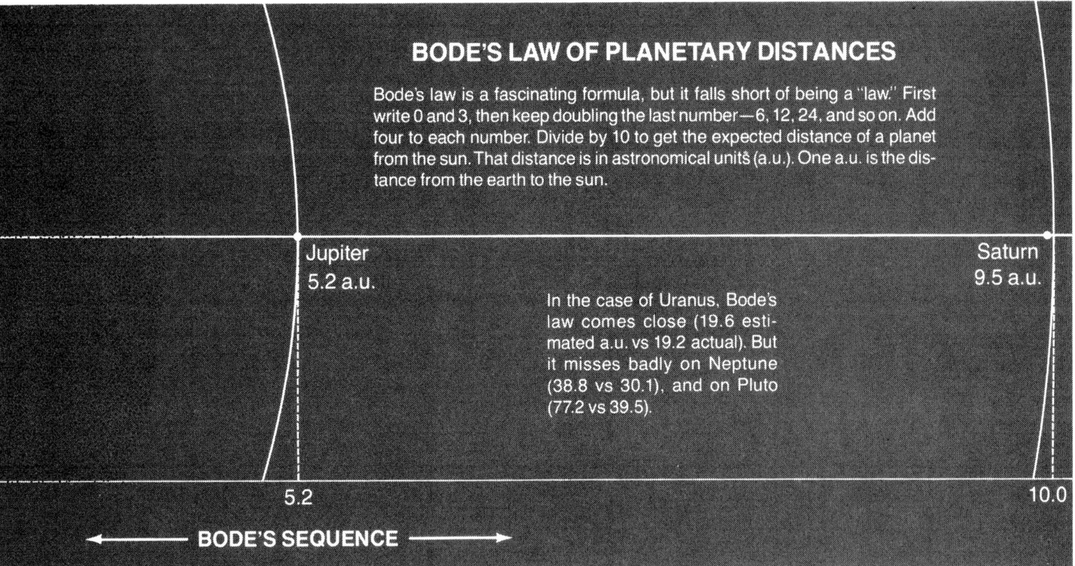

its surface. The amount of heat a body can hold is roughly proportional to its volume. A big body cools down much more slowly than a small one. Think for a minute: a young baby may freeze to death where an adult would feel only chilly. For meteorite material to have cooled as slowly as a degree in a million years, it must have been at one time in a body at least 160 km (100 mi) across.

With this sort of support, the idea of an exploded planet became generally accepted knowledge by the 1940's. As late as 1955, the Dutch astronomer Jan Oort suggested that comets too might have come from the same exploded planet. It surely is a dramatic picture—comets, meteorites, asteroids and all the rest of the interplanetary debris being spewed into the solar system in one gigantic explosion of a planet. Still, the idea that planets may from time to time explode does not comfort the more sensitive among us.

But there are fashions in science, no less than in dress. In recent years some scientists have suggested another theory of planet formation. According to this theory, the planets probably did not cool off from a molten state at their formation but rather grew by the sticking together of smaller meteorite-sized pieces, known as planetesimals. It therefore became more natural to think of the asteroid belt as material that failed to stick together to make a planet. After some asteroids stuck together and the mass became almost the size of a planet, they began to collide with one another and were again broken up into smaller pieces. The average distance of the asteroids from the sun is close to 2.8 times earth's distance—just where Bode's law says a planet should be.

LAW OR CHANCE?

So, is Bode's law really a law? Is it due to chance? Chance is a curious concept. In everyday life we use it either because we don't know the laws governing the behavior of things, or (more usually) because we ignore a wider context of influences that are actually bearing upon the course of local events. However, we do have one important clue. The distances separating the various moons of Uranus from the planet and the distances separating the inner satellites, or moons, of Jupiter can also be predicted by a mathematical formula. This formula is similar to Bode's law. The moons near the planet are bunched together, while those more distant are farther apart. While

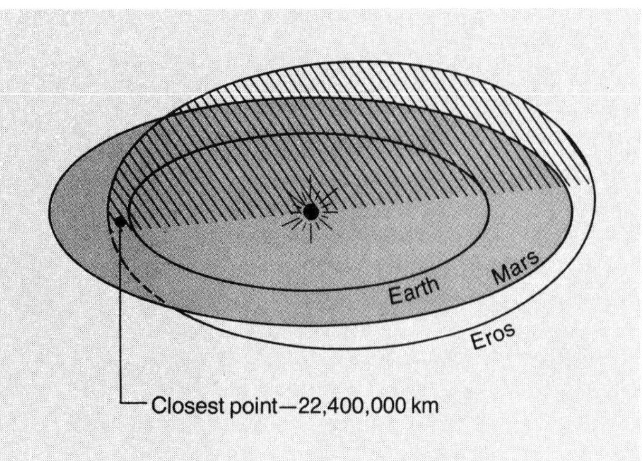

The asteroid Eros swings close to earth in 1975, becoming for a short time our nearest neighbor.

Bode's law itself may not have any precise physical significance, the general way in which planets and satellites are distributed surely has some meaning.

What meaning? There are two possibilities, or a combination of them. Either the planets have stayed where they were formed—in which case their distribution tells us something about what was going on in the early days of the solar system—or the planets have moved to their present positions.

Why should the planets move? A single planet revolving around the sun, if left to itself, would not change its orbit. But the planets do not leave each other alone. Just as the sun and a planet attract each other by the force of gravitation, so two planets also attract each other. The sun is much heavier than the planets so it has a stronger force of attraction than do the smaller planets. The effect of one planet on the motion of another is very small. This small effect is called a perturbation of the affected planet's orbit. These perturbations are too small to cause a significant change in a planet's distance from the sun in a million years. But the planets have existed for hundreds of millions of years. What then? Could even small perturbations gradually over hundreds of millions of years significantly affect a planet's orbit?

Curiously enough, we don't really know. In principle, if we know where every planet is at a given time and how it is moving, the future and the past of the planet's orbit can be determined. But our mathematics isn't powerful enough to enable us to write down a formula telling us what happens. No general solution exists even for the simple case of the sun and only two planets. This case is the famous "three body problem" that gave Newton a headache. Such formulas as we have are only approximate, and cease to be reliable if we use them for working too far back in time. They suggest that significant changes may occur in the solar system over periods of a hundred million years or so, but perhaps we are stretching the formulas too much.

On the other hand, some very general arguments show that over an infinite time either the pattern of the solar system repeats itself again and again, or else one or another of the planets escapes from the solar system. But this idea assumes that the solar system is isolated from the rest of the universe—and it isn't. In fact, the rest of the universe can influence the solar system. For example, passing stars may be responsible for sending comets with very long orbital paths near to the sun.

SNAPSHOT OF THE SOLAR SYSTEM

Why don't we settle the question using modern computers to calculate the past history of the solar system? We do, but there are limitations to the computers and to the mathematical formulas we can use. The longest calculation of the solar system's evolution that has been made with reasonable accuracy covers less than a million years. It is not enough.

Let's suppose that given enough time the mutual attraction between the planets does change their distances from the sun by large amounts. Where then would we expect to find the planets? When two planets come close together, they will perturb, or change, each other's orbits violently so the orbits will change rapidly. On the other hand, when they are far apart their mutual perturbations are small, and their orbits will change slowly. So, if we could take just one snapshot of a system of planets—and that is all our thousands of years of observation really amount to—we would expect to find the planets as far away from each other as they possibly can be.

A simple idea? Yes. That's why it is interesting. The problem is to find the distribution where the planets are as far away from each other as possible. At first sight, you might think that you could just let some of the planets escape from the solar system. They would certainly be far apart then. But the system as a whole has certain constraints. Among other things, its energy has to remain constant. It turns out, for example, that if you had three planets and the sun, and you took one planet off to infinity, you would have to put the other two closer together.

The problem, then, is: Given a star and a set of planets or a planet and a set of satellites, what is the configuration available to the system during its evolution in which the planets are, on the average, as far apart from each other as possible? This would then be the "equilibrium" configuration that we would be most likely to find the system in. It turns out that it is possible to discover this configuration, at least approximately. In fact, we have examples in our solar system.

MOST LIKELY CONFIGURATION

The configurations of the satellites of Uranus and the inner moons of Jupiter are very close to the calculated patterns. The system of Saturn is difficult to calculate as a whole, because of the great range of satellite masses. But parts of the Saturnian system seem to obey the principle also. But when the theory is applied to the planets of the solar system, it doesn't work at all. Other calculations reveal that the 5,000,000,000 years the solar system has existed is plenty of time for the planets to get into their "most likely" configuration. So what's wrong? It might just be that we are, now, in a phase of evolution of the solar system between one "critical" configuration and another.

At this point the old idea about the origin of the asteroids emerges again. Is it possible that the solar system *was* once close to its "expected" distribution, or most likely configuration, with a planet between Mars and Jupiter, and that now

Some of Jupiter's moons are thought to be asteroids captured by the planet's gravitational pull. These photos show Jupiter and its four largest moons emerging from behind the earth's moon. In the left photo only two of the moons have emerged; in the middle photo Jupiter with another moon almost touching its left side appears; and in the last photo, the fourth moon makes its appearance.

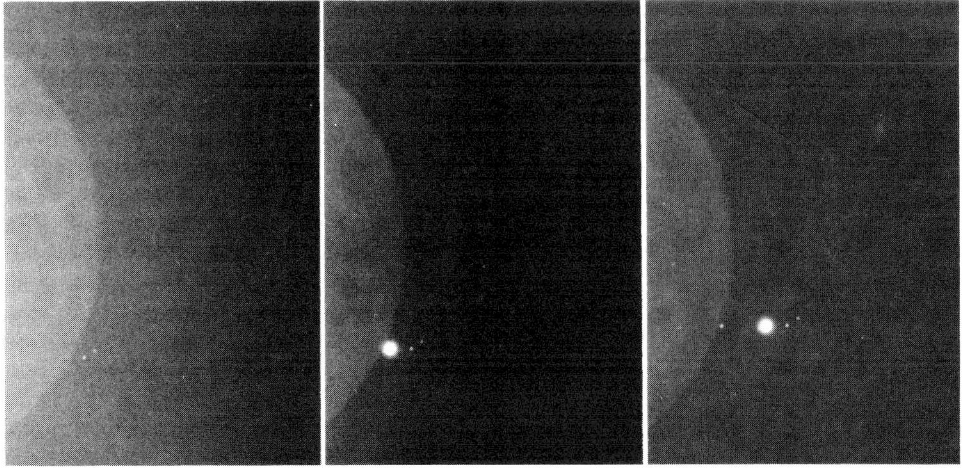

it is changing to a new "expected" distribution? The answer to the question is yes—if the missing planet had had a mass of about 100 times the mass of earth, and if it had disappeared within the last hundred million years, which is just yesterday in the history of the solar system.

Did it really happen that way? No one can tell. The remote past is as hypothetical as the future, and any statements made about it are speculative. So, remembering that the whole investigation is necessarily speculative, how does the new perspective stack up?

EVIDENCE FOR A LOST PLANET

There are some facts that tend to support the idea of a lost planet between Mars and Jupiter. First, we have seen that the material of meteorites has been heated in the past and then slowly cooled. What heated it? The obvious explanation is the energy of fall-in of material as the original small bodies, or planetesimals, collected into bigger bodies. The aggregate bodies must have been at least several thousands of kilometers, or miles, in diameter in order for the heating to have been sufficient.

Second, analysis of the material inside many meteorites shows that it cooled in a magnetic field of the size that we would expect only on large rotating planets. We could suggest several ideas, but the simplest explanation is that the meteorite material was once near the surface of a large rotating planet that automatically would have had a magnetic field.

Third, the outer satellites of Jupiter move in the opposite direction to the other satellites. It is very difficult to see how such opposite-moving satellites could have been formed that way. Almost everyone has supposed that these satellites are captured asteroids. In other words, that they are asteroids that were captured by the force of Jupiter's gravity. However, they are too deeply held by Jupiter's gravitational field to have been captured into their present orbits. In fact, the orbits of Jupiter's satellites can be understood in some detail if we assume that these moons

originated from a single body and were temporarily in the region of Jupiter when Jupiter suddenly increased its mass by about 100 earth masses. Is this where most of the missing planet went? If so, how was Jupiter able to collect so much of it? Here is a field for future work.

Fourth, by looking at the chemical composition of meteorite material, we can find out how long the material has been in solid form and hence how long since the last "melting." We do this by looking for products of radioactive decay in the meteorite. This age always comes out to about 4,500,000,000 years. This is presumably the time since the original planet was formed.

Another age can be found from the effect of cosmic rays on meteorites. Cosmic rays can penetrate only about a meter, or yard, of meteoritic material. So the cosmic ray-exposure age is the time since the meteorite became less than a meter in diameter. It happens that two quite different cosmic ray-exposure ages turn up. Stony meteorites and a few iron meteorites show ages less than 40,000,000 years. This age is consistent with the

Meteorites are stray asteroids that collide with earth. The structure and age of some meteorites lend support to the theory of a lost planet between Mars and Jupiter. Left: a stony meteorite. Above: an iron meteorite.

theory of the explosion of the planet and the resulting sudden production of meteorite fragments at this time. However, most of the iron meteorites show a much greater cosmic ray-exposure age—about 600,000,000 years. The ages are found assuming that all the meteorite material has been irradiated by the same, constant cosmic ray intensity. In a large planet, the stony material would lie nearer to the surface than the iron. If the planet did indeed explode, a lot of energy would have to have been released in its interior. Perhaps the iron material was exposed to radiation from the internal explosion. This might give the iron the characteristics of 600,000,000 years of exposure.

AND, IF YES—A NAME?

Did a large planet once orbit between Mars and Jupiter? Does the evidence presented here stand up? Right now we simply cannot say for sure, and it probably will be many years before the question is settled. Actual exploration of the asteroids should ultimately give the answer. Such exploration will certainly eliminate some of the theories of asteroid origin, just as lunar exploration has reduced the number of theories concerning the origin of our moon.

Suppose we are right—suppose the planet did exist. Shall we propose a name? My first thought was Aztex in recognition of the aerospace expertise at the University of Texas where I did most of my calculations and of the Instituto de Astronomía de la Universidad Nacional Autónoma de México where I did most of the thinking for the subsequent calculations. But my unfamiliarity with popular mythologies soon became apparent when I learned that Superman came from an exploded planet called Krypton. So, in keeping with the tradition of naming the planets from mythology, the lost planet should be named Krypton□

 SELECTED READINGS

Moons and Planets by W. K. Hartman. Bogden and Quigley, 1972.

The Tiny Planets: Asteroids of Our Solar System by David C. Knight. Morrow, 1973.

An artist's rendition of the surface of Titan, Saturn's largest satellite and the only moon known to have a dense atmosphere.

Titan

by Gregory Benford

THE planets are obvious, brilliant beacons in our night sky. Venus, Mars, Jupiter, and Saturn usually are among the brightest points of light in the heavens. This prominence has led astronomers to devote much time to them. In fact, many astronomy texts tend to leave the student with the impression that the sun and planets make up all of our solar system.

There are, however, other, just as interesting objects in the solar system: the moons. Because our own satellite is obviously barren and lifeless, the possibility of life on any satellite in the solar system has typically been dismissed with little thought. But some astronomers are coming to believe that this dismissal is hasty. We are gradually learning that these other moons are definitely not carbon copies of our own.

The 33 natural satellites in the solar system range from large bodies, comparable in size and mass to the planet Mercury, to others that would not even be visible from the surface of their primary planet. Some of the satellites follow circular orbits in the same planes as the equators of their planets, while others follow elongated ellipses inclined at steep angles to the equatorial plane of their planet.

Although there are more moons than planets, little is known about them. They are smaller than planets, harder to see, and at first glance seem unlikely places to study the early chemical processes that lead to life. Yet conditions on one of these moons, Titan, may be reminiscent of those of the early earth.

LIKE EARLY EARTH

A small, inconspicuous body in the solar system, Titan is Saturn's largest satellite. It has twice the volume of our moon, 1.9 times the moon's mass, about half the mass of the planet Mercury.

Titan is the only moon known to have a dense atmosphere. In 1944 the late Gerard P. Kuiper of the University of Arizona found methane in its atmosphere. For the next quarter of a century this was nearly all that was known about Titan's atmosphere. In the last few years, however, attention has focused on this satellite.

Because Saturn is more than nine times as far from the sun as earth is, one would expect Titan to be cold, about −191° C (−312° F). But detailed study of Titan's infrared emissions shows some regions of the atmosphere may be much warmer—at least −128° C (−198° F). Even more surprisingly, we now have a measurement of Titan's surface pressure—a startling 0.4 earth atmosphere. This high surface pressure—hundreds of times greater than that on the surface of Mars—is startling for a body with so little mass.

An important key to the mystery of Titan may be its distance from the sun. It is much farther than that of our own moon, and we can expect the warming influence of sunlight to have played a different role in the evolution of any possible atmosphere.

Near the top of an atmosphere a high-velocity molecule moving directly upward has a good chance of escaping from the atmosphere. At a given temperature, the lightest molecules escape most readily. Thus, hydrogen, helium, and other relatively light gases should be lost rapidly from less massive objects, such as Titan. Heavier gases, such as methane, nitrogen, and ammonia, may cling to large moons, however, and provide a fairly thick atmosphere. What matters is the temperature at the top of the atmosphere because the temperature affects the velocity of gaseous molecules. The temperature at the top of the atmosphere is determined primarily by the amount of sunlight falling upon it. The temperature of the lower atmosphere may be considerably different, a fact with important implications.

GREENHOUSE EFFECT

How can we account for Titan's warmth? One reasonable explanation seems to be that a greenhouse effect operates there, trapping the sun's heat. This process begins when visible light passes through Titan's atmosphere and warms the surface of the satellite. Once heated, the surface radiates infrared waves outward. These infrared waves do not pass through the atmosphere, but rather are absorbed by the gases. This process acts somewhat like a greenhouse, where a glass or plastic ceiling traps warm air.

Since 1944 Kuiper and others have closely studied Titan. They observed that it has dark and light markings, which change with time. Cornell University's Joseph Ververka has noted that sunlight reflected from Titan is reminiscent of the reflection from clouds, rather than from a solid surface. Titan is also red, a property not fully understood. Until recently these facts fit together into a fairly consistent view. Although Titan has only one-sixth the earth's gravity, the top of its atmosphere is relatively cold, so it should retain slow-moving heavy gases such as the methane Kuiper found, but not the faster moving lighter gases such as hydrogen. Thus, astrophysicists were surprised when Lawrence Trafton of the University of Texas announced in 1972 that he had found hydrogen, the lightest gas of all, in Titan's atmosphere.

RECYCLED ATMOSPHERE

Hydrogen, like methane, efficiently absorbs infrared radiation and seems a good candidate for a greenhouse agent. The presence of hydrogen in Titan's atmosphere is a mystery, however. Why doesn't it diffuse away? Or, is it steadily replenished by the moon itself? Cornell University's G. Mullen and Carl Sagan believe volcanoes on Titan may give off large quantities of liquid ammonia, methane, and water. These fluids could percolate to the surface, evaporate, and enter Titan's atmosphere. Ultraviolet sunlight would then break them down into hydrogen and several types of organic compounds. This

Saturn and six of its ten satellites

would be a continuing source of hydrogen in Titan's atmosphere.

Thomas McDonough and Neil Brice of Cornell University have speculated that hydrogen may appear in Titan's atmosphere because, although it escapes, it must inevitably return. A hydrogen molecule that leaves the top of Titan's atmosphere goes into orbit around Saturn. It does not, however, have enough velocity to leave the vicinity of Saturn's deep gravitational "well." Thus, a doughnut-shaped ring of hydrogen would accumulate around Saturn in the region of Titan's orbit. Eventually, a wandering hydrogen molecule will encounter Titan again and, if conditions are right, be recaptured within its atmosphere. This process could greatly increase Titan's hydrogen concentration. This theory raises the interesting possibility that Titan may recycle its atmosphere.

WARM BLANKET

Whatever the mechanism, methane and hydrogen combine to form a warming blanket around tiny Titan. Recent studies have tried to sketch the formation of such small worlds. These sketches assume that these moons began as large clumps of the dust and various ices that seem prevalent in the outer solar system. According to such studies, the heavier, rocky portions of the mix then sank inward and formed a core surrounded by a thick mantle of liquid water and ammonia. Gravitational compression probably warmed the interior somewhat, providing the heat to keep most of the water and ammonia slush from freezing. Overlying this is a crust of solid ice perhaps 48 km (30 mi) thick. Meteorites falling on this crust would cause extensive cracks and spectacular craters. Volcanic magma boiling up through the liquid mantle would warm parts of the surface, perhaps providing pools of liquid methane.

Saturn is surrounded by rings. Upper left photo shows rings at their maximum tilt of 27° to the earth. Lower right shows rings turned edgewise to earth and not visible.

There are probably no ponds of water or liquid ammonia, for although Titan is anomalously warm, it is still quite chilly by earthly standards. Ammonia freezes at −78° C (−108° F) on earth and Titan is much colder than that. In chemical composition our picture of Titan's surface resembles the early earth. It is a much colder place, however, and at first glance seems an unlikely site for important biological processes.

OTHER LIFE FORMS

But our ideas about the chemistry of living things are based on a narrow range of experience. In the early earth, there were probably many more avenues available for chemical evolution. We know that life without oxygen once held sway on our planet and has now virtually vanished. It lost out to those organisms that could use oxygen for various life processes. There were probably other incipient living systems, based on the different biochemistry of that age, but the oxygen-based system was highly successful, literally devouring its competition. The winner in this early struggle among life systems was probably dictated by chance ingredients on earth at that time. As far as we know, there is no reason why our particular biochemistry is the only one that should survive in a wide range of planetary environments.

All living creatures on earth are made up of complex carbon compounds con-

How a NASA artist envisions the encounter of Pioneer 11 with Saturn scheduled for September 1979. Plans call for the spacecraft to fly between the inner ring of Saturn and the planet's surface and then to move out for a look at Titan.

taining nucleic acids and proteins. The nucleic acids carry the blueprint of inherited characteristics, and the proteins do the many tasks of transmitting this information. These ingredients live in a bath of water. All life we know has evolved to use water wherever possible. Life is essentially supported by a welter of complex organic molecules immersed in water. But water is not the only solvent that promotes chemical reaction. Many of ammonia's properties—heat capacity, heat of evaporation, versatility as a solvent, and tendency to liberate a hydrogen ion—are, in the biological sense, almost as good as water's.

If there were liquid ammonia on Titan, many biological reactions analogous to those that occur in water would be possible. But it is likely that conditions do not permit liquid ammonia, and that there are, instead, ponds of methane on Titan. Methane, however, is not the same sort of liquid as water. Water's special properties as a solvent encourage substances to react chemically and to form complex structures. But in a totally inert background, such as methane, substances receive no help from the solvent. Methane cannot dissolve many substances, such as salt, that water can dissolve. This would seem to destroy any analogy we wish to make between life in a water ocean and life in a methane pool. But methane can dissolve other types of substances, such as fats or oils. Water cannot do this—thus "oil and water don't mix."

In a water based environment, proteins serve to carry a great deal of information in their complex chains. This variety and versatility seem necessary to communicate the vast library of genetic information that life requires. To imagine a methane environment that is not hostile to the formation of complex structures we must search out long organic molecules that can interact in methane. There are already some molecules on earth that could conceivably react in a methane environment. Our brains, in fact, contain such molecules that form long chains of complex and unknown function.

BUT IT'S COLD

The obvious drawback to liquid methane as a background for chemical evolution is its coldness. Life uses marginally stable compounds that can react quickly and variously in many subtle fashions. Temperature has a great influence on these reactions. Our earthly biochemistry would be sluggish indeed in a cold methane ocean. But we cannot rule out the possibility that fat chains can be quite reactive in cold methane surroundings. These molecules would be so unstable at earthly temperatures that we probably do not even know of them, but they could possibly exist in a colder environment.

There must, of course, be sources of energy to drive chemical reactions, in addition to a hospitable solvent to contain them. Although we know little of surface conditions on Titan, there are probably energy sources resembling those that existed on the primitive earth. High-energy particles from the sun bombard the surface of Titan, lightning may fork between the methane clouds observed above Titan, and volcanoes could be a continuing source of heat and raw material percolating up from its core.

Remember that reactions at low temperatures require less energy to drive them than do reactions at higher temperatures. We can speculate that complex organic chemistries may proceed at respectable rates in methane ponds. Long molecules, such as the fats and oils we know, could combine in subtle fashion to set the stage for life itself.

OTHER MOONS

What of other large moons in the solar system? According to earthbound observations and the results of the Pioneer space probes, two of Jupiter's moons, Io and Ganymede, also have atmospheres. But the gases clinging to their surfaces are a million times thinner than Titan's.

Io is an odd object. It circles close to Jupiter, and after it emerges from Jupiter's shadow, it is unusually bright. But the luster fades within fifteen minutes. This leads some observers to speculate that Io's atmosphere condenses out in the cold shadow. Like Titan, Io is red.

Jupiter's fourth moon, Ganymede, has 0.16 earth gravity. Because it is closer to the sun than Titan, the top of its atmosphere should be warmer. Perhaps this is why it has not retained as much gas as Titan has: the gaseous molecules are moving faster. Ganymede reflects light well and shows light and dark patches. Since this reflected light seems characteristic of snow or rock powder, the moons may contain snowfields among areas of dirty ice or bare rock.

Our reasoning that ammonia or methane could be life-supporting solvents holds equally well when applied to the large Jovian planets—Jupiter, Saturn, Uranus, and Neptune—themselves. There is good evidence that a greenhouse effect operates within Jupiter. Some layers deep within these planets are probably at earthlike temperatures. Possibly ammonia and methane seas exist on them. Recent experiments have shown that complex organic structures form readily in conditions such as those on Jupiter.

Studying oceans deep inside the giant planets, however, will be extremely difficult. Clouds at the top of Jupiter's great atmosphere move faster than the velocity of sound. Our space program cannot muster rugged probes capable of surviving entry far into the Jovian cloud belt. In terms of energy requirements and landing conditions, though, the moons of Jupiter and Saturn are comparatively easy to reach. If elementary biochemistries have evolved on these moons, we could investigate them at relatively small cost.

Within a decade we may have preliminary answers to questions of life on Mars and among the clouds of Venus. But to gain more knowledge about the prevalence of life in the universe, space exploration may turn to the moons of Jupiter and Saturn, particularly Titan. There we may find circumstances reminiscent of the early earth and solve many riddles otherwise impossible to explore, since present conditions on our planet are radically different from those that occurred before life began. Although we customarily think of the planets as possible hosts for life, it may be that we will finally learn more about life's origins by studying Titan□

Thirty-two Moons: Natural Satellites of the Solar System by David C. Knight. Morrow, 1974.

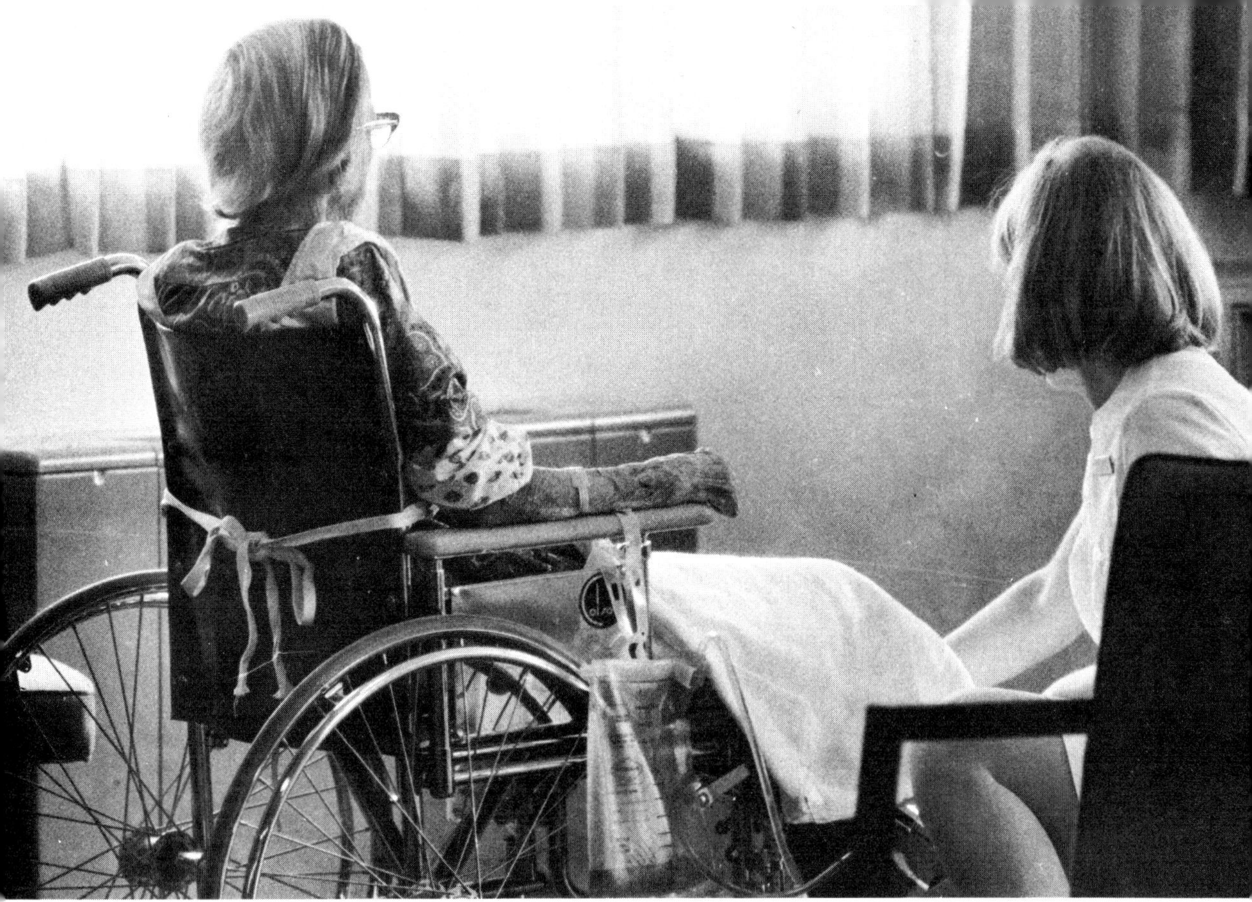

behavioral sciences

Tied to her wheelchair, an elderly woman sits alone in a nursing home. Reports of the poor quality of care in many of the nation's nursing homes—particularly those for the elderly—shocked the country in 1974 and 1975.

review of the year behavioral sciences

Psychology and the Law. Some of the most dramatic advances in the behavioral sciences in the last few years have been in the treatment of psychological disorders. But with these new powers come new responsibilities. Indeed, the ethical questions raised by today's technology to affect and control behavior rival those problems faced by the physicists who developed the atom bomb.

In the public eye, the term behavior modification conjures up images of *1984* and *Clockwork Orange.* However, its principles are as old as the first mother who smiled at a well-behaved child. Behavior modification involves reshaping behavior through the systematic application of rewards and (less frequently) punishments. Undesirable habits ranging from stuttering to sexual fetishes have successfully been eliminated using this approach. Most behavior modification techniques require the active cooperation of the patient. Dr. Albert Bandura of Stanford University summed it up this way in his 1974 presidential address to the American Psychological Association, "Reflexive conditioning in humans is largely a myth."

A photo of patients in a mental hospital. The care and treatment of the mentally ill and their legal rights is a growing concern.

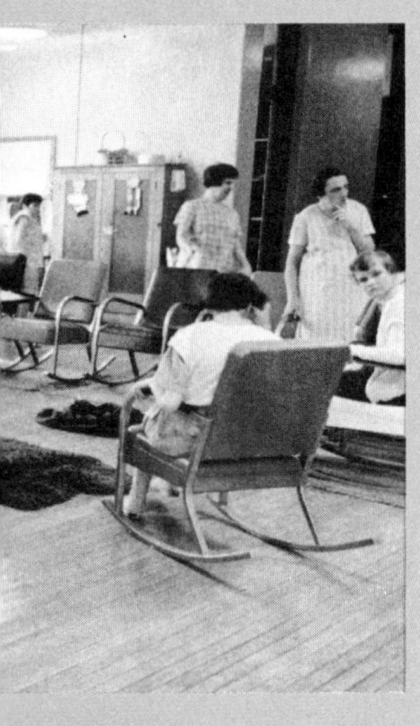

Psychosurgery, or brain surgery aimed at changing a person's thoughts and actions, may be an area fraught with even more ethical problems. Technical advances now allow neurosurgeons to alter structures deep within the brain. Proponents of psychosurgery argue that, for example, some persons with a history of attacks of uncontrollable violence are actually victims of a form of epilepsy that can be treated only surgically. But the relatives of one such patient recently launched a $2 million malpractice suit against his psychosurgeons, contending that he was disabled by the operation. While this case was still pending, a Michigan court ruled that involuntarily confined persons (like prisoners and most mental patients) cannot give legally adequate consent to a high-risk operation like psychosurgery.

These are not the only areas in which scientists and lawyers are facing new moral dilemmas. In New York, one woman sued her psychiatrist to prevent him from publishing a disguised description of her case, a practice common to all medical fields. Still another controversy is brewing at the Harvard Medical School over a study of the genetic makeup of all newborn infants at a Boston hospital done with the hope of predicting behavior problems that might later develop.

Fundamental issues of privacy, rights to treatment, and the limits of human experimentation are now being debated in courts, legislatures, and classrooms. A U.S. Senate Subcommittee on Constitutional Rights recently completed a three-year investigation of this area. It concluded, in part, "It may be that Congress may have to define by law the limits of scientific research in these fields as they affect the constitutional guarantees of liberty." Virtually all mental health workers agree that the powerful new tools for the prediction and control of human behavior demand stricter safeguards against the potential for abuse.

The Fallible Eyewitness. Some lawyers are suggesting that society reconsider the legal process in the light of recent findings from the research laboratory. Psychologists have known for some time that the human memory does not provide a literal recording of our experiences but depends on personalities and expectations as well. And yet criminal courts treat eyewitness testimony as if each person carried a tape recorder in his head. When a crime is committed, the eyewitness is typically confused and under stress. To demonstrate the effects this can have, Dr. Robert Buckhout of Brooklyn College recently staged purse snatchings in some of his classes. Students were later asked to pick out the "thief" from a videotaped lineup. Only 13 per cent of the eyewitnesses were able to identify the culprit. Even more disturbingly, 67 per cent accused one of the innocent men.

How reliable are eyewitnesses? Results of a test by Dr. Robert Buckhout of Brooklyn College had disturbing aspects, with 67 per cent accusing an innocent person.

The Hemispheres of the Brain. Observations of patients with head injuries convinced physicians as early as Hippocrates that the two sides, or hemispheres, of the brain were not exactly the same. We now know that, for most right-handed people, the left hemisphere is involved with logical, verbal thought processes while spatial, emotional, and intuitive thoughts depend on the right hemisphere. The implications of this split for normal conscious experience were the focus of many of the most exciting studies of 1974.

In general, the right side of the brain controls the left side of the body and vice versa. This contralateral design of the human nervous system serves as the basis for many sensory differences. At McGill University, researchers recently demonstrated that infants as young as five months of age show greater sensitivity to musical sounds in the left ear (right hemisphere of the brain) and to speech sound in the right ear (left hemisphere). In adults, another researcher found that this left ear superiority for the recognition of simple tunes applies only to the "musically naive"—professional musicians show a right ear (left hemisphere) superiority. This is consistent with a growing body of evidence that suggests that the right hemisphere is concerned with the whole (intuition), the left the parts (logic).

The hemispheres of the brain. There is growing evidence that the right hemisphere is concerned with intuition, the left with logic.

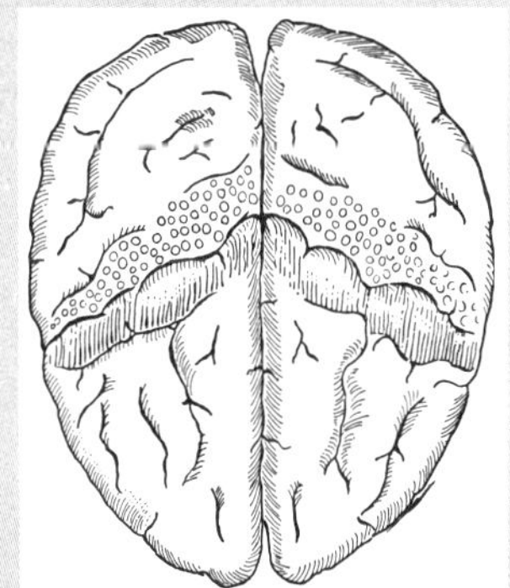

Such differences can also be detected by noting the direction in which a person's eyes move as he considers a question. If you ask a right-handed person to "define the word 'abstract'," you will typically see that his eyes move to the right as he considers this logical, verbal question, indicating that the left hemisphere of his brain generates the answer. But you may ask the same individual a right hemisphere spatial emotional question, such as, "If you were crossing a street from west to east, and a car coming from the south smashed into you, which leg would be shattered first?" In this instance, you will more frequently find him looking to the left. These specific questions were first used in a study by psychologist Gary E. Schwartz and his colleagues at Harvard University, and similar findings have been reported in many other laboratories.

On the other hand, the 6 to 11 per cent of the population born "lefties" usually have a pattern of "mixed cerebral dominance"—that is, the differences between the two hemispheres are not so clearly defined. Recent studies suggest that this physiological ambiguity may have advantages and disadvantages for the left hander. Some reports indicate that "lefties" tend to have more problems with reading, speech, and arithmetic but that they also tend to be more creative and to perform better on certain visual tasks. Dr. Theodore Blau, a clinical psychologist, has also found that many left-handed children develop an early pattern of rebellion as they resist attempts to force them to use the "more normal" right hand.

James Hassett

One form of behavior modification is desensitization. Here patients with an irrational fear of dogs view a series of slides of dogs—starting with slides of small cuddly dogs, then larger dogs and finally hostile dogs—until they overcome their fear.

Behavior Modification

by Peter Chew

"TODAY a bag of M&Ms, tomorrow—the world!" Such is the motto of that fast-growing school of psychology known as "behavior modification." For years behavior modifiers have been trying to change people's lives by "reinforcing" constructive behavior patterns and breaking "maladaptive" habits. The heart of "behavior mod" beats at the University of Kansas. There practitioners of behavior modification have:

Raised the reading scores of 8,000 disadvantaged elementary-school children to scores well above the national norm for middle-class children.

Created neighborhood homes for 8 to 10 "predelinquent" children that cost far less to operate than big state institutions, seem to produce a higher success rate, and serve as models for homes popping up elsewhere in Kansas and in other parts of the country.

Taught retarded persons and mental patients how to talk, become more self-sufficient, and to work and play.

Behavior modifiers are at work on a wide array of human problems: excessive smoking, eating, drinking, and limitless phobias, or irrational fears. Dr. Nathan Azrin, an Illinois practitioner of behavior modification, has become so adept at quick-curing nervous habits that "he could probably franchise the service," says one admirer.

Dr. Morris Parloff, an official of the U.S. National Institute of Mental Health (NIMH), says of the movement, "It's important; it's big; it's growing fast; and it's now widely dispersed."

The Association for the Advancement of Behavior Therapy says it has 1,500 members. Four behavior-modification journals have been born in the last decade. Papers on the subject proliferate in the clinical literature. And there's a disciple or two at most university faculties.

GROWING PAINS

The movement is also suffering growing pains, reversals, and opposition. While the National Institute of Mental Health and the U.S. Office of Education continue to support behavior modification, the U.S. Bureau of Prisons and the Law Enforcement Assistance Administration have recently started shutting off money for such programs in penal institutions. At issue is the right of a prisoner *not* to have his behavior modified. Also, age-old methods of prisoner abuse have been cropping up under the guise of "behavior modification." Such practices have at times given behavior modification a bad name.

Behavior modifiers have incurred the resentment of traditional psychologists, psychiatrists, and psychoanalysts, into whose domains they have been steadily moving. Finally—to the acute distress of behavior modifiers, who consider their basically nonphysical therapy to be benign—they have become lumped in the minds of many with therapy involving behavior-changing drugs and brain surgery, or "psychosurgery." Moves are afoot in the U.S. Congress to legislate far stricter controls over all human experimentation than now exist.

"The widely publicized theories of B. F. Skinner and the riveting drama of *A Clockwork Orange* have suggested grim visions of 'mind control,' " observes a recent issue of APA *Monitor*, the journal of the American Psychological Association. "Such visions have been followed by allegations of prisoners' groups, and groups of mental patients, that the dangers are far more real than imaginary."

Dr. Perry London, a professor of psychiatry and psychology at the University of Southern California, puts the problem in these terms in his book *Behavior Control:* "There is an intrinsic ambiguity about behavior control. Whether its implications are more ominous or more promising to the individual than to society depends on how it will be understood, prescribed, exploited, and contained as it emerges in the future."

FEARS OF '1984'

Behavior modification appears anything but ominous as practiced at the University of Kansas' Department of Human Development and Family Life. The department, headed by Dr. Francis Degan Horowitz, includes many members who joined in the mid-1960's. "Community supervision and control of behavior-modification programs is absolutely essential," says Dr. Montrose Wolf, a key member of the department. Thus Achievement Place—the family-style homes for predelinquent boys and girls that he helped establish—are under control of the town of Lawrence, Kansas.

Behavior modifiers are also keenly sensitive to the fears of *1984* and *Brave New World* that they inspire in many people. "All you need to start practicing behavior mod is a bag of M&Ms and a kid," says KU's Dr. Todd Risley.

Drugs are used in some behavioral modification techniques. A problem drinker, for example, may be given a drug that induces nausea when combined with any liquor. Thus the person develops an aversion to alcohol.

Behavior modification is easy to grasp, though more subtle than it appears at first glimpse. Jargon aside, it boils down to the carrot-and-stick principle. And while behavior modification—also known as behavior analysis, behavior therapy, and action therapy—is nearly all carrot, it should not be confused with permissiveness.

REWARD FOR RESPONSE

The roots of behavior modification go back to the beginning of the 20th century when the Russian physiologist Ivan Pavlov successfully produced conditioned reflexes in animals. Later animal experimenters also studied learning and the role of reward in the development of desired behavior. Most notable among them was the American psychologist B. F. Skinner.

Skinner discovered that when one of his hungry laboratory rats accidentally stepped on a lever that released food in his specially designed "Skinner Box," the animal soon learned to step on the lever when hungry. Similarly, a child will do a teacher's bidding if rewarded with M&Ms —assuming that he likes M&Ms.

Suppose a child refuses to settle down in class and read. The behavior-modification teacher says, "Okay, Billy, if you'll read for five minutes I'll give you five M&Ms."

Billy reads. Behavior modifiers call the M&Ms "reinforcers"—the stimuli that cause him to read. Before long it should be possible to withdraw the M&Ms. The teacher's praise, the pleasure the student will derive from reading, and his improved grades will prove reinforcement enough.

Wolf states the reinforcement principle this way: "A stimulus-reward, if given contingent upon a response-behavior, will strengthen that behavior."

In lieu of candy, the teacher might give the child tokens that he can later exchange for five minutes' "free play." This is called a "token economy."

This is hardly revolutionary. Grandmother, and her grandmother before her, used similar stratagems with rock candy and lollipops.

"Yes," reply the behavior modifiers, "but what we have done is systematize what every good parent has always known."

Isn't this simple bribery?

"Does your employer 'bribe' you with your paycheck?" they reply.

Behavior modifiers stress that while the reinforcement principle is straightforward enough, each person's behavior pattern is invariably extremely complicated, the result of untold interactions with his environment. Moreover, it is one thing to motivate a child to read with candy or "free play," but it is quite another thing to motivate a "normal" adult and even more complex to try to change the behavior of people with serious mental or emotional problems.

Traditional psychologists and psychiatrists are concerned with leading an individual toward a discovery of the subconscious roots of his behavior. The behavior modifier, on the other hand, generally cares little about root causes. He considers himself a "sharpshooter," gunning for symptoms. It doesn't matter whether a person has, say, "an unresolved Oedipal problem," is an obsessive drinker, or suffers from claustrophobia. The behavior modifier attacks the symptom, not the cause.

A MORAL FACTOR

"We take complex behaviors and try to break them down into components that can be studied and measured, then we try to develop an environment that will strengthen the proper behavioral components," says KU's Wolf.

Traditional psychologists reject this as overly simple. Dr. Howard Shevrin of the University of Michigan says: "The symptom is the tip of the iceberg. The main problem is what gives rise to the symptom."

Shevrin sees behavior modification as too dependent upon animal research. "Human beings are more complicated than animals, as the behavior-mod people are finding now that they've come out of their laboratories."

Achievement Place scenes. Left: professional teaching parents live in the facility with their own children as well as with youths they are trying to help. Upper right: a family conference where youths can air their grievances and discuss their problems. Lower right: youths being taught family and community living skills.

Dr. Howard Farber, former president of the Washington, D.C., Society of Existential Psychiatrists, has written in the magazine, *Commentary*: "I would agree that, unlike morality, behavior—objective, visible, measurable behavior—is bodily conduct we share with animals. But the moral imagination to consider such matters as good and evil, including of course the behavior associated with these human realities, is not a capacity we share with animals. To treat an animal as though he possessed this capacity is merely silly, but to treat a human being as though he were only his behavior is, I am afraid, wicked."

Behavior modifiers are adamant. "Change the behavior and you change the individual," says KU's Dr. Daun Martin. "I've seen it time and time and time again."

To the question, "Who's going to control the controllers?" Dr. Ivar Lovaas of the University of California at Los Angeles has replied in a recent issue of *Psychology Today:*

"We need to ask ourselves what kind of society we want. I don't want 1984; I don't want a brave new world. I don't want another Hitler. I don't want Skinner to engineer my society. . . . And we won't produce that kind of society, because most of us don't want it. . . ."

HELPING THE CASTOFFS

Lovaas is best known for his work with autistic children. Autism is a form of schizophrenia. Autistic children are often uncommunicative and sometimes self-mutilating. Lovaas has used standard reinforcement to reward desired behavior and "negative reinforcement," such as one or two electric shocks during self-mutilative behavior, to punish undesired behavior. He has succeeded in improving autistic children's behavior so they can be freed from physical restraints.

Behavior modifiers are particularly proud of their work with cases that are often castoffs of society. They see traditional psychoanalysis as too time-consuming, too costly, and too often ineffective with disturbed individuals. They speak angrily of mental and criminal institutions as "warehouses" that do little for their inmates.

KU's Dr. James Sherman specializes in curing "language defects." He recalls helping a man in his mid-50's who had been diagnosed by a psychiatrist as a paranoid schizophrenic. In more than 25 years of institutionalization, the man had uttered only a few dozen words; he communicated by writing notes.

One day the man appeared in Sherman's office with a note. He had sent off for a magazine reprint that had not come, and he feared the reason was that his return address was a mental institution. Would Sherman write for him?

Sherman made a "contract" with the patient: Come to my office regularly, reply to oral questions with a nod or shake of the head. I'll pay you a few pennies per session and send off to magazines for you, he said. In time the nods became grunts, then "uh-huh" or "uh-uh," then "yes" or "no," then complete sentences. And the man began talking—with Sherman, the attendants, and with other patients. His life brightened.

"Then a funny thing happened," recalls Sherman. "He continued to talk with everyone but me, and I asked him why. He said that I wasn't a very interesting conversationalist!"

KU's Daun Martin recalls a little boy diagnosed as suffering from anorexia nervosa, a mental state characterized by a refusal to eat, withdrawal, and a tendency to sleep almost continuously. She counted the number of the boy's bites of the evening meal. They came to a half dozen or so. She drew up a contract with the boy and his family. The boy's favorite pastimes were working on model airplanes and watching television. These pastimes were made contingent upon increased bites. Privately she instructed the parents to praise the boy when he ate extra bites but to ignore him when he failed to eat.

The father used an automatic counter to keep track of the bites. The boy took just enough bites each time to get the reinforcement he wanted—permission to work on model airplanes or watch television. The bites gradually increased to 30, 40, and more. Then presto! No more anorexia nervosa.

EXCEPTIONAL RESULTS REPORTED

Dr. Don Bushell, Jr., Dr. Gene Ramp, and colleagues at Kansas University oversee a program involving 8,000 deprived children. The children range in age from kindergarten through third grade and live in nine states. They are part of a nationwide program, called Project Follow Through. It is a follow-on to Project Head Start, which is for preschool children.

The Kansas behavior modifiers use the full range of behavior-modification methodology—instructional films, workshops, and team teaching. They say that they have been able to raise their children "head and shoulders" above the national norms for all children their age in reading, writing, and arithmetic. For example, they say, their children are three months ahead of the national norm in reading.

The Kansas behavior modifiers say they have statistics to demonstrate that the boys and girls that live at Achievement Place fare far better upon release than their peers on parole or in state institutions. The two homes for the children are just that: homes, pleasant frame houses in big yards, overseen by obviously dedicated "teacher-parents" whose own children live with them.

The so-called predelinquent children attend local schools and live on a complicated token-economy system. In this system they earn points toward weekends at home with their families, an afternoon downtown, or time to watch television. If they misbehave, they can lose points temporarily. Every evening there is a meeting where they can air any grievances.

PSYCHOSURGERY'S TWO FACES

Though Kansas is considered the world center of behavior-modification studies, important work is going on at other universities, including Indiana, Illinois, Oregon, Drake, and Western Michigan, and at private or semiprivate research institutes. Although the Kansas practitioners' motives are entirely benign, there has been ample criticism of behavior modification and its potential for Orwellian social control.

Early in 1974 the U.S. Law Enforcement Assistance Administration announced that it will no longer finance any kind of behavior-modification program for hard-core prisoners at its Medical Center for Federal prisoners at Springfield, Missouri. It is, however, continuing programs at three institutions for juveniles.

The ultimate form of behavior modification is psychosurgery. This type of brain surgery has been criticized on ethical grounds when it has been used principally to make patients more docile and thus more manageable. In July 1973 three Detroit judges ruled in a highly publicized case that psychosurgery may not be practiced on inmates of Michigan institutions, even with the inmates' consent.

With behavior modification, as with all such therapies, society faces the imperative of balancing the technique's potential for good against its potential for misuse and invasion of human rights□

SELECTED READINGS

Behavior Modification: Theory and Practice by Robert A. Sherman. Brooks-Cole, 1973.

"Explosive Youngsters: What to Do About Them" by Edwin Kiester. *Today's Health*, January 1974.

Behavior modification techniques have been used in programs to help people stop smoking. Left: in a "SmokEnders" seminar, a smoker continues to puff on her cigarette as an instructor describes ways of becoming more aware of the smoking habit. Right: a smoker monitoring her own habits and behavior by recording the time of each cigarette on a specially designed "pack strap."

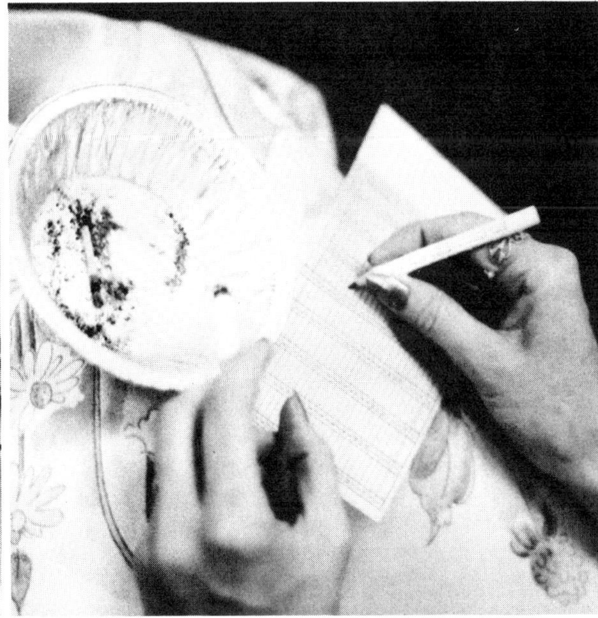

Parapsychology

by Joan Schuman

• Traffic is heavy and you are late for an appointment with friends. You drive the car onto the shoulder of the road and beam a mental message to them, explaining what is happening. When you arrive one hour late, your friends—"informed" of the delay—are smiling.

• You and your family are planning a cross-country trip by car this year. As you go over the maps together, you "see" your family in an auto accident. You cancel your cross-country drive.

You are not in the land of science fiction but, perhaps, in the not-too-distant realm of science fact. Scientists have a special vocabulary for these strange happenings that can't be explained in physical terms. They are parapsychological or psychic phenomena. Psychic phenomena collectively are called "psi," after the first letter of the Greek word *psyche*, meaning "soul."

Uri Geller, the most flamboyant psychic of our time, seems to bend metal objects, such as keys, without using any physical force.

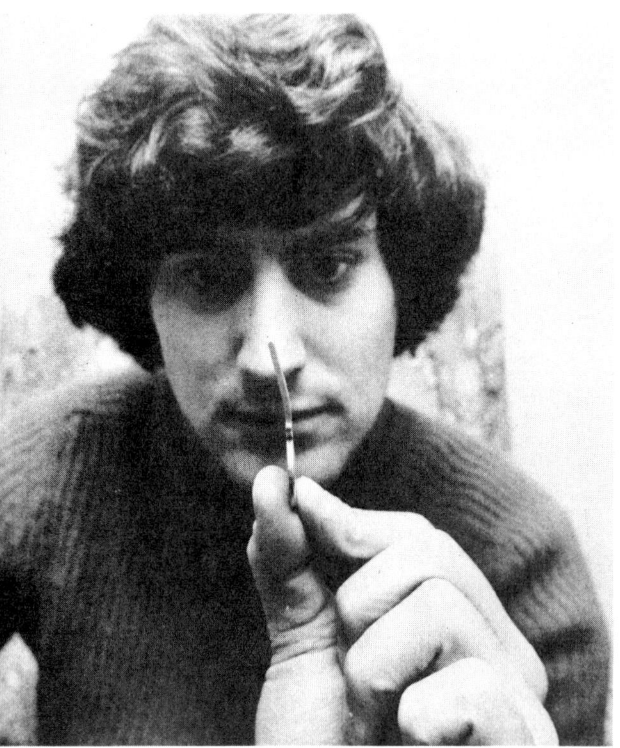

THREE CATEGORIES

Psi can be classified in three major categories. The most familiar to you is extrasensory perception (ESP). ESP includes mental telepathy, the perception of another person's thoughts; clairvoyance, the perception of events or objects not present to the senses; and precognition, or seeing into the future. Communicating with friends with only your mind is an example of mental telepathy. "Knowing" that an accident will occur in the future is an example of precognition.

A gambler influencing the fall of die with his mind is an example of psychokinesis, sometimes abbreviated PK, or mind over matter. Psychokinesis is the ability to move or change matter without using physical force.

Some parapsychologists think that there is a third category of psi—a category known as the survival phenomenon, or "theta." This category includes events influenced by deceased persons. Mediums and seances, haunting spirits, possession by spirits, and reincarnation are all part of "theta" for some. Other parapsychologists, however, do not think that there is a third category of psi but rather that the events of "theta" can be explained by other more widely recognized psychic phenomena.

To some, the world of psi is a world of words and little reality. To others, it is a mistaken reality. These skeptics have adopted the attitude of one researcher who defined ESP as "Error Some Place." But to many psychologists and other interested scientists, psi is alive and real.

FLAMBOYANT PSYCHIC

Psi was never so prominently publicized as it was in 1974, when Uri Geller appeared on the scientific stage. Geller, an Israeli in his late 20's, is the most flamboyant psychic of our time. The tall former paratrooper has been an enter-

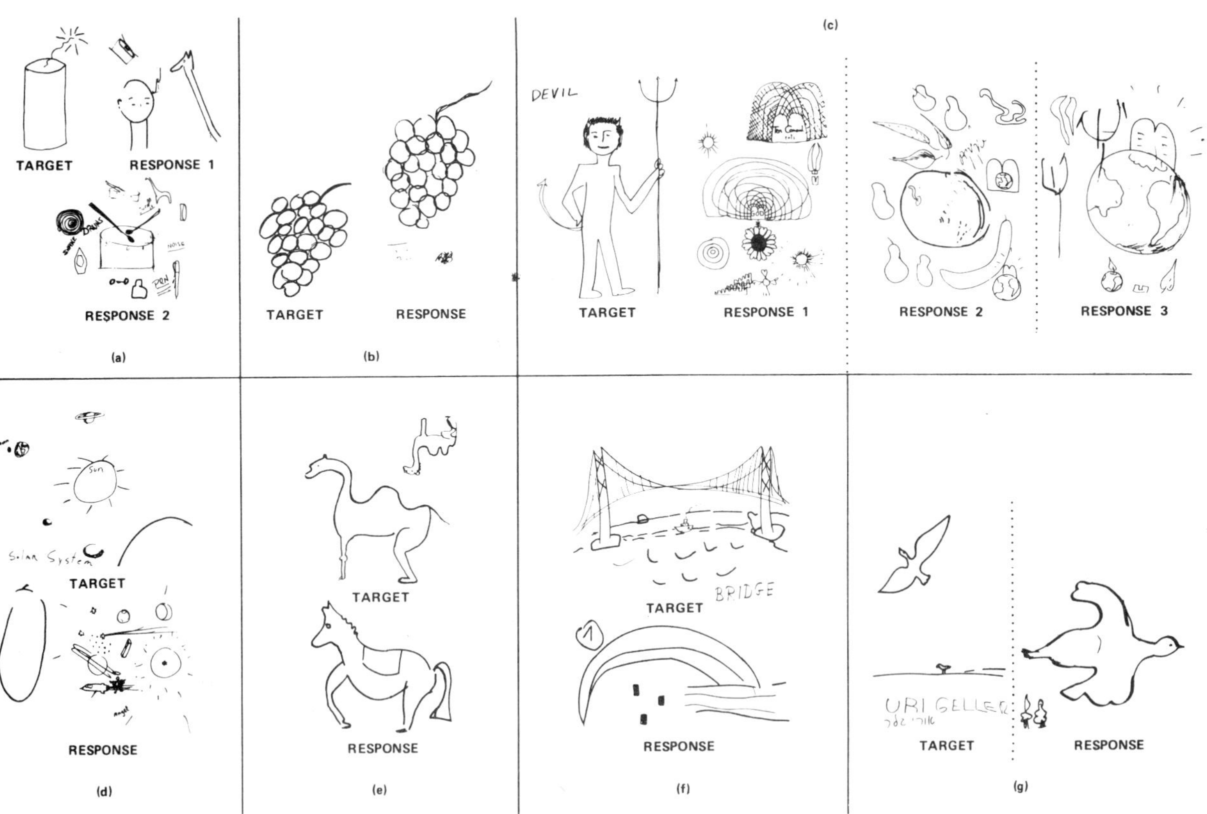

Seven target pictures (drawn by a scientist) and the responses drawn by Uri Geller in a locked soundproof room. Geller correctly drew seven out of nine pictures. The chance probability of his doing this is one in a million.

tainer and television performer known for his abilities in psychokinesis. He seems to bend metal objects, such as keys, with no visible effort and without using any physical force.

None of Geller's public demonstrations created as much wide-scale excitement as those performed for science in a small room at the Stanford Research Institute (SRI) in Palo Alto, California. Two scientists, Dr. Harold Puthoff and Dr. Russell Targ, put Geller through the most trying tests they could devise. The results were published in one of the world's most prestigious and conservative scientific journals, *Nature*, a British weekly. The fact that *Nature* published the report was in itself a feat for the field of parapsychology.

In one of three documented series of experiments reported in the magazine article, Geller was locked in a soundproof room lined with metal cabinets. A group of scientists was placed in a nearby room. Randomly, one of the scientists picked a word in a dictionary and drew a picture representing the word. At the same time Geller was asked to draw the same picture without, of course, being given the word. Nine words, including "seagull," "grapes," "bridge," and "camel," were chosen. According to the scientists, Geller accurately drew seven of the nine pictures. The chance probability of his doing so is one in a million.

In a second experiment, images stored in a computer and known only to the computer operator were displayed on a screen. While still isolated in his room, Geller drew pictures remarkably similar to all three computer images.

The last experiment, and the most difficult, was conducted before a group of scientists and recorded by camera in an effort to spot any possible tricks that Geller might have performed undetected

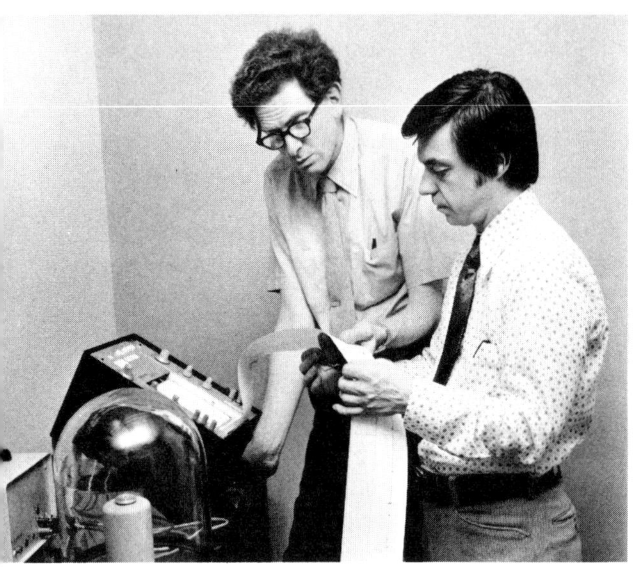

Physicists Russell Targ (left) and Harold Puthoff studying data from an experiment in which Geller apparently interacted with a precision laboratory balance covered with a bell jar causing the balance to respond as though a force were applied to the pan of the balance.

by the scientists. On eight successive occasions, Geller correctly identified the uppermost face of a die that a scientist had shaken in a steel box. This, again, was a million-to-one shot.

NO IMMEDIATE EXPLANATIONS

The chief researchers, Drs. Puthoff and Targ, said of the Geller experiments, "We have presented evidence for the existence of a perceptual ability." At a Columbia University Physics Colloquium, Dr. Puthoff added, "We have observed certain phenomena with the subject [Geller] for which we have no scientific explanations. All we can say at this point is that further investigation is clearly warranted."

Drs. Puthoff and Targ contend that the psi phenomena performed by Geller and other so-called psychics "will be explained by science and math. At the present time we don't have the explanations. We feel that we will either have to extend our scientific laws or conduct more research to learn how these phenomena work."

David Davies, editor of *Nature,* said that by "publishing the paper we are serving notice to the scientific community that there is something here worthy of scrutiny."

SOME STILL SKEPTICAL

Even though the experiments were conducted under rigidly controlled conditions and published in a well-known science journal, some scientists remained skeptical about psi phenomena and Geller's performances. One was Dr. Joseph Hanlon, a physicist.

Dr. Hanlon pointed out that Geller was discovered in Israel by Dr. Andrija Henry Pucharich, who holds 56 patents in the field of medical electronics. One patent is for a receiver so small that it can be hidden in a tooth. Could it be, Dr. Hanlon asked, that Geller "is simply a good magician" rather than a psychic?

Martin Gardner, a mathematics writer for *Scientific American,* argued that Geller is "so skillful a magician that only another magician, and not a group of scientists, can determine whether Geller uses trickery or not."

Former astronaut Edgar Mitchell, a believer in psychic phenomena, contends that scientific breakthroughs will soon show these phenomena to be "natural events that can be as easily explained as sunlight bending around the moon."

But until this does occur, there will probably still be two avenues in the world of psi. One avenue is that mainly traveled by scientists in laboratories, where subjects are tested and retested again and again. The other is crowded with thousands of psi-cult followers who attend institutes, classes, lectures, and performances, and buy special kits that promise followers some psychic knowledge and insights.

PSI RESEARCH

For centuries, there have been folk tales about human beings who possess mysterious powers that go beyond those of the five normal senses. For just as long, learned men have demanded proof of these powers. Today, some of the most respected scientists in the world are seeking that proof.

Nobody can say exactly what psychic research is. The phenomena being investigated include unidentified flying objects (UFO's), acupuncture, Kirlian photography, and perception in plants. The famous Duke University parapsychologist, Dr. J. B. Rhine, believes these phenomena do not fall in the category of psi research, because they may be physical—not psychic—in nature.

No matter which psychic phenomenon a researcher is studying, there are problems that are common to all. First, only a few "psychic" individuals seem to be able to demonstrate psi ability to any significant extent. And in these "unique" individuals, sometimes it works, and sometimes it doesn't. Moreover, the individual does not always "know" whether his or her psi is turned on or off on that particular day at that particular moment. Results are often inconsistent. During one experiment at the SRI, Geller threw back his head, covered his eyes, and said, "I don't know if I can do it. I'll try, but don't be disappointed if nothing happens." Despite his doubts, he was successful.

Researchers have made progress. In 1969, the American Association for the Advancement of Science (AAAS) granted membership to the Parapsychology Association, and the National Institute of Mental Health has awarded grants for the study of psi phenomena. For a long time, private donations and grants were the main support of psi research. No longer.

Examples of funded psi research are as varied as they are numerous. In Durham, North Carolina, for example, the Psychical Research Foundation operates as a spin-off from Dr. Rhine and his group of researchers at Duke University. In its laboratories, W. G. Roll, a philosopher, and Dr. Robert Morris, a psychologist, are investigating "out of body experiences," known as astral travel. Also in Durham is Dr. Ed Kelly, who is conducting computerized card-guessing experiments with a Yale Law School student, who appears to be a gifted psychic.

Finding out more about psi means finding and working with psychics. Who is most likely to be psychic? Dr. Gertrude Schmeidler of the City University of New York has been conducting an extensive study of the personality of persons with greater-than-average psychic talents. She has found them generally to be outgoing, self-confident, sensitive, and warm people. They also have good memories—especially when it comes to recalling their dreams.

"SENDING" A PICTURE

Dreams have played a major role in psychic research, especially at Maimonides Medical Center in Brooklyn. Approximately 15 years ago, Dr. Montague Ullman had the then-wild idea that

Some parapsychologists are interested in Kirlian photography, a technique that involves photographing high-frequency electric discharges from the surfaces of objects.

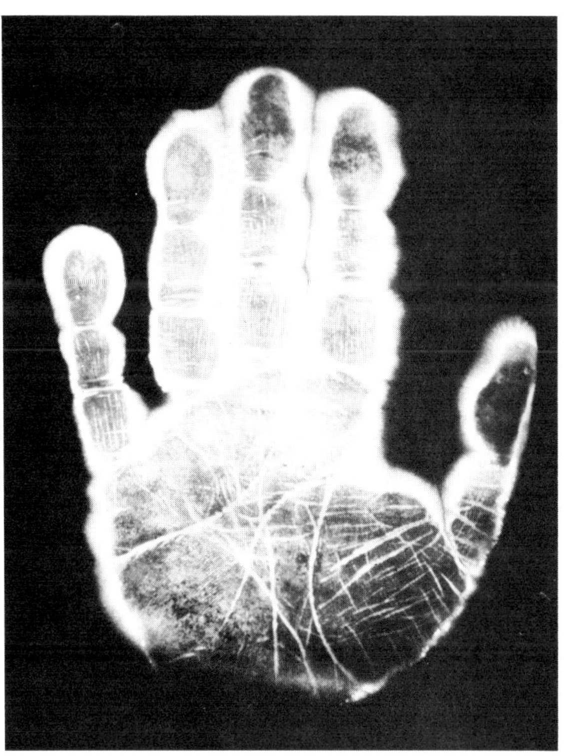

telepathy could be induced during a dream—when the mind is in an "altered state of consciousness." His laboratory is now called the Division of Parapsychology and Psychophysics. The research performed there by Dr. Ullman and associates Charles Honorton and Dr. Stanley Krippner has attracted much attention. The three researchers have been attempting to show how ESP works, not that it works.

Here is how one ESP and dream study works: The person being studied—the subject—sleeps at the dream lab. Electrodes attached to his scalp provide an indication to the researchers in the next room when the subject is dreaming. At the end of each dream, a researcher wakens the subject, who then reports his dream into a tape recorder.

Meanwhile, throughout the night, a "sender" sits a considerable distance away, focusing his attention on an art print he has chosen that night from a selection of four pictures. Only the "sender" knows which of the four prints he has chosen.

In the morning, the subject is given his taped recordings to review, and all four pictures. More often than not, the picture the subject chooses as the one he believes matches his dreams is the one the "sender" chose and focused on.

According to the dream lab researchers, these experiments show that altered states of consciousness, such as dreaming, make ESP events, such as telepathy, possible. The mind is more "receptive" then, they say. As a result of the dream experiments, the researchers are now studying other altered states of consciousness and ESP.

In some of these experiments, the subject's eyes and ears are covered so he cannot see or hear. In others, the subject is suspended in a sort of "cradle" in a lightless, soundproof room. After several minutes of not seeing, hearing, or feeling, the subject begins to hear and see things that are not in the room. A part of all these experiments is the "sender"—a student, scientist, or other volunteer—who sits a considerable distance away, viewing a picture he has chosen.

In one series of these experiments, the subjects saw the picture the senders were looking at 76 per cent of the time, the researchers reported. In another experiment, when the expected chance level was 25 per cent accuracy, the subjects scored 43 per cent.

A SETBACK

Researchers are also exploring psi abilities in other animals. But one such researcher is believed to have caused a setback in the field of psychic research. Dr. Jay Levy, until recently the director of the Institute for Parapsychology in Durham, had devised a complicated experiment to test whether rats possess the power of psychokinesis. He published reports maintaining that rats do have this power. But in the middle of 1974, other scientists at the Institute reported that they had discovered that Dr. Levy was "faking" his experimental results.

"This whole thing serves as a reminder that you can't always take research findings at face value," said Dr. Robert Morris, president of the Parapsychology Association.

Many serious psi researchers feel that they won't be able to offset this scandal for some time. And they're afraid that other scientists who didn't quite believe in psi research before definitely do not believe in it now. Research, they believe, is going to be more demanding than ever.

PSI CULTS

While philosophers, psychologists, physicists, and even magicians continue to work in laboratories investigating the mysteries of psi, thousands of people are finding out for themselves what psi may be all about. They are flocking to people who promise to teach them how to alter their states of consciousness and open their minds to new forces.

Most people who are excited about the psychic get involved in transcendental meditation, yoga, hypnosis, scientology, or biofeedback.

Ex-astronaut Mitchell feels, as do many other psi believers, that most programs or

Famous parapsychologist J. B. Rhine and his wife, Louisa, at the Foundation for Research on the Nature of Man in Durham, North Carolina.

movements that end up being a "cult" with followers dependent on one person are harmful or even dangerous. "Ideally," Mitchell said, "a person should sample the techniques used to open the mind by each of these organizations and then move on to another."

But even this, according to Dr. Allen Cohen, might not be safe. He explained: "Some groups have learned how to open a person's mind up, but then they simply don't have the spiritual direction or depth to give the person direction. Some end up hurting a lot of people." Dr. Cohen, who is director of a drug-abuse institute at the John F. Kennedy University in Martinez, California, has seen psychic study and experiences replace dependence on and interest in drugs. Many drug experts are learning that the expanded consciousness that comes with psychic experiences is the alternative to drugs for many young people. Dr. Cohen foresees laws by the late 1970's to regulate psychic experience and abuses, just as we now have laws to regulate drugs that change our perception of things.

Most commercial operations get little support from the federal government and psi researchers. In fact, at the 1975 AAAS meeting researchers warned the public against psychic fraud. According to Dr. Honorton, serious parapsychology research confines itself to scientific laboratories and excludes persons seeking publicity. And the experiments can be repeated only in other laboratories by other scientists—not the mass public.

Dr. Rex Stanford of St. John's University in Jamaica, New York, who studies psi research and whose twin is a gifted psychic, focused on biofeedback and alpha states, at the AAAS meeting. He criticized the so-called mind control courses that teach a person to get his mind in the alpha state. Supposedly, when the brain produces alpha waves it is in its most receptive and creative state. According to Dr. Stanford, no one has proved a relationship between alpha waves and psi ability. He calls these mind-control courses bizarre and dangerous.

GUIDELINES

A panel of AAAS researchers did come up with guidelines for the public. First, beware of anyone who succeeds in demonstrating psi ability again and again in public. That person is more likely a magician than a true psychic. Second, beware of people who have psychic phenomena simply labeled into "states,"

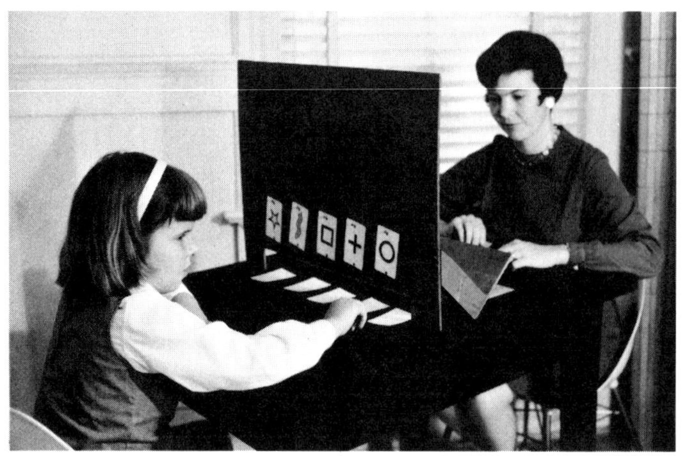

A young child being tested for ESP, or extrasensory perception, one of the categories of psi.

"stages," and "dimensions." Psi is not, scientists believe, that easily controlled and categorized. And third, beware of political predictions, especially if first announced after the fact. The person making the prediction might have inside information, or the prediction may be ambiguous—and therefore never subject to being proved incorrect.

Knowing what is truly a psi phenomenon and what is magic or trickery is difficult even for scientists. While some parapsychology researchers were suggesting these guidelines, others reported bizarre experimental discoveries. These included mice being healed psychically and baby chicks that could perform psychokinesis.

EXCITING POSSIBILITIES

With all this research and demonstration of psychic abilities and talents, where do we stand today?

The Soviet Union and the United States lead the world in the amount of attention paid to psi study, and yet explanations of what is "going on" physically are still to come from researchers in those nations. No one knows the physical nature of psychic phenomena.

But almost everyone agrees that the psi revolution presents exciting possibilities. Regardless of how the experiments with Geller eventually turn out, they represent a significant change in scientific attitudes toward a subject that was once regarded as a joke.

Some people see psychic phenomena as Sigmund Freud, the father of psychotherapy, did. Freud suggested that psi phenomena are fading. He believed that all humans once had these powers, such as telepathy, but began to lose them as we evolved and developed other methods of communication. Freud saw ESP as a way for humans to communicate before we developed our present methods—our present five senses.

Is psi growing and developing, as many people believe? Or, is it fading, as Freud believed? Will you some day communicate through telepathic messages with a friend? Or, will a technologically advanced telephone with viewing screen be "the way" of the 21st century? Researchers don't know now, but they are definitely interested in trying to find out□

SELECTED READINGS

Experimental Parapsychology by K. Ramakrishna Rao. Charles C. Thomas, 1966.

From Anecdote to Experiment in Psychical Research by Robert H. Thouless. Routledge & Kegan Paul, 1972.

Mind Over Matter by Louisa E. Rhine. Macmillan, 1970.

New Directions in Parapsychology by John Beloff. Elek Science, 1974.

"New Flap Over Uri." *Time*, Nov. 4, 1974.

Parapsychology: Frontier Science of the Mind by J. B. Rhine and J. G. Pratt. Charles C. Thomas, 1957.

"Psychokinetic Fraud." *Scientific American*, September 1974.

Shoplifting

by Ann W. Appelbaum, M.D.
and Herbert Klemmer, M.D.

Trying to avoid being caught, a shoplifter sneaks a glance at clerks before taking slacks off the rack of a dry goods store and putting them into a shopping bag.

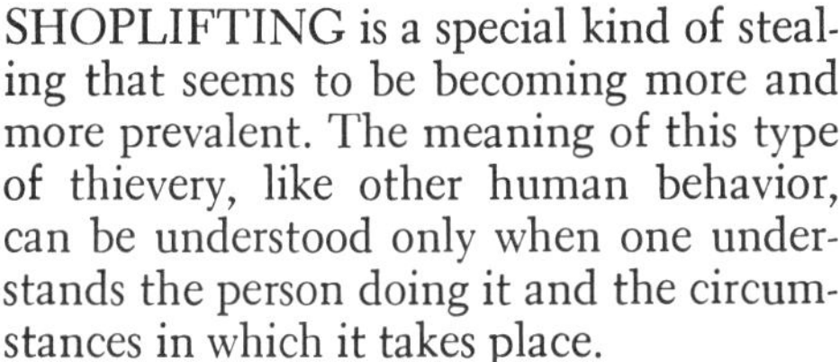

SHOPLIFTING is a special kind of stealing that seems to be becoming more and more prevalent. The meaning of this type of thievery, like other human behavior, can be understood only when one understands the person doing it and the circumstances in which it takes place.

In our society, for example, we prepare children to be competitive. We place high value on money and material possessions. Nevertheless, our society is paradoxical because, with all our affluence, many people still cannot acquire enough money and material goods to satisfy their basic needs. As a result they feel helpless and frustrated. Our society is also increasingly unstable. The contradictory forces of economics and morals clash, and the search for power increasingly seems to dictate actions and undermine values.

The causes of shoplifting may be grouped as primarily social or psychological. Keep in mind, however, that causes rarely exist in pure form but usually are mingled.

POVERTY AND REBELLION

Some of the social causes of shoplifting are familiar to everyone. One example is poverty with its accompanying despair and rage. In the 19th-century French novel *Les Misérables* by Victor Hugo, Jean Valjean, basically a normal and healthy man, stole the bishop's silverware to keep from starving. So today basically healthy people can be driven to steal because they and their families are desperate and in need.

Groups of children and teenagers sometimes take up shoplifting as a competitive sport. The object is to see how much one can get away with, and kids are pressured by one another to take chances. It is a way for the youngster to raise his status with his peers. It is also a way to rebel against the rules set down by parents, teachers, and others in authority. A youngster may also see it as a way of defining himself as an independent person, no longer tied to mother's apron strings.

Something similar takes place in groups of adults who feel that they are an oppressed minority with the right to steal from the society that oppresses them. Here again, shoplifting does not necessarily indicate psychological illness. Rather, it expresses the shoplifter's identification with a group rebelling against society, completely rejecting "the establishment's" rules and standards.

OUT OF TOUCH

What so often puzzles law enforcement officials as well as the general public is that a great many individual acts of shoplifting cannot be attributed to a social cause, such as poverty or belonging to a criminal group. More often than not, the offender does not need what he steals, and he is usually able to pay for it. The wealthy are shoplifters too.

The psychological causes of shoplifting are not always complex. For example, the offender may not know what is expected of him. A three-year-old child who pockets an item from the grocery shelf doesn't understand the meaning or the consequences of his act. Nor does a mentally retarded adult. The same holds true for the absent-minded pilfering that almost everyone can engage in when preoccupied and temporarily out of touch with what is expected of him at the moment. Many a person has returned home from the grocer's to find something that he picked up without paying for. Whether or not the person promptly makes good his mistake depends on his integrity. Most healthy adults return or pay for the item.

A safety-detection mirror in a supermarket reveals a shoplifter in the act of stuffing a can of hair spray into her roomy handbag.

POOR IMPULSE CONTROL

Poor impulse control is a common personality defect that some authorities believe is more common currently than it may have been half a century ago when people were brought up with greater strictness. Certainly children whose parents have never consistently expected them to stick to the rules, to wait their turn or to tolerate frustration when necessary do not develop the internal controls that prevent them from taking what they want without considering the consequences.

Beyond these defects in upbringing, however, there are many people who, from birth, show great difficulty in tolerating frustration. As adults they typically act before they think. Often they develop various rationalizations to ward off the loss of self-esteem and the accompanying feelings of guilt and shame for their ill-considered actions.

Many shoplifters fall into this category. They may say they shoplift to get back at society, to fit into their group, or to show their courage. But the fact is that they simply can't help it. These people also show a great many other kinds of impulsive behavior besides shoplifting.

ANTISOCIAL PERSONALITIES

There are other shoplifters who are psychologically very ill but who don't exhibit clear-cut symptoms of mental illness. Nevertheless they commit a broad variety of antisocial acts without feeling concern or guilt. The causes of this personality disorder are not well understood. Certainly not all people who commit antisocial acts are antisocial, or sociopathic, personalities. On the contrary, many antisocial acts are committed by people who already feel extremely guilty and are seeking punishment. This is not true of the antisocial personality. These individuals may be extremely skillful at avoiding punishment and certainly do not seek it. They are resentful when apprehended and punished, because they assume they have a perfect right to do as they please no matter how much they may harm others.

Above: in an "inside job," a clerk in a camera store is wrapping merchandise for an accomplice. Right: meanwhile the transaction is seen by the store's manager on closed-circuit TV installed to prevent thefts.

A DEEP GRUDGE

Still other shoplifters are people who harbor deep unconscious feelings of envy and deprivation. These hidden feelings impel them toward shoplifting. Shoplifting may be their only obvious symptom of emotional disturbance; otherwise they may have generally high moral standards and good self-control. When apprehended, these people are at a loss to account for their actions. Usually they don't need the object they steal. However, the stolen item often has some special emotional significance of which they are unaware.

For example, a woman who believes she is ugly and unlovable may steal cosmetics or pretty lingerie even though she is quite able to afford them. By doing this she takes, by force, things that she somehow feels she has a right to have. Careful psychological study of such unhappy people often reveals a deep grudge against the mother who didn't bestow upon them the attributes they feel they should have. For these individuals, shoplifting fulfills the dual function of getting back at the mother as well as taking what they feel is rightfully theirs.

TO BE PUNISHED

In others, shoplifting may be one of several antisocial acts carried out in an effort to be caught and punished. In a sense it is penance for other unconscious "crimes"—such as forbidden masturbation and feelings of hatred toward brothers and sisters or parents. The guilt associated with these childhood acts and feelings may linger deep inside a person throughout his life. This hidden guilt eventually may lead him to behavior that elicits punishment from the people who represent his parents—shop owners, the law, or society itself.

OTHER CAUSES

A certain amount of shoplifting is done by people who are under the influence of drugs or alcohol. Shoplifting also may be part of a broad range of symptoms in individuals who are out of touch with reality because of severe mental disorders. Such people may feel that higher forces command them to commit certain acts, or that by stealing they are stamping out the evil in society. Some may even believe something unfortunate may happen to them unless they fulfill their needs by whatever measures they deem necessary.

Sometimes shoplifting is associated with severe emotional illnesses in which the major symptoms are alternating periods of overeating and self-starvation. These patients may be quite aware that shoplifting is against the law, yet they are driven to it by the irrational fear of starvation or by overwhelming attacks of greed, against which they are unable to struggle successfully.

TREATMENT

The way one handles a shoplifter should depend upon one's understanding of the individual case. A small child should be dealt with through his parents. A group of children who have taken up shoplifting as a sport are best dealt with by working with their parents as a group. Skilled social workers often are able to be extremely helpful in these cases. Referring families to the mental health center in the community is a good way to deal with a group of young shoplifters.

Teenagers usually are much more responsive to one another than they are to adults and sometimes are helped by group psychotherapy. If such an approach is contemplated by the court, however, it is wise to decide on the appropriate punishment first, carry it out, and *then* see what can be done to provide the youngsters with an opportunity to help each other stay out of trouble in the future. An understanding judge can do a great deal to prevent further lawbreaking among adolescent groups.

Any apparently normal person apprehended for shoplifting more than once should have the benefit of psychological examination before being sentenced. If the person is found to be suffering from impaired impulse control, he may be helped by psychological treatment. If the disorder is severe, he might even need to be hospitalized.

The sociopathic shoplifter lacks interest in changing his behavior and thus is not receptive to psychological treatment. Neither psychiatry nor the law has yet found an adequate way to deal with this disorder.

A great number of offenders who shoplift because of needs and fears hidden even from themselves stop stealing after being caught the first time. Some, however, cannot stop. They are driven by irrational forces to risk punishment again and again. Punishment does not help these individuals, but often they do benefit from skillful psychotherapy.

The more serious cases of shoplifting, in which offenders have severe mental illness, toxic conditions, or even certain forms of epilepsy, are usually so obvious that the offenders are referred by the courts to medical or psychiatric facilities.

It is interesting to speculate why more people do not steal—especially when faced with the contradictions within our society. Certainly the majority are not prevented merely by the fear of punishment. It seems that, in the past, we have relied on the development of a special kind of social conscience that tells us that it is not right to do certain things. Now it seems that many people think the opposite. Psychiatric treatment can sometimes alleviate, but not always solve, the problem. Preventive measures are desperately needed even though they are untested. What we do know is that such measures cannot be given a fair trial until the social factors involved have been corrected□

SELECTED READINGS

"Truth About Teenage Shoplifting" by G. W. Weinstein. *Parents' Magazine*, April 1974.

Animal Behavior

by M. A. Freiberg and J. A. Roze

AN opossum closes its eyes and lies very still. A chameleon suddenly changes its color. A chimpanzee punches keys on a computer.

All startling and fascinating observations of animal behavior. Is the opossum dead? How can an animal change its body color? An intelligent chimpanzee?

The observation of how animals behave is probably one of the oldest sciences. Indeed the survival of early man depended to a large extent on his observation of animals. He needed animals for food, for clothing, and for shelter. And he had to protect himself from attacking animals.

Today, man is becoming more and more aware that he must live in harmony with all forms of life and with his natural surroundings. For his own survival and for the survival of many animals, man must prevent further destruction of the environment. Many species of animals have already become extinct because their environment has been changed. The passenger pigeon is an example. The feeding and migrating habits of the passenger pigeon were interfered with. It became extinct: the last individual—named Martha—died in the Cincinnati Zoo on Sept. 1, 1914.

Many species of birds engage in complex courtship rituals. Upper: male frigate bird proudly displays bright red inflated throat pouch. Lower: courting albatrosses.

INSTINCT OR LEARNING

The study of animal behavior is called *ethology*. For many years this science has been divided into two main schools of thought—one stresses heredity, the other emphasizes learning.

Early in the 20th century some keen observers noticed that every species has definite ways of acting in certain situations. Each species seems to have inherited a certain way of acting. These ways are called *fixed action patterns*.

Ethology, the study of animal behavior, is also the name most often used for the school of thought that stresses the importance of heredity in animal behavior. One of the most important scientists in this field is the Austrian biologist Konrad Lorenz.

Ethology is based largely on the idea that an animal must be observed in its natural surroundings. A duck must be observed in a pond, a penguin in the Antarctic region, a camel in the desert. Only when an animal is in its natural surroundings, or habitat, can we see how that animal responds to its environment. How does a duck act when it can no longer find food in its pond or when other ducks are put into the pond? Ethologists believe that the way an animal acts—its fixed action patterns—is as important a characteristic of the animal as its shape or

Lionfish, brightly striped, has long sharp spines with which it fends off enemies.

how its body functions. For example, pigeons suck water, while most other birds lift their heads and swallow water.

Other scientists take a different approach to the study of animal behavior. They stress the importance of learning in animal behavior. This school of thought is called behavioral psychology or comparative psychology. Behavioral psychologists explain how an animal learns to act in certain situations in its environment. Like ethologists, they also study animals in their natural environment but will also study them under laboratory conditions.

The Russian physiologist Ivan Pavlov did much to further this way of thinking. In a famous series of experiments, Pavlov rang a bell each time he put food out for dogs. After this process was repeated several times, the dogs began to connect the sound of the bell with food. Then whenever the bell sounded, the dogs expected food. In fact, they even salivated, waiting for food. The dogs continued this response to the sound of the bell even after food was no longer offered. The dogs had developed a *conditioned reflex*. The dogs had learned, or were conditioned into, a certain way of behaving by the repetition of a certain stimulus—the bell—and a certain reward—food. Later, other experiments showed that similar conditioned reflexes could be developed in other animals using other stimuli.

The two schools of thought try different approaches to explain behavior. Both present accurate points and must be considered together to get a full picture of behavior. For the ethologists, behavior is "written down" before birth. It is inherited, not primarily learned. The animal acts by instinct in a certain way that is determined before its birth.

For behavioral psychologists, behavior is learned. External stimuli determine the reflexes and development of behavior.

Today we know that both automatic reflexes and learning are important in the development of behavior.

CERTAIN COMMON FEATURES OF BEHAVIOR

Behavior differs with each species. As some observers were quick to point out, certain patterns of behavior can be as important a characteristic of an animal species as the animal's body form. Certain types of behavior, however, occur in many species. Animals communicate with each other, defend themselves, mate, and produce young. A brief look at how some animals go about these activities will show us some common features of behavior.

HOW ANIMALS "TALK" TO EACH OTHER

Animals communicate, or "talk," to each other through signals. Each animal uses certain signals to communicate with other members of its species. It uses these signals to recognize other members of its species, to attract mates, to call for food, to warn of danger, and for other reasons. The signals differ with the species.

Calls and songs are important ways of communicating. A hen "talks" to her baby chicks with several types of calls. Among fur seals, cows, goats, rabbits and many other species, mother and young communicate by voice signals. Other animals "call" other members of their species when they find food. They also warn others of danger. A prairie dog, for example, will give an alarm call if it sees danger, thus telling others to take cover.

Vocal noises are also a very important way of communicating between the sexes. Some species have definite vocal calls or songs in courtship. Male frogs, for example, peep and croak during the mating season. Females recognize the croaks of their own species and go to find the male. Many birds "sing" to attract mates.

Odor is another way of signaling. Many mammals "mark off" a territory, or home region that they consider theirs, by odor. They urinate around the boundary of their region. The odor tells other animals not to intrude. Odor is also often a sexual message. The male silkworm moth has an extremely sensitive sense of smell. He will pick up the odor of a female at a distance of 3.2 km (2 mi) and follow the odor.

Some species have developed very unusual ways of communicating. Bees, for example, use various "dances" to tell other members of their hive where food is. A bee who has found a food source returns to the hive and performs a "dance." The form of the dance tells other hive members the direction of the food and how far away it is. Dances are also a part of courtship for many.

TO LIVE ALONE OR IN A GROUP

Some animals live alone, avoiding contact with other members of their species, except in the mating season. Other animals typically live in a group. Some animal groups—a school of herring, for example—may include several thousand individuals, none of which is the leader. They all just live and travel together. In other groups, such as a flock of sheep, there is one leader, and all other members of the group follow. In a flock of chickens, there is a "pecking order." The hen leader pecks all members of the flock without being pecked back. The next ranking hen pecks all but the leader and so on.

In other types of animal groups, there is a complicated social organization. Ants, for example, live in large colonies that have a complex organization. Each member has a special job and rank.

Baboon group life has been the subject of much study. Generally, one older male baboon is the acknowledged head of the group. He is supported by a core of "central males"—elder statesmen, so to speak. Younger males and adolescent males fight for rank and for the females. The females are protected by the males and spend most of their time caring for and playing with the young. Each member knows its place within the group. Rank is recognized through different types of rituals, such as grooming. A lower-ranking group member will groom a higher ranking individual of the group.

TO BUILD A HOME OR TO WANDER

Some animals build permanent elaborate homes. Bees, for example, live in large colonies and build complicated hives. The hives may have many connecting rooms and passageways, with some of these rooms used as nurseries and some for honey.

Beavers are well known for their home-building talents. They typically use sticks and mud to build a dam and a comfortable lodge along a stream. They are able to fell trees with a diameter of 45 cm (18 in) to use for their homes. They hide the entrance to their lodge and store food in the lodge for use during the winter months when they hibernate.

Other animals make use of "temporary" homes. A hermit crab, for example, uses

Land hermit crab emerging from snail shell it has used as a temporary home.

Hognose snake avoids battle with an enemy—it simply rolls over and plays dead.

the empty shell of a sea snail as a home. As the crab grows too large for the shell, he simply moves to another, larger, temporary home.

Still other animals, most typically fishes and birds, move about almost constantly, stopping only for nest building.

Many vertebrate, or backboned, animals and at least some lower animals establish a home territory even if they don't build a home. For some species, the territory is a certain area that the animal or animals living together consider their own—where they live, eat, sleep, reproduce, and raise their young. Other species establish a territory only during the breeding season. For them the territory is the area for courtship, mating, and the care of the young. For a lizard the home territory may be simply a small area around a tree log. For a mountain lion the territory may be very large—almost 39 km^2 (15 mi^2). Most animals defend their territories from intruders, using various forms of attack to do so.

Some animals have two widely different home regions, like winter and summer homes. Birds such as the Canada goose, sandpiper, and the arctic tern often travel tremendous distances and have remarkable abilities to sense direction between their two homes. Lemmings and some other mammals also migrate between two home regions.

HIDING FROM AN ENEMY

Every animal must protect itself. For some animals this means hiding from an enemy or trying to fool it. Some play dead. The opossum, for example, closes his eyes and lies very still even if bitten gently. An attacking enemy thinks the opossum is dead, loses interest, and moves on. The hognose snake is another animal that "plays dead."

Other animals hide by blending into their background. This type of behavior is called camouflage. The green mantis, for example, has a long narrow green body. It looks like a blade of grass. In a similar way, the brown mantis blends in among twigs. The vine snake of the American tropics is another example. It looks like a hanging branch or jungle vine and moves gently as if it were a branch swaying in the wind. Among many animals, the arrangement of bands or stripes, the shape of parts of their bodies, and their overall coloring all serve to camouflage them.

Some animals are even able to change their color to match the background. Some fish are especially known for this ability. The Nassau grouper can change its color into eight different patterns in a few minutes. It changes color to match the tropical reef background of its habitat. Chameleons are well known for their ability to change color, although other lizards are even better at it. The little tree lizard *Anolis* can change very rapidly from dark brown to green.

WARNING AN ENEMY

Other animals do not hide from an enemy but warn it of their own dangerous nature. In that way they often avoid attack. Here again, color is one method used. The North American cottonmouth, for example, assumes a threat posture and opens its mouth wide revealing a white lining that contrasts with the snake's darkly patterned body. The South American frog *Dendrobates tinctorius* is very brightly colored and makes no effort to hide itself. Its bright coloring warns other animals of its very dangerous, highly venomous, nature.

Some animals use other methods to warn or threaten an enemy. Cobras, for example, often spread their head region into a "hood" shortly before striking. During the mating season male birds often erect head feathers, call, and show other signs that attract a female but also warn all other males to stay away.

DEFENSE AND ATTACK

Some animals try to get away from danger as fast as possible. Some—the impala, the deer, the rabbit, and many others—can often outrun their attackers. Birds take to the air, flying away from a ground attacker. Some small animals flee into burrows, thickets, or small openings where larger predators cannot follow them.

In some cases, animals cannot hide from or avoid attack, and they themselves seek out battle. Each species has certain ways of fighting, and most are equipped with certain "weapons." Some snakes, for example, inject a poisonous venom that paralyzes or kills a victim. Many mammals and lower animals have very sharp teeth, and some have sharp claws and sharp horns. Birds often use their beaks in fighting.

TRYING TO FIND A MATE

During the breeding season many species use different methods to attract a mate. As mentioned before, some animals, such as frogs, use vocal signals to call and attract a mate. Some, such as the silkworm moth and snakes, use odor to attract and find a mate.

Many animals use camouflage for protection. Right: a blenny blending into its background. Lower left: Stick insect—its long, thin, brownish body just like a stick or twig. Lower right: chameleon closely matching the green of the leaf.

In still other species, elaborate courtship rituals have been developed. In many birds, for example, the males are brightly colored. At the mating season, the males display their colorful feathers. Some, such as the peacock, open and erect special feathers to attract attention. Others like the grouse have colored sacs on each side of the head. They quickly inflate and deflate the sacs, making an audible noise to attract mates. Some male and female birds also engage in mutual pecking, nibbling, and dancing before mating.

Complex courtship rituals are not limited to birds. Some snakes perform complicated and very graceful dances before mating. In some species of spiders, males must perform a fixed courtship dance as they approach the females or else risk being eaten by the females. Some fish also perform certain rituals. The stickleback male, for example, dances around the female and then begins to nibble at her tail to nudge her into the nest he has built.

NEST BUILDING AND CARE OF THE YOUNG

In many kinds of animals the young must care for themselves shortly after they hatch from eggs or are born. In other species, however, one or both of the parents build a nest and care for and protect the young for a period of time.

Nest building is most elaborate among birds. The nests may be built on the ground or in a tree, or they may hang from a roof or branch. Some species construct the nests of twigs and leaves and carefully line them with feathers. Once the eggs are laid, one parent, usually the female, incubates the eggs. Sometimes, the male supplies the female with food while she incubates the eggs. As the young hatch the parents may give them food, often food that has been partially chewed.

The stickleback fish mentioned earlier also constructs an elaborate nest. The male builds the nest of plantlike material and glues it together with a threadlike substance that he secretes from his own kidney. After the female lays the eggs, he swims around them. Later he cares for the young.

Other animals have different ways of taking care of their young. Among ants and bees, certain members of each colony have the task of caring for the young. Kangaroos, opossum, and a few other mammals keep their newborn in a special pouch on the front of the mother's body.

A cardinal feeding its young in a well-concealed cup-shaped nest.

ARE ANIMALS INTELLIGENT?

Intelligence is a very difficult word to define. It is sometimes explained as the ability to learn, or as the ability to respond to new circumstances, or as the ability to solve a problem. But these explanations do not really define the word. Learning, response to a situation, and problem solving can all exist without true intelligence. Intelligence, as we are using the word, is probably best defined as the ability to reason.

Many animals can learn certain ways of behaving. Like Pavlov's dog, they can be "taught" a particular way of acting. Many animals can also be presented with a problem and solve it through trial and error.

Scientists have developed several ways of testing an animal's ability to learn, to respond to circumstances, to adapt, to have an idea, and to reason. In most cases the tests reveal that animals develop conditioned reflexes or learn by repeated trial and error experiences and not through intelligence. A brief explanation of some of the tests will help explain the ability of some animals and also the nature of intelligence.

Pygmy marmoset being given a three-object discrimination test. Tests such as this are being used to determine the intelligence and learning ability of many animals.

LEARNING THROUGH TRIAL AND ERROR

Many tests involve the use of a maze. A rat or other test animal is placed at the entrance of a maze. It must find the exit. As the animal moves along the maze, it finds a series of branches or forks. It must decide which fork to take. If it chooses the wrong fork and comes to a dead end, it must go back and try the other fork. It continues until it reaches the exit. After many errors the animal "learns" how to go through the maze without any wrong turns.

Some mazes are simple. Some are difficult, involving as many as 25 turns. Animals vary greatly in how quickly they learn how to go through a particular maze. In at least one test, white rats did better than college students. However, this proved only that rats are good at learning through repeated trial and error. It did not prove intelligence.

SOLVING A PROBLEM AND "REMEMBERING" THE SOLUTION

In another type of test, animals must solve a particular problem. Some birds, squirrels, cats, and other animals have learned to open a door, open a lock, or solve other "problems" to get at what they want—usually food. Still other tests determine whether an animal is just repeating a certain way of acting or whether it can remember a correct way. For example, can an animal, once it has learned the answer to a problem, remember the answer and use it at a later date? Monkeys seemed to do well in these types of tests.

Such abilities are impressive. Even more impressive is adaptability. Some scientists think adaptability shows at least some intelligence. Monkeys seem to be able to adapt: they are able to change their normal patterns of behavior to adjust to new situations. When monkeys were presented with a series of problems, they solved the problems through trial and error, but each time they were given a new problem, they solved it faster and faster. In other words, the monkeys learned how to solve problems; they learned how to learn.

TO USE A TOOL

For many years the use of tools was considered a sign of intelligence. In fact, for many years scientists who trace the history of early man considered the use of tools as the beginning of modern man. Recent research, however, has cast some doubt on whether tool use can be considered a sign of high intelligence.

Primates are a group of animals that includes monkeys, chimpanzees, and large apes as well as man. Some primates, beside man, can use tools, and so can some other mammals and at least one bird.

Chimpanzees put in a room where food is placed on a high shelf, too high for

Family group of Gibraltar apes. Rank in a social group is recognized through certain rituals, such as the grooming seen here.

them to reach, will pile boxes one on top of the other and then climb on the boxes to reach the food. The chimps, in other words, adapt to the situation and solve the problem by using the boxes as tools to get what they want. If necessary, they will carry tool use another step. After piling up the boxes and climbing on them, they will use a stick to pull the wanted food closer to them.

Sea otters also use tools. They favor clams as food. A sea otter will hold the clams against its chest and use a rock to smash open the shell. In a very surprising finding, scientists at the University of Massachusetts have shown that a northern blue jay will use a feather or straw to rake food pellets closer to its cage where it can then reach them. Such findings hint that tool use is probably more widespread than has been thought.

USE OF SYMBOLS AND OF LANGUAGE

The understanding of symbols shows an ability at abstract reasoning. Chimpanzees were given a series of tests involving the use of a vending machine and poker chips. The chimps learned that one grape came out of the machine each time they put a white chip into a slot. They next learned that two grapes came out when they used a blue chip. The chimps soon learned that blue chips were more valuable. They also learned that a red chip brought water, and they used it when they were thirsty. This experiment showed that the chimpanzees were able to understand symbols—in this case, chips. One color chip symbolized, or stood for, one thing, another for something else. The chimps understood this and remembered it at least for a time.

The understanding of symbols is essential for the use of language. In a series of experiments being conducted in several centers throughout the United States, chimpanzees are being taught language. Not a verbal language, but a sign language. Some of the chimps, including one called Washoe, is being taught American Sign Language (ASL), the same language that deaf people use. Other chimps are being taught to "read" plastic chips that symbolize different words. And another chimp, named Lana, has been taught a special language, called Yerkish, which she uses on a special computer typewriter.

INBORN ABILITY PLUS LEARNING

Adaptability, the use of tools, the understanding of symbols, and, lastly, language—all seem to be signs of intelligence. The field of exploring animal intelligence is fascinating. Animals are being observed in their natural habitat to see if they naturally display signs of intelligent behavior. Animals are also being taught in laboratories to see what they can learn□

The Marvels of Animal Behavior by National Geographic Book Service. National Geographic Society, 1972.

biology

Snowball, the first polar bear to be born at New York's Bronx Zoo, goes on public display at the age of about five months. Olga, the mother, towers above and lets no one near—and so Snowball's sex is not known.

review of the year

biology

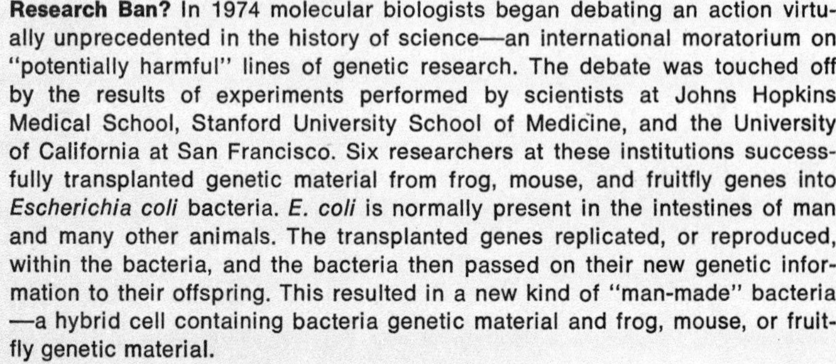

Research Ban? In 1974 molecular biologists began debating an action virtually unprecedented in the history of science—an international moratorium on "potentially harmful" lines of genetic research. The debate was touched off by the results of experiments performed by scientists at Johns Hopkins Medical School, Stanford University School of Medicine, and the University of California at San Francisco. Six researchers at these institutions successfully transplanted genetic material from frog, mouse, and fruitfly genes into *Escherichia coli* bacteria. *E. coli* is normally present in the intestines of man and many other animals. The transplanted genes replicated, or reproduced, within the bacteria, and the bacteria then passed on their new genetic information to their offspring. This resulted in a new kind of "man-made" bacteria—a hybrid cell containing bacteria genetic material and frog, mouse, or fruitfly genetic material.

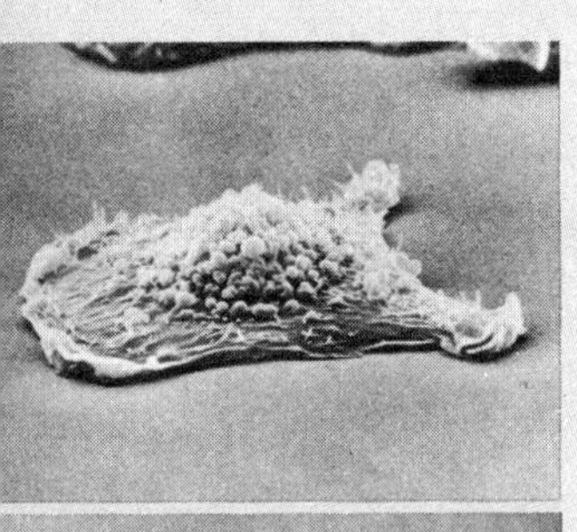

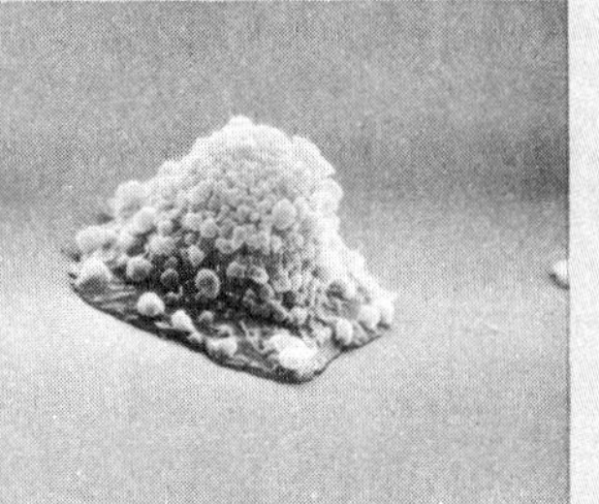

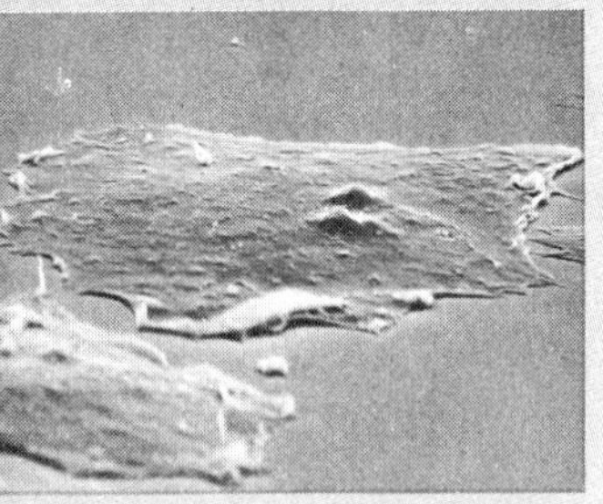

Scanning electron micrographs of a mouse cell. Top: whole cell. Middle: isolated nucleus surrounded by small amount of cytoplasm. Bottom: cytoplast, or enucleated cell.

The implications and promises of this discovery excite many researchers. Some hope it could shed light on the processes that control genes function. Others see these hybrid cells as tools in cancer research. Practical applications of the research have also been foreseen. For example, the gene responsible for the production of the hormone insulin could be transplanted from human cells to bacteria. The insulin molecules produced could then be inexpensively harvested from the bacteria and used as a drug to treat diabetes. However, a committee of renowned molecular biologists, backed by the U.S. National Academy of Sciences, decided that the potential risks of this line of research outweigh its promises at this time. Among the committee members are four scientists who were involved in the original research. These scientists fear the creation of super-bacteria that could carry new types of infections and other diseases which could provoke epidemics and be resistant to all known forms of medical treatment. The committee asked all scientists to voluntarily refrain from experimenting with genetic transplants until the public hazards could be assessed.

Genetics. The puzzle of how genes are turned "on" and "off" is well on its way to being solved. Every body cell in an organism has an identical genetic makeup. Yet, most of the genes in most cells are turned "off" most of the time. For example, a nerve cell is specialized to conduct impulses and its genetic ability to be a muscle cell or blood cell is turned "off." What turns "on" a particular gene so that a cell has a specialized function—for example, as part of an eye and not as part of a kidney? Dr. Gobind Khorana, a 1968 Nobel Prize winner, and his colleagues at Massachusetts Institute of Technology have succeeded in synthesizing the double-stranded DNA (deoxyribonucleic acid) that makes up one gene in the common bacterium *E. coli*. The gene is made up of 126 units called nucleotides, and the researchers have recently identified 29 nucleotide units that they believe make up most, and perhaps all, of the "on" switch, and are part of the "off" switch. The next step is to synthesize the "on" and "off" switches and link them to the already synthesized gene. If this gene then operates in a colony of growing bacteria, the first "functioning man-made" gene will have been created.

Other researchers at Harvard University, the Laboratory of Molecular Biology in Cambridge, England, and the University of Cologne, Germany, have also made headway in understanding the "on" and "off" switches of genes. These researchers have been studying a gene in *E. coli* and a gene in the lambda virus. They have identified the chemical sequences of the "on" and "off" switches and have discovered that chemicals in the cell's environment can control these switches.

Scientists at the University of Colorado at Boulder succeeded in taking living mouse cells apart—separating the nuclei and cytoplasm—and putting them back together, in laboratory flasks, within a span of several hours. The researchers plan to transfer nuclei from normal cells to cancer cells, and from young cells to aged cells. They hope to answer two questions: Will a normal nucleus make a cancer cell normal? And, will a young nucleus make an old cell young?

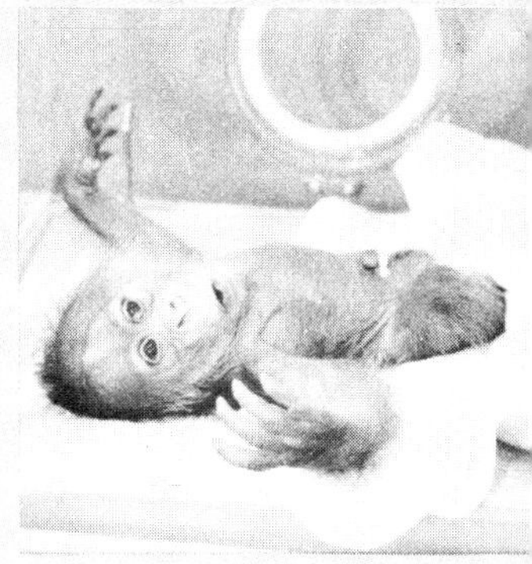

An infant orangutan, the subject of scientific research at Yerkes Primate Research Center. This photo was taken as part of the documentary "Primate."

Bacteria. Dr. Ray E. Cameron and Frank A. Morelli of the Darwin Research Institute in Dana Point, California, recently retrieved bacteria from permanently frozen Antarctic sediment samples. The bacteria, which are at least 10,000 years old, were put into a broth of nutrients, and to the researchers' surprise, some of the bacteria grew and reproduced. This discovery is of great interest to space scientists, particularly those involved in the planned 1976 attempts to determine if life has ever occurred in Martian soils.

Hormones. There were several advances in hormone research in 1974. The chemical structure of a human sex hormone—the follicle stimulating hormone (FSH)—was unraveled by University of California scientists. Researchers now think it possible to use FSH as a male contraceptive and as a means to correct infertility in both men and women who lack sufficient FSH. FSH stimulates the growth of eggs in the ovary and spermatozoa in the testes. ■ In early 1975, researchers in New York claimed to have isolated a hormone from the thymus, a gland known to be involved in the body's immune system. If the claims are proved valid, it will be the first evidence of a hormone involved in immunity. ■ The newly discovered role of hormones in leukemia was termed a "pivotal discovery" by the researcher, Dr. Charles D. Higgins, a 1966 Nobel Prize winner. In his experiments, leukemia in male rats disappeared four or five days after the pituitary gland, which produces hormones, was removed.

Insects. The African honeybee (*Apis mellifera adansonii*) caused much concern in the United States in 1974 and early 1975. African bees are hard-working honey producers, but they are ferocious, vicious, and aggressive. African bees often attack without provocation and have been blamed for thousands of human and animal deaths in South America. The bees are swarming northward at a recently reported rate of 320 km (200 mi) a year.

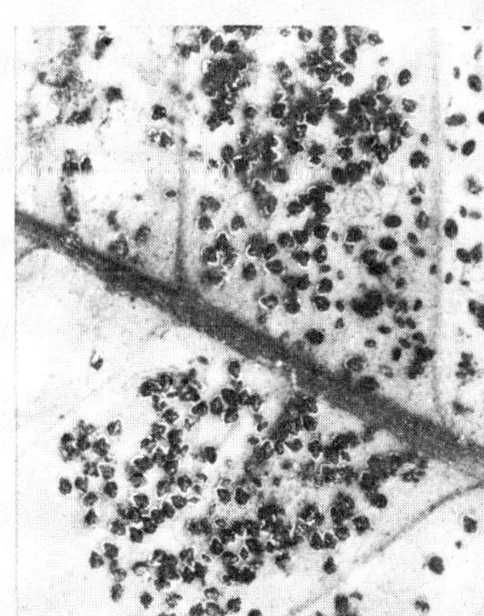

Black citrus fly on an orange leaf. The black citrus fly entered the United States for the first time in 1974 and is causing serious problems to citrus crops.

Primate Research. The basic and to a large extent unquestioned assumption in American society that scientific research with animals is good was vividly and controversially brought to the attention of researchers and the general public by the film "Primate," which was presented on television by the Public Broadcasting Service in December 1974. "Primate" was filmed, directed, and produced by Frederick Wiseman at Yerkes Primate Research Center in Atlanta, Georgia, as part of his film studies of American institutions. Without explaining any of the research, Wiseman filmed men and women apparently tormenting and mutilating apes and monkeys. Many primate researchers, especially those at Yerkes, were appalled at what they considered to be a prejudiced and misleading film.

Joan Schuman

The 1974 Nobel Prize in Physiology or Medicine

by Barbara Tchabovsky

THREE biologists whose work opened the field of cell biology were awarded the 1974 Nobel Prize in Physiology or Medicine. The two Americans, Albert Claude and George Emil Palade, and the Belgian, Christian Rene de Duve, shared the award equally. The work of these three men, all trained as physicians, provides a detailed description of the structure and function of the cell and its specialized parts, or organelles. Much of the award-winning work was done at the Rockefeller Institute for Medical Research (now Rockefeller University) in New York City.

The cell is the basic unit of structure and function in virtually all living things. In the late 1930's Albert Claude, the senior scientist of the group, began to use the newly invented electron microscope to study the cell. He discovered ways to prepare cells so that they could be observed through an electron microscope without damage to their delicate structure. The magnification provided by the electron microscope made it possible for the first time to see the detailed architecture of the cell. Claude also developed techniques whereby the chemistry of the newly discovered cell parts could be studied. He made use of a centrifuge, or spinning technique, to separate the solid particles of the cell. By spinning the cells in a liquid he obtained layers of different kinds of particles. The layers could then be separated and studied chemically.

In 1945 Claude published the first description of the detailed anatomy of the cell. He discovered two organelles: the mitochondrion and the endoplasmic reticulum. Mitochondria are cigar-shaped bodies found scattered throughout the cell. Often called the "powerhouses" of the cell, mitochondria store the cell's energy. The endoplasmic reticulum is a network of fibers that extends throughout much of the cell, supporting the various organelles. In further electron microscope studies of the cell, Claude and his colleague Keith R. Porter showed cancer virus particles in tumor cells.

George Emil Palade, after joining Claude at the Rockefeller Institute, improved the techniques of preparing cells for electron microscopy. He also developed biochemical techniques for studying cell organelles. He discovered ribosomes, which are very small organelles on the endoplasmic reticulum. Through biochemical analysis he found that the ribosomes were the sites of protein synthesis in the cell. Palade characteristically found an organelle through examination of electron micrographs of cells and then set to work to determine the chemical actions going on in the organelle.

Christian Rene de Duve typically pursued his investigations from the other direction. Trained as a biochemist, de Duve would find a chemical activity going on in a centrifuged cell and then search for the organelle responsible for the activity. In this way he discovered the lyso-

Albert Claude

some. He observed that something seemed to consume, or "eat," a chemical that he artificially introduced into a test tube containing centrifuged cell parts. Searching for the organelle responsible, he found tiny baglike structures, now called lysosomes, that take in and break down foreign material introduced into the cell. According to de Duve, lysosomes function as the "stomachs of the cell."

The detailed study of the cell begun by these three scientists has led many other investigators to look at the complex machinery that governs all cell activities. Dr. de Duve has said, "We are sick because our cells are sick." Researchers are now seeking the causes of diseases at the cellular level and a new, cellular approach to medical treatment.

Albert Claude was born in Luxembourg in August 1899. He was educated in Belgium, receiving his M.D. from the University of Liège Medical School in 1929. He then traveled to the United States, beginning his long association with Rockefeller University (then the Rockefeller Institute for Medical Research). In 1950 Claude returned to Belgium and pursued cancer research at the University of Belgium. He now heads the Institut Jules Bordet in Brussels.

George Emil Palade was born in Jassi, Rumania, in 1912. He received his M.D. from the University of Bucharest in 1940. After serving in the Rumanian army he went to the Rockefeller Institute on a two-year fellowship program. He returned to Rumania for a while, but later moved to the United States and again became associated with the Rockefeller Institute in 1946. He remained there until 1972 when he took over the cell biology section of Yale University School of Medicine.

Christian Rene de Duve was born in Thames Ditton, near London, on Oct. 2, 1917, of Belgian parents. He received his M.D. from the University of Louvain in 1941 and a M.S. in chemistry in 1946. He then did research at the Nobel Institute in Stockholm and at the Carl Cori Institute of Washington University in St. Louis, Missouri, before returning to Louvain. In 1962 he became associated with Rockefeller University but maintained his affiliation with Louvain. Now a transatlantic commuter, de Duve has research teams at both Rockefeller University and the University of Louvain in Brussels. His efforts to coordinate research at the two places have contributed much to the exchange of ideas in the field of cell biology.

George Emil Palade

Christian Rene de Duve

Gardens Under Glass

by Lillian Strohm

MORE than a century ago, smoke belching from the factories of London led to the development of miniature greenhouses that are now found in so many American homes, offices and classrooms. Today, the glassed-in gardens are called "terrariums." Back in the 1800s, though, they were called "Wardian cases," after Dr. Nathaniel Ward, an English surgeon and amateur horticulturist.

Ward was dismayed to find that the bog ferns in his London garden were being killed by industrial pollution. Then, while inspecting a moth chrysalis he had covered with soil in a sealed glass jar, Ward found bog ferns actually thriving in their protected environment. After experimenting with other plants in similar containers, he arrived at a remarkable conclusion. If plants have light, still air and the proper amount of moisture, Ward determined, they can live encapsulated for years without care.

Subsequently, practical application of that discovery made it possible for countries to exchange plants that previously could not stand long ocean voyages. New tea plants were sealed in glass cases and sent from Shanghai to India. Brazilian rubber trees were introduced into Ceylon, and botanical gardens exchanged rare and exotic plants from all parts of the world.

More recently, ecology-minded home owners have found that gardens under glass can be made into tables, hung from the ceiling, planted in clear bowls and grown in everything from antique bottles, old fishbowls and brandy snifters to Steuben crystal cracker jars and plastic containers sold in commercial terrarium kits.

CONSERVATIONIST'S DREAM

Terrariums demonstrate how a closed ecological system works. Energy supplied by sun or artificial light triggers the plants to use carbon dioxide from the air, plus water and plant food from the soil, to produce plant sugars. That process, of course, is called photosynthesis. At the same time, the plant takes oxygen from the air and gives off carbon dioxide. That is called respiration. The carbon dioxide is recycled back into the terrarium to make more plant sugar.

The terrarium is a conservationist's dream, for it efficiently uses and reuses the elements it needs. Moisture is taken into the root system, passed through the leaves and then evaporated into the air. Eventually, the closed container makes miniature clouds that rain the water back.

Happily, anyone can make a terrarium. And the possibilities are almost unlimited, from a traditional New England berry-bowl made with moss, tiny ferns and creeping partridgeberry to a grouping of tropical plants, a woodland scene or a cultivated garden. Here are some pointers on how to set up a Wardian case.

THE CONTAINER

A glass container is preferable to plastic for creating a suitable microclimate for houseplants. Plastic has a tendency to retain water droplets instead of dropping them back into the soil. Clear glass is better than tinted because it will transmit all available light. A glass bowl with an opening large enough to accommodate your hand is as easy to plant as a rectangular aquarium tank and the lustrous glass is equally decorative on a table or hanging from a bracket. Clear glass strips leaded together make a beautiful container to use with antique furnishings, and a 50-cm (20-in) glass globe on a metal stand blends with modern furnishings.

THE GARDEN

Plants grouped in a terrarium should provide a contrast in color, form, texture and growth habit, yet they need to be compatible enough to thrive in the same light, temperature, soil and humidity.

The woodland garden reproduces a natural scene in miniature by using native plants and rocks. Hemlock, spruce and laurel seedlings, wintergreen, club mosses, rattlesnake plantain and partridgeberry are recommended for woodland scenes. Flowering plants might be violets, hepatica, bloodroot or wild strawberries. Lichens and fungi give color and contrast, but need to be watched for mold.

The bog garden needs acid soil and a cool location. Carnivorous plants that catch and eat flies and insects include: purple pitcher-plant, sundew, huntsman's-horn and venus flytrap. Other bog plants are sheep laurel, swamp blueberry seedlings and cranberry.

The cultivated garden is easiest for a city dweller to create since these plants come from a florist or department store. There are several types of plants that are popular for cultivated-garden-type terrariums. *Fittonia*, for example, a wild plant from Peruvian jungles, has pink or white veins. *Peperomia*, from South America, comes in 15 varieties; one popular choice is emerald ripple. Club moss or rainbow moss is difficult to grow outside a terrarium. Hoya wax plant has fragrant pink flowers. *Pittosporum*, of Japanese origin, is a shiny evergreen that can be trimmed into any shape. *Podocarpus*, an evergreen, will stay compact if pruned regularly.

The genus *Begonia* includes more than 1,000 species; for terrariums, the dwarf varieties are required. *Croton* is a tropical plant that needs bright light for best color. *Maranta* from Africa has beautifully marked leaves in shades of green, white and pink. For ground cover, use baby tears, philodendron, grape ivy or moneywort.

Some steps in setting up an attractive terrarium. After you have laid the foundation and arranged the soil in varying depths to create a landscaped effect, place stones to hold the soil and give structure to the arrangement. Then start to position the plants. The top photo shows tentative placement of a fern to see how it looks in relation to the other plants. The middle photo shows plants positioned on the right; in the bottom photo, a fairly flat plant fills in the center.

The terrarium is given some finishing touches. Whitish oval stones are added to form a valley floor and some darker stones are added to the back of the valley to create an impression of shade and distance.

THE PLANTING

First, at least a day before planting, wash the container in hot soapy water, rinse it thoroughly and allow it to dry completely for 12 hours.

If you want to hide soil and roots, line container with sheet moss up to one-fourth the height of the container, placing the top of the moss toward the glass. Then, add 5 cm (2 in) of white pebbles for soil drainage, and spread a thin layer of hardwood charcoal bits over the pebbles. The charcoal bits absorb chemical salts and decay gases.

Next, use a layer of sphagnum moss to prevent the soil from washing into the drainage pebbles. Or, use a layer of nylon net that serves the same purpose and will not decay.

Now, add soil mix to fill the container one-fourth to one-third full. Pasteurized mixes are ready to use. If you make your own mix, you will need one-third pasteurized garden loam, one-third builders' sand and one-third milled sphagnum moss. Have it moist but not soggy.

Arrange the soil in varying depths to create landscaped effects. A bowl lends itself to a hillside planting with a focal point in center front. Usually, it is easiest to place the largest plant in the center, and space smaller plants around it, allowing room for growth and also for accessories if used. Bare soil between plants should be mulched with bark chips, small stones, or sheet moss. This prevents low leaves from rotting when they rest on moist soil.

Accessories in a planted terrarium fascinate small children. Most terrariums made in schools include metallic animals, small ceramic mushrooms or animals, driftwood, rocks, pretty shells or coral.

To make a bottle garden, the same materials are used, but special tools are needed. A funnel made of rolled paper should reach almost to the bottom of the bottle to allow you to pour in the growing medium. A wire coat hanger can be fashioned into a plant placer by using straight wire with an open loop on one end. Plant roots are washed, then lowered into the bottle with this positioner.

Long tweezers made from split bamboo are needed to hold the plant in the bottle until the soil is tamped down with a cork attached to the end of a dowel.

To water a bottle terrarium, run the water down the inside of the glass, using a kitchen baster. The water level can reach the top of the drainage pebbles. Then, close the bottle. Usually, no ventilation is needed. When plants need trimming, a razor blade taped to a dowel makes clean cuts.

THE GROWING

Most gardens encased in glass do best with filtered light, not direct sun. If artificial light is used, special fluorescent tubes developed to simulate actual sunlight rays are more effective than regular light tubes. A standard amount of light is 20 watts for 0.09 square meter, or 1 square foot, of growing space.

Although sealed terrariums are possible, some ventilation is usually needed to keep the glass from fogging and obscuring the plants inside. Inserting a small pebble between the lid and container is one easy way to ventilate. Use very little fertilizer to encourage slow growth and trim back plants that become overgrown. Mold is the most common terrarium plant disease. Remove all infected plants and treat the garden with a fungicide spray. Too much water, not enough light or poor ventilation will encourage mold.

One final thing: *talk* to the plants in your terrarium. If you do, they'll grow better—especially if you remove the lid first. For as you talk, you will breathe carbon dioxide into the container, and, as we have seen, green plants thrive on carbon dioxide□

SELECTED READINGS

Successful Terrariums: A Step-by-Step Guide by Ken Kayatta and Steven Schmidt. Houghton Mifflin, 1975.

The Complete Book of Terrarium Gardening by Jack Kramer. Scribner, 1974.

The Terrarium Book by Charles Evans and Roberta Pliner. Random, 1973.

Terrariums can be made in a variety of containers. The tall vase is planted with *Gesneria, Columnea,* and *Sinningia.* The jug has an assortment of greenery, while the rectangular terrarium limits its display to a *Seemannia latifolia* in full bloom, set off by a fern and a pebble beach.

A dahlia in full bloom. Dahlias are widely cultivated autumn-blooming garden flowers.

Flowers

by Jenny Tesar

FLOWERS are found almost everywhere. In the tropics flowering vines grow on trees, competing with other lush vegetation for sunlight. Colorful flowers brighten dull expanses of hot desert. Lakes and even salty marshes can also be home to flowers. Water hyacinths and water lilies float aimlessly in lakes and ponds, while pickerelweed and pond lilies stay anchored to the bottom but show off their flowers above the water line. Meadows and fields explode with color as dandelions, bluebonnets, thistle, and cowslip give way to wild roses, black-eyed susans, and goldenrod. In woodland areas, violets and bloodroot fade away as azaleas and rhododendron bloom. Even mountainous areas with snow-capped peaks have flowers, with edelweiss and mountain heather following snowdrops that break through the snow.

Many of the flowers that are familiar to us are large and brilliantly colored. Other flowers are tiny and inconspicuous —so small that you do not notice them unless you search for them. All, however, are built on the same basic pattern. And all have the same function: to reproduce the species.

A flower exists for only a short while. Then, parts of it develop into a fruit. Within the fruit are the seeds, which will produce a new generation of plants when they return to the soil.

THE PARTS OF A FLOWER

A typical flower has four main parts: the sepals, petals, stamen and pistil. These parts are attached to a stem tip, called the receptacle, which is slightly enlarged.

If you look at a typical flower bud, you'll see that it is covered by green, leaflike structures. These are the sepals. Their function is to enclose and protect the other parts of the bud, before they are fully developed. In an open flower, the sepals can be found beneath, or outside, the petals.

Many flowers are known by their color. We talk of red roses, goldenrod, and purple asters. In some cases, the sepals provide the distinctive color. Usually, however, the bright, showy parts of a flower are the petals. Their main function is to attract insects, which play an important role in pollination.

Petals attract insects in several ways. The glistening white or bright colors of many flowers are inviting to insects and even to certain birds. The petals of some flowers have glands that secrete nectar. This sugary liquid is greedily sought by bees, butterflies, and other flower-visiting insects, which use the nectar as food.

The odors of oils and other substances produced by the petals of many plant species are still another way of tempting insects. People, too, often find these odors very pleasant. As a result, the oils secreted by flowers such as roses, lavender and jasmine are used in making perfumes.

Some plants, such as skunk cabbage, have very unpleasant floral odors. Often, these plants also have purplish- or reddish-brown petals or other structures that resemble decaying animal flesh. Bees and other insects that visit pleasantly scented, brightly colored flowers are not attracted to these plants. But other insects are, especially those that frequent rotting flesh and other foul-smelling organic matter.

Within the enclosure formed by the flower petals are the stamens. These are the male organs of the flower. A stamen usually consists of a slim stalk, or filament, which bears at its tip a single, enlarged anther. Pollen grains are produced

Left: the Oriental poppy, an easy-to-grow, hardy species. Right: two well known spring-blooming flowers—forsythia (top) and Darwin hybrid tulips (lower).

Left: American cowslip (*Dodecathon*), a wild flower of woodlands, prairies, and mountainous areas. Center top: Flowering dogwood—the white petal-like structures are modified leaves surrounding a tiny greenish flower head. Center bottom: a Royal Highness rose. Right: a flowering plum in full bloom.

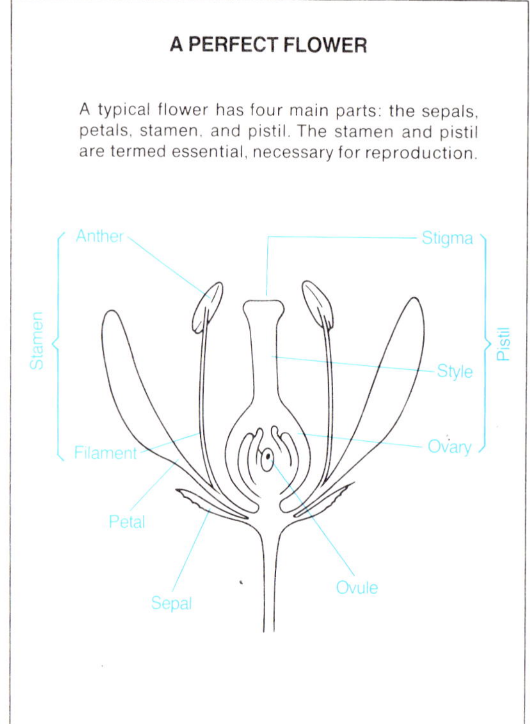

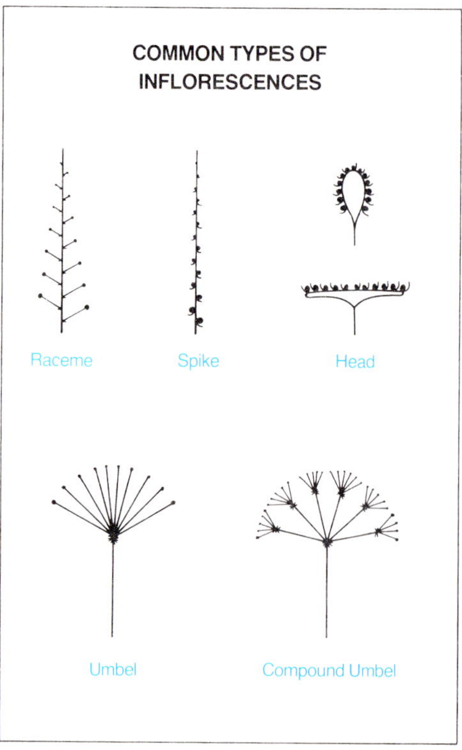

in the anther. Later, these grains will form the sperm, or male reproductive cells.

In the center of the flower is the pistil —the female organ. A pistil often looks like a flask with three fairly distinct parts. At the base is a sphere-shaped ovary. This is where the eggs develop and, later, the seeds are formed. A slender stalk, the style, rises from the top of the ovary. At the top of the style is a slightly enlarged stigma.

Before seeds can form, pollen grains must pass from the anthers to the top of the stigma. To ensure that the pollen will stick to its surface, the stigma is often rough or sticky. Similarly, the outer wall of the pollen grain is usually covered with spinelike structures.

In roses and many other flowers, the floral organs are all separate and distinct from each other. In other flowers, some of the parts are joined together. In morning glories and petunias, for example, the petals are fused into trumpetlike structures.

The parts of a flower usually occur in multiples of 3, 4, or 5. A lily, for example, has 3 sepals, 3 petals, 6 (2×3) stamens, and 1 pistil with 3 sections in the ovary. The evening primrose is an example of a flower with 4 sepals, 4 petals, 8 stamens, and an ovary with 4 sections.

TYPES OF FLOWERS

Most of the flowers that you see in a garden have all the parts that we just described. They are complete flowers. Some flowers, however, do not have all four floral parts and are known as incomplete flowers. The tiny flower of a grass plant, for example, has neither sepals nor petals. The flowers of corn and other grains and

Top left: Common garden petunia, often used for bedding and borders. Top right: a rhododendron. Bottom left: a rock aster, a wild flower of mountainous areas. Bottom center: night-blooming cereus (*Hylocereus*). Bottom right: *Impatiens*.

of many trees are also incomplete, lacking at least one of the four parts of a complete flower. Sepals and petals are often termed accessory parts of a flower because they are not concerned with reproduction.

When a flower contains both stamens and pistils, it is said to be perfect, or bisexual. Orchids, lilies, roses, and sweet peas are all perfect flowers, containing both male and female reproductive organs in each flower. When a flower does not contain both stamens and pistils, it is said to be imperfect, or unisexual. It may be a pistillate, or female, flower or it may be a staminate, or male, flower.

In some species such as corn, pumpkin, oak, and squash, the pistillate flowers and the staminate flowers are born on the same individual plant. The plant is then said to be monoecious. In other cases, including the willow tree, the asparagus, hemp, and date palm, the pistillate and staminate flowers are borne on separate plants. These are said to be dioecious.

Red poinsettia, a favorite Christmas decoration. In this plant, the showy part is the leaves —bright red bracts—surrounding a small yellowish flower.

A flower may be perfect but incomplete. A calla lily, for example, is perfect because it has both stamen and pistils, but it is incomplete, lacking sepals.

FORMING A FLOWER

A flower starts as a bud. In many plants the same stem tip that forms leaves will later form a flower. Small projections form along the sides of the stem tip. These develop into the various parts of the flower.

What causes flowering? What determines when a plant will produce flowers rather than leaves? Many factors seem to be involved. The plant must have an ample supply of food. Also, certain hormones must be produced.

Environmental factors can also affect the start of the flowering period. The relative length of day (light) and of night (dark) is one such factor.

The daily period of light to which a plant is exposed is called a photoperiod. Plants that bloom in the spring or fall are short-day plants. Violets, poinsettias and chrysanthemums are examples. Long-day plants, such as clover, potatoes and most grains, usually bloom in the summer. They flower only when the day length is comparatively long.

Other plants bloom only when the day length is neither too long nor too short. And some, such as dandelions and tomatoes, will bloom during a wide range of day lengths.

Another environmental factor that influences flowering is temperature. Plants such as lettuce, cotton and peppers flower only (or best) at relatively high temperatures. The flowering of celery, carrots and onions is favored by low temperatures. Some plants flower best at intermediate temperatures. Still others blossom under a wide range of temperature conditions.

Knowledge of the effects of temperature and light on flowering is used by florists. By regulating environmental conditions in greenhouses, they can make plants such as chrysanthemums and carnations bloom on any chosen day of the year.

POLLINATION

We have been talking about many different kinds of flowers. Certainly there is much variety among them—in size, color, shape, number of parts, periods of blooming and so on. In every case, however, the flower has just one function: to make seeds.

If seeds are to be made, pollen must get from the anther to the stigma on the tip of the pistil. This transfer of pollen is called pollination. In a perfect flower, pollen from its own stamen may reach the pistil. Or the pollen from one flower may land on the pistil of another flower on the same plant. This is self-pollination. When pollen is carried from the stamen of one plant to the pistil of a flower on another plant, the transfer is called cross-pollination.

Cross-pollination depends on an outside agent to carry the pollen from one plant to another of the same species. The most common agents are insects and wind, though birds and water also sometimes carry the pollen. Plants that depend on insects advertise their presence with bright colors or strong odors. Insects visit the flowers to feed on nectar and pollen. The pollen is sticky and easily adheres to an insect's hairy body, and when the insect then moves on to another flower of the same species, some of the pollen rubs off.

In many other plants, the wind carries the pollen from one plant to another. In most of these plants the stamens and stigma are exposed to air currents. The pollen grains are light-weight and easily carried by the wind. Among the many plants that are wind-pollinated are grasses, corn, oak, pine, and fir.

In cross-pollination the characteristics of two plants are mixed. This often results in plants that are superior to those that result from self-pollination. This is true for certain varieties of apples, cherries, pears and other kinds of fruit. People who grow these fruit trees usually keep bee-

Top left: amaryllis. Top right: iris, a popular ornamental flower. Bottom left: a fishhook cactus. Bottom right: a giant sunflower. Sunflowers turn to follow the sun's path.

Left: a garden of annuals that includes marigolds and petunias. Upper right: water lily floating in a pond. Lower right: violets, started indoors.

hives in their orchards to insure cross-pollination of the blossoms.

Pollination is the first step in making seeds. The next step is fertilization—the union of egg and sperm. This occurs in the ovary. The sperm, which is formed from a pollen grain, travels down the pistil through a pollen tube. When the sperm reaches the ovary, it fertilizes an egg and seeds are formed.

After it is fertilized, the egg begins to grow. The ovary grows, too. In time, the ovary becomes a fruit, containing one or more seeds. When the fruit is ripe, it may drop to the ground and the seeds develop into new plants. In many cases, however, the fruit or seeds are carried by wind, water, insects, birds, and other animals before they take root. In some cases, the fruits "explode," scattering the seeds. Seeds sprout, or develop, if temperature, moisture and other environmental conditions are favorable.

INFLORESCENCES

The many differences between flowers are useful to people who are interested in identifying plants. If you were given a rose and a dandelion, you could tell them apart because you have learned to identify these two flowers. What differences between the rose and the dandelion do you use to identify them?

One important characteristic used in identification is the relative position of the flower on the plant. In some plants, such as roses, magnolias and violets, each flower is solitary, borne on a stem that is some distance from other flowers on the plant. In most flowering plants, however, the flowers are borne in clusters. These flower clusters are called inflorescences.

There are many types of inflorescences. We'll just look at some of the most common ones:

1. Raceme. The main axis of this inflorescence is elongated. The flowers are borne on short stalks known as pedicels. The pedicels are all approximately the same length and are more or less equally distributed along the main axis. This simple type of inflorescence is found in such plants as currant, radish, hyacinth and snapdragon.

2. Spike. This is similar to a raceme, but the individual flowers do not have stalks. They are sessile, attached directly to the main axis. Wheat, cattail, gladiolus, and common plantain have spiked flower clusters.

3. Simple umbel. Here, the main axis is very small. The stalks that bear the flowers all seem to arise at the same point and all the stalks are of about the same length. Thus an umbel looks rather like an umbrella. Examples include ginseng, bluelace flower and onion.

4. Compound umbel. In a compound umbel, the branches grow from the tip of the main axis. Each branch then bears an umbrellalike cluster of flowers. Carrot, dill, and Queen Anne's lace have this type of inflorescence.

5. Head. In this disk-shaped inflorescence, both the main axis and the pedicels are very reduced in size. The flowers are crowded close together forming a disk-shaped arrangement. Examples include the daisy, sunflower, and thistle.

The head is one of the most unusual and interesting types of inflorescence. In a head, the flowers are usually very small and tightly crowded on a flattened receptacle. The daisy is a good example; it isn't a single flower but a whole cluster of flowers! Marginal flowers, called ray flowers, are large and brightly colored. Their function is to attract insects. The flowers in the center of the daisy head are much smaller and less conspicuous. These are the disk flowers. They produce the seeds.

Dandelions are also examples of head inflorescences. Here, however, the entire head is composed of ray flowers, each of which produces a tiny one-seeded fruit.

The next time you walk through a garden, look at the flowers. Can you identify different inflorescences? Can you find flowers with fused parts? Can you tell which flowers are pollinated by insects and which by the wind?

You will find many floral designs in the garden. Each is a thing of beauty. But what is really remarkable is that nature has found so many ways in which to ensure the formation of seeds and, hence, of flowering plants on our planet□

SELECTED READINGS

Flowers of the World by Sandra Holmes. Bantam, 1974.

Recognizing Flowering Wild Plants by W. C. Grimm. Hawthorne, 1974.

What's in the Name of a Flower (grade 6 to 8) by Peter Limburg. Coward, 1974.

Left: camelia-flowered balsam, a bedding favorite that blooms in summer and early fall. Center top: an Easter lily. Center bottom: torch zinnia, a popular garden and cut flower. Right: tree peony.

Whales

by Nicholas Rosa

MUCH of what you will read here about whales will seem incredible. Your common sense may revolt—"it can't be happening that way." Surely, you may suppose, this man is crying wolf? But everything I have to report is dolefully true. The facts are even admitted by the "bad guys" in the situation, which itself may seem incredible.

First, some background. Modern whaling is carried on by means of harpoon cannon, explosive harpoons, and fast diesel-powered catcher boats serving gigantic factory ships. Sonar, helicopter scouts, and efficient radio communications tie all flotilla elements together. Old Captain Ahab with his pigsticker harpoon and flimsy rowboat does not come into this at all. With all his dreams, Ahab could not have dreamt of what is going on today.

TEN EASY STEPS

What is going on today? Where does it stand with the whales and the whalers? The situation can be outlined in ten easy steps.

1. All species of "great" whales—the truly large ones—are in danger of extinction. Not a remote danger. Not a hypothetical danger. The real thing. Now.

2. There is just one reason for this: intensive commercial whaling.

3. Several species of large whales are already "commercially extinct." That is, they are too few and too scattered to be worth the expense of deliberately hunting them. A few species are protected according to international convention, and a few by gentleman's agreement among some whalers. The most recent examples are the blue whale, which has been protected since 1965, and the humpback whale, which has been protected since 1963. Both of these whales remain on the verge of true extinction.

4. Whales are not killed for the sake of feeding hungry people. Hardly anybody eats whale meat. "Whales vs. people" would be a false issue. Whales are killed for cash.

5. Whale bodies are processed into cosmetics, luxury soaps, car wax, lubricants, automatic transmission fluid, margarine, fertilizer, hog and cattle feed, and pet food.

6. Adequate substitutes for all whale products exist at reasonable prices. This makes a chronic competition problem for the whaling companies.

7. Whaling is not economically important to any nation. Even the largest whaling fleets—those of the Soviet Union and Japan—are minor subsidiaries of large shipping and fishing combines.

8. As one species of whale becomes

This Japanese wood-block print by Kuniyoshi, circa 1840, shows a right whale being butchered at a shore station.

depleted, the industry turns to the next smaller species and kills still larger numbers.

9. The whaling industry has ignored the warnings of scientists, including those it has employed, in full awareness that it is committing economic suicide.

10. All large-scale whalers expect to stop within a few years, since all whales worth chasing will be commercially extinct by then.

These ten statements, plus many more to come, are not open to question. They are among the admissions of whaling industry spokesmen around the world. They hardly leave any room for wolf-crying or for indictments by "emotional ecology fans." The situation is analogous to nuclear war: the bare facts are so bad that exaggeration is hardly possible.

An eleventh observation: the International Whaling Commission (IWC), a self-regulatory consortium of the whalers of the major whaling nations, has been ineffective in carrying out its chartered purpose—the conservation of whale stocks for perpetual yields. We'll look into why, later.

The situation, while dire, is not quite hopeless. Grass-roots pressure has had some surprising effects since 1972. With enough pressure on enough governments, a long-proposed ten-year moratorium on whaling could be adopted by the IWC. That will not be enough—it is a necessary but not sufficient condition. Some drastic things will have to be done now, if the whales are to survive.

INCREDIBLE BUT TRUE

The tenth outline statement—namely, that all large-scale whalers expect to stop within a few years since all whales worth chasing will be commercially extinct by

BOTTLENOSE WHALE
SPERM WHALE
BLUE WHALE
HUMPBACK WHALE
KILLER WHALE
BOWHEAD WHALE,
OR GREENLAND RIGHT WHALE

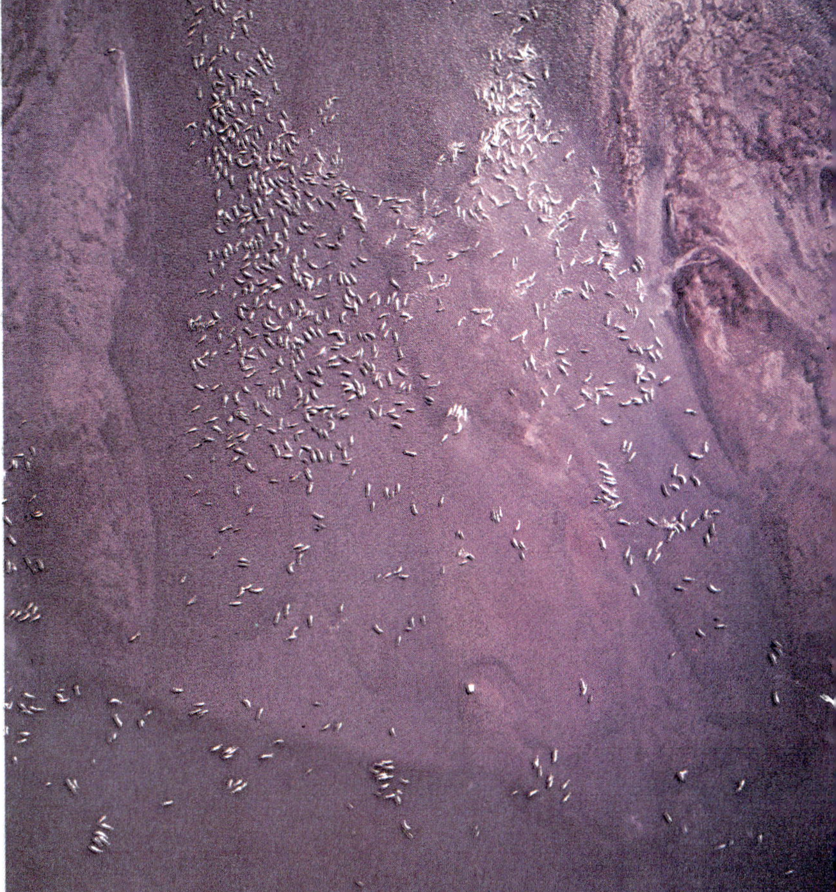

Great numbers of white whales in their breeding grounds in Canada's Northwest Territories. This rarely seen view, taken with special water-penetrating film, shows the adult and young whales as well as the physical characteristics of their breeding grounds.

then—reflects the industry's replies to recent conservationist pressures. Whether the pressure comes from scientists, the United Nations, or conservationist groups, whalers reply "Why don't you leave us alone? You know we'll have to stop in a few years anyway."

The ninth statement—that the whaling industry has ignored the warnings of scientists in full awareness that it is committing economic suicide—is likely to strain your credulity. "Hard-headed businessmen don't kill the goose that lays the golden egg." But they do. They have. Historical examples include furs and timber.

In any enterprise involving a "free" resource, once the resource is gone the investment moves into something else. In whaling, ships can be converted or sold. This, indeed, has been happening.

The fourth statement, about whale meat not feeding people, is vulnerable to hair-splitting. Actually, some whale meat is eaten in Japan. It is a fairly recently introduced, and partial, substitute for fish. A whale, remember, is not a fish but a mammal—and its meat resembles beef. Japan's fisheries have been experiencing declining outputs due to overexploitation and ocean pollution. Whale meat now provides eight to ten per cent of the animal protein consumed by the Japanese people each year. Substitutes for this substitute, however, will have to be found within a few years. The Japanese whalers admit they are going to have to quit (but not before the Russians do). Many others have quit, leaving the field to Russo-Japanese domination. Japan and the Soviet Union, between them, carry on 88 per cent of the world's deep-sea whaling.

NO GUARANTEE

The third point mentions commercial extinction, at which point deliberate, large-scale hunting of a species stops. Stopping at this point, however, is no guarantee against biological, or true, extinction. Whales can be too few and too scattered to mate frequently enough to offset natural loss of numbers. This may already be the case for the great blue whale.

A whale in the process of diving deeply, a behavioral characteristic known as sounding. At the start of the dive, the flukes are raised in the air. Then the whale slips below the surface at a nearly vertical angle.

The blue whale (*Balaenoptera musculus*) is the largest, heaviest animal ever to live an earth. A fully mature female blue whale weighs up to 150 tons and can be over 30 m (100 ft) long. No dinosaur was ever like this. But no fully mature blues have been reliably reported since the 1950's. Whalers' estimates vary, but there now seem to be between 600 and 2,000 blue whales left in the world, mostly in the Southern Hemisphere. The original population probably exceeded half a million. The survivors are scattered over the oceans.

Female blues come into heat once every four years. They must encounter their mates within a brief annual mating season. A female blue is not sexually mature until she is more than 23 m (77 ft) long. She may not be able to produce viable young until she is 25 m (83 ft) long—this is "effective sexual maturity." For many years, the minimum "size limit" for blue whales, set by the IWC, was 21 m (70 ft). Therefore, many adolescent females were killed before protection was accorded all blue whales in 1965. That protection, which contains many loopholes, is still not honored by all whalers.

In his 1971 book, *The Blue Whale*, George L. Small of the City University of New York declared that the number of blue whales in the world as of that year might actually be between 0 and 200.

In the 1931 whaling season close to 30,000 blue whales were taken in the Antarctic alone. The whalers wanted no other species. This was the "cream" whale —one carcass delivered two to six times the oil and meat of any other whale.

THE REPEATING PATTERN

With the blue whales effectively out of the picture since the 1950's, whalers turned to the smaller fin whale (*B. physalus*) as the whale of commercial choice. They also began to take the still smaller sei whales (*B. borealis*). Since 1972 they have taken increasing numbers of the diminutive mincke whales (*B. acutorostrata*), only 9 m (30 ft) long and for decades spurned as too small to bother with. In recent seasons, Japanese whalers returning home from the Antarctic Ocean have taken up to 220,000 man-sized dolphins a year. Fin whale populations, meanwhile, have crashed.

International statistics on the Antarctic catch of major species of whales began to be tabulated in 1934. Then the blue whale was practically the exclusive target. Through the mid-1930's the whalers were still taking about 17,000 blues a year, but were phasing in the fins. The peak in fin whale catches came in 1938 as the blues began a definite decline. This occurred for two reasons. First, the available blues were younger, smaller, and giving less oil. Second, once attention turned to the fins, these were pursued with a vengeance. During World War II, pelagic whaling stopped, giving the fin whales a brief breeding respite. However, the decade 1953–1962 was the jackpot for fin whale catches. This reflected increased whaling effort, not increased populations.

Catching a whale. A whaler waits for the whale to approach closer before firing a harpoon (right). After it has been harpooned, the bleeding whale is brought to the side of the ship (below). Then a hole is cut into its fin so that it can be roped to the side of the ship (lower right).

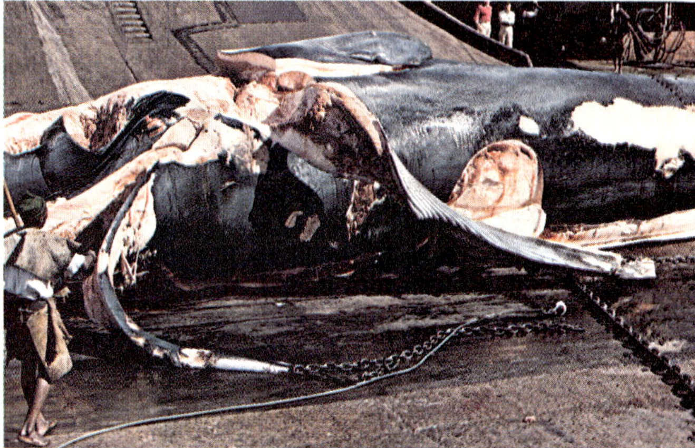

Whales being flensed, or stripped of skin and blubber. Large factory ships on which whales are flensed and the bodies processed into various products are part of modern whaling fleets.

Because of their four-year breeding cycle, the blue whales' stocks made no significant wartime recovery. After 1951 blue whales became targets of opportunity as the chase shifted to the fins. So did the 18 m (60 ft) sei whales. In the 1960's, however, more and more sei whales were taken as the catch of fin whales plummeted.

The original Southern Hemisphere fin whale stock was probably about 380,000. The 1971 estimated population was about 77,000. Population dynamics experts judge that a population of 222,000 would permit a maximum sustained yield (MSY) of 10,000 whales annually. The 1974 IWC quota for fin whales was only 2,000—all that can be caught without serious further depletion of the stock. Until 1972, the IWC rejected any sustained-yield recommendations.

The sperm whale (*Physeter catodon*) was ignored by whalers from the end of the *Moby Dick* era in the nineteenth century to the end of World War II. Kerosene and then electricity had destroyed Captain Ahab's market for sperm oil. Sperm oil is actually a liquid, inedible wax, and modern whalers were at first looking just for edible oil. A factory ship would accept a sperm whale carcass only if she had special tankage for its oil. This was unusual before 1945.

Since 1945, industry has come to appreciate certain unusual properties of sperm oil. It does not oxidize unless ignited; it does not film over; it does not turn rancid; it is not seriously affected by temperature changes or mechanical churning. So, factory ships now carry the special tankage to hold sperm oil. In terms of numbers and tonnage taken, inedible sperm whales are commercially the most important whales today.

In 1971, the United States legally outlawed whaling from American-flag ships or ports, and banned the importation of all whale products.

THE ECONOMICS OF WHALING

Whaling is not even profitable. The whalers are always caught in a squeeze between rising labor costs and other expenses, and the sinking price and demand for whale oil and other whale products. The annually shrinking supplies of these products do not call forth increasing market prices, or encourage demand. Substitutes are all too available, usually more reliable in supply and always competitively priced.

Whale oil, for example, has long been used in the making of margarine in Europe. But margarine can be made from a large number of common vegetable oils—cottonseed, corn, soy, safflower, coconut, and others—as it has been for decades in the United States. For pet food, cattle feed, and fertilizer, Peruvian fish, fish meal, and fish oil tend to crowd out whale meat and oil.

Norway, a whaling giant only recently, now sends its attenuated fleet out every other year. The Norwegians explain they cannot afford to send it out every year. Obviously business is terrible. The Japanese whaling fleets are reported to be virtually bankrupt, always operating in the red, bolstered by subsidies from their parent companies. Information on the economic condition of the Soviet whaling fleet is not available. Its whale oil, meat, and other products appear on the European and world markets. There must be something of an internal market, but whaling can hardly be more profitable for the Russians than for the Japanese or Norwegians.

THEN WHY IS ANYBODY WHALING?

There seem to be only two reasons that make even remote fiscal sense. The first is amortization of expensive equipment. The second reason is, as the Japanese put it, that even if the equipment were amortized, it would be "economically wasteful" for them to refrain from using it.

As the number of whales dwindled and the big-time whalers trimmed their fleets or dropped out, equipment was sold here and there around the world—and the amortization problem was generated anew.

MUSICAL CHAIRS

In 1946, Norway was dominant, operating more whale factory ships in the Antarctic than any other nation. Japan and the USSR were minor participants. Over the years, Norway became weaker, while Japan and the USSR became dominant. The ships of "other" nations disappeared.

Did they really? "Other," by and large, sold its ships to nations not considered important whalers, or registered them under flags of convenience. The ghost "other" fleet hunts opportunistically outside as well as in the Antarctic. Even the Japanese have resorted to flags of convenience, as total annual IWC catch quotas have fallen. Flags of convenience are usually those of countries not represented in the IWC or signatories to the old Whaling Convention. Thus regulation is circumvented; the ghost "other" fleet can be considered as pirates.

The term "pirates" is used loosely here. There is no international law requiring whalers to accept regulation, or to report their catches. And this brings us to the regulatory body, the IWC, and how it functions.

THE PAPER TIGER: IWC

The International Whaling Commission was founded in the aftermath of a treaty-like agreement, the International Convention on Whaling of 1946. It had its first meeting in 1949. The delegates for the most part represented the whalers, not the governments, of twenty interested nations. Its chartered purpose was and is "to provide for the conservation, development, and optimum utilization of the whale resources. . . ."

Built-in self-defeating mechanisms hamstring the effectiveness of the IWC. In practice, all regulations require unanimous agreement. Any nation that does not agree to a regulation has ninety days in which to register an objection. Having registered an objection, that nation is not bound by the regulation. The IWC was consciously modeled on the UN Security Council, and while officially an objection is not a veto, it usually has the effect of one.

There is no way to override an objection. Not even signatories to the convention are obliged to belong to the IWC or to accept its regulations. Members have left the IWC at will. The original twenty has shrunk to fourteen. Until Japan and the USSR agreed, as of 1973–74, to accept each other's observers on their factory ships, there was no real way to monitor, much less enforce, regulations that survived the objection process. Certain matters, like a moratorium, require a three-fourths majority and are still subject, at least indirectly, to objection.

THE QUOTAS

The IWC has no authority to restrict the numbers or nationalities of factory ships, or to set individual quotas on ships or nations. All it can do is set an overall catch quota each year.

Almost immediately the IWC hired committees of scientists to work on the problem of dwindling stocks and catches. To guide annual total catch quotas, the scientists chosen were not experts on whales or whaling, but on population dynamics. This made for objective reports.

Ecologists support the concept of *sustained yield* as safeguarding the conservation of species and also allowing optimum utilization of the stocks. Sustained yield can be obtained if no more biomass—be it of whales or petunias—is harvested each season than the processes of growth and reproduction can replace. Surely, one would suppose, hard-headed businessmen would buy that concept. But the whalers rejected sustained-yield recommendations, despite the fact that in the early 1960's economists had offered figures showing that whaling would be more profitable under sustained yield. Seasons would be shorter, fuel and labor costs lower, overall efficiency higher, and so forth. The whalers remained insistent on maximum possible harvesting.

THE BLUE WHALE UNIT

By 1949, it was plain there could never be another bonanza season like that of 1931, which produced nearly 30,000 blue whale carcasses. Taking smaller whales, after all, could not be as profitable. It takes about as much effort to catch and process an 80-ton fin whale as it does for a 100- or 150-ton blue whale.

Yet fin whales had to be taken. Now, how about catch limits or quotas? Species limits were rejected out of hand, for blues or anything else. A total numbers limit would be risky, since even large numbers of smaller whales could give an unprofitable harvest. A tonnage limit was impossible: there is no way to heft a whale onto a scale. (Those that have been weighed have been weighed piece by piece, a process taking many hours.)

After much thought, the idea of the Blue Whale Unit (BWU) was put forward. All whales would be counted in terms of the blue whale. Going by average oil yields per carcass for each species, it came out like this:

1 BWU = 1 blue whale *or*
2 fin whales *or*
2½ humpback whales *or*
6 sei whales

The annual quota could be set in BWU, with the species mix left unspecified. No BWU value was assigned sperm whales, which were still of marginal interest in 1949. Nor were BWU values given the little piked or mincke whales.

The BWU scheme was deplored by scientists at the time and has been ever since. As the numbers of blues and humpbacks fell alarmingly, scientists in and out of the IWC pleaded for species limits. Partial regional protection did begin in 1960. Humpbacks received full worldwide protection in 1963 and blues in 1965, but no measurable increase in their numbers has occurred since.

THAT MORATORIUM

Through the 1960's, scientists and conservationists pelted the IWC with urgings for a ten-year moratorium on all whaling.

This 19th century German engraving depicts whaling boats attacking sperm whales. Sperm whales, valuable for their oil, are now partially protected by an IWC quota.

Presumably, ten years of freedom from predation would give stocks a chance to recover somewhat. Only presumably, since a decade of protection has not yet done much for the populations of blues or humpbacks. It would also allow time for intensive scientific study of whales. Such study would be needed for the setting of realistic species quotas if whaling later resumed. But, even more important from the scientific point of view, it would allow time to learn more about whale ecology and physiology. Very little is now known. What role do the various species of whales play in the web of life in the sea? Nobody knows. Why have malignant tumors never been found in the various whales "dissected" by whaling crews? Nobody knows. And the whales are disappearing before anyone can find out.

Year after year, the IWC refused even to consider a moratorium. Each year, it reduced its catch quota for the forthcoming season—but always to an unrealistically high level. For example, one year it declared a quota of 10,000 BWU. Its own scientists predicted that no more than 8,500 BWU would be caught. The actual catch was 8,429 BWU. The quota was accordingly reduced the next year, with scientists again accurately predicting a still smaller catch; and so it went until 1972 when the BWU was abandoned.

TANTRUM DIPLOMACY

Several nations within the IWC, including the United States, favored the moratorium, but were afraid to press for it. A successful vote might destroy the IWC, leaving the active whalers—Japan, the USSR, and Norway—going their own way with no hint of regulation.

At the June 1972 annual meeting, the moratorium finally came up for a vote, but the USSR and Japan blocked passage. At the 1973 meeting, the moratorium passed in committee, but failed to achieve a three-quarters majority on the open floor.

At the 1974 meeting the proposal for a ten-year moratorium on killing all whales again failed to pass. The IWC did consider a selective moratorium in which any whale population falling below sustainable yield levels would be automatically protected. Japan and the USSR cast the negative votes, and the idea is now being further studied in an IWC committee. In one important shift, the IWC did agree to manage whale stocks by ocean areas rather than by the whole ocean.

The 1972 and 1973 meetings set species quotas for the first time, abandoning the Blue Whale Unit. Even the sperm whale was finally included in these quotas. At the 1974 meeting, the fin whale quota was reduced to 1,300 and the sei whale to 6,000. The sperm whale quota was kept at 23,000. In 1975 the fin whale was given almost total protection and the quota for whales was reduced by 10,000, but the moratorium was not brought up.

POPULAR PRESSURE

International popular pressure is what put the moratorium proposal onto the IWC floor the last few years. The IWC isolates itself from public opinion, but most of its member nations' governments are not so isolated. In Australia, Britain, Canada, Denmark, France, and the United States, at least, the governments have been hearing from their citizens about whaling. So have the ambassadors to these countries from the USSR, Japan, and Norway. Also, a wave of pressure is rising within Japan. Popular pressure moved the UN Stockholm Conference to urge the moratorium on the IWC in 1972, and has emboldened the American and other IWC delegates to push the moratorium in the face of Soviet and Japanese intransigence.

A number of conservation organizations have generated this pressure, but the most outstanding job has been done by Project Jonah, whose letter-writing campaigns are having noticeable effects.

WHAT WILL BE NEEDED

An IWC moratorium would be only a first and largely symbolic step. A new convention or treaty on whaling would be needed to ensure that all IWC nations honored the moratorium, and that equipment was duly mothballed or converted—not sold to unregulated pirates. A cessation of whaling would have to become, immediately, a priority matter for the UN General Assembly. Countries that are now markets for whale products, such as West Germany and the Netherlands, would have to follow the examples of the United States and United Kingdom and outlaw their importation. New treaties or conventions would have to reserve the decision on whether or not to resume whaling after ten years.

IS WHALING WORTH SAVING?

Economically, whaling is a piddling small business. Its total income is under $150 million a year. Worldwide, it probably accounts for fewer than 14,000 jobs. Substitutes for these jobs, or pensions, will have to be provided in a few years anyway, as commercial extinction of all target species brings whaling to a stop. Those substitute jobs and pensions may as well be provided now.

Whaling's contribution to human nutrition has also been piddling. Even in 1931, when the industry could take 30,000 blue whales and get two to three times the oil it now gets by killing more whales, the world knew hunger and malnutrition, and whaling made no dent in this. Except for margarine in well-fed Europe, and a little whale meat eaten here and there, practically all resources from whales were put into trivial products. They still are, only more so.

The population of the world has doubled since 1931. It is due to double again by the year 2000. Even with "wise management," sustained yields for whalers never will be what they could have been had good management been applied thirty, twenty, or even ten years ago. Therefore whaling never will make a significant contribution to the nutrition needs of a hungry world.

There are several ways of regarding whales. One way is as a food resource for hungry people. Another way is as important elements in the oceanic ecosystem, on which man depends for food and other resources. Another way is as fellow inhabitants of this planet with us, having as much right to existence and freedom as human beings have. A final way is as a free resource possibly convertible to the monetary profit of a few entrepreneurs. The reader may make his own choices□

The Year of the Whale by Victor B. Scheffer. Scribners, 1969.

"Vanishing Giants" by David O. Hill. *Audubon*, January 1975.

Sugar

by Joan Schuman

MANY of us have the sugar habit.

When in 1969 the U.S. Food and Drug Administration banned the use of the sugar substitutes, cyclamates, because of their possible cancer-producing potential, most people became aware that the sweetener is habit-forming as they went back to the real thing. In 1974 sugar lovers were jolted again: the price of the sweetener rose more than 300 per cent. Prices climbed, naturally, for cereals, candy, cakes, ice cream, canned fruits, and baby foods, among other sugar-rich foods.

Sugar is a common part of the American diet. The average person eats about 46 kg (102 lb) of it a year. Most of it is "hidden," as in jams and jellies. But if it were "straight" sugar it would fill two thirds of a cup per person per day. That is about 450 calories.

ONE WEEK'S SALARY

People were not always hooked on sugar. In the 14th century, the average European had to spend one week's salary to buy less than 0.5 kg (1 lb) of sugar. Therefore few people became accustomed to it. Then in 1493 Christopher Columbus carried sugarcane from the Canary Islands to the New World. Soon the cane, a giant grass that thrives in warm climates which have plenty of rain, was growing abundantly in the West Indies. Today these canes—2.4 to 7.3 m (8 to 24 ft) high—rise in fields throughout South and Central America, Africa, and Asia.

Not until the late 1800's did sugar become inexpensive and a big seller—all because of new, improved industrial methods of refining sugar. The granulated white sugar we know is an industrial product, the result of milling, shredding, extracting, chemical processing, and refining. From the late 1800's through the 1930's, sugar cost only about a nickel a pound. For a time in 1974, however, the price was more than 14 times that high.

A crop of tall, thick, and heavy sugarcane grows on silt loam soil in Louisiana.

The sugar beet, too, contributes to the world's sugar output. Either kind of commercial sugar—cane or beet—is known to chemists as sucrose.

THE SWEET NERVE

How much do you know about the taste that we call sweet? If you touch all the areas of your tongue with a piece of sugar, the tip will probably be the most sensitive. That is because the "sweet nerve" runs from the tip to the back of your tongue, and on to your brain. Sugar can also be tasted in other parts of the tongue. Children even have these sweet taste receptors inside their cheeks.

Many people's built-in liking for sugar and for sugar-rich foods and drinks can bring on health problems. For one, there is tooth decay (caries, dentists call it). Fossils of prehistoric humans show little tooth decay; its occurrence coincides with man's big-scale use of sugar. Sugar alone does not cause tooth decay. Bacteria found in the mouth ferment sugar, forming an acid that slowly dissolves and destroys the enamel covering of teeth.

If you eat sugar at mealtime and then brush your teeth, there's little chance that teeth will decay. But continuous nibbling of sweets throughout the day increases the danger. Dr. James H. Shaw, professor of nutrition at Harvard School of Dental Medicine, says that hard candies and caramels are the worst culprits, since they stick to the teeth and are difficult to remove even with a toothbrush.

HAZARDOUS FAT

Sugar is blamed for another common health problem—obesity. If a person gets very little exercise and eats too much, he gets more calories than he needs. And sugar provides about 15 per cent of the total calories consumed by the average American. All this all too frequently adds up to excess fat.

In comparison with a person of normal weight, an overweight person runs a higher risk of developing high blood pressure, diabetes, and atherosclerosis, an abnormal thickening and hardening of the arterial walls. In persons who inherit a tendency toward diabetes or atherosclerosis, excessive sugar intake can trigger the onset of the disease. These people are called "carbohydrate sensitive," because an excess of sugar (which is a carbohydrate) can be harmful to them. Some people develop a condition that is the direct opposite of diabetes. It is hypoglycemia—too little sugar in the blood. These victims may suffer weakness, hunger, nausea, and rapid heartbeat.

MORE FATTY CHEMICALS

In his book *Sweet and Dangerous,* Dr. Yudkin, emeritus professor of nutrition at Queen Elizabeth College, London University, has virtually nothing good to say about sugar. He claims that men who have suffered heart attacks have eaten larger quantities of sugar than those who have not had heart attacks. And Dr. Yudkin contends that sugar triggers the production of body chemicals that lead to heart disease. Other authorities, including Dr. Jeremiah Stamler, chairman of the department of community health and preventive medicine at Northwestern University Medical School, say that there is little reason to believe that sugar plays a specific role in causing heart trouble.

Dr. Yudkin has performed many experiments on how sugar affects the body. In one experiment 18 young men ate a normal diet for two weeks as Dr. Yudkin studied samples of their blood. Then, for two weeks, the men ate more sweet foods than usual. They substituted sugar for starch—say, a candy bar instead of a slice of bread. Tests then revealed that the levels of triglycerides and cholesterol—fatty chemicals—in the blood had increased for many of the men.

Scientists still are debating whether or not high levels of fatty chemicals in the blood cause heart disease. Most researchers believe they do. Meanwhile, evidence from some animal experiments also shows that sugar causes an increase in the level of these possibly dangerous chemicals in the blood. U.S. Department of Agriculture researchers fed one group of rats a 65 per cent sucrose diet after weaning, and they fed a second group a 65 per cent starch diet. When both groups reached adult age, the rats on the high-sugar diet had much higher cholesterol levels than those on starchy diets.

Researchers consider these results significant for humans because (1) rats and humans have similar body functions, and (2) though these rats were particularly sensitive to carbohydrates, so are about one in 20 Americans. Other scientists are searching for simple tests that will indicate who is especially sensitive to carbohydrates and who, therefore, should cut out sweets.

A LINK TO INFECTIONS

One recent scientific report links sugar with an increase in infections. Dr. U. D. Register, chairman of the department of nutrition at Loma Linda University in California, has studied the effects of sugar on white blood cells—the body's primary defense against all infections.

Dr. Register found that after a person eats from 18 to 20 spoonfuls of sucrose at one time there is a 50 per cent drop in the number of white blood cells. The quantity of sugar may sound large—but it is what the average person eats daily. According to Dr. Register, the white blood cell count returns to normal only after five or six hours. Until it does, the person—especially if a very young child—is very vulnerable to infections.

ABOUT QUICK ENERGY . . .

We have been told that sugar provides quick energy. It does get into the bloodstream and supply energy to tissues a few minutes faster than, say, a slice of bread and butter. But normally the body has a store of fuel in its tissues. So, unless a person is really weak and starving and has no fuel reserves, sugar is not a unique source of strength and energy. What most of us need is a balanced diet and the right amount of rest and exercise. The diet may, of course, include some sugar, such as the sugars in fresh fruits.

THOSE SUBSTITUTES

What about satisfying your sweet-tooth cravings? Many people have turned to sugar substitutes—artificial sweeteners. After cyclamates were banned, people turned to saccharin. But saccharin has a bitter aftertaste. Besides, it may be dangerous. In 1971 researchers at the Wisconsin Alumni Research Foundation Institute reported that some rats developed bladder tumors after a two-year diet containing 5 per cent saccharin.

In 1972 a committee sponsored by the National Academy of Sciences and the FDA began research on the safety of saccharin. So far it has not come up with conclusive results. Its chairman, Dr. Julius M. Coon, believes that pure saccharin may be safe but that the contaminants in commercially prepared saccharin may not be.

There is a potential newcomer to the sugar-substitute market, a synthetic prod-

U.S. Agricultural Research Service laboratory scientists comparing the consistency and texture of high-grade and low-grade raw sorghum sugars.

uct known as Aspartame. Because it is composed of two amino acids, the building blocks of proteins, it even has some nutritional value. And because Aspartame is 180 times sweeter than sugar, FDA officials believe that few people could eat enough of it to add up to more than eight calories a day. In mid-1975, sale of this sweetener was being held up by the FDA while it reexamined the safety of the product.

Perhaps, for your sweet tooth, nothing will ever quite take the place of sugar. But if the real thing is the culprit that some people believe it is, possibly a safe substitute will be the answer for you. It could be easier on your wallet and on your body, too□

SELECTED READINGS

"How Sweet It Is." *Newsweek*, Aug. 5, 1974.

"Saccharin Study: No Substitute for Data." *Science News*, Jan. 25, 1975.

Sweet and Dangerous by John Yudkin. Peter H. Wyden, Inc., 1972.

Soybeans

by Jenny Tesar

A soybean-based imitation meat dish. Clockwise from upper left: ham-flavored diced "meat," Bac-Os, chicken-flavored dices, and granules with a beef flavor.

A friend recently prepared a fine lunch that featured vegetable soup, chiliburgers, butterscotch pudding, and coffeecake. All his guests happily overate. And all were surprised to learn that the dishes had a common ingredient: soybeans. The soup contained pureed soybeans; the chili had whole soybeans; the burgers, mashed soybeans; the pudding, soy milk; and the coffeecake, soy oil.

In the last few years, interest in soybeans has jumped. Two trends account for much of this: (1) the desire of many people to switch from overly processed, additive-filled foods to natural foods; (2) increased concern over world food and energy problems.

Though the American public has just recently discovered the soybean, it has been a staple in East Asian diets for thousands of years. The soybean was introduced to Europe by a German botanist, Engelbert Kaempfer, who had visited Japan in the 1690's. The first mention of soybeans in the United States occurred in 1804—a physician named James Mease noted that Pennsylvania's climate was favorable for the cultivation of the plant. It wasn't until late in the 19th century, however, that U.S. agriculturists really began to realize the species' potential. Since then, the U.S. Department of Agriculture has evaluated more than 10,000 varieties and has been instrumental in developing new varieties.

A PROTEIN POWERHOUSE

The soybean plant (*Glycine max*) is in the pea, or legume, family. It ranges in height from less than 30 cm to more than 180 cm—about 1 ft to 6 ft. It generally has a deep branched taproot system. Like other legumes, the roots are invaded by nitrogen-fixing bacteria from the soil. The bacteria produce small swellings, or nodules, on the roots. Within the nodules the bacteria convert the free nitrogen of the atmosphere to a form usable by the plant.

As the plant matures, it produces small, inconspicuous white or purple flowers. The flowers give rise to fuzzy green pods, each of which contains two, three or four pea-sized beans.

From 40 to 45 per cent of a soybean may be protein—an unusually high fraction. This is double the percentage found in beef, three times that in eggs, and 11 times that in whole fresh milk. Nutritionally, soy protein is similar to animal protein. Thus it can take the place of animal protein in human diets. It contains insufficient amounts of the amino acid methionine, but this can be corrected by including corn, wheat, or milk in the diet.

The soybean is an important source of lecithin, a fatty substance found in all living cells. Lecithin contains important amino acids, and some evidence indicates it aids in lowering cholesterol levels in the body.

FOOD AND INDUSTRIAL USES

In Asia, soybean plants have always been raised primarily for the beans, which are used in food. But in the United States, soybean was first used as a forage crop, green manure, and cover crop. Not until 1935 did the acreage of plants raised for processing of beans equal that for forage; thereafter, however, the acreage for processing increased rapidly.

The products from soybeans can be divided into three categories:

Whole bean products that are used for cereals, flours, and other foodstuffs.

Meal products. The meal that remains after the oil has been extracted is an extremely valuable product. Approximately 95 per cent of the soybean meal produced in the United States is used as a feed for poultry and livestock; 66 per cent of the total vegetable protein meal consumed by such animals is soybean meal.

Soybean meal is used to improve the body and flavor of beer, in pet foods, and in imitation meats. Soybean flour is used in a wide variety of edible products such as baked goods and cereals. It serves as an emulsifier and binder in sausages and other meat products, as well as in ice cream and whipped toppings.

Soybean meal products are also used in the manufacture of antibiotics and printing inks, as sizing in papers and textiles, and for finishing leather.

Oil products. Many Americans were first introduced to soybeans during World War II, when they turned to margarine made with soybean oil as a substitute for butter. Today, the use of margarine leads butter use by 2 to 1. Soybean oil is also used to make salad oils and shortening.

About 85 per cent of the soybean oil consumed in the United States is used in food products. The rest is used in industry —in, for example, the manufacture of high-grade paint enamels and the production of insecticides, adhesives, linoleum, soap, caulking compounds, cosmetics, and synthetic rubber.

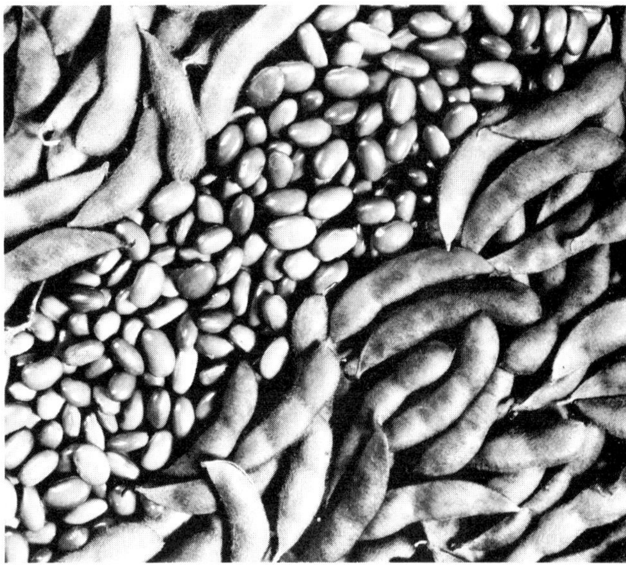

Soybean pods and beans. The beans are made into a wide variety of nutritious foods.

AT YOUR SUPERMARKET: TVP

What makes bacon taste like bacon, chicken like chicken? Scientists have isolated many of the chemicals that make up meat flavors. By adding these chemicals to flavorless and odorless soy flour or concentrated soy protein, they have created imitation meat that tastes a lot like the real thing.

When meat prices climbed to record highs in the mid-1970's, supermarkets began adding soy extender to chopped meat, offering this "beef patty mix" to consumers at prices well below the price of a comparable amount of beef. Soy extender is also available separately so that people can add it to dishes prepared at home.

It is also possible to spin the soy protein into meatlike fibers, which can then be flavored. Such fibers are called textured vegetable protein (TVP) and are used to make imitation meat, or meat analogs. These products look and taste like meat even when cooked. Imitation bacon bits, sausagelike breakfast links, frozen chicken à la king and escalloped potatoes, and canned baked beans—these are only some of the products containing TVP-based analogs, and the use of TVP is predicted to increase.

WARM SUMMERS AND WATER

The soybean plant prefers regions with summer rains but will also do well under irrigation anywhere with warm summers. Approximately one half of the U.S. soybean crop is grown in the Corn Belt: Ohio, Indiana, Illinois, Iowa, and Missouri. The crop is becoming increasingly important in the southeastern states and in the lower Mississippi Valley. In 1973, U.S. farmers harvested over 1,500,000,000 bushels of beans. This was about 75 per cent of the world's production, making the United States the major soybean-producing nation. China was second, Brazil third.

RESEARCHERS LOOK AT YIELDS

Biologists are concentrating efforts on trying to increase the crop's yield. The Program for International Research, Improvement and Development of Soybeans, located at the University of Illinois, coordinates research. It is directed by Earl R. Leng, who indicates that current soybean yields are generally limited by the following factors: (1) insufficient productive potential of local varieties; (2) low soil fertility; (3) very low plant populations; (4) the absence of effective bacterial populations in the roots; (5) damage by insects, plant diseases, and weeds; and (6) growing the crop during unfavorable weather conditions.

Soy protein can be spun into fibers. These textured vegetable protein (TVP) fibers are then colored and flavored for meat analogs.

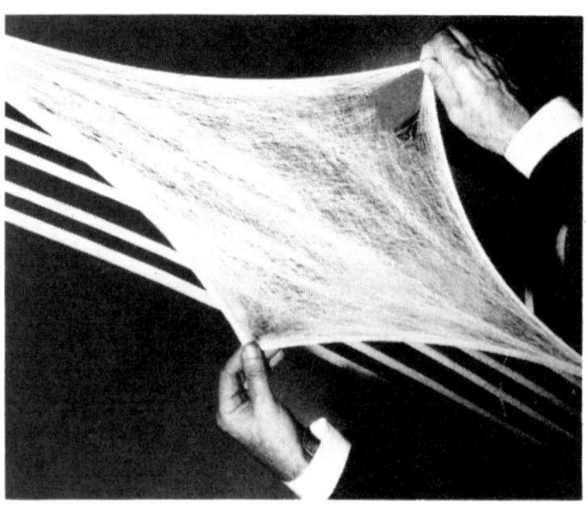

CHEAPER AND MORE HEALTHFUL

There are advantages of a diet that substitutes soybean products for meat products. First, it is cheaper. When judged by the amount of protein, vitamins, minerals, and energy provided per unit of cost, soybean meal is one of the cheapest foods available. A 1973 study conducted at Kansas State University indicated that 70 per cent protein soy flour cost 21¢ per pound of food, or 30¢ per pound of protein. Beef at 75¢ per pound of food cost $4.20 per pound of protein. This cost differential is due in large part to the fact that farmers must feed about 45 kg (100 lb) of plant protein to a steer to produce 2.2 kg (5 lb) of edible meat protein.

Second, eating soybean is more healthful than eating meat because one ingests less fat and fewer calories, and soy oil is very low in cholesterol.

Third, it requires the use of less land. For example, 10 times more land is needed to produce natural (pig) bacon than is needed to produce the same amount of bacon analog from appropriately processed soybeans.

Fourth, because the plants contain nitrogen-fixing bacteria, they require less fertilizer than other crops. And, since the production of fertilizer involves the use of a large amount of oil, legumes are energy-saving□

"A Bean to Feed the World?" by Richard Rhodes. *The Atlantic*, January 1975.

Modern Soybean Production by Walter O. Scott and Samuel R. Aldrich. S&A Publications, Champaign, Ill., 1970.

The Professional Chef's Soy Protein Recipe Ideas by Nance Snyder. Cahners Books, 1971.

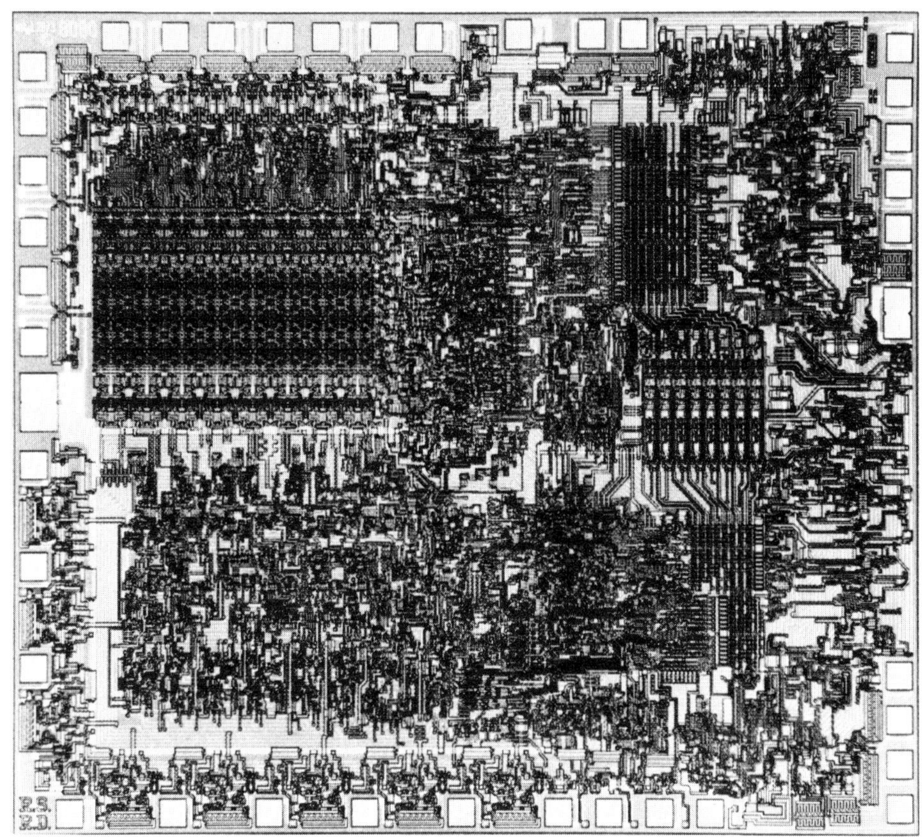

computers and mathematics

contents

Photomicrograph of an 8-bit microprocessor integrated circuit. This incredibly complex circuitry fits into a tiny chip, the size of the rectangle at the lower left edge of the photo.

review of the year

computers and mathematics

Computers. The trend toward smaller and smaller computers continued in 1974 with the rapid development of the microcomputer. The heart of the microcomputer is a tiny chip of silicon packed with thousands of transistors. This chip, called a microprocessor, functions in the same way as the central processing unit in a standard computer. Thus small-scale memory systems and other units can be linked with the chip to produce a complete micro-computing device. The general-purpose design of a microprocessor permits it to be adapted to a wide range of control and automation functions. It cannot handle many operations at once and does not perform as rapidly as larger computers. But its size and inexpensiveness make it useful to small businesses and laboratories that cannot afford or do not need large-scale systems. In an automated factory of the future, each machine could be fitted with its own microcomputer "brain," linked with the factory's hierarchy of mini-computers and a central computer. It could also function alone. Similar set-ups may come to be applied to the business machines in a large office, the traffic lights in a city, and many other systems.

The market for calculators that can be programmed is also growing rapidly, even as the sale of calculating machines in general has begun to level off. While programmable calculators are more complex than ordinary models, they are still simpler to operate than computers. They do not require specially-trained personnel, and they use the familiar decimal system of numbers rather than the binary system of standard computers. Very complex programmable calculators are already beginning to compete in the minicomputer market. International Business Machines Corp. (IBM) has brought out its smallest general-business computer yet. Called "System 32," the desk-size computer includes a central processing unit, memory and storage system, and an operating console with a display screen, keyboard, and printer. It can be used alone or as a terminal for a larger computer. Another IBM innovation is its "3850" system for mass storage of data, to be used with its System 370 computers. The "3850" system will be especially useful for businesses that handle enormous amounts of data, such as insurance companies. It uses a new kind of magnetic tape, which comes in cartridge-like reels that can hold six times as much data as standard tape reels. The cartridges are stored in honeycomb-like cells in cabinets. When needed, they are retrieved by a robot device and loaded for use within three or four seconds.

IBM's desk-sized System/32 computer was designed for use by small businesses and institutions such as hospitals.

An experiment at Stanford Research Institute attempted to feed commands directly from a human brain into a computer. The subjects of the experiment —25 in all—wore an electrode-studded helmet that was linked to the computer by an electroencephalograph, a device for recording brain waves. The computer was also linked to a television screen on which a white dot was displayed. When a subject thought one of seven simple commands—up, down, left, right, slow, fast, or stop—the dot on the screen was supposed to obey this order. It would do so because, prior to the test run, electroencephalograph recordings had been made of the subject as he thought each of the commands. These specific brain-wave patterns were then stored in the computer's memory. Thus when the subject was linked to the computer and told to rethink one of the commands, the computer was to search its memory, identify the brain-wave pattern being emitted, and move the dot accordingly. The result of the experiment was that the computer moved the dot correctly 60 per cent of the time. Lawrence Pinneo and his colleagues, who conducted the project, think that computers eventually will be able to read brain waves efficiently. Indeed, the time may come when information can flow the opposite way—from computer to brain—thus realizing the "thinking caps" of fable.

In IBM's 3850 storage system, data cartridges housed in honeycomb compartments can be retrieved by a robotlike device.

A New Form of Mathematics. A new way to handle the infinitely large and infinitely small was the subject of much attention at the annual meeting of the American Mathematical Society in Washington, D.C., in January 1975. The new system, known as "nonstandard analysis," was mainly the work of the late Abraham Robinson of Yale University. Nonstandard analysis adopts an "infinitesimal" approach. For example, it conceives of a line as consisting of an infinite number of points separated by infinitely small distances. An "infinitesimal" approach to calculus was first developed in the 17th century by Sir Isaac Newton and Gottfried W. von Leibniz, but it resulted in mathematical paradoxes, and "modern calculus" with its concept of limits was devised. Nonstandard analysis returns to the infinitesimal approach and seeks to avoid the paradoxes. It does this by conceiving of each infinitely small interval as, in itself, consisting of a complete series of "nonstandard" numbers that can be handled as in conventional mathematics. Similarly, infinite terms can be expanded into complete series of nonstandard numbers. (See "A New Form of Mathematics" on page 92.)

Steven Moll

Mathematics and Social Problems. A group of 30 mathematicians and medical experts gathered in Utah in the summer of 1974 to consider the problems of disease epidemics. The meeting was arranged by SIMS, the SIAM Institute for Mathematics and Society, which was formed in 1973 to assist social scientists and public administrators in their work. (SIAM stands for The Society for Industrial and Applied Mathematics.) The association between mathematics and the study of epidemics began more than a century ago, during a cholera outbreak in London. A British scientist found that deaths from cholera clustered suspiciously close to a certain public well in London, and concluded that the well was somehow causing cholera. City officials sealed off the well and, sure enough, the epidemic soon died out.

A subject wearing an electrode-studded helmet is asked to say or think specific words. Her brain's electrical signals are transmitted to a computer for analysis.

Strangely enough, until the SIMS meeting, mathematicians had done little more in solving the problems of how epidemics start, spread, and finally dwindle. Some relations suggest themselves. For example, the waves of flu epidemics that often sweep around the world resemble the flow of heat or of fluids. And mathematicians have studied heat and fluid flow for many years. Other, less contagious diseases "jump" from place to place through chance contacts between persons. Hop-and-skip problems like these are also familiar to mathematicians, but they are usually more difficult to handle.

Perhaps the most important discovery of the SIMS meeting was that many theoretically-inclined mathematicians need to learn how public health agencies function. Such agencies are often bogged down in political or financial problems. Public health officials need to make difficult choices in deciding how to use the funds they obtain. Mathematicians, well trained in the tools of decision-making, can help in such matters. Once they have learned the biology of epidemic diseases—and the political and financial complications that may be involved—they can be of great help in dealing with epidemics.

George A. W. Boehm

A New Form of Mathematics

by Walter Sullivan

THERE'S big news in the world of numbers. The men who work in that world are talking about a new form of mathematics—a new approach that adds to the store of numbers they can use. The new approach also seems to clear up certain old mathematical paradoxes. And it may be of wide importance for economics, physics, biology, and our concept of time.

Therefore it is no surprise that this new development has aroused a good deal of interest. It was the subject of four special lectures at the annual meeting of the American Mathematical Society, held in Washington, D.C., in January 1975. The lecturer was H. Jerome Keisler of the University of Wisconsin, who has written a calculus text using the new approach.

The name of this new approach is "nonstandard analysis." It was developed by Abraham Robinson, a Yale University professor who died in 1974. Robinson was best known for his work in mathematical logic, but he also directed his attention to practical problems. Born in Germany and educated in Jerusalem, he served as a scientific officer with the British Royal Aircraft Establishment in World War II. There he became an authority on wing design. He is credited with laying the mathematical foundations for the design of the triangular "delta" wing used on high-speed aircraft.

LOOKING AT THE INFINITE

Robinson's method of nonstandard analysis is also a combination of the theoretical and the practical. As Keisler's book indicates, it makes a new approach to calculus possible. And calculus is a very widely used branch of mathematics. It can deal with changing situations of all sorts—for example, biological and economic growth, the movement of bodies, and the burning of fuels.

Nonstandard analysis involves the concept of the infinitely large and the infinitely small, or infinitesimal. The roots of this new approach reach back into antiquity. The speculations of the Greek mathematicians and the paradoxes of the philosopher Zeno dealt with the infinitesimal. But nonstandard analysis approaches this concept in a way that enables it to deal with mathematical problems that previously had seemed impossible to handle.

Robinson's approach is in some ways a return to the original "infinitesimal" calculus developed by Isaac Newton and Gottfried Wilhelm von Leibniz in the 17th century. In this early form of calculus, a line was thought of as being made up of an infinite number of points separated by infinitesimal distances. But at the same time, these distances were considered larger than zero.

These two descriptions seemed to lead to an unavoidable paradox. That is, both were apparently true, and yet they contradicted each other. For example, suppose that the infinitesimal distances *are* larger than zero. No matter how small they are, it would appear that a number of them added together would have some length. Yet the way that infinitesimals were used in calculus implied that any number of them would still be infinitely small. This contradiction led Newton's contemporary, the philosopher George Berkeley, to call the idea of infinitesimals "obscure, repugnant, and precarious."

Over the next two centuries, a new calculus with a concept of limit was devised. This "modern calculus," which is in use today, avoided recourse to infinitesimals and thus avoided the above paradox. But some mathematicians consider the infinitesimal approach more "intuitive"—that is, closer to the way the human mind actually conceives infinities. Nonstandard analysis seems a move back toward this more intuitive approach. That is why Keisler wrote his new calculus text based on Robinson's work on nonstandard analysis.

NUMBERING INFINITIES

Robinson saw the "infinitesimal" problem as a problem in the "language"—particularly the numbering system—now being used in mathematics. In the course of his work in model theory—a relatively new field of mathematical logic which Robinson helped to found—he formulated a new approach to numbering.

In Robinson's system, an infinitely small interval within a series of standard numbers can be looked upon as a complete series of numbers in itself. Seen from "within" the interval, these "nonstandard" numbers can be thought of as ordinary real numbers such as 1, 2, 3, and so on. That is, within the interval, they behave as numbers do in conventional mathematics. Seen from "outside" the interval, however, the series of nonstandard numbers shrinks to the infinitesimal.

According to Robinson's system, the same numbering idea can be applied to the infinitely large. That is, what appears as an infinite term in conventional mathematics can be expanded into a series of nonstandard numbers that then can be handled as numbers ordinarily are.

Some mathematicians—though as yet by no means all of them—think that this new, "nonstandard" way of looking at numbers will prove very useful. They believe that for the first time it will become possible to deal effectively with practical problems involving numbers so large that they border on the infinite. Among many such problems are the behavior of molecules in a fluid, and economic projections that include huge numbers of buyers and sellers. For example, in 1973 Robinson and Donald J. Brown, a theoretical economist at Yale, were using nonstandard analysis to attack the relationship between bargaining and the competitive price system.

AN AID TO QUANTUM THEORY?

Robinson also sought to apply nonstandard analysis to quantum theory in physics. In considering the behavior of atomic particles, quantum theory states that it is impossible to predict the actions of one particular particle. It is only possible to predict the average behavior of a large number of particles. For example, one can predict how fast a certain radioactive element will decay, but not when any particular atom of that element will in fact decay.

This "uncertainty principle," set forth by Werner Heisenberg in 1927, also holds

In nonstandard analysis both the infinitely small interval (left) and the infinitely large (right) can be viewed as composed of a series of nonstandard numbers.

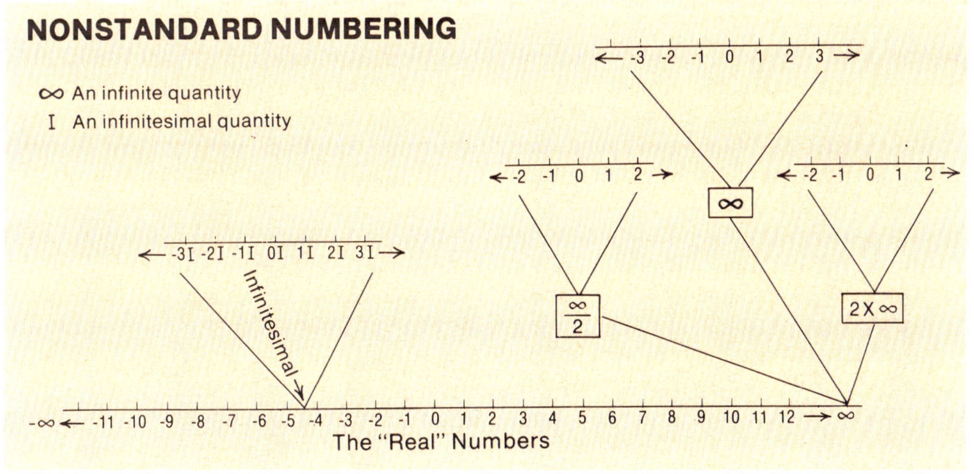

that it is impossible to determine both the position and the velocity of a particle at the same time. To some physicists the uncertainty principle merely states a present shortcoming of human ability. But the stronger belief among physicists is that the uncertainty principle is a basic part of the nature of things. Robinson's nonstandard formulations lead toward this same outlook. They indicate that there are limits to the precision with which mathematical language can describe a situation. For this reason, some theoretical physicists are hopeful that nonstandard analysis will help in understanding some of the puzzling aspects of quantum theory. This sort of use of mathematics is similar to the way that advanced forms of algebra have been used to recognize natural laws in classifying atomic particles.

AN OLD PROBLEM OF TIME

Nonstandard analysis may also help to resolve an ancient problem relating to time. The problem dates back almost 2,500 years, to the days when Greek philosophers such as Democritus and Zeno debated the nature of time and motion.

The paradoxes of Zeno were concerned in various ways with the problem of the infinite and the infinitesimal. The most famous paradox involves an imaginary race between Achilles and a tortoise. Supposing that the tortoise had a head start, Zeno theorized that Achilles would never catch up. His argument was that while Achilles covered the distance from his starting point to the tortoise's position when Achilles began, the tortoise would have advanced a certain distance. While Achilles covered this farther distance, the tortoise would have advanced still farther, and so on. Not that Zeno actually thought Achilles would never pass the tortoise. It was the way that the problem was stated that made this seem logically impossible —and a paradox.

The solution to this paradox was stated in terms of distances that shrank toward the infinitesimally small. The reasoning involved in the solution was closely related to the reasoning that gave birth to calculus. However, two conflicting concepts of time emerged. One concept saw time as an unbroken flow, a continuum. The other, widely used in practical problems, saw time as a series of individual moments defined in terms of minutes and seconds and fractions of seconds.

In the continuum concept, there is no such thing as "a moment later." But in the other view, time is seen as a succession of moments separated by finite intervals —finite, to meet the old argument against infinitesimals. With the use of nonstandard analysis, it is believed that these two concepts can be combined. This would resolve the difficulty of having two different approaches to situations involving the flow of time.

A USEFUL FICTION FOR THE FUTURE

At a memorial service for Robinson in the fall of 1974, Yale philosophy professor Stephen Korner noted that Robinson did not believe that infinite totalities really exist. Mathematicians should act "as if" they are real, he said. But nonstandard numbers are actually no more than a useful fiction.

An international gathering of mathematicians at Yale University in May 1975 was slated to examine the implications of Robinson's work. This would include his role in developing that branch of logic known as model theory. One notable assessment has already been made. Kurt Godel, a German regarded by some mathematicians as the world's leading logician, has called Robinson's contributions lastingly important. He has also predicted, "There is good reasons to believe that nonstandard analysis will be the analysis of the future"□

SELECTED READINGS

The Lore of Large Numbers by Philip J. Davis. Random House, 1961.

Modern Science and Zeno's Paradoxes by Adolf Gruenbaum. Wesleyan University Press, 1967.

Non-Standard Analysis by Abraham Robinson. Humanities Press, 1966.

Number: The Language of Science by Tobias Dantzig, 4th edition. Free Press, 1967.

Teams of experts are seeking ways to make computer networks secure from tampering. Douglas Engelbart, director of the Augmentation Research Center, Stanford Research Institute, tests procedures for revising a displayed text.

The Computer Rip-off

by Tom Alexander

ONE morning in the fall of 1973 a computer operator on duty at Honeywell Information Systems Inc. in Phoenix, Arizona, was startled to see the output printer on the computer's console start up all by itself. Out rattled a message that referred derisively to a recent Honeywell press release about the company's new computer system, called "Multics." When it finished sniping at Multics, the mysterious message signed off with the words "ZARF is with you again."

ZARF is the code designation for part of a joint project of the U.S. Air Force and MITRE Corp., a defense-research company. The project is concerned with computer security, and a favorite pastime of people involved in it is cracking "uncrackable" computers. The day before the Honeywell computer acted up, two ZARF men, Air Force Major Roger Schell and Steven Lipner of MITRE, visited Honeywell to look over the security features of prospective systems for classified Air Force computing chores. After seeing the press release about Multics, Lipner quietly placed a long-distance call to a ZARF colleague, Lieutenant Paul Karger, in Massachusetts, nearly 5,000 km (3,000 mi) away. Karger, in turn, sat down at his teletypewriter computer terminal, dialed into Honeywell's private Multics system, and typed in a few subtle instructions. These instructions subverted every one of the system's safeguards, giving Karger effective control of the computer system.

The ZARF prank was particularly embarrassing because Multics was designed with security as an uppermost consideration. Of all large commercial computers on the market, Multics probably incorporates the most elaborate safeguards against unauthorized tampering.

GROWING FEARS OVER SECURITY

The kind of vulnerability indicated by ZARF's little joke is beginning to disturb the keepers of modern electronic-data-processing (EDP) systems. Most EDP systems consist of one or more large, multipurpose computers and banks of stored data. These are usually accessible by means of telephone circuits from individual terminals, such as the teletypewriter that Lieutenant Karger used. Until not long ago, computer manufacturers and users saw little reason to fear that an unscrupulous person at one terminal would be able to read, alter, or delete another user's data, or tamper with the intricate programs that manipulate the data. But by now, even the computer manufacturers have more or less come to acknowledge that it is not really very difficult for someone with a lot of skill to do things like that, even with the most secure systems now in existence. According to one expert, it's about as difficult "as solving a hard Sunday crossword puzzle."

Computers, of course, have come to be deeply and pervasively involved in basic functions of our society. Top executives may die, factories blow up, or foreign subsidiaries get nationalized, but if you really want to see a company president blanch, ask him what he would do if the magnetic tapes with his accounts receivable got erased.

Electronic and magnetic data have not only replaced manually kept books, but have also gone a long way toward replacing tangible assets, including money itself. Today's credit-card system, for example, is an offspring of computerization. In the words of a former top computer expert who is now a banker, "The base form of an asset is no longer necessarily a 400-ounce gold bar; now assets are often simply magnetic wiggles on a disk."

KINDS OF COMPUTER CRIMES

Gold bars in vaults, notations in a ledger, or, for that matter, written reports from a corporate research project are unchangeable and immovable things compared to magnetic wiggles on a computer tape. Computer-stored data can be read, altered, or destroyed at the touch of a teletypewriter key. For criminal purposes, funds can be fraudulently credited to an account, a bank balance can be programmed never to fail, the record of ownership of very large sums can be changed, and so on.

This is not to say that computer crime is an overwhelming source of loss as yet. Robert Courtney, who is the man responsible for the safeguards that go into I.B.M. equipment—and who is therefore likely to be one of the first people called

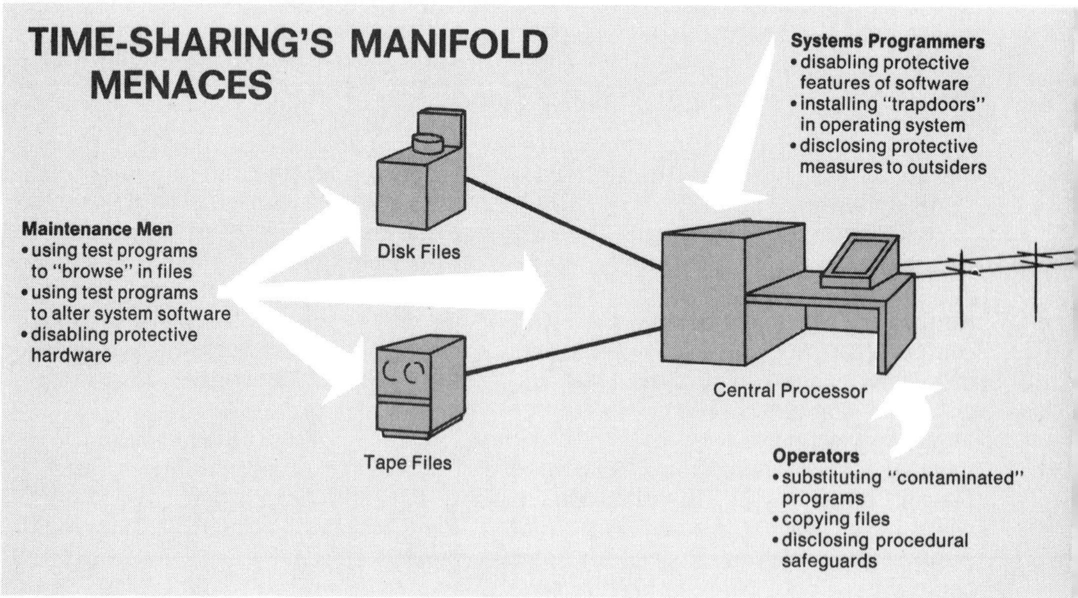

when something goes wrong—ranks computer-related losses in six categories in decreasing order of occurrence. The largest category, accounting for about one half of all losses, consists of errors and omissions by clerical and data-processing employees. Next in order is employee dishonesty. Then come losses of data and equipment in fires; sabotage by disgruntled employees; and water damage such as may result from floods and sprinkler-system malfunctions. Lastly, an "other" category includes remote manipulation of the computer system by outsiders—that is, by people not employed by the company.

But there seem to be reasons to fear that criminal losses—whether the work of insiders or of outsiders—will grow much larger as time goes by. For one thing, Courtney has found that employee dishonesty has risen from fourth place to second since 1972. This may mean that it just takes time for dishonest people to learn how to take advantage of their opportunities.

Most of the present concern about computer security seems to have emerged since the widely publicized Equity Funding insurance swindle that broke open in 1973. The swindle was really more an instance of old-fashioned fraud than a feat of computer manipulation. But it pretty well demonstrated that conventional auditing practice is all but helpless when confronting deception involving computers. The auditors have lost their traditional "paper trail" of orders, invoices, bills, and receipts to pore through on the track of irregularity.

TEACHING COMPUTERS TO LIE

The main group to benefit from the Equity Funding revelations has been the small but growing corps of specialists who claim to be able to write programs to make the computer do the auditing. That is, they program the computer to perform various accounting cross-checks and to throw up a warning when certain suspicious transactions occur. This sort of auditing, however, like everything else that goes on inside a computer, is only as dependable as the computer itself. And unfortunately, computers can be programmed to lie or conceal as easily as they can be programmed for truth.

Inklings of the computer's special potential for fraudulent use began to surface in the 1960's. The earliest federal prosecution, in 1966, involved a young program-

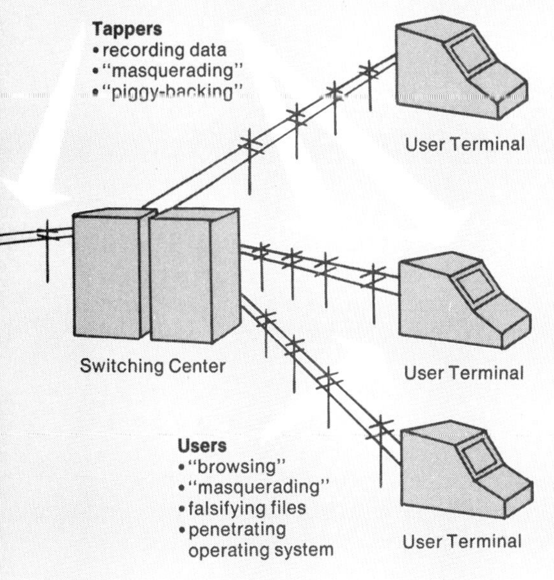

The programmers who write the software can subvert supposed protective features or install "trapdoors" for subsequent entry. Operators may have daily opportunity to tamper with data or files. Maintenance men may incorporate subversive instructions into the test programs they employ to test for malfunctions. Wiretaps and various bugging devices can intercept data transmissions or even pick up electromagnetic emanations from wires and terminals. The tappers may use intercepted passwords to "masquerade" as legitimate users, or may even insert "piggyback" data into legitimate transmissions. Sometimes legitimate users borrow passwords to masquerade or browse in other people's files. And persons posing as legitimate users may employ a large variety of tricks to penetrate operating systems from afar.

mer in a Minneapolis bank who instructed the computer to ignore all overdrafts from his account. In that case, discovery occurred when the computer failed one day and the bank had to go back to manual processing.

One of the more disturbing aspects of computer crime, in fact, is that detection, when it occurs, usually occurs by accident. Early in 1973, New York police raided a bookie and learned that one of his best customers was a man who for weeks at a time had gambled $30,000 a day. When detectives looked into the man's background, they discovered that he was an $11,000-a-year teller at New York's Union Dime Savings Bank. It turned out that he had access to one of the bank's computer terminals. For more than three years, he had been using the device to milk hundreds of savings accounts, netting $1.5 million.

Combining workaday larceny with computer skill, he would accept a customer's deposits at the teller window and pocket most of the money. Later, he would go to a computer terminal and type in false information to the machine. Or he would instruct it to transfer money into the customer's account from one of hundreds of other accounts that had shown little activity over several years.

TIME-SHARING AND NETWORKING

Cases like this involve comparatively simple manipulations of the computer toward narrow aims. These crimes are fundamentally no different from what a dishonest bookkeeper might try to accomplish. Furthermore, they are the kind of thing that computer auditing should be able to prevent. In the last couple of years, however, it has come to be recognized that the newer generations of computers, by the nature of their design, are vulnerable to more cunning forms of subversion.

The leading expert on the history of computer crime is Donn Parker, a former computer manager who is now a researcher at Stanford Research Institute in Menlo Park, California. Parker points out that "computer technology, over the years, was based upon the assumption of a benign, nonhostile environment." The machines were designed to provide maximum efficiency and easiness of use by friendly, honest employees, within secure computer rooms to which access was limited.

In addition, newer computers were put to uses that were not clearly anticipated by the designers. At the same time as these new computers were being developed, the Massachusetts Institute of Technology (M.I.T.) and other institutions were perfecting the concept of "time-sharing." Time-sharing makes it possible for many individuals in remote locations to use the same machine at the same time by means of terminals and telephone lines. It has placed the advantages of computer use at the fingertips of people who might never have been able to afford a computer of their own. Another development, called "networking," has made it possible to link several computers and data banks together. This allows widely separated installations to share data.

Time-sharing and networking are "multi-access" systems. Several individuals or companies have access to and can use a single computer system. In all such systems, each user has the impression that the entire computer is at his disposal. Actually, the machine may be serving many users at once. It is reading each user's typed commands and parceling out milliseconds of time as it enters and removes pieces of programs and data in and out of its circuits and memory banks. While it is doing all this, the system is supposed to keep each user's data separate from those of every other user. This is done by means of a system of secret passwords or code numbers, together with "access controls" programmed into the system itself. Each person types in his number or password at the beginning of his session to identify himself as a legitimate user. The access controls then specify what data and programs he is authorized to use. They "tag" and keep track of his work as it moves through the stages of processing.

These housekeeping functions are controlled by a very complex collection of special supervisory programs called the "operating system." These programs are permanently stored in the computer and are altogether distinct from the "applications programs." The applications programs are the instructions for carrying out special tasks, such as a payroll run, a bank's daily accounting, or a scientific problem.

THE PERILS OF COMPLEXITY

The troubling fact is that the typical operating system of today is pathetically exposed to tampering. For one thing, manufacturers and users have to be able to make changes in the system's programs and data contents. Such changes may involve the passwords or privileges granted to any user. For this reason, the manuals that come with each system contain a number of standard code words that act as keys to unlock or bypass the access controls or safeguards. These standard code words are called "systems commands."

In many systems, therefore, all that a would-be wrongdoer needs is to be familiar with the manufacturer's manuals, know the telephone number of the target installation, and have access to a terminal. He can dial in and identify himself somehow as a legitimate user. He can then type in commands that make the system reveal its passwords, the names of other users, their privileges, data files, and so forth. Once he has the passwords, any user can masquerade as another user. Or he can pose as a staffer with authorization to make changes in the system's password-privilege list—or, for that matter, in the operating system's own programs.

Like the passwords, the systems-command code words are arbitrarily chosen and can be changed as easily as the lock on a door. That would foil inexpert intruders. Crack programmers, however, have demonstrated that it is not necessary to know the systems commands in order to take over any major operating system that now exists. For one thing, each of

A key lock (projecting from the right side of this IBM 3270 information display system) restricts access to stored data.

the command code words is really a shorthand symbol that stands for a prewritten "miniprogram" stored in the computer. When the word is used, this program carries out the various steps required to unlock the system's safeguards. A skilled would-be penetrator with access to the proper manuals can figure out everything he needs to write his own program, type it in, and subvert an operating system.

Another weak point derives from the sheer complexity of today's operating systems. Some operating systems contain hundreds of thousands of separate instructions. Thus hundreds of errors inevitably creep in—either oversights in the design of the safeguards or simple mistakes in the writing of the instructions. Many of these errors must be located and corrected before the system will work at all, but some remain hidden—or annoyingly evident—for years.

Under certain circumstances, these errors will let data leak from one user's domain into another's. They may even open a way into the supposedly very secure territory of the operating system itself. Many a subscriber to a commercial time-sharing service, having accidentally pressed a certain combination of keys, has found someone else's data rattling out unbidden. By now, a lot of people have learned how to exploit "software," or programming, errors deliberately—not only to read data stored in the machine, but also to type in changes in safeguards, data, and programs.

ATTACKS BY TIGER TEAMS

The first delighted exploiters of these software quirks were the "systems hackers"—students at universities where some of the first time-sharing systems had been installed as far back as the mid-1960's. Among other things, faculty members stored grades and examinations in some of these systems. Systems hackers then became adept at changing their own grades or reading upcoming exam questions.

A computer controls access to this door. The "key" is a thin card with a magnetic stripe that tells a computer to release the lock.

By the late 1960's, computer experts at Rand Corporation were warning their government patrons that all the multi-access systems on the market were vulnerable to tampering. Since then, under contracts with the U.S. Defense Department, Rand and a number of other organizations have been seeking methods to improve operating-system security and ascertain whether any system is really secure. The most glamorous phase of this activity is the work of the "tiger teams," who actually try to penetrate systems being considered for defense uses. So far, no major system has withstood a dedicated attack by a tiger team.

The disturbing implications of all this are only now coming to be widely recognized. In principle, the ability to take over a computer's operating system implies having access to all data and all programs on the machine, together with the ability to change them at will. Properly done, such tampering is likely to go undetected. For criminal purposes, such control would be something like having a small army of corrupt bookkeepers at one's command, but without all the risks of exposure that relying on the cooperation of human beings entails.

Multi-access systems are being used increasingly for the storage and transfer of valuable assets and data. Therefore a number of computer professionals have begun speculating about the grave potentialities for criminal manipulation of computer systems. Among them is Clark Weissman, a manager of computer-security research with System Development Corporation. Weissman believes that a lot of criminal activity could already be going on, leaving no external evidence. "Sherlock Holmes," he says, "can't come in and find any heel marks. There's no safe with its door blown off. Many companies wouldn't even know their data's been manipulated." As for auditing programs, "the first thing the interloper would do is corrupt the audit-trail software itself."

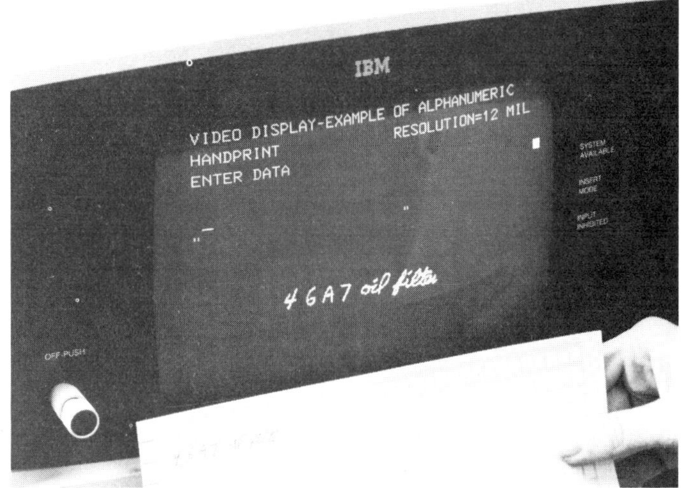

An optical character reader introduced in 1974 is able to capture, store, and display letters, numbers, and even signatures that are normally unreadable by optical scanning devices.

THE EXTENT OF THE PROBLEM

No one has valid statistics as to how much of this sophisticated subversion goes on, but from all indications, a lot more goes on than is ever detected. Donn Parker concludes that of nearly 175 cases of computer crime he has looked into, hardly any were uncovered through normal security precautions and accounting controls. Nearly all were exposed accidentally. One expert guesses that the ratio of undiscovered to discovered crimes may be on the order of a hundred to one.

A lot of the computer crime that is detected, moreover, is never publicly announced. Most security experts have collections of incidents that they have investigated but that were never reported to the police. Furthermore, some banks and companies candidly admit that when an incident is discovered, the corporate victims usually try to avoid the embarrassment and loss of confidence that publicity might bring. According to I.B.M.'s Robert Courtney, "It's generally accepted in this business that about 85 per cent of detected frauds are never brought to the attention of law-enforcement people. The companies just eat 'em. Of the 15 per cent announced, a fair number are brought in from the outside by police."

What often happens is that the offender, once detected, is required to make restitution and then leave. Sometimes he even gets severance pay and letters of reference to speed him away. One consequence, no doubt, is a circulating population of unpunished, unrepentant, and unrecognized embezzlers going from company to company. Probably a more serious consequence, though, has been to suppress recognition of the extent of computer crime, and thereby to lull both makers and users of computers into minimizing the problem.

Computers appear to have magnified the potential rewards to the criminal. Parker analyzed 12 cases of computerized bank embezzlement that occurred in 1971 and found that the losses averaged $1.09 million apiece, or about ten times the average embezzlement loss. And ever larger amounts of credit and other assets are moving onto EDP systems. Thus it seems inevitable that more criminally inclined people with more elaborate resources will grab for the prizes so temptingly exposed. "There are something like a million programmers in the country right now," observes Willis Ware, a pioneer computer-security expert at Rand, "and if only one per cent of these were inclined to be dishonest, that's 10,000 dishonest programmers."

Especially troubling is the thought of even a one per cent incidence of dishonesty among the "systems program-

Project RISOS (Research in Secured Operating Systems) at California's Lawrence Livermore Laboratory seeks to develop better guidelines for computer security.

mers" who write the operating systems for the computer vendors or modify them to fit the needs of particular users. These programmers are the people most knowledgeable about the intricacies and weaknesses of specific systems. Robert Jacobson, a vice president of Sentor Security Group, Inc., jokingly said, "Ideally, the first step in securing a system would be to shoot the programmer."

In a really big job, the programmer or programmers would probably have accomplices with other skills. A somber prediction along this line comes from Robert Abbott, director of an Advanced Research Projects Agency computer-security project at Lawrence Livermore Laboratory. "It's only a matter of time," he says, "until somebody mounts a team-directed approach, involving programmers, accountants, and maybe wiretappers and burglars. When it happens, it's going to be awful."

LACK OF PROPER SECURITY

One problem for would-be perpetrators is the difficulty of obtaining detailed knowledge about a given organization's EDP system, procedures, and accounting controls. Aside from that problem, the principal defenses against computer frauds right now are the passwords. And passwords often turn out to be a laughably weak defense, even against those without fancy programming skills. A lackadaisical attitude toward security persists in many EDP installations. For instance, it is apparent to the casual visitor to the offices of the average time-sharing company or service bureau that he would have little trouble walking in—posing perhaps as a prospective customer, a delivery messenger, or even a legitimate but confused user—and scooping up proprietary tapes, printouts, or passwords.

It has also been demonstrated on more than one occasion that a persuasive liar on a telephone can entice employees of a time-sharing system into giving out passwords. In all sorts of computer installations, people bandy passwords about or write them down. Wastebaskets galore are stuffed with printouts on which passwords are visible. And often there will be some employee who will provide passwords for a bribe. Everything else failing, a prospective intruder has technical means at his disposal. For example, he might dial up a system, plug a small computer into the line, and set it to trying out passwords until he finds the correct one.

Generally speaking, computer security is obtained only at some cost, part of which is the inconvenience to the ordinary people who must use the machines. Many organizations, in seeking a proper balance, often put convenience to their harried, forgetful users ahead of airtight security. In the case of commercial time-sharing services, at least, it appears that if customers are really concerned about the privacy of certain information, they had better keep it out of those systems.

Other defenses besides passwords have been devised. One possibility is to program the computer to identify legitimate users by asking random questions—for example, about family background. "The trouble with that," says Robert Courtney, "is that if you're running thousands of transactions a day, you don't much care to spend ten seconds or so every time arguing with the computer about who you are." I.B.M. is currently trying out, among other things, the use of magnetically striped cards that users can insert into terminals to prove their identity. Already, though, tinkerers have found that it is no great feat to counterfeit such a card, using ordinary magnetic tape. A number of companies are working on devices that will recognize personal characteristics such as the shape of a hand or the unique motions an individual makes as he signs his name.

INGENIOUS CRIMINALS

Even with elaborate screening procedures, honest employees, and guarded computer rooms and terminals, most multi-access systems still have a huge sector of vulnerability: the telephone lines that stretch from one facility to another. Experts contend that it is technically a simple matter to tap into phone lines and thereby learn passwords and identifying signals, transmit false data, or penetrate an operating system. One ingenious wiretapping tactic, called "piggybacking," involves hooking another computer onto the tapped line. This computer then intercepts legitimate messages and modifies them. For example, a piggybacker could insert additional credit transfers into accounts during a bank-to-bank transmission.

About the only defense against wiretapping is some method of scrambling or coding messages. It happens that this is something a computer can do quite handily. It also happens, however, that computers are very handy at breaking encoding and scrambling schemes, often in a matter of minutes or hours. Staying ahead of a sophisticated wiretapper would take both elaborate coding schemes and provisions for changing the keys to the encoding frequently. This would impose considerable costs, together with the potential for chaos if keys get lost or mixed up.

Furthermore, while ignorance of the computer system and accounting controls will probably stop the casual intruder, it is not likely to deter for long the dishonest employee or the sophisticated and highly motivated thief. As Donn Parker puts it, "The most dangerous threat is the penetrator who knows as much about the system as you do."

Such was the case in one of the more ingenious computer crimes so far, the work of a young Californian named Jerry Schneider. Around four years ago, at the age of nineteen, Schneider spent some months learning the necessary codes and procedures of the system that Pacific Telephone & Telegraph Company used to handle field orders for communications equipment in Los Angeles. Among other

Once jailed for computer crime, Jerry Schneider now teaches businesses how to prevent it.

things, he posed as a magazine reporter to gather information. He also used his own computer terminal to probe the system.

Eventually Schneider learned enough to pose as a field-supply foreman. Using a pushbutton phone, he tapped in orders for equipment—phones, Teletypes, switchboards, and so forth—to be delivered to field locations, including manholes. Then, with an old phone-company truck, Schneider or one of his employees would pick up the goods and sell them. Schneider used his entry into Pacific Telephone's computer to keep track of current inventory. On occasion, after spotting shortages, he sold the company some of its own equipment.

One of his thirteen employees eventually turned him in after a wage dispute, but not until he had operated for nearly two years and stolen nearly a million dollars' worth of equipment. After serving forty days in jail, he went into the business of advising clients on how to prevent computer rip-offs. His motto: "It takes a computer thief . . ."

NO QUICK SOLUTIONS

Computer manufacturers are trying hard to develop systems that will be more resistant to manipulation. The consensus of the experts seems to be that it is possible to design penetration-proof operating systems, but that they are not likely to be commercially available in large systems before 1978, at the earliest. When they are available, the problem will then be what to do about the existing systems. According to International Data Corp., something like $17 billion has already been invested in remote-access computer hardware, or equipment, and probably even more in software. Most of this stuff has ten years or more to go before the investment will be paid off.

Right now, expert opinion is divided on the question of whether, even in principle, any of the existing systems can be made sufficiently secure to handle assets or information of very high value in the face of a sophisticated attack. Steven Lipner, one of the perpetrators of that ZARF prank in Phoenix, contends "There are two difficulties with trying to retrofit one of these large monolithic operating systems to get better security. One, it's expensive, and two, it doesn't work."

Others, however, believe that security can be significantly strengthened. As one measure, some advocate the use of separate minicomputers and software as "gatekeepers," to handle the chores of user identification and access control. The main purpose is to remove these sensitive functions from the intricate maze of a main operating system.

Manufacturers are showing more and more interest in these new developments. But they contend that it is fairly pointless to bring out systems capable of resisting sophisticated attack until their customers adopt better physical security measures in their own installations, as well as better screening of computer employees. And while customer interest in the problem has picked up a lot since the Equity Funding scandal, people are still reluctant to spend much money for computer security. It may take the shock of dramatically expensive and well-publicized computer crimes to start the money flowing in any abundance.

There is talk in the trade of numerous large rip-offs. One story tells of a young swindler who arranged false credit transfers into two major banks from two other banks within a span of two weeks and escaped with nearly $5 million. But no really big computer crimes involving tens of millions of dollars have surfaced in the public domain. A great many people in the computer-security business wonder aloud when that huge rip-off is going to happen—if it hasn't already, undetected□

Computer Abuse, a research report, by Donn Parker. Stanford Research Institute, 1973.

"Computer Raped by Telephone" by W. Thomas Porter, Jr. *The New York Times Magazine*, September 8, 1974.

Databanks in a Free Society by Alan F. Westin and Michael A. Baker. Quadrangle/The New York Times Book Company, 1972.

Swiss mathematician Jean Bernoulli who wondered what path joining two points on a surface and lying wholly on the surface has the shortest length.

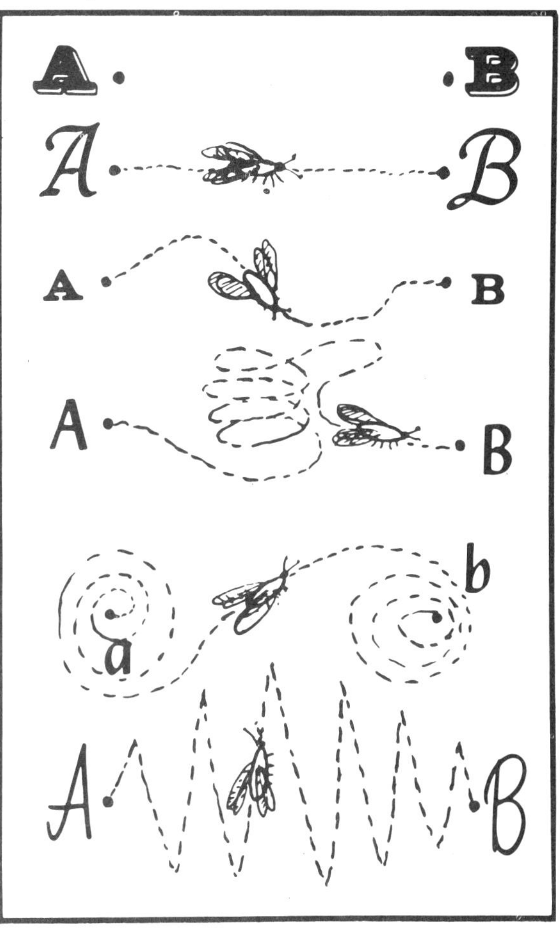

Fig. 1. Testing the obvious: the shortest distance between two points is a straight line.

The Band-Aid Principle

by Philip J. Davis

IT is always a delight when simple ideas lead to great consequences. Sir Isaac Newton's observation of an apple falling to the ground led to the law of the mutual attraction of bodies, or gravity. The consequences of this cannot be set forth adequately in fifty volumes. The story that I'm going to tell here is not so well known as Newton's apple. Its consequences are not so great. But the story is easier to understand: all that is required is a bit of geometrical and mechanical intuition. And the story is a fine illustration of how mathematics tries constantly to understand and explain a complicated situation by an appeal to a related simple situation.

SHORTEST DISTANCE

The shortest distance between two points, said the ancient geometers, is along a straight line. This is a simple enough statement to begin with, and one that is intuitively obvious. In Figure 1, the artist seems to be testing out this proposition to make sure that it is correct.

When we come to put this principle into practice, complications intervene. The principle may be applied when we take a short cut across a field, but in going, say, from New York to Tokyo, we are not likely to go in a straight line, unless some kind government provides us with a tunnel through the crust of the earth. A meaningful question that relates to travel on the surface of the earth is:

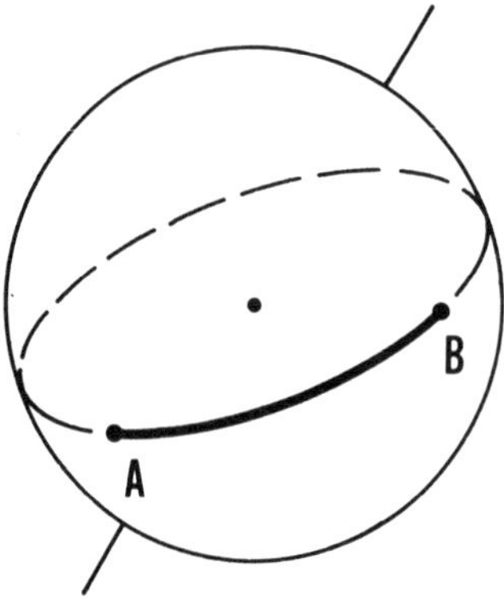

Fig. 2. The shortest distance between two points on a sphere is an arc of the great circle.

given two points A and B on the surface of a sphere, what curve joining A to B, *and lying entirely on the surface of the sphere*, has the least length? The answer, as you may know, is an arc of the great circle that joins A to B. Great circles are circles that lie on the surface of the sphere and whose centers coincide with the center of the sphere. (See Fig. 2)

But a more general question than this can be formulated. For while a sphere is undoubtedly of great importance to us earth dwellers, it is certainly not the only curved surface that mathematicians have thought about. There are many kinds of curved surfaces: a cylinder, a cone, a sphere, an ellipsoid, a piece of tin that has been twisted into a shape that has no special name. Given two points A and B on the surface, what path joining B to A and lying wholly on the surface has the shortest length? This problem was posed more than 250 years ago by the famous Swiss mathematician Jean Bernoulli. In August 1697, Bernoulli invited—or perhaps challenged—all geometers to solve this problem.

A path of minimum length is known as a *geodesic*. Today, the study of geodesics is carried out in the subject known as *the calculus of variations* as well as in the branch of geometry known as *differential geometry*.

If you would like to get a feeling for what geodesics are, you can think of them physically. Suppose that the surface is a football or fancy bottle. Hold a piece of string at one point on the surface with the left thumb, and with the right thumb and forefinger located at a second point on the surface, pull the string taut. If the string lies on a convex, or bulging, portion of the surface, then it will be pulled into a position of minimal length between its two end points. If the surface is not completely convex, but in some portions is concave, curving inward, the string may leave the surface and go off into space. In this case, the construction of geodesics with a string would be rather difficult. This is a mechanical way of constructing geodesics, and it tells us little about how to figure out their paths. (See Fig. 3)

THE SPIDER AND THE FLY

To try to understand somewhat how geodesics are determined, let's consider some simple surfaces. The simplest surface of all is the plane, and we know the answer there. The next most simple surface (from the point of view of our problem) is that formed by two planes intersecting. This leads to the famous problem of the spider and the fly. A spider at point A on the west wall of a room spies a fly at point B on the north wall. The spider, who is mathematically inclined and does not like to build webs, would like to determine the shortest path along the walls to the fly. The fly, who is also mathematically inclined, is far more interested in seeing the problem solved than in pre-

Fig. 3. Stretching a string between two points can produce a geodesic, or shortest path.

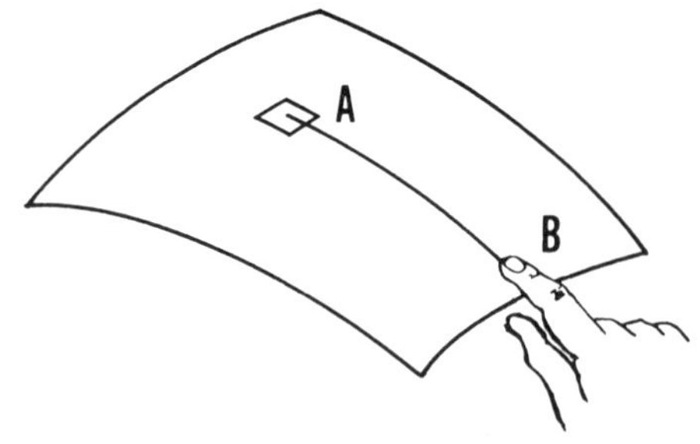

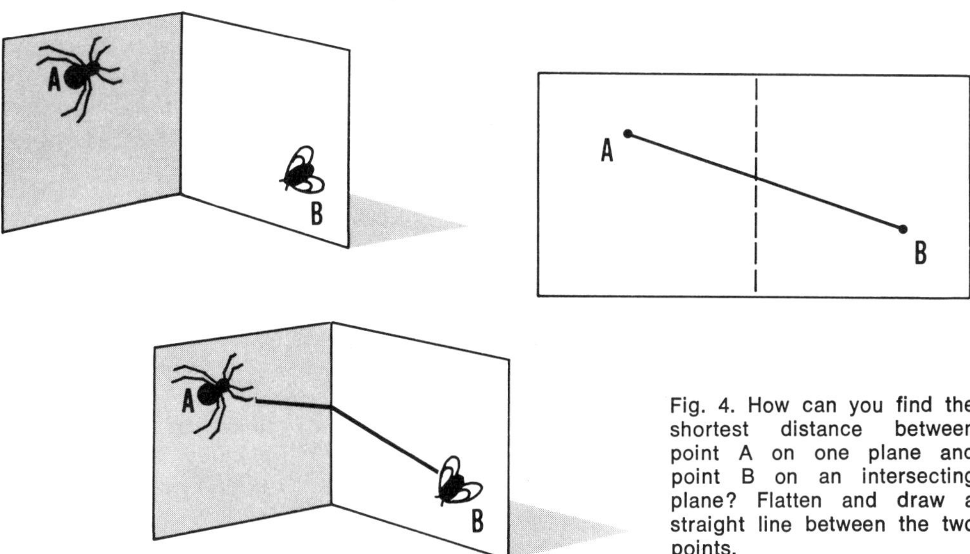

Fig. 4. How can you find the shortest distance between point A on one plane and point B on an intersecting plane? Flatten and draw a straight line between the two points.

serving its identity. The problem can be solved by reducing it to that of two points in a single plane. Think of the two perpendicular walls as being hinged together. Flatten them out so that they form one plane. Then draw a straight line joining *B* to *A*. Fold the walls up again, and the path of minimum length, or geodesic, is drawn in proper position. To prove this statement, suppose that some other path along the walls were shorter. When the walls are flattened to one plane, we would then have a path joining *A* and *B* that is not a straight line, but whose length is shorter than the straight line path. This would be impossible. (See Fig. 4)

UNWRAP AND FLATTEN

Now, it does not take a great stretch of the imagination to go beyond this. The principle of the spider and the fly can be applied more generally than to the walls of a room. What makes the principle tick? The fact that we can flatten out the

Fig. 5. To find the shortest path between two points on a developable surface such as a cylinder or cone, unwrap, flatten, and again draw a straight line.

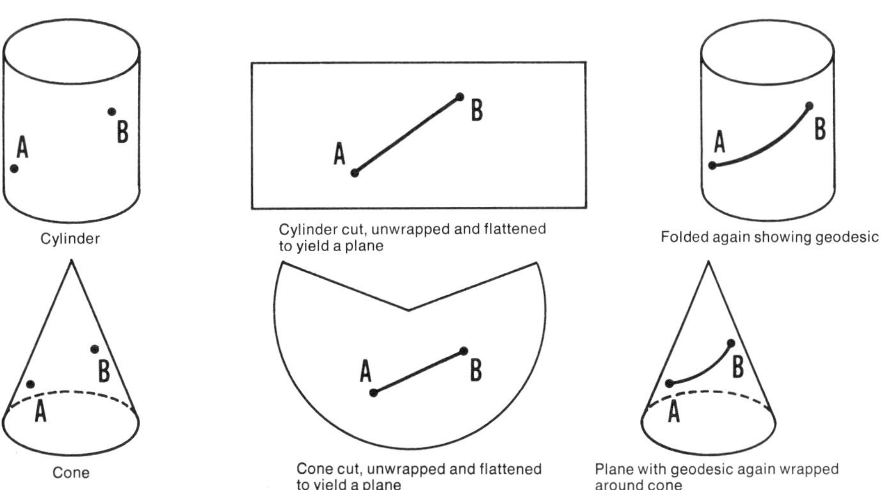

surface so that it lies in a plane without stretching or tearing it in any way. The principle is therefore applicable to any surfaces that can be flattened in such a way. In addition to surfaces formed of sections of planes joined together, there are two common surfaces with this property: the cylinder and the cone.

In order to find geodesics on a cylinder or a cone, we "unwrap" the surface and flatten it to a plane. Then we draw the relevant straight line in the plane and then wrap the plane up again. (See Fig. 5).

A surface, such as a flexible piece of paper, that can be flattened to a plane without tearing or stretching, is known as a *developable surface.* The spider-and-the-fly principle can be used only with developable surfaces. To draw geodesics on such a surface, flatten it out, draw a straight line, and then bend it back to its original shape. This would end my story, but for one crucial fact: not all surfaces are developable. In fact, most surfaces are not. A sphere, for example, is not developable. Anyone who has tried to flatten out an orange peel knows this. And so we are back to Bernoulli's original problem without, apparently, having achieved much success.

BUT AN ORANGE PEEL?

Let's go back to the story and see what happened. Bernoulli's challenge caught the eye of the great Leibniz. Baron Gottfried Wilhelm von Leibniz was both a philosopher and a mathematician and he was coinventor with Isaac Newton of calculus. Rising to the bait, Leibniz wrote Bernoulli in July 1698 that he had thought of the problem even before seeing Bernoulli's challenge, but had not yet been able to solve it. However, he did have this idea: suppose that the surface on which we want to draw a geodesic is thought of as composed of many tiny bits of planes. If R and S are two nearby points on the surface, then in order to draw the geodesic between R and S, we allow the planes on which R and S are located to intersect. On their line of intersection, we locate a point T such that the sum of the distances from T to R and S is a minimum. Note what Leibniz is attempting to do here. He would like to use the spider-and-fly principle on a certain developable surface that approximates a very small portion of the true surface.

Jean Bernoulli answered Leibniz somewhat patronizingly that though Leibniz's idea was a good one, and Bernoulli had also worked with it, it did not lead him to a proper goal. But he admitted proudly to Leibniz that he had found the secret of geodesics. It consisted of the fact that "*planum transiens per tria quaelibet puncta proxima lineae quaesitae debeat esse rectum ad planum tangens superficiem curvam in aliquo istorum punctorum.*" In English, Bernoulli had discovered that "the plane that passes through three neighboring points of the geodesic curve, must be perpendicular to the tangent plane to the surface at these points." Bernoulli's mathematics is not easy to understand, for by "the plane that passes through three neighboring points of the curve," he is referring to what is now called the *osculating plane* of the curve. This is a notion that is difficult to explain without the use of differential calculus.

But there is another way of explaining the law of the geodesic curve that does not require use of differential calculus. In a sense, it lies halfway between Leibniz's idea and Bernoulli's idea. These two men lived in a day of string and spiders and flies. If they had lived in the day of the Band-Aid and had had occasion to spread one over a skinned knuckle, they undoubtedly would have thought of it.

THE SOLUTION

To try to understand the Band-Aid principle for geodesics let's begin by noticing two things. First, if two surfaces are tangent, or touching, along a curve, and the curve happens to be a geodesic on one surface, it will also be a geodesic on the second surface. Imagine an infinitely thin string lying between the two surfaces and stretched between A and B. If the string is stretched taut for one surface, it will be taut for the other as well.

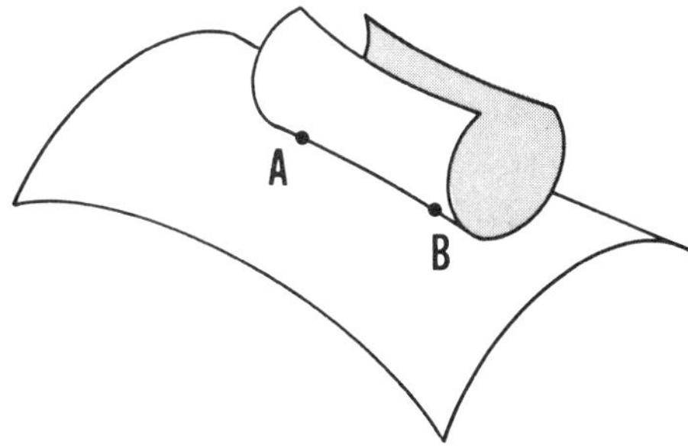

Fig. 6. Two surfaces touching along a geodesic.

Hence, if it lies along a geodesic on one, it will lie along a geodesic on the other. (See Fig. 6).

Second, if a surface has a short geodesic drawn on it, then along this curve we can apply a thin strip of flexible paper so that the paper is tangent to the surface along the curve. Just think: a geodesic comes about by stretching a string on a surface, but if the string is "widened," it becomes a strip, and the strip will be tangent to the surface. (See Fig. 7).

Putting these two observations together, we obtain what may be called the Band-Aid principle for geodesics:

> Take a piece of paper and draw a straight line on it. Along a sufficiently small portion of a geodesic, we can glue a portion of this paper in such a manner that the piece of paper is tangent to the surface along the geodesic, and the geodesic coincides with the deformed straight line lying on the paper.

Fig. 7. Band-Aid applied to geodesic arc.

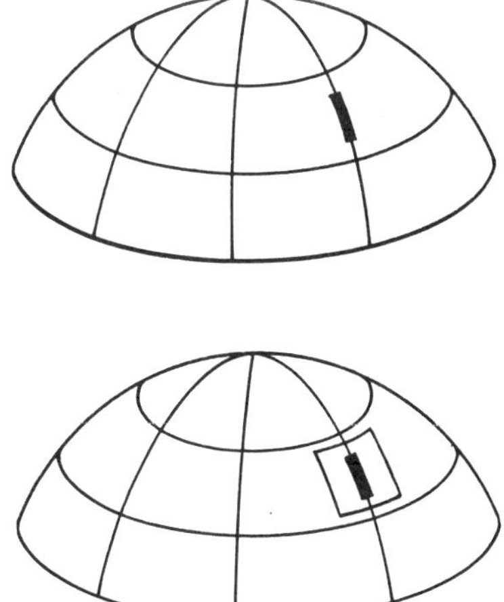

In order to get a feeling for what this principle says, try this experiment. Take a strip of paper that has a straight edge. Now try to apply this edge to, say, the 60-degree parallel of latitude on a globe. It can be done, but notice how: you must lift the paper up at an angle to the surface of the globe. It cannot be done with the paper tangent to the surface.

Leibniz simply did not go far enough. Instead of applying planes to the curve at nearby points, he should have noticed that he could apply a developable surface to whole arcs of the geodesic.

What does higher mathematics make of all this? Quite a bit. Bernoulli's principle, or the Band-Aid principle, leads to the exact mathematical description of the differential equation of geodesics on a surface. Bernoulli did not prove his principle. A quarter of a century later, in 1728, another Swiss mathematician, Leonhard Euler, gave a proof that was based on certain ideas of mechanics. It was not until 1806 that a first completely mathematical proof was given by the French mathematician Joseph Louis Lagrange.

Geodesics are of great importance in pure mathematics, in cartography, or map-making, and in mathematical physics. One of the high points came in the middle of the nineteenth century when the Irish mathematician William Rowan Hamilton formulated a principle that can be interpreted as saying that the universe goes through its gyrations along a geodesic of a certain sort. Although this is a direct descendant of stretching strings on globes, it requires a great deal of knowledge to be made comprehensible. I mention it here only to whet the appetite□

SELECTED READINGS

Introduction to the Calculus of Variation by Hans Sagan. McGraw Hill, 1969.

Shortest Paths by Lazar A. Lyusternik. Macmillan, 1963.

The Reporter's New Tool: The Computer

by Robert Reinhold

UNTIL fairly recently, all a bright young man or woman needed to know to get ahead in the news business was how to write clear sentences, find the way to City Hall, and handle a fearsome city editor. Today, the young reporter is more likely to make it if he knows something about chi square, Kendall's tau, variance, and standard deviations. And if he does know about such things, it is he who will probably scare the city editor.

All these strange terms are the lingo of statistics. And statistical method is quickly becoming almost as much a part of journalism as the note pad, typewriter, and television camera. About 20 years ago, political science, sociology, and the other behavioral sciences began to move heavily into "quantification"—that is, the use of statistical data—as a means of testing armchair intuition against reality. Now journalism is cautiously adapting some of these "scientific" techniques of polling, surveys and analysis for its own ends.

THE LURE OF HARD FACTS

"One of the main reasons for what is happening is that editors want to improve their credibility," said Philip Meyer. Meyer is probably the leading exponent of the new trend, by virtue of his book, *Precision Journalism,* published by the Indiana University Press. He is a national correspondent of the Knight newspaper chain, which has pioneered in survey journalism.

At large and small newspapers all over the country, political reporters are doing

Computers are now also being used in typesetting. At the Detroit *News,* reporters view their work on cathode-ray screens as they type and edit on keyboards (close-up at left) linked to a typesetting computer.

sophisticated samplings of voter opinions to help them interpret election trends and results. Crime reporters are sifting criminal justice records with computers to detect patterns in law enforcement. Others have rummaged through census data and analyzed traffic accident patterns, the background of rioters, political campaign contribution lists, and countless other kinds of data. With this information they can tell readers more about their cities and what makes people act the way they do.

At the root of all this is a growing dissatisfaction among many journalists with the traditional tools of their trade. Reporting is sometimes a haphazard enterprise. The writer draws inferences about reality from a few interviews, official statements, and plain intuition. Sometimes the conventional wisdom has proved to be wrong. The vision of even the most penetrating journalistic eye can be distorted by its own experiences.

Through exact measurement and computer speed, the new techniques enable reporters to be more precise and accurate. These techniques also hold out the possibility of testing the truthfulness of official pronouncements or the claims of political candidates.

In 1973, for example, *The Philadelphia Inquirer*, part of the Knight chain, explored allegations by the local District Attorney, Arlen Specter, that too-soft judges were letting criminals loose. Through a massive computer analysis of some 1,000 criminal cases, the newspaper was able to demonstrate that inefficiencies and failures in the prosecutor's office, not lenient judges, were the main reasons so many accused criminals went free. Specter lost his bid for re-election that fall.

GETTING ON THE BANDWAGON

Such successes have not been lost on other newspapers. In August 1974, 22 reporters and editors attended a three-week crash course in statistics and experimental method at Northwestern University, where they formed the first organization of "precision journalists." Some other reporters, like Jay Harris of *The Wilmington News-Journal* and Howard Covington of *The Charlotte Observer*, have taken leaves to study survey methods at major universities.

Harris had already discovered the power of computers in 1972, while trying to do an article on heroin traffic in Delaware. Court records there yielded about 2,000 names, a quantity of information that could be digested only by a computer. He later conducted a major statewide public-attitude survey in collaboration with the University of Delaware. Explaining the purpose of the survey, Harris said, "We realized how very little we knew about the electorate in general, and we thought it would be nice to have people tell us what their concerns were rather than have the candidates tell us."

The use of statistics in reporting the news, particularly for pre-election polling, is not entirely new. What is new is the aggressive use of such methods for analytical and not just descriptive purposes. In the first half of 1974, both *The New York Times* and *The Washington Post* carried series of articles based on surveys

Another journalistic task being computerized is the selection and cropping of photographs.

of New Yorkers and Washingtonians, respectively. The articles explored the things that pleased and displeased city residents and the ways in which different ethnic and social groups differed in their concerns and perceptions.

And in August, *Time* magazine began a quarterly feature, called "Soundings," that is designed to monitor, statistically, the changing national mood on such matters as economic distress, social resentment, and political conservatism.

Computer journalism is not confined to big-city newspapers. Even such a small daily as *The Dubuque Telegraph-Herald* has mounted a sophisticated effort, using its business computers. The paper's managing editor, James Geledas, has handed out copies of Meyer's book to some of his reporters. One of them, John McCormick, is now analyzing the records of thousands of traffic accidents in Dubuque to find out why and where accidents occur.

HAZARDS OF COMPUTEREPORTING

All of this new fascination with numbers and "precision" is not without problems. Social measurement is at best a crude science. The numbers are really just gross approximations of reality. But once they are cranked into computers and emerge in neat tables, they begin to take on a reality of their own and tend to give a false sense of scientific accuracy. What is statistically significant, however, is not necessarily socially significant or especially newsworthy.

Already some papers have fallen into mechanistic and simplistic uses. One small Midwestern daily recently polled the seven members of the City Council and created a numerical "irritation" rating to gauge what bothered the city fathers most. The figures were then averaged and carried out to two decimal places, with "public apathy" coming out at the top of the list. The article said nothing about how irritated the public was with the council members.

It is also hard to determine when it is justifiable to draw the inference that one social factor directly causes another. That is, it is possible to find all kinds of statistical correlations in human behavior. But it is hazardous to conclude that some particular factor is the cause of a given social situation, without first examining an enormous number of "variables." Scholars spend months or even years digesting data. Reporters may have only hours or days. Harvey Kabaker of *The Washington Star-News* concedes that "I may be accused of going beyond the data" in his analyses. But he contends that it is a lot better than the sheer guesswork that marks a good deal of political analysis in general.

Another difficulty is that numbers are dull. Few editors would want to let numbers substitute for well-written, impressionistic reporting filled with color and human interest. For these and other reasons, most newspapers are moving with caution. "We have been making use of these techniques in a variety of ways," said Seymour Topping, assistant managing editor of *The New York Times*. "We are now addressing ourselves to a more systematic application because new opportunities have been opened up in terms of technology."

Like many other editors, John G. Craig Jr., executive editor of *The Wilmington News-Journal*, feels that statistical methods are valuable but should not be oversold. He believes they should be used to validate customary reporting and suggest new ideas. "Statistics are just a check on things," he said. "We just start from there."

Thus there are drawbacks as well as advantages to the use of computers in the news business. Used with intelligence and plain common sense, however, they are a valuable new tool for the reporter□

SELECTED READINGS

Data Bases, Computers, and the Social Sciences by Ralph L. Bisco. John Wiley, 1970.

Let's Talk about Computers by Gerald Snyder. Jonathan David, 1973.

Those Amazing Computers: Uses of Modern Thinking Machines by Melvin Berger. John Day, 1973.

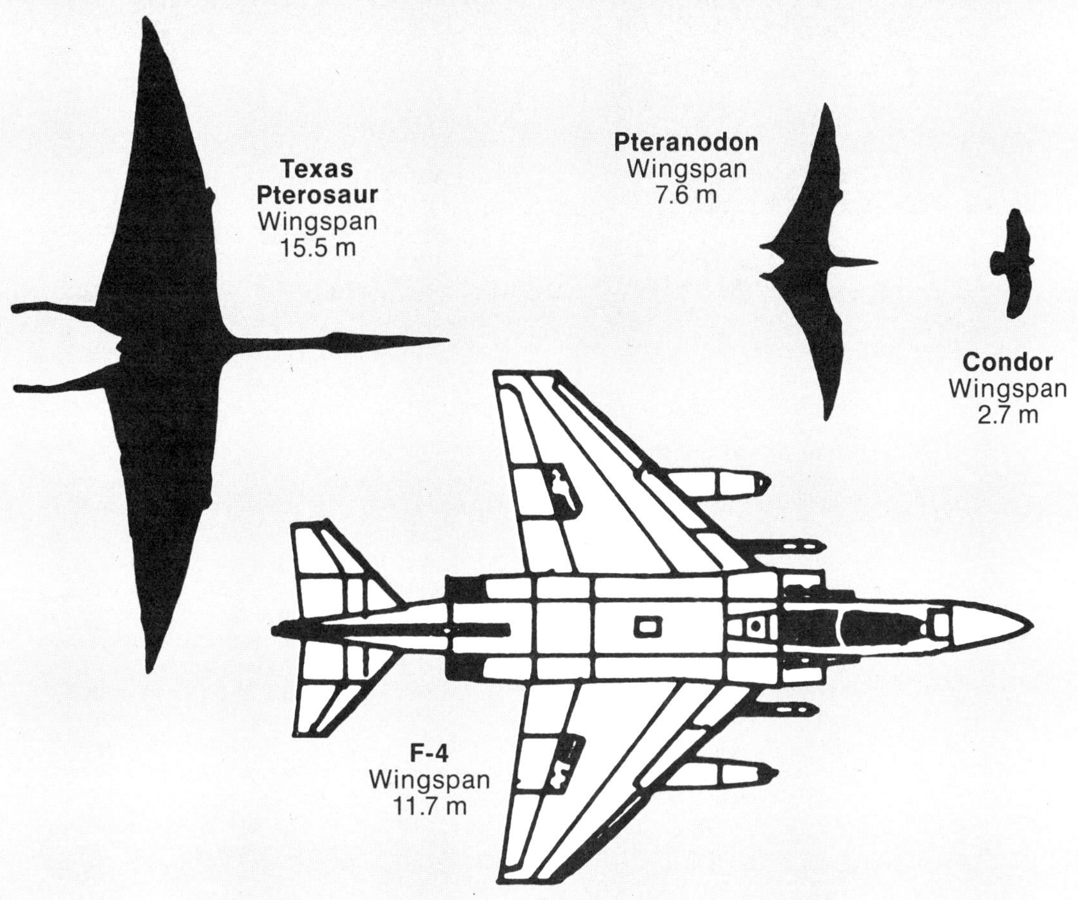

earth sciences

contents

The discovery of the fossils of the largest known creature ever to have flown was announced in March 1975. Study of the pterodactyl fossils, found in southwestern Texas, revealed that the flying reptile had a wingspan of 15.5 m (51 ft).

review of the year

earth sciences

Drilling in the South Atlantic Ocean, the *Glomar Challenger* discovered a submerged tongue of land. It is the last piece in a "jigsaw puzzle" of Gondwanaland, a supercontinent some geologists believe once existed.

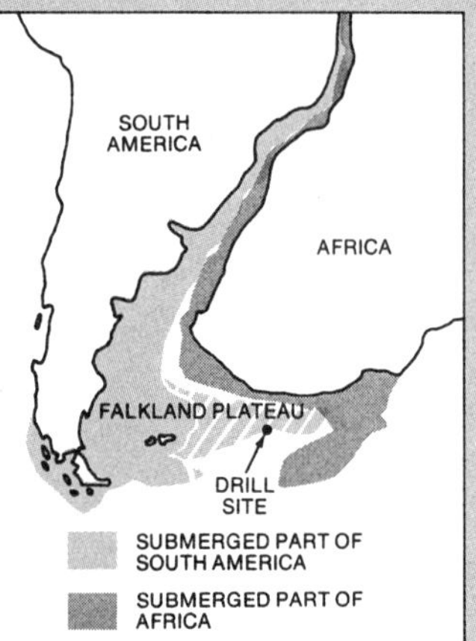

Geology and geophysics. Our understanding of the earth as a whole is rapidly expanding through recent studies of the other earthlike members of the sun's family. As one scientist put it: "The scope of what have been called the earth sciences has expanded to include the entire inner solar system." Meanwhile, geological research continues to be dominated by the so-called "new geology," which features the concept of continental drift and plate tectonics. This concept holds that the earth's outer shell is divided into huge plates that move about slowly and collide with one another, reshaping the continents and seas and mountains as they move. Many geologists look upon plate tectonics as a unifying theory for earth sciences in general. For example, theories trying to account for the present distribution of plant and animal species tend to make much use of the idea of continental drift. Yet sharp criticisms of the new geology have also been advanced. Critics feel that events are being fitted into a unified picture all too easily and that things are just not that simple. Such adverse opinions tend to be heard at scientific meetings and in the professional literature rather than in the new textbooks on earth sciences.

One important discovery in 1974 does seem to lend support to the theory of continental drift. It was made by the research ship *Glomar Challenger* during Leg 36 of the ongoing Deep Sea Drilling Project (DSDP), which was begun in 1968. While drilling off the Falkland Islands in the South Atlantic Ocean, the ship discovered a submerged tongue of land some 1,200 km (750 mi) long. The rock core brought up contained the oldest granite yet found at the bottom of the sea. Granite is continental rather than ocean-floor rock, and the tongue of land was later identified as an eastward extension of the submerged Falkland Plateau. For continental drift theorists, it was also the final piece of land needed to complete the Gondwanaland "jigsaw puzzle." That is, according to the theory, South America, Africa, Antarctica, and India had once been joined together as a single southern supercontinent, Gondwanaland. The newly found tongue of land fits neatly into an empty place in theoretical reconstructions of this ancient supercontinent.

Among other developments in the study of plate tectonics, a German scientist, Kurt Lemcke, measured the water pressure in sandstone strata in the Alps. He found that the pressure is higher on the northern side of the mountain chain. This could indicate that the Alps are still being moved northward as the African continent presses up against Europe. ■ One of the more remarkable aspects of the new geology has been the determination that the earth's magnetic poles have reversed themselves from time to time in the geological past. In 1974, geophysicists C. E. Helsley and M. B. Steiner of the University of Texas, studying rocks of Colorado dating from the Mesozoic era, more than 65,000,000 years ago, discovered that the spacing of these reversals has not been uniform. And Japanese geophysicist Masaru Kono found that the intensity of the magnetic field appears to have remained nearly uniform for the past 70,000,000 years. There also seems to be growing evidence for the idea that magnetic reversals have been linked to large-scale extinctions of species in the past.

International projects. Also related to plate tectonics studies was an important French-American program that took place last summer. Its name, FAMOUS, stands for *F*rench-*A*merican *M*id-*O*cean *U*ndersea *S*tudy. Small submersible craft from both countries were used to make repeated dives to the Mid-Atlantic Ridge, some 2,750 meters (9,000 ft) below the ocean surface. The divers brought back thousands of photographs and many rock samples from the trench running down the middle of the ridge. The trench is thought to be the site of sea-floor spreading. Evidence now indicates that the rate of spreading may amount to a little more than two centimeters—about one inch—per year. The story of this daring project is told in detail in "Window on Earth's Core." ■ Another international project, called GATE, also took place last summer. GATE stands for *G*ARP *A*tlantic *T*ropical *E*xperiment, and GARP in turn stands for *G*lobal *A*tmospheric *R*esearch *P*rogram—a decade-long effort by the World Meteorological Organization and the International Council of Scientific Unions. GATE studied a vast area of land and sea, centered on the South Atlantic Ocean, in order to gain a better understanding of atmospheric processes. The efforts and achievements of this program are surveyed in "Project GATE."

Operating at depths that would crush an ordinary submarine, the three-man *Alvin* made repeated dives to the Mid-Atlantic Ridge during Project FAMOUS.

Earthquakes and volcanos. Several further attempts were made to test an earthquake-prediction method based on the "dilatency-diffusion" theory that has been developed over the past few years. The theory arose from Soviet recordings of seismic pressure waves prior to an earthquake. The scientists noticed an unusual slowing down of the waves and then a return to normal speed before a quake. American scientists theorized that the effect was caused by changes in the rocks of the fault where the quake occurred. Strain on the rocks caused pressures to increase to a critical point and the rocks began to develop cracks. The cracks made the rocks dilate, or swell, more rapidly than groundwater could seep into them. Since seismic pressure waves travel faster through water-filled rocks than through those without water, they slowed down as they passed through the swollen rocks of the fault. But eventually groundwater did diffuse into the cracks, and the speed of pressure waves passing through them returned to normal. By this time, the rocks were at critical pressure, and an earthquake occurred. For very large faults, the dilatency-diffusion process could take many years. Quake-prediction attempts made in 1974 on the basis of this theory met with mixed results, but there have been successful predictions of small tremors. The U.S. Geological Survey is undertaking an extensive experimental program in Bear Valley, California, which is crossed by the huge San Andreas fault.

As part of Project GATE, the Jet Propulsion Laboratory's giant antenna at Goldstone, California, picked up earth satellites' data on weather in the South Atlantic Ocean.

Many scientists think that as part of the dilatency-diffusion process, the earth's surface swells up where a quake is about to occur. If this movement could be detected, it would provide another means of quake prediction. But the swelling could amount to only a centimeter, or less than one half of an inch, or so, and would be nearly impossible to detect with land-based instruments. An experimental system that uses radio telescopes, the instruments that detect radio waves emitted by objects in outer space, is now being developed to try to detect such small swellings. Two radio telescopes are placed on either side of a major fault, many kilometers, or miles, apart. Both are focused on one of the very distant radio objects known as quasars. The tiny difference in the time when a given radio wave from the quasar reaches the two different telescopes can be measured to 0.0000000001 second. Thus if any ground swelling changed the distance between the two telescopes, the change could be detected. A program is now under way to explore this quake-prediction technique. It centers on the Jet Propulsion Laboratory's fixed radio facility at Goldstone, California. The other, portable telescope will be placed at various sites.

As for seismic and volcanic activity during 1974, the strongest earthquake occurred in Peru on Oct. 3. It had a magnitude of 7.8 on the Richter scale and caused considerable damage and loss of life. Probably the most conspicuous volcanic activity was that of Sicily's Mount Etna, which began erupting on March 11 and continued at intervals throughout the year. ■ Earthquakes that accompany volcanic eruptions are seldom severe. However, events in the Leeward Islands of the South Pacific Ocean proved an exception. Beginning in April, a swarm of seismic and volcanic events caused widespread damage. An undersea volcano was involved in some of the activity.

Some scientists believe that josephinite-containing rocks (above) were "scooped up" as the earth's Pacific plate slipped beneath the North American plate.

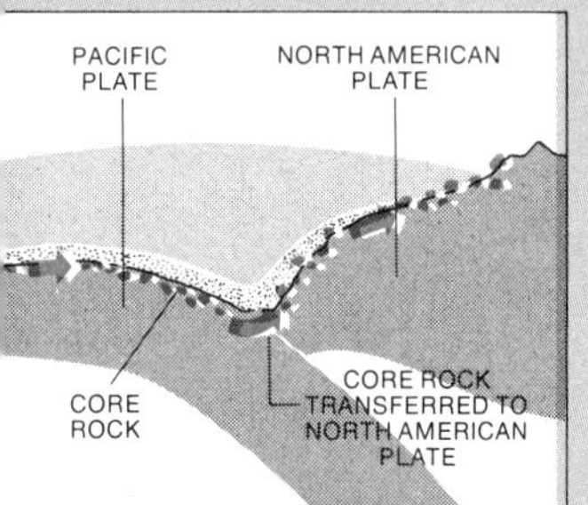

Rocks and minerals. At the annual meeting of the American Geophysical Union, held in Washington, D.C., in April 1974, four Cornell University scientists suggested that rocks found many years ago in Josephine County in Oregon are actually material from the earth's outer core. The rocks consist mainly of an apparently unique iron-nickel alloy named josephinite. The density of these rocks corresponds to the calculated density of the earth's outer core, some 2,900 km (1,800 mi) below the surface. Their structure also indicates that they were formed deep within the earth, under extreme temperatures and pressures. The scientists suggested that the rocks arrived at the earth's surface as a result of two processes, both controversial. The first involves the "plume" theory, which suggests that hot funnels of core rock can move upward through the overlying rocks of the earth's mantle. In the case of the Oregon samples, the material was brought to the surface of the plate underlying the North Pacific Ocean. Secondly, according to plate tectonics theory, this plate is colliding with and slipping beneath the neighboring North American plate. In the process, the core material was "scooped up" by the overriding plate and now lies at the surface in southern Oregon. Not all geologists accept this reconstruction of events, by any means, but it has attracted much attention.

Of the new kinds of minerals established last year, one is found on the moon but not on the earth. The Soviet scientists who described it from their lunar samples named it "armstrongite" for Neil Armstrong, the first man to walk on the moon. ■ The few dozen minerals, in all, that have been returned from the moon have now been enumerated by mineralogist Joseph V. Smith of the University of Chicago. He predicts that all of the minerals found in meteorites will eventually be found on the moon. ■ Urea, an organic compound, was established for the first time as a naturally occurring mineral. P. J. Bridge, a scientist of Australia's Government Chemical Laboratories in Perth, described its occurrence in Western Australia. Its acceptance by the International Mineralogical Association's Commission on New Minerals means that the standard textbook definition of minerals as solely inorganic in nature will have to be rejected.

Other developments. In California's White Mountains, scientists J. Wyatt Durham and Jean B. Firby discovered cone-shaped fossil "teeth"—actually denticles—of a large, squidlike mollusk that lived in Lower Cambrian time, over 500,000,000 years ago. The mollusk's chief food seems to have been the ancient crustacean, the trilobite. ■ In measuring the deterioration of the West Antarctic Ice Sheet, University of Maine geologists found that it was once much larger and that it is now either dropping at the surface or being undercut by the sea, or both. One geologist, George Denton, calculated that the extensive ice sheets of some 18,000 years ago began to shrink about 14,000 years ago. They either reached their present limited extent some time in the past—perhaps some 6,000 to 10,000 years ago—or else they entirely disappeared and have since returned.

Richard M. Pearl

Project GATE

by Henry Lansford

The earth's tropical zone—the source of most of the world's weather—was the subject of project GATE. This U.S. ship was equipped with tethered balloons that carried instruments into the atmosphere.

IN the summer of 1974, nearly 6,000 scientists and workers from about 70 countries took part in the largest and most complex international experiment ever attempted. The project involved research ships, airplanes, land stations, balloons, radar systems, and earth satellites. The common goal of all these people and research facilities was to develop a better understanding of the world's weather.

The name of the gigantic project was GATE. These letters stand for GARP Atlantic Tropical Experiment. GARP, in turn, stands for Global Atmospheric Research Program, a long-term effort sponsored by the United Nations' World Meteorological Organization and the International Council of Scientific Unions.

WHERE, WHAT, AND WHO

GATE was designed as a study of the earth's tropic zone—the equatorial region that is the breeding ground of much of the world's weather, including the huge storms known as hurricanes and typhoons. GATE scientists wanted to learn more about the ways in which weather events are related to conditions in the ocean and the atmosphere. The region under study ran from the western Indian Ocean, across Africa, the Atlantic Ocean, and Latin America, to the eastern Pacific Ocean—some 50 million km^2 (20 million mi^2). Within this area, the study ranged from the top of the atmosphere to more than one and a half km (about a mile) below the ocean surface. The most intensive work was done in an area of about 520,000 km^2 (200,000 mi^2), centered at 10° north latitude, 23° west longitude off Africa.

The ships and airplanes that took part in GATE were supplied by many countries. Thus, of 38 research ships, two came from Brazil, one from Canada, four from France, three from the Federal Republic of Germany, one from the German Democratic Republic, one from Mexico, one from the Netherlands, 12 from the Soviet Union, four from the United Kingdom, and nine from the United States. Of 12 research planes, one each came from France and the United Kingdom, two came from the Soviet Union, and eight came from the United States.

In addition to this, six kinds of U.S. and Soviet satellites formed part of the GATE effort. They provided photographs of the earth's cloud cover and measurements of the upper atmosphere. Another vital part of the program was carried out by about 40 ocean buoys. Many were placed in the high-interest area in the eastern Atlantic, while others were set out along the equator to measure deep ocean currents. Finally, about 1,000 land stations of the World Weather Watch were included in the GATE activities.

The international control center of this great effort was located at Dakar, Senegal, on the western coast of Africa. A U.S. scientist, Joachim Kuettner, directed GATE. The deputy director was Yuri Tarbeev of the Soviet Union.

THE IMPORTANCE OF THE TROPICS

Why was the earth's tropic zone selected as the first center of interest of the GARP program? The tropics are the source of most of the world's weather. They receive about half of the heat energy coming from the sun. Much of this heat is first stored in the oceans there. It is then transferred to the atmosphere, where it produces the clouds and winds that carry solar energy all around the world.

However, much of the earth's tropic zone consists of oceans and jungles and deserts. As a result, the tropics have not been as well observed as most other areas on the earth. Meteorologists do not have a very good understanding of this region of the atmosphere. GATE was designed to provide some of the information that is needed. In particular, it was to provide a better understanding of tropical "cloud clusters" and how they affect weather.

The amount of data gathered in such a project is enormous. It takes years and years to work through the material and develop useful theories from it. In order to make the data from GATE easier to manage and accessible to scientists all over the world, it was divided into five areas of interest. At Hamburg, Germany, data will be stored pertaining to that portion of the atmosphere extending from the ocean surface to the bases of clouds. Data related to how the sun's energy is absorbed by the atmosphere will be archived at Leningrad. All of the measurements of events occurring within the ocean will be stored at Brest, France. Data pertaining to clouds and their effects will be kept at Washington, D.C. Finally, at Bracknell, England, data will be archived that are useful in studying large-scale and long-term processes at work in the atmosphere.

STUDYING THE WEATHER BY COMPUTER

Of particular importance to meteorological work as a whole is the development of computer models of the atmosphere. The behavior of the atmosphere is very complex. There are many motions and processes under way at the same time, and all of them are related to one another. To understand these processes better, meteorologists develop mathematical models of the atmosphere—mathematical equations that represent the motions of the air, its change in temperature, and so forth. The equations can be handled with a computer so as to simulate events taking place in the atmosphere itself. In this way, scientists try to learn how to predict the behavior of the atmosphere. They hope in time to be able to make long-term weather forecasts.

To make their mathematical models as realistic as possible, meteorologists must test the predictions of the models against observations of how the atmosphere actually behaves. This was the primary purpose of GATE—to obtain data that will make such tests possible. Research with mathematical models is going on at several institutions in the United States, including the National Center for Atmospheric Research in Boulder, Colorado; the Geophysical Fluid Dynamics Laboratory of the National Oceanic and Atmospheric Administration (NOAA) in Princeton, New Jersey; and the University of California at Los Angeles.

Even after all the information provided by GATE has been thoroughly studied, atmospheric scientists will still need to know more about the tropic zone. The next step planned by GARP is a study of worldwide weather activities□

"Atlantic Tropical Experiment." *Space World*, August 1974.

"Home from the Warming Sea—and Into the Computer" by Jonathan Eberhart. *Science News*, November 23, 1974.

Introduction to GARP, prepared by the World Meteorological Organization. Unipub, 1969.

Instant Islands

by Robin Burton

EARLY in the morning of Tuesday, Jan. 23, 1973, Iceland experienced the dramatic beginnings of a major disaster. At about 2 a.m. the inhabitants of Vestmannaeyjar—a small but important fishing port on the island of Heimaey—were awakened by a noise rather like that of a low-flying jet airplane. Springing from their beds, they were horrified to see the land close to their houses literally splitting apart and belching fire.

A great, livid glow spread eerily over the landscape. Heimaey's volcanic peak, Helgafell, had begun to erupt after being dormant for many years. Fearing the worst, the townspeople made for the fleet of fishing vessels moored in the small harbor. Within hours the town was virtually deserted.

Volcanic debris was raining on Vestmannaeyjar. A gaping fissure had appeared with up to 20 active vents. At its greatest extent, the fissure stretched across one corner of the island and 300 m (1,000 ft) out beneath the sea. In the days that followed, the fissure contracted and many of the vents stopped erupting. But the bombardment of the town with volcanic ash increased. A new volcanic cone arose, and a slow but steady wall of lava began to creep toward the harbor.

BATTLING THE ERUPTION

From the safety of the mainland and the open sea, Heimaey looked like a huge bonfire. The glow from the eruption was reflected from the underside of the towering cloud of volcanic ash, which climbed some 9,000 m (30,000 ft) into the air. The incandescent lava fountains from the vents sometimes spouted nearly 300 m (1,000 ft) skyward. In its way, the sight was incredibly beautiful—and also danger-

A spectacular smoke pillar heralds the birth of an island, Surtsey, off Iceland. This 1963 undersea eruption is shown in its third day.

ous. Red-hot stones were being hurled some 600 m (2,000 ft) into the air, crashing down on the town and setting fire to factories and houses. During the most violent phases of the eruption, some of these natural missiles were thrown for distances of more than a kilometer (over six tenths of a mile).

The molten rock was a kind of basalt known as hawaiite, which is somewhat like glue and flows relatively slowly as a lava. Therefore the invasion of Vestmannaeyjar was gradual, giving the 5,300 inhabitants time to escape. A few hundred people remained behind for a while to salvage what they could.

In the following days, the people of Iceland joined battle with the eruption as they tried to keep their chief fishing port from being destroyed. Men shoveled volcanic ash from rooftops to keep buildings from being crushed. They set up shields at windows to prevent the hurtling rocks from crashing through and starting more fires. But the major battle was with the advancing stream of lava, which poured into the harbor and threatened to block its entrance. Squads of workers valiantly sprayed the lava with water to make it congeal, or become hard, thereby halting or diverting the flow of molten rock. Explosives were considered for a while, but the idea was given up as too risky.

In about a month the volcano had belched forth 115,000,000 m³ (150,000,000 yd³) of lava, and the area of the island had increased by nearly 3¼ km² (1¼ mi²). But the harbor, though partially blocked, was still usable. In fact, it had been improved—as the lava cooled it formed a new, natural breakwater! As for the town, about one third of the buildings of Vestmannaeyjar lay buried beneath volcanic ash or were destroyed by fire. Volcanic gas, which tended to collect in cellars and in hollows of the land, had

By the 13th day of its activity in 1973, a volcano known as Helgafell had almost buried the homes in the fishing port of Vestmannaeyjar, on the island of Heimaey.

Night and day, incandescent lava fountains presented a sight of incredible beauty—and great hazard—to the villagers of Vestmannaeyjar late in January 1973.

claimed one victim by the time the battle was over. But by the summer of 1973 the citizens of Heimaey were beginning to return and rebuild their battered town. Four fifths of the original population now live there.

NEW ISLANDS FROM THE SEA

Heimaey is one of a group of islands that hug Iceland's southern coast. The whole Icelandic region is a volcanologist's paradise. Strange, subterranean mutterings and rumblings are often heard there. From time to time, major eruptions take place—the most famous being those of Mount Hekla on Iceland itself. The region also abounds in volcano-related features such as hot springs, geysers, and bubbling mud pools. All these make Iceland a fascinating country.

Probably the most striking of all the phenomena in the region is the occasional birth of a new island. One such island rose from the sea in 1963, only 19 km (12 mi) southwest of Heimaey. The violent activity ended four years later. By that time the island, named Surtsey, was about 150 m (500 ft) high and had an area of about 3 km^2 (1 mi^2). The smaller islets of Syrtlingur and Jölnir also appeared in the course of the eruptions. And another islet, Surtur, later emerged from the ocean

Jets of lava rose about 300 m (1,000 ft) when the volcano Helgafell began to erupt. On the second day, homes are not yet covered.

near Surtsey. All three of these islets quickly sank beneath sea level again. Then things remained relatively calm until the eruption on Heimaey.

Iceland is not the only site of such activity, by any means. For example, in the same year as the Heimaey disaster, a new volcanic isle surfaced amid the Volcano Islands of the Pacific Ocean, about 1,000 km (600 mi) south of Tokyo. In all, there are more than 400 volcanos currently active, to one degree or another, around the world. But Iceland remains one of the most volcanic regions of them all. The ongoing activity helps to explain the island's lack of good soil and its sparse vegetation. The place has a strange beauty that tends to appeal to persons with rather Spartan instincts. Looking across the interior of the island, one sees an almost lunar landscape. On some days the air is crystal clear and the sun sparkles brilliantly on the surrounding waters. But on gloomy days, Iceland looks to some people like the end of the world.

SITTING ON A SHAKY RIDGE . . .

Why is there all this activity in the North Atlantic Ocean? Geological discoveries in recent years help to provide an explanation.

First of all, Iceland sits astride the mighty Mid-Atlantic Ridge. This massive, scarred, and fissured ridge runs the entire length of the Atlantic Ocean. It is, in fact, part of a ridge system that extends beneath all the oceans of the world. Along the length of the Mid-Atlantic Ridge is a central rift where rock material is welling up from below. The rift is the site of many earthquakes and much volcanic activity.

The emerging rock material spreads out to either side of the rift to form new sea floor. This means that the Atlantic Ocean is growing wider and that the continents that border it are drifting apart. The rate of movement is quite slow, but it can be measured by sampling sea-floor rocks and finding out how old they are. The rocks grow older the farther they are from the central rift. These measurements indicate that the continents are drifting apart at a rate of about 10 km (6 mi) per one million years.

According to the theory of continental drift, the continents were once joined together some 125 million years ago. Thus the rocks that make up present-day Iceland were once directly bordered by the rocks of Scotland and Ireland to the east, and of Greenland to the west. The breaking-apart process did not begin in the region of Iceland until about 65 million years ago, although it began much earlier to the south.

The path of this mid-Atlantic activity cuts right through the center of Iceland. It passes through Surtsey, Heimaey, Mount Hekla, and on in the direction of the Norwegian island of Jan Mayen, about 640 km (400 mi) to the north. The forces at work along this line are literally tearing Iceland apart. That this is so is confirmed by measuring the age of Iceland's rocks. Like the rocks of the Atlantic sea floor, they are found to be older the farther they are from the central region of activity.

Continental drift is linked to the general theory of plate tectonics. According to this theory, the thin outer layer of the earth is divided into large plates that slowly move about in relation to each other. They carry the continental masses with them, thus reshaping land and sea areas all around the world. The plates bearing the continents that border the Atlantic Ocean are moving outward as new material wells up from the Mid-Atlantic Ridge. The plates that border the Pacific Ocean, on the other hand, are generally moving in toward that basin. As a result, the Pacific floor is disappearing beneath the plates in a number of great ocean deeps known as trenches. These trenches, like the Mid-Atlantic Ridge, are the scenes of many earthquakes and much volcanic activity.

. . . AND PERCHED ON A HOT SPOT

But there is still more to the story of Iceland and its instant islands. The recent Heimaey eruption was not simply a product of Mid-Atlantic Ridge activity. For instance, the erupting fissure ran almost directly south to north, rather than following the general southwest-northeast line of mid-Atlantic activity in the North Atlantic region. Nor was the lava typical of the kind of material that comes up along the Mid-Atlantic Ridge.

Another factor is involved as well. That is, Iceland is perched above a "hot spot" in the earth. A number of such hot spots have been observed around the world,

Four years after eruptions began under the Atlantic waves, a volcanic crater on the new island of Surtsey sends a stream of lava to the ocean.

underlying the earth's outer crust. These hot spots are associated with chains of volcanic activity. Besides Iceland, for example, there is a hot spot near Hawaii.

Over the last few years, scientists have developed the theory that the hot spots represent narrow "plumes" of molten material. The material is rising up from far below the earth's crust. When these plumes, or volcanic fountains, come into contact with the bottom of the earth's crust, they spread out. From time to time the material forces its way through the crust and produces a volcano. The volcanos tend to form in chains—such as the Surtsey-Heimaey chain—because the plates of the crust are sliding over the hot spots all the while. Indeed, the activity of the hot spots may be the very force that causes the plates to move.

The theory is a complicated one. It may eventually provide a unified picture of the geological events that have shaped our world. But it will require much further investigation by earth scientists. The study of such major features of the earth's crust as the Mid-Atlantic Ridge has only really gotten under way. In the last decade, British, American, Canadian, and Russian ships have made detailed maps of the Ridge and placed sonar buoys to aid in underwater work. In 1973 the French bathyscaphe Archimède set out to explore the Ridge. The three-man submersible craft took rock samples and made magnetic, pressure, acidity, and other measurements some 320 km (200 mi) southwest of the Azores. And 1974 saw the joint French-American effort described in "Window on Earth's Core" (page 140).

The results of this project are being analyzed now. Much research still lies ahead. But in the end we may gain a better understanding of the forces at work beneath us in the earth—forces that are able to lift instant islands above the surface of the sea□

SELECTED READINGS

Continents in Motion: The New Earth Debate by Walter Sullivan. McGraw-Hill, 1974.

The Making of the Earth: Volcanos and Continental Drift by Haroun Tazieff. Saxon House, 1974.

Volcano: Ordeal by Fire in Iceland's Westmann Islands by Árni Gunnarsson. Iceland Review Books, Reykjavik, 1973.

"Volcano Watchers." *Newsweek*, March 5, 1973.

Up from the sea comes the volcanic island of Surtsey. Photo was taken in late 1963.

In search of sea-floor riches: an underwater television camera on launch ramp of a vessel designed to gather nickel-bearing manganese nodules from the ocean floor.

Mining the Seas

by B. D. Loncarevic

BY the time the 21st century arrives the major source of metal ores may well be the deep ocean floors.

There are at least two types of deep-sea mineral resources. One consists of lumps, or nodules, sitting on top of ocean floor sediments. The second, and more recently recognized type, consists of metalliferous, or metal-containing, deposits that have settled on the sea floor. These deposits are confined to small sediment ponds and basins in zones near the crests of oceanic ridges.

Methods of exploiting both types are being developed rapidly, but it seems likely now that the recovery and processing of the lumpy material will bring the first payoff. At the sites where they occur, the nodules cover the sea floor in a single, tightly packed layer. They have rarely been found below sea-floor sediments, instead sitting on top of them.

The big mysteries about the nodules today are what makes them precipitate and why the nodules rest on top of sediments. In the center of some nodules a grain of sand, a shark's tooth, or any other stray object may be found. Thus it appears that a nucleus is required before the precipitation starts.

Our present knowledge of the distribution of nodules is incomplete, but at least we know that they are not uniformly spread over all the ocean floor. Concentrations vary greatly. Deep Pacific basins appear to be a favorable location.

A RENEWABLE RESOURCE

Any estimates of the amount of nodules on the sea floor must be treated as very tentative. The sort of estimates that have appeared suggest that there might be as much as 1.5 trillion tons, a staggering amount. As an ore deposit, sea-floor nodules are a renewable resource, for it is estimated that 6 million tons precipitate from sea water every year.

The nodules consist largely of useful metals, but in a combination that is a metallurgist's nightmare. The main constituents are manganese (30 per cent) and iron (26 per cent). Ores of both of these metals are still abundant on dry land, so nobody can make money out of deep sea deposits yet. The prospect of economic recovery of some of the minor constituents of the nodules is the main reason for the considerable effort that a few industrial giants are willing to take to develop practical and economic recovery methods.

The most important minor constituents are:

Cobalt	0.2—2.7 per cent
Copper	0.6—1.3 per cent
Nickel	0.8—1.5 per cent

There are local fluctuations in grade that are thought to occur during the initial formative process or to result from erosion or possibly the action of bacteria on the nodules. There are indications that the grade improves with depth.

FOUND IN THE RED SEA

Because the occurrence of manganese nodules has been known for a long time, the discussion of the economic prospects in the deep sea has revolved around this type of resource. Since about 1970 new knowledge has been accumulating that suggests that even vaster reserves might be found within the metalliferous sedimentary deposits. Such deposits have

The research vessel *Prospector* sets out on an exploratory mission, looking for ocean sites where manganese nodules can be mined profitably. Special cameras (right) that scan the ocean floor are an essential part of the effort.

been found in the middle of the Red Sea between Sudan and Saudi Arabia. But the understanding of continental drift and a few previously unrelated observations suggest that these types of deposits might be worldwide. If this is the case and if the questions of ownership, recovery, and extraction can be solved, then deep-ocean mining may become a real competitor to any land-based operation.

As our knowledge of geology increases, the solid earth on which we live appears to be less and less solid. We now recognize that there is a worldwide pattern to earthquakes and that their distribution over the earth follows defined zones. These active zones occur along the edges of plates, or sections, of the earth's crust, where adjoining plates are rubbing against each other. Where the plates are moving away from each other, new material rises up to fill in the cracks. Thus chains of young mountains are formed, following with a remarkable regularity the center lines of the Atlantic and Indian oceans and extending across the southern Pacific Ocean from Australia to the Gulf of California. As the plates move apart at a very slow speed of a few centimeters per year, the mountains gradually grow. The rocks near the central gap in the mountains are quickly solidified, leaving numerous cracks through which the water can seep, thereby circulating beneath the bottom of the

Workers aboard the *Prospector* keep an eye on television monitor screens (left) that show what the underwater cameras are viewing. At a good mining location, the metal-rich nodules pepper the ocean floor in the millions (right).

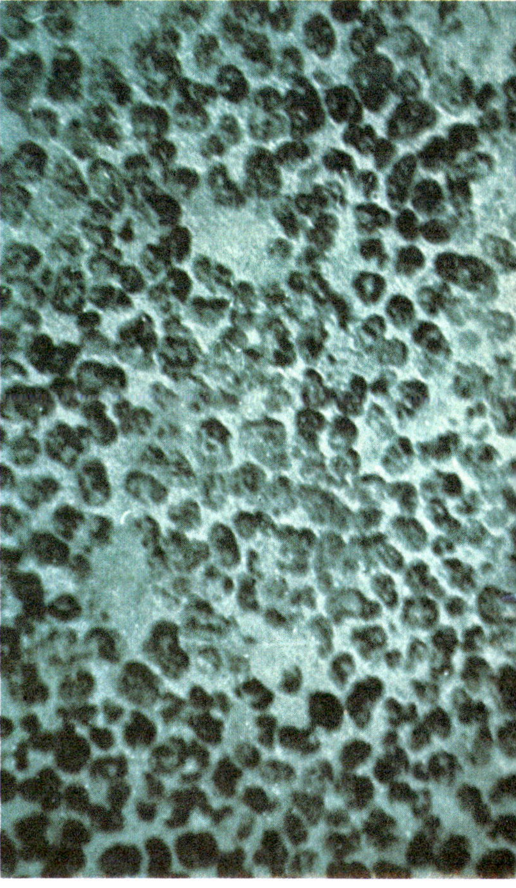

sea. We do not have direct evidence from the ocean floor for this circulation and we do not know how deeply the water might circulate. But in Iceland—which in effect is a surface appearance of such mid-ocean mountains—rain water seeps into ground perhaps to a depth of 30 to 50 km (20–30 mi) and eventually returns to the surface in thermal springs.

METALS IN HOT BRINE

The seeping water takes heavy metals into solution and is heated by the host rock. The hot brine, with its heavy metal content, eventually finds a vent to return to the ocean floor, there to mix with the normal sea water. Because of the reactions that follow this mining process, various metals are precipitated. If this takes place in a hollow of the ocean floor, metal-rich sediments will accumulate.

Three such basins have been found in the middle of the Red Sea about halfway between Port Sudan and Jidda in Saudi Arabia. They have been named after the ships that discovered them: Atlantis II, Discovery, and Chain Deeps. All three were discovered by measuring the temperature of bottom water. In the Atlantis II Deep the bottom temperature is 58° C (136.4° F), the temperature of a rather uncomfortably hot bath. The Deep is elongated, a few km wide and less than 20 km (12½ mi) long. Seismic probe

A dredge scoops up samples of the nodules (left) and brings them back on deck. In a later test-mining operation, the nodules are conveyed to a collection area (upper right). The size of the nodules is indicated by the ruler (lower right).

records indicate a possible thickness of sediments between 25 and 30 m (27–33 yd). Only the uppermost 0.8 meter (31 inches) has been sampled with coring devices—and the assays of these samples turned out to be exceedingly interesting and unexpected.

The cores show a number of different sedimentary arrangements and compositions. Iron montmorillonite (a group of clay minerals) is near the sediment surface. Under that is a goethite (bog iron ore) layer. Next comes a sulfide layer. Interspersed are layers primarily of manganese and also of detritus (rock fragments). It is supposed that changes in the rate of flow and composition of the brine and changes in the chemical environment of the overlying water cause—over a period of time—the precipitation of the different minerals.

The average metal components of the sediments of the Atlantis II Deep are: iron, 29 per cent; zinc, 3.4 per cent; copper, 1.3 per cent; silver, 54 parts per million (ppm), and gold, 0.5 ppm. The grade of the sediment varies greatly from layer to layer, with the highest grade in the sulfide layer. The highest values found thus far are 11 per cent zinc, 7 per cent copper, and 0.02 per cent silver on a dry-weight, salt-free basis.

It is not easy to estimate the total size of this orebody. The latest survey results

The metallic content of the nodules can be determined quickly by means of an atomic analyzer aboard the *Prospector* (left). The geological conditions at the dredged site are also studied by analyzing core samples (right).

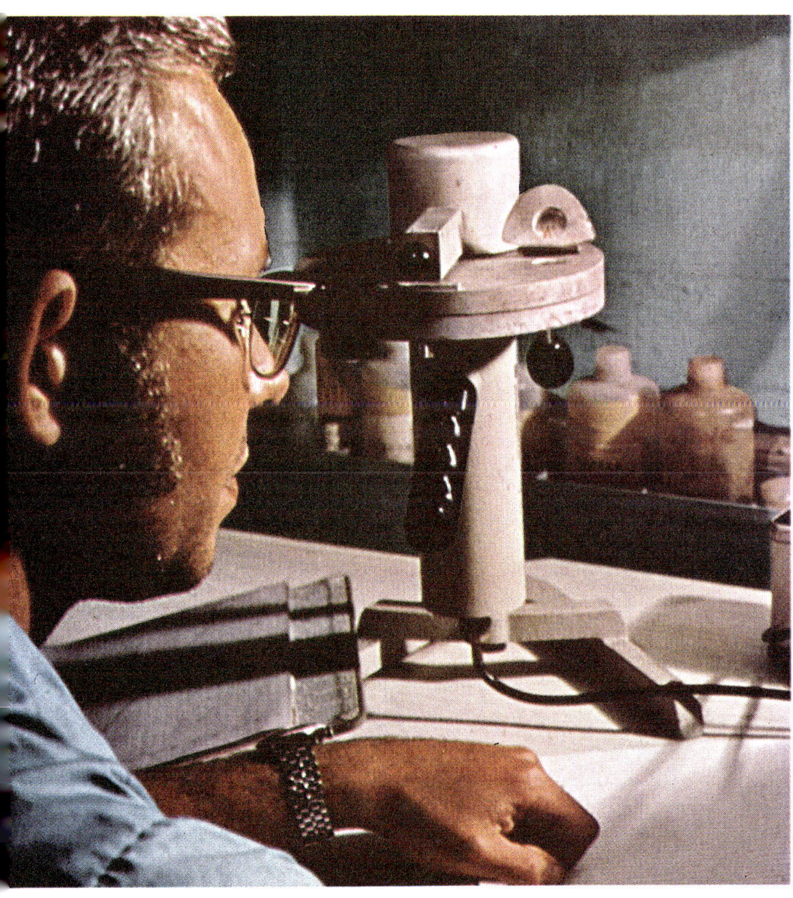

Four metals can be obtained from deep-sea nodules. Shown here on a bed of nodules are a manganese slug and sheets of copper, nickel, and cobalt.

have become a closely guarded commercial secret. This was not always the case. Up until the early 1970's the mining concerns of the world largely ignored the discovery of metal-rich sedimentary deposits in the Red Sea. They were considered rare and the area was politically troubled.

The picture started changing, however, as a result of the deep-ocean drilling conducted by the United States government 500 km (about 310 mi) east of Cape Hatteras, North Carolina, in water 5,180 m (more than 17,000 ft) deep.

Some 600 m (about 2,000 ft) of sediment were found overlying typical oceanic basalt. The lowest sediment, just above the basalt, was 153 million years old. And buried beneath 350 m (about 1,150 ft) of these sediments, there is a layer 60 m (about 200 ft) thick that resembles the mineralized zone of the Red Sea. The sediment contains zinc sulfide, which, in patches, constitutes 50 per cent of the material. The amount of copper so far analyzed is less than $\frac{1}{10}$ of 1 per cent. It is unlikely that this ore will be worked for many years. Its discovery is mainly of interest in showing that these types of ores are not a peculiarity of a particular site and time but are an example of a general process.

DEPOSIT OFF CANADA?

Where are other likely localities for the occurrence of such sediments?

The Red Sea is a narrow sea and the central crack with its metalliferous sediments is not far from the adjoining continents. There are other places where cracks in the oceanic plate are close to the continents. A particularly interesting region for exploration might be off Canada's Vancouver Island, where Juan de Fuca ridge strikes at an oblique angle toward the continent. A Canadian expedition in 1970 measured the world's highest recorded rate of heat flow at one station near that ridge—perhaps not an insignificant factor in considering the possibility of useful deposits on the ocean floor there.

The occurrence of Red Sea deposits might be due to a process associated with the growth of mid-oceanic mountain ranges and nothing else. In this case they might occur anywhere along the chain of mid-ocean mountains. If this is indeed so, the amount of metals available to the miners of the future is truly staggering, simply beyond comprehension. Even speculation about the exploitation of this resource would sound like science fiction today, when so much well-grounded concern is being voiced over the dwindling supply of the earth's available resources.

To resolve the nature of the occurrence of the metalliferous sediment deposits and to develop methods of finding them, detailed and painstaking surveys of mid-ocean ridges will be required. Here Canada has an unquestioned lead. Since 1965, five trips have been made with the Canadian ship *Hudson* to carry out intensive investigations over a small area of the mid-Atlantic Ridge near 45° north. This small region is probably known better than any other comparable area anywhere in the oceans. The metalliferous sediments have not been found there yet, but knowledge has been accumulating.

SOME BIG "IF'S"

As John L. Mero says in his book, *The Mineral Resources of the Sea:* "Economic systems, technology, political climates, governmental decisions, taxes, and a myriad of other factors are involved in the equation with which we attempt to determine whether or not a mineral deposit is a mineral resource. . . . Mineral deposits may be economic mineral resources, or at least potential mineral resources in one location but not in another, at one time in history but not in another, and by political decision in one country but not in another."

The "if's" are big ones and the uncertainties many. It is clear, however, that science and technology are moving forward. Potential mineral resources of the deep sea are great and cannot be ignored by anybody concerned with resources□

SELECTED READINGS

The Mineral Resources of the Sea by John L. Mero. American Elsevier Publishing Co., Inc., 1965.

"Tapping the Lode on the Ocean Floor." *Business Week*, Oct. 19, 1974.

A model of the kind of deep-sea rig that will be used in mining the seas. The model shows a section of the ship's hull that will support a drilling rig, which will lower a pipe to the ocean floor. A pickup mechanism at the end of the pipe will sweep up the nodules.

Sea level changes for many reasons. The best known is tidal action. At the right is a photo of France's famous Mont-Saint-Michel in the Bay of St. Michel. At low tide the Bay is almost dry but at flood tide fills with treacherous rapidity.

The Ever-Changing Sea Level

by Alan P. Carr

WAVES and tides are the most obvious features which show that the surface of the sea varies in height, but they are by no means the only ones. In fact, looking at a geological time scale, such short-term changes are not even the most noteworthy.

Yet variations in the height and frequency of waves, whether wind-driven or in the form of swell, are important. By making records of such information it is possible to predict the range of conditions likely to be encountered by offshore oil rigs and engineering works, and whether sea defense schemes will be adequate or are unnecessarily elaborate.

Superimposed on such wave data is the effect of the tide. Spring tides occur following the new and full moon when sun, moon, and earth lie in the same line; this gives rise to the maximum tidal range. At neaps, when sun and moon pull at right angles to each other, the tidal range is less. But it is not just gravity that influences tidal range. The coastline is also important. Thus tides may be amplified by a narrowing estuary. The Bay of Fundy, and the Severn Estuary, England, are good examples. Tides reaching about 12 m (40 ft) occur in both areas.

One tide may complement the next. For example, a tide traveling around the north of Scotland meets the succeeding one traveling up the English Channel. On parts of the North Sea and English Channel coast, they are in phase and augment each other. Elsewhere, such as along parts of the Dutch coast, they cancel out.

Periodic changes appear to occur over the longer term. Oscillations in the height of sea level are thought to take place at 18⅔-, 93-, and 525-year intervals.

SURGES

Less regular changes in tide height are caused by weather conditions. Storms have the effect of altering predicted tides as well as of generating waves. Extensive flooding may result as a consequence of excessive or prolonged high water. In an estuary these effects may be increased by additional freshwater flow from rivers after a heavy rainfall. Such increases in tide level are called surges and have attracted attention for some time. More recently, negative surges, where tides do not reach prediction, have begun to cause concern too. With the increasing number of supertankers, and the smaller and smaller clearance in navigable channels, this aspect looms large because of possible dangers to the environment through oil spillage. Other fluctuations, such as tsunamis (tidal waves caused by an earthquake), are of a particularly chance nature.

RECOGNIZED BY LEONARDO

Leonardo da Vinci was one of the first persons to recognize that the relation between land and sea had varied over time. Many of the geological rock types that form the land masses of the world are made up of limestones, sandstones, and clays that were originally laid down below what was then the sea level. How have they now risen above the sea?

There are three types of change in relative height between land and mean sea level—tectonic, isostatic, and eustatic. The most dramatic of these is the first. In tectonic change, an area of land may be suddenly elevated above sea level as a result of an earthquake. The Alaskan earthquake of 1964 is one example. It left boats stranded well above extreme high-tide level. Isolated coastal features, such as stacks (chimneys entirely removed from the mainland), were no longer affected by subsequent wave attack. Tectonic effects may also be slower, as in the gradual subsidence, or sinking, of parts of the seabed when sediment is deposited upon it.

Snow and ice-covered beaches of Marble Point, Antarctica, reveal the area's past—once submerged by the weight of glaciers.

RISING LAND

Isostatic change is most marked in areas that were submerged or are recovering from having been submerged under many hundreds or thousands of feet of ice following the last of the various glacial stages which have been typical of the last 2 million years or so. It is as if the land acts like a gigantic pair of kitchen scales—the weight (the ice) is put on and the pan (the land) drops. When the load is re-

A nearly horizontal surface at Blackdown Hills, England, molded by land or sea processes.

Rio de Janeiro, situated on Brazil's Guanabara Bay, has a partially submerged coast and long stretches of flat shoreline.

moved, the pan goes back to its original position. The process is slow compared with the effects of an earthquake but, even so, parts of the Baltic and northern Canada are thought to have risen some 275 m (900 ft) since the last glaciation, a period of about 20,000 years or less.

Both tectonic and isostatic effects are most important in a regional context, but the third type of relative change between the land and the sea, that of eustasy, is apparent on a worldwide scale. As a glacial stage begins—and the cause of such changes in climate is still very much in dispute—water from the sea gradually becomes locked away in the growing ice sheets of the polar regions. Such ice sheets and glaciers increase both in thickness and area extending into what had been temperate lands.

As a result, relative sea level falls throughout the world, but the most obvious effects are apparent in the nonglaciated areas. It is believed that in the last glaciation sea level was perhaps as much as 145 m (475 ft) lower than that of the present day. Similar low sea levels probably occurred during other glacial stages. A large part of the continental shelves would have been exposed and, indeed, there is considerable evidence for this. It includes borehole data which indicate former soil profiles, submarine canyons, and the tracks of ancient icebergs that became grounded on the seabed.

In many cases the effects of isostatic and eustatic change may have worked against each other so that the whole picture is difficult, if not impossible, to unravel. Some dramatic "raised beaches" in the Antarctic may be of this type.

These remains of an interglacial pebble beach in Devonshire, England, reveal a drop in sea level—in this case, a eustatic change with water locked up in glaciers.

Scotch Cap Light Station on Unimak Island in the Aleutian Chain, Alaska. Left: lighthouse in 1946 before it was destroyed by a tidal wave. Right: remains after tidal wave. Tidal waves—a tectonic effect—dramatically affect sea level.

THE SEA-LEVEL ARGUMENT

Change over the last 40,000 years or so can often be dated by the radiocarbon technique. With this method, the amount of carbon-14 isotope in a sample of material is measured under controlled conditions in the laboratory. Since the isotope decays in proportion to its age, the date when the deposit was first formed can be calculated. Peat beds are most suitable for analysis, but shells may be used.

Even with peat, care is needed to be sure that the material is in its original position and that it does, in fact, reflect sea level at the time at which it was laid down. Evidence for earlier periods may be obtained by dating with other isotopes. Sometimes the sequence of events, if not absolute dates, can be determined by microfossils and pollen.

Although there is general agreement that up to 5,000 to 7,000 years ago sea level had been rising—at one stage by as much as 1.5 m (5 ft) in 100 years—there is great argument, strangely, as to what has happened over the last few thousand years. There are two main views. Some scientists believe that about 7,000 years ago the rise in sea level slackened off and its position has remained broadly stable thereafter; others think that sea level has been at, or above, the present-day level on at least one occasion during the past few millennia. Local variations often tend to obscure any worldwide picture.

Present-day trends are studied principally by installing especially accurate tide recorders on what are believed to be stable land sites. The information is later analyzed by averaging out the tides to obtain mean sea level. From this it may be possible to recognize a small, but critical, trend from one year to another. Allowances have to be made for the widely varying weather pattern between successive years, so that the task is by no means easy. In Britain, between 1920 and 1945, there were only three tide gauges of the required accuracy and only one of these operated throughout the whole period. Extensive flooding along England's east coast in 1953 emphasized the need for more, and accurate, information, especially since land surveys and tide data were in conflict.

Maximum tide levels recorded at London Bridge increased about 1 m, or 3 ft, in the last 180 years, and there is evidence to suggest that relative sea level is now about 4 m, or 13 ft, above that of Roman times, some 2,000 years ago. Much of this change can probably be attributed to compaction (packing down of the land) as a result of the weight of buildings, effects of drainage, and so on. Whatever the cause, it has become necessary to construct an emergency barrier across the Thames to reduce the flood hazard to central London. The problem is by no means unique to that city. Similar difficulties apply to Venice, Italy, and along parts of the Japanese and Dutch coasts. Over half of the Netherlands is subject to flooding, and the country's whole history is one of struggle against the sea.

GAINS AND LOSSES

The changing relationship between the level of the sea and the land has many other effects, not all of a harmful nature. On the negative side, rising sea level may result in the filling of valleys by peat and unconsolidated sediments. These provide problems for the foundations of civil-engineering structures such as bridges. Similarly, higher sea level may permit larger waves to reach the coast and may therefore increase erosion. In contrast, along rocky coastlines, deep harbors may be provided. In addition, waves and tidal currents can sort material. This property is of value in producing sources of well-graded building aggregate. Heavy minerals may be concentrated in particular deposits, thus making them economically worthwhile to work both in areas now above sea level and in those below. Iron, tin, and even diamonds are cases in point.

Changing sea level has affected our surroundings, too. Sometimes it is difficult to tell just what proportion of the horizontal surfaces in the landscape are marine in origin; in other places the evidence is clear. Along the southeast seaboard of the United States, there is a whole staircase of former barrier coastlines about 80 km (50 mi) wide and several times as long. Elsewhere there are cliffs no longer affected by present-day wave action. Around many parts of the British coast these may be fronted by so-called raised beaches, characteristically about 7.5 m (25 ft) above current sea level. The features are probably legacies of more than one interglacial stage when sea level was similar to that of the present. Unfortunately, neither the relationship between such features and sea level at the time of their formation, the effect of exposure, nor the processes by which they developed are known accurately.

The sea and the land are restless. They are restless from wave to wave, from tide to tide, from millennia to millennia, and over geological time. The changing interrelationship of the two is of interest in terms of pure and applied research, but it has special significance in its environmental and economic implications□

Oceanography (grades 7–12) by Jerome Williams, Franklin Watts, Inc., 1972.

Recent Sea Level Changes by Joseph R. Curray and others, Geological Society of America, 1970.

A remarkable stairway of marine terraces and old cliffs marks the Palos Verdes peninsula in southern California. These features have resulted from tectonic changes in this earthquake prone region.

The Bermuda Triangle

by Steven Moll

IN 1945 five U.S. Navy planes on a training flight vanished over the Atlantic Ocean without a trace. They disappeared over an area of the Atlantic known as the Bermuda Triangle, or, sometimes, as the Devil's Triangle. A search plane sent after the five planes also disappeared. Three years later the same fate befell two large airliners in the same area; although skies were clear, they never reached their destination.

Equally strange things have happened on the ocean surface in this area. Ships have vanished, often within sight of land, leaving no sign of debris. Or they have been found drifting without any passengers or crew aboard and no indication of what happened to the people. The most famous abandoned ship of all, the *Mary Celeste*, was found in 1872, but similar events are taking place today.

These are the kinds of stories that make up the mystery of the Bermuda Triangle, off the North American coast. The area is so called because of its triangular shape, roughly bound by a line running from Miami to Puerto Rico to Bermuda and back to Miami again. In the last 150 years, more than 40 ships and boats and 20 aircraft have disappeared or been found abandoned within this area. About 1,000 lives may have been lost in these incidents.

Some people think that there must be something very strange about the Bermuda Triangle. Even though organizations such as the U.S. Navy and Coast Guard put the events down as coincidence, there are groups and individuals who talk about sinister forces that may be at work there.

Scary stories about the sea are hardly new. People have sailed across the ocean for centuries, but it remains a somewhat mysterious and unpredictable place. So it is not surprising that strange and seemingly hard-to-explain events in the Triangle have aroused the interest of many people. At present this interest seems to be growing rapidly. Many books and articles have appeared by now, and television shows have been devoted to the subject. The name "Bermuda Triangle" itself seems to be only about 10 years old.

OTHER WORLDS AND UNDERWORLDS

Several "explanations" for the things that happen in the Triangle are strange themselves. One of the strangest is that the Triangle must be some kind of "trap" used by beings from another world. For unknown reasons, according to such notions, these beings are believed to be gathering up samples of humanity, or at any rate, looking for living things that can make talking sounds. Cats and dogs are sometimes found in abandoned ships in the Triangle, but pet parrots disappear along with their masters.

This otherworldly idea is linked to the many reported sightings of unidentified

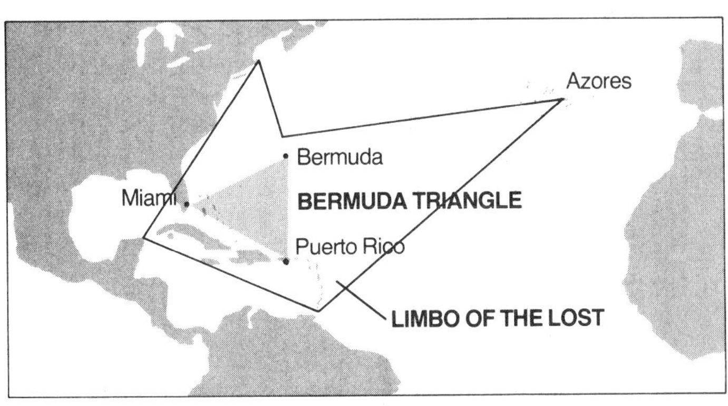

The Atlantic area bounded by Miami, Puerto Rico, and Bermuda is called the Bermuda Triangle and is, according to some stories, a mysterious and unpredictable region.

flying objects (UFO's) in the area. The UFO's are said to have been seen entering and leaving the sea there, as though visiting a base on the ocean floor. Some people who think UFO's exist blame the vanishing ships and planes on them. One such writer is John Wallace Spencer, a UFO researcher who wrote *The Limbo of the Lost*. This is his name for the Bermuda Triangle—or actually, for a larger area that extends all the way to the Azores.

An equally imaginative "explanation" for events in the Triangle is that a very ancient—and legendary—human civilization is causing the trouble. The people who write about such notions tell their story as follows. Underwater structures that—according to them—look manmade have been found around the Bahamas. Therefore, they say, the whole region may have been above water long ago. If it was, it may have been the site of the legendary country of Atlantis. According to such writers, the people of this mythical Atlantis were very advanced scientifically. Perhaps some signalling device of theirs lies buried under the Atlantic Ocean. It may still turn on and off now and then, perhaps because of a passing plane or ship. As a result, the instruments aboard the craft are somehow disrupted. Or there may even now be a living civilization down there, underneath the waves. . . .

Other people have suggested that there is a "hole in the sky" in the Triangle region, a place that one can enter but cannot leave. It may be some kind of fourth dimensional "space warp" that will some day return all the lost travelers and ships and planes.

THE SARGASSO AND THE GULF STREAM

These fancy explanations obviously are not useful if one tries to explain events inside the Triangle in a more ordinary way. Usually one would begin by looking for natural forces that could be causing the strange accidents.

For example, what about sea and weather conditions in the area? To the east and south, the Triangle merges with the Sargasso Sea. This region of the North Atlantic Ocean is noted for its calm weather and its masses of floating seaweed. In the days of sail, ships were sometimes stranded there for weeks or months. Thus strange tales have grown up about the Sargasso, dating back even to Christopher Columbus's first voyage.

To the west and north, the Triangle is crossed by the Gulf Stream. This warm ocean current can carry drifting boats and debris over long distances in a surprisingly short time. Storms blow up suddenly here, and the weather can be treacherous. Waterspouts—ocean-going tornados—tend to occur during certain seasons. Such tornados are as dangerous on sea as they are on land. In addition, pilots crossing the area often experience clear-air turbulence—that is, violent air motions even when the sky is free of clouds. Many of the Bermuda Triangle stories talk of "absolutely calm" seas and skies. Yet when some of the stories are checked further, it appears that bad weather conditions did exist after all. Such misleading stories have added their share to the Bermuda Triangle mystery.

MISBEHAVING COMPASSES

Another natural phenomenon often mentioned in Triangle stories is the earth's magnetism. It is often contended that there is something "wrong" about magnetism within the Triangle—something that makes compasses work strangely.

Compasses almost everywhere on earth point toward the magnetic north pole, not toward the true north pole. The difference between the two directions is known as the magnetic variation. Pilots must take this variation into account.

However, in the Bermuda Triangle, a compass points toward both magnetic north and true north. There is nothing odd about this. The magnetic and true north poles are simply in line with each other, as seen from the Triangle. What some writers say that they find odd is that there is a region on the opposite side of the world where compasses also point toward both magnetic and true north, for the same reason. And this area, they say, is a patch of ocean off the coast of Japan that is known as the "Devil's Sea." It is so called because it is as strange a place as the Bermuda Triangle. Thus these writers believe that the matter of compass direction must be important after all.

The problem with this is that the Japanese themselves do not seem to think there is a "Devil's Sea" mystery. The most mysterious event in the area may have been the disappearance of a research vessel, *Kaiyo Maru,* in 1952. Evidence indicates that the ship was destroyed by an undersea volcano that it was studying. Yet some Triangle writers mistakenly report that *Kaiyo Maru* disappeared in 1955, and that its very mission was to explore the strange "Devil's Sea."

Finally, some writers speak of the mysterious way that compasses tend to spin when inside the Bermuda Triangle. The fact is that it is not hard to set compass needles spinning, and they always tend to swing back and forth in rough weather. And this happens anywhere.

THE MYSTERY OF THE MYSTERY

Which leads to a more basic question: is there really anything so odd about the Bermuda Triangle itself? Certainly many of the things that have happened there are very odd. For example, what happened on the *Mary Celeste* remains unexplained today. But the *Mary Celeste* story is also an example of one of the problems about the Bermuda Triangle mystery—it did not take place inside the Triangle. The ship was found 800 km (500 mi) east of the Azores. This places it within the "Limbo of the Lost" mentioned earlier. But when a "mystery region" is made to include much of the North Atlantic Ocean, the "mystery" of the region itself seems to fade. There may only be a very strange sea tale left to explain.

Several other Triangle events besides the *Mary Celeste* also actually seem to have taken place outside the Triangle. In addition, stories can sound quite different according to the way they are told. For example, the most famous airplane mystery of the Triangle is the disappearance of the five Navy planes in 1945. An Arizona State University librarian named Lawrence David Kusche checked this story out carefully. He found that official records of the pilots' radio conversations do not contain the strange comments that appear in some of the Bermuda Triangle accounts. And the story unfolds as a series of understandable and tragic mistakes. By the time the planes were last heard from, night and bad weather were approaching —unlike some accounts that describe a perfectly clear sky. What happened to the five planes at the end is still unknown. But what probably happened to them is not hard to imagine. It is not unlikely that they simply were completely lost, and too low on fuel, and crashed into the ocean.

Waterspouts—tornadoes at sea—endanger ships and planes within the Bermuda Triangle.

The Bermuda Triangle is a heavily traveled area. Many strange disappearances have occurred there over the years. But strange disappearances also occur all over the world, on land as well as at sea. Do the events in the Bermuda Triangle make it a strange place in itself? Some people think so. Others believe that there is no real mystery. Which viewpoint is right? Anyone who is interested in that question will find plenty to read about the matter□

SELECTED READINGS

The Bermuda Triangle by Charles Berlitz. Doubleday, 1974.

The Bermuda Triangle—Solved by Lawrence David Kusche. Harper & Row, 1975.

The Elusive Bermuda Triangle, 3d edition of *Bermuda Triangle Bibliography* by Lawrence Kusche and Deborah Blouin. University Library, Arizona State University, 1975.

Project FAMOUS gets under way as *Alvin*, a deep-ocean submersible carrying a crew of three, maneuvers into position to be hoisted aboard the *R. V. Knorr.*

Window on Earth's Core

by Alan Anderson, Jr.

ONE day in the summer of 1974, in a tiny submarine named *Alvin*, three men cruised slowly over a stretch of ocean floor never before seen by man. That by itself was not unusual. Man has examined very little of the sea floor, even that close to the continental shores where he lives. And the stretch that the men were traveling over could scarcely have been more remote. It lay nearly 2,700 m (9,000 ft) beneath the waves of the Atlantic Ocean, between Cape Hatteras and Gibraltar.

The divers were not interested in sheer adventure. The great trenches in the Pacific Ocean would have offered them a dive four times as deep. The bleak, rubbly landscape that they were exploring was unique for another reason: it lies along a huge "seam" called the Mid-Atlantic Ridge. This ridge can be thought of as a single, gigantic, linear volcano. It is here that the floor of the Atlantic Ocean is thought by many of today's geologists to have been created by the spreading out of lava from persistent, small volcanic eruptions for millions of years.

A beam of light from *Alvin* broke the blackness of the near-freezing water surrounding the craft. The pilot and his two geologist passengers peered out at dark, often jagged rocks. The rocks were sprinkled irregularly with the whitish skeletons of minute calcium-bearing organisms. Every 30 m (100 ft) or so there were "stretch marks"—rips or fissures—of varying size in the sea floor. The fissures, which were all nearly parallel to the ridge, seemed to indicate enormous forces pulling the sea floor away from the seam. The geologists studied these fissures with excitement, because their parallel position provided a major clue to the movement of the sea floor.

As the submarine approached one of the fissures, the pilot applied the craft's reverse thrusters. *Alvin* slowed from a cruising speed of a half-knot to full stop. The geologists sat transfixed. They realized that they had come to the lip of the largest crevasse they had yet seen. It was the last dive of the summer, and they knew that they would probably never again see such an impressive monument to the giant forces that seethe beneath the earth's rigid skin.

"We could see as much as 80 ft [25 m] down into that fissure," recalls Dr. Robert Ballard of Woods Hole Oceanographic Institution, one of the diving scientists aboard the *Alvin*. "Do you remember the old movies in which the earth opens up and swallows everyone in huge cracks? Well, that is geological fiction on land, but down there it happens. My reaction was just to sit still and look. We didn't say anything or do anything. Seeing that crack was like getting a lollipop too big to fit in your mouth. We realized that we were the first human beings to see that fissure, and because of its remoteness, we'll probably be the last. It is a heavy feeling to realize you are witnessing the spot of the first creation of the crust of the earth."

THE RIDGE AND PLATE TECTONICS

It would be difficult to exaggerate the significance of the Mid-Atlantic Ridge for geology. Since the mid-1960's this science has seen the development of a number of fascinating theories that embrace the earth as a whole.

The theories may be lumped together under the heading of "plate tectonics." The word "tectonics" is related to the name "Tecton," a carpenter in Homer's *Iliad*. It has come to refer to the art or science of construction. In geology it is the study of how the earth's structures are formed. As for "plate," geologists have hypothesized that the earth's entire outermost layer is constructed of about a dozen rocky plates. These plates are continuously assembled, moved, and destroyed over geological time by vast, mysterious processes taking place deep within the earth.

The movement of these plates is the best understood aspect of the theory. The North American plate, for example, is known to be moving away from the European plate at the rate of more than two centimeters (about an inch) a year. The movements of the other major plates—South American, African, and so forth—are equally well charted. Destruction of the plates is not so well understood. It is thought to occur at the sites of the great ocean deeps known as trenches. From the evidence provided by seismic and other instruments, it seems reasonable to assume that the plates are somehow forced down these trenches. There they are recycled through the hot, somewhat pliable

Great forces appear to be pulling the sea floor away from the Mid-Atlantic Ridge. The two dark lines in this photomontage are "stretch marks"—fissures, or openings—in the sea floor. These fissures run parallel to the sides of the ridge.

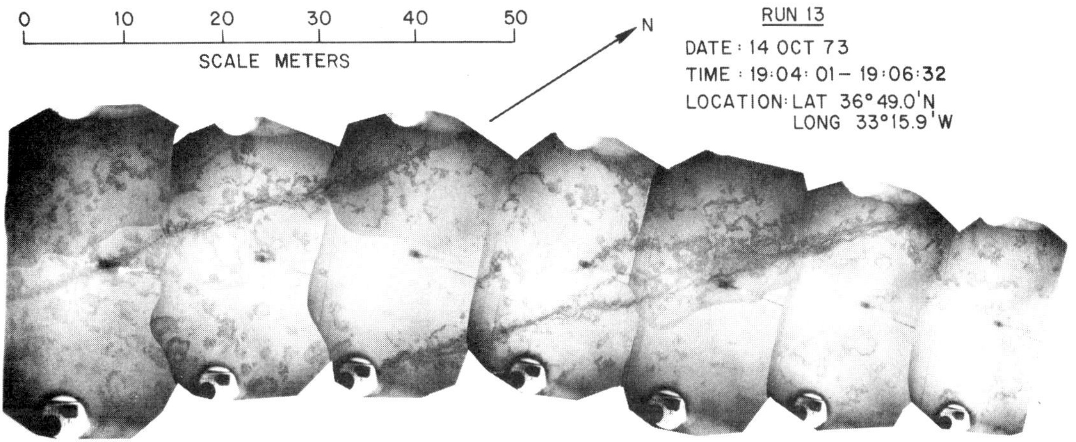

Alvin's mechanical claw picks up a small rock in front of some "toothpaste lava" that has squeezed up through the sea floor.

layer of rock material called the mantle.

Meanwhile, new material from the mantle emerges elsewhere to replace the plate edges that are sinking. This new material is thought to rise steadily to the surface of the earth's crust along the entire extent of the Mid-Atlantic Ridge. Actually, this ridge is part of a worldwide underwater ridge system. It runs beneath the Pacific and Indian oceans, girdling the globe like the seams of a giant baseball. It is the largest geographic feature on the face of the earth, winding continuously for about 75,700 km (47,000 mi). And as the site where the earth's crust is formed the mighty ridge system seems to offer geologists a unique chance to sample fresh mantle material. Thus it may prove to be a kind of "window" to the interior of the earth. It could offer an opportunity for gaining clues about the nature of the geological "engine" that actually moves the plates of the earth's crust.

A MOONLIKE ADVENTURE

Several dozen geologists gathered at Princeton University in 1971 to plan a diving assault on this window. They agreed to collaborate with French scientists, who, since the early days of Auguste Piccard and Jacques Cousteau, have pioneered in the field of deep ocean diving. The French-American Mid-Ocean Undersea Study—Project FAMOUS—became operational in the summer of 1972. The French sponsors of the project were the National Center for Exploitation of the Oceans, the Oceanological Center of Brittany, and the French Navy. The chief French scientist was Xavier Le Pichon. The American sponsors were the National Oceanic and Atmospheric Administration, the National Science Foundation, and the Office of Naval Research. Dr. James Heirtzler of Woods Hole, an old hand at plate-tectonics investigation, was selected to direct the U.S. attempt to verify, by eye, the spreading of the sea floor.

In many ways Project FAMOUS was as great an adventure as man's recent journeys to the moon. Thus, in talking of the results of the U.S. part of the project,

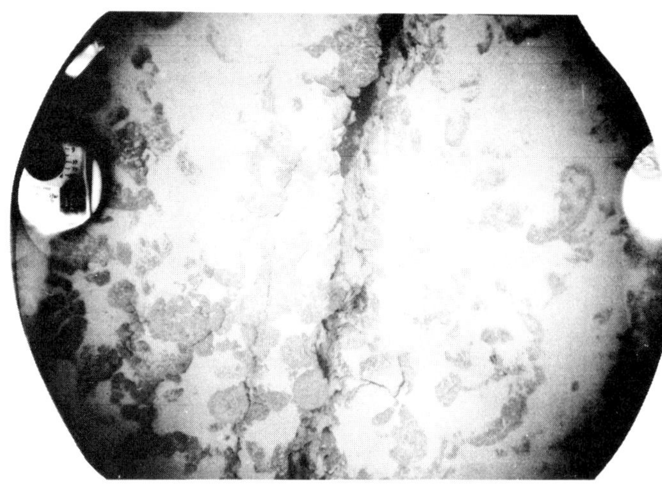

Detail of a fissure in the sea floor inside the median Rift Valley. This fissure is about 1.5 m (5 ft) wide. Photos such as this have been made possible by the U.S. Navy's LIBEC photographic system, which allows light to be directed to larger areas of the sea floor than was possible with conventional equipment.

Heirtzler was able to describe a series of accomplishments that sounded very much like those of the Apollo astronauts. "Last summer the *Alvin* made 17 dives, covering 29 km [18 mi] of sea floor in 81 hours of submerged time. She stopped at 81 sampling stations, brought back 867 lb (393 kg) of rock, and took 17,000 photographs. The surface ship *Knorr* made 45 dredging stops and covered 80 km [50 mi] on the sea floor with a camera towed just above the bottom. Altogether we have about 50,000 photos of the sea floor as well as videotape and moving pictures."

Other parallels between the moon program and Project FAMOUS include the similarity between the lunar surface and the surface of a valley running down the crest of the Mid-Atlantic Ridge. Like the moon, the bottom of the valley bears no vegetation, displays little coloring, and is littered with rocks. When the *Alvin* moved, it stirred up a cloud of sediment, just as the lunar module threw up a shroud of moon dust as it settled onto the lunar surface. And the rocks retrieved by the *Alvin* were all basalt, as have been moon rocks.

On the other hand, despite the crushing pressures outside the hulls of their vessel, the FAMOUS divers found the *Alvin* to be a more reassuring place than a spaceship and more congenial than solitary terrestrial exploration. "We had a few awkward moments when we tried to go down in a couple of the biggest fissures," said Ballard, "but we never really had a feeling that we were in danger. Having done 12 years of scuba diving, I felt a lot safer and more comfortable in the submarine. The most important thing was being able to talk with someone else about what we were seeing. You sometimes get off on a funny idea underwater,

Project FAMOUS dive sites near the Azores. The U.S. ship *Alvin* operated in slashed areas A, B, and C, while the French ships *Archimède* and *Cyana* made dives at sites I, II, and III. The *Glomar Challenger* drill site is marked at upper left.

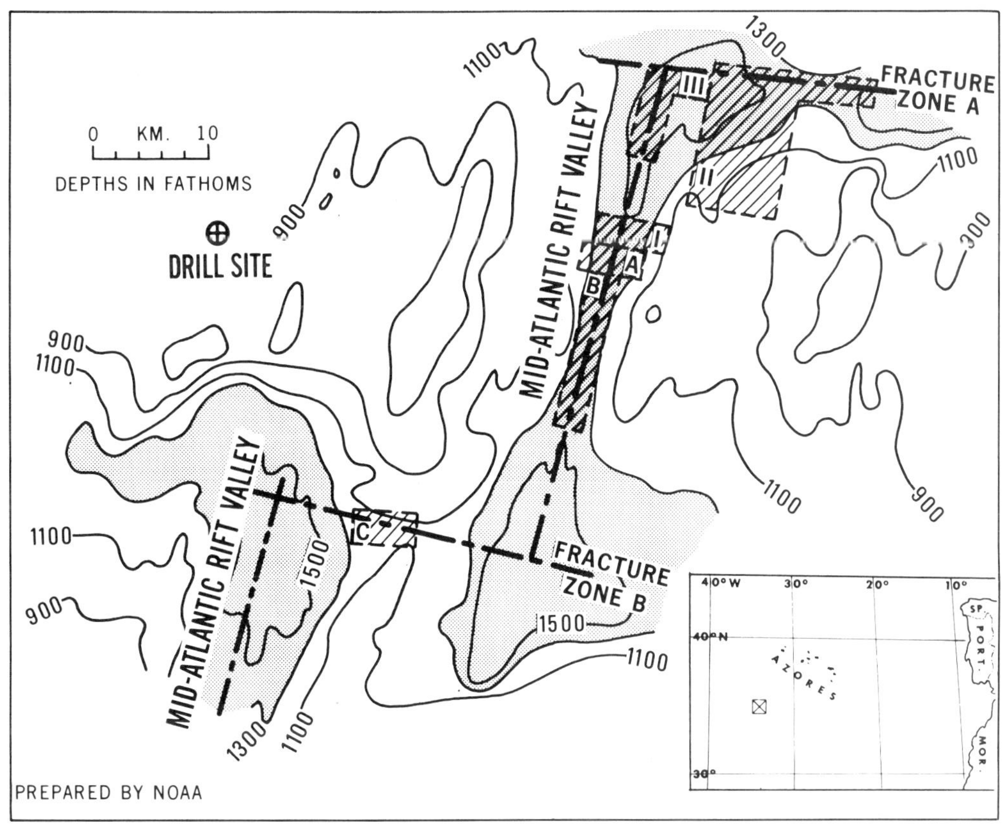

The *Cyana*, a highly maneuverable "diving saucer," explored an undersea canyon and took scientists close to the steep walls of the rift valley for visual observations.

and it is good to have someone around who can bring you back. We could even eat lunch down there . . ."

Is "flying" the *Alvin* like maneuvering a spacecraft in orbit? "It's more like flying a helicopter—you don't want to tip over on your side. Everything would spill."

DARKNESS, QUAKES

The divers noticed one problem that was unique to the sea floor. "We never got any perspective on where we were," said Ballard. "We'd think, 'wouldn't it be nice to perch ourselves up on the rim of the Mid-Atlantic Valley and look down, as you can do above the Grand Canyon or in orbit around the moon?' Well, it can't be done. All you can see through the porthole is a little bit of ground 3 or 4 ft [about a meter] away, which is moving by so fast that it takes all your concentration to assimilate it. It's like standing so close to a tree that all you can see is the bark—and from that information trying to make deductions about the nature of not only the whole tree but also the forest itself. That's why the surface work of the *Knorr* and other ships is so important—to sketch the forest."

After several decades of surface work, oceanographers are now reasonably familiar with the appearance of the "forest." The "bark," however, provided some surprises. "My impression of the sea floor," said Heirtzler, "is that a giant has been walking around crushing things. It's obviously a horrendous place to be, very busy with earthquakes and volcanic eruptions. We recorded hundreds of tiny earthquakes. Big earthquakes and volcanic eruptions are less frequent if you're measuring by our everyday lunchtime time scale. But on a geologic time scale, they are very common.

"A big mystery is the absence of any very large or very small features. The biggest rocks we saw were about this big [he stretched his arms wide]. You don't find any marble-sized rocks or any house-sized rocks. Everything seems to be broken up—but only into several pieces, a few inches to a few feet in diameter. They're not crushed, and they're not eroded. It's a very simple geological environment in that sense."

TOOTHPASTE LAVA

Another mystery is the origin of the "toothpaste lava," so named because it looks like rough, blackened toothpaste that was slowly squeezed out of small openings in the sea floor. Whereas the cracks from which the lava issues are presumably of many shapes, all of the toothpaste lava is tubular in shape. A single piece looks like the leg of a monstrous submarine elephant. Heirtzler said of the phenomenon: "We are guessing that the tremendous water pressure controls the shape of toothpaste lava, but this is just a guess. We haven't even begun to look at the rock samples or photographs or any of the data. For quite some time we are going to have more questions than answers."

Heirtzler also commented about the results of FAMOUS in general: "I have asked myself what we would have concluded if we had made these dives without knowing anything about sea-floor spreading. I think we would have said the same thing we are saying now. There is clear evidence of volcanic activity, and the fissures seem to indicate that the ridge area is being pulled apart, rather than pushed apart, by magma upwelling along it. We wouldn't have raced home from the expedition coining phrases like 'sea-floor spreading,' but what we saw certainly seems to support that idea, and I suspect that when we have analyzed the rock samples we collected, the picture will be even clearer."

The French teams also produced an impressive body of new data, through the dives of the bathyscaphe *Archimède* and the "diving saucer" *Cyana*. Supported by its mother ship, the *Marcel le Bihan*, the bulky *Archimède* made 16 dives into the main rift valley. The more maneuverable *Cyana* explored the valley's steep walls and one of the transverse canyons in four series of dives. Perhaps the most exciting of *Cyana*'s discoveries was evidence of possible ore deposits along the rift valley.

CRITICS OF FAMOUS

Some geologists outside of Project FAMOUS have voiced criticisms of it. They argue that there is more publicity than science involved and that diving to the Mid-Atlantic Ridge is a frivolous goal. "It's kind of like a blind man's feeling his way over the skin of an elephant," says John Sanders of Barnard College. "It doesn't tell you much about evolution."

Others say that unmanned instruments sent to the ocean bottom can do the job more cheaply. They point out that the *Knorr* was able to take bottom photos and collect rock samples from the surface as well as to deploy floating earthquake detectors.

"Some of us regard FAMOUS as a huge sink for resource funds," says an oceanographer at Columbia's Lamont-Doherty Geological Observatory. "There are a lot more things you can do with the amount of money they are spending, and you can cover a lot more distance. But FAMOUS is exciting for the general public, and it gets the funding."

"A VERY SPECIAL PLACE"

Heirtzler, who is "not entirely surprised" by all the commotion, defends the approach of FAMOUS as consistent with classic geological technique. "Much of geology is an observational science, but it's a primitive science in the ocean, carried over from what you can see on land. This, of course, doesn't necessarily apply in the sea. We do know the Mid-Atlantic Ridge is one of the most energetic areas on earth, and yet it has never been examined in detail." The great mystery of the moment is the driving mechanism for sea-floor spreading. What is the force that is great enough to move the sea floor and whole continents thousands of kilometers? Virtually everyone agrees that this mechanism is located in the mantle. The Mid-Atlantic Ridge, whose yet-to-be-analyzed rocks could provide the nearest thing to a "window to the mantle," may indeed offer the best hope for clues to this deep geological riddle.

"It is," says Heirtzler, "a very special place"□

SELECTED READINGS

"A Famous Project," *Time*, June 17, 1974.

The Drifting Continents by Alan Anderson, Jr. G. P. Putnam's Sons, 1971.

First Book of Submarines (grades 4–6) by Joseph B. Icenhower, Franklin Watts, Inc., 1971.

Two Hundred Million Years Beneath the Sea by Peter Briggs. Holt, Rinehart & Winston, Inc., 1971.

One particularly dangerous industrial pollutant is sulfur dioxide. This gas pollutes the air we breathe and once in the atmosphere joins with water molecules there to form sulfuric acid, which comes back down to the surface as acid rain.

Acid Rain

by Ian C. T. Nisbet

WHAT goes up must come down. This is as true of pollution, unfortunately, as of anything else. Yet for years we seem not to have believed this. The common "answer" to pollution from our factories and plants has been to send the pollutants up the smokestack and let them blow away. They blow away, all right, but sooner or later they land somewhere.

THE CAUSE

There are many kinds of pollutants to worry about. One of the worst of them is sulfur dioxide. This industrial waste is dangerous to living things in itself. It presents an added danger when it enters the atmosphere. It joins with water molecules there to form sulfuric acid, a very reactive and corrosive chemical. Most of the sulfur dioxide that goes up a stack is transformed into sulfuric acid within three or four days. And it eventually comes down in the rain—hence, "acid rain." This acid rain usually descends within a few hundred kilometers, or miles, of the source. Tall chimneys have little effect on this process. They merely disperse the sulfuric acid more widely.

Sulfuric acid also enters the atmosphere from natural sources. It originates mainly as hydrogen sulfide from decaying vegetation, together with some sulfur dioxide from volcanoes. Thus, even without human contributions, rainwater would be slightly acid—about 5.8 on the pH scale. This scale is a measure of how many hydrogen ions are present. It runs from 1, which would be a very strong acid, to 14, a very strong base. A pH of 7, therefore, indicates a neutral substance, and 5.8 is not too far from neutrality.

The total emissions of sulfur dioxide that humans add to the atmosphere—primarily from burning fossil fuels—have been estimated to be 100 to 150 million tons per year. That amount would yield roughly 200 million tons of sulfuric acid. This is very roughly half the input from natural sources. But more than 90 per cent of these emissions are in the Northern Hemisphere, where they must be approaching in total magnitude the natural contribution.

The introduction of this additional sulfuric acid to the Northern Hemisphere's annual rainfall would suffice to make the rain more acid by a full pH unit, even if fully mixed. In practice, however, most of the major sulfuric acid sources are localized within the industrial belt of the temperate zone. Thus, most acid fallout is concentrated into relatively limited areas downwind from these sources. There are three main areas: eastern Canada, the northeastern United States, and northern Europe. Most of these areas have poor glacial soils and a natural cover for coniferous (evergreen) forests. These soils tend to be somewhat acid anyway, and they are poorly buffered against additional leaching or loss of important minerals that they contain, minerals that are essential to life.

DEATH FROM THE SKY

The most detailed studies of acid rain and its consequences have been carried out in Norway and Sweden. These two countries have special reasons to feel aggrieved, because most of their pollution is derived from other industrial countries to the south and west. The average pH in most Swedish and Norwegian rivers and lakes has fallen steadily in recent decades—that is, they have become more acid. This was especially true in the late 1960's, when the rate of decline in most Swedish rivers was between 0.1 and 0.4 pH units per year.

This change has a direct and drastic effect on animal life in the water. Salmon and trout are first affected around pH 5.5, and reproductive failure and death occur if the pH falls much below 5. Already these fish have ceased to breed in other-

One serious effect of acid rain is thought to be a slowing down of the growth rate of trees, due to the effect of increased acidity on soil nutrients.

wise unpolluted Norwegian rivers. If present trends continue, most rivers in Scandinavia will be similarly affected within a few decades.

Although data are scanty, the present situation in eastern North America is probably at least as bad. Fish kills have been reported in acidified lakes in northern Ontario. In rural New Hampshire the pH of rain now averages less than 4.1, and the pH of forest runoff is often below 5.

THE LOSS OF VITAL MINERALS

Perhaps an even more serious result of acid rain is the leaching of essential nutrients from environments that scarcely contain enough of them anyway. The most important of these nutrients is calcium. Others are magnesium and potassium. A recent study in a deciduous (seasonal) forest in New Hampshire showed that, in the summer, most of the acidity was neutralized in the tree canopy. In the process, substantial quantities of calcium and potassium were leached from the leaves. In winter, and in coniferous forests, there is further leaching from the soil and from leaf litter on the forest floor.

Swedish studies have indicated net losses from forest soils that were already poor in calcium. In the New Hampshire study, the minerals leached from the forest system were more or less being replaced by weathering of subsurface rocks. This indicates a very uncertain natural balance at best. There is no build-up of mineral reserves taking place there, to protect the system against future losses.

Although not quite conclusive, certain evidence strongly suggests that Scandinavian forests are growing less well as a result of increased acidity. Tree-ring studies in Norway have revealed a decline in the growth rate of the trees during this century. The productiveness of such a forest is known to be related to the calcium content of soils. And this content is being reduced by acidification. Experiments have confirmed this. The only contrary evidence is that treatment with lime, a calcium compound, failed to restore full productivity. But this could have been due to other factors. On agricultural land, productivity of acid-leached soils can probably be maintained by liming, but at increased expense.

A somewhat strange defense has been put forward by one of the polluters, the electric power industry. The argument is that sulfur, which is also a plant nutrient, is not present in sufficient amounts in some areas and that therefore sulfur dioxide emissions, if sufficiently well dispersed, are actually beneficial. If we could locate sulfur-emitting power plants upwind from the sulfur-deficient ecosystems, we might then gain the best of both worlds. Unfortunately, this argument ignores the existence of natural sulfur compounds in the atmosphere. If sulfur-limited ecosystems actually exist—which is in dispute—they exist primarily because

Although most of the western United States is not yet seriously affected by acid rain, the area is not immune. Here a huge cloud of polluted air hangs over part of Denver near a public service generating station.

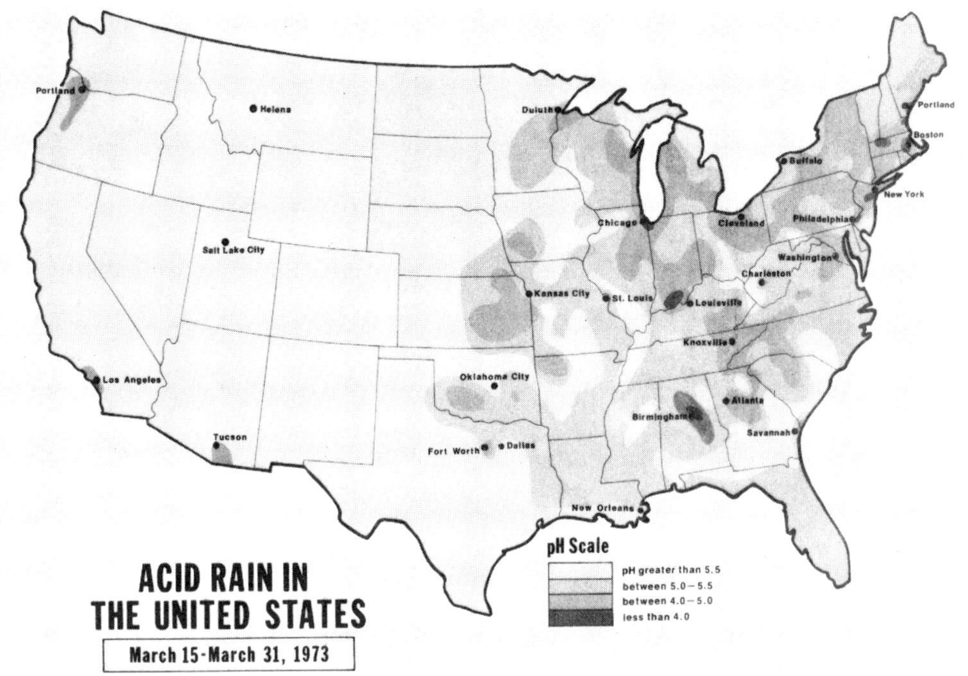

This map shows acid rainfall in the United States during a two-week period in 1973. Large parts of the eastern United States show rain with a pH below 5.5, the point at which some forms of animal life in water begin to be affected by the acidity.

there is not enough rainfall to bring down these compounds. Adding more sulfur dioxide would do little to relieve this problem. It would simply pass on the sulfur, and hence the acid-rain problem, to other areas.

DILUTION IS NO SOLUTION

What we know of acid rain is thus enough to tell us it is a major economic problem. And it is growing steadily worse in proportion to the growth in sulfur dioxide emissions. The resulting economic losses, since they are gradual and widespread, are hard to evaluate. Rough estimates based on the Swedish study, however, suggest that losses from acid rain to forestry alone could outweigh the costs of emission controls in western Europe.

In the United States, the effects of acid rain were not taken into account in setting air quality standards. But until 1973, it had seemed likely that the problem would be solved anyway, even if by accident. This would have come about through the adoption of fuel sulfur standards as the best way to avert direct damage to human health and to vegetation. However, the United States is now in the process of relaxing fuel standards to meet the short-term energy crisis. Thus we are simply relying once again on the atmosphere to dilute sulfur emissions. But dilution will not eliminate acid rain. Without fuel standards, the only solution is to install sulfur recovery systems in smokestacks. Either that, or we will continue to pass on the deadly problem of acid rain to our fishermen, farmers, and foresters□

SELECTED READINGS

Clean Air by Beulah Tannenbaum and Myra Stillman. McGraw-Hill, 1974.

"Tall Stacks: Sewers to the Sky" by W. L. Forestell. *American City*, June 1974.

Your Environment and You: Understanding the Pollution Problem by Elliott H. Blaustein and others. Oceana, 1974.

The high winds and seas of a hurricane show nature violent and destructive.

Hurricanes

by F. G. Walton Smith

WHAT is the most violent and destructive of all the forces of nature on earth? Volcanoes, avalanches, earthquakes, tornadoes, and tsunamis or seismic waves all take fearsome toll, but the damage wreaked by a hurricane over widespread areas of shore and sea may well qualify it for this unenviable distinction.

On Dec. 17 and 18, 1944, the U.S. Third Fleet, caught in a Pacific typhoon, lost 790 men, 146 planes, and three destroyers; the remainder of the great fleet was scattered and broken. In 1789, only 20 people survived out of the 20,000 population of Coringa, India, after the passage of a tropical cyclone. Perhaps the record is that of a Chinese typhoon which caused the loss of over 300,000 lives in 1881. But, as recently as 1970, a close runner-up moving from the Bay of Bengal across low-lying islands of Bangladesh killed nearly 300,000 persons.

All these major storms, and the lesser ones that are reported every year, are tropical cyclones, though they go under various names. In the Atlantic they are hurricanes, in the Pacific Ocean typhoons, in the Indian Ocean cyclones, in Australia willie-willies. They all have enormous destructive potentials and justifiably are causes of concern for loss of human life and property. Nevertheless, hurricanes are of special interest because they demonstrate the fundamental way in which the main energy source of the planet is distributed by the oceans. Spread over areas up to some 482 km (300 mi) or more in diameter and blowing strongly for several days, the larger hurricanes release energy equal to that of several hundred atomic bombs.

THE GREAT HEAT ENGINE

The sun, a huge generator of nuclear energy, directs a very small portion of its energy upon the earth. Even this small portion is vastly greater than man can possibly use—and most of it is absorbed by the ocean. The ocean, in turn, releases part of the energy to the atmosphere, where it drives the wind systems. The hurricane is the outward and visible sign of this great weather engine.

Hurricanes and other tropical cyclones are storms with winds in excess of 121 km per hr (75 mph) that circulate around low-pressure areas, counterclockwise in northern latitudes and clockwise in southern latitudes. Their power is derived from the energy of evaporating water, the carrier of solar heat. Water evaporates continuously at varying rates from the surface of the warm tropical seas, but most of the time there is no visible evidence of the enormous energy potential involved. Only when the process is concentrated into the self-perpetuating heat engine of a tropical cyclone does its strength become awesomely apparent.

Essentially, the structure of a fully developed hurricane is that of heavy rain clouds, rushing in a spiral fashion around a central low-pressure area, in which lies the eye or calm core. The winds and accompanying clouds of water vapor would be sucked directly in a straight line, to fill the low-pressure core, were it not for the effects of the earth's rotation and the friction forces involved. These effects cause the circular motion.

Toward the center of the core, rising moist air in the cloud systems, as they gain altitude, becomes cooler. This causes the water to condense as rain and, in doing so, to release heat. The release of heat causes the air mass to rise more quickly and this, in turn, reduces the pressure. Thus, a chain reaction sets in. Moisture-laden clouds are sucked into the system by the low-pressure center. As they arrive at the center, they form heavy rain, rise upward, and suck in more damp air to replace them.

THE FUELING PROCESS

The heat energy released in the condensation of water vapor to form rain is the same energy that was used to form vapor from liquid water in the first place. It requires somewhat less than an ounce of fuel such as gasoline to turn a pint of water into vapor, that is, to boil it. In condensing, the heat released by each pint of water is similarly equivalent to the energy released by burning an ounce of gasoline. In a large hurricane, the amount of water that condenses could amount to more than 18 billion metric tons per day. Thus, the total energy released by the storm each day is equivalent to that of a billion tons of flaming fuel or, to put it differently, the equivalent of several hundred 20-megaton hydrogen bombs.

The structure of a hurricane. Heavy rain clouds rush in a spiral fashion around a central low-pressure area, known as the eye of the storm. The clouds rise, cool off, and release rain.

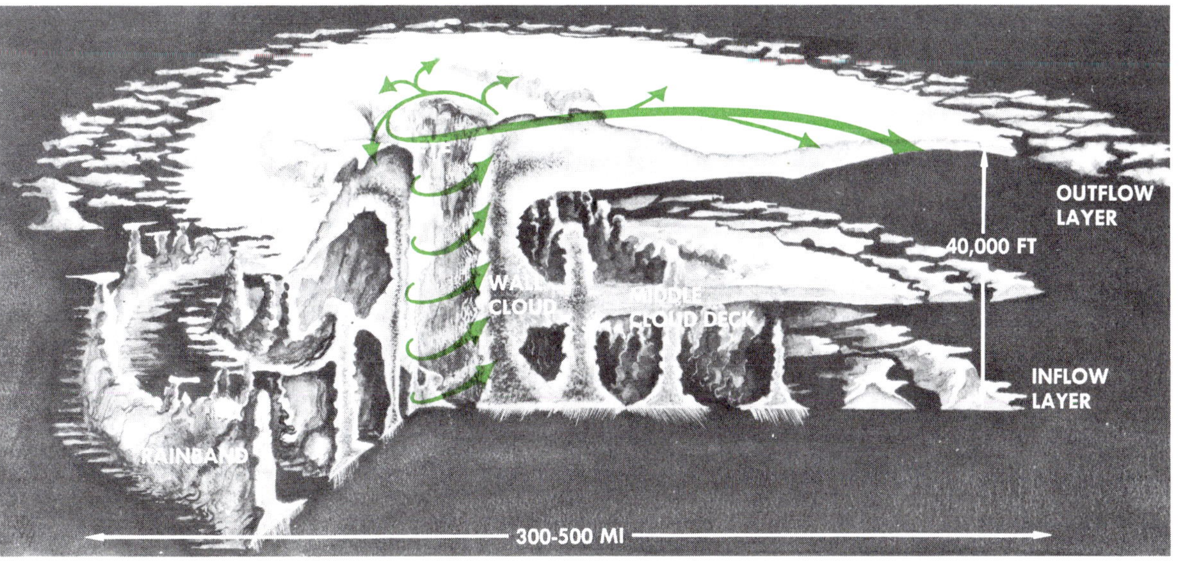

A condition favorable to the development of a hurricane is the presence of heat and water vapor. This condition exists in the tropical trade-wind region, extending from Africa to the Caribbean. During the summer months, the easterly trades, flowing westward across the tropical seas, become laden with moist warm air. This is the initial fueling process. The air becomes heated and rises. As the moisture begins to condense, the familiar cumulus clouds form. If they are able to rise to a sufficient altitude, thunderheads grow, and rain falls. Above the lower layer of moist warm air, however, is a layer of dry warm air. Air usually becomes cooler as the altitude increases, so that warmer

Left: the "eye" of a hurricane. This photo was taken from an altitude of 18,000 m (60,000 ft). Below: a satellite photo of the 1972 hurricane Agnes as it hangs over the southeastern United States. Agnes left 118 dead and over $3 billion of damage in the United States.

air, being more buoyant, will rise. The warm layer in the trades, however, forming an inversion layer, prevents the convective cumulus from rising very far. As the flow of air moves westward, the inversion layer becomes weaker, the latent heat of the lower layers begins to be released, and the cloud heights increase.

IGNITING SPARKS

The existence of sea temperatures at 26.6° C (80° F) or more and of winds to evaporate seawater and of a weakening of the inversion layer are not in themselves sufficient to spark a hurricane. A low-pressure center is also required. Sometimes low-pressure troughs develop in the easterlies flowing toward the Caribbean. These characteristically move from east to west at intervals of a few days apart. They are known as easterly waves, which are preceded by descending air and fine weather. Behind the wave, ascending air gives rise to thunderstorms.

Very few of the easterly waves develop into severe storms, but they are carefully watched. Any further disturbance that may lead to a cyclonic movement around the low-pressure area increases the possibility of a major development.

A further factor may now contribute to the development of the storm. As air is sucked into the low-pressure area and rises upward, it will tend to fill the vacuum, as it were. Winds at high altitudes may help to disperse the upper layers, however, and redistribute the air beyond the limits of the storm. They act as an exhaust to the engine of the storm.

In addition to easterly waves, two other possible sources may be involved. These are polar troughs, low-pressure areas that move out of the westerlies toward the trades when the Bermuda high-pressure area is temporarily weakened. Some of these may give rise to easterly waves, others may become isolated centers of disturbance. There are also disturbances that originate in the doldrums, the band of low pressure between the trades of the North Atlantic and South Atlantic. Disturbances from this area, the equatorial

Darwin, Australia, was 90 per cent destroyed by a cyclone on Dec. 25, 1974.

trough, or intertropical convergence, may move northward until the effect of the earth's rotation, which increases with latitude, assists in the development of a cyclonic movement.

With ample fuel from the warm tropical ocean to fire the engine, the fully developed hurricane consists of tall cumulus and cumulonimbus thunderclouds arranged in spiral bands converging on the center. At the center, the clouds become denser, forming a cloud wall that reaches altitudes of over 12,000 m (about 40,000 ft). The center itself is a calm region surrounded by the roughly circular cloud wall. It is within the cloud wall that the vertical movements are greatest and the heavy rain signals release of energy aloft. In the upper part of a hurricane, the heat released may be considerable and the temperature of the air may be as much as −6.6° C (20° F) above normal. In the eye, surrounded by the cloud wall, there is a downward movement of air, which accounts for the lack of rain in that area.

VERY DELICATE BALANCE

Powerful though a hurricane may be, it is really a very delicate balance of forces and, even though for several days it may be self regenerating, eventually part of the mechanism fails. The most generally known of the causes of a hurricane's death is its passage over land. Deprived of its ocean source of warm moisture-laden air, the engine falters, the rising air in the cloud wall begins to slow down, the pressure in the center begins to rise, and the strongest winds near the center begin to wane.

A failure of the circulation at the top of the cloud wall, which may be a part of a distant anticyclonic system (high-pressure center), may result in a slowing down of the vertical movement with resulting starvation of the engine. Friction forces may also tend to destroy the cyclonic organization. Movement into higher latitudes may also reduce the force of a hurricane as it loses its fuel source, the warm sea.

The first weak beginnings, the growth, and the final death of a hurricane are phenomena that cannot easily be ignored. As a giant heat engine, the cyclonic storm is awesome and intensely destructive, but it is also a reminder of the manner in which solar energy is channeled through the ocean to the atmosphere. Perhaps, with more precise understanding of the balance of forces that sustains a hurricane for its 10 or 12 days of existence, it may become possible, eventually, to disturb the balance and bring it to a premature end□

SELECTED READINGS

"Benefits of Hurricanes: Effect on Earth's Heat Balance," *Time*, Sept. 24, 1973.

"Darwin Is Gone," *Time*, Jan. 6, 1975.

Typhoon: 1944 (grade 7 and up) by John Clagett, Julian Messner, Inc., 1970.

Cyclone Tracy made Darwin, Australia, almost unrecognizable. Tall office buildings suffered little damage but houses were unroofed and trees stripped.

energy

This huge refuse-to-energy plant in Saugus, Mass., expected to be operational in the fall of 1975, will burn an average of 1,200 tons of refuse a day in special furnaces that will produce steam, which, in turn, will be used to generate electricity in a nearby power plant.

review of the year

energy

Colorado's oil shale holds some promise as an alternative energy source. However, work on a pilot plant has been suspended because of high costs and uncertainty over energy policy.

Solar cells that can convert the sun's energy into usable electricity are the subject of much research. Here two Bell Laboratories scientists test a promising new type of solar cell.

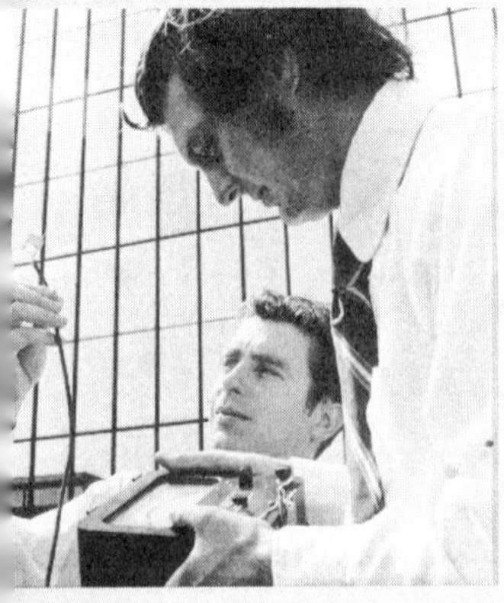

Political and economic aspects of the world energy picture dominated headlines in 1974 and promised to continue to do so in the remaining years of the seventies. The year, however, also saw a number of noteworthy developments concerning scientific and technological aspects of the energy situation.

Oil. Many nations, hoping to move toward greater energy self-sufficiency, were looking for and developing energy supplies within their own boundaries. In many cases, this move centered on a search for oil and natural gas, both on land and in offshore waters. Drilling activity in the United States increased more than 20 per cent during 1974. Such activity is not, however, to be equated with oil production, which has dropped some 5 per cent in the United States since late 1973. Potentially great oil reserves lie in the Outer Continental Shelf (OCS) along the U.S. coasts. However, environmental dangers of OCS drilling are varied and could be severe. Oil spills could damage beaches and marine life, including fish and other seafood that have significant economic importance. The drilling of sites in the Gulf of Alaska would occur in waters often subject to severe storms; in addition, the gulf is prone to earthquakes. ■ Improved recovery methods and increased oil prices make it economical to recover much more oil from wells than had previously been possible. When a well is drilled into oil-saturated rock, the oil is forced to the surface by natural underground pressures. Such pressures, however, yield an average of only 15 to 20 per cent of a field's oil. *Secondary recovery* methods, such as pumping water into the oil-bearing rock in a process known as "waterflooding," increase the yield to an average of approximately 35 per cent. Now, oil companies are testing a number of *tertiary recovery* techniques to get at previously unrecoverable reserves. In places where the oil is too thick for waterflooding, it can be thinned by injecting steam into a well so that oil flows more freely. By injecting air into oil-bearing rocks, it is possible to ignite some of the oil, making the rest thin enough for waterflooding. A third method involves the pumping of surfactants into the rock. These compounds, which function like laundry detergents, remove oil droplets that would otherwise remain in the rock. ■ Construction of the Colony oil shale plant in northwest Colorado, America's leading oil shale pilot project, was suspended "indefinitely" in late 1974. The four oil companies that sponsored the project blamed higher costs and "energy policy uncertainties" for the suspension. Another factor may have been a Federal Energy Administration study that indicated that almost as much energy might be needed to produce the oil as would be obtained as a product. Other potential problems include increased salinity in the Colorado River and how to dispose of oil shale wastes. ■ In early 1975 the Canadian government announced plans to help support a project to extract oil from tar sands. (See "Athabasca Tar Sands," page 185.)

Nuclear Energy. Though its potential as a source of electrical power is great, nuclear energy presents several unresolved problems. One major difficulty is how to dispose of the radioactive wastes produced by nuclear reactors. Three commercial reprocessing plants were to have been in operation in the United States by 1979. These plants would receive spent, or used, reactor cores from nuclear power plants and extract whatever uranium remains, plus the byproduct plutonium, for later recycling in fresh reactor fuel. However, problems have arisen in designing and building the plants and delays are expected. The U.S. Atomic Energy Commission (AEC) estimated that the United States could have a backlog of more than 8,300 tons of used but unprocessed reactor fuel by 1979. Because of limited storage capacity at nuclear power plants, government storage and reprocessing facilities may have to be opened to commercial use. ■ In October, President Ford signed the Energy Reorganization Act of 1974, which dissolved the AEC. Nuclear development programs have been shifted to the Energy Research and Development Administration, which is expected to spend more than $10 billion on energy research and development before 1980. The AEC's regulatory machinery, including the safety and licensing of nuclear plants, is now the responsibility of the Nuclear Regulatory Commission.

Energy Conservation. Unnecessarily high lighting standards, gas-guzzling cars, inadequate insulation in homes—these are some of the many ways that energy is wasted. The U.S. Federal Energy Administration estimates that Americans waste as much energy each year as Japan uses. "The time has come when [Americans] have got to kick the energy habit," says John R. Quarles, Jr., of the Environmental Protection Agency. "In the past we have always met problems of shortages by reaching out for more production. We have never really tried to scale down the demand." A study conducted by Allan Mazur and Eugene Rosa of Syracuse University indicates that current U.S. living standards can be maintained even if energy consumption is cut. "We suggest that so long as America's per capita energy consumption does not go below that of other developed nations, we can sustain a reduction in energy use without long-term deterioration of our indicators of health and health care, of education and culture, and of general satisfaction." ■ A study conducted by the Charles Stark Draper Laboratory, Inc., and MIT's Center for Policy Alternatives concludes that some relatively simple changes in refrigerator design would cut that appliance's energy consumption by 50 per cent. Refrigerator power consumption has increased over the years, especially since the introduction of frost-free equipment. Today, refrigerators use more energy than any other appliance in the average home. Substituting polyurethane for fiberglass insulation and increasing the copper winding in the compressor motor would improve refrigerator efficiency.

General Electric has reported reaching 20 per cent efficiency with a new type of MHD generator (foreground of photo). Below: diagram of a basic MHD system.

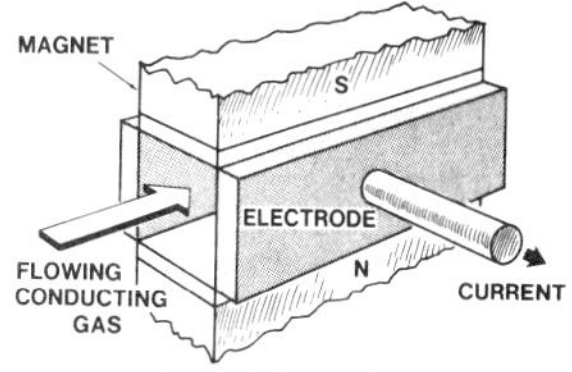

Magnetohydrodynamics (MHD). A major shortcoming of current electricity generation systems is their inefficiency. Fossil-fuel electric power plants have an efficiency, at best, of 40 per cent—that is, they turn only 40 per cent of the fossil-fuel's energy into electricity; the rest is waste heat. Nuclear plants are only about 33 per cent efficient. In a conventional fossil or nuclear power plant the heat produced when fuel is burned is used to make steam, which drives a generator to produce an electric current. In October 1974 the General Electric Company announced a breakthrough in MHD research that may lead to much more efficient production of electricity. In an MHD system burning of the fuel produces a hot gas that is "seeded" to increase its ability to conduct electricity and is then passed through an electromagnetic field to produce an electric current. MHD systems have been under study for more than 15 years but were stalled at efficiency levels of only 8 per cent. Now GE reports achieving 20 per cent efficiency with a radically different type of MHD system. An MHD system, combined with a conventional electricity generation system and making use of its waste heat, would, it has been estimated, have the potential of achieving overall electric power plant efficiency of almost 60 per cent.

Jenny Tesar

Solar Heating

by Marguerite Villecco

MANKIND has revered and praised the power and beauty of the sun through the centuries. Aside from times of drought and injury, the sun has become a synonym for joy, productivity, intelligence, majesty, life, and even God.

In ancient civilizations in Egypt, South America, the British Isles, and other lands, the sun was divine. Today, civilization may be coming full circle. The sun is being resurrected as an ultimate power—not by priests performing religious rites, but by scientists, engineers, architects, governments, and peoples who see its inexhaustible, nonpolluting energy as a possible solution to the world's suicidal depletion of resources.

Our challenge now is to harness our nearest star so that it can provide us with even more benefits than it has on its own—domestic water heating, climate control systems for our buildings, and electrical power generation. Our problem is that the sun performs its life-sustaining duties on its own terms, demanding partnership rather than mastery by mankind. We must find how best to use its energy.

One of the most important frontiers for the use of solar energy is just now being given widespread serious attention. It is the use of solar energy to provide reliable and substantial space heating and air conditioning, or, in other words, the use of the sun's energy to heat and cool homes and other buildings. The potential is vast. In the United States, for example, almost 25 per cent of current energy production is consumed in heating and cooling buildings.

Solar space-heating systems that can assume a large portion of a building's temperature control requirements are already technically feasible, but they are not in most cases cost competitive with conventional systems. However, the rising costs of fossil fuels, advancing technological progress, the application of mass production methods, and increasing energy conservation practices that reduce load requirements may very well change this cost picture by 1980.

The basic physical components of a solar-powered thermal system are a collector to absorb the sun's heat, a transfer medium, and a storage system for sunless days and nights.

THE COLLECTOR

The collector is the single most important element in determining both thermal and cost efficiencies. The most common type of collector is a flat plate designed to absorb both direct and diffuse radiation. Collectors are generally modular panels of aluminum, copper, or steel, but the use of more exotic materials is also being studied. The collector plate may have a surface coating of flat black paint, or it may have a selective surface designed to reduce reradiation (emissivity) of heat away from the collector and maintain solar ray absorption. Insulation protects the rear of the collector from heat losses. A typical collector for a 110-sq m (1,200-sq ft) house, could easily take between 50 per cent and 100 per cent of that area itself, depending on load requirements and systems design.

The collector is usually covered with transparent glass or plastic. This type of cover prevents efficiency-lowering condensation from accumulating. One to three layers thick, the cover protects the face of the collector, reduces heat losses by conduction and convection, and creates a greenhouse effect within the unit.

The greenhouse effect is the term given the phenomenon in which a transparent ceiling or cover traps and retains warm air. In all such cases, the transparent cover allows short-wave solar radiation to pass through it to the collector (or plants or people) inside, where the solar heat is absorbed. The transparent cover is, however, opaque to long-wave, or infrared radiation, which the collector reradiates away from its surface. Thus the cover reduces any heat loss. The heat remains trapped, thus raising inside temperatures.

GLASS VS. PLASTIC

Scientists and engineers are still debating the relative merits of glass vs. plastic covers. Glass is usually transparent to a larger portion of the sun's spectrum, especially glass with a low iron content. But glass is also easily broken in transportation, during installation, or by vandalism—a legitimate concern with a mechanical system as exposed as a collector. Glass is also heavy and rigid, requiring significant structural support. Plastics, on the other hand, are usually lighter and more flexible, and some are resistant to vandalism. However, they are also more transparent to long-wave reradiation and more likely to deteriorate as a result of exposure.

Collectors are usually tilted to achieve greatest operating efficiencies. The angle of the sun's incidence (how it hits a surface) is crucial to performance. At an angle of incidence of 60° or below, transmission of the solar energy to the collector is high; beyond 60° transmission drops sharply to zero at 90°, or "grazing" incidence. Most collectors, then, are mounted to face south at a slope perpendicular to the sun's rays. A familiar formula for tilt is latitude plus 10° to 20° for winter heating, when the sun is relatively low in the sky, or latitude minus 10° to 20° for cooling in the summer, when the sun is high in the sky. With a stationary collector, tilt must be selected for optimum performance in most, if not all, times and seasons for a particular building.

The size of a collector requires sensitive calculations. Overestimating load requirements, and therefore collector dimensions, can be very expensive. Generally loads must be figured to achieve a balance between the capacity of a collector and the amount of time that capacity is needed. For example, Arthur D. Little (ADL), a Cambridge, Mass., research and engineering firm, has estimated that solar systems should usually be sized to assume 50 per cent of a building's thermal load in most sections of the United States. The number of times such load capacity would be

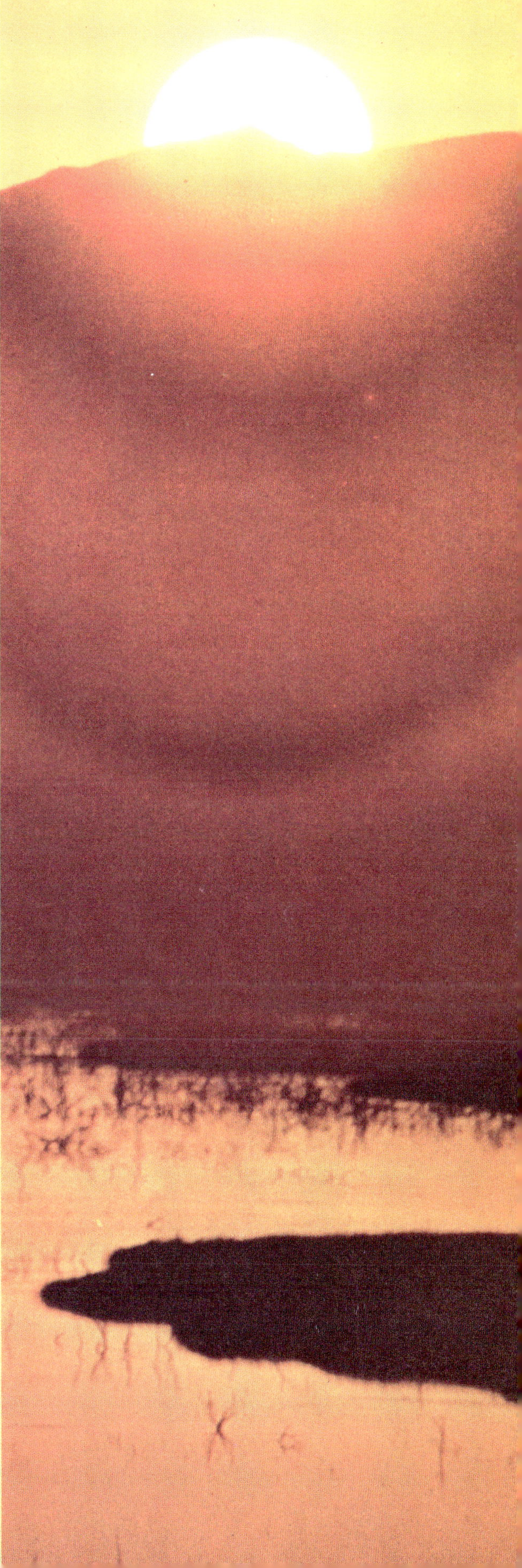

Solar energy for buildings

Large wind generators

Ocean power plant

SOLAR ENERGY FOR BUILDINGS

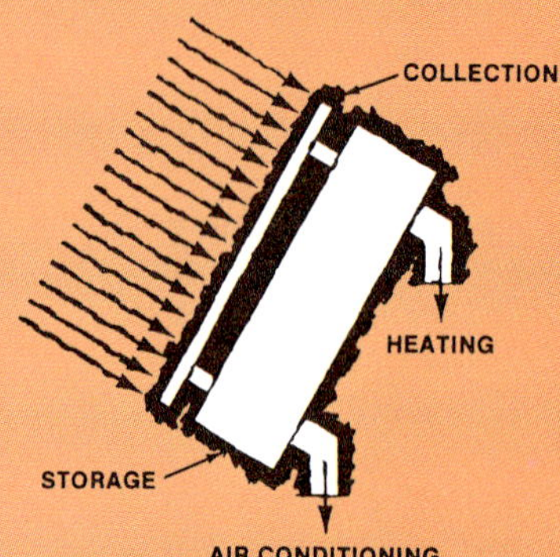

WORKING PRINCIPLE—Solar energy, in this concept, would be used (1) to heat and cool buildings by means of a solar collector and (2) to provide electric power by means of a small wind generator or "windmill." In the solar collector, thermal radiation is transmitted by glass covers and absorbed by a blackened metal sheet. Temperature of fluid circulated in collector can reach 100-200°F. System includes a heat storage tank, an auxiliary heater, and an air conditioner.

A 25-ft-diameter wind generator would meet a typical house's average power demand of about 2-3 kw.

POTENTIAL – Provide 50-75% of future buildings thermal energy needs.

TECHNOLOGY GAP – Main need is for well-engineered, economical solar collectors. Also need more efficient heat and electric storage devices and air conditioners operated with lower temperature inputs. System preferably would include its own storage and peaking capability to span variations in available wind energy and consumer home demand.

LARGE WIND GENERATORS

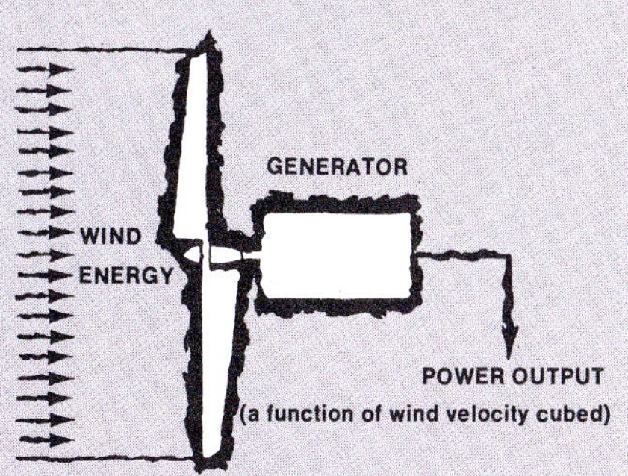

WORKING PRINCIPLE—As our atmosphere is alternately heated and cooled by earth's day/night cycle, winds storing the sun's energy as momentum move over the surface of the globe. Momentum-interchange devices (wind turbines) driving A.C. generators can extract this energy and convert it to electricity. Huge 200-ft diameter wind generators erected in selected coastal areas or on the Great Plains could operate with the strong, steady winds in these areas to supply electricity for large areas of population. The electric output of such generators might be fed directly into a local or national grid, used for pump storage in a hydroelectric system, or for water electrolysis to produce hydrogen as a fuel. Main requirements: steady, high-average-speed winds.

POTENTIAL — Supply 50% of total U.S. electricity needs in 2000.

TECHNOLOGY GAP — While no technology breakthroughs are needed, emphasis must be directed toward developing system designs that produce energy at competitive prices. Also need efficient storage devices for large scale applications.

OCEAN Δ_T POWER PLANT

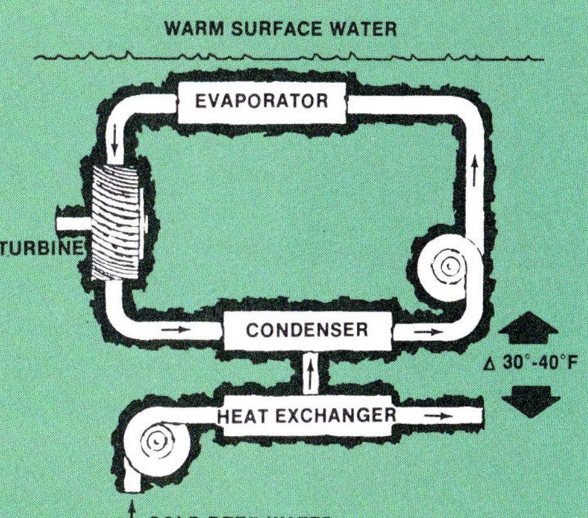

WORKING PRINCIPLE — The oceans' warm surface waters store a huge untapped reserve of the sun's thermal energy below which, at depths of more than 1,000 ft, lies a nearly infinite heat sink — a stable layer of much colder water. This temperature difference, or gradient, can be utilized indirectly by means of a heat engine to produce electricity. Rankine-cycle heat engine shown here could, when operating on a temperature difference of about 30-35°F, achieve a theoretical maximum conversion of heat into useful work of about 5%. An overall practical efficiency of 2% is a reasonable estimate. Main requirements: an ocean thermal gradient (OTG) of 30-40°F such as is found in tropical and near-tropical waters and in warm ocean currents. This is the only ground-based application of solar energy that does *not* require energy storage.

POTENTIAL — An estimated 182 trillion kwh of electricity could be generated with array of OTG plants along the length and breadth of the Gulf Stream. This would be enough to meet the total energy demand projected for the year 2000, with less than 0.3°F drop in Gulf Stream.

TECHNOLOGY GAP — Development of efficient, low-cost heat-exchangers, compatible with the seawater environment, is the key to making this concept work at a competitive price.

Solar thermoelectric system

Photovoltaic power system

Satellite solar power station

SOLAR THERMOELECTRIC SYSTEM

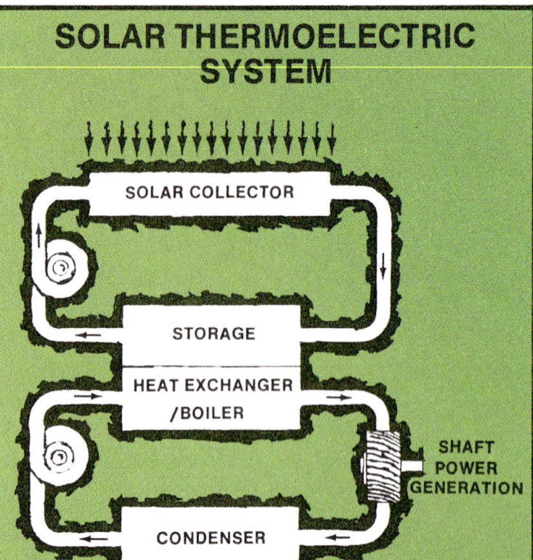

WORKING PRINCIPLE—Thermal conversion systems consist of solar collectors, such as the trough-type shown above, and thermal storage devices delivering heat to a turbine power plant. With high-temperature selective solar absorber coatings developed for the space program, temperatures needed to run standard steam turbogenerators can be achieved with relatively low solar concentration. Conversion efficiencies (direct solar energy to electric energy) of 20-30% are estimated. In the southwestern U.S. about 10 square miles are needed for 1,000-megawatt power plant operated at an average of 70% capacity. Main requirements: Large land areas, maximum solar insolation.

POTENTIAL — A roughly 60 x 60 mile area of our southwestern desert would provide total estimated electrical needs in the year 2000.

TECHNOLOGY GAP — Key problem is to find an economical design for long-life operation with a minimum of maintenance. Such optical components as the concentrator and absorber surfaces must perform for many years while exposed to the elements. Efficient heat transfer and storage devices must be developed.

PHOTOVOLTAIC POWER SYSTEM

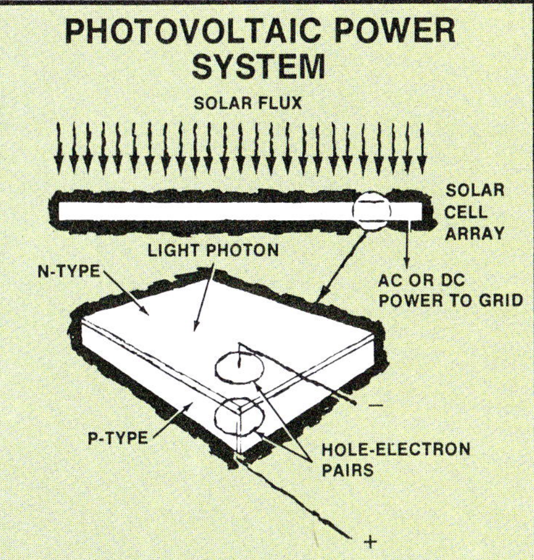

WORKING PRINCIPLE—This concept of converting solar energy to electricity is based on the photovoltaic effect in solid-state devices (solar cells) laid out in huge arrays on the earth's surface. The theoretical limit efficiency for the conversion process is about 25% for a single device operating at room temperature. At present, the two leading solid-state materials for large-scale power generation are silicon and cadmium-sulfide. The U.S. currently produces about 100 tons of single-crystal silicon per year, but about 2 million tons would be needed to match present U.S. power needs. Roughly 1% of the total U.S. land area, or 35,000 square miles, would be needed for this total energy system. Main requirements: Large land area, maximum solar insolation.

POTENTIAL – A total area of 100 x 100 miles of our southwestern desert could supply total estimated U.S. electric needs in the year 2000.

TECHNOLOGY GAP – Reducing cost and increasing life of solar arrays in the earth environment are the key to making the photovoltaic system competitive with commercial sources. The concept also requires lower-cost, longer-life energy storage devices.

SATELLITE SOLAR POWER STATION

SOLAR FLUX
PHOTOVOLTAIC CELL ARRAY
DC TRANSMISSION
ANTENNA
MICROWAVE BEAM
(average density is 8 mw/cm² on ground)
+
–
AC POWER
RECEIVING ANTENNA
(rectifying diodes)

WORKING PRINCIPLE—Space offers the one location with constant access to the sun's energy. The Satellite Solar Power Station (SSPS), positioned in a synchronous orbit (19,350 miles high) around the earth's equator, would receive solar energy for 24 hours a day except for short periods near the equinoxes. It would receive six times the solar energy available on earth to an equivalent array. Assembled in space, a typical SSPS might be composed of lightweight solar cells forming a huge solar collector about 7 miles long by 2.5 wide. The electricity produced would be fed to a microwave antenna which directs a beam to a receiving station on earth where the microwave energy can be safely converted back to electricity. Efficiency of microwave energy conversion on earth is estimated at 90%. SSPS designs currently being considered would provide 5,000 MWe to the power grid.

POTENTIAL – One hundred SSPS's could supply the estimated total U.S. electrical power demand in 2000.

TECHNOLOGY GAP – Key to making this concept practicable is development of a lightweight, mass-produced, low-cost, thermally-insensitive solar cell and efficient high-volume space transportation systems.

exceeded during a year does not usually justify the extra cost of a larger installation. On this basis it would be foolish to insist on a system designed for peak seasonal loads in Washington, D.C., for example. Such capacity could only be used a few days a year—a very expensive luxury. It is cheaper to operate auxiliary conventional systems during peak load periods or long stretches of insufficient sunlight.

CHOOSING A LOCATION

Location of the collector on or off a building is another important factor in solar systems design, and a problem of particular importance to architects. Integrating a collector into a building roof or wall is common, but the practice places restrictions on building design. If the collectors are built into the building roof, the roof must face south, and have appropriate tilt, size, and structural strength to accommodate a specified collector. If the collector is designed as a building wall, similar problems must be solved and the collector may suffer because it does not tilt. Integrated design also leaves an owner with the state of the art of his installed solar system because the system cannot be easily removed or changed. Alan Balfour, an architect with ADL, says this could leave an owner with an obsolete system, especially while solar-energy technology is still developing.

The use of solar energy for heating homes is starting to increase. Here, a photo of a solar-heated suburban house with solar collectors on the roof of the house.

Balfour is convinced that a solar-energy system independent of a building's structure, or serving several structures, offers greater flexibility in the design of both solar system and building, and greater potential for using, and therefore developing, standardized components. Balfour also notes that independent solar collectors could be deemed the responsibility of a utility company rather than a building owner.

Other designers, however, will argue that "billboard"-type collectors are ugly in themselves, requiring an independent structural system that might otherwise be part of the wall or roof of a building. These critics also note that an integrally designed solar collector can act beneficially as insulation, or that any heat loss from the collector can perhaps be used to advantage in a building.

HEAT TRANSFER AND STORAGE

The second element of a solar system is the heat transfer system, or the way heat is carried from a collector into a building. The most common transfer media are air or water, which circulate through tubes mounted in or on the collector and carry its heat away for immediate use or to storage facilities. Air systems have some advantage over water versions in their elimination of corrosion problems (especially in noncopper collectors), but air is a less efficient thermal medium than water and so requires either higher collector temperatures or larger storage facilities. Water is generally the more frequent selection.

Storage systems are the third component. "The night has a thousand eyes and the day but one yet the light of the bright world dies with the dying sun," wrote Francis Bourdillon. So with the solar-

A new building at the New York Botanical Garden's Cary Arboretum in Millbrook, New York, will be solar heated. The collectors face south and the back of each collector row is reflective, thus increasing the solar radiation on the row of collectors behind.

energy system. When the sun doesn't shine, the solar collector doesn't work, and the system must rely either on stored heat or on conventional auxiliary systems.

Most storage systems are sensible heat units, which means that they store the kind of heat we feel, or "sense," on our bodies. For systems in which air is the transfer medium, crushed rock is usually used to absorb heat from the hot air, often in a well-insulated basement area. In water-transfer systems, the water is its own best storage system. Because water is more efficient thermally than air, water storage systems may be only one quarter the size of a crushed rock counterpart. Water systems, however, are not necessarily cheaper. They require the use of rust-resistant storage tanks that can be quite expensive.

An alternative to sensible heat storage is latent heat storage. Theoretically such a storage system occupies little space and is reasonable. Latent heat is heat that is stored by materials as they change from one form to another. It does not require a rise in sensible heat temperatures. An example of latent heat is the heat, or energy, involved in changing ice to water.

In the case of solar-energy systems, the usual latent heat storage media are eutectic, or phase-changing, salts, that turn from liquid to solid form at a given temperature. But problems remain to be solved, despite some experimental installations. So far at least, eutectic salts cannot endure enough phase changes reliably enough to make them practical for long periods.

PROPHETS FULFILLED

Work to develop thermal building systems did not start until the 1930's. These early efforts are primarily responsible for the state of solar art today. In the 1960's, the moon and space became the nation's primary scientific frontier. Solar thermal systems were already regarded as economically impractical. Work was largely abandoned until recently, except by those dedicated enough to continue despite low funding or interest. Today, these pioneers are again at the scientific forefront. Some have grown sophisticated with the times and are competing in modern solar research efforts independently or as consultants. Some others are still fighting for recognition in a modern technological world. But all can cast themselves as prophets fulfilled□

SELECTED READINGS

Direct Use of the Sun's Energy, by Farrington Daniels. Ballantine, 1974.

First Book of Solar Energy (grades 4–6), by John Hoke. Watts, 1968.

"Solar Derby: Who'll Control Sun Power?" by Peter Barnes. *New Republic*, Feb. 1, 1975.

"Tapping the Sun's Energy," by David G. Lee, *National Wildlife*, August–September 1974.

Offshore Oil

by Les Gapay

TALK about future fuel sources often dwells on the exotic side—development of solar and geothermal energy, extraction of oil from shale, conversion of coal to gas. But the main hope emerging for adequate fuel in the next decade is not quite so unconventional. This is drilling for oil and gas off shores, partly in new areas of the highly productive Gulf of Mexico but also—for the first time—in waters off the Atlantic coast and in the Gulf of Alaska.

The Atlantic and Alaska areas alone, by conservative government estimates, may hold enough oil to meet U.S. needs for two to four years and enough gas to last even longer.

U.S. Interior Department officials, among others, look upon new offshore drilling as offering the best chance for the nation to achieve self-sufficiency in fuel. Under Secretary John C. Whitaker says development of new Outer Continental-Shelf areas "is the only way to get energy self-sufficiency short of any major research-and-development breakthroughs." Government and private experts expect that new energy sources won't contribute much for at least 10 years.

The Interior Department has speeded up the leasing of federal tracts in the Gulf of Mexico. Parts of the Gulf of Alaska are likely to be the first of the frontier areas to be developed. And a 1975 ruling by the U.S. Supreme Court has cleared the way for the government to lease Atlantic tracts.

NIGHTMARES OF OIL SPILLS

But even before leasing starts in new offshore areas, controversy is sure to come. Critics say the planned drilling raises unprecedented environmental dangers. The President's Council on Environmental Quality warned of grave problems, with the Gulf of Alaska seen as the highest risk area for drilling. Wells in the Atlantic, off the populous East Coast, could also pose problems. Some environmentalists and members of Congress already have nightmares of oil spills sullying Long Island beaches and of refineries and petrochemical complexes defiling Cape Cod.

Others say, though, that dangers to the environment can be minimized with proper planning. Administration officials note that since the famous Santa Barbara leak of 1969, the oil industry has improved its technology and work practices, stricter federal regulations have been issued for offshore drilling, and enforcement has been strengthened.

LARGE SUPPLY

Whatever the environmental risks, there is little doubt that lots of oil and gas lies in the Outer Continental Shelf beneath the Atlantic and the Gulf of Alaska. The shelf is generally considered to extend underwater to a depth of 200 m (650 ft). In the Atlantic, that point ranges from as little as 16 km (10 mi) out from the southern Florida coast to as far as 480 km (300 mi) off New England.

The government estimates that there may be 7 billion to 13 billion barrels of oil off the Atlantic coast and three billion to six billion barrels in the Gulf of Alaska. Besides, it is estimated, there are about 1.5 trillion to 3 trillion m^3 (55 trillion to 110 trillion ft^3) of natural gas in the Atlantic and about 0.4 trillion to 0.8 trillion m^3 (15 trillion to 30 trillion ft^3) in the Gulf of Alaska. In one year, the United States consumes about 7 billion barrels of oil and about 0.7 trillion m^3 (25 trillion ft^3) of gas.

The Interior Department reckons that the 1.1 million barrels per day now being produced offshore might be boosted to 4 million by 1980 if new areas in the Gulf of Mexico, the Gulf of Alaska, and the Atlantic are tapped. But there is ordinarily a lag, ranging from two to 10 years, between the granting of a lease and actual production. Moreover, some experts caution that there may be some bottlenecks, including shortages of drilling rigs, other materials, and manpower. Others respond that the essentials could be concentrated in the most promising places.

Standard practice calls for the Interior Department to ask the oil companies to nominate tracts they want offered for lease. The companies have exhibited an eagerness to tap new offshore areas. They have told the department they are most interested in additional leasing in the central Gulf of Mexico, an area where they are already drilling. The industry's next choice for fast development is the environmentally risky Gulf of Alaska. "They think there's another Prudhoe Bay up there," one Interior Department official says. (Prudhoe Bay on Alaska's North Slope, opening on the Beaufort Sea, is the scene of the biggest recent oil find in the United States.)

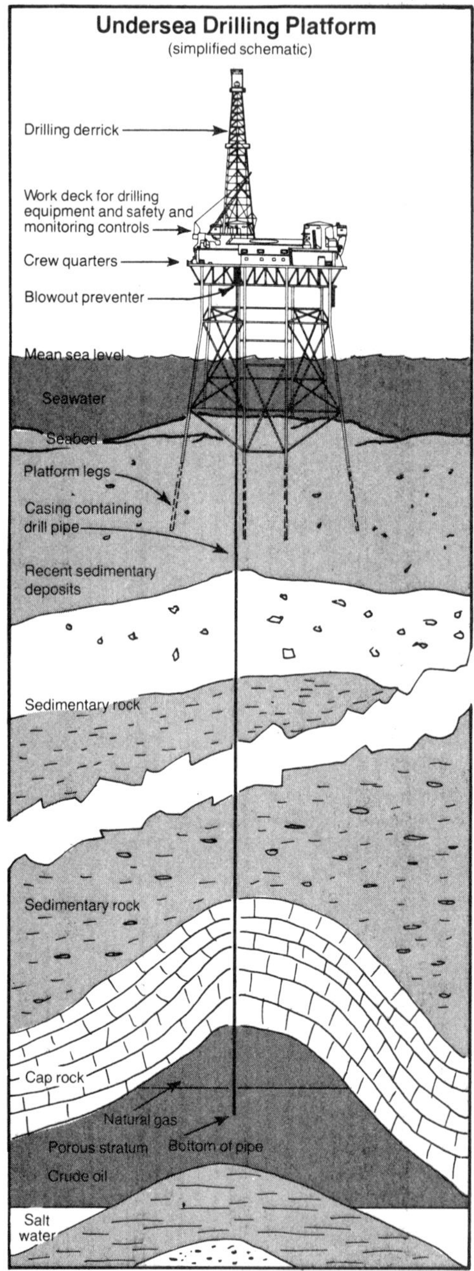

Simplified diagram of a typical offshore drilling platform showing key sections.

HOME FOR SALMON AND SEALS

A report by the U.S. Council on Environmental Quality, released in 1974, stopped just short of recommending an outright ban on drilling in the Gulf of Alaska. The study found that the eastern part of the gulf was the riskiest of all new offshore areas, with the western part (Bristol Bay) coming next. It foresaw a high probability of oil spills washing ashore in the gulf and of severe storms, earthquakes, and tidal waves wrecking drilling operations. It said that conditions there would be "more severe than the industry has yet experienced anywhere in the world."

Moreover, conservationists note that the gulf is rich in fish and marine mammals, ranging from the pink salmon and king and snow crabs to sea lions, seals, and otters. More than 200 species of birds can be found there. The estuaries are habitats for species ranging from common geese to rare trumpeter swans. Nonetheless, Under Secretary Whitaker says a sale of leases in the Gulf of Alaska could probably be held by the end of 1975, after preparation of an environmental-impact statement and completion of other studies.

QUESTIONING THE PACE

Next on the oil companies' list of tracts desired comes the western Gulf of Mexico, where leasing now is going on, followed by the Pacific off Southern California and then the mid-Atlantic region between Cape Cod and Cape Hatteras. Part of that area, off Long Island, is listed by the Council on Environmental Quality as having high environmental risk.

[Thirteen Atlantic coast states unsuccessfully pressed a claim to title for oil and natural gas rights in the Outer Continental Shelf beyond the 4.8-km (3-mi) limit. Their pressure led the Interior Department, on Feb. 12, 1975, to abruptly withdraw invitations to the major oil companies to designate sites in the Baltimore Canyon on which they intended to submit bids for leases. However, the U.S. Supreme Court ruled, 8–0, on March 17, 1975, that the federal government had exclusive right to any oil and gas in the Outer Continental Shelf. Seven days later, the Interior Department asked the companies to name the tracts they wanted in the Baltimore Canyon. This opened the prospect for large-scale oil and gas production off the East Coast by the 1980's.]

Because the Interior Department's leasing timetable is too fast to suit many environmentalists, the general controversy is expected to be fierce. Groups are gearing up to assure that there is adequate protection of ocean life, beaches, coastal wetlands, and estuaries from oil spills. Bills have been introduced in Congress for this and other conservation purposes.

Most major environmental organizations are not opposed to development of the Outer Continental Shelf, but "we question the premise of maximum speed in consumption and depletion of (these) resources," says Leonard C. Meeker, a Washington attorney who has represented the Sierra Club and other groups in testimony before congressional committees. Many questions about U.S. energy requirements, fuel conservation, and alternative sources of power should be answered "before we decide to strip the Outer Continental Shelf of the fossil fuels it contains," he says.

MORE STUDY NEEDED

Concern about drilling in new offshore areas, especially off the Atlantic coast, involves not just pollution but the possibility that vast development of the Outer Continental Shelf would drastically alter

Above: *Glomar Grand Isle,* a drilling ship that operates under its own power in the North Sea. Below: A semi-submersible drilling rig, *Sedco 1,* being towed to the Grand Banks off Canada.

many coastal areas and towns. The Council on Environmental Quality said in a study that New Bedford, Mass., a onetime whaling port, could turn into a booming oil town. In South Carolina, if offshore drilling reaches maximum potential, the state could have three oil refineries, two gas-processing plants, and two or three petrochemical complexes by 1985, the council said.

Also feared, of course, are oil spills devastating to beaches and to fishing. With that in mind, several governors of Atlantic states have urged the Interior Department to develop the Gulf of Alaska first. "Virginia cannot afford a major oil spill," says William Hargis, director of the state-run Virginia Institute of Marine Science.

Although the Council on Environmental Quality study said that offshore Virginia was a relatively low-risk area, Mr. Hargis, who has done research work for the council, says he wants three more years of data before development begins. One need that he sees is to examine carefully the regions through which undersea pipelines might be laid from drilling areas to the shore.

Critics also are challenging the Council on Environmental Quality's rankings of environmentally risky drilling areas. Its study predicted high risk in the Southeast Georgia Embayment (a baylike area near the Blake Canyon) off northern Florida and Georgia, and in the northern part of the underwater Baltimore Canyon off Long Island. Less risk would result, the council said, from drilling in the central and southern Baltimore Canyon from New Jersey to Virginia and in the Georges Bank trough off New England.

But Democratic Sen. Edmund Muskie of Maine says the study "might not have focused adequately on the need to preserve our fisheries resources off the New England coast. The Georges Bank is especially rich in fishing." And a National Academy of Sciences panel has said the criteria used for ranking the dangers in various areas were "inadequate and incomplete."

In at least one area where drilling is proposed—Alaska—many citizens seem unworried. Among the Alaskans who support drilling off his state's coast is Republican Sen. Ted Stevens. He says the great Alaska earthquake of 1964 didn't hurt oil-drilling platforms in the Cook Inlet near the Gulf of Alaska. But even in that state, the Alaska Conservation Society, for one, says more study is needed. It charges that the oil industry wants to start as many projects as possible while energy shortages persist□

SELECTED READINGS

"Life on a Rig" by Robert Gannon. *Oceans*, November 1974.

"Offshore Drilling" by E. Marshall. *New Republic*, Dec. 28, 1974.

"Oil and Influence: The Rush to the Sea" by E. F. Hollinger. *Nation*, Jan. 18, 1975.

"Oil and Water: Can They Mix?" by Paul Kalman. *Field & Stream*, March 1975.

A new device called an SPS—Submerged Production System—is released from a barge in the Gulf of Mexico and heads for the seabed in 52 m (170 ft) of water. In an 18-month test, Exxon will use this remote-controlled device to drill three wells.

Peat, wet and spongy when cut, is heaped up and left to dry out in this bog near Ballinakill in Ireland's County Galway. A number of countries now are looking to peat as a fuel that will help ease their energy shortages.

Peat—The Forgotten Fuel

by Michael Cusack

"WE just don't have enough fuel," my Irish cousin said. He was telling me why Ireland couldn't develop many big industries. "We have no oil at all," he continued. "And the little coal that we have is of poor quality."

"But," I asked, "what about peat?"

"Peat? Peat? That's not a decent fuel," he snorted. "That stuff's only good for smoky fires in cold country cabins." He paused. "We'd be better off to forget all about peat as a modern fuel."

That talk with my cousin took place many years ago, when I was visiting Ireland. At that time peat was an almost forgotten fuel—even in most of Ireland, where it was once in common use. Today the situation has changed a lot. Peat as a fuel is being well remembered now, and particularly in Ireland. The reason, of course, is the energy crisis and the need for alternatives to petroleum. There are about 151 million hectares (375 million acres) of peat bog in the world. And about 250 tons of good-quality peat can be dug out of each hectare (about 100 tons in each acre). That's a lot of fuel, and the search for fuel resources is going on everywhere.

Peat sounds, then, like a promising added resource. But in fact, people have known about peat for centuries. One wonders why it has been looked down on as a fuel for so long, whenever other forms of fuel are available. What kind of fuel is peat, and how good is it, really?

HOW PEAT IS FORMED

To answer this, let us first see how peat is formed. Peat is plant matter—trees, grasses, bushes, rushes, reeds, and mosses—that has decayed in water. Thus peat could be called "baby coal." It is the first stage in the long, slow process of change from dead plants to coal. All present-day peat could in time become coal—that is, if tons of rock and soil were to press down on it for a few million years.

The making of peat requires water. Therefore, peat is found only in wet places—in damp, cool bogs—where the weather is damp most of the time. A bog, like a swamp, is a place where water collects on or near the surface of the soil. But unlike a swamp, a bog has no outlet for the water to escape. Instead, bog water slowly seeps into the soil.

The bogs that are the best sources of peat are also usually found in areas that were once covered by great sheets of ice. At the present time, vast peat bogs cover large areas of the Soviet Union, Scandinavia, Germany, and Ireland. In fact, one seventh of Ireland's land surface is one big peat bog. Somewhat smaller peat bogs can be found in Britain and North America.

Most of today's large peat bogs started to form around 12,000 years ago. That was shortly after the end of the most recent great ice age. As the huge ice sheets melted, many low-lying land areas were flooded. Forests and grasslands were "drowned." Waterlogged trees and bushes collapsed into the flood waters. These "drowned" plants partly decayed. Their remains formed a layer of organic debris in the water. This layer of debris tended to trap and hold some of the flood water.

Later on, reeds, rushes, and mosses took root in the soggy mess and sprouted out above the water surface. These surface plants, and the organic debris beneath them, acted as a huge sponge to soak in and hold additional rainwater. And that was the beginning of a peat bog.

In time, the plants on the bog surface became waterlogged. They also sank, decayed, and became part of the organic debris. As each layer of plant life sank, it was replaced by new mossy growths on the surface. This process was repeated time and again. In fact, it is still going on. Peat is still being formed in most peat bogs.

As layers of waterlogged organic debris pile up and squeeze together in a bog, many chemical changes take place in the

Old and new ways blend in the Irish peat bogs. A worker cuts turf by hand, and a machine loads it into railroad cars.

debris. Some chemical compounds in the plant tissue change by combining with oxygen from air, water, and other substances. This is called oxidation-reduction, and it is part of the decay process. At the same time, bacteria, yeasts, molds, and fungi "attack" the soggy plant tissue. They help break down the plant tissue and change it, an action called fermentation. This is also part of the decay process.

As plant tissue decays, various combinations of carbon, hydrogen, oxygen, nitrogen, and a few other elements are given off. When plant matter decays in dry air, most of these decay products drift into the air in the form of gases, vapors, and tiny solid particles. All that usually remains on the ground is a little ash consisting of mineral salts. However, when plants decay in water, as they do in bogs, the result is very different. The decay process in water is much slower than it is in air. What's more, when the process takes place in water, most of the decay products do not escape. They mix into the changing, waterlogged debris. And they add to the changes taking place.

As a result, the decaying organic debris becomes rich in hydrocarbons—various chemical compounds of hydrogen and carbon. Hydrocarbons are "great for burning." Add enough heat, and they will readily combine with oxygen from the air. In other words, materials containing hydrocarbons can be used as fuels. Coal is rich in hydrocarbons. So is oil. So is natural gas. And so is peat.

THE PROBLEM OF WATER

Peat is also rich in something else, however: water. And this presents a problem. A freshly dug peat sod may be 70 per cent water. This is only natural, since the peat could not have formed without water. But all that water is a problem when it comes to burning the peat. The water content of peat must be reduced so that it is not more than 25 per cent water before the peat can be used as a fuel. That means a lot of drying. And as any bog person can tell you, the job of drying peat may be far from easy.

This harvester turns out cylindrical peat sods for use as a fuel in some of Ireland's electricity-generating power plants.

For thousands of years, people living near bogs have used peat to keep their home fires burning. They still do, in parts of Ireland. In the peat harvest, brick-sized turfs, or sods, of the wet, spongy fuel are cut out of bogs. Then, on sunny days, the soggy sods are spread on the ground to dry in the warm air. But remember, peat forms only where the weather is cool and damp. So the sunny days needed to dry the peat are few and far between in those same places. And that is one simple but basic problem with the use of peat.

When the sun does shine, the sods are spread out to dry. Then, if the rain falls, they are gathered into stacks. When the rain stops, the sods are spread out again, and so on. It's a slow process. Indeed, it is so much of a bother that many bog people stopped using peat long, long ago.

THE RETURN TO PEAT-BURNING

Yet despite all these difficulties of harvesting and drying, many nations are now betting on peat to ease their energy shortages. Several years ago, for example, the Irish government decided to use peat in a big way. They sent giant machines into the bogs. These machines cut more peat in a day than an army of men with spades could cut in a month. Millions of tons of peat a year are harvested in Ireland now. Most of this peat is burned in factories and power plants. About 25 per cent of Ireland's electricity comes from peat-burn-

Peat mining in the Soviet Union, which reportedly has about 65 per cent of the world's peat deposits. Seventy Soviet electric power plants burn peat as fuel.

ing power plants. Irish officials plan to use more and more peat in the next few years.

The Soviet Union is also burning peat to generate electricity. Today there are 70 large peat-burning power plants in the USSR, and many more are planned for the future.

Finland recently decided to use its peat resources, as well. Sweden is considering a similar move. So peat, the almost forgotten fuel, is being remembered once again.

The use of huge machines has made peat harvesting practical and economical. Getting the water out is still a problem, however. Irish scientists have experimented with methods of shaking, baking, squeezing, and tossing peat sods, but none of these approaches works very well. In the end, the scientists found that the easiest way to dry peat sods is to spread the sods to dry in the sun. The spreading and turning can now be done by machines.

This drying method limits the harvesting of peat sods to certain times of the year. Peat doesn't have to come in sods, however. Soviet scientists discovered this fact, and they developed a method of peat harvesting that is good for all seasons. This method is called milling. It involves "shaving down" the surface of a peat bog to provide peat dust, which dries very rapidly. Milled peat dust can be used only in power plants. But Irish scientists then found that milled peat could be squeezed into little bricks, or briquettes, that are suitable for use in homes and factories.

THE COST TO THE ENVIRONMENT

What are the environmental values of using peat? For one, peat burns cleaner than coal. There is practically no sulfur in peat. Therefore, unlike coal, it does not give off the poisonous pollutant called sulfur dioxide. And that's not all. Dry peat tends to burn more completely than coal. That means less ash, less carbon monoxide, and much less soot.

Unlike coal mining, peat harvesting is easy on the land. The peat is usually cut away to a depth of just a few meters, or yards. And in the process, the peat bog is drained and aerated, that is, its surface is loosened so that air can get into the soil. When the peat is gone, grass and trees will grow there. Thousands of acres of Ireland's peat bogs have become forests and farmlands.

Many people like this change, but there are also conservationists who object to it. They say that the loss of a bog means the loss of certain bog animals. In reply to this, Irish Peat Board officials say that few animals live in peat bogs. And, the officials argue, most of these animals can adapt to life in moist grasslands or forests.

The environmental benefits of peat to human beings thus seem to far outweigh the environmental costs. At any rate, we can probably expect a greater use of peat in the future. Indeed, we may come to value peat for more than its usefulness as a fuel. Peat may also play a part in feeding our hungry world. How? The organic compounds known as humic acids are obtained from peat, and humic acids are necessary fertilizers for dry, worn-out soils. The story of peat may have to add some interesting new chapters□

SELECTED READINGS

Peatlands by P. D. Moore and D. J. Bellamy. Springer-Verlag, 1973.

A tanker specially equipped to carry liquefied natural gas docks at a U.S. port. The American oil industry is seeking to import more liquefied natural gas to supplement domestic supplies.

Oil and Gas: How Much Is There?

by Robert Gillette

IN 1922, the vast pool of oil under eastern Texas had not yet been discovered. At that time, the U.S. Geological Survey solemnly predicted that the nation's cumulative oil production would not exceed 15,000,000,000 barrels. This figure suggested that the United States might soon run out of oil. Happily, the Geological Survey was wrong. However, its low estimate was not unreasonable, considering the infant state of petroleum geology at that time.

In 1974 it looked as if the Geological Survey may have erred again—this time on the high side. It had estimated that reserves amounted to 200,000,000,000 to 400,000,000,000 barrels of oil and to 2.8 to 5.6×10^{13} m^3 (1 to 2×10^{15} ft^3) of natural gas. But according to a survey put out in 1975 by the National Academy of Sciences (NAS) the amount of oil and gas left to be discovered and produced with current technology in the United States is "considerably smaller" than that.

A more realistic estimate, in the opinion of the NAS Committee on Mineral Resources and the Environment, is that 113,000,000,000 barrels of oil and 1.5×10^{13} m^3 (5.3×10^{14} ft^3) of gas remain to be found and produced onshore and offshore, mostly in Alaska. The main implication of these lower estimates, which are in addition to proved reserves, is that a large increase in annual production of oil and gas in America is "very unlikely."

Two years in the making, the NAS report broadly reviewed national supply-and-demand prospects for fossil fuels and essential metals. One of its main conclusions was that industrialized nations could face a "series of shocks of varying severity" in the not-so-distant future as shortages crop up in one critical material after another. The shortages will occur not because of any international politics but because there are physical limits to the earth's

Oil geophysicist M. King Hubbert and his "pimple," a graph showing his estimate of the rise and fall of oil production in the United States.

resources. The committee recommended nonmilitary stockpiling of "threatened materials."

Beyond that, committee chairman Brian Skinner, a Yale geologist, urged the adoption of a conservation ethic "as a kind of national religion," both for fuels and for scarce industrial materials. Skinner and the resource committee also made a point of trying to free policymakers of the notion that technology can always come quickly to the rescue whenever shortages develop. "The theses that technology is infinitely improvable and that substitution is infinitely possible, we feel, are highly suspect," the report observed.

WERE ESTIMATES TOO HIGH?

Probably the report's most controversial aspect was its judgment on oil and gas resources. The Geological Survey's estimates of these resources have been a major basis for federal petroleum policy and for the common opinion that supply would increase uniformly with price. And for more than a decade these estimates have stood conspicuously above estimates developed by major oil companies. For just as long one of the Survey's more prominent researchers, M. King Hubbert, has been saying that the Survey's numbers were wrong. To Hubbert, now in his 70's and a past president of the Geological Society of America, the NAS judgment came as vindication.

Hubbert seems to have started the dispute in 1956 with a widely discussed speech in which he predicted that U.S. oil and gas resources would turn out to be smaller than generally presumed. It was his opinion that oil production would reach a peak and begin to decline in 10 to 15 years. (And in fact, oil production in the United States has been declining since late 1970 and gas production appeared to have reached a peak in 1974.) At the time, Hubbert was one of Shell Oil Company's leading exploration geophysicists. But his gloomy predictions marked him as a maverick, out of step with the outlook of the oil industry. "My grandchildren may have to worry about oil shortages, but I won't have to," was more or less that outlook.

The industry's first reaction to Hubbert's speech was one of dismay and disbelief. The second reaction was to try to prove him wrong. Within a year, other industry experts were coming out with higher and higher estimates of oil and gas reserves. The Geological Survey trumped them all in 1961 with an estimate that U.S. oil production would eventually exceed 500,000,000,000 barrels—more than five times the amount produced in the industry's first century.

Most of the industry's estimators kept their methods to themselves. Hubbert derived his own figures from a straightforward statistical analysis of past records of discovery and production. His basic assumption was: given the fact that conventional oil resources cannot be endless, then "what goes up must come down." That is, a chart showing oil production over many years would look like a roughly bell-shaped curve of rising and then falling amounts of oil. The span of the curve would be an almost insignificant blip, compared with the whole span of human history.

HOW THE SURVEY SAW IT

The Geological Survey took a simpler approach. Their method required nothing more sophisticated than a geologic map of the country and an adding machine.

The technique was first advanced in about 1960 by A. D. Zapp, a Survey researcher. Zapp was being frustrated by resource estimates that always turned out to be ultraconservative. In 1918, for instance, the Survey had said the U.S. was on the threshold of running out of oil. He sought a method of estimating that would break away from the old system of basing estimates on proved reserves. The size of such reserves, after all, had as much to do with economics as geology.

Zapp's new method led him to the following conclusion. Only 20 per cent of the nation's sedimentary rock—either on or off shore—had been thoroughly explored. (All major deposits of oil occur in sedimentary rock.) Therefore, 80 per cent of the recoverable oil resource, or more than 460,000,000,000 barrels, remained to be discovered. Zapp's reasoning went like

Lengths of flexible steel pipe waiting to be welded to form part of the Alaska oil pipeline. The Prudhoe Bay oil field on Alaska's North Slope may be one of the last big oil finds in North America.

The route of the Alaska pipeline. When completed the pipeline will carry the oil of Prudhoe Bay south to Valdez for transshipment.

this. Thick sedimentary rock covers 4.82 million km² (1.86 million mi²) of land and nearshore seabed. To explore this area thoroughly would require one well to be drilled to an average depth of 1,800 m (6,000 ft) every 5 km² (2 mi²)—for a total of 1,500,000,000 m (5,000,000,000 ft) of exploratory drilling. By the late 1950's, cumulative exploratory drilling added up to just under 20 per cent of the necessary total. According to Zapp, this left 80 per cent of the rock to be explored —and the same proportion of oil to be found.

Zapp wrote in 1962, shortly before his death, that, with all that oil, the size of the resource would not limit domestic production capacity "in the next 10 to 20 years at least, and probably not for a much longer time." Except for minor refinements, this was the official position of the Geological Survey from that time forward. And so, in effect, it was the position that was also assumed by the government as a whole.

It is hard to tell just how this optimistic forecast affected federal energy policy during the 1960's. It may have contributed to Federal Power Commission decisions to hold down the price of natural gas, a contributing factor in the present shortage. A 1968 energy policy report by the Interior Department noted that if the Survey's oil and gas estimates turned out to be too high "we certainly should know about it in time to decide intelligently among the available alternatives." The report went on, however, to indicate that the Survey's estimates were probably valid. On the other hand, one Washington energy analyst with long experience in the Interior Department has said that the Survey's predictions were generally taken with a grain of salt. "I don't know anyone who used these estimates for planning public policy," he said.

HUBBERT AGAINST THE SURVEY

They were, in any case, promptly questioned by Hubbert. In a report on national energy resources produced by NAS in 1962, Hubbert pointed out that Zapp's approach implied that oil had been—and would continue to be—found at a uniform rate per meter or foot of drilling. Yet this was not actually so. "Finding rates" had fallen sharply since the late 1930's as oilmen skimmed the cream off the prospects in Texas, Oklahoma, and California. From a high of 84 barrels per meter (276 barrels per foot) of exploratory drilling, discoveries had fallen to about 11 barrels per meter (35 barrels per foot) by 1965 and to 9 barrels per meter (30 barrels per foot) in 1972.

Over the years the disagreement evolved into a professional feud between Hubbert and defenders of the Survey estimates. Chief among the defenders was the Survey's present director, Vincent E. McKelvey. In an interesting contrast with the usual practices of government agencies, the Survey hired Hubbert in 1964. During the next decade he kept up his criticism from within, largely without effect. In 1965, however, the Survey did concede Hubbert's point about "finding rates" and note a "definite decline" in discoveries. The Survey then suggested that oil would, on the average, prove to be only half as abundant in unexplored rock as in explored rock.

NAS ENTERS THE DEBATE

However, this entire debate over oil and gas resources was generally regarded as rather academic for a number of years

—until 1973, when the Arab oil embargo struck. Then talk began to be heard about the need for achieving "self-sufficiency" as a nation, at least partly through dramatic increases in domestic oil and gas production. The Project Independence report released in November 1974, for example, accepted the National Petroleum Council's contention that holding the price of oil at $11 a barrel could more than double the present production rate of 9 million barrels a day by 1985. But the 1975 Academy report, in effect, says this is probably impossible. With the disagreement no longer academic, and with revised industry estimates in hand that were close to Hubbert's numbers, the NAS resources committee agreed to arbitrate the dispute between Hubbert and the Survey.

The central point of the disagreement was the finding factor used by the Survey. This factor was the average ratio of oil found in thoroughly explored sediments, to the oil expected to be found in a volume of unexplored rock. A finding ratio of 1—that is, equal concentrations in explored and unexplored rock—would lead to a prediction of 400,000,000,000 barrels of undiscovered, recoverable oil. A finding ratio of ½, everything else being constant, would reduce the Survey's estimate to 200,000,000,000 barrels.

In discussions with the committee's resource estimation panel, McKelvey acknowledged that the figure of one half was largely a "subjective judgment." Another official described it as "mostly a guess." Hubbert, not one to guess, applied a little calculus to drilling statistics. He came up with a finding factor of only ⅒, not ½, for the thoroughly drilled lower 48 states. Plugging this into the Survey's arithmetic gave an oil resource estimate of 120,000,000,000 barrels—nowhere near the Survey figures.

How the NAS committee arrived at its own estimate of 113,000,000,000 barrels was not entirely clear. Besides consulting with the Survey and Hubbert, the committee spoke at length with researchers from several oil companies whose estimates were well below the Survey's. None was identified, but one certainly was Mobil Oil, whose former vice-president for research and production, John Moody, was a member of the resource estimation panel.

In making its own estimates, Mobil has used an elaborate computer program that combines data on the geologic and production characteristics of known and possible oil and gas reservoirs with the instincts of Mobil's explorers out in the field. The result is a series of "probability profiles" that project the output of known and suspected deposits in each of the 14 "oil provinces" in the nation.

Moody has said that this technique is "as sophisticated as we know how to make it" and that it covers all U.S. territory, onshore and offshore. McKelvey and other Survey experts are convinced, however, that Mobil's method has its faults. They say it cannot avoid reflecting the major oil companies' tendency to look for giant oil-bearing structures, like the one

Special equipment such as this diamond drill that cuts through permanently frozen soil has been built for the Alaska pipeline project.

at Prudhoe Bay on Alaska's North Slope. In doing so, the companies tend to overlook small and scattered deposits that could add up to a lot of oil. Many geologists, McKelvey among them, firmly believe that huge amounts of oil are hidden in small and subtle "traps" between layers of rock. Our best hope, McKelvey says, is that with improved technology we will soon begin finding these traps.

BETTER METHODS NEEDED

Weighing these various and conflicting opinions, the NAS committee, as indicated, settled on a position much closer to Hubbert than to the Survey. After all their deliberations, the panel decided that an estimate of 105,000,000,000 to 120,000,000,000 barrels remaining to be found—the median of which is 113,000,000,000—"appears realistic." With present technology, in the committee's view, these future discoveries plus past production and known reserves should add up to 247,000,000,000 barrels. An additional 100,000,000,000 barrels might someday be recoverable with new technology. Hubbert's comparable estimate, published in 1974, is 253,000,000,000 barrels.

Offshore oil-drilling rigs, such as these in the Gulf of Mexico, are becoming more common as oil companies explore the rock of the near-shore seabeds.

What does all this imply for estimates of world petroleum resources? The true picture is not easy to come by. The fact is that methods of prediction differ from one substance to another. Petroleum, being one of the least accessible of these substances, is one of the hardest to measure. No standard method exists for estimating this resource. The NAS committee, however, accepts industry estimates that the world's undiscovered recoverable oil amounts to about 1,130,000,000,000 barrels and its natural gas to 1.4×10^{14} m^3 (4.9×10^{15} ft^3). In addition, reserves of shale oil in the United States alone are said to eclipse these figures at an estimated 4,000,000,000,000 barrels.

The Geological Survey, by mid-1975, was itself bringing its estimates closer in line with those accepted by the NAS. It now says that the United States may possibly have between 50,000,000,000 and 127,000,000,000 barrels of undiscovered recoverable oil—quite a sharp drop from the estimates published in 1974. The figures for natural gas have also dropped markedly, to 9.12 to 18.55×10^{12} m^3 (3.22 to 6.55×10^{14} ft^3).

Nevertheless, as the Survey's chief geologist, Richard Sheldon, has pointed out, different methods are based on different premises and are therefore hard to compare. Most estimates include economic factors in one way or another, for example. In contrast, notes Sheldon, in the past the Survey has aimed for relatively "price-free" figures that include a larger amount of possible, if unmarketable, resources than most estimates do. All would probably agree that the art of resource estimation is, in Sheldon's words, "in a very unsatisfactory state of affairs right now" □

SELECTED READINGS

The Mineral Position of the United States, 1975–2000 edited by Eugene N. Cameron. University of Wisconsin 1973.

Mineral Resources and the Environment. National Academy of Sciences 1975.

Natural Gas

by Joel Legunn

THERE is much talk these days about the ongoing energy crisis. A large part of this talk deals with the world's supply of natural fuels: who has them, and who needs them most.

One of the major fuels being discussed is natural gas. This mineral resource is found in deep underground reservoirs all around the world. Natural gas accounts for 21 per cent of the energy being consumed in the world today. In the United States, it accounts for 31 per cent.

Natural gas has several advantages. It burns efficiently; it is odorless; and it does not produce carbon monoxide or other dangerous oxides. The least expensive of the fuel gases, it is used both in homes and in industry.

In the home, natural gas is used for space heating, gas furnaces, gas incinerators, and stoves. Some large building complexes and hospitals use "total energy" systems based on the burning of natural gas. The heat thus obtained is used to generate electricity, provide hot water, and heat rooms. Such self-contained systems do away with the need for power lines.

In industry, the high heat value of natural gas makes it valuable for many kinds of metallurgical processes, such as the making of steel. The gas is ideal for industrial processes involving ceramics, which require a clean-burning fuel. And in many areas of the world, natural gas is used to generate electricity by means of gas turbines.

Natural gas serves as a raw material in many chemical industries. Among the compounds produced from natural gas are ethyl and methyl alcohol, formaldehyde, acetone, ethylene, and acetylene. The gas is also important in the production of nitrogen fertilizers, pesticides, herbicides, solvents, and plastics. Synthetic fibers such as Acrilan, Dacron, and nylon use natural gas as a prime ingredient. And there has been experimental work done on the use of natural gas in the synthesis of protein.

Special tankers that can store and transport more than 750,000 barrels of liquefied natural gas (LNG) have been designed.

Finally, many valuable substances are obtained in the purification of natural gas. For example, natural gas is the only commercial source of helium. It is also a source of carbon black, from which printer's ink is made. The hydrogen sulfide present in some natural gas reservoirs is a source of elemental sulfur. The propane and butane contained in natural gas are used in making liquefied petroleum gas (LPG). Other, heavier hydrocarbons are obtained from the purification of natural gas, as well.

COMPOSITION AND PROPERTIES

As this would indicate, natural gas is actually a mixture of several different gases. The mixture varies from reservoir to reservoir. The chief gaseous component is methane, a hydrocarbon that in some reservoirs makes up as much as 90 per cent of the mixture. Other hydrocarbons present in natural gas include ethane, propane, butane, and the heavier compounds that make up "natural gasoline." Small amounts of different kinds of hydrocarbons such as cyclohexane and benzene are also present.

In addition, natural gas often contains substantial amounts of foul-smelling hydrogen sulfide. Nitrogen, carbon dioxide, and helium may also be present, along with water vapor and solid matter that escapes from the gas reservoir. None of these substances burn, so their presence reduces the heating value of natural gas. They are removed both to increase the efficiency of natural gas as a fuel and because many of them are themselves valuable minerals. Substances such as hydrogen sulfide and water would also corrode the pipelines used in transporting natural gas. Water vapor would form compounds with other gas components and would clog the lines.

Natural gas with a high concentration of hydrogen sulfide—sometimes as much as 9 per cent—is called a "sour gas," whereas one with a low concentration is called a "sweet gas." Hydrogen sulfide is a highly poisonous compound. It is removed by chemical absorption, as are carbon dioxide and water vapor. Liquid water and solid particles are removed by mechanical separators. "Scrubbers"—tanks of oil through which the gas is bubbled—may also be used for purifying the gas. The valuable hydrocarbons are removed by low-temperature distillation.

Many natural gas purification plants dot the landscape of the southwestern United States, the main producer of the valuable resource.

Purified natural gas is colorless and odorless. It is about one half as dense as air. The gas becomes a liquid when it is cooled below −161° C (−258° F). When it is compressed to liquid form, one cubic unit of the liquid is equivalent to about 625 cubic units of the gas. The heating value of purified natural gas, as obtained from a pipeline, ranges from about 9,000 to 9,800 kilocalories/m^3 (about 1,030 to 1,100 British thermal units/ft^3). Because the purified gas is odorless, it is difficult to detect potentially explosive leaks in pipelines. For this reason, highly odorous substances known as mercaptans are introduced into the pipelines to make such leaks apparent.

HOW GAS RESERVOIRS ARE FORMED

Natural gas is probably the result of the decay of tiny marine animals and plants in ancient oceans. The decaying remains settled on the floors of the oceans, along with other sediments such as sands and clays. As more and more layers of sediments built up, over long periods of time, pressure and heat converted the organic remains into coal, oil, and gas. The other sediments became rocks.

Because the natural gas was less dense than the surrounding rock, it seeped upward through rock fissures and through porous sediments. It continued to rise until it encountered rock through which it could not seep. Thus natural gas is found in porous sedimentary rock, such as sandstone or limestone, that lies underneath nonporous rock such as shale or anhydrite. Such gas reservoirs usually collect in anticlines—rock layers that are folded concavely downwards, forming a natural trap. Such formations account for 80 per cent of the world's known reservoirs of gas and oil.

Every oil reservoir is, in fact, a gas reservoir as well. Gas that is found with oil is known as "associated gas." But there are also large gas reservoirs that contain no oil. Such gas is known as "nonassociated gas." The latter makes up three fifths of the world's major gas reservoirs. A third type of accumulation is also found, in which the natural gas is dissolved in the oil. This is known as "dissolved gas."

LOOKING FOR NATURAL GAS

People who explore for natural gas pay special attention to anticline formations and to sites of ancient oceans. Because drilling for gas is expensive, very thorough geological and geophysical surveys are made beforehand.

Aerial photography provides topographic maps of a given region. A ground survey provides a rough idea of what kinds of geological formations lie below. Sometimes there is also surface evidence of the presence of an underground gas reservoir. It may be as obvious as gas seepage or surface rocks that are impregnated with oil, asphalt, or tar. Otherwise the explorers must look for more subtle clues.

There is no way to test directly for hidden gas reservoirs from above ground. Geophysical surveys, however, can provide a fairly accurate picture of subsurface structures. These will indicate whether or not gas is likely to be found there. An instrument known as a gravity meter is also used. It detects small differences in the strength of gravity, indicating differences in rock densities below. Another instrument, the magnetometer, detects small differences in the earth's magnetic field, such as would be produced by variations in rock structure.

A seismic survey will also likely be made of the region. Small explosions are set off to send shock waves through the earth. The waves are recorded and studied. Changes in the strength and direction of wave movement indicate differences in the density and the structure of the rocks below.

However, the only direct way of learning what lies in the earth is to drill and find out. As exploratory drilling proceeds, workers keep track of the characteristics of the rock through which the drill is passing—its density, porousness, and so forth. Cuttings from the drill are recovered and analyzed. Special instruments are lowered into the drill hole to test the rock in various ways. For example, electrical conductivity tests are made because oil- and gas-filled rock conducts electricity poorly. In addition, the fluid pumped down into the well during drilling is repeatedly analyzed to see if it contains gas.

New pipelines are being built across the vast Siberian reaches of the Soviet Union, to make fuller use of the world's largest gas fields.

MINING AND DISTRIBUTING

Once a promising reservoir is found, wells are established to tap it. Drilling for gas is essentially the same as drilling for oil. The most common method is rotary drilling. A hollow drill pipe is attached to a drill bit that has rotating teeth to crush and grind rock as the pipe turns. Drilling mud—a special fluid that lubricates the drill bit—is pumped down through the pipe. It rises back to the surface by passing between the pipe and the walls of the drill hole, carrying away cuttings from the bit as it does so. Its pressure also prevents the blowouts, or sudden discharges of gas and oil, that were common in early days of drilling.

The well is completed by placing a wide steel pipe, called casing, in the hole. The casing is surrounded by cement in order to prevent gas and oil from seeping up around it. Tubing is inserted inside the casing to conduct the gas to the surface. Attached to the tubing and casing at the earth's surface is an assembly of valves and gauges known as a "Christmas tree" because of its appearance. This assembly controls the flow of gas from the well. The gas moves from the "Christmas tree" into the purifying systems already mentioned. It is then ready for shipment to the consumer.

There are several ways of handling the processed gas. Some nations have built long-distance pipelines that carry the natural gas to cities and towns that may be thousands of kilometers, or miles, away. One such network, for example, extends 6,900 km (4,300 mi) from Texas to New York. The gas travels under high pressure through pipes that are about a meter, or yard, in diameter. The initial pressure of about 110 kg/cm^2 (1,600 lb/in^2) is maintained along the pipeline route by pumping stations. When the gas reaches a city, a local utility takes over its distribution to consumers.

Not all the gas produced at wells goes directly to consumers, however. Pipeline companies use huge storage facilities to maintain reserves for periods of peak demand. Often these facilities are natural geological formations such as salt caverns or porous rocks that originally contained water. And sometimes gas is pumped back into exhausted oil and gas fields, to be kept there until needed. Within city limits, utility companies maintain reserves in storage tanks that are often placed underground.

Natural gas can also be transported and stored in liquid form. This is most often the practice in places such as Algeria, where extensive pipelines do not yet exist. It costs additional money to produce liquefied natural gas (LNG). And the LNG must be stored in special containers, of high insulating quality, that are able to stand the stress of extreme cold. However, storage of LNG does offer the advantage of taking up much less space.

RESERVES FOR TOMORROW

The value of natural gas as an energy resource is apparent from this account. The question then becomes: how much natural gas remains for us to use?

There are two basic ways to calculate proven—that is, known and recoverable—reserves. One, the volumetric method, is based on a detailed knowledge of the extent, thickness, and porousness of the rock containing the gas. From this knowledge, the amount of gas that the rock is likely to contain can be calculated. The other method is to measure the drop in gas pressure when a known volume of gas is removed from a reservoir. The smaller the drop, the greater is the volume of natural gas at that site.

Total proven reserves around the world are estimated at 62.9×10^{12} m^3 ($2,220.4 \times 10^{12}$ ft^3). The countries with the largest reserves are the Soviet Union, Iran, the United States, Algeria, the Netherlands, and the United Kingdom.

Worldwide production of natural gas at the end of 1974 stood at 11.13×10^{11} m^3 (393×10^{11} ft^3). The amount produced by a country, however, did not necessarily correspond to its proven reserves. The United States, for example, was the largest producer that year, whereas Iran, with larger reserves, hardly tapped them.

Gas production also varies from year to year. In the United States in 1974, for example, gas production declined for the first time in 25 years. In other parts of the world, the situation was quite the reverse. In some areas, gas could not be transported away from the wells as fast as it accumulated. What happens in such cases is that large amounts of the gas are vented into the atmosphere or burned up —a process called "flaring." Such differences mean that the picture of natural gas as an energy resource is constantly changing□

"Bright Spot: Better Seismological Indicators of Gas and Oil" by A. L. Hammond. *Science*, August 9, 1974.

Fundamentals of Natural Gas. Consumers Power Company, 1970.

Liquefied Natural Gas by W. L. Lom. Halsted Press, 1974.

The Outlook for Natural Gas—A Quality Fuel edited by Peter Hepple. Halsted Press, 1973.

At the site of the Great Canadian Oil Sands operation in Alberta's Athabasca region, a drainage ditch cuts through the bleak and boggy landscape.

Athabasca Tar Sands

by W. L. Dack

RAPIDLY changing world events have swung the development spotlight onto Canada's huge untapped energy resources locked up in the Athabasca tar sands. In recent years, skyrocketing oil prices and the continuing decline in North American supplies have converted tar sands from an uncertain, energy possibility into an exciting here-and-now actuality.

The presence of the Athabasca tar sands—located in northeastern Alberta and extending into Saskatchewan—has been known for centuries. Nearly 200 years ago an explorer, Peter Pond, watched the Cree Indians along the Athabasca River mix the oily substance with spruce gum to waterproof their canoes. The sands are beds, or layers, of a mixture of sand, water, and bitumen, a natural hydrocarbon. The water and bitumen form a film around each tiny grain of sand. The material looks black and oily and usually has the consistency of very coarse brown sugar. When you squeeze a handful, it leaves a discernible oily stain and a definite oil smell.

Serious scientific evaluation of the material started only some 60 years ago. Since then there has been a long list of abandoned experimental projects until the one continuing commercial venture came into operation in 1967—that of Great Canadian Oil Sands Ltd. (GCOS), near Fort McMurray.

Other new production plants are expected to be coming into being by the early 1980's. Spaced about two years apart in starting time, they will each produce about 100,000 to 125,000 barrels of petroleum supplies daily.

THREE MAJOR DEPOSITS

The main deposits of tar sands are located in three areas—in the Athabasca region about 370 km (230 mi) northeast of Edmonton; at Peace River, about the

Athabasca tar sand is black and has an oily smell. When the bitumen is removed, however, the sand becomes the same white, powdery material found on any ocean beach.

same distance northwest of Edmonton; and at Cold Lake, about 242 km (150 mi) northeast of Edmonton. The Athabasca deposit is by far the largest. It covers an area of some 23,300 sq km (9,000 sq mi).

Along the banks of the Athabasca River the sands extend from the surface to a depth of about 46 m (150 ft). Farther from the river, where most of the deposits are located, they can be buried as deep as about 610 m (2,000 ft).

There are a number of theories as to how the tar sands were formed in the first place. A popular and long-held one is that something happened—earthquakes or land-subsidence—to cause oil from deep pools to migrate upward and spread throughout the existing sand beds. Another popular geological belief today is that the oil was squeezed somehow out of extensive surrounding shale source beds into ancient delta sand deposits that were formed more than 65 million years ago.

The Athabasca deposits are estimated to contain about 600 billion barrels of oil. Of this, about half may eventually be recovered, based on current technology. That is close to the entire reserves of the Arab oil-producing nations and is some 30 times Canada's present known reserves of conventional oil.

But only 10 per cent of the deposits have a thin enough overburden, or layer of earth and rocks—up to 90 m (300 ft) —to permit recovery by open-pit mining operations. The Alberta Energy Resources Conservation Board has estimated that these mineable reserves contain some 38.8 billion barrels of bitumen (oil sands), from which some 26.6 billion barrels of oil are recoverable.

These surface deposits alone would support nine or 10 separate giant recovery projects operating over a 30-year cycle.

UNDERGROUND RECOVERY

To obtain oil from the deeper deposits, industry must use underground recovery techniques that leave the sand in place. Among methods proposed to liquefy the oil are controlled underground fire, steam injection, emulsion injection, and underground atomic explosions. In all these plans the idea is to heat the reservoir and apply pressure sufficiently to cause the heavy oil to migrate to drilled recovery wells.

Considerable experimental work has already been carried out on both steam injection and fire-flooding methods—the first by both Imperial Oil Ltd. and Shell Canada Ltd. and the latter by Amoco

Canada Petroleums Ltd. as well as other companies.

To develop and exploit the tar sands for the maximum benefit of his province, Alberta's premier, Peter Lougheed, set up a special research agency that was granted $100 million in funds. This sum was added to a $40 million research and development commitment by Canada's federal government to develop new technology for *in situ* (in place) operations and for expanding surface mining recovery of oil.

In announcing the new provincial body Mr. Lougheed said: "Too much effort might be channelled into new commercial surface recovery projects at the risk of delaying development of the greater portion of the tar sands potential."

Oil industry officials say that Canada's existing tar sands technology is about five years ahead of comparable oil shale research in the United States. This is regarded by some Canadian observers as less than a comfortable lead-time in view of the greatly stepped-up U.S. research program into oil shale recovery methods for the huge shale deposits in Colorado.

While the oil industry knows that oil can be produced *in situ* from conventionally drilled wells by injecting steam into the underground reservoir, it remains to be proved by controlled field pilot testing that the process is technologically and economically viable on a large commercial scale. The great rise in world oil prices since 1973 improved the prospects of economically viable production from the deep-seated tar beds.

PIONEERING VENTURE

The first commercial plant complex for recovery of oil from the tar sands—that of Great Canadian Oil Sands Ltd.—started operating in 1967 on Lease 86, covering 1,600 hectares (4,000 acres) at a location some 34 km (21 mi) north of Fort McMurray. The lease is estimated by Alberta petroleum authorities to contain more than one billion barrels of bitumen and recoverable reserves of 630 million barrels of synthetic oil. A combination of economic and operating problems has plagued this big pioneering tar sands venture, owned mainly by Sun Oil Co., centered in Philadelphia.

Basically, a tar sands recovery operation using a surface mining technique is a simple process. But the tremendous tonnages of material that have to be moved every day make it a truly formidable undertaking. The economics of the operation depend on a steady flow of tar sands through the mining extraction process. Slowdowns or stoppages through equipment breakdown are very costly because of the great sums invested.

To start with, vast quantities of overburden have to be removed from the tar sands deposits. Then the tar sands must be scooped out of the deposit at a hefty and continuous rate and transported to the extraction plant, which can be as far as 3 km (almost 2 mi) away.

Tar removal demonstrated: the sand settles in the hot-water vat while the tar overflows it.

The pioneering GCOS project removes the over-burden by large front-end loaders and scoops out the tar sands by two giant bucketwheels, each weighing 1,700 tons. Together the bucketwheels dig out an average 108,000 tons of tar sands a day. The tar sands are deposited on wide conveyor belts, which transport them to the extraction plant at a rate of 19 km per hr (12 mph). There the material is treated with a hot water flotation process that was developed by Alberta scientist Karl Clark almost 50 years ago.

The sands are funneled into slowly revolving drums and mixed with hot water. This strips the bitumen from the sand. The bitumen is then heated and fed to tall coker drums, where it is broken down into coke and lighter hydrocarbons. The coke is used to supply fuel for the project's powerhouse. In various other units the other coker products are upgraded into naphtha, kerosene, and gas oil. Every day, about 300 tons of sulfur are separated out. Finally, a high-quality synthetic crude is made by blending these petroleum products that can be refined into a range of finished products.

THE SYNCRUDE PROJECT

The second major tar sands recovery project, that of Syncrude Canada, Ltd., is under way. It is owned by a team made up of Imperial Oil Ltd., Canada–Cities Service Ltd., and Gulf Oil Canada Ltd. Atlantic Richfield Canada Ltd., a fourth member of the team, withdrew in late 1974, but additional capital was provided by three Canadian governments—$300 million from the federal government in Ottawa, $200 million from Alberta, and $100 million from Ontario.

Syncrude will be a surface mining operation, but it will have a production twice as large as that of GCOS, at 125,000 barrels per day. It is also located on the Athabasca deposits, near Mildred Lake, 42 km (26 mi) north of Fort McMurray.

In the Syncrude project the tar sands will be scooped out by four giant drag-

The two gigantic bucketwheel excavators being used to strip-mine the Athabasca deposits are over 60 m (200 ft) long. Left, one of the bucketwheels in operation.

Tar sands are mixed with hot water and steam in revolving drums at the GCOS plant. This process removes the tar from the sand.

lines. These will be located on the surface of the overburden and will drag the tar sands from the exposed deposits up the steep sides of the pit to piles on the surface. The material will be transported to the plant complex from the piles by a conveyor belt system.

SHELL'S PROGRAM

Shell Canada Ltd. is the third company to enter the tar sands picture. Along with its U.S. affiliate, Shell Explorer Ltd., it is seeking provincial government approval to build a 100,000 barrels-per-day tar sands complex in the Athabasca area. Plans are to reach first production in 1978–79. This would also be a surface mining operation. Following preliminary hearings before the Alberta Energy Resources Conservation Board, the board approved the application as feasible and has recommended approval to the Alberta government.

Evaluation drilling on Shell's Lease 13 has defined some 3 billion barrels of reserves that can be surface mined. The reserves are sufficient to support three 100,000 barrels-per-day projects for some 25 years, a Shell official said.

But Shell's program for tar sands development is a two-pronged one involving eventual development of deeper tar sands deposits in both the Athabasca and Peace River regions by *in situ* processes. Up to now most of the company's *in situ* tests have been concentrated in its Peace River lease holdings, where a steam injection program is under way. If the results of this test are encouraging they would provide the basis for expanding to a large pilot project costing $40 million and involving about 40 production, injection, and observation wells. This in turn would provide the basis for design and economic evaluation of a full-scale project which could come into being by 1983.

The fourth group to reach the application stage with a new planned tar sands project is one comprising Petrofina Canada Ltd., Pacific Petroleums Ltd., Hudson's Bay Oil & Gas, Murphy Oil, and CanDel Oil Ltd. The group applied to build a 122,500 barrels-per-day plant complex involving surface mining technology to begin operating in 1982□

 SELECTED READINGS

"The Future Arrives in Tar Sands Country" by Reggi Ann Dubin. *Business Week*, March 31, 1975.

"Oil Shale: Bonanza or Bust for the Rockies" by James Bishop, Jr. *National Wildlife*, June–July 1974.

It is possible to save almost 25 per cent of the energy used to run a household without a drastic change in life-style. One way is reduce heat loss—for example, by caulking windows.

Cutting Your Home Energy Budget

by James K. Page, Jr., and John P. Wiley, Jr.

IF you are a regulation-size adult you give off about the same amount of heat as a 100-watt light bulb. It takes about 306 kg (675 lb) of coal to fuel the bulb if left on all year and it takes about 635 kg (1,400 lb) of food to fuel you for a year.

Your main function is not to produce heat. Neither is it the bulb's. But the waste heat is not incidental in either case. It is an absolute necessity, thanks to the laws of thermodynamics. If you take fuel of any sort and make power from it of any sort, you have to waste energy along the way. The question is how much is wasted and how much has to be wasted.

Take the American home. The 70 million living units of the United States account for one fifth of all the energy used in the nation. This does not include the energy used to build the houses and make the appliances. In response to pleas from the U.S. government and other organizations, most Americans have turned down the heat in their houses and turned off a few lights.

There is a great deal more that one can do, however. One can save something like 25 per cent of the energy used to run a household without making a radical change in life-style. And if everyone did so, that would mean an enormous decrease in the nation's energy needs. Somc of the advice on how to make such savings will be good and some of it will be bad.

For example, one hears that if all the pilot lights in U.S. gas stoves and water heaters were turned off when not in use, the nation would save an enormous amount of energy. Not necessarily. The pilot light gives off heat—not much but a little—and during most of the year the heating system would have to replace this heat. And no matter what kind of heating system you have, it is less efficient than the flame burning in the stove. So one should only turn off the pilot light when the kitchen is too warm—that is, during the summer.

Other advice is unquestionably good, however. Many suggestions concern small things which, taken together, add up to significant savings. For example, a 0.6 cm (0.25 in) crack along a 90 cm (3 ft) attic access hatch will cost you over 76 liters (20 gal) of fuel oil in a winter in a moderate climate, even more in a severe one. The rule of thumb is that for an inside-outside temperature difference of 35 degrees, your home loses 55 BTUs per hour through every square inch of such openings. Or, in metric, a temperature difference of 20 degrees for every 6.5 cm^2. The idea is to learn to visualize those BTUs disappearing.

Think of it as a game—the game of household thermodynamics. It is a game anyone can play and one that everyone will have to play. The trick is to see the energy that flows all around us, just as a photographer or an artist sees light spilling over a building or bouncing off a wall. If we learn to make choices in terms of energy consumption as we now do in terms of money, we will have stretched the limited energy resources of the planet—and we will save ourselves a good deal of cash in the bargain.

THE LANGUAGE OF ENERGY

The language of energy is filled with words we have heard all our lives, but don't always fully understand. We buy light bulbs rated in watts, cars rated in horsepower, food rated in calories and air conditioners rated in BTUs. All these units are ways of saying the same thing, and all can be converted and compared.

One *BTU*, or British thermal unit, is equal to the amount of heat needed to raise the temperature of one pound of water by one degree Fahrenheit. In terms of fuel sources there are 5,000 BTUs in a pound of wood, 1,000 in a cubic foot of natural gas, 13,000 in a pound of coal and 125,000 in a gallon of gasoline. Or, in metric: there are approximately 11,000 BTUs in 1 kg of wood, 1,000,000 BTUs in 1 m^3 of natural gas, 28,700 in 1 kg of coal, and 33,000 in 1 liter of gasoline.

An advantage of thinking in BTUs is that they are readily convertible to other units. For example, 3.4 BTUs equals one watt-hour—that is, the power of one watt for one hour. However, this is perfect conversion, which is only theoretical. In practice, it takes about ten BTUs at a power plant to produce one watt-hour.

A *kilowatt* is equal to 1,000 watts, or about one-and-a-third horsepower. A kilowatt-hour is 1,000 watts of power expended for an hour, or, for example, ten 100-watt bulbs burning for an hour. This is the unit used on your electric bill.

Knowing these conversions, one can calculate how much energy and fuel are used by appliances. Suppose an electric dryer takes 4,000 watts and it runs for 45 minutes to dry a load of wash. The 45 minutes is three quarters of an hour. So take three quarters of 4,000 watts to get the watt-hours, 3,000, or three kilowatt-hours. From the conversions above it is shown that it takes about 10,000 BTUs to produce a kilowatt-hour, so it will take about 30,000 BTUs to produce the power needed to run the dryer once. This, in turn, converts to more than one fourth of a gallon of gasoline or nearly two-and-a-half pounds of coal. Or, to approximately 1 liter of gasoline or a little more than 1 kg of coal.

How many watts does an appliance use? You can find out by multiplying the voltage of the house current—usually 120—by the current consumed by the appliance. This current is measured in *amperes*. The ampere rating of an appliance is usually given near the serial number. For example,

Solar water heaters are commercially available and can be fitted into many houses.

Annual Energy Requirements of Electric Household Appliances

	average wattage	est. kwh consumed annually
food preparation		
Blender	386	15
Broiler	1,436	100
Carving Knife	92	8
Coffee Maker	894	106
Deep Fryer	1,448	83
Dishwasher	1,201	363
Egg Cooker	516	14
Frying Pan	1,196	186
Hot Plate	1,257	90
Mixer	127	13
Oven, microwave (only)	1,450	190
Range		
with oven	12,200	1,175
with self-cleaning oven	12,200	1,205
Roaster	1,333	205
Sandwich Grill	1,161	33
Toaster	1,146	39
Trash Compacter	400	50
Waffle Iron	1,116	22
Waste Disposer	445	30
food preservation		
Freezer (15 cu ft)	341	1,195
Freezer (Frostless 15 cu ft)	440	1,761
Refrigerator (12 cu ft)	241	728
Refrigerator (Frostless 12 cu ft)	321	1,217
Refrigerator/Freezer		
(14 cu ft)	326	1,137
(Frostless 14 cu ft)	615	1,829
laundry		
Clothes Dryer	4,856	993
Iron (hand)	1,008	144
Washing Machine (automatic)	512	103
Washing Machine (non-automatic)	286	76
Water Heater	2,475	4,219
(quick-recovery)	4,474	4,811

	average wattage	est. kwh consumed annually
comfort conditioning		
Air Cleaner	50	216
Air Conditioner (room)	860	860*
Bed Covering	177	147
Dehumidifier	257	377
Fan (attic)	370	291
Fan (circulating)	88	43
Fan (rollaway)	171	138
Fan (window)	200	170
Heater (portable)	1,322	176
Heating Pad	65	10
Humidifier	177	163
health & beauty		
Germicidal Lamp	20	141
Hair Dryer	381	14
Heat Lamp (infrared)	250	13
Shaver	14	1.8
Sun Lamp	279	16
Tooth Brush	7	0.5
Vibrator	40	2
home entertainment		
Radio	71	86
Radio/Record Player	109	109
Television		
black & white		
tube type	160	350
solid state	55	120
color		
tube type	300	660
solid state	200	440
housewares		
Clock	2	17
Floor Polisher	305	15
Sewing Machine	75	11
Vacuum Cleaner	630	46

*Based on 1000 hours of operation per year. This figure will vary widely depending on area and specific size of unit.

Electric Energy Association

the small electric motor on a rock tumbler is rated at 0.40 amps. Multiplying this by the house voltage gives 48 watts, which is in the range of a light bulb. If the motor is run 24 hours, it uses 48 × 24, or 1,152, watt-hours. Rounding it off to one kilowatt, the motor used 10,000 BTUs, or not quite one twelfth of a gallon of gasoline, two pounds of wood or less than a pound of coal. Or, in metric, the motor used 10,000 BTUs, or not quite one third of a liter of gasoline, less than 1 kilogram of wood, and less than one half of a kilogram of coal.

Leaves, grass clippings, and vegetable waste made into a compost pile that can later be used as fertilizer for the garden.

APPLIANCES

Have you ever tried to count the appliances in your house? To do so is something of a shock for anyone who has grown up believing in the tradition of American self-reliance. Just scan a list of typical appliances found in most homes and their energy use. Armed with the conversions previously mentioned, you can make your own list and calculate the total energy used in a week, say, by all of the machines in your house. And then you can compute fairly precisely how much energy you could save by being more selective in their use. For example, dishes dry perfectly well at room temperature, so why not stop putting the dishwasher through its drying cycle?

Even more significant savings can be made if you are about to replace an appliance with a new one. Often the higher priced machine is less expensive in the long run because it is cheaper to run. A Harvard University study compared two refrigerators of similar size. One cost $292 to buy but would cost $746 to operate over its 20-year lifetime. The other cost $359 to buy but only $392 to operate over 20 years. Thus the expensive one is $287 cheaper to own. The same principle applies to virtually every appliance.

The greatest savings, of course, lie in doing without wherever possible. It takes energy to make an appliance and transport it as well as to use it. It even requires energy to take it to the dump.

HEATING

Outside of fueling the family car, most Americans spend more energy to heat their homes than for any other single purpose. Residential heating takes something like 11 per cent of the national energy budget, and a much bigger bite out of the family energy budget—up to 40 per cent in northern parts of the country—not to mention an increasingly larger bite out of the family money budget as well.

A home loses heat in three ways, and all can be managed so we get the most for the least. Home heating plants are relatively efficient, some as much as 75 per cent. That still means a lot of waste heat goes up the chimney, and some of that can be tapped—for example by attaching fins to the flue pipe, whose outside temperature may reach several hundred degrees. The fins would have to be removed in summer if the burner also heats your water. Those building a new house can go a step further by having heat exchangers installed right in the chimney.

Of the heat that reaches the radiators, about two thirds is eventually lost to the outside while the remaining third is lost in heating cold air that infiltrates from the outside.

There are at least four ways that you can reduce the amount of energy you now use to heat your home.

First, reduce the amount of heat you require. Lowering the temperature six degrees Fahrenheit, or 3⅓ degrees Celsius, can save you approximately 20 per cent of your fuel bill in cities like New York, Washington, St. Louis, Wichita, Denver, Boise, or Walla Walla. The figure will be lower for areas colder than these, and higher for warmer areas. Raising the humidity will make a lower temperature a good deal more tolerable.

Second, make sure your heating plant is working at top efficiency. In an oil-fired system, for example, not only should the burner be serviced, but the boiler should be vacuumed. A very thin layer of carbon inside combustion chambers can reduce efficiency by as much as 20 per cent. In any home, the heating system should be balanced so that it does not work overtime to keep one room warm while others are too warm.

Third, keep the heat in the house as long as you can. Heat is continually being lost through walls, windows, ceilings, and the roof. Insulation and storm windows significantly cut this loss, and quickly pay for themselves. Evergreen trees planted to form a windbreak around the house slow the rate at which winter winds suck heat from your house.

Fourth, reduce the amount of cold outside air that gets in and must be heated. Caulking and weatherstripping around doors and windows can eliminate a lot of infiltration. Check for leaks around air conditioners and pull-down attic doors and seal them. If vapor forms on the inside of windows on the downwind side of your house on cold days, you know the house is properly sealed and that you have provided the highest feasible humidity for maximum comfort.

Another important part of the heating bill is for hot water. About three per cent of the U.S. energy is used to heat water in homes. Here, too, there are a number of things you can do: First, make sure your water heater is working efficiently. Second, in many homes, you can adjust the temperature of the hot water. Turn this down 10 or 20 degrees F (5 or 10 degrees C). Third, Make sure hot water pipes are insulated, particularly when they run long distances. Fourth, use cold water whenever possible. Finally, in a new home it may be possible to arrange the drains so that they heat incoming water. Also, if you happen to be designing a new house, look into such equipment as solar water heaters.

INSULATION

Insulation and storm windows slow the flow of heat out of your home. The difference between inadequate and proper insulation in a temperate climate can easily be 40 per cent of your fuel bill. And insulation has the additional advantage that it can make you feel comfortable at a lower temperature than would otherwise be the case.

The human body loses heat by conduction through clothes, by air currents moving past the skin (convection), by evaporation of moisture from the skin, and by radiation. The body also loses heat by respiration and evacuation, but these are relatively insignificant.

Drafts make us feel cold, because they increase the rate at which we lose heat by convection. And low humidity inside a house in winter makes us feel cold, because it increases the rate at which perspiration evaporates. Moving air also increases this rate.

Perhaps least familiar is how we lose heat by radiation. When walls, ceilings and floors are cooler than 80° F (27° C), which is the average surface temperature of a normally clothed adult, we lose heat by radiation of heat directly to these surfaces, regardless of the temperature of the intervening air. If we feel comfortable at 71° F (22° C) in a room with one outside wall, we need an air temperature of 73° F (23° C) to feel equally comfortable in a room with two outside walls.

Insulation behind walls, ceilings and floors means their inside temperatures are warmer. Storm windows or double panes do the same for windows. Thus they make lower temperatures tolerable.

The secret of good insulators is that they contain many tiny air spaces. In large air spaces, heat is readily transferred by convection, but in tiny spaces, air is a very good insulator. A dense material, such as brick, with little or no air space, will conduct five BTUs per hour through a 2.5 cm (1 in) thickness for every Fahrenheit degree of temperature difference between one side and the other. Wood, with more air spaces, will conduct only one BTU in an hour. A mineral-wool blanket will conduct only three tenths of a BTU in the same time. And insulation is not limited to 2.5 cm (1 in), of course. The optimal amount is generally considered to be 7.6 cm (3 in) in the walls and at least 15 cm (6 in) between attic floor joists. In addition, reflective foil will bounce the heat being lost in radiation to where you want it.

Storm windows also create an air space, of course, large but still useful. There is some convection in the space between inside and outside windows, but nothing like the convection of winter winds. Storm windows cut in half the heat loss through windows, and they cut in half the difference between air temperature in the room and the window temperature.

COOLING

Keeping a house cool by running air conditioners is the hard way in terms of energy. There are plenty of things that can and should be done first. Insulation keeps heat in during winter and out during summer; it is therefore the first order of business.

Hot air rises and the sun burns down on your roof. Your attic temperature can be 40 degrees F (22 degrees C) hotter than the rest of your house, burdening the entire cooling system. Simple ventilation of the attic will help. An inexpensive attic fan will do much more. It will keep the attic at about the same as the outside temperature during the day, and quickly circulate cooler night air through the house. Most days, in most parts of the country, that is enough to keep things reasonably cool. It takes about 300 kwh annually to run an attic fan. A central cooling system in a house that is 139 m^2 (1,500 ft^2) may take nearly 4,000 kwh.

Windows are often kept shut tight even when the wind is blowing. Wind-tunnel tests show that if you open the windows on the windward side of the house a little and those on the leeward side more so, you get better ventilation.

On the other hand, you want to keep the sun out. Light-colored shades or draperies will cut the solar energy inflow (dark ones simply absorb more). Better yet, put awnings on the south side of the house. Then you can open the shaded windows.

Plant deciduous trees around the southern portion of the house. In summer they give shade. In winter they let the sun stream in through the windows.

The difference in ground-level temperature between grass and concrete or flagstone around a house may be as much as 40 to 50 degrees F (22 to 26 degrees C). Plants respire water and its evaporation has a cooling effect. Do not, therefore, build a sunlit patio next to the house. Bushes, which are taller, have more leaf area and respire yet more water, provide a greater cooling effect.

The difference between inadequate and proper insulation can be 40 per cent of your fuel bill. Left: insulating an attic. Right: closeup of insulating material.

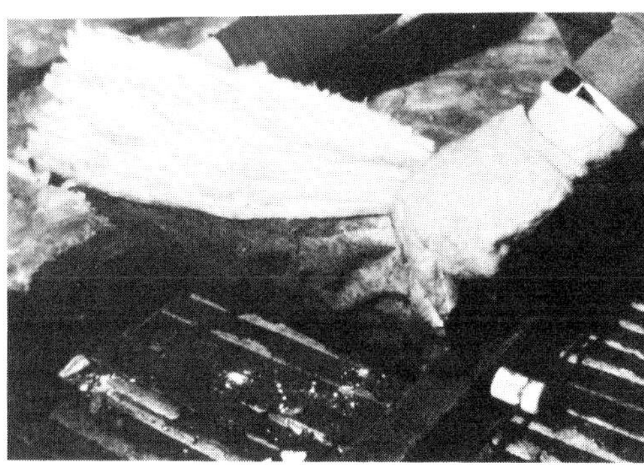

BUYING AN AIR CONDITIONER (IF YOU INSIST)

Many brands of air conditioners now come with a number called the energy efficiency ratio (EER). The EER is derived by dividing the number of BTUs of cooling capacity by the unit's wattage. You can do it yourself if the dealer doesn't have the number available. A 10,000 BTU unit that draws 1,000 watts would have an EER of 10, which is good. If it draws 2,000 watts, the EER is 5 and that is terrible.

Generally, the higher the EER, the higher the initial purchase price, but the savings on the electric bill can be as much as $18 a year, which is enough to pay you back in three or four years.

How many BTUs? Most dealers have charts to estimate the load you will need. (Or you can write the Association of Home Appliance Manufacturers at 20 North Wacker Drive, Chicago, Illinois 60606, and ask for their detailed information on the subject.) Given the choice, buy an undersized unit rather than an oversized one. If you need 9,000 BTUs, it is better to buy an 8,000 unit rather than a 10,000 unit. An oversized unit will cool the room so quickly that the compressor turns off too frequently, thus eliminating an air conditioner's second function: dehumidifying the air.

Maybe you don't need another air conditioner. If you have hot-air heat, you can run the furnace fan and circulate cool air from two or three units throughout the house.

THE LAWN AS ENERGY SINK

To grow grass is to engage in a vast struggle against nature. It is fine in damp England, but grass was simply not "supposed" to grow in many parts of the United States.

Except for the cooling effect of grass as opposed to concrete, a lawn is a classic model of the negative energy system. It takes 162,000 BTUs worth of natural gas to produce the nitrogen in a 22.5 kg (50 lb) bag of fertilizer. A 930 m^2 (10,000 ft^2) lawn requires as much as five bags a season. It then takes about half a million or more BTUs worth of gasoline to mow that much lawn, and the only product of all this energy input—the grass clippings —is usually thrown away instead of being put to use.

As food shortages continue and prices climb, more Americans will learn to see a vegetable garden as a far more attractive bit of landscaping than grass. Also the garden's taller plants cool things off better and one doesn't throw away its products. Further, the garden provides a need for the grass clippings from whatever lawn area is retained. Grass clippings placed between rows of vegetables keep weeds down and fertilize the soil. They contain the same amount of nitrogen that you are paying cash for in 22.5 kg (50 lb) bags.

While you're at it, save the leaves in the fall instead of having them hauled away. With leaves, grass clippings, eggshells, vegetable waste and a little dirt you can start a compost pile which will give you a supply of beautiful humus for the garden.

CREEPING TOWARD AUTONOMY

Anyone contemplating building a new house is in the catbird seat in terms of energy. Proper insulation, roof overhangs and a host of other well-known but little-used principles can be specified. Find an architect who understands how to design a house that works with, rather than fights against, the climate. Better yet, wait a year or two and see what happens with the many experimental houses now being built in various parts of the country—houses that will employ the energy of the sun directly and test techniques for recycling household wastes and reclaiming energy.

Meanwhile, such equipment as solar hot-water heaters and wind generating plants is already available commercially and some of this can be fitted onto existing houses. It is worth exploring. Below are some sources of information. Imagine being the first person on your block to run the refrigerator with a windmill! (If you write these sources, be patient. Interest is growing rapidly and there may be a backlog of inquiries.)

Solar power. Information on Beasley Solapak water heaters can be obtained from *Solar Energy Digest*, P.O. Box 17776, San Diego, California. These are of Australian manufacture and are at present being tested here in the United States. For similar devices, as well as solar space heating and cooling modules and designs, write Mr. Everett Barber, Sunworks, Inc., 669 Boston Post Road, Guilford, Connecticut 06437. A book entitled *Solar House Plans* by Harry Thomason is available from Edmund Scientific Co., 555 Edscorp Building, Barrington, New Jersey 08007. You can even find out about a solar mobile home by writing to Fred Rice Productions, Inc., 6313 Peach Avenue, Van Nuys, California 91401.

Wind power. Information on a variety of wind generators and their use can be obtained from Windworks, Route 3, Mukwonago, Wisconsin 53149; Solar Wind Company, East Holden, Maine 04429; Real Gas and Electric Company, Main and Armstrong Streets, Guerneville, California 95446; and Brace Research Institute, McGill University, Montreal, Quebec, Canada.

Hydroelectric power. If you have a stream running through your property, you might want to install a small water-powered turbine to produce electricity. James Leffel & Co. of Springfield, Ohio 45501, is probably the only U.S. manufacturer of such equipment—ranging from 3 to 99 horsepower. Their Pamphlet A, called *Hints on the Development of Small Water Power*, is available on request.

Continuing information. Two periodicals provide a regular dosage of encouragement and advice about how to live a less energy-intensive life: *Mother Earth News* (P.O. Box 70, Hendersonville, N.C. 28739) and *Alternative Sources of Energy* (Route 1, Box 36B, Minong, Wisconsin 54859). Both are directed primarily at rural life, but many of the ideas and schemes can be employed by more urbanized citizens.

A home vegetable garden has several advantages for energy-saving families.

Two general information publications are available with overall suggestions for energy conservation. One is *Hidden Waste, Potentials for Energy Conservation*, edited by David Large and available from the Conservation Foundation at 1717 Massachusetts Avenue, N.W., Washington, D.C. 20036. The other is *Citizen Action Guide to Energy Conservation* from the Citizens' Advisory Committee on Environmental Quality, 1700 Pennsylvania Avenue, N.W., Washington, D.C. 20006□

SELECTED READINGS

"At the Heart of the Garden: the Old Compost Pile." *Organic Gardening and Farming*, May 1974.

Composting by Clarence Goleuke. Rodale Press, 1973.

"Doggone It, Our Heating Fuel-Oil Bill Is Up to $6 This Month," *American Home*, September 1974.

"Solar Heating for the Handyman," *Mechanix Illustrated*, September 1974.

Alternative Automotive Fuels

by Jerry E. Berger

EVER since the gasoline shortage in the winter of 1973–74 there has been a surplus of suggestions about how the United States could augment its gasoline supply. Many of these suggestions revolve around the use of gaseous fuels and alcohols.

GASEOUS FUELS

The gaseous fuels—compressed natural gas, liquefied natural gas (LNG), and liquefied petroleum gas (LPG)—immediately come to some people's minds as being suitable candidates as alternative fuels. The technology for operating spark-ignited internal combustion engines on gaseous fuels is well known. Indeed, more than 300,000 U.S. vehicles now use LPG, mostly in fleet operations.

In addition, the gaseous fuels have been heralded for several years as a means of reducing exhaust emissions. Air–fuel mixtures are more uniform with these than with gasoline and leaner mixtures can be burned—factors that tend to produce lower emission levels.

There are, however, serious problems and at present little hope that gaseous fuels can become a replacement for gasoline. The physical properties of the gases present an immediate hurdle. First, it is technically difficult and would be expensive to maintain the temperature and pressure conditions necessary to keep natural gas or petroleum gas in a liquid state. Second, the gaseous fuels have less heat energy volume-for-volume than gasoline. Their use therefore would require very large fuel tanks, and the costs associated with installing new fuel tanks and new fuel-induction systems on conventional cars would probably be high.

The availability of natural gas is another problem. It is not readily available in a liquid form. The availability of LPG is somewhat more favorable but an appreciable growth in demand for LPG as an automotive fuel would produce disruptions in the existing applications of LPG—including its use in chemical feedstocks and for heating.

METHANOL

Methanol, or wood alcohol, is also often considered as a possible automotive fuel. The technology for producing it exists from several non-petroleum sources. One interesting possibility is being pursued by the city of Seattle. Like many other cities, Seattle is running out of space for landfill garbage disposal. A preliminary study of the problem led to the tentative conclusion that the best strategy would be

French mechanical engineer Jean Chambrin displays an invention—an engine that he claims can run on 60 per cent water, 40 per cent alcohol.

ALTERNATIVE LIQUID FUELS

Sources and Uses

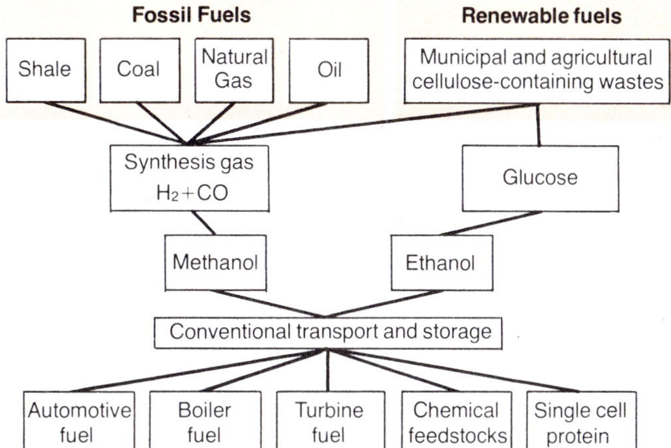

Chart showing possible ways of producing and using alternative fuels. As the availability and costs of fossil fuels increase, more research is being devoted to a search for substitute fuels.

burning of the waste to produce carbon monoxide and hydrogen, which, in turn, form feedstocks for methanol production. The city's annual solid waste production of about 550,000 tons could yield about 40 million gallons (151 million liters) of methanol each year. This is more than the fuel being consumed by all city-owned vehicles. Hence Seattle officials envision converting all municipal vehicles to operate on 100 per cent methanol and perhaps inviting private fleet operators such as taxicab companies to do the same. It's an intriguing concept, attacking the two problems of solid waste disposal and fuel supply.

The garbage concept works especially well in Seattle where hydroelectric power is used in great quantity. But the methanol route might not be so appropriate for cities such as St. Louis where garbage can be substituted for a portion of the coal in coal-fired electric generators. Direct use of solid waste as fuel, where feasible, avoids the expense required to build methanol plants.

Lumber and agriculture wastes—millions of tons—could be used as raw materials for methanol production, but this is unlikely because the costs of collecting such widely scattered supplies appear too high.

Natural gas is another possible raw material for producing methanol. But since the demand for natural gas far exceeds the current domestic supply, it would seem unwise to consider converting much of it to less energy-intensive methanol. One could consider imported natural gas, but this doesn't make any contribution toward the U.S. goal of greater domestic self-sufficiency in energy.

Coal may be the best bet for producing methanol. Coal can be gasified by means of known technology and the resulting gas converted to methanol; the maximum rate today is about 5,000 tons per day. The United States has enormous reserves of domestic coal, but we also have the major problem of being able to mine enough of it to fill projected demands with minimal environmental damage.

Some U.S. governmental agencies favor pushing ahead rapidly on the coal-to-methanol concept. The Bureau of Mines, for example, has recommended that a 5,000 ton/day demonstration plant be built as soon as possible. Segments of the U.S. Energy Research and Development Administration that are concerned with coal research tend to agree. It is estimated that such a demonstration plant could be in operation by 1980, or even by 1978 if the project were assigned a "crash basis" priority. The consensus of expert opinion indicates that, in terms of today's dollars, methanol derived from synthesis gas could be available in the early 1980's for about 12 to 22 cents per gallon, or about 3 to 6 cents per liter.

ETHANOL

Another alcohol with potential fuel applications is ethanol, or grain alcohol. Scientists at the U.S. Army Laboratory at Natick, Massachusetts, have isolated a mutant fungus that is capable of producing an enzyme which is relatively effective in converting cellulose to glucose, a form of sugar. Once the glucose is available, it can be fermented to yield ethanol.

The annual production of cellulose—most of it in paper products—in the United States is staggering. Although waste paper was used as raw material in much of the Natick development, researchers believe that garbage can also be used. They are seeking money to construct a demonstration plant capable of handling 500 tons of trash per day. If the glucose is free, it is estimated that a ton could yield 68 gallons (257 l) of ethanol, costing, in 1974 money, about 20 cents per gallon (5 cents per liter). If the glucose costs, say, a penny a pound, the alcohol cost would be 34 cents per gallon. Or in metric, if glucose costs about 2 cents a kilogram, the alcohol cost would be 9 cents per liter.

If ethanol can eventually be produced in significant quantities it probably could be employed as a minor—10 per cent or less—gasoline blending component without causing insurmountable problems.

GASOLINE/ALCOHOL BLENDS

Mixing alcohol with gasoline has popular appeal since it would appear that the gasoline pool will expand in volume to whatever degree alcohol is added to existing gasoline. Furthermore, methanol and ethanol have high anti-knock properties and this fact seems attractive, at a time when gasoline suppliers have to curtail the use of alkyl lead anti-knock additives. Proponents also argue that modest quantities of alcohol can be blended into gasoline without requiring carburetor adjustments on today's cars.

However, studies have shown that ten per cent methanol cannot simply be added to existing gasoline without concomitant adjustments in gasoline composition. When methanol is added to gasoline, the volatility becomes too high. To correct for this, butanes and pentanes have to be taken out of the gasoline. The net result of these changes is that the energy content of the gasoline pool will diminish when methanol is added.

The question of operating an automobile on gasoline/alcohol blends also has some subtleties associated with it. Cars manufactured before about 1968 were equipped with carburetors that provided "rich" fuel mixtures—that is, more fuel and less air than the chemically correct ratio. Mixing alcohol and gasoline for these older cars yields an apparent increase in fuel mileage. Newer cars, however, have carburetors designed to prepare fuel/air mixtures that are much "leaner," and cleaner. The use of alcohol/gasoline blends in such carburetors can produce excess exhaust emissions and driveability problems. According to Dr. Ronald Bradow, an EPA spokesman, a carburetor can be set up to operate on either gasoline or a *single particular* alcohol-in-gasoline blend, but once so tuned, it cannot be used on *any other fuel* without retuning.

Solubility is another problem. Methanol is sparingly soluble in motor gasoline, especially at low temperatures. More important, however, is the fact that methanol/gasoline blends are intolerant of small amounts of water that can enter the gasoline distribution system accidentally or unavoidably. Contamination by water causes the blend to separate into two phases. Methanol also is reported to cause rusting of fuel tanks, corrosion of aluminum or magnesium components in the fuel handling system, and deterioration of certain plastics and elastomers.

The problems associated with solubility and compatibility with construction materials are present to a lesser degree with ethanol/gasoline blends. These will not provide any near-term solutions since not even the Natick Laboratory demonstration plant is expected to be operational before 1980□

environmental sciences

There is increasing concern over the possible release of the extremely toxic chemical plutonium from nuclear reactor facilities. Catastrophic accidents, slow leakage from overloaded disposal facilities, thievery, and sabotage—all of these are possible disasters.

review of the year environmental sciences

Chemicals in Our Drinking Water. During 1974 several chemicals—some in use for many years and considered harmless—were discovered to be hazardous. A major new threat identified involves chlorination, the common water purification treatment. The chlorine added to kill bacteria in water can increase the levels of some hazardous chemicals, including carbon tetrachloride and chloroform. Chlorine also reacts with industrial and agricultural wastes to create new compounds that produce cancer in laboratory animals.

An investigation by the Environmental Defense Fund, a nongovernmental group, suggested that drinking water from the Mississippi River could have produced cancer in some Louisiana residents. Significantly higher death rates from cancer of the urinary organs and intestinal tract were found in communities that used chlorinated Mississippi River water than in those communities that used well water. On April 18, 1975, the U.S. Environmental Protection Agency (EPA) announced that it had found traces of organic chemicals in the water supplies of the first 79 cities tested in a nationwide survey. Some of the chemicals found are suspected of being causes of cancer.

High-altitude supersonic transports, including the British-French Concorde, could cause depletion of the earth's ozone layer, an MIT report declared.

Many environmental disease specialists believe that 85 per cent of all human cancers result from exposure to pollutants in the air and water. Hope is held that the Safe Drinking Water Act of 1974 will help to reduce the incidence of cancer. One possible solution—already in use in Canada and Europe—is to use ozone instead of chlorine as a water purifier. (See "How Safe Is Our Drinking Water?" on page 227.)

Ozone Problem. The most newsworthy chemical of 1974 was ozone, a gas that is more poisonous than cyanide but vital to life an earth. There is a thin layer of ozone in the lower stratosphere, about 32 km (20 mi) above the earth. It absorbs the sun's ultraviolet rays that can cause skin cancer. Scientists have warned since 1971 that depletion of the ozone layer would have serious effects on the earth, including possible climate changes.

Beginning in September 1974, a series of scientists—from Harvard University, the University of Michigan, and the Massachusetts Institute of Technology (MIT)—reported evidence that supersonic transports (SST's), nuclear explosions, and even spray from aerosol cans may destroy ozone in the stratosphere. (For details of the aerosol threat, see "Aerosols and the Ozone Layer" on page 223.)

The ozone problem first came to general public attention in the U.S. Congressional debate of 1971 that led to a cutoff of governmental funds for the U.S.'s SST development. (Despite the warnings, development continued on the British-French Concorde and the Soviet TU-144 supersonic craft.) In 1971 the U.S. Department of Transportation commissioned a team of MIT researchers to set to work to see if there is any truth to environmentalists' claims that nitric oxides in the high-flying SST's could deplete ozone. A three-year, $20-million study used mathematical models to simulate the effect on the lower stratosphere if a fleet of 500 SST's made regular flights. In a 1975 summary the MIT researchers predicted that under such conditions a 12 per cent depletion of ozone could occur within 25 years.

Nuclear Reactors Under Attack. Opponents of nuclear reactors kept up a strong attack based on a variety of issues—safety, reliability, cost, waste disposal, and the possibilities of sabotage and theft. They asked for a halt in the building of new reactors until these issues are settled. So far, the United States has in operation 55 nuclear reactors, which now produce 7 per cent of the nation's generating capacity. Critics directed their heaviest blows at such safety issues as fears of radioactive leakage and catastrophic accidents. Another problem is liquid wastes, which environmentalists said will remain lethal for at least 250,000 years. Concern also was expressed over U.S. efforts to develop the breeder reactor, which would produce more plutonium fuel than it burns in the form of uranium. Plutonium is the most dangerous material in nuclear weapons and is very toxic to humans, and there is fear that thievery or sabotage will release it.

French experts assemble the Phenix breeder reactor at the Marcoule Nuclear Center. Critics attacked such reactors on safety and other grounds in 1974.

Environmentalists kept suggesting that oil and coal be supplemented with solar, wind, tidal, and geothermal energy. Meantime, the U.S. Congress was expected to spend considerable time debating the issues, leading L. Manning Muntzing, a former Atomic Energy official, to observe, "1975 will be the go or no-go year for nuclear power."

Solution to Garbage Disposal? The idea of disposing of garbage by using it as fuel is catching on. In St. Louis, Missouri, the Union Electric Company, after two years of testing, began accepting 8,000 tons of garbage daily from six counties. To fire its power plants, Union Electric is using one part garbage to nine parts coal. ■ Several metropolitan areas in the United States are planning to use a new process called pyrolysis. It converts garbage to gas or oil in oxygen-free furnaces. ■ Connecticut, through its new Resources Recovery Authority, is planning to recycle the garbage of the entire state.

Long-Term Investment. Though expensive in the short run, environmental controls are seen as a good long-term investment. A study by the National Academy of Sciences forecasts that the cleaning up of noxious auto emissions may eventually cost $8 billion. Yet, it says, the savings in work days not lost to respiratory disease alone will be $10 billion annually. ■ The U.S. Council on Environmental Quality, in its fifth annual report, predicted that expenditures for pollution control would reach $80 per capita in 1976, equivalent to 2 per cent of the average family's income. This sum, the report added, is "not expected to have significant impact on gross national product, growth, inflation, or unemployment."

Exit Two DDT Relatives. As a result of an EPA ban, no aldrin nor dieldrin will be produced in the United States in 1975. These two chemicals are relatives of DDT, banned by EPA in 1973. Used on 10 per cent of the U.S.'s farmland, these long-lasting chlorinated hydrocarbons get into animal food, then into the fatty tissues of livestock, and finally into human beings. EPA tests have found that 99.5 per cent of U.S. residents have some dieldrin in their body fat. Other tests show that mice develop cancer if given food containing amounts of dieldrin similar to that in human foods. ■ Dr. G. M. Woodwell of the Ecosystems Center of the Marine Biological Laboratory, Woods Hole, Massachusetts, believes that use of DDT is increasing in the tropics. Worldwide use, he added, probably equals or exceeds that of a decade ago when the United States production of DDT reached a peak.

Frank W. Knight, Jr.

Raw refuse, in a step toward its use as a fuel, is pushed to a receiving conveyor at a Union Electric power plant in St. Louis, Missouri.

Old and new travel methods: a dog-sled team and a cargo plane transport explorers.

The Race Is On for Antarctica

by Erwin A. Bauer

ONE blinding bright January morning, I waded onto the uninhabited shore of a land so strange that it might well have been on another planet. Steam and sulfur fumes hissed from beneath the coarse black sand as I crunched inland, past bleached whale skeletons. Slowly I climbed for 300 meters (1,000 ft) or more, until reaching a rim-rock of crisp new lava. Standing at the edge of that snow-covered (but still active) volcano, I looked back with amazement at a bizarre landscape, part inferno and part frozen barrens, surrounded by a great blue sea flecked with icebergs. So this was Antarctica!

More specifically, according to the map, this far-off place was Deception Island in the South Shetland archipelago at the very edge of the continent. It was named about 150 years ago by the captain of an English sealing vessel desperately seeking shelter from a storm. Since then, only a relative handful of humans, most of them whalers and sealers, have landed on Deception. But this lonely continent isn't going to be lonely much longer.

Unhappily, the last and largest of the earth's untouched land masses is about to be invaded. The first small vanguards of tourists have already landed but that is just the beginning. Next will come the exploiters—the cutting edge of a mineral-hungry, energy-thirsty world that is just now turning an eye to the frozen south.

LOCKED UP

It is not difficult for a visitor to see why the Antarctic has thus far eluded development. It is the coldest, highest and windiest continent in the world, largely covered by a blanket of ice about 3.2 km (2 mi) thick. Temperatures that plummet as low as −88° C (−126° F) help make Antarctica the world's most hostile human environment. Thus, even in this age of sophisticated transportation, most of Antarctica has remained locked up to serious exploration.

Only during the fleeting summertime, from January through mid-March, has one region been fairly accessible, and that is the northern "tail" of the 1,125-km (700-mi) long Antarctic, or Palmer, Peninsula. Pointing toward South America, this piece of land has been the location of most tourist visits. It is also here that much of the scientific research has been conducted by the 12 nations involved in the Antarctic Treaty of 1961.

Though limited in scope, those initial probes have indicated, in no uncertain terms, that Antarctica's forbidding exterior conceals a cornucopia of riches. In addition to supporting a remarkable abundance of wildlife, the continent's perimeter appears to contain some of the most lucrative mineral deposits known to man. Notwithstanding the Antarctic Treaty, however, which deals basically with scientific research and environmental matters, international jurisdiction over these resources is far from certain. In effect, therefore, the continent is up for grabs. At a time when oil shortages have underscored the worldwide political and economic implications of natural resource distribution, Antarctica suddenly looms as a potential international powder keg.

How mineral-rich is the region? Though no major find has yet been made, a great number of minerals and fuels, from gold and diamonds to oil, are believed to exist there. One estimate, compiled by the U.S. Geological Survey, pegs the potential fuel resources of Antarctic continental shelves alone at 45 million barrels of oil and 3.25 trillion m^3 (115 trillion ft^3) of natural gas. Those amounts are roughly comparable to the proven reserves of the entire United States. A National Science Foundation research vessel found support for that earlier estimate when it discovered traces of ethane and methane—indicators of the presence of natural gas and oil—near the middle of the Ross Sea west of the Antarctic Peninsula. In the early 1960's U.S. researchers found coal in the Horlick Mountains. Evidence of porphyry copper, chromium, platinum, and other valuable minerals has also been found.

Playful Weddell seals in Antarctic ice hole.

FREE FOR THE TAKING

To date, the technical problems of resource exploration and exploitation in Antarctica's harsh and dangerous environment have been the major deterrents to opening up the new frontier. Scientists now predict, however, that the technology

Adélie penguins, out for a stroll, fearlessly let a photographer approach closely.

for offshore drilling in Antarctica's ice-bound water will be available before 1980. Meanwhile, many other mineral resources of Antarctica are virtually free for the taking right now.

The Antarctic Treaty neither permits nor bans exploration for oil and minerals. Consequently, government officials in many of the signatory nations are increasingly fearful that, without a broad international framework to regulate oil and mineral exploration, the continent will inevitably fall prey to massive degradation. Or, worse, competition for its riches could lead to major conflict. In anticipation of a possible mineral rush, the White House's National Security Council reportedly is considering proposals to revise the historic treaty.

In the meantime, the United States has 65 projects involving 175 scientists under way in the Antarctic. The projects range from how glycoprotein keeps fish from freezing to measuring how much global air pollution is present at the South Pole. There are wildlife studies as well as geological and glacial research. And to complicate matters further, another kind of resource has been found in abundance throughout Antarctic waters: plankton.

The richest of all waters, the Antarctic seas are the liquid equivalent of the tropical rain forest. For despite their frigid temperatures, they contain the most essential elements for marine plants: "fertilizer" salts such as phosphates and nitrates. Thus the blue tropical waters of the world, poor in fertilizer salts, are virtual "deserts" compared to the green polar waters. And the lush pastures of diatoms and other phytoplankton support a food pyramid that goes from krill right up to whales, seals, and sea birds. As the worldwide search for food escalates, some scientists believe the plankton they contain could become a major source of sustenance.

Shrimplike krill abound in the Antarctic seas, the richest waters in the world.

FEARLESS PENGUINS

It is this remarkable abundance of plankton that makes icy Antarctica attractive to a variety of other wildlife. Sea birds and marine mammals populate the region in droves. After navigating the Drake Passage, which connects the Atlantic to the Pacific, a traveler will find King George Island one of the most densely inhabited wildlife areas. A sheltered anchorage in Potter's Cove provides the first encounter with penguins—Adélie, chinstrap and gentoo—in what seem to be astronomical numbers. The fearless birds allow cameramen to approach within a few feet for photos and probably nowhere else in the world is bird photography any easier or more rewarding.

Other wildlife share the shorelines of King George Island with the penguins. Herds of elephant seals lolling on a gravel beach are also tolerant of human intrusion; most only belch at visitors who poke cameras toward their large faces. On a windswept rock just above the elephant seal beach is a nesting colony of giant petrels, also called giant fulmars, with wingspreads up to 2.4 m (8 ft).

Weather and ice floes permitting, Hope Bay on the Antarctic mainland is another place where a beachhead is possible, and where a half-million Adélie penguins nest in a fairly confined area. Here, many life activities can be seen almost simultaneously, from parading to the sea en masse for food, to brooding and feeding chicks.

A majestic ice formation towers over a U.S. Navy technician rowing in Paradise Bay, one of the most beautiful spots in Antarctica.

A cliff rises abruptly at Deception Island in the South Shetland archipelago, a lonely spot visited mostly by whale- and seal-hunters.

Men from the *USS Glacier,* an icebreaker, get ready to set off an explosive charge.

Also at Hope Bay, visitors encounter two more interesting birds. One is the white sheathbill, a scavenger and ptarmiganlike bird exclusive to extreme southern latitudes. The other is the remarkable brown, or south polar, skua, a large and aggressive predator and the only wildlife ever to have been observed at the extreme South Pole. Both skuas and sheathbills prey almost entirely on penguins.

SCULPTURED ICE

Even in a region of the earth where almost everything is spectacular, movement by ship from one point to another is extraordinary. Places such as Paradise Bay, which is really an elongated channel or strait, become indelible memories for every visitor, no matter whether he sees them in brilliant sunlight (as I did) or during an angry snow squall. The bay is punctuated with ice of all shapes and sizes, sculptured and shattered, some fantastically colored. Some bergs, which have recently broken off the sheer cliffs of Anvers Island or the Palmer Peninsula, may be several times as large as the ship. Others are only flat slabs, perfect platforms for a cargo of penguins or Weddell or leopard seals. The consensus of our well-traveled group was that the Antarctic constituted the greatest scene of natural beauty anywhere in the world. Indeed, some of us considered the voyage through Paradise Bay the single greatest adventure of our lifetime.

I had my own comparison to make. Back home in Jackson Hole, Wyoming, the dark Tetons are perpetually tipped with white. But in the Antarctic, typhoon winds have accomplished the opposite by exposing the bare rock peaks which surround Paradise Bay, while the rest of the mountain ranges in the area remain covered with snow.

How long such moving scenes of pristine beauty will last is a moot question. It is entirely conceivable that, in virtually no time at all, parts of the frozen continent will suffer the fate of other exploited lands, their vitality sapped and their natural beauty ruined for decades to come. One practical way to head off that tragedy, beyond treaty measures to regulate exploitation, has already been suggested—the concept of an international park in the Antarctic. More and more environmentalists are convinced that this notion should be pursued with all possible haste, because another race—the race to get in, clean up and get out—is already well under way□

 SELECTED READINGS

Antarctica: Authentic Accounts of Life and Exploration by Charles Neider, ed. Random House, 1972.

First Book of the Antarctic (grades 4–6) by Joseph B. Icenhower. Franklin Watts, Inc., 1971.

The Last Continent by Ian Cameron. Little, Brown & Co., 1974.

This Is Antarctica (grades 5–8) by Joseph M. Dukert. Coward, McCann & Geoghegan, Inc., 1972.

As part of survival training program, researcher uses ice axe to test for safe footing.

Superstition Wilderness, Arizona. Earthcare is promoting campaigns "to safeguard the world's irreplaceable natural heritage."

Earthcare

by William E. Kennedy

WILL World Environment Day of June 5, 1975, mark the beginning of a string of successes for "Earthcare"? Can the international friends of conservation unite to achieve Earthcare's goal: "global protection of natural areas"?

The Sierra Club and the National Audubon Society, which jointly sponsored World Environment Day to kick off a four-day Earthcare conference, hope so. For heartening proof that environmental campaigns sometimes do pay off, they can look back to Earth Day of April 22, 1970. Earth Day got its start when U.S. Senator Gaylord Nelson of Wisconsin suggested that colleges shut down for a day while faculty and students sift through the problems of dirty air, dirty water, and the misuse of dwindling natural resources. As an aftermath, an awakened public persuaded the U.S. Congress to pass the Clean Air Act, the Water Pollution Act, and other laws for conserving natural resources.

In contrast to Earth Day, World Environment Day had a carefully structured start. It served to open a privately sponsored conference, held June 5–8 in the New York Hilton Hotel and in the United Nations headquarters.

For the San Francisco-based Sierra Club, it was also the 14th Biennial Wilderness Conference. (Its 1951 conference brought forth the idea of a U.S. Wilderness Act, a proposal that became a reality 13 years later.)

For the New York-based National

Pisgah National Forest, North Carolina. All ecosystems, says René Dubos, must be protected from "unwise management . . . by technology."

Audubon Society, the Earthcare conference provided an opportunity to present the global conservation story on the club's home grounds—the capital of U.S. press and television, the capital of corporate finance, the home of influential foundations that could grant funds, and, not least, the home of the United Nations. The Audubon staff long has been accustomed to working in this heady world of media, money, and political activity.

A CALL FOR WISDOM

"Unwise management of nature by technology," René Dubos once said, "can destroy civilization in any climate and land, under any political system." An eminent bacteriologist and a professor emeritus of The Rockefeller University, Dubos was chosen by the Sierra-Audubon leadership to speak on World Environment Day. U.N. Secretary General Kurt Waldheim also was enlisted, and he welcomed the conferees to the U.N. headquarters.

Just what does Earthcare involve? In advance of the conference, its sponsors said: "The aim will be to encourage the inauguration of several campaigns to safeguard the world's irreplaceable natural heritage of forests, mountains, and seas, with emphasis on the fragile tundra, grasslands, wetlands, and urban open space."

Traditionalists may have been jolted when the conference planners added: "The concept of wilderness as viewed in North America may not be applicable elsewhere. New definitions for ecosystem protection need analysis, articulation, and support."

THREE MAJOR DANGERS

Earthcare speakers warned of three ways in which ongoing alteration of natural systems threatens the existence of the human race:

• Excessive consumption of energy. Dr. Dubos observed that, should global energy consumption keep on doubling every 10 years, consumption would "overtake the production of new energy by green plants within a century. . . . It would probably mean the destruction of life."

• The obliteration of animal, plant, and insect species. "Each natural area," Dr. Dubos noted, "constitutes a unique reservoir of biological species. The multiplicity of these reservoirs is the best and indeed the only insurance we have against ecological catastrophes inherent in the oversimplified ecological systems resulting from industrialization, urbanization, and modern agriculture."

• The upsetting of regional balances by chemicals or by other manmade innovations. "Super-pests," said Taghi Farvar, an Iranian ecologist, "were unleashed as the result of pesticide use" in many underdeveloped countries. In addition, a highly acclaimed engineering feat, the Aswan High Dam in Egypt, served to spread schistosomiasis, a disease that is carried by snails.

EARLY WARNING SYSTEM

Meanwhile, global cooperation on environmental matters has been moving along. There exists a United Nations Environmental Program (UNEP), complete with a 58-member Governing Council. That council met in Nairobi, capital of Kenya, in March 1974 and again in March 1975. The biggest single action was the authorizing of an "early warning system" to trace 15 pollutants around the globe. This setup will be known as GEMS —the Global Environmental Monitoring System.

UNEP cooperated in staging the Earthcare conference and sent its liaison officer, Dr. Noel Brown, to speak on "ecologically sound development." The UNEP's Governing Council, in its Nairobi sessions, had urged that priorities be given to research on helping arid lands. In particular it called for medium-range and long-range plans to stop the spread of deserts, which is most dramatic in famine-ravaged Africa but is a process also under way in Asia and South America.

Another area of concern for the UNEP is what it calls "human settlements," or better living conditions for the people. The United Nations body will contribute money for and take part in still another international gathering, to be called "Habitat: Conference on Human Settlements." That session will be held in the spring of 1976 in Vancouver, British Columbia, Canada.

Slowly, international conference by international conference, the world appears to be coming more receptive to environmentalists and their ideas. Some persons continue to dismiss environmentalists as faddists or "ecofreaks," unacquainted with the realities of business and political action. Now, however, the literature that scientists have been compiling for years has been gaining broader acceptance rather than being ignored as "scare talk"□

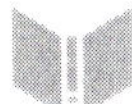

SELECTED READINGS

"It's Your Hide": environmental impact statement. *Outdoor Life*, November 1974.

"Yes—the Environment Can Be Saved" by William Ruckelshaus. *Saturday Review/World*, Dec. 14, 1974.

Glacier Peak Wilderness Area, Washington. Earthcare conferees warned against reckless alteration of natural systems.

This crowded beach on Spain's Mediterranean coast seems headed for ecological destruction and yet still more construction goes on.

Europe's Cesspool

by Alan Linn

VISIT the centuries-old Greek temple of Poseidon, god of the sea, and you will see the ancient columns crumbling from the corrosive bite of air pollution. The sun will be setting behind a man-made smokescreen, and the once-azure Mediterranean waters will be lapping the shore in sickly gray waves. Cross over the Adriatic Sea to Italy and you will be warned not to eat the local shellfish. Check in at some resort hotels in Marseille or Cannes and you may find the beaches closed to swimmers.

Today, the glorious Mediterranean of Homer and Vergil, the sensuous Mediterranean of the good life and the beautiful people, is becoming, inexorably, a sea of pollution, waste, and deterioration. The same people who have loved it over the ages—for selfish or generous reasons—have turned the Mediterranean into a cesspool. As a result, the world's largest inland sea is dying.

French oceanographer Dr. Alain Bombard gives the Mediterranean 25 years. Jacques-Yves Cousteau and many other experts agree with him. But whether or not their timetable proves accurate, the condition they have diagnosed is irrefutable. And, even more frightening, what is happening to the Mediterranean today will almost certainly happen to the rest of the world's large bodies of water tomorrow.

MODEL FOR ALL OCEANS

It is precisely this omen that makes the Mediterranean's survival crucial. On a planet covered more than 70 per cent with water, a planet whose oceans contain nearly 80 per cent of all life, the fate of any international sea cannot be ignored. And this particular sea, which is bordered by 21 nations and used by dozens more, is reacting more rapidly and more irreversibly to ecological stress than any other sizable body of water in the world.

Some 3,200 km (2,000 mi) long from Gibraltar to Syria, the Mediterranean is a model for all of the great oceans. The name "Mediterranean" comes from Latin words meaning "middle of the earth," and throughout history it has formed a great inland sea for the three continents of Asia, Europe, and Africa. On its shores, Western civilization took root. The systems of agriculture, art, philosophy, religion, law and city-building that define our society today began here. The first seagoing ships crossed the Mediterranean for fishing or trade or conquest. The first Western empires came to life and matured as one Mediterranean nation coveted the riches of another.

And as long as man has lived on the Mediterranean, he has been changing it—building on its shores, altering its landscape, using its resources, and polluting its waters. The inverted columns of the Minoan palace of Knossos on Crete were probably hewn from towering cypress trees which, along with pine and holly, once forested Mediterranean shores. Centuries before Christ, people were burning and clear-cutting the forested areas to make room for agriculture and herding. Then, in unwitting collaboration with the hot dry climate, thousands of grazing goats prevented reforestation.

IMPOVERISHED SEA

Homer called the Mediterranean "fish-infested," and there are still some 500 different species in the sea today. Relatively few are edible, however, and most of those have relentlessly been fished out. Today Sicilian fishermen still manage to trap a few of the Mediterranean's most important food fish, the bluefin tuna, or "tunny," with the same kind of nets their ancestors used. At a maximum length of 3.6 m (12 ft) and weight of 545 kg (1,200 lb), the tunny is the largest mackerel in the world. As it heads swiftly out to the open Mediterranean, it encounters a series of net chambers ranging from shore. Driven by instinct, the tunny proceeds from chamber to smaller chamber toward the sea, although it could escape merely by turning back. Finally it reaches the "chamber of death," where waiting fishermen spear it and haul it in.

This practice may soon disappear because, with commercial demands for the

Tourists, such as these at the Acropolis, are adding to Europe's growing pollution problems.

fish higher than ever, overfishing is finally taking its toll. At one time the Mediterranean was teeming with abundant schools of tunny. But now the middle-aged, welterweight bluefins of 40–115 kg (85–250 lb) that have provided the bulk of each year's spawning are quickly disappearing. When the last of these 15-to-20-year-olds, which produce most of the new fish, die or are fished-out, there will not be anything left to produce more tunny. As a result, in recent years harvests of the bluefin have declined considerably throughout the entire Mediterranean region.

Other beleaguered inhabitants of the Mediterranean are not faring much better. The sponges once used as cushions in Greek armor are nearly gone. Divers have been collecting these invertebrates since prehistoric times. The lustrous brown and white monk seal mentioned by Homer, Pliny, Plutarch, and Aristotle once flourished along most of the Mediterranean coast. Now, it numbers no more than a few hundred. Such majestic creatures as the dolphin, the sperm and rorqual whales, and the green and leatherback

Fish harvests have declined in all the seas of the Mediterranean region. Above: preparing fish for study aboard a Yugoslav hydro-biological research ship. Below: Greek fishermen.

turtles, still appear there. But by and large, the Mediterranean is an impoverished sea.

WINE DARK SEA

The total yield of food fish for the Mediterranean and the Black seas together is only 1.1 million metric tons a year. This is one fourth what the northwestern Atlantic produces, and one tenth the yield of the northeastern Atlantic. The Mediterranean, however, never was as prolific as its reputation suggests. That famous Mediterranean blue—the color Homer called "wine dark"—is actually the color of poverty. Seas rich with plankton, the basis of the marine food chain, are green, and the deeper the green, the richer the sea. The Mediterranean is blue and clear—where it has not yet been polluted—because there is little plankton to reflect the light.

A combination of natural factors contributes to this acute anemia. For one thing, the tides rarely exceed 5 cm (2 in). Consequently, there are almost no tide pools or intertidal zones to serve as nurseries of marine life, as in other oceans. Beyond that, shallow continental shelves—the richest zones of most oceans—are nearly absent in the Mediterranean. The coastline drops relatively sharply and steeply instead of slanting gently as most sea coasts do. Finally, the Mediterranean is saltier than most seas—4 per cent, compared with the Atlantic's 3.5 per cent—and much warmer. This is because it loses so much more water through evaporation (about 1000 tons a second) than it regains from fresh-water rivers. The result is an inhospitable natural environment for many life forms. But a variety of unnatural causes—basically industrial and municipal pollution—compound that problem almost beyond repair.

INDUSTRIAL POLLUTION

The Greek city of Eleusis, for example, the birthplace of Aeschylus and the celebrated site of ancient rituals, is now an industrial city of 20,000 people, dominated by the Petrola oil refinery and by

This photo of part of Venice shows an all-too-familiar scene—industrial complexes spewing wastes into the air creating a blanket of dirty air.

steel and cement works. Alarmed at the noticeable dimming of the famous sunlight of the region and the dismaying grayness of the once-blue Aegean Sea—that fabled arm of the Mediterranean stretching up Greece's eastern coast—2,500 citizens of Eleusis staged an emotional demonstration in September 1973. Fearful that expansion of the oil refinery and lack of waste treatment facilities for the cement and steel plants would do irreparable damage, they demanded more stringent controls. And yet, the dilemma of Eleusis is a mere fraction of the total problem.

From Spain to Syria, industrial complexes are spewing deadly chemical wastes into the air and water. As much as 1,000 million tons of industrial and untreated household wastes are dumped into the Mediterranean annually. Alain Bombard hardly needed to comment that "this waste blankets and kills all living things." Buildings that have withstood thousands of years of weathering are now blackening and crumbling from noxious fumes. Early in 1973, ominous gray and yellow clouds enveloped Venice and 50,000 factory workers had to wear army-style gas masks.

According to the UN Educational, Scientific and Cultural Organization (UNESCO), some 300,000 tons of oil residue are discharged into the Mediterranean each year—and this amount could be doubled in the next few years. If left unchecked, crude oil residue will literally strangle the Mediterranean. On the sea's surface, the oil film prevents the take up of oxygen and further takes oxygen from the water during its own breakdown. It also interferes with the photosynthesis of plant plankton. This, in turn, disrupts the entire marine food chain. Already the United Nations reports that the fish harvest from the Mediterranean has begun to decline. Anchovies have practically disappeared and sardines are getting scarce. Some of the pollutants constitute a direct threat to human life when they are ingested along with food fish. Mercury, for example, travels along the food chain to swordfish and other fish eaten by people.

AND THE TOURISTS

But in many areas, the tourists who flock to Mediterranean shores to enjoy the good life pose an even greater threat to the sea than oil residue. Along the Riviera, even modern sewage treatment plants cannot cope with the doubling or tripling of population—and the resulting raw sewage—that occurs every summer. Jacques-Yves Cousteau says that tourists are the real "heavies" of the oil pollution problem. Spills from huge tankers grab all the headlines, but, as he warns, unnoticed private boaters contribute far more oil—as well as garbage—than all the tankers combined. And the evidence is everywhere.

Cans and bottles cover the banks of the Arno River and float into the Mediterranean.

Plastic throw-away bottles bob in the sea far from sight of land. Detergent foam disfigures formerly unspoiled beaches. On the sea floor, plastic shopping bags snuff out life. Globs of petroleum waste the size of grapefruits form "tarbabies" on the sand.

OUTBREAKS OF DISEASE

Just as scientists believe the Mediterranean foretells the fate of other oceans, the Adriatic and Tyrrhenian seas around Italy may forecast the way the Mediterranean will go. "We shouldn't be surprised if some great ecological change were to take place within the next two years," Dr. Carlo Mortarino said in an interview. A professor of hydraulics at Italy's Turin University, Mortarino added: "Our coastal waters are already dead as a source of food and as an amenity. It's not a question of when the sea will be dead; for the Italian it has already happened."

For Italy, the problem is more than a matter of aesthetics. Typhus is endemic, and hepatitis is threatening too. No Italian in his right mind eats local shellfish. Of Italy's 8,000 km (5,000 mi) of coastal waters, more than 6,900 km (4,300 mi) are polluted by municipal and industrial runoff. In addition, the high radioactivity of some waters has caused outbreaks of rashes among bathers. In the summer of

Heavily polluted rivers such as this one near Naples flow into the Mediterranean.

1973, incidents of cholera began in Naples and soon spread as far north as Milan, eastward to Bari on the Adriatic, and westward to Sardinia. The disease claimed more than 20 lives. Italian Health Ministry officials blamed the outbreak on contaminated mussels taken from polluted waters off Italy and North Africa. In a drastic bid to prevent an epidemic, police frogmen uprooted entire shellfish beds in the Bay of Naples.

EVERYONE'S RIGHT, NO ONE'S RESPONSIBILITY

Though by now the facts of the Mediterranean's crisis are well known to experts and laymen alike, surprisingly little has been done to avert the disaster. The sad fact remains that the Mediterranean is "everyone's right, no one's responsibility." To get any kind of effective action, the concerted effort of all the nations using the Mediterranean is necessary.

All nations bordering the Mediterranean have signed preliminary agreements to study ways to eliminate pollution. And each of them has passed antipollution laws which are largely unenforceable. In the summer of 1973, representatives from most of the major Mediterranean cities met in Beirut, Lebanon, to urge their governments to put teeth into existing laws. The Mediterranean's pollution, they concluded, "has reached the danger point for the survival of the populations living around it." The resultant Beirut Charter called for the creation of an international antipollution code for Mediterranean cities. The United Nations supports related efforts. The experts stress that nothing will be done unless antipollution measures drawn up by the Mediterranean governments are honored by all the countries of the world whose tankers use the Mediterranean waters. And, of course, by all the tourists who annually visit the Mediterranean region.

Whether the many nations that have exploited the Mediterranean can now save it is one of the most urgent questions of our time. Some people say that it's already too late to turn a cesspool back into a clean and healthy sea. If that is true, what hope is there for the rest of the oceans that wash up on every continent and that serve us all? A recent UNESCO report emphasizes that "the Mediterranean can no longer wait." Neither, it seems clear, can the rest of the world□

A Venetian palace—hundreds of years old—now succumbing to the effects of air pollution.

SELECTED READINGS

"Mediterranean: Danger! Oil Pollution" by C. Munns. UNESCO *Courier*, January 1973.

Must The Seas Die? by Colin Moorcraft. Gambit, 1973.

Opposition to the Transafrican Highway stems in part from fear that the habitat and behavioral patterns of much of the wildlife will be threatened.

Here Comes the Transafrican Highway

by Norman Myers

SOMETIME in 1975, work will begin in central Africa on a monumental construction project—an awesome undertaking that, its proponents insist, will shed more light on the continent than the great dams of Kariba, Volta, Aswan, and Cabora Bassa combined. Unfortunately, its opponents emphasize, it will also create more environmental havoc than all of those other massive enterprises. The project in question is the Transafrican Highway.

Already more than three years in the planning, the highway will take at least that long to build. When it is finally completed, it will connect Lagos, Nigeria, on the Atlantic Ocean with Mombasa, Kenya, on the Indian Ocean, 7,080 km (4,400 mi) to the east. Passing through at least six nations, the new corridor will link the giants of tropical Africa—Nigeria, Zaire (formerly Congo-Kinshasa), and Kenya—for the first time. It will traverse rain forests, savanna grasslands, thorn scrublands, and deserts. It will scale mountain passes 3,350 m (11,000 ft) high, and it will cross the equator.

ECONOMIC OPPORTUNITY

Few deny that the passageway will present an unparalleled economic opportunity for Africa's developing countries. But the price of such progress, many environmentalists warn, will be forbiddingly high. The highway will pave the way for traumatic development in some of the most complicated and sensitive wilderness areas in the world. In fact, critics charge, it will constitute a far greater threat to wildlife than the controversial Transamazon Highway in Brazil, the Baja Highway in Mexico, and the Alaska-Canada roadway in North America.

Barring any unforeseen political difficulties, however, the highway is going to be built. In the summer of 1971, the Transafrican Highway Bureau was set up in Addis Ababa, Ethiopia, and the nations along the proposed route assigned a feasibility study. To no one's surprise, the study concluded that the roadway was indeed feasible. Since then, the project has been endorsed by most African leaders—for obvious reasons. Of all the continents, Africa is by far the worst off in

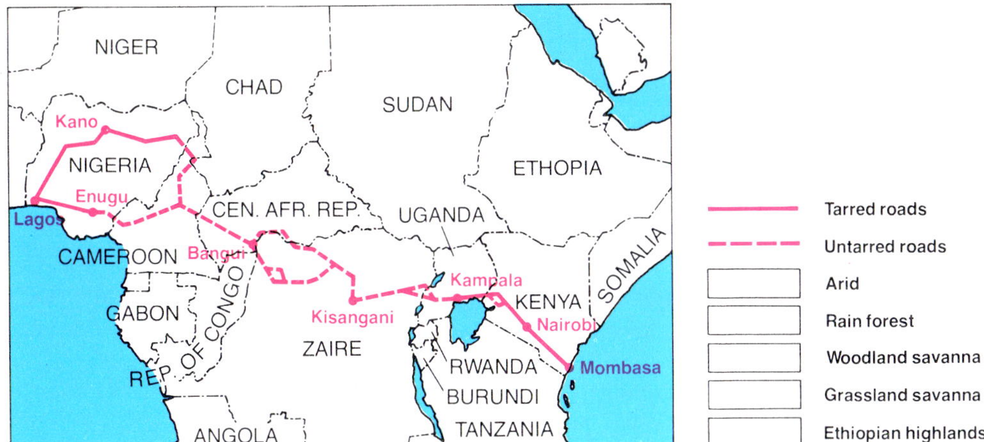

terms of transportation and communications in general.

Within Africa's English- and French-speaking zones, transportation networks are bad enough. But to get from one zone to another is a major undertaking. If you are in Niger, for example, and you want to get over the border south into Nigeria, you have a problem. There are plenty of airlines flying out of Niger to Europe and even to Asia, but only one (Air Algeria) flies from Niger to Nigeria. There are no trains or buses. It would not be at all unusual if you ended up making the trip in a contraband dealer's truck.

For the emerging African nations, however, the transportation problem is more than a matter of inconvenience. It strikes at the very heart of their crushing economic difficulties. Of Africa's total trade, only 5 per cent is internal. But there is massive potential for exchange between the East Africa nations of Kenya, Uganda, and Tanzania, and the West Africa nations of Niger, Nigeria, and Cameroon. Refined oil and timber could be sent from West Africa eastward, and textiles and other products from East Africa westward, into the heart of the continent. Africa's view of the gap between the haves and have-nots in the rest of the world is that Latin America and parts of Asia are achieving some degree of advancement, while Africa is falling further behind.

One major medium for development is international trade. But Africa faces prohibitively high tariffs and other trade barriers in more advanced nations. Hence, anything that enhances Africa's economic well-being by stimulating internal trade will benefit at least 100 million people in the countries directly affected by the highway. By and large, these people see as little cash in a year as most Americans spend on ice cream and soda pop.

WILDLIFE OR PEOPLE?

In the intensifying confrontation over the Transafrican Highway, the economic plight of the people bears special emphasis. For many Africans today insist that

The life style of these Masai-related tribesmen and of others will be seriously affected by the construction of the highway.

Giraffes are not seriously threatened by the road, but they will probably find some of their acacia tree-studded savannas altered.

those who oppose the highway place a higher value on wildlife than on people. Thus, the challenge confronting conservationists is to convince Africans that the principal aim in safeguarding wildlife is to better man's lot. And the conservationists might be advised to face the fact that the highway—though it will cause wide-scale disruption of wildlife in some areas—could operate, in the long run, to protect the best interests of those same species.

The double-laned tar or gravel road will range through widely different types of regions—from some of Africa's most arid

The road will cross semidesert areas like this as well as savanna, woodland, and rain forest.

environments to the wettest. From Mombasa on the Indian Ocean, the highway will head west through coastal hotlands and into Tsavo's thornbrush scrub country. After 240 km (150 mi) or so, the baobabs and acacia thorn trees give way to the plains of Masai land, with Kilimanjaro to the south and Mt. Kenya to the north. Beyond Nairobi, the roadbed will cut across the Great Rift Valley, with its ranching savannas, before climbing the western wall to the 270 m (900 ft) Mau forests and their cool pine plantations. From there, the road will cross into Uganda, a land of lush vegetation watered daily by storms off Lake Victoria. And at the border of Zaire, just north of the Ruwenzori mountain range, the road leaves East Africa.

Since the highway will follow already well-established routes in East Africa, it will have little direct effect on the great spectacles of wildlife in that part of the continent. In Zaire, however, the present forest tracks must be upgraded to highway standards. That means open season for bulldozers and chain saws through several hundred kilometers of complex rain forest. And yet, the ecological effects of a cleared strip approximately 90 m (100 yd) wide will, in and of itself, be trifling in the immediate locale.

If the road were abandoned, Zaire's forests would reclaim the land within a few years. Elephants will lose only one millionth part of their forest forage. The occasional okapi will lose its patch of forest completely, but the result will be so marginal as to be insignificant. The same will be true for gorillas, pangolins, and a host of forest animals. The amounts of habitat and food to be lost to the road itself are simply not worth bothering about.

WITHIN REACH OF HUNTERS

What does matter, however, is the impact of the human communities that will follow the road through Zaire and settle the opened-up countryside. Within the first year, at least 16 km (10 mi) on either side of the road will almost certainly be colonized. Within five years, 80 km (50 mi) on either side will probably suffer from gross disruption. Not only will the forests be chopped, burned, and otherwise adapted to accommodate settlers, but in addition, resident wildlife will be brought within reach of hunters.

From northern Zaire, the highway will enter the woodland savanna zone of the Central African Republic (CAR), where, fortunately, it will traverse the heavily populated southern sector. Its immediate impact there will be far less dramatic than in the rain forests of Zaire. However, the highway will almost certainly increase ivory trade out of CAR's animal-rich northern sector to the markets of East Africa.

Passing from CAR into Cameroon, the road will take one of two possible routes. It will run directly through the Cameroon rain forest, which is home to endangered gorillas and chimpanzees, or it will go along a lengthy northern route toward Lake Tchad. Whichever route is followed, the pressure to exploit wildlife populations for meat, ivory, skins and trophies will be intense.

Nor will those pressures abate as the road crosses into Nigeria, the last country along its route. There, one third of all meat consumed is wild game. A porcupine sells for five U.S. dollars. In Ghana, a cane rat will not stay on a market stall for twenty minutes. Previously, transporting game from Africa's animal-rich areas to distant markets has been no easy task. But now, with the prospect of making quick money, a truck driver is unlikely to pass up a chance to buy an illegally killed antelope in Cameroon to sell in Nigeria.

How northern Africa's droves of wild animals will fare in the face of such new challenges remains to be seen. Elephants, antelopes, cats, and giraffes will probably not be threatened as continent-wide or regional species, but they will definitely be reduced in number and range. In Zaire, the northern strain of the white rhinoceros will find itself within 160 km (100 mi) or so of a major roadway for the first time. But the most threatened life forms of all may well be birds, insects and plants.

VULNERABLE BIRDS AND INSECTS

Many bird species of the tropical forests are highly susceptible to disturbance. They now find what they need in the way of food, shelter, and warmth within the forest all year round. Consequently they have not evolved the migratory traits that characterize many temperate-zone birds. A "sanitized" strip of human settlements only 1.6 km (1 mi) wide is enough to split a bird population into two segments. These segments may be more prone to further, perhaps critical, disturbance than a single, composite population. Certain localized forest species, occupying a tract

A typical Masai village—a group of homes, called a *boma,* surrounded by thorn barriers. Such scenes will probably become less frequent as the highway changes the economic status of the people so that fewer are "living off the land."

The new road will permit the transportation of products to distant markets, thus decreasing dependence on local markets such as this.

of only a few hundred square kilometers, could disappear altogether within five years of the highway's intrusion into their habitat. In fact, the highway may well eliminate some bird species even before they have been identified.

This danger applies more directly to very localized species of insects and plants in the rain forests. Conceivably, forest-clearing bulldozers could sweep away one such species after another. Over thousands of years different species of plants, insects, and birds have adapted to slight variations in their habitat. Far more than the savanna grasslands of Africa, with their millions of wildebeest, zebras and gazelles, the rain forests present the orchestration of wilderness forces at their most differentiated—and vulnerable. The disruption of that delicate balance may well prove to be the chief cost of the highway.

A Masai girl looking across the Great Rift Valley in western Kenya.

BEST HOPE?

Ironically, however, the highway could also be wildlife's best hope. Currently, Africa's population growth rates are higher than those of any other continent and the prospects for checking them are not good. Already, people are spilling out of the fertile agricultural areas into the savannas and anywhere else they can scratch out a living. In the near future, wildlife could well be driven to and confined to deserts and mountaintops—unless fundamental changes are made in the continent's economy. The highway will make those changes possible. It will facilitate the growth of modern trade, industry, and cities. Thus it will significantly reduce the inevitable strains of an economy based on "living off the land."

But a highway alone is not enough. Africans will reap few benefits from manufacturing textiles, footwear, and electronic products unless the nations with the most purchasing power lower their trade barriers. If the United States, for example, continues to refuse to accommodate competitive African goods in a truly open marketplace, some Africans must, perforce, return to the land.

These economic and social imperatives may sound far removed from "conservation" to the wildlife devotee who prefers to donate funds for catching poachers. But whereas the conservation methods of the 1950's served Africa's needs well enough into the 1960's, the 1970's must anticipate the problems of the 1980's. The serious conservationist had better adjust his sights accordingly. The future of wildlife lies as much with trade and balance-of-payment ratios as with gatherings of animal lovers. In a very real sense, the Transafrican Highway is an apt symbol of that pragmatic new outlook□

Aerosol spray cans, such as hair sprays, are thought to pose a serious threat to the earth's protective ozone layer. The chemicals that serve as propellants in the aerosols cause the removal of ozone molecules from the upper atmosphere.

Aerosols and the Ozone Layer

by George Haber

THE fragile ozone layer of the upper atmosphere is essential to life on earth. Over the past few years, atmospheric scientists have been studying the chemistry of this layer, which is still little understood. And they have come to the conclusion that it is definitely in trouble. The researchers differ in their notions of the severity of the trouble. But they agree that certain twentieth century technological "advances" are the cause.

THE IMPORTANCE OF OZONE

Ozone is a minor but important component of the atmosphere. It exists to some degree at virtually every altitude. Mostly, however, it is found as a "layer" in the stratosphere between 19 and 48 km (12 to 30 mi). It is most concentrated around 20 to 25 km (12.5 to 15.5 mi). At that height, most of the sun's relatively short ultraviolet rays break down molecular oxygen (O_2) into atomic oxygen (O). The atomic oxygen then combines with molecular oxygen to form ozone (O_3). A surplus of ozone gas does not build up because nitric oxides found naturally in the stratosphere act as a catalyst to destroy the gas.

The continued existence of the protective ozone layer has influenced the very nature of life and its evolutionary path, according to atmospheric researchers. In fact, some scientists believe that life would not have evolved on the seas and on the land if the ozone layer had not come into being.

Relatively little attention was paid for many years to the effect that human activities were having on this layer. It was generally assumed that there were none. Then, in 1970–1971, investigations into possible environmental consequences of a fleet of SST's indicated that this assumption was not true. It was found that nitric oxide emitted in the exhaust fumes of the aircraft could accelerate the ozone layer's breakdown.

Another source of ozone-destroying nitric oxide was discovered soon after this bad news: thermonuclear explosions. Under the intense heat generated by these explosions, said some investigators, oxygen and nitrogen are broken down and large quantities of nitrogen oxides are created. Could the series of nuclear tests conducted by the United States and the Soviet Union in the early 1960s—and by other nations since—have done serious damage to the ozone layer?

Another question also came to be asked. Could the fact that the reported rising incidence of skin cancer over the past decade be attributed to ozone layer breakdown? According to the American Cancer Society, there is a well-defined causal relationship between skin cancer in fair-skinned people who have had excessive exposure to the ultraviolet radiation from the sun. Scientists are reluctant to pin the blame for increased reports of skin cancer on ozone depletion, however. One reason is the poor reporting of skin cancer cases over the years.

A NEW THREAT: AEROSOLS

At any rate, it became evident that there are good reasons to be concerned about the ozone layer. And even as the public was absorbing the news about SST's and thermonuclear explosions, researchers began publishing studies that cited an even more serious danger to the ozone layer from a seemingly innocuous source: aerosol spray cans and refrigerants.

The first warning appeared in the June 28, 1974 issue of the British scientific journal *Nature*. The authors, F. Sherwood Rowland, professor of chemistry at the University of California, Irvine, and Mario J. Molina, a research associate, charged that certain substances called chlorofluorocarbons are a threat to the earth's ozone. Chlorofluorocarbons are manmade chemical compounds that serve as propellants in aerosol sprays. That is, they are pressurized gases that release and spread the contents of an aerosol can in the form of a fine mist when the valve of the can is pressed. The gases are also used as refrigerants and in air conditioning units. Rowland and Molina reported that these compounds are actually six times more efficient than the nitrogen oxides in breaking down the ozone layer.

Chlorofluorocarbons are commonly known by their DuPont trade name of Freon, but the chemicals are manufactured under various trade names by a large number of chemical firms. Colorless and odorless, Freon-11 ($CFCl_3$) and Freon-12 (CF_2Cl_2) are composed of chlorine, fluorine and carbon. Relatively inert, they do not react with the paints, deodorants, perfumes, insect killers, or other substances with which they are used. A typical aerosol hairspray may contain 64 per cent of the inert compounds, a typical insecticide spray 80 per cent.

EFFECTS IN THE STRATOSPHERE

The stability of chlorofluorocarbons makes them desirable to manufacturers. It is this quality, however, that makes them a threat to the ozone layer, according to the article in *Nature*. Once they are released, they gradually ascend in the atmosphere—perhaps over a period of years—to stratospheric heights. There they are dissociated, or broken apart, into their separate atoms by the strong ultraviolet radiation of the sun. No published data support the fundamental premise that the most widely used compound, fluorocarbon, CF_2Cl_2, can decompose, but Rowland and Molina say that they have actually decomposed it.

The problem that results, if this is so, is that the breakdown of a chlorofluorocarbon molecule releases a highly reactive chlorine atom. A single such atom can act as a catalyst and, according to Rowland, cause the removal of thousands of molecules of ozone. Thus, very minute traces of chlorine in the ozone layer can have an extremely large effect.

Furthermore, if the aerosol compounds remain stable until they reach the stratosphere, far more than very minute traces of chlorine may be released into the ozone layer. From 1950 to 1973 inclusive, say Rowland and Molina, an estimated 5,897,000,000 kg (13,000,000,000 lb) of fluorocarbons were produced worldwide. More than 377,000,000 kg (831,000,000 lb) of the principal chlorofluorocarbons were sold last year in the United States alone, according to the U.S. Tariff Commission.

Normally, the ozone layer undergoes a continuous buildup and breakdown by natural processes. But if man goes on pumping these aerosol gases into the atmosphere at the present rate, says Rowland, it will only be a matter of two or three decades before the artificial destruction processes are comparable to the natural ones. In other words, destruction of the ozone in the stratosphere will go on at a greatly accelerated rate because of man's interference. But natural production of ozone will not increase in proportion.

So far, the fear of ozone layer destruction is based mainly on theoretical calculations. However, measurements of increasing chlorofluorocarbon concentrations in the troposphere have been recorded in the 1972–1974 period. A team of researchers from the U.S. Naval Research Laboratory (NRL) and the National Oceanic and Atmospheric Administration's (NOAA) Air Resources Laboratory monitored levels of Freon-11 in the upper troposphere over remote ocean sites. They found 61 parts of the compound per trillion (10^{12} parts) of air in November 1972, and 85 parts per trillion (10^{12}) in February 1973. These findings indicate that the chlorofluorocarbons are collecting in the troposphere at a rate approaching the increase in worldwide production. This in turn suggests that the total amount of the aerosol compounds dispersed in the troposphere is about equal to the amount produced to date. The NOAA and NRL report also confirms the belief that the compounds are unaffected by natural "sinks," such as rainfall, which act as regulators in removing other gases from the atmosphere.

MORE DIRE PREDICTIONS

No measurements have been made of the presence, much less the breakdown, of the chlorofluorocarbons at stratospheric levels. Just as difficult is the measurement of any ozone increase or decrease. But can we wait until such studies are made? Many concerned scientists think not. Time does not seem to be on the side of investigators of the ozone layer. Thus, Rowland believes that any attempt to monitor fluorocarbon dissociation and ozone layer depletion right now will not yield very significant results. According to him, one of the troublesome aspects of the situation is the delayed-action effect while the fluorocarbons are diffusing upward. If the destruction of the ozone because of the chemicals ever becomes measurable, it will by then have become too late to reverse the situation. Instead, the problem will remain for decades.

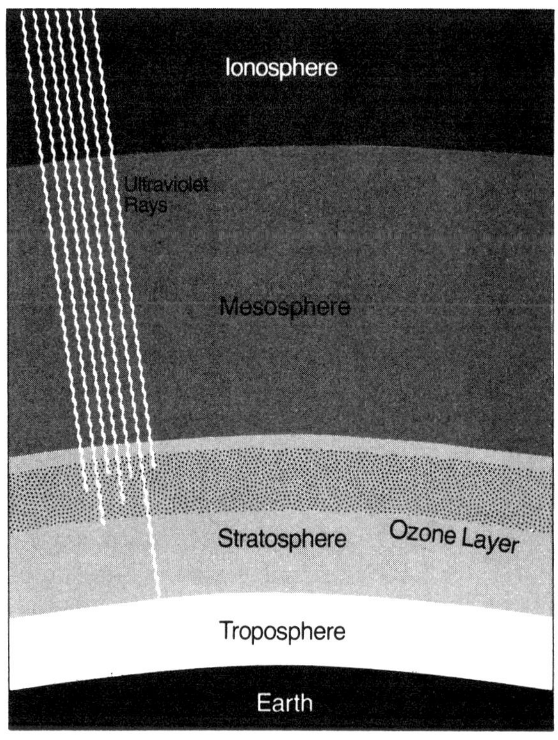

Rowland believes that if the use of chlorofluorocarbons continues at the present rate, their harmful effect on the ozone layer will be felt for 50 years or more. A group of investigators at Michigan's Space Physics Research Laboratory is also pessimistic. They gloomily predict that calculations based on current use of chlorofluorocarbons indicate widespread destruction of the ozone layer by the early 1980s. Even if chlorofluorocarbon emissions were curtailed now, they declare, the resultant ozone destruction would reach its peak around 1990 and would remain significant for several decades.

Still another prediction came from Harvard atmospheric scientists Michael B. McElroy, Steven C. Wofsy, and Nien Dak Sze, who performed various computer calculations assuming different rates of worldwide chlorofluorocarbon production. In a model describing the worst situation—an uninterrupted annual growth rate of 22 per cent—the researchers forecast a 40 per cent decrease in the ozone layer within 20 years. Even in a model based on an unrealistically low fluorocarbon increase, the researchers found the result would be a 5 per cent decrease in the ozone layer by the end of the century. This is enough to cause more than 8,000 additional cases of skin cancer a year, according to a 1973 study by the National Academy of Sciences (NAS).

As a response to all these ominous warnings, the NAS formed a five-man committee to study the fluorocarbons and the ozone layer. The group's chairman, Donald Hunten, an atmospheric chemist at Kitt Peak National Observatory, ominously summarized their findings: "The best opinion is that a problem is well on its way." Subsequently speaking for himself and not as a committee member, he said that he believed an immediate halt to the purchase of spray cans using the ozone-destroying fluorocarbons is in order.

In addition to the NAS committee, research groups formed by industry are conducting studies of their own. The Manufacturing Chemists Association of Washington, D.C., on behalf of chlorofluorocarbon manufacturers, has investigated possible reactions of these chemicals with other atmospheric components.

WHAT SHOULD BE DONE?

Whatever industry concludes, many independent scientists have already made a judgment. "There are only about a half a dozen people who are really qualified to have an opinion on this—certainly fewer than a dozen," said Kitt Peak's Hunten. "And they're all absolutely unanimous that the present indication is the ozone layer is being destroyed." The University of California's Rowland is not particularly pessimistic, however, despite sharing this opinion. He thinks that it will not be too long before substantial changes are made in the policy of the chlorofluorocarbon industry. Those compounds that are particularly dangerous, he expects, will probably be phased out. Freon-11 and Freon-12 are able to rise through the troposphere, according to Rowland, because they are not attacked by hydroxyl (OH) radicals, hydrogen, and oxygen compounds. "There are other fluorocarbons that *can* be attacked by hydroxyl radicals," he says, "and that would be removed primarily in the troposphere. These can be used in aerosols and should be much less of a threat to stratospheric ozone."

The task of finding alternative substances may not be so easy, however. And in the meantime, some scientists believe that society will have to weigh the benefits and risks of those presently in use. Windblown hair and overheated car interiors may seem out-of-date in the last quarter of the twentieth century. In the very near future, however, we may be forced to consider the price we are paying for our "modern" ways□

"Aerosols" by Janice Crossland. *Environment*, July/August 1974.

"The Crumbling Shield" by George Haber. *The Sciences*, December 1974.

"Why Aerosols Are Under Attack." *Business Week*, February 17, 1975.

How Safe Is Our Drinking Water?

by Eugenia Keller

AMERICANS have long considered clean, safe drinking water as a natural heritage. When they travel to other countries, they are often warned that the water there is not as safe. But now the tables are being turned. Visitors to the United States are sometimes well advised not to trust American drinking water. Its quality is becoming as uncertain as that.

From 1960 to 1970, 128 outbreaks of disease or poisoning were attributed to U.S. drinking water. In 1969, a study was made that covered nearly 1,000 public water systems supplying some 18 million users. The study showed that about 2.5 million people were drinking substandard water and about 360,000 were drinking water considered potentially dangerous. The smaller the community, the worse the problem seemed to become. One out of every five smaller water systems was found to deliver substandard water. And in 1975, a survey made by the U.S. Environmental Protection Agency (EPA) of the drinking water of 79 American cities revealed the presence of chemical pollutants in all cases—a clear indication of a nationwide problem.

Results of a 1975 EPA survey indicated "nationwide problems" in U.S. drinking water systems.

PICKING UP POLLUTANTS

Why should this be so? The answer is basically simple: water is an excellent solvent. It can dissolve more substances than any other known liquid—especially if it contains carbon dioxide. This is the property that renders water so necessary for life. And water travels everywhere. It evaporates from the land and the ocean. In vapor form, it is carried by wind currents to other parts of the world. It forms clouds, which condense and fall as rain or snow. On the earth's surface, water continues its journey by re-evaporating, flowing as runoff into lakes and streams, or seeping into the ground to join groundwater there. Eventually it returns to the oceans and the atmosphere again.

These two facts about water—its ability to dissolve substances, and its long cycle of travels—tell us why our drinking-water problems can exist. In its long journeys, water comes into contact with and thus has a chance to dissolve many substances. For example, during its fall from the clouds, rain dissolves gases and collects particles of matter. In a clean atmosphere it dissolves mostly nitrogen, oxygen, and carbon dioxide. But in a dirty atmosphere, it dissolves pollutants as well. Thus drinking water begins to become contaminated during the very first leg of its journey from clouds to our faucets.

One example attracting recent attention is "acid rain." Acid rain occurs mainly where large amounts of sulfur dioxide are discharged to the atmosphere. But recent studies have shown that rural areas, especially those downwind from industry, are also being affected by these discharges. Sulfur dioxide reacts with water to form sulfurous acid. This in turn is rapidly converted to sulfuric acid, a highly corrosive acid. When the water containing this acid falls as rain, it has serious effects on wildlife and vegetation. (See also "Acid Rain" on page 146.)

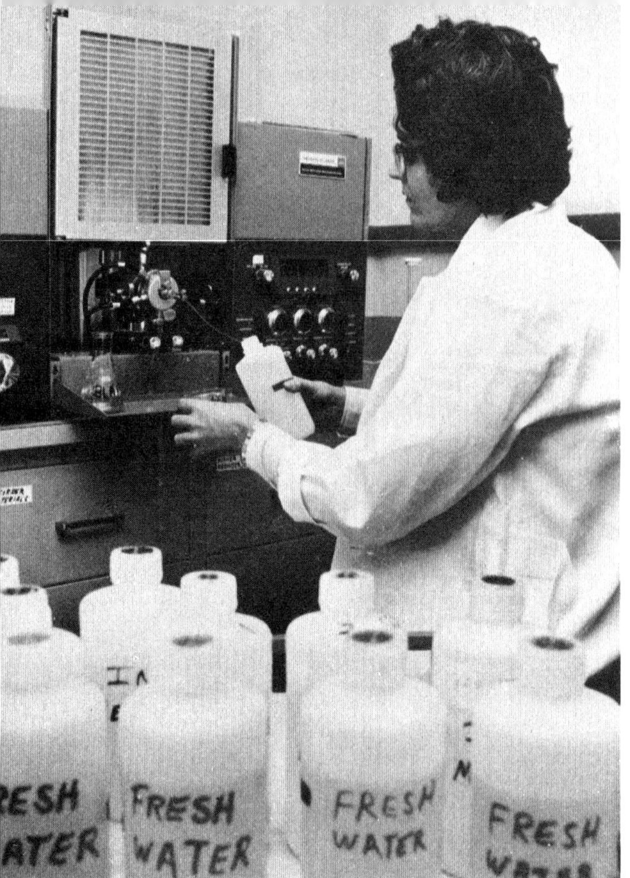

Metal contamination of surface waters is a serious problem. Here a Suffolk County, N.Y. researcher uses an atomic absorption spectrophotometer to test for 18 metals.

Heavy metals injected into the atmosphere, such as lead from automobile exhaust and cadmium from smelting operations, are also a matter of concern. In ice from cores drilled out of the Greenland icecap, scientists have found that the lead content increased about two and one half times from 1900 to 1950. In contrast, the lead content of ice scarcely increased at all over an earlier span of nearly 25 centuries of human history.

Airborne pollutants, such as pesticides sprayed by airplanes, and dust from vast expanses of agricultural lands, also are washed down by rain and snow. A question can be raised about certain chemicals, called chlorofluorocarbons, in aerosol spray cans. These chlorofluorocarbons, when breathed, are said to be a health hazard. (Also note the article, "Aerosols and the Ozone Layer," beginning on page 223.) Imagine their effect, then, if they are washed down in rain and ingested in drinking water. And in areas near plants that make the plastic known as polyvinyl chloride, vinyl chloride, a highly dangerous chemical, has been detected in the air in average concentrations of 0.5 to 1 parts per million. This chemical has been identified as a cause of angiosarcoma, a rare and fatal form of liver cancer.

SURFACE WATER AND SEWAGE

Contamination of drinking water continues during the successive legs of its journey. As runoff from agricultural lands, water dissolves or carries along materials such as animal wastes, fertilizers, pesticides, and minerals naturally present in the soil. Then, after it reaches lakes or streams, it picks up more contaminants from industrial and municipal wastes discharged into those bodies of water.

The repeated reuse of surface water by towns and industries adds many pollutants to the water. That is, a community or manufacturing plant draws water from a stream and discharges wastes downstream. Another community or plant still farther downstream draws in more water and discharges its own wastes, and so on. About 60 per cent of American public water supplies rely in this way on used water.

The magnitude of the problem is shown by the Mississippi River. Along the nearly 3,900 km (2,400 mi) of the river, water is withdrawn and discharged hundreds of times by cities and industry. For example, it has been estimated that besides industrial wastes, St. Louis alone discharges more than 800,000 liters (210,000 gallons) of liquid body wastes and 400 tons of solid body wastes each day. Yet in New Orleans, not too far from the mouth of the Mississippi, drinking water is still being drawn from the river.

Sewage contributes phosphates, nitrates, and organic matter to our water supplies. Disease-producing bacteria and algae are also to be found in sewage-polluted streams. Indeed, even the methods used in municipal sewage systems to deal with the pollution problem are now suspected of presenting hazards of their own. Chlorine, for example, has been widely used as a disinfectant in such systems since 1909. But studies have now revealed traces of chloroform and carbon tetrachloride in the drinking water for Cincinnati and New Orleans. These two compounds have been suggested by some studies as potential causes of cancer, in situations of long-term exposure. And they are believed to have been formed by reactions of pollutants with the chlorine used for disinfecting the water. In addition to forming toxic compounds, reactions of waterborne materials with chlorine trap the chlorine that would normally be available for disinfection. This does not mean that the use of chlorine is bad and that it should stop. Much more needs to be learned before any such decision is made. But it does mean that a problem exists, perhaps a serious one.

HAZARDOUS CHEMICALS AND METALS

Industrial pollutants in surface waters present a complex picture. For example, the organic chemical industry has discharged enormous quantities of chemicals —many of them not yet even identified— into lakes and streams. Some are known to cause cancer. In addition to their own toxicity, these chemicals can react with each other—and perhaps with chlorine— to form new toxic compounds. Few water-treatment plants are equipped to deal with these problems.

One such substance is the metal mercury. Tons of mercury used in making caustic soda have been discharged into surface waters. Because it is heavier than water, the metal was thought to settle on the bottom of lakes and remain inert. But suddenly mercury was discovered in fish. Later studies showed that, through the action of bacteria in the water, metallic mercury is converted to methylmercury, a soluble and poisonous compound. Thus the mercury that now resides in sediments may be gradually released into our waters in this dangerous form.

Even in our water pipes, water can become contaminated. In this connection, cadmium and lead are of concern. If the water is soft, it usually contains dissolved carbon dioxide. This forms carbonic acid which, when flowing through zinc pipes, extracts cadmium. (In nature, cadmium and zinc occur together, and many zinc products also contain traces of cadmium.) In the body, cadmium replaces zinc and is believed to play a role in some circulatory diseases such as high blood pressure.

Boston is an example of a city where lead is a problem. In some parts of the city, old lead pipes are still used. The drinking water, with its carbonic acid content, leaches out the lead. This hazard is said to have been discovered when a physician observed that a dog died of lead poisoning as a result of drinking daily from a certain water tap. In some of Boston's water, lead levels five times the maximum set by the U.S. government were found. In the Beacon Hill area of the city, lead pipes are being torn out.

CONTAMINATED GROUNDWATER

Pollution reaches underneath the surface of the land, as well. Groundwater is sometimes as contaminated as surface water, even though the earth itself is a natural purifying system for the water

Industrial pollution, such as that in the James River at Lynchburg, Va., presents complex problems for water-treatment plants.

passing through it. Nature's method of purification, like man's, includes filtration, adsorption, neutralization, and oxidation. These processes remove many natural contaminants such as carbonic acid—which, for example, can react with calcium ions in the soil and be precipitated out as calcium carbonate. Bacteria in the soil can decompose materials of biological origin. Thus, for the most part, harmful materials of natural origin can be removed. Two notable exceptions are the evil-smelling hydrogen sulfide (H_2S) present in some waters and excessive amounts of salts in brackish groundwaters.

However, man's activities are now overloading nature's purification system. Some of the added materials are of natural origin. Others are completely foreign to the system, such as pesticides, detergents, radioactive wastes, oil spills, and landfills. Of the many kinds of problems that now exist, only two examples will be given here. In one county on Long Island, New York, detergents have been found in groundwater, and their use has been banned. But some heedless families are said to purchase their detergents in neighboring counties. The other example is the asbestos-fiber pollution of Lake Superior. Each day some 67,000 tons of mining residues containing asbestos are dumped into the lake. Before 1955, Lake Superior contained no asbestos pollution. Today about 5,180 km^2 (2,000 mi^2) of the lake are contaminated with these fibers. Water samples have contained up to 12.4 million fibers per liter, or quart, whereas well water taken from near the lake showed only 20,000 fibers per liter. Thus, although most of the fibers were removed by nature's purification system, some did get through. Similar problems have been found in other areas, such as San Francisco, the Rocky Mountains, and Vermont. Asbestos is known to cause cancer in humans. And the number of fibers ingested by a person drinking Lake Superior water for 15 to 17 years can equal the number inhaled by a person who is exposed to asbestos at work.

Disposal of wastes by landfills and by dumping into deep wells or abandoned salt mines also troubles many scientists. Little is known about the circulation of groundwaters. Some waters move very slowly, traveling fewer than 15 m (50 ft) per year. Thus, contamination from deep-well disposal might not become apparent for years. A notable example of this problem occurred in a New Jersey area where no industry is nearby. A company dumped petrochemical wastes into a landfill a good hour's drive away. Not until two years later was contamination discovered in surrounding wells. But there it was, indeed. The water contains petrochemicals but their identities are unknown. It has neither odor nor taste, and so far no sickness has appeared. But what might happen in the future, scientists can only guess. Some 148 of the wells have been closed. And in any given location, contamination might appear one day and be gone the next. Of three houses in a row, water in the middle house might test negative while that in the two end houses might be contaminated.

From this brief survey, one can easily see why many scientists feel that our drinking water supplies are in serious trouble. Help may come before it is too late. The EPA, as indicated, is conducting a systematic study of the chemical and bacterial content of all municipal drinking water supplies in the country. And legislation permitting the federal government to set standards for all water supplies has been passed by both houses of Congress. But it remains to be seen what real steps will be taken, and how quickly and on how large a scale. The problems are not small, and left to themselves they will only continue to grow worse□

SELECTED READINGS

"Drinking Water: Another Source of Carcinogens?" by Jean L. Marx. *Science*, November 29, 1974.

"How Safe Is Your Drinking Water?" by Jack Ryan. *Family Health*, September 23, 1974.

Our Dirty Water by Sarah M. Elliott. Messner, 1973.

health and disease

1975 has seen several protests by physicians. In March some New York interns and residents struck over long working hours in hospitals (above). In June many private physicians went on strike to protest the sharply rising costs of malpractice insurance.

review of the year

health and disease

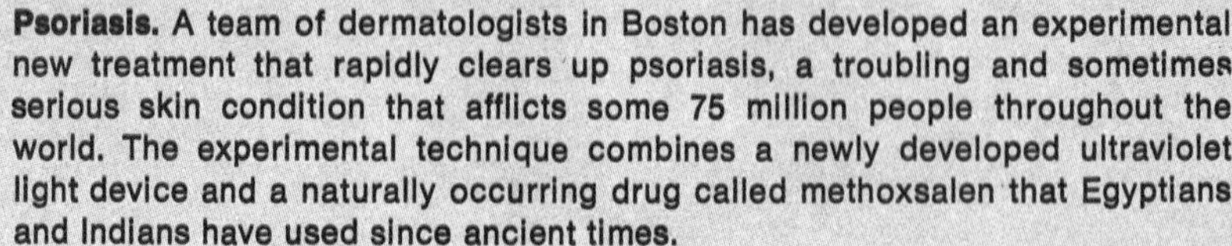

Psoriasis. A team of dermatologists in Boston has developed an experimental new treatment that rapidly clears up psoriasis, a troubling and sometimes serious skin condition that afflicts some 75 million people throughout the world. The experimental technique combines a newly developed ultraviolet light device and a naturally occurring drug called methoxsalen that Egyptians and Indians have used since ancient times.

The new therapy is not a cure for psoriasis, whose name is derived from the Greek word for itching. The chronic, relapsing skin disorder is a genetic disease that is inherited in a poorly understood pattern. Nevertheless, the new technique achieved complete clearing of the red, scaly patches that covered more than half the body of the first 85 patients that were treated by researchers at the Massachusetts General Hospital in Boston and by an Austrian co-investigator in Vienna. The patients selected had severe cases of psoriasis that had not cleared with standard therapies. The side effects of the new treatment—nausea and itching—were reported as minimal.

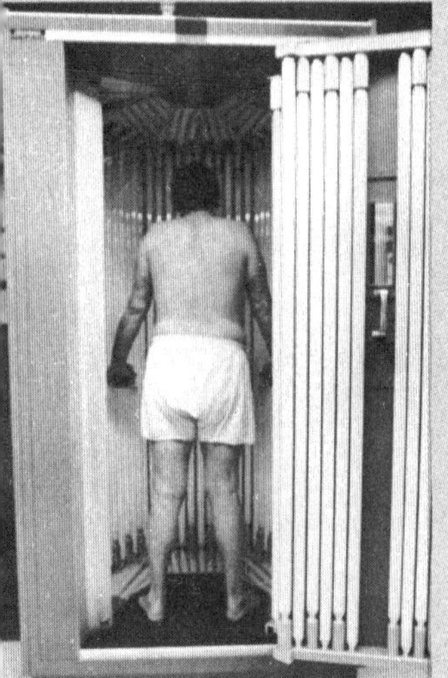

In a chamber about as big as a small shower stall, ultraviolet light—along with a drug called methoxsalen—is used in an experimental new treatment of psoriasis at Massachusetts General Hospital, Boston.

Psoriasis patches characteristically appear on the scalp, elbows, knees, back, and buttocks. But they can break out at any time anywhere on the body. Though psoriasis seldom causes death, the appearance of the patches is embarrassing and leads to serious psychological problems for many patients. Psoriasis, for example, can limit sexual intercourse for those with patches in the genital area.

For many patients, psoriasis is confined to such a small area that it requires no treatment or only periodic applications of coal tars and similar ointment preparations. But in others, the psoriasis clears after long, costly hospitalizations, only to come back after a patient goes home. One patient who benefitted from the new therapy had been hospitalized 36 times for psoriasis.

Drs. John A. Parrish, Thomas B. Fitzpatrick, Lewis Tannenbaum, and Madhukar A. Pathak, who developed the new therapy at the Massachusetts General Hospital, said that it is effective only if both pills and the high-intensity, long-wave ultraviolet light system are used. The new system does not work if the pills are combined with use of a sunlamp. Methoxsalen belongs to a family known as the furocoumarins, or psoralens. They are derived from celery, carrots, parsnips, parsley, figs, limes, and other plants.

The ultraviolet light system was made by GTE Sylvania of Danvers, Mass., at the specific request of the Boston investigators. Just two devices existed at the time the doctors made their experimental results public, and they expect that it will be 1976 at the earliest before the therapy can be generally available.

The devices can be used in two ways. The patient either lies in a bed that is slid under a horizontal device lined with rows of 48 specially designed light tubes, or the patient stands in a cylindrical chamber about the size of a small shower stall. Two hours after swallowing the pills—when methoxsalen is at its peak intensity in the skin—psoriasis patients are exposed to the ultraviolet light for from eight to 30 minutes.

In psoriasis, for reasons doctors do not understand, skin cells replicate up to 10 times faster than the usual 28-day cycle. The drug interferes with the skin's molecular biology. Within the range of long-wave ultraviolet light, the drug inhibits the synthesis of DNA (deoxyribonucleic acid) in the skin cells. Because the effects of the treatment stop at the skin and ultraviolet light cannot penetrate deeply, interior parts of the body are unaltered.

The number of treatment sessions varies with the individual. After about a dozen such treatments, the psoriatic lesions disappear, leaving a deep tan in the skin of the patients. Just how often the treatment must be repeated to maintain psoriasis-free skin cannot be determined until doctors gain further experience with the new therapy. Ultimately, the investigators hope the devices can be made at a sufficiently low cost so that dermatologists can have them in their offices and some patients in their homes.

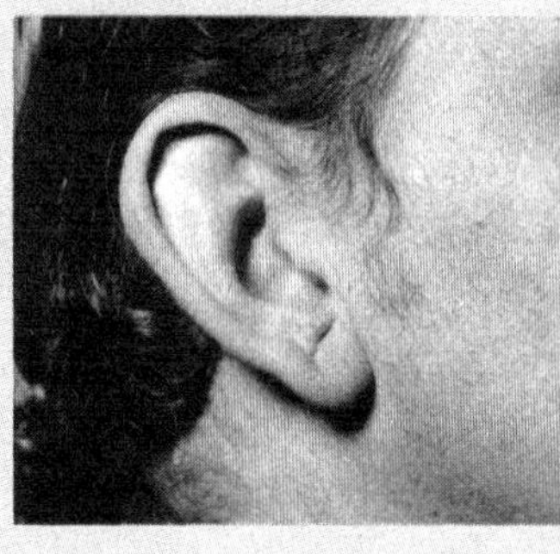

In a study of 144 patients with suspected heart disease, Mayo Clinic researchers found 133 had creased earlobes—and for 120 of them the diagnosis of heart disease was confirmed. However, no one has established a physiological link between creased lobes and heart disease.

Heart Disease. Heart disease remained the No. 1 killer in the United States in 1974. An epidemic of heart attacks continues to cause premature deaths among Americans and people living in other developed countries. Several studies have left little doubt that cigarette smoking contributes significantly to the risk of heart disease and death. American researchers have documented in a long-term study that men under 65 who gave up smoking cigarettes suffered fewer heart attacks and lived longer than men who continued to smoke. Though doctors have long suspected a link between quitting smoking and reducing the incidence of heart attacks, these findings from a study made among residents of Framingham, Mass., are believed to be the first that document the hypothesis. The investigators could not determine whether the cardiac benefits from stopping smoking had their full impact immediately, or only after some time had elapsed. But there was an apparently prompt drop in the incidence of coronary heart disease when men stopped smoking. This suggested that smoking has a noncumulative, reversible triggering effect rather than a direct influence on the promotion of arteriosclerosis, the process that underlies heart attacks.

Two Hearts in Parallel. In South Africa, Dr. Christiaan Barnard, the cardiac surgeon who did the first heart transplant in 1967, devised another experi-

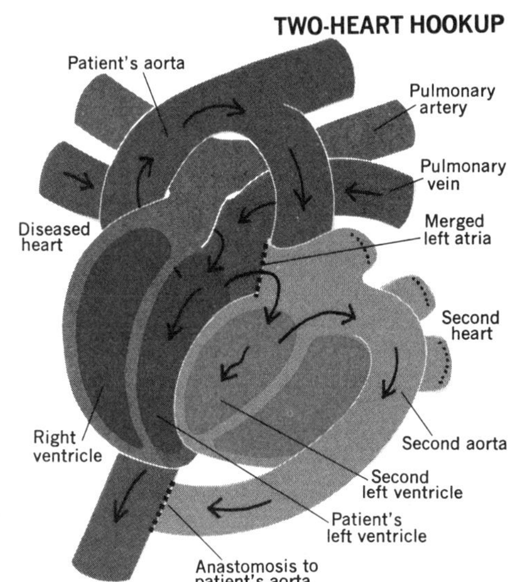

The diagram shows basically how Dr. Christiaan Barnard connected the circulation of two hearts in parallel. It was the first time the donor heart was sewn to the recipient's heart, giving the patient two hearts working together.

mental surgical technique in an attempt to extend the lives of some patients with terminal heart disease. In two patients, Dr. Barnard implanted a second heart, leaving the patient's diseased heart in place, and connected the circulation of the two hearts in parallel.

"It's like two farm dams adjoining one another. When the first dam fills up, it overflows into the side dam and so relieves the pressure on the walls of the main dam," Dr. Barnard said. American experts in heart disease, surprised by Dr. Barnard's latest feat, applauded the Capetown surgeon for his imagination but pointed out that the new technique does not overcome the immunologic rejection phenomenon that has limited the usefulness of heart transplant surgery. The first patient to have the twin hearts died four months after the procedure.

Cancer. Discovery of a link between exposure to polyvinyl chloride (PVC), a widely used chemical in the plastics industry, and a rare type of cancer of the liver, called angiosarcoma, focused attention on the importance of occupational health. More than a score of chemical workers have been found to have died from angiosarcoma since Dr. John L. Creech, Jr., a physician for the B. F. Goodrich Co. in Louisville, Ky., first made the association between the chemical and the cancer. Dr. Creech found that all the original group of affected workers were directly involved in the production of polyvinyl chloride from vinyl chloride, a gaseous chemical known to damage the liver at high concentrations. Vinyl chloride, a simple molecule, is the foundation for much of the modern plastics industry. Large numbers of vinyl chloride molecules are joined to form the polymer polyvinyl chloride.

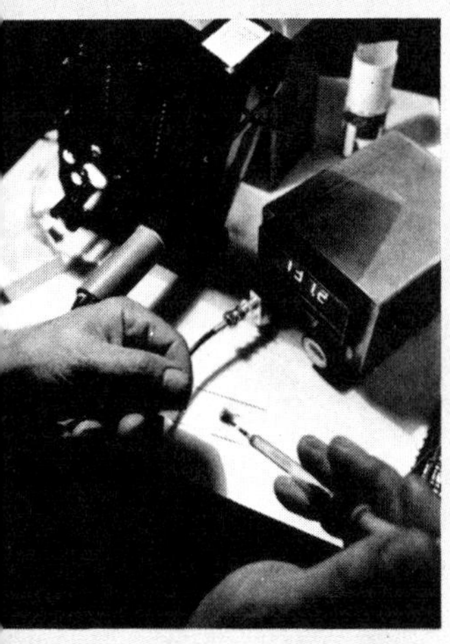
A quick, easy, and inexpensive blood test for lead poisoning has been devised at Bell Labs.

Tens of thousands of American workers participate in the conversion of the raw materials, vinyl chloride and polyvinyl chloride, into countless products such as paints, furniture, upholstery, draperies, toys, clothing, phonograph records, dentures, bottles, and pharmaceutical products. It takes many years of exposure for the cancers to form. Angiosarcoma has also been found in workers who convert the polymer into finished products. Accordingly, federal officials regarded the situation as a serious emergency requiring immediate action. Subsequent medical investigations in the United States and elsewhere have pointed to an increased risk of other types of more common cancers among PVC workers. (See also "Vinyl Chloride" on page 263.)

Ultrasound. Doctors are beginning to rely more on ultrasound as an aid in diagnosing heart conditions. Animals such as bats use ultrasound to communicate and to sense their environment. In medicine, the technique's advantage is in being noninvasive—that is, it does not require inserting tubes and chemicals into the heart as is done in cardiac catheterization. The ultrasound technique involves bouncing sound waves off the heart. The sound waves are of such high frequency that they cannot be detected by human ears. Using equipment that costs $20,000, cardiologists can view the anatomical features of the heart in a form called an echocardiogram.

Echocardiography is rapid and involves no pain, needles, or radiation hazards. It can be done on an outpatient basis to get information that otherwise must be derived from X-ray tests called angiograms and other complicated procedures. In some cases, echocardiography can provide information not obtainable by any existing technique. However, echocardiograms are not routine tests, nor a substitute for all heart catheterizations.

A decade ago, ultrasound's chief use in cardiology was to detect abnormal collections of fluid in the pericardial sac that surrounds the heart. Such pericardial effusions, which can impair the heart's ability to pump enough blood, can be caused by several conditions like tuberculosis, viral infections, and collagen diseases like lupus. Now, echocardiograms have become in some instances an important diagnostic aid in detecting heart valve damage, like mitral stenosis, which is a frequent complication of rheumatic fever and infections called bacterial endocarditis. With the echocardiogram, doctors are collecting further evidence that one type of obstruction of the aortic valve results from a genetic disorder.

Echocardiograms can also help a doctor confirm a suspected diagnosis of atrial myxomas, which generally are noncancerous tumors of the heart. Though benign, myxomas can cause fatal complications. They can be cured by open-heart surgery.

Pediatric cardiologists are using the technique to help diagnose many of the birth defects that affect the heart, and doctors are using it as a research tool in coronary care units. The technique also is used by neurologists, neurosurgeons and obstetricians, among others, to diagnose noncardiac disorders.

Epidemics. Thousands of visitors who drank tap water while visiting Leningrad, Soviet Union, returned home with an intestinal parasitic infection that can last months unless it is treated with a drug specifically effective against the ailment. Giardiasis, which is caused by the parasite *Giardia lamblia,* is one of the most common parasitic infections throughout the world. Just why the infection now seems to be concentrated in the Soviet Union is puzzling. Giardiasis is not the same condition as traveler's diarrhea, which comes at the beginning of a trip and generally disappears without treatment. Giardiasis often does not begin until after the trip has ended. Doctors can diagnose giardiasis by looking through a microscope at a stool specimen to detect the pear-shaped parasite which thrashes around in the small intestine to sap the body of vital nutrients.

A person with giardiasis can have prolonged diarrhea, abdominal cramps, severe weight loss, fatigue, nausea, and flatulence. Fever is unusual. Others have no symptoms yet pass the parasite in their stools. Symptoms usually disappear promptly after treatment with either of two drugs—Atabrine or Flagyl. Giardiasis cannot be prevented by taking pills.

DMSO. Dimethyl sulfoxide, an inexpensive byproduct of paper pulp processing, has been hailed by some people for its allegedly startling powers in helping to provide rapid relief from cold sores, ankle sprains, bursitis, shingles, skin ulcers, and a vast array of other conditions, common and rare. But the U.S. Food and Drug Administration, acting on reports of eye damage in animals given DMSO, clamped down on human testing a decade ago. As a result, DMSO has become one of the most mysterious and controversial drugs known. Now, in a hard second look at DMSO, FDA officials have made it clear that the key obstacle to licensing DMSO for prescription use in humans in the United States is not toxicity, but scientific proof of its efficacy. To this end, the FDA says it has approved more investigators' applications to study the myriad of benefits claimed for DMSO. The drug causes the body to give off a strong garliclike odor for an hour or two after it is rubbed on, swallowed, or injected. DMSO soaks through the skin instantly with the apparent ability to speed the healing process and carry other drugs with it to virtually all organs except the teeth and nails. Accordingly, some researchers are studying DMSO with the idea of using it to deliver cancer drugs to selected sites and to combine it with antiviral drugs that cannot penetrate the skin.

Lawrence K. Altman, M.D.

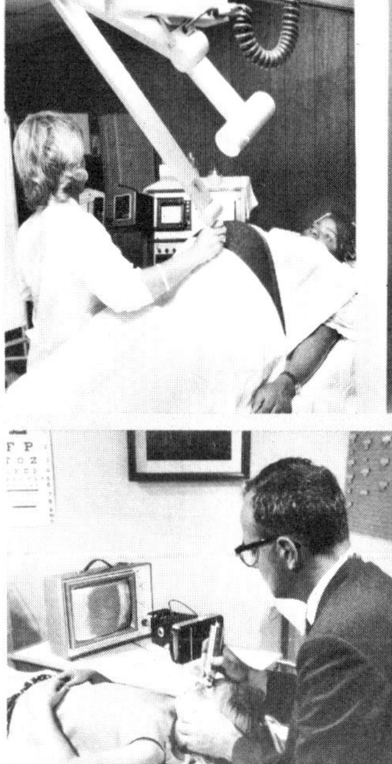

The ultrasonic scanner is becoming an important tool in diagnosis. One scanner is used in examining a pregnant woman at a high-risk obstetrics clinic; the other aids in an eye examination.

Herpes VD

by Richard R. Leger

A 19-day-old infant was admitted to Atlanta's Grady Memorial Hospital, an affiliate of Emory University School of Medicine. She wasn't eating well, was lethargic and had a yellowish discharge from her left eye.

The child was treated with antibiotics but her condition worsened. Finally, after a fruitless search of more than two weeks for the cause of the illness, doctors cultured germs from her throat. They discovered an infection by a virus—herpes simplex Type 2. Despite efforts to treat her, the infant now is in a home for brain-damaged children.

The child's tragedy is a rare but important consequence of a growing national medical problem. Until recently the problem—venereal disease caused by herpes virus Type 2—was almost unrecognized by doctors and the general public. The Atlanta infant contracted the disease at birth from her mother, whose venereal affliction had gone unnoticed.

VD caused by herpes virus differs importantly from the better-known venereal diseases such as gonorrhea and syphilis. The latter diseases are caused by bacteria. These diseases, if treated promptly with strong doses of antibiotics, almost always can be cured. But venereal herpes, like nearly all virus diseases, cannot be cured by antibiotics or any known medication.

LINKS TO CANCER?

Herpes VD may be reaching pandemic proportions in the United States. In early 1974 medical experts estimated that some 250,000 Americans would contract or experience recurrent episodes of venereal herpes during the year. The virus that causes venereal herpes is similar to the virus—herpes simplex Type 1—that causes cold sores or fever blisters on the face. But Type 2 is almost always acquired through sexual contact, doctors say. It is highly contagious.

There is growing evidence, too, that herpes venereal disease may lead to cancer of the cervix and perhaps the prostate. Dr. Paul Wiesner of the U.S. Public Health Service's venereal disease control unit, part of the Center for Disease Control in Atlanta, remarks, "The morbidity for babies plus the association with cancer makes the cases very significant."

Herpes VD may trail only gonorrhea as the most prevalent venereal illness in the United States. No one knows for sure, because reporting of cases isn't required by the U.S. Public Health Service. Dr. William E. Josey, associate professor of gynecology and obstetrics at Emory, estimates there has been a threefold-to-fourfold increase in venereal herpes in the past 10 years.

"There has been a marked change in sexual behavior patterns," Dr. Josey says. "The casual sexual encounter is now prevalent in the middle class. On top of that, you've got a disease that recurs, and intercourse may be one of the things that activates it. There's no treatment, you've got the disease for life, and every time it recurs you can potentially infect other people. It's as simple as that."

STEPPED-UP RESEARCH

Much of what is known about herpes Type 2 has been gleaned only in recent years. Before 1967, doctors believed that herpes venereal infections were caused by the same virus that causes cold sores. But then a pioneer in herpes research, Dr. Andre J. Nahmias, professor of pediatrics and chief of infectious diseases and immunology at Emory's medical school, and associated researchers in Atlanta made an important discovery. They found that one type of herpes virus caused most of the facial infections and a second caused some 90 per cent of those in genital areas—hence the designations Type 1 and Type 2. Either herpes virus, however, can infect any part of the body.

Since then, doctors have been stepping up their research on the scope and seriousness of Type 2 infections. And the medical and social implications are unpleasant.

For example, about 1 per cent of Grady Memorial's maternity cases have active genital herpes infections during their pregnancies. As many as one-fourth of these women have the infection at the time of childbirth. Present data suggest that if a baby from such a patient isn't delivered by Caesarean section, it stands at least a 25 per cent chance of dying from a herpes infection. And of those infants who survive, about one-third will have serious medical problems, Dr. Nahmias says. In addition, pregnant women with herpes Type 2 have about three times as many spontaneous abortions as women who don't, he says.

Several studies have shown a definite link between venereal herpes and cancer of the cervix, although it hasn't been proven that herpes actually causes cancer. In one Emory University study under way for several years, 900 women with herpes Type 2 infections have been compared with a control group of 600 women who haven't had the infection. So far the results indicate that the women with herpes infections are eight times more likely to develop localized cervical cancer than the control group. The study is being conducted by Emory's herpes research team, led by Dr. Nahmias, Dr. Josey and Dr. Zuher M. Naib, director of cytology.

The studies also indicate that 6 per cent of women who get herpes Type 2 infections will contract cervical cancer within five years, Dr. Nahmias says. The association between cervical cancer and herpes Type 2 infections is as strong as that linking cigarette smoking and lung cancer, he asserts.

In the controversial "dye-light" treatment for herpes simplex, the external lesion is coated with a special dye (left) and then exposed to fluorescent light (right). The lesion dries and forms a crust within two days.

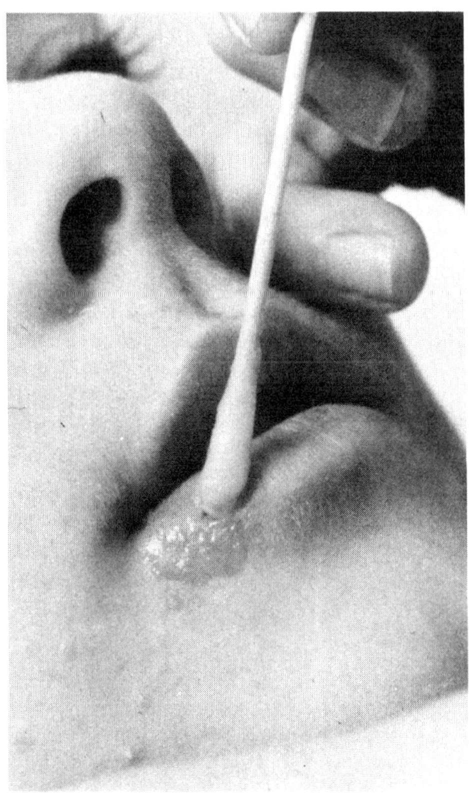

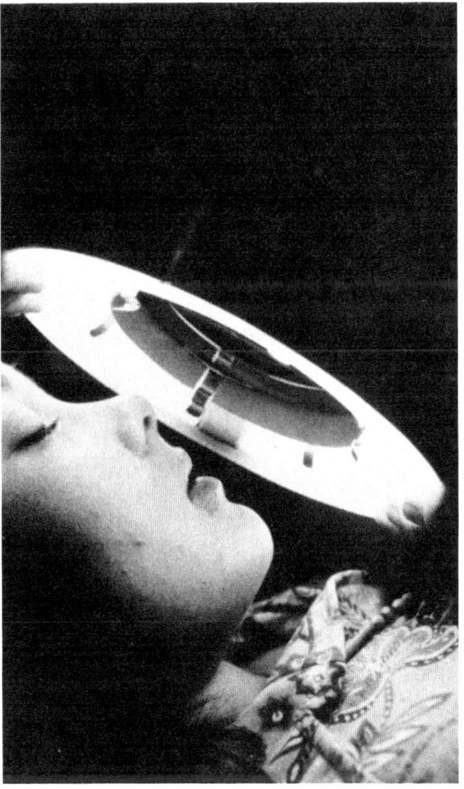

SYMPTOMS

Symptoms of venereal herpes usually appear within two to 20 days after exposure. About six days is average. In the male, small lesions or blisters usually appear on the outside of the penis, although the urethra may also be infected. In the woman, the lesions may be external, even on the buttocks, but they usually occur internally, in the cervix. Cases frequently are mild and even unnoticeable. But they can be more serious, lasting for as long as six weeks, with fever, headaches and other symptoms.

"I have one patient, a divorced woman, who was hospitalized for over a week, to whom I gave narcotics because of the pain," says Dr. Ellis Mitchell, a dermatologist in Greenbrae, California, and president of the Bay Area Venereal Disease Association. "She lost her job as a clerk in a store because she was away from work, and she had to get neighbors to take care of her kids. The psychological trauma can be enormous and the physical pain tremendous." He adds: "Ten years ago it was an uncommon event to see a patient with genital herpes. Today, there are days when I see up to 10 patients a day with it."

Part of the reason for the current outburst of genital herpes cases, doctors say, is that many infected persons don't have obvious symptoms and thus are unknowing carriers.

RECURRING, CONTAGIOUS ATTACKS

Herpes also is spreading because it frequently recurs after the initial infection, just as cold sores do. Dr. Wiesner of the Center for Disease Control estimates an average patient may have four or five relapses the first year and two or three the second year before symptoms stop coming back. The victim is contagious to others when the symptoms recur and may be contagious without knowing it if a recurrence is so mild as to be unnoticeable, he says. After active episodes of the disease it's believed that the virus retreats to nerve cells. There it is sheltered from being attacked by antibodies produced by the body in reaction to the virus.

There is no cure for the viral disease. And there is growing argument over whether there is any safe treatment to reduce the severity of the symptoms and the number of potential recurrences. Many doctors, including Dr. Wiesner and the Emory team, argue that good hygiene and perhaps some medicine to ease the

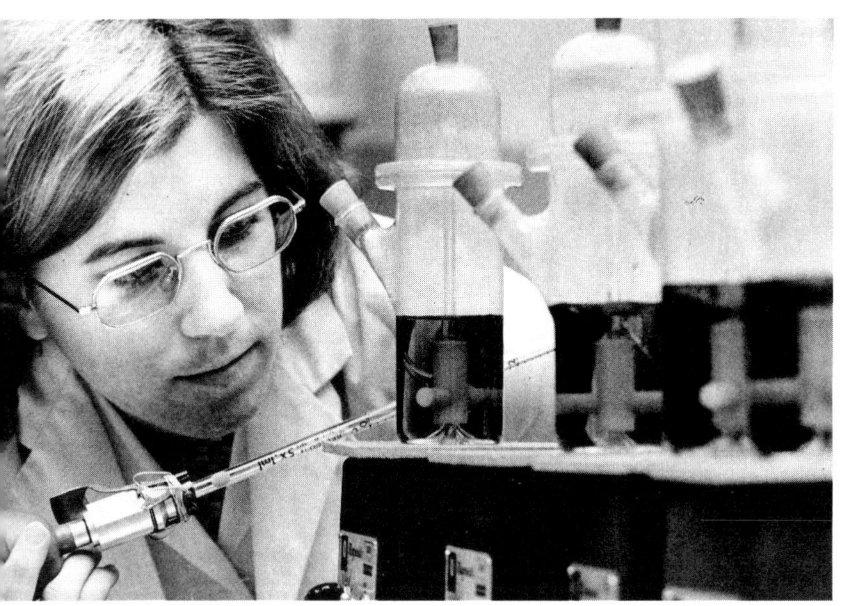

Drug companies are trying to develop a vaccine against herpes Type 2. Here a virologist removes samples of herpes virus grown in a laboratory culture.

pain or prevent secondary bacterial infections are the best medical practice.

One controversial form of treatment is being espoused, however, by a herpes virus research team at the Baylor College of Medicine in Houston, Texas. The team includes Dr. Joseph L. Melnick, professor of virology and epidemiology, and Dr. Raymond H. Kaufman, chairman of the obstetrics and gynecology department. The Baylor doctors coat external lesions with a dye that has the ability to make the herpes virus sensitive to light. Then the doctors expose the lesions to ordinary light, which they believe inactivates the virus. "In our experience, it shortens the clinical course of the disease," Dr. Kaufman says. He adds, however, that there isn't any conclusive evidence yet that the treatment reduces the number of recurrences.

BETTER THAN RECURRENCES

The treatment is controversial, however. Experiments with such photo-inactivated herpes Type 2 viruses in hamster-tissue culture cells suggest that the inactivated viruses may cause cancer. But Dr. Kaufman says: "It's our opinion at the Baylor group that the risk of using (the treatment) is no greater than allowing these patients to have the risk of letting the disease run its natural course and the risk of having repeated recurrences."

A few doctors recommend even more extreme treatment for their patients with genital herpes infections—trips abroad for injections with a German-made inactivated herpes Type 2 vaccine. The vaccine hasn't been cleared by the U.S. Food and Drug Administration. Proponents of the vaccine say it works after repeated injections by helping patients build their immunity to the virus in much the same way that a patient is given injections to combat an allergy. The vaccine is made by the Hermal-Chemie Co. of Hamburg under the name Lupidon G.

"It should be available in this country for experimental purposes, but you can't get it here," says Dr. James Lewis Pipkin, clinical professor of dermatology at the

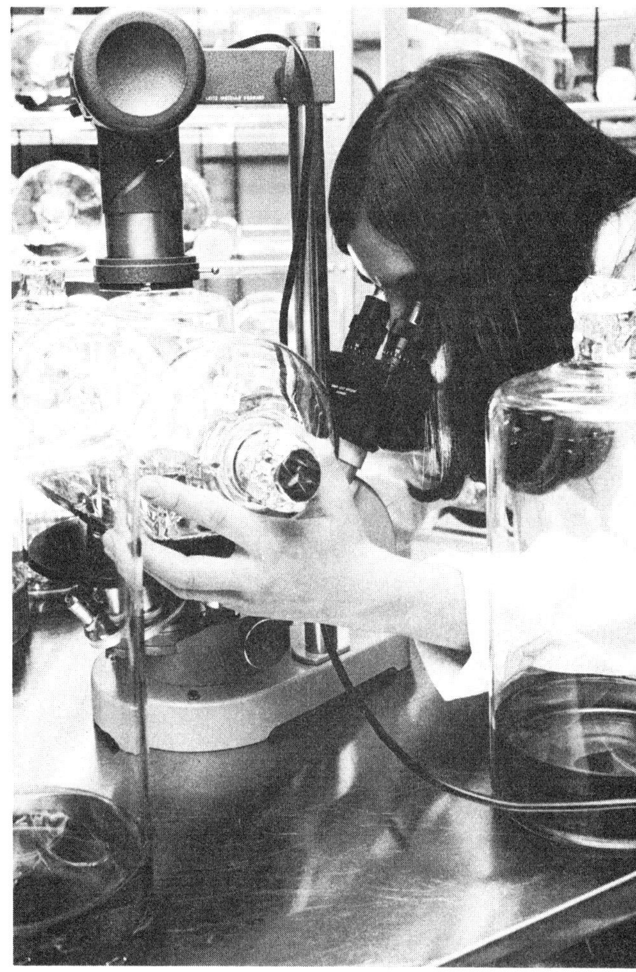

A virologist examines a culture of cells that have been infected with herpes virus to determine how much the cells have been damaged.

University of Texas Medical School at San Antonio. "Results have been very spectacular with the patients I've sent to Germany. We know the virus is potentially carcinogenic (cancer-causing), so the patient is no worse off being treated. The patients have received hundreds of injections, and we've never seen any reaction from it or any evidence of it producing cancer." He says he has been sending patients to Germany for the vaccine treatment for about six years, and he says the vaccine prevents recurrences in 90 per cent to 95 per cent of cases.

WORK ON U.S. VACCINES

Scientists also are working on making a herpes Type 2 vaccine in the United States. Dr. Nahmias says his group is focusing on the immunological defense mechanism. One major hurdle was cleared in 1971 when he and some other Atlanta-based scientists succeeded in infecting monkeys with the herpes simplex Type 2 virus. This gives them a nonhuman primate on which to study immunological responses to the infection as well as the effectiveness of vaccines or other drugs.

One pharmaceutical company, Eli Lilly & Co., has had a herpes Type 1 vaccine available for investigational use for about 10 years. It has a Type 2 vaccine "in the laboratory stage," says Dr. F. Bruce Peck Jr., director of the company's regulatory affairs. "Type 2 virus has been associated with cancer. This gives some people pause," he says. "Until the theoretical virologists arrive at some conclusion, we'll have to wait and see about anybody working with a Type 2 vaccine in humans."

Dr. Maurice R. Hilleman, director of virus and cell biology research for Merck, Sharp & Dohme Research Laboratories, says his pharmaceutical laboratory is working under a U.S. government contract to develop a vaccine against herpes Type 2 "because of its probable association or role in cervical carcinoma (cancer) or prostatic carcinoma and possibly others."

"If everything works out right, we hope to be in early clinical testing (on humans) in two years," he says. "Theoretically, everybody could get it as a child. Our first goal is a vaccine to prevent the primary virus infection. You should be able to prevent (certain types of) cancer if cancer is caused by this virus. A second use would be for bolstering immunity for therapeutic purposes for recurring herpes"□

SELECTED READINGS

"Grim New Venereal Disease in Our Midst: Herpes Simplex Virus II" by D. R. Reuben. *Readers Digest*, November 1974.

Venereal Disease and Its Avoidance by R. Richard. Holt 1974.

Dr. Maurice R. Hilleman, working with Dr. Vivian M. Larson to develop a vaccine against herpes Type 2, hopes to begin tests on humans in two years.

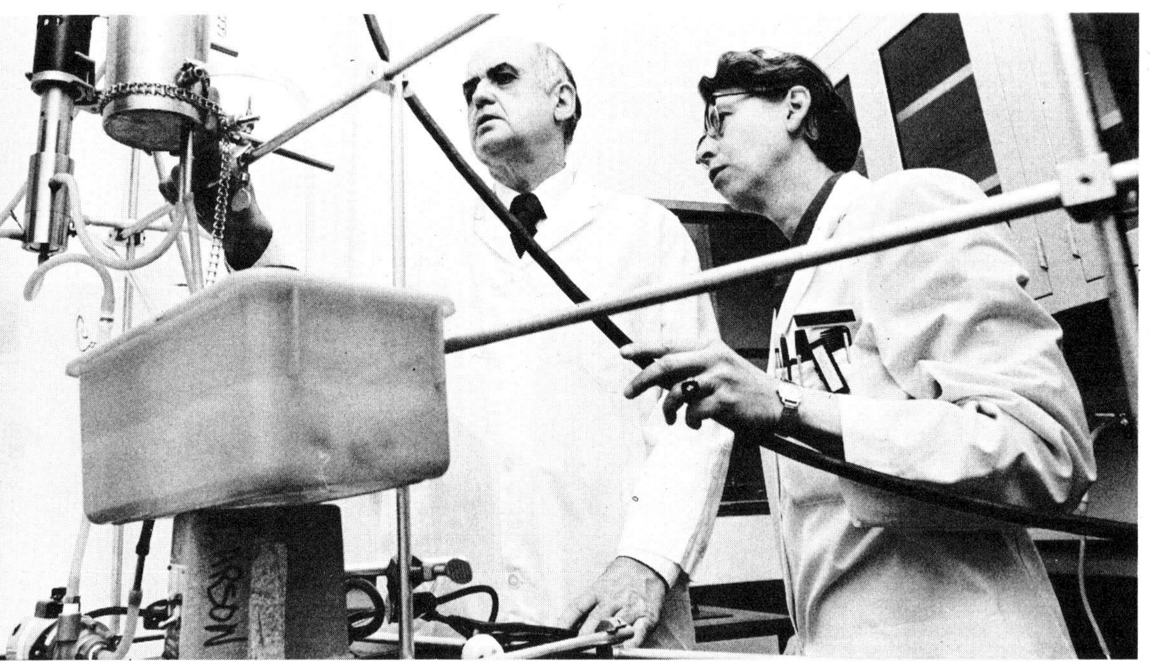

A Primer on Vitamins

by G. Edward Damon

VITAMINS are organic compounds that are necessary in small amounts in the diet for the normal growth and maintenance of the life of animals, including man.

They do not provide energy, nor do they build any part of the body. They are needed for transforming foods into energy and body maintenance. There are 15 or more of them, and if any is missing, a deficiency disease develops.

Vitamins are alike because they are made of the same elements—carbon, hydrogen, oxygen, and sometimes nitrogen. (Vitamin B_{12} also contains cobalt, an essential mineral—that is, a mineral that the body needs and cannot synthesize.) Vitamins differ from one another because their elements are arranged in different combinations. Each vitamin performs one or more exclusive functions in the body.

In the early 1900's, it was thought that three compounds were needed in the diet to prevent beriberi, pellagra, and scurvy. They originally were believed to be a class of chemical compounds called amines. They were named from the Latin *vita*, or life, plus *amine*: vitamine. Later, the "e" was dropped when it was found that not all of the substances were members of the amine class of chemicals.

At first no one knew what vitamins were chemically, and they were identified by letters. Later, what was thought to be one vitamin turned out to be many, and numbers had to be added to the identifying letter. The vitamin B complex is the best example. Then, some vitamins were found unnecessary for human health and were eliminated from the list, which accounts for the gaps in the numbers. The present trend is to use the chemical names and eliminate the confusion of the past.

SMALL AMOUNTS

Vitamins are measured in extremely small amounts, because a very little is effective in generating the needed chemical reactions. Some vitamins are measured in I. U.'s—International Units. Others are expressed by weight only, in milligrams or micrograms.

To illustrate the small amounts needed by the human body, let's start with an ounce of vitamins, which is 28.3 grams. One gram, then, is about 35/1,000 of an ounce; a milligram is 1/1,000 of a gram, and a microgram is 1/1,000 of a milligram, in turn.

To look at it another way—the recommended allowance of vitamin B_{12} for adults is 6 micrograms a day. Just 1 ounce of this vitamin would satisfy the daily needs of 4,724,921 people.

United States Recommended Daily Allowances

	Unit	Infants (0–12 mo.)	Children under 4 yrs.	Adults and children 4 or more yrs.	Pregnant or lactating women
Vitamin A	IU	1500	2500	5000	8000
Vitamin D	IU	400	400	400	400
Vitamin E	IU	5	10	30	30
Vitamin C	mg	35	40	60	60
Folacin	mg	0.1	0.2	0.4	0.8
Thiamine (B_1)	mg	0.5	0.7	1.5	1.7
Riboflavin (B_2)	mg	0.6	0.8	1.7	2.0
Niacin	mg	8	9	20	20
Vitamin B_6	mg	0.4	0.7	2	2.5
Vitamin B_{12}	mcg	2	3	6	8
Biotin	mg	0.05	0.15	0.3	0.3
Pantothenic acid	mg	3	5	10	10

IU = International unit
mg = milligram
mcg = microgram

The U.S. RDA system was developed by FDA for its nutrition labeling and dietary supplement programs. This table for use in the labeling of dietary supplements lists only vitamin requirements, for the purpose of this article.

NO NEED FOR INSURANCE

Getting enough vitamins is essential to life. But the body has no use for excess vitamins. Many people believe, however, in insurance. So, fearing that they are not eating a well-balanced diet, they take extra vitamins.

So-called normal eaters probably never need supplemental vitamins, although many think they do. People eating diets known to be deficient in one or more vitamins require supplemental vitamins, as do those recovering from a specific illness or suffering from certain vitamin deficiencies that have been identified by a physician.

Every adult consumer interested in nutrition and good health should become familiar with the initials U.S. RDA, which stand for "United States Recommended Daily Allowances." The recommended allowances were established by the U.S. Food and Drug Administration (FDA) for use in nutrition labeling. They are the amounts of vitamins, minerals, and other nutrients from food that a person should eat every day to stay healthy.

The accompanying table lists the U.S. RDA's for vitamins. The table is used in nutrition labeling of foods, including foods that are also vitamin supplements. The table is not complete because it lists only vitamins and not minerals and other nutrients.

ITEM-BY-ITEM REPORT

Here is a rundown of the vitamins, with a short summary of how each helps the body, the effects of a deficiency, and the main natural sources.

Vitamin A—Retinol

Vitamin A, like vitamins D, E, and K, is soluble in oil. It is stored principally in the liver. This vitamin is necessary for new cell growth and healthy tissues and is essential for vision in dim light.

Vitamin A deficiency causes night blindness and other eye problems, and a dry, rough skin that may be more susceptible to infection. Too much vitamin A

causes headache, nausea, and irritability. More severe ailments include growth retardation in children, enlargement of the liver and spleen, loss of hair, rheumatic pain, and disturbance of the menstrual cycle.

In some instances, children and young people who have been given large doses of vitamin A have developed an intracranial pressure that mimicked a brain tumor so realistically that unnecessary surgery was performed.

Vitamin A is found most abundantly in liver, fortified margarine, eggs, butter, and whole milk. Green and yellow vegetables and yellow fruits are the best sources of carotene, which the body converts to vitamin A.

Vitamin B_1—Thiamine

This vitamin is water soluble as are all in the B group. Thiamine is required for normal digestion. It is necessary for growth, fertility, and lactation, and for the normal functioning of nerve tissue.

Vitamin B_1 deficiency causes beriberi, a dysfunctioning of the nervous system. Other deficiency problems are loss of appetite, body swelling, growth retardation, cardiac problems, nausea, vomiting, spastic colon, and pain in the calf and thigh muscles.

Thiamine is found abundantly in pork, beans, peas, and nuts, and in enriched and whole-grain breads and cereals.

Vitamin B_2—Riboflavin

Riboflavin helps the body to obtain energy from carbohydrates and protein substances. A deficiency causes lip sores and cracks, as well as dimness of vision. This vitamin is found abundantly in leafy vegetables, enriched and whole-grain bread, liver, cheese, lean meat, milk, and eggs.

Niacin

This vitamin has been called B_5 as well as PP (pellagra preventive). Both terms are obsolete.

Niacin is necessary for the healthy condition of all tissue cells. A niacin deficiency causes pellagra, which was once a common deficiency disease. Pellagra is characterized by rough skin, mouth sores, diarrhea, and mental disorders.

Niacin is one of the most stable of the vitamins, the most easily obtainable, and the cheapest. The most abundant natural sources are liver, lean meat, peas, beans, whole-grain cereal products, and fish.

Pantothenic Acid

Once called B_3, pantothenic acid is needed to support a variety of body functions, including proper growth and maintenance of the body.

A deficiency causes, among other things, headache, fatigue, poor muscle coordination, nausea, and cramps.

Pantothenic acid is found abundantly in liver, eggs, white potatoes, sweet potatoes, peas, and peanuts.

Folic Acid (folacin)

Folic acid helps to manufacture red blood cells. It is also essential in normal metabolism which is, basically, the converting of food to energy. A deficiency causes a particular type of anemia.

The most abundant sources are liver, navy beans, and dark green leafy vegetables. Other good sources are nuts, fresh oranges, and whole wheat products.

Vitamin B_6—Pyridoxine-Pyridoxal-Pyridoxamine

This vitamin is involved mostly in the utilization of protein by the body. Like other vitamins, B_6 is essential for the proper growth and maintenance of body functions. Deficiency symptoms include mouth soreness, dizziness, nausea, weight loss, and sometimes severe disturbances of the nervous system.

Pyridoxine is found abundantly in liver, whole-grain cereals, potatoes, red meat, green vegetables, and yellow corn.

Vitamin B_{12}—Cyanocobalamin

Vitamin B_{12} is necessary for the normal development of red blood cells and the functioning of all cells, particularly in the bone marrow, nervous system, and intestines.

A deficiency causes pernicious anemia. If the deficiency is prolonged, a degeneration of the spinal cord occurs.

Abundant sources are organ meats, lean meats, fish, milk, and shellfish. B_{12} is not present to any measurable degree in plants, which indicates that strict vegetarians should supplement their diets with this vitamin.

Biotin

"Biotin" is now the sole descriptive term for what was once called vitamin H. It is actually a member of the B complex. Biotin is important in the metabolism of carbohydrates, proteins, and fats.

Most deficiency symptoms involve mild skin disorders, some anemia, depression, sleeplessness, and muscle pain. As with many vitamins, deficiency is very rare.

Abundant sources include eggs, milk, and meat.

Vitamin C—Ascorbic Acid

Vitamin C is the least stable of the vitamins. It promotes growth and tissue repair, including the healing of wounds.

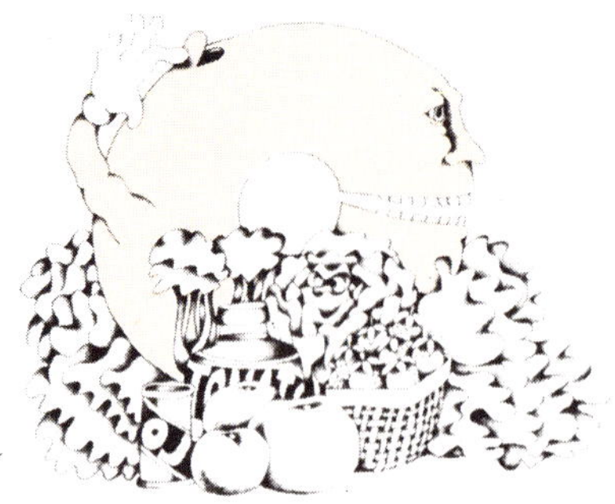

It aids tooth formation, bone formation, and repair. When used as a food additive, vitamin C acts as a preservative.

A lack of this vitamin causes scurvy, one of the oldest diseases known to man. The signs of scurvy include lassitude, weakness, bleeding, loss of weight, and irritability. An early sign is bleeding of the gums. Long before the 16th century, American Indians knew that scurvy could be cured by a tea made with spruce or pine needles.

Abundant sources are citrus and tomato juices, strawberries, currants, and green vegetables such as lettuce, cabbage, broccoli, kale, collards, mustard and turnip greens, and potatoes. You can get all the vitamin C your body can use, for example, by drinking 140-170 grams (5 or 6 ounces) of orange or tomato juice a day.

Vitamin D—Calciferol

Vitamin D aids in absorbing calcium and phosphorus in bone formation.

Vitamin D deficiency causes rickets. The earliest obvious signs are skeleton deformation—bowed legs, deformed spine, "potbelly" appearance, and sometimes flatfeet and stunting of growth.

Too much vitamin D causes nausea, weight loss, weakness, and excessive urination, and the more serious conditions of hypertension and calcification of soft tissues, including the blood vessels and kidneys. Bone deformities and multiple fractures are also common.

Abundant sources are canned fish such as herring, salmon, and tuna; egg yolk, and vitamin D fortified milk. People who spend time in the sun need no other sources of vitamin D, since it is formed in the skin by the sun's ultraviolet rays. Foods that are fortified with vitamin D are intended mainly for infants and the elderly who lack outdoor exposure to sunlight. The daily dietary requirement of vitamin D is very small, and any excess is stored in the body.

Vitamin E—The Tocopherols

Vitamin E in humans acts as an antioxidant; that is, it helps to prevent oxygen from destroying other substances. In other words, vitamin E is a preservative, protecting the efficiency of other compounds such as vitamin A. No known clinical symptoms are associated with very low intake of this vitamin in man. A rather rare form of anemia in premature infants, however, responds to vitamin E medication.

Abundant sources are vegetable oils, beans, eggs, whole grains, liver, fruits, and vegetables.

Vitamin E is not the most important vitamin, but it is one of the most talked about. To some extent the wild and unsubstantiated claims made for vitamin E have come from a combination of misinterpretation and hope. The Committee on Nutritional Misinformation of the National Academy of Sciences has issued a report about vitamin E. Three statements are quoted here:

"Surveys of the United States population indicate that adequate amounts of vitamin E are supplied by the usual diet."

"Careful studies over a period of years attempting to relate these [test animal] symptoms to vitamin E deficiency in human beings have been unproductive."

"Self-medication with vitamin E in the hope that a more or less serious condition will be alleviated may indeed be hazardous, especially when appropriate diagnosis and treatment may thereby be delayed or avoided."

Vitamin K

There are several scientific names for vitamin K, which is essential for clotting of the blood. One type is found naturally in food. Another is made in the intestinal tract, and a third is made synthetically.

A deficiency causes hemorrhage and liver injury. Vitamin K is found in spinach, lettuce, kale, cabbage, cauliflower, liver, and egg yolk.

CLEARING UP MISCONCEPTIONS

No primer about vitamins and their proper functions would be complete without clearing up some misconceptions. The clarifications:

- "Synthetic" vitamins manufactured in the laboratory are identical to the natural vitamins found in foods. The body cannot tell the difference and gets the same benefits from either source. Statements to the effect that "Nature cannot be imitated" and "Natural vitamins have the essence of life" are without meaning.
- Vitamins will not provide extra pep, vitality beyond normal expectations, or an unusual level of well-being.
- Excess vitamins are a complete waste, both in money and effect.
- Anyone who eats "all over the store," meaning a reasonably varied diet, should normally never need supplemental vitamins. Vitamin sources are varied and abundant and have been for centuries.

MULTIPLE SOURCES

The abundant sources that have been listed give some idea of how difficult it is to be undernourished from lack of vitamins. Each of these is an abundant source of one or more vitamins:

Liver, eggs, cheese, fortified margarine, butter, whole milk, fortified milk, fish, egg yolk, yellow vegetables, green leafy vegetables, yellow fruit, beans, peas, nuts, whole-grain foods, red meat, lean meat, pork, shellfish, fresh vegetables, white potatoes, sweet potatoes, yellow corn, rice, strawberries, currants, citrus fruit and juices, tomatoes and juices, other fruits, juices, and berries, canned herring, salmon, and tuna, lettuce, fresh oranges, cabbage, spinach, cauliflower, and vegetable oils of several kinds.

Even though the widely seen and identified vitamin deficiency diseases of 30 years ago have all but disappeared, the American consumer is approached from all sides with misinformation about the almost-universal "need" for supplemental vitamins. Is there really a need? Each person can answer this only after learning what vitamins do and do not do□

SELECTED READINGS

"Safe Use of Vitamins and Minerals." *Good Housekeeping*, November 1974.

"Vitamin A: Potential Protection from Carcinogens." *Science*, Feb. 14, 1975.

Insomnia

by John Peterson

WHILE doctors debate such esoteric questions as whether sleep is truly necessary, nearly one in every three American adults just wishes for a decent night of it. They suffer from some degree of insomnia, all 45 million of them.

For insomniacs, getting enough sleep can become a desperate struggle. It may mean powerful, addictive sleeping pills, sessions with a psychiatrist, and costly expenditures for such things as new beds, sound machines, humidifiers, and air purifiers. All together, about $2 billion is spent annually in the pursuit of sleep, yet relief is fleeting.

ANXIETY AND DEPRESSION

"There is strong evidence that even among people without a situational or medical disturbance in their lives, 80 to 90 per cent of all chronic insomniacs show a psychiatric disorder," says Dr. Anthony Kales, the foremost investigator of insomnia among the growing number of sleep researchers. "Some people say insomnia causes the psychiatric disorder, but we believe that insomnia isn't causative, that it's a symptom."

The primary reason people are emotionally or psychologically unhealthy, and restless sleepers, is shifting. In the 1950's and 1960's, psychiatrists say, they were seeing more people suffering from anxiety and its attendant worries. Now they say more and more people are suffering from depression. Says Leon Marder, a Los Angeles psychiatrist: "Estimates are that there are about 10 million depressed people walking the streets, and a huge number of them have trouble sleeping."

Insomnia is, of course, either the inability to fall asleep at night, periodic reawakenings throughout the night, premature waking at 3 or 4 A.M., or any combination of the three. "There's one thing about insomnia I tell all my patients," says Gerald Jampolsky, a Tiburon, California, psychiatrist. "You don't die from it."

There has always been a great fascination with sleep and dreams, and what they both mean and do for us or to us. We are forever reading about them, and it seems strange to learn there are few solid data in the field. Just recently, however, sleep researchers began learning so much from their studies that they now contend they know really very little at all. The new research keeps knocking all of the old ideas out of whack. For instance: remember the theory that you would go insane if you didn't dream? Nonsense. Or the idea that held it was not so terribly important how much you slept, but how much quality, or deep, sleep that you got? Again, nonsense. Or even that you dream only during the stage of sleep called REM, the acronym for the rapid-eye-movement stage? Not true. And there really is a serious debate about whether sleep is necessary.

SOME AGREEMENT

"It is clear that many of our earlier conceptions about sleep are proving to be wrong," says Dr. William Dement, head of the Stanford University sleep disorders clinic and laboratory. "A lot of people, for example, believe that they're piling up poisons in the body that only sleep can handle. But right now it seems sleep is only necessary to reduce sleepiness. We simply don't understand the brain mechanisms that dictate sleep."

Still, doctors allow that they are gleaning significant facts about sleep and how you can get more of it. For example, if you suffer only mildly from insomnia, there are a number of things you can do that may alleviate your problem. Doctors such as Kales, Dement, and Laverne Johnson at the U.S. Navy's Balboa Hospital in San Diego, California, though often in professional disagreement, speak generally of the same changes insomniacs should make in their behavior. Among these changes:

• Regulate your schedule. Many people confuse their biological rhythms, get their

body out of synchronization by trying to go to bed one night at 11 P.M., the next night at 3 A.M., then at 10 P.M. It can be as unsettling as the jet lag that comes from cross-country plane rides. Too, the body seems to work on a 90-minute rhythm, so you are likely to be the most susceptible at, say, 11 P.M. and then again at 12:30 A.M.

• Exercise can help. You can increase how deeply you sleep through exercise, though doctors caution that if you exhaust yourself you may have even more trouble sleeping. They recommend that the exercise come earlier in the day, counseling that exertion just before bedtime is not as beneficial.

• Relax your mind before retiring. Don't get involved in mentally stimulating or disturbing activity late in the evening. For example, don't get involved in the corporate books, family finances, or any other kind of homework. Instead, read a neutral book.

• If you can't sleep, get up. Don't lie in bed longer than perhaps 10 minutes at a stretch. Johnson says the greatest cure for insomnia is to keep people awake, to keep them out of bed until they're ready for sleep.

• Your sleeping environment can be important. Flotation or water beds can help some people, firmer beds still others. The darker the room, the easier it is to sleep. Early-morning sun in the face has its effect, so blackout curtains might be in order. Too, distracting and unexpected noise can awaken the insomniac who normally enjoys a much lighter sleep anyway. Chester Pierce, a professor at Harvard University, says the ghetto could be the model of an environment that deprives people of sleep because of its noise and crowding.

Sleeping pills—hypnotics—are of increasing concern. Sleeping pills sold over-the-counter are usually antihistamines and they aren't as strong as the barbiturates prescribed by doctors. The widely advertised over-the-counter sleeping aids can be helpful if you expect to have trouble sleeping for only a night or two. They are of little help for longer periods of time.

GETTING WORSE ON PILLS

Kales, who has established a sleep clinic at Pennsylvania State University's Hershey, Pennsylvania, Medical Center, has been investigating the effect of the most commonly prescribed sleeping pills. He contends that hardly any of them are effective in inducing sleep after a week or two of use. "The effect of prolonged usage of the pills is to create a drug-dependent insomnia and a poorer night's sleep," he says.

He cites the results of a 1973 Los Angeles Metropolitan Area Survey, conducted by the University of California at Los Angeles (UCLA), where he formerly worked. The study indicated that about one third of insomniacs are taking drugs. He says another survey of about 50 Beverly Hills, California, doctors showed that about one half of their insomniac patients had been prescribed pills for one month, about one third for three months.

Drug-dependent insomniacs have another set of problems. "They suffer severe withdrawal symptoms," explains Kales. He says that drugs reduce the amount of rapid-eye-movement (REM), or dream-stage sleep. When a person suddenly quits taking the drugs he experiences a "marked increase" in his dreams and nightmares. This experience then creates a psychological dependence on the drugs.

A PAINFUL CHOICE

This becomes a serious dilemma to the doctor when a patient has a medical disturbance that will interfere with his sleep. Often people take the pills because they can't sleep because of pain, for example, and if they didn't have insomnia before the onset of the pain-producing condition they wind up with it because of the pills.

Sleep researchers agree that insomniacs —both those on drugs and those suffering along without them—should see a doctor. "A person should have a doctor's guidance and help when he starts withdrawing from drugs," says Stanford's Dement.

For the chronic insomniac whose plight is not compounded by drugs, doctors contend that a combination of psychotherapy and pharmacological treatment is normally required. "Insomniacs tend to deny their problems and focus on the symptom, their sleeplessness," says Kales. "They nearly all want an exotic, quick cure."

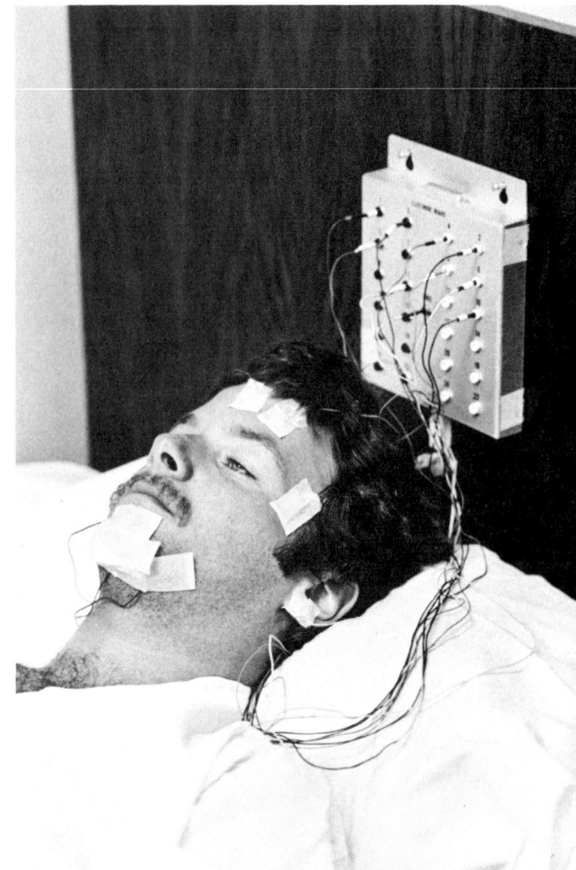

Sleep disorders result from anxiety, depression, tension, neurosis, or poor physical health, adds Johnson. "There is even a question that a sleep disorder is a medical problem. We have no data to say that the loss of sleep is detrimental, other than how it makes a person feel for having less of it than he feels he needs."

THEORIES AND GIMMICKS

Many theories have been advanced as to how insomniacs can get more sleep. Since the mid-1960's there has been great interest in such things as "electric sleep," in which a tiny electrical current is passed

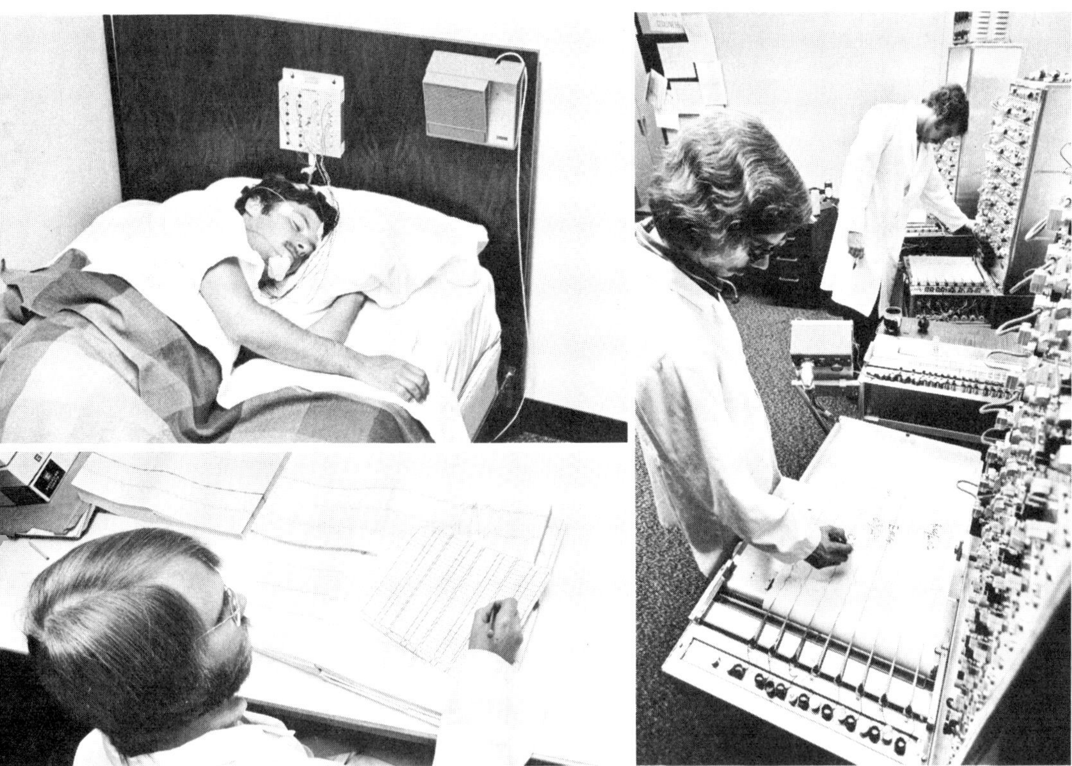

Electrodes are attached to a study subject to record brain-wave activity, eye motion, and facial-muscle activity during different stages of sleep. This research is part of attempts to understand sleep and sleep disorders such as insomnia.

through the sleeper's brain. This method is most popular in Russia and other Communist-bloc countries. "There was a time that we thought it might be a breakthrough," says Kales, "but studies show that its effects aren't that beneficial."

Too, biofeedback and other relaxation therapies have helped some people, but doctors warn that the therapy can harm a person with a severe psychological or medical problem. It can even make some psychiatrically disturbed persons a lot worse.

A number of people are cashing in on insomnia. Tom Snyder, host of NBC's wee-hours *Tomorrow* show, says projections when the show premiered in October 1973 were for two million viewers each night. "We've been reaching about three million," says Snyder, "and our audience is growing."

Bill Steed's sleep learning center in San Francisco gets about one half of its business from people suffering from either anxiety or depression. "They've already been through the psychiatrists," he says. "Good psychology is good common sense. We lead a life of suggestion, and the message on our records gives you a good image of yourself. Depression, after all, is learned feedback from experience. We simply reprogram people to feel good about themselves." His records for a 30-week course cost $469.

One of the leading water-bed marketers has its own in-house sleep expert. That's Dr. Irving London of Innerspace. "Not all water beds are flotation beds," the in-house expert contends, "and it's important to own a flotation bed, which can cut your tossing and turning by at least 25 per cent."

TECHNOLOGICAL TEDDY BEARS

London says that until recent years no one has questioned the sleeping environment. "I suffered from insomnia myself," he says, "hopping back and forth from barbiturates to stimulants." The answer for him was in his sleeping environment. But purchasing all of what London now says is available and possibly helpful would approach what Kales would call a "fetish."

London describes some of the accessories that can enhance a sleep environment: the flotation bed, of course; a "white-sound" machine to reduce noisy distractions; a cold-air humidifier; an air purifier to remove dust and pollutants; a clock that slowly changes colors and produces a relaxing, hypnotic effect; and blackout curtains. He says that each may have its place.

All of these sleeping aids, even if effective for many people, would have little impact upon people with serious sleep disorders, and many times insomnia indicates those severe problems. Stanford's Dement says that there is "absolutely no relation" between the amount of sleep a person actually gets when studied in the clinic and the severity of his complaint. Too, he says there is no way to determine whether a person has a severe medical problem without long and costly study of his sleep.

Dement says sleep apnea—a condition where a person stops breathing during his sleep because the brain fails to order it—may have been the cause of death for some people taking heavy doses of sleeping pills. At the very least, he says that sleep apnea can put a huge strain on a person's heart and lungs, when he awakens frequently, gasping for air.

DON'T COUNT HOURS

Studies at the three leading sleep clinics in the United States—Stanford University Sleep Clinic, the Hershey sleep center in Pennsylvania, and Dartmouth College sleep center in New Hampshire—are doing more to knock down previously accepted theories than to prove them out. Some of the more-significant investigations are in areas such as just how much sleep a person needs, whether sleep is necessary, and the effect of a limited amount of sleep upon a person. "We can reduce a person's time sleeping until he is overwhelmed by exhaustion, but if the reduction is only an hour or two a night, though the person may feel tired, his performance on the job or at school doesn't suffer," says San Diego's Johnson.

Psychiatrist Jampolsky contends that a person suffering from insomnia should forget that a specified period of sleep is a prerequisite to feeling well. "People should sleep when they are ready," he says. "The body is a good manager. It isn't so necessary to place such a great value on sleep."

Yet all sleep researchers and psychiatrists agree that sleep disorders such as insomnia probably are symptoms of a more serious disorder. "Our biggest effort right now," says Kales, "is to educate the general practitioner who is prescribing the drugs." The fear is that the pills now taken by about 10 million people merely camouflage the real disorder, perhaps even making it more severe.

So, despite the debate about whether sleep is necessary, whether so many hours a night are needed, and precisely what function sleep plays, sleep—or lack of it—remains a major problem for millions. There is no easy cure for most people, particularly since researchers have become so dissatisfied with the current batch of sleeping medications. One thing the doctors are convinced of is that the loss of sleep isn't as harmful as generally believed.

Writes Dr. John Stevens in the British Department of Health's *Prescriber's Journal*: "Those who regularly lose most sleep throughout their lives—seamen, nurses, and doctors—remain resilient, healthy, and hard working, in spite of such losses over long periods."

And if that doesn't hearten the insomniac, it's well to remember that doctors also agree that warm milk or Ovaltine, just as mom knew, does help□

Vegetarianism

by Daniel Grotta-Kurska

WHEN the Russian woman accepted Leo Tolstoy's invitation to dinner, she was hardly prepared for what she found at the table—a live chicken tied to her chair. "My conscience forbids me to kill it," Tolstoy, a committed vegetarian, told his meat-eating visitor. "As you are the only guest taking meat, I would be greatly obliged if you would undertake the killing first."

The story, which does not go on to tell if the woman did kill the chicken, is tribute to the dedication that many vegetarians bring to their adopted life-style. For some, the pursuit of vegetarianism is almost a noble commitment. "I hold flesh food to be unsuited to our species," said Gandhi. "We err in copying the lower animal world—if we are superior to it."

The register of vegetarians reads like a diversified *Who's Who:* Voltaire, Milton, Newton, Shelley, Schweitzer, and George Bernard Shaw were all vegetarians. More recently, such celebrities as Dennis Weaver, Clint Walker, Paul Newman, Dick Gregory, and Samantha Eggar have converted to nonflesh diets.

MANY REASONS

To the meat eater, the first, and very puzzling, question is why. Why give up the steak, the barbecued spareribs, the pork roast, the Thanksgiving turkey, the hamburger, and the hot dog? There are many reasons why people do so:

- Most vegetarians live below the poverty level. They simply cannot afford the high price of meat.
- Followers of certain religions and philosophies exclude flesh foods from their diets because they believe eating meat hinders their spiritual development, or because it is contrary to their religious edicts.
- Health enthusiasts think that meat, as well as all processed or refined supermarket foods, is harmful to the body.
- Some pacifists believe that killing and eating animals is inconsistent with their ethical or social consciences.
- Recent emphasis on ecology has convinced many that using meat as a primary protein source is an arrogant exploitation of the earth's finite resources.

NUTRITIONALLY SOUND?

The United States Department of Agriculture estimates that less than 5 per cent of the country's population is predominantly vegetarian. Even so, that figure represents more than 10 million people. A second question comes naturally: Is a vegetarian diet nutritionally sound?

It certainly didn't hurt the Danes during World War I, when Denmark virtually became a meatless country because of the British naval blockade. Nutritionists who studied the people during the war concluded that general health had significantly improved. Similarly, Norway had to adopt a vegetarian diet during World War II, and there was a drop in heart disease. But both nations reverted to meat diets as soon as the crises passed and later studies showed that the temporary health advantages subsided.

Americans, too, have been conditioned to believe that only a meat-based diet can provide the adequate nutrition necessary for good health. Traditionally, we have been a nation of carnivores, consuming an average 227 grams (one-half lb) of meat, per person, every day. (The Japanese eat an average of only that much meat per month per person.) In 1973, Americans devoured 80 kg (176 lb) of meat per person—66 times more than in the average Indian diet. In fact, McDonald's—the fast-food hamburger franchise—uses more beef per year than is consumed by the entire populations of countries such as Ghana and the Ivory Coast.

THINNER AND HEALTHIER

Until recently, even many scientists were accustomed to classifying meats as "first-class" proteins and vegetables as "second-class" proteins, thereby implying that nonanimal sources of protein were somehow inferior in quality. The most current medical and scientific evidence, however, points to other considerations:

- Man can subsist perfectly well on a proper nonflesh diet.
- Statistically, vegetarians in the United States are thinner, healthier, and may live longer than meat eaters.
- Meat, especially in the large quantities Americans are accustomed to eating, may be harmful to the body.
- Protein from nonflesh foods can be an adequate nutritional substitute for meat protein.

Protein is essential to life: It is the substance that the body uses to build and replenish its organs, skin, cartilage, nails, hair, muscles, and the organic framework of bones. The proteins that our bodies use are composed of 22 amino acids, not all of which must come from the diet. The human metabolic system can synthesize (combine by uniting chemical elements) 14 of these 22 amino acids, but the remaining 8 must be obtained regularly from food sources outside the body. These amino acids that the body cannot synthesize are called the essential amino acids for that reason.

MUST BE COMPLETE

To be useful to a person, the totality of food proteins must be "complete"—that is, all eight essential amino acids must be ingested simultaneously, and in the right proportion. Incomplete proteins cannot be used to build muscle and tissue; they often end up as stored fat or are utilized for energy.

Meat is a complete protein because all eight essential amino acids are present in the proper proportion. Vegetable foods, however, may be incomplete proteins, lacking the minimum requirement of one or more of these eight amino acids.

But it is possible to satisfy your protein needs by a proper intermixing of vegetable proteins, according to Elwood Speckmann, Ph.D., director of the nutrition research program for the National Dairy Council. "You have to be careful and make sure you use the right combinations," explains Dr. Speckmann. "It's simply easier to meet your protein needs with animal foods, such as meat, milk, and eggs."

In *Diet for a Small Planet,* Frances Moore Lappé offers some suggestions for combining vegetables to good advantage. Wheat, which has a deficiency in the amino acid lysine but an abundance of sulfur-containing amino acids, can be combined with beans, which have the opposite enrichment combination. Taken together, they complement each other to form a "complete" protein.

"Certainly some vegetable proteins, if fed as the sole source of protein, are of relatively low value for promoting growth," the editors of the British medical journal *Lancet* wrote in 1959. "But many field trials have shown that proteins provided by suitable mixtures of vegetable origin enable children to grow as well as children provided with milk and other animal protein."

TWO CRITERIA

Nutritionists use two criteria in evaluating protein sources: quality and quantity. Quality refers to the useability of proteins by the body (not all of them can be used). This factor is expressed on a scale of 0 to 100. Quantity is the proportion of useable protein to total weight and is expressed as a percentage. The United Nations World Health Organization gives meat a protein quality rating of 67—higher than that of most plant proteins, with the exception of whole rice (70), but below that of cheese (70), fish (80), milk (82), and eggs (95). In terms of quantity, 20 to 30 per cent of the total weight of flesh food is useable protein—lamb rates the lower figure and turkey the higher one. The rest is water, fat, and trace minerals.

On the other hand, soybean flour is 40 per cent protein; Parmesan cheese, 36 per cent; many nuts and seeds, between 20 and 30 per cent; and peas, lentils, and dried beans, between 20 and 25 per cent. Grains are fairly low in quantity but, surprisingly, so are milk (4 per cent) and eggs (13 per cent).

There are other rating systems for food protein, also. The Food and Drug Administration uses a protein efficiency ratio (PER) as a quality standard for protein in nutritional labeling. Foods, such as meat and eggs, which are above a 2.5 PER, are considered excellent sources of protein; those, such as vegetables, which are below a 2.5 PER, are considered poor sources. The National Livestock Meat Board rates meats, both raw and cooked, for protein quantity. A serving of broiled, lean round steak is 31 per cent protein; raw, the same meat contains 22 per cent. Choice-grade leg of lamb, cooked, is 25 per cent protein; raw, 18 per cent.

DISADVANTAGES OF MEAT

What all this means is that, in general, one has to eat proportionately less meat in order to obtain the same amount of useable protein than if relying on vegetable sources, but that nonflesh alternatives are perfectly adequate. Balanced against this, however, are the disadvantages of a heavily meat-laced diet.

The first problem most American meat eaters face is not a deficiency of proteins,

Some of the world's most remarkable people have been vegetarians, among them the novelist Leo Tolstoy (left) and the playwright George Bernard Shaw (right).

but an excess. Nutritionists have established that a 70-kg (154-lb) man needs 43.1 grams of useable proteins and 2,800 calories per day for adequate nutrition; a 58-kg (128-lb) woman also needs 43.1 grams of protein, but only 2,000 calories.

A number of nutritional studies have concluded that lacto, lacto-ovo, and pure vegetarians (see "Vegetarian Vocabulary" on this page) who eat a proper diet consistently meet their protein and caloric needs but do not exceed them. Most meat eaters, however, exceed their limits and so tend to weigh more.

Vegetarian Vocabulary

Vegetarianism is a general term that applies to those who do not use flesh foods in their diets (although some vegetarians will eat fish). There are, however, different kinds of vegetarians. Here is a brief glossary relating to vegetarianism:

Lacto-vegetarians use dairy products such as milk, cheese, and butter.

Lacto-ovo-vegetarians also include eggs in their diet.

Macrobiotics is a Zen Buddhist dietary system that strives for a progressively limited diet according to spiritual development. The ultimate objective is a mono diet of brown rice.

Mono-vegetarians eat only one food, such as brown rice or soybeans.

Natural foods are pure, unrefined, and unprocessed foods without additives or artificial ingredients.

Natural vegetarians will not eat refined or processed foods, such as sugar or bleached flour. Some will eat only raw, uncooked foods.

Organic foods are those that are grown without the use of chemical fertilizers or pesticides.

Pure vegetarians use only grains, legumes, nuts, fruits, and vegetables. Some pure vegetarians will not eat honey, but others will.

Vegans are pure vegetarians who, for ethical reasons, refrain from using any animal products, such as leather. Vegans often refuse vaccinations because they are prepared from animal cultures.

"Forty per cent of the fat in our diets comes from meat," says Frederick Stare, M.D., chairman of the department of nutrition at the Harvard School of Public Health.

Meat is about 4 per cent saturated fat, or cholesterol. With the exception of eggs, nonflesh foods have no cholesterol. The consequences of meat and nonmeat diets were measured in a study conducted by Dr. Stare and Mervyn Hardinge, M.D., dean of the Loma Linda School of Health, Loma Linda, California. The results showed that vegetarians had consistently lower levels of serum cholesterol than did meat eaters. And high levels of serum cholesterol have been linked with some disease processes.

DISPUTE OVER ADDITIVES

The effect of meat additives on human health also is a point of contention among scientists. In 1971, for example, Charles Edwards, M.D., former commissioner of the Food and Drug Administration, testified before a House committee on nutrition that sodium nitrite, a meat preservative, is potentially dangerous to small children, can deform the fetus in pregnant women, and can cause serious damage in anemic persons. Dr. Edwards, currently secretary of health in the Department of Health, Education, and Welfare, also said the additive may be carcinogenic.

But Harvard's Dr. Stare says no carcinogenic agents are used in preserving meat. "Sodium nitrite and sodium nitrate have probably been used longer than any other type of preservatives," he explains. "And there is no evidence which I know of that they are carcinogenic."

Some studies, however, indicate a strong correlation between a meat diet and cancer of the colon. "Animal protein tends to create anaerobic bacteria in the intestinal tract, and these anaerobic bacteria tend to convert bile acids into carcinogenic compounds," explains U.D. Register, Ph.D., chairman of the nutrition department at the Loma Linda School of Health. (Anaerobic bacteria do not need oxygen to survive.)

And there are some indications that meat is highly susceptible to bacteria growth and food spoilage.

Meat eaters also may be bothered by poor absorption and elimination. Food with a low fiber-content, such as meat, moves sluggishly through the digestive tract, making stools dry and hard to pass. But vegetables retain moisture and bind waste bulk for easy passage.

FINDINGS OF ANTHROPOLOGISTS

But still the question remains: Is a vegetarian diet healthier than a meat diet? Nutritionists have yet to agree on an answer. Advocates of vegetarianism frequently cite unsubstantiated evidence and present "testimonials" about the relative superiority of a nonmeat diet, often claiming "miraculous" cures for asthma, poor eyesight, and even cancer. Though such claims may be sincere, they have not been proved.

Scientific evidence suggesting the superiority of a vegetarian diet is offered, not by nutritionists, but by anthropologists. Field investigations of certain nonmeat cultures have documented the excellent health and longevity enjoyed by people such as the Hunzas of northern Pakistan and the Otomi Indians of central Mexico. Heart diseases and many forms of cancer appear to be Western diseases in that they are practically unknown in some underdeveloped countries where meat is not a regular part of the diet. That lower incidence, however, may result from the very different life-style.

In 1973 the National Institutes of Health began a $1 million, five-year study to determine what role vegetarianism plays in health. The subject: 100,000 Seventh-Day Adventists who neither drink nor smoke nor eat meat and who use limited amounts of coffee and tea.

"Our studies have revealed that the Seventh-Day Adventist vegetarians are healthier than the average Californian," says Dr. Mervyn Hardinge. "There is virtually no lung cancer—in fact, a lower incidence of all forms of cancer. Heart disease is significantly less and, when it does occur, it is an average of 10 years later than in other Californians. Adventist males live 6.2 years longer than the average California male, and women 3.5 years longer."

Helen and Scott Nearing, leaders in the vegetarian movement, are active gardeners even though Scott is over 90. The Nearings' vigor is a good advertisement for their way of life.

The differences have been substantiated, says Dr. Hardinge. The purpose of the NIH study is to see if they are linked, in any way, to a meatless diet.

UNCONVINCED

Other nutritionists are unconvinced of the superiority of vegetarianism. "From a standpoint of nutrition, I don't think vegetarianism is superior," says Hilda White, Ph.D., a consultant in nutrition and instructor at Northern Illinois University. "However, there is no reason why vegetarianism cannot be an alternative to a meat-based diet. It's just that I can't think of any nutritional reason that would stop me from eating meat."

Unfortunately, certain vegetarian diets can lead to serious nutritional problems. A strict macrobiotic diet, for example,

Vegetable gardens must be carefully tended. Man at left peers at seedlings through protective plastic coverings. Woman at right picks green beans with a deft touch.

can induce scurvy, hypoproteinemia, anemia, hypocalcemia, emaciation, and loss of kidney function.

Other equally ill-advised exotic vegetarian diets have resulted in kwashiorkor (a rare protein deficiency that became endemic with children who were victims of starvation during the Biafran-Nigerian war), marasmus, beriberi, rickets, pellagra, and severe vitamin deficiencies.

BASIC GUIDELINES

There are a few basic guidelines that nutritionists recommend for people who are following, or plan to adopt, a vegetarian diet. For those who wish to include dairy products or eggs, or both:

- Cut "empty" (sugar, fats, oils) calories in half.
- Replace meat with increased intake of legumes, nuts, or meat analogs (textured vegetable protein such as soyburgers).
- Give up as many refined or processed foods as possible—whole foods have greater nutritional value.
- Eat more grains and cereals.
- Eat a salad every day, adding such things as raw carrots, beet roots, and dried fruits.
- Include cottage cheese and low-fat milk in your daily diet, and restrict eggs to no more than four per week.
- To retain vitamins and minerals, cook vegetables for the shortest time and in as little water as possible.

EAT MORE OF EVERYTHING

Pure vegetarians should make a special effort to:

- Increase intake of leafy green vegetables;
- Increase general caloric intake, eating more of everything;
- Use either fortified soy milk preparations or take some form of vitamin B_{12} supplement.

Perhaps it is good to remember that the word vegetarian is not, as one might think, derived from the word vegetable, but from the Latin *vegetus*, which means "whole, sound, fresh, lively."

"Vegetarianism is a divine crusade," says Jay Dinshah, president of both the North American Vegetarian Society and the American Vegan Society in Malaga, New Jersey. "It is a part of the practice of Ahimsa (nonkilling, noninjuring), an expression of the oneness of all life." And, from a nutritional standpoint, it may not be such a bad idea either□

SELECTED READINGS

Diet for a Small Planet by Frances Moore Lappé. Ballantine, 1973.

Great Meatless Meals by Frances M. Lappé and Ellen B. Ewald. Ballantine, 1974.

"Meatless, Guiltless" by Maya Pines. *The New York Times Magazine*, Nov. 24, 1974.

Recipes for a Small Planet by Ellen B. Ewald. Ballantine, 1973.

The Ritual of the Hearth by Roberta Sickler. Macmillan, 1973.

False Teeth

by Jean Butler

WHEN Louise Barrett's dentist informed her that all her teeth would have to be extracted and replaced by dentures, the 55-year-old woman welcomed the news. Louise's youngest son had just gone off to college, leaving only Louise and her husband at home, and she felt both old and neglected. A bright new smile, she thought, would bring back her youthful appearance and might also revive her husband's waning interest in her. But when the new teeth achieved neither goal, she was utterly dejected.

John Keith, a 50-year-old executive, received his new dentures just a few days before he lost his job in a corporate economy wave. The new "plates" changed the lines of his face and seemed to interfere with the way he talked. They made John so self-conscious that he fell silent in job interviews and finally stopped job-hunting altogether. He complained bitterly that the dentures and the dentist had destroyed his life and career.

For most of us, the odds are 2 to 1 that we will be wearing dentures by the age of 65. Twenty-five million Americans now masticate with molars not their own, according to the American Dental Association, and although their proportion in the population is declining, thanks to better dental care and treatment, the ranks still increase by millions every year.

Fortunately, prosthodontics, the specialty of dentures, can now reduce much of the pain and discomfort once associated with "store teeth." Yet for many first-time denture-wearers, the chief difficulties originate not in the mouth, but in the mind. Their problems aren't dental—they're mental.

"A LIFE-CRISIS EXPERIENCE"

"Getting your first set of dentures is a life-crisis experience," says William F. Fitzgerald, Ph.D., assistant professor of psychology at the University of Michigan

A dentist counseling a patient as she selects an arrangement of teeth that can be modified to satisfy her particular needs and wishes.

School of Dentistry and a crusader for better recognition by dentists and patients of the emotional stresses of denture wearing. "On the one hand, you have the people to whom it's a symbolic admission of 'old age' and reminder of other losses they've suffered or are about to suffer—loss of job, prestige, authority, health, sexual potency, perhaps of family and friends. On the other hand, you have the people with glowing expectations of what the new teeth will do—take away the wrinkles around the mouth, make them more attractive sexually, get them a promotion or better job—and these people are going to be bitterly disappointed. Either way, it's a traumatic period."

Dr. Fitzgerald's opinions are echoed by dentists who recently participated with him in a symposium on the psychological aspects of denture wearing. "Patients who are faced with the necessity of complete denture treatment for the first time are confronted with a host of new experiences: physical, emotional, social, psychological," says Dewey H. Bell, D.D.S., of Virginia

George Washington often complained about his false teeth. At that time artificial teeth were wooden and often did not function properly.

Commonwealth University School of Dentistry.

Adds Hazen Baron, D.D.S., of Warner-Lambert Research Institute: "The period of adjustment for most people will probably be extremely trying, affecting their whole life-style and perhaps even altering their personality."

William Codwin, D.D.S., Dr. Fitzgerald's colleague at the University of Michigan, puts it crisply: "Fitting dentures is 80 per cent psychology and 20 per cent dentistry."

EMBARRASSING TO DISCUSS

Unfortunately, it is a proportion that dentists have not always been aware of—and patients may have been too embarrassed to talk about. According to a survey of dental schools conducted in 1971, only one-tenth of 1 per cent of a dental school curriculum was devoted to training in interpersonal communication—even though dentistry, in Dr. Fitzgerald's words, is "a labor-intensive profession characterized by talking between dentist and patient." The number of psychology courses being taught doubtlessly has risen since 1971, but it is still a minor aspect of dental education. And as for patients, many have never confronted nor been encouraged to openly face their feelings about dentures. "Most of them treat it as though it were a toilet thing," says Dr. Baron.

Yet many of the emotional problems of a first set of dentures could be overcome with better understanding and better interpersonal communications on both sides, according to Dr. Fitzgerald. (Dr. Baron says a first set of dentures should require no more emotional adjustment than a first set of eyeglasses.) What is necessary, Dr. Fitzgerald says, is for both dentist and patient to discuss fully and frankly all the expectations and realities of the new "plates." Such a discussion is at least as important as how well the teeth fit, Dr. Fitzgerald adds. And it is a "communications" program that should begin long before the dentures are actually needed.

Dr. Fitzgerald, an educational psychologist by background, became interested in the psychology of the denture-wearer after being told by prosthodontists of patients who returned again and again, taking up "chair time" with vague complaints that seemed only tangentially related to how well the teeth functioned. With the aid of dental students, Dr. Fitzgerald conducted interviews of several hundred patients, prosthodontists, and dentists about the expectations and feelings of first-time denture-wearers. One result has been a series of videotaped "psychodramas" which Dr. Fitzgerald uses to show prospective dentists how to recognize nonverbal cues and unspoken questions and hesitations on the part of the patient.

MISADVENTURES

A typical psychodrama depicts the dental misadventures of Mrs. Jones and Dr. Smith, the new dentist in town—a classic example of mutual misunderstanding, in Dr. Fitzgerald's view.

The scene opens in a cornflower blue dentist's office. Mrs. Jones's thoughts are heard in a voice-over as she enters and sits: "It looks new. I wonder how long he has been in practice. But I won't ask him that." To the dentist, she says: "You're new in town, aren't you, doctor?"

"Yes, I am, Mrs. Jones. Now what can I do for you?"

"Well, I've had these dentures for about 12 years and it seemed time for a new pair. I thought maybe you could make a new set for me that would make me happy." The voice-over continues with her thoughts: "My husband hasn't paid much attention to me lately. Maybe a new set of dentures would change that." But Mrs. Jones doesn't express these thoughts aloud.

However, the dentist replies: "I'll do my best, Mrs. Jones."

At this point, Dr. Fitzgerald usually stops the videotape and asks: "You see what the doctor and patient were doing wrong? Mrs. Jones wasn't being honest with the dentist about her expectations and the dentist wasn't being sensitive to Mrs. Jones. He should have recognized the subtlety in her questions and arranged a clear understanding of what he's going to do and what she expects.

"Because Mrs. Jones has unreasonable expectations of what the new dentures would do for her, she is going to be bitterly disappointed if her husband continues to pay no attention to her. And she's going to blame the dentist and the new set of teeth."

Then Dr. Fitzgerald starts the tape again and, sure enough, Mrs. Jones is back in the dentist's office complaining that the dentures don't fit properly, she still can't chew comfortably and, well, they just don't look good. There is still no mention of her disappointment at her husband's reaction, only her dissatisfaction with the dentist.

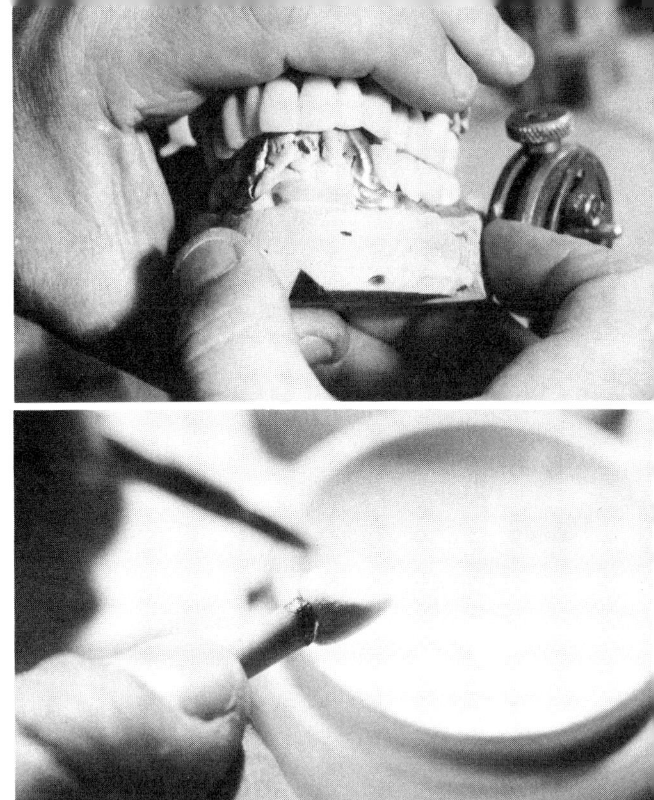

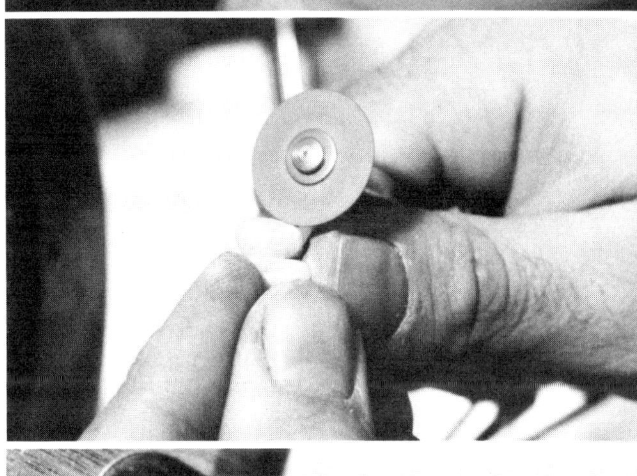

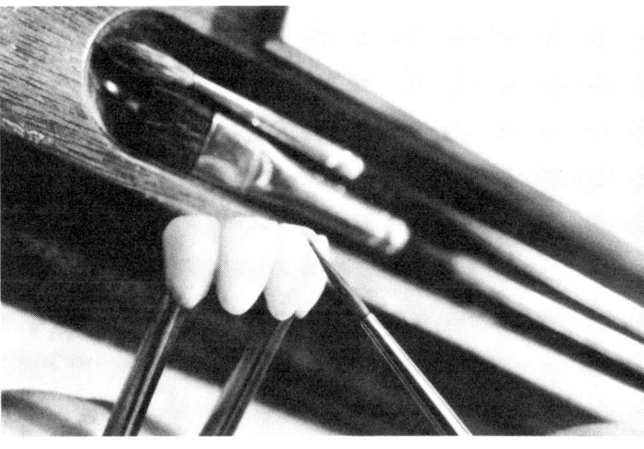

Steps in making artificial teeth. Right from top: a plaster cast of a patient's jaw being used as a guide in fitting new teeth; building up and forming the shape of an artificial tooth; delicate shaping with a file; coloring and shading to match the person's natural teeth.

UNSPOKEN HOPES AND FEARS

Yet, according to Dr. Fitzgerald, even the patients themselves often do not recognize their unspoken hopes or fears related to the new teeth. It is part of the legacy of a society that idolizes youth and beauty and dismisses old age as a problem to be dealt with rather than gracefully accepted. Television commercials, he says, repeatedly drum out the message that a gleaming smile and a mint-sweet breath are ingredients essential to romance and to the glow of youth.

"I saw an ad on television recently," Dr. Fitzgerald says, "where this young kid runs up, grabs a woman around the waist, throws her in the pool, and says, 'Oh, I'm sorry, Mrs. Davis, I thought you were Paula.' She answers, 'Oh, I get confused with my young daughter all the time!' That's sick! The values in this culture are so fantastically reinforced by these commercials.

"How often do you see a television show where the characters are happily middle-aged and in which growing older is natural and accepted as part of life?"

Indeed, Dr. Fitzgerald says, new dentures often confer many positive benefits on older patients—such as easier chewing, more comprehensible speech, an end to bleeding gums, a firmer jawline—and these pluses may be overlooked because of the emotional overtones. The younger the person, and the closer he is to what he perceives as the peak of life, the more likely it is that the prescription of dentures will be a psychological setback. Yet even an older person may undergo some personality change. It is not uncommon for a once gregarious person to become withdrawn, a voluble one to fall silent. In one case, a woman whose nature appeared sunny and optimistic became obsessed with age and fear of death.

"A DOWNHILL SLIDE"

According to Dr. Fitzgerald, the psychological problems of first-time denture-wearers fall into a few general groupings. (Those being fitted for their second or third set, he says, are more likely to be concerned with how the teeth function.) Most common, of course, is the association with advancing age and one's mortality. "Frankly," says Dr. Fitzgerald, "most first-time denture-wearers are either at or past their professional peak. If they're at it, they see false teeth as the beginning of the downhill slide. If they're past it, they see the teeth as one more sign of the downward plunge. Either way, they're depressed about it."

Among women, Dr. Fitzgerald says, the emotional difficulties are most marked when the diagnosis of dentures coincides with menopause, when signs of other physical changes may make the woman feel that she is no longer attractive. Among men, needing dentures at a time when their careers are often highly successful is disturbing, reminding him that he is getting older.

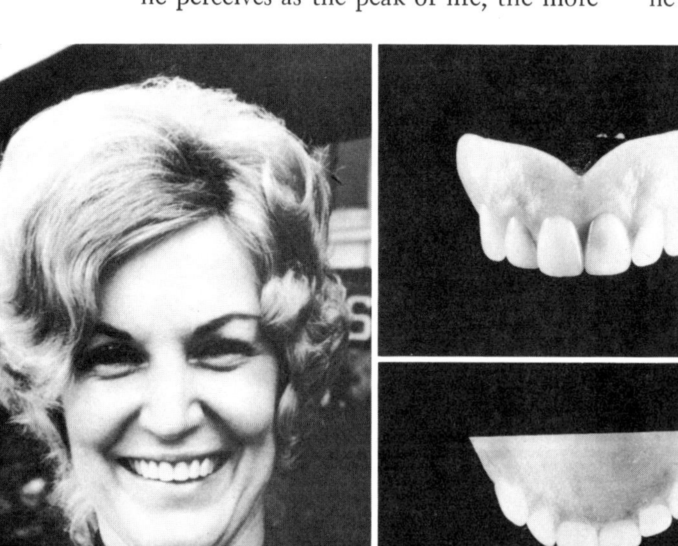

Artificial teeth are personalized by modifying size, shape, color, and arrangement so that they fit the facial structure and expression of the individual.

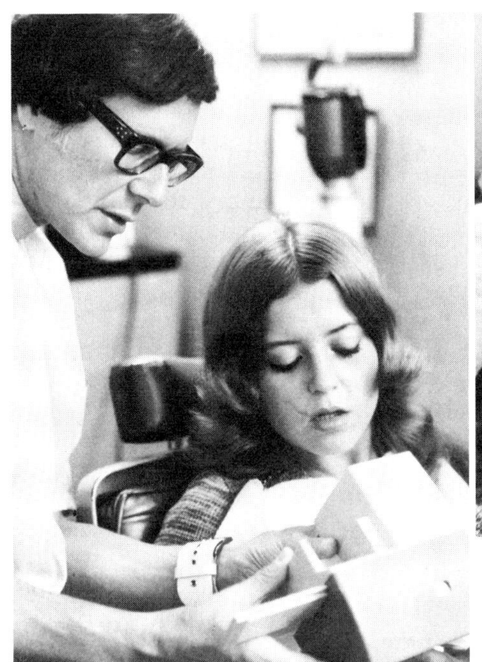

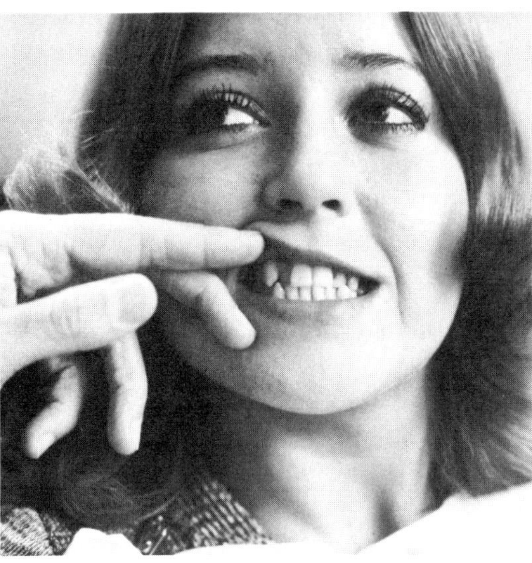

A dentist using a slide viewer to help explain to a patient what can be done. Visual aids such as this can help her to understand the possibilities and limitations of treatment.

ALL THAT BRUSHING IN VAIN

A second large group of first-time denture-wearers sees the diagnosis as a kind of betrayal. All their lives, they've diligently brushed and flossed, visited the dentist regularly, paid for the crowns and bridgework—and now they need dentures anyway. Dr. Fitzgerald compares the reaction to buying a new automobile covered by a warranty. The owner scrupulously follows the manual for service, pays for all the essential repairs and equipment, and the moment the warranty expires, the car falls apart. "Here you've played by the rules all your life, and now you're being cheated," Dr. Fitzgerald says. "It makes you feel worthless and defeated."

For both men and women, the anticipated loss of physical attractiveness can be the most crushing problem. The diagnosis of dentures can be especially devastating for those, such as salesmen, who consider their appearance important to career success. Dr. Fitzgerald recalls one man in his late 50's who was widely known for and took great pride in his distinguished mien and bearing. The new teeth, which he felt would change his facial contours, depressed him.

NOT A FACE-LIFT

Conversely, another large group of denture-wearers expects the teeth to provide a form of rejuvenation. "A woman may mistakenly assume that what she's getting is a face-lift and relief from hot flashes," Dr. Fitzgerald says, "and a man thinks he's getting a youthful new look that will stimulate his career and maybe bring him a promotion." The Michigan psychologist recalls one salesman who welcomed dentures, believing that the diagnosis explained why his sales had been slipping. When he got new teeth and still couldn't meet his quotas, he kept coming back to the dentist in the hope that some adjustment would at last provide the necessary magic.

How can denture-wearers—and dentists—anticipate and minimize the emotional problems of a first set of dentures? According to Dr. Fitzgerald, dentists themselves must take the first step, creating an atmosphere in which the patient is encouraged to talk, drawing out of him his hopes and concerns about the new teeth. "All too often," Dr. Fitzgerald says, "the patient starts to unload his worries, and then the dentist says, 'That's very interesting. Open wider, please.' Then he pops in a bite log and the patient can't even talk! Yet, unless everything is brought out on deck and made clear between them, there's going to be trouble."

For the dentist himself, Dr. Fitzgerald believes that a failure to communicate is counterproductive. The patient will continue to return with vague complaints that can't be completely identified nor treated and that will waste the dentist's time.

SUGGESTIONS FOR THE PATIENT

As for the patient, Dr. Fitzgerald suggests these guidelines:

• First, keep your teeth as long as you possibly can. "I would rather spend thousands of dollars on periosurgery and crowns and bridges than $400 to have my remaining teeth pulled and get dentures," Dr. Fitzgerald says. "The person who walks into a dentist's office and says, 'OK, I've had it. Give me a set of plates, it will be easier,' doesn't know what he's in for!" Some patient fears about dentures are justified: He may indeed have slurred speech, loss of sensation, less chewing efficiency, and changes of appearance. Naturally, he should avoid getting dentures for as long as possible.

• If dentures become unavoidable, choose a prosthodontist with whom you feel relaxed and able to discuss all your fears and concerns. Although some dentists protest a move "to make shrinks out of us," many understand and respond to the psychological needs of their patients. Obviously, you are more likely to have rapport with some persons than with others, and you should make the final choice carefully.

• Postpone the installation of dentures if you are upset by other matters. A period of unemployment, divorce, the death of someone close, a career change—these are not times to undergo additional trauma. Wait until the immediate period of stress has passed.

• Tell the prosthodontist all your fears and expectations about the teeth, however trivial or embarrassing they may seem. Dr. Fitzgerald suggests making a list of your questions and concerns, pointing out that in the dentist's chair an "anxiety reaction" sets in, so that you may forget what you meant to ask.

• Cooperate with the dentist in deciding on your new teeth. Several studies have shown that the most satisfied denture-wearers are those who helped choose the color, shape, and configuration of their teeth. Remember that your goal should be to have teeth as similar to your own as possible. Teeth become uneven and yellow as one grows older. If you insist on teeth that resemble your smile at the age of 20, they will look exactly like what they are—false teeth.

• Discuss the dentist's bill and all aspects of the treatment fully before it begins. A new set of teeth can produce enough problems, without your being hit with financial surprises as well.

EMOTIONAL READINESS

Thanks to increasing fluoride treatment, better dental techniques, greater use of dental services, better patient education, and a more alert public, the number of persons who'll need "store teeth" continues to drop. Perhaps such developments as tooth implants may reduce the number even more in the future.

But as Dr. Fitzgerald points out, most of us, if we live long enough, can expect to need dentures, and we should be emotionally ready for that moment. It's a subject that both dentists and patients should confront—and open their mouths about□

"The Fashionable Tooth" by Charles I. Stoloff. *Natural History*, February 1972.

"Medicine today: tooth implantation" by D. R. Zimmerman. *Ladies' Home Journal*, November 1973.

Workers in many chemical plants are exposed to substances known to be dangerous to health. Since news that vinyl-chloride gas, which is used to make many common plastics, can cause a rare form of liver cancer in humans was made public, increased attention has been focused on the problem of occupational health hazards. Here a worker in a chemical plant wears a protective helmet and goggles and dons a disposable smock before starting to handle a known dangerous chemical.

Vinyl Chloride

by Barry Kramer

IT'S a simple molecule: two atoms of carbon, three atoms of hydrogen and a single atom of chlorine. At room temperature it is a gas. The molecule is commonly known as vinyl chloride.

The chemical structure of vinyl chloride has been known since the 1830's. Since a decade after the Civil War, scientists have known how to link, or polymerize, the vinyl-chloride molecules like beads on a chain to form a plastic called polyvinyl chloride, or PVC. Since the late 1930's, when B. F. Goodrich perfected a commercial process for polymerizing vinyl chloride, the plastic has come to be a staple in thousands of products.

In January 1974, the world learned something else about vinyl chloride: it can cause cancer in humans. Twenty-six cases of a rare liver cancer have been discovered among workers in polyvinyl chloride plants. All the workers were exposed over many years to large quantities of vinyl-chloride gas. In late 1974, further evidence came to light indicating that the gas is also responsible for an increase of other cancers among the workers in the PVC plants. As a result, there now are U.S. government standards regulating vinyl-chloride emissions in factories. Vinyl-chloride gas has also been banned for use as an aerosol propellant. And the U.S. Food and Drug Administration is toughening the restrictions on the amount of vinyl chloride in PVC food wraps.

POTENTIAL DANGERS

Vinyl chloride, of course, is far from the only man-made chemical known to cause cancer or, for that matter, other human ailments. Industry regularly works with toxic substances of all types known to cause ill effects ranging from skin disorders to damaged lungs, kidneys and livers. In fact, the findings about vinyl chloride point up the potential dangers of an entire group of similar chemicals. Like vinyl chloride, they contain hydrogen, carbon and chlorine. The chlorinated hydrocarbons, as the chemicals are collectively called, are used in a broad range of products to which every human being has multiple exposures.

It would be difficult to find a person anywhere who hasn't come into contact with products such as plastics, anesthetics, insecticides and herbicides, solvents and pharmaceuticals, all of which can be made from chlorinated hydrocarbons. Molecules from these products can be found everywhere on earth and in the upper atmosphere. Such molecules are also commonly found in human tissues.

What is of particular concern to some scientists is the fact that the compounds are rarely found in natural systems unless those systems have been exposed to man-made pollution. "Although all living things contain considerable amounts of chloride ion . . . very few chlorinated organic compounds actually occur in living things," says Dr. Barry Commoner, director of the Center for the Biology of Natural Systems at Washington University in St. Louis, Missouri.

TRIAL AND ERROR

Dr. Commoner further notes that biologic evolution is a process of trial and error over millions of years. Therefore, he says, the assumption can be made that since the chlorinated hydrocarbons are virtually absent from all living things, the compounds are likely to be "evolutionary rejects." And that means, he says, that if such compounds invade a natural system like that of man, they are likely to be toxic.

"This means that industrial operations that synthesize or make use of such substances, and agricultural and other operations that disseminate them into the en-

Many workers in textile plants, press rooms, and the construction trades breathe toxic chemicals. Here two workers being given medical tests.

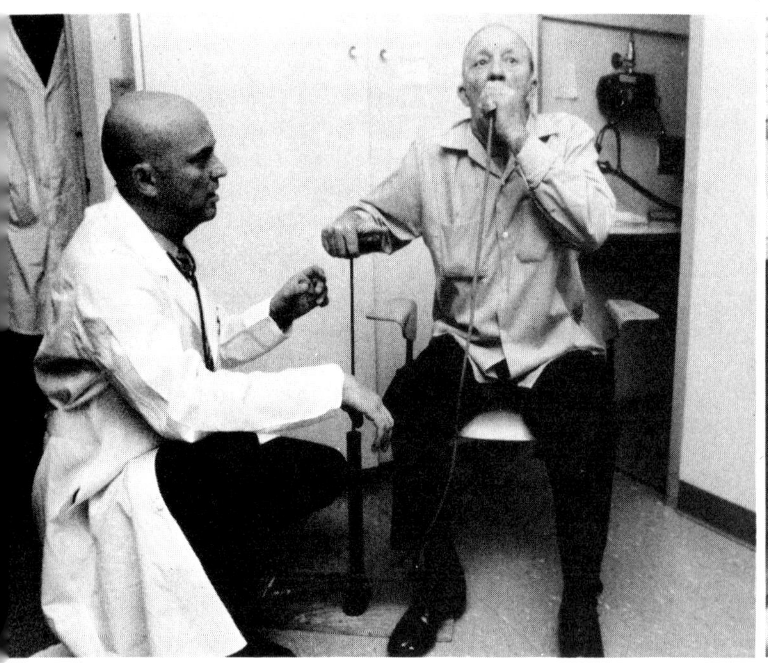

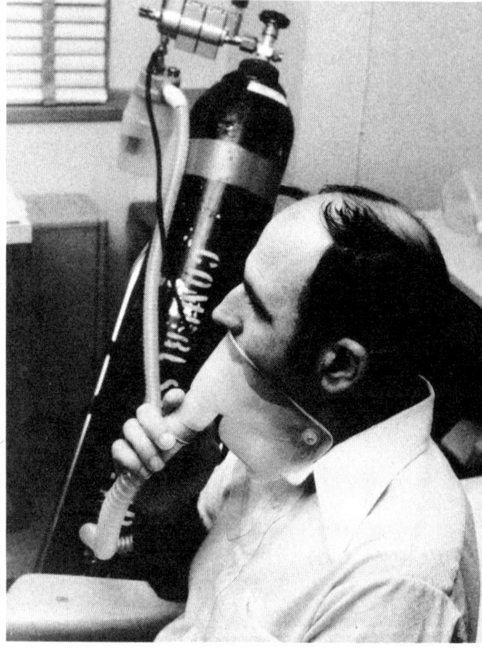

vironment, ought to be governed by the level of prudence that is demanded by the inherently dangerous situation," Dr. Commoner says. "That we now are discovering, with increasing frequency, health hazards due to dissemination of synthetic organic substances, both in the workplace and the general environment, is evidence that we have thus far failed to appreciate the need for such care."

It is interesting to consider that vinyl chloride, in the early days following its discovery, was actively considered as an anesthetic for surgery. But animal tests showed that the gas caused heart irritation, and it was abandoned for that use in favor of other substances. However, many anesthetics in use today are chemically related to vinyl chloride—and there is growing evidence that they are not without harmful side effects.

For the last several years, for example, there have been scattered reports of ill effects suffered by those who administer anesthesia and among others continually exposed to anesthetic gases while working in hospital operating rooms. It has also been known for some time that there is greater-than-expected incidence of spontaneous abortion among female anesthesiologists and nurse-anesthetists and, more tellingly, a greater than expected rate of certain types of fatal cancer among anesthesiologists of both sexes. There is no evidence that such anesthetics pose long-term dangers to surgical patients.

One recent survey of nurse-anesthetists in Michigan showed that of those who worked in the operating room during pregnancy, more than 16 per cent delivered infants with birth defects, compared with a birth-defect rate of under 6 per cent among nurse-anesthetists who stopped working during their pregnancy. Other surveys have found higher-than-expected rates of miscarriage and stillbirths among the wives of anesthesiologists, even though these wives presumably didn't enter an operating room during their pregnancies. One possible explanation is that the anesthesiologists somehow carried home sufficient amounts of anesthetic gas in their breath or on their clothes to affect their spouses.

The 1975 fire at the New York Telephone Company exposed firemen to vinyl-chloride gas because the plastic PVC was used in insulating telephone cables.

Studies are under way to determine whether or not the wives of vinyl-chloride workers have been affected by minute amounts of the gas unwittingly carried home by their husbands from the plants. Of particular interest is the rate of stillbirths and miscarriages among these women. The studies are by no means simple, since the true rate of fetal wastage —stillbirth and miscarriage—throughout the United States is not exactly known and therefore a basis of comparison is difficult. Furthermore, the women's husbands are also ordinarily exposed to a wide variety of chemicals other than vinyl chlorides, hampering direct correlations.

There are, of course, other carcinogens, or cancer-causing agents, and toxic chemicals in widespread industry use that are even more dangerous than vinyl chloride. The U.S. Labor Department issued standards in January 1974 for 14 other carcinogens. [In May 1974 the department also set standards for vinyl-chloride emissions in factories, and later it set "permanent" standards that took effect on April 1, 1975, a day after the U.S. Supreme Court refused an industry request for delay.]

The implications of these studies and standards are clear: industry will no longer be able to assume blithely that untested chemicals in the work environment are safe simply because they have never demonstrated any overt harm. Like vinyl chloride, which took years to take its toll on worker health, many chemicals thought to be harmless may be equally insidious. This may well mean that there will have to be extensive animal testing of new chemicals before they are introduced and that workers' health will have to be continually monitored to detect disease.

MAMMOTH TASK

The task of such testing and monitoring would be mammoth indeed. There are currently 25,000 industrial chemicals. More than 500 new ones are introduced every year. With an array like this, it's likely that other vinyl chlorides are lurking in the background.

Allied Chemical Corp. and Dow Chemical Co., for example, recently reported to the Labor Department's Occupational Safety and Health Administration (OSHA) that they had found excess cancer mortality among workers at two plants that made pesticides with inorganic arsenic. One study, conducted by Johns Hopkins University's School of Hygiene and Public Health, found that of the 22 retired male workers from Allied's Baltimore pesticide plant who died between 1962 and 1972, 17 had died of cancer. At Dow's Midland, Michigan, arsenical pesticide plant, which was closed down 20 years ago, Dow researchers found that of 173 workers who died between 1940 and 1972, 57 died of cancer. Both studies show higher-than-expected rates of cancer death.

Based on previous, less-conclusive evidence linking arsenic with cancer, the National Institute for Occupational Safety and Health in 1974 recommended reducing maximum levels of arsenic in the air of factories from the present 0.5 milligrams per cubic meter of air to 0.05 milligrams. Industry has opposed that reduction, but there is growing pressure on OSHA to impose a "no detectable" limit on arsenic.

Obviously, it is not enough to learn that workers exposed decades before to vinyl chloride, arsenic and asbestos—to name a few carcinogens—are dying today of cancer or of other effects of those substances. But the question of how to go about determining whether chemicals are indeed lethal in the long term is the subject of some dispute.

SUGGESTED SOLUTION

One suggested solution is to test all chemicals already in the workplace and to test other chemicals before they are used. However, Dr. Irving J. Selikoff, an expert on environmental carcinogens at Mount Sinai School of Medicine in New York

A technician at the National Cancer Institute uses a gas chromatograph to analyze a compound suspected of being carcinogenic.

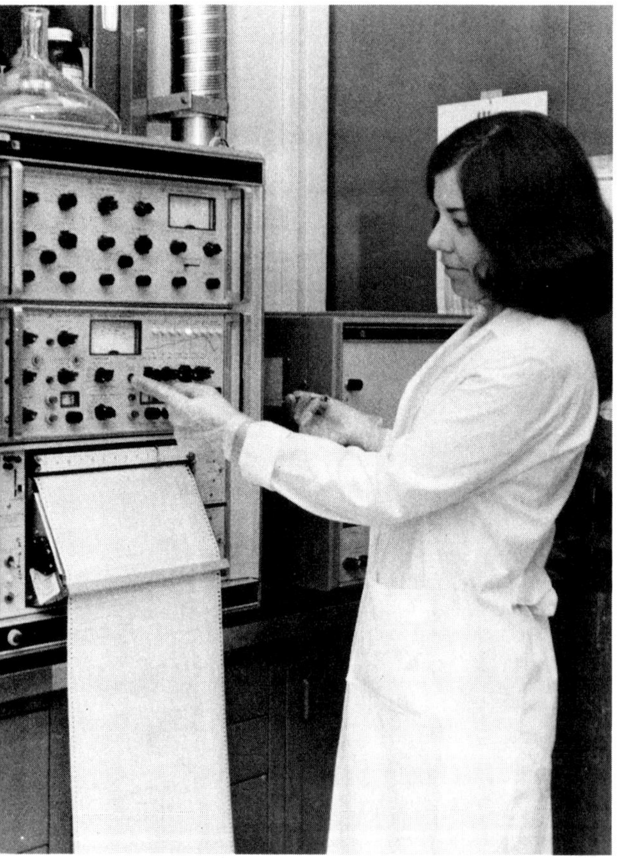

City, claims that this would be "unrealistic and scientifically impossible.

"Resources are limited," he says, "so we can't go charging off in all directions at once." Instead, Dr. Selikoff says that he and Dr. E. Cuyler Hammond, the chief health statistician of the American Cancer Society, have worked out some tentative testing guidelines. First, he says, chemicals to be tested should be those to which large numbers of workers are exposed. If many consumers are exposed to the chemical as well, he adds, the substance is an even likelier target for study.

An example of one such chemical is carbon black, an ingredient in rubber tires and, consequently, a widespread air pollutant. "We ought to be taking a look at what's happening to carbon-black workers," the doctor says. Scientists currently know that massive doses of carbon black painted on the skin of mice have caused tumors. Other prime study targets, he says, are substances whose chemical structure is "suspicious," or not unlike the structures of known carcinogens.

The testing envisioned by Dr. Selikoff would be a combination of animal trials, in which hundreds of animals would be exposed for long periods to the chemicals being studied, and statistical surveys of working populations that have handled the chemicals. "There are agents to which millions of people have been exposed which now can be evaluated in terms of long-term human experience," he says. "The human data is there waiting for us to evaluate it." Because animal studies do not always predict what will happen in humans exposed to the same substances, he says, the human monitoring is essential.

All this testing would be complicated by the possibility that some chemicals in the workplace cause cancer only in combination with other chemicals. And the exposure of most workers to many chemicals at the same time would make it difficult to pinpoint the offending chemical.

The cancer danger of vinyl chloride was spotted only because it caused an exceedingly rare tumor, liver angiosarcoma, of which there are only slightly more than

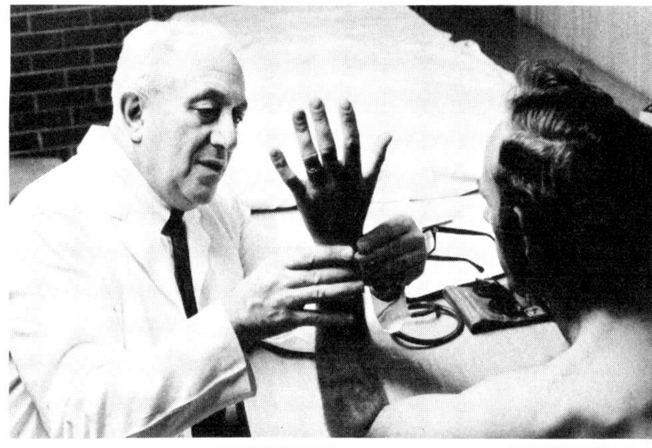

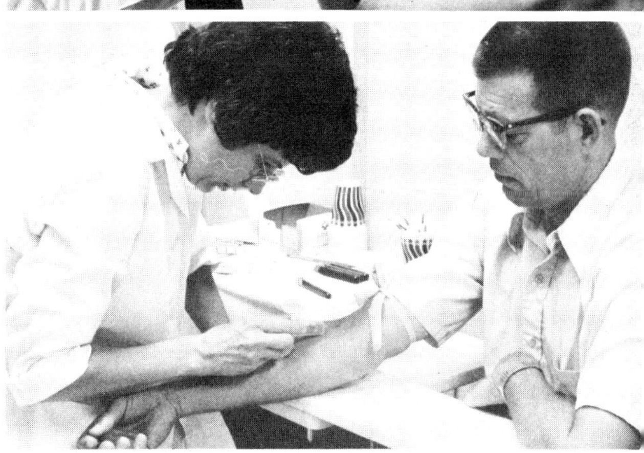

A team from Mount Sinai School of Medicine in field work investigating the effects of vinyl chloride. Top: Dr. Paul Milvy taking a chemical worker's exposure history. Center: Dr. Selikoff testing the blood circulation of a vinyl chloride worker. Bottom: Mrs. Joan Oswald taking blood samples from a vinyl-chloride worker.

Another occupational health problem: roofers who breathe benzopyrene, a chemical that is known to be a potent cancer-producing agent in animals.

100 cases in medical literature. If vinyl chloride caused a more common malignancy, such as lung cancer, it wouldn't have been so readily detected.

WHAT IS ACCEPTABLE?

Testing is only one part of the problem, the other part being what to do about toxic substances once their dangers are exposed. There is some risk in almost every activity, meaning that "acceptable" risks have to be determined for various substances. For example, even sugar, if injected in sufficiently large doses, will cause cancer in laboratory animals.

To arrive at a balance between risks and benefits, the risks must be fully understood. But very little is known about the dangers posed to workers by the thousands of substances they work with, and there is little optimism that such substances will be fully tested in the near future. Government agencies are understaffed and working with limited funds. A Toxic Substances Control Act, which the Labor Department says it needs to strengthen its control of industrial chemicals, is in a House-Senate committee.

Of course, even if such an act were to be passed, even the most sanguine aren't suggesting that the workplaces of American industry will be cleared of danger. Nevertheless, it is becoming more and more evident that there is less willingness simply to accept chemical dangers.

"Whatever happens," editorializes *Lancet*, the British medical journal, "the vinyl-chloride episode will have provided a salutary lesson. It will not be quite so easy in the future as it has been in the past for any chemical manufacturer to assume, until proved otherwise, that a chemical to which workers are exposed is carcinogenically safe. There must surely be more systematic evaluation of industrially used chemicals for carcinogenic risk to workers" □

SELECTED READINGS

"Hidden Plague" by Alan Anderson, Jr. *New York Times Magazine*, Oct. 27, 1974.

"On the Horns of the Vinyl Chloride Dilemma" by Paul H. Weaver. *Fortune*, October 1974.

"Vinyl Chloride Hazard." *Chemistry*, November 1974.

Arthritis

by Suzanne Loebl

ARTHRITIS is mankind's oldest known chronic disease. The disease plagued the Java, Lansing, and Neanderthal men who lived more than 400,000 years ago. Arthritis is also one of mankind's commonest chronic diseases. Today in the United States, arthritis, or rather "the arthritides," a group of arthritis-like diseases, affect over 20 million people seriously enough to require medical care. Another 35 million Americans have the disease to a minor degree and manage on their own.

The word arthritis means joint (*arthro*) inflammation (*itis*). Painful, swollen joints are one of the major characteristics of a group of about 80 different arthritis-related conditions that includes osteoarthritis, rheumatoid arthritis, and gout as well as some less well-known disorders such as systemic lupus erythematosus, scleroderma, and ankylosing spondylitis.

Arthritis-related diseases are not restricted to humans. Evidence of joint deterioration has been detected in the skeleton of the 100-million-year-old swimming reptile, platecarpus, and man's close friends the horse and the dog suffer from the diseases.

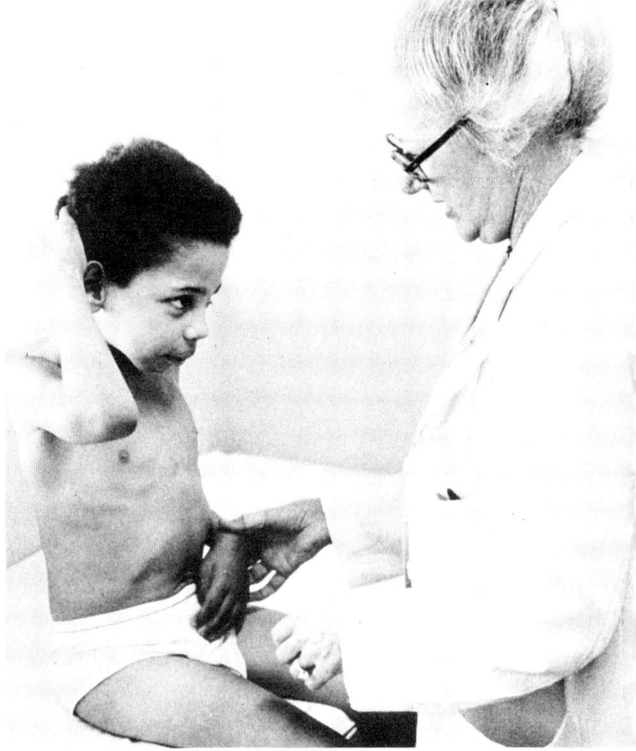

This boy is one of 250,000 children in the United States who have rheumatoid arthritis.

OSTEOARTHRITIS

Osteoarthritis is the most common form of arthritis. It is sometimes called the wear-and-tear disease. Indeed the X rays of 95 per cent of persons over the age of 65 show some evidence of joint erosion. The changes that take place in an osteoarthritic joint are very similar to those seen in other forms of arthritis.

Osteoarthritis can be primary, starting without any apparent provocation, or secondary, occurring as a result of one-time or repeated trauma. Football players commonly have arthritic knees, ballet dancers arthritic toes, and keypunch operators trouble with the index finger joint.

Osteoarthritis often affects only a single joint in the body. The cartilage, or soft elastic tissue surrounding the joint, is often the first part affected. The first noticeable change is a softening, pitting, and fraying of the smooth cartilage surface, followed by loss of elasticity. Pain and impaired mobility are common early symptoms.

Treatment of osteoarthritis is aimed at suppressing the inflammation. If only one joint is affected this is sometimes handled by local injection of an anti-inflammatory drug. Much progress has been made in the surgical treatment of osteoarthritis, and total joint replacement has been highly successful.

RHEUMATOID ARTHRITIS

Rheumatoid arthritis is the second most common form of arthritis. It affects about five million persons in the United States—three times as many females as males. It may occur at any age, frequently starting in early adulthood.

Unlike localized osteoarthritis, rheumatoid arthritis is systemic, meaning that it affects the entire body, sometimes causing fatigue and weight loss. An abnormal protein called the rheumatoid factor is present in about 75 per cent of patients with rheumatoid arthritis.

Rheumatoid arthritis usually affects symmetric joints; thus if the joint in the third finger of the left hand is affected, so usually is the corresponding joint in the right hand. The disease, like all forms of arthritis, is highly variable, its symptoms and course differing greatly among individuals. No two patients are exactly alike. This makes the diagnosis of the disease difficult.

Rheumatoid arthritis is a chronic disease. Fortunately, however, one of its startling features is that it often comes and goes. Even patients with severe disease have periods during which they are entirely "in remission" and feel free of symptoms.

Damaged joints can now be replaced with artificial ones. At top is a knee and from left to right are a hip, fingers, and an elbow.

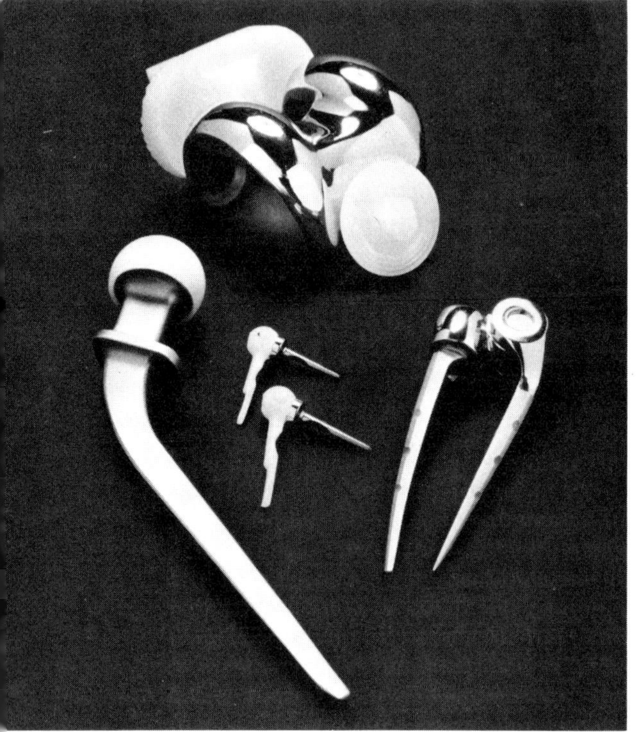

The treatment of rheumatoid arthritis is complex, involving the use of drugs such as pain killers and anti-inflammatory agents as well as rest and exercise.

Rheumatoid arthritis sometimes affects children. In the United States about 250,000 children are afflicted with juvenile rheumatoid arthritis. The great majority of these children outgrow the disease, but often only after many years of suffering.

GOUT

Gout is a metabolic disease associated with acute attacks of arthritis. It is a form of arthritis that can be treated very successfully. Patients suffering from gout have a defect in the way they handle uric acid, a key degradation product of proteins and purines.

For a variety of reasons—mainly either an overproduction of uric acid or too little urinary excretion of uric acid—gout patients have too much acid in their blood. This acid can crystallize out, much as sugar crystals collect at the bottom of a jar of honey. During an acute attack of gout, uric acid crystals become lodged in a joint—the big toe joint being a favorite target. There the crystals initiate the inflammatory process.

Some drugs, such as allopurinol, colchicine, and probenecid, can correct the defect in uric acid metabolism—either by preventing excess formation of uric acid or by speeding up its elimination in the urine. Today few patients with gout need to suffer any of the overt symptoms of the disease.

INFECTIOUS ARTHRITIS

Common infectious agents, such as those that cause tuberculosis, gonorrhea, or staph infections, can become lodged in joints where they cause intense inflammation. The recent upsurge in venereal disease has led to an increase in infectious arthritis. Infectious arthritis is a medical emergency, because it can lead to rapid cartilage destruction. It is, however, easily treated with suitable antibiotic agents.

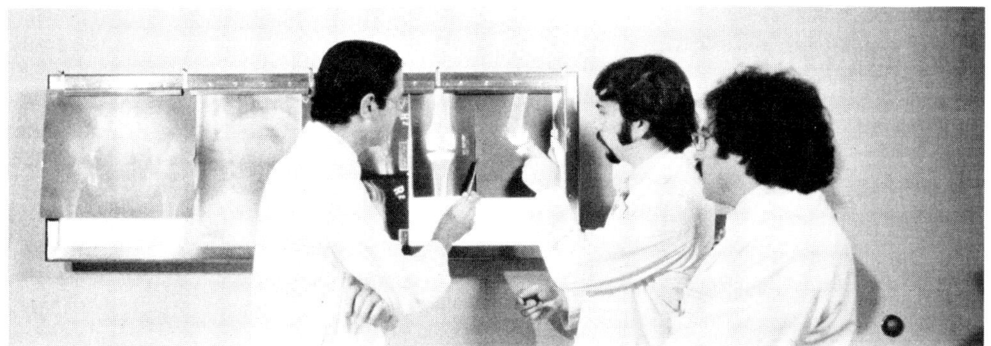

A group of doctors examine X rays of joints for signs of arthritic disease.

OTHER FORMS OF ARTHRITIS

Ankylosing spondylitis, systemic lupus erythematosus, and scleroderma are all serious forms of arthritis that fortunately occur rarely.

Ankylosing spondylitis occurs ten times more frequently in men than in women. It usually begins in adolescence or early adulthood. Untreated, it results in total fusion of the spine. In 1973 it was discovered that the great majority of patients suffering from ankylosing spondylitis have a characteristic "genetic marker," HA W-27. This marker could be used to identify persons at risk of developing ankylosing spondylitis.

The finding of HA W-27 is also an important discovery from a research point of view, since it and other yet-to-be discovered genetic markers may give a clue as to what type of person is at risk of developing arthritis.

Systemic lupus erythematosus is a cousin of rheumatoid arthritis and like rheumatoid arthritis affects more women than men. It is associated with a disorder of the immune system and affects many organs.

Scleroderma means a "hardening of the skin." It involves an overproduction of the protein collagen, the main constituent of cartilage and other types of connective tissue. Such overproduction eventually results in the choking of vital organs. Skin that looks and feels too tight is a characteristic of this disease.

THE INFLAMED JOINT

Joint inflammation is the "common ground" of the arthritis-type diseases. A joint is the junction between two or more bones. Bone ends are usually capped by cartilage, a soft, elastic tissue, which is the precursor of fully mineralized bone. The joint itself is enclosed in a joint capsule that is lined by a thin lining—the synovium—and filled with a lubricant—the joint fluid. The joint is "operated"—flexed, stretched, rotated, opened, and closed—by a system of muscles and tendons.

The initial step that triggers inflammation is not known for most forms of the arthritide diseases, but much of what happens once the inflammation is underway has been elucidated.

Any type of inflammation—including an inflamed arthritic joint—is characterized by heat, pain, swelling, and redness. The joint feels hot when touched, is exquisitely painful, swells, and may appear red.

Inflammation is a normal physiological mechanism, an attempt of the body to rid itself of something it considers foreign. The "enemy" can be many things—a splinter, a foreign protein, a transplanted organ, a particle of some sort, or a virus.

KINDS OF RESPONSES

The body reacts to such provocation with both "humoral" and "cellular" responses. The humoral response refers to the special proteins—antibodies—that the body manufactures when it encounters a foreign substance, or antigen. An *antibody* is generated against a specific antigen and combines with it, thus neutralizing the antigen. In the normal course of events, the antibody-antigen complex is somehow disposed of. Antibodies are made by specialized white blood cells called "plasma cells."

The cellular response of the body also involves the white blood cells—one type of white cell in particular, the phagocyte, or "eating cell." Phagocytes are supposed to physically remove an offender, including the antigen-antibody complexes, from the scene of the battle. The phagocytes have been compared to foot soldiers. Their function is to "swallow" and "digest" the enemy. To this end they are equipped with special corrosive enzymes—the lysosomal enzymes—inside special little sacs called lysosomes. Unfortunately sometimes the phagocytes swallow more than they can chew. Instead of neatly digesting their prey, they burst open, and the contents of the cells, including the corrosive lysosomal enzymes, escape into the surrounding tissues.

DESTRUCTION OF CARTILAGE

In arthritis the lysosomal enzymes escape into the joint cavity and attack the synovial membrane. This initiates the inflammatory process. The synovial membrane thickens. More white cells come to the battle scene. More lysosomal enzymes pour into the joint cavity. Sometimes the confrontation results in a "pannus," or pileup of synovial lining cells and defender cells. The inflammation is then feeding on itself.

Eventually the cartilage becomes inflamed and is gradually destroyed. It too may attempt a repair, which sometimes takes the form of overstimulation and overgrowth. In some cases arthritic joints become fused.

Inflammatory processes are seldom allowed to run their course today. There is a whole armamentarium of anti-inflammatory agents that suppress inflammation. Some of the more familiar drugs used for this purpose are aspirin, gold salts, and cortisone. Some of the newer cytoxic agents, which suppress the white blood cells, are being used to treat rheumatoid arthritis on an experimental basis at present.

Unfortunately none of these drugs can do more than suppress the inflammatory process of arthritis. They do not cure the disease, because the factor that triggers the whole process of the arthritic attack is still unknown.

IMMUNE FACTORS

There is increasing evidence that some but not all forms of arthritis are associated with a disorder of the immune system of the body. The details of the immune disorder are not yet known, but patients suffering from rheumatoid arthritis, for example, are known to have abnormal antibodies. In addition, a portion of the antibody-antigen complexes in these patients then reacts with some of sensitive receptor sites located along the blood vessels, in the kidneys, and in the synovial membranes. In turn, the body also may make antibodies against these antigen-antibody complexes; the rheumatoid factor mentioned earlier is one example of such an antibody.

There is still more evidence that the immune system may be involved. The white blood cells of patients suffering from some forms of arthritis have lost the ability to tell "self" from "non-self." In other words, they do not clearly recognize an "enemy." These patients then make antibodies against some of their own tissues. This is perhaps why their antibody-antigen complexes are not cleared away as they would normally be. In some forms of an immune system disorder—systemic lupus erythematosus, for example—patients make antibodies against their own nucleic acids. Such anti-nuclear antibodies are important for the diagnosis of these diseases. These abnormal immunological complexes may very well play an important role in triggering self-perpetuating joint inflammation□

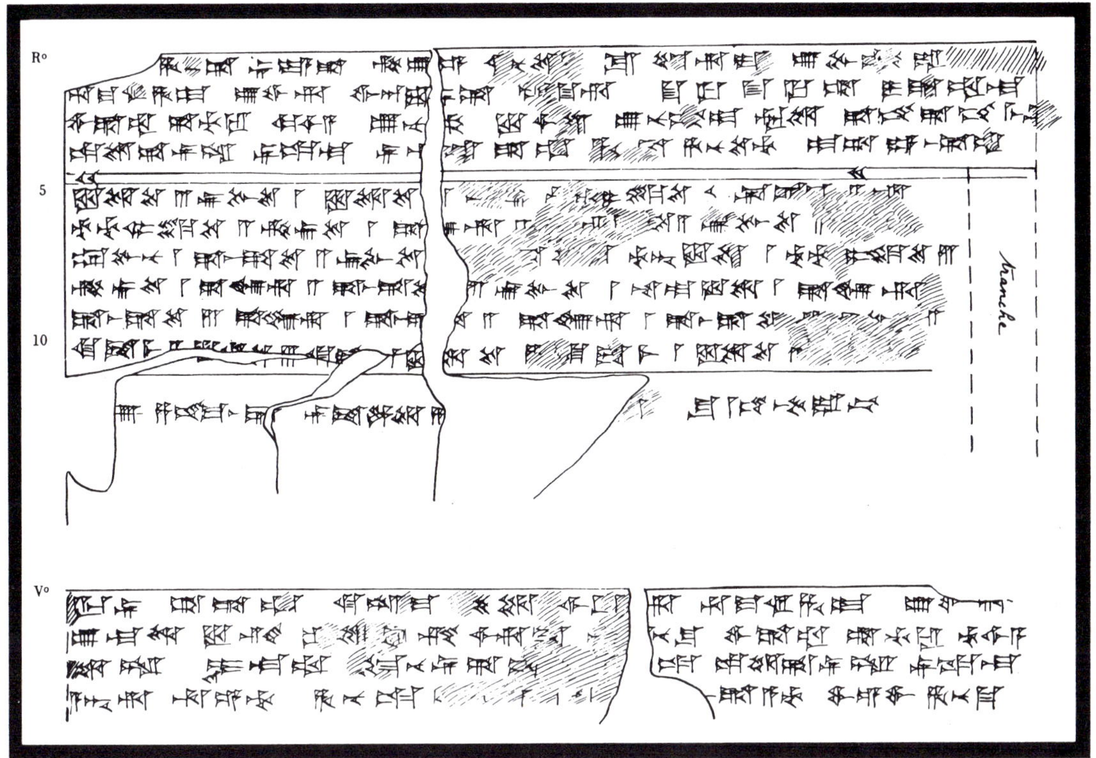

man and his world

contents

This is the oldest known piece of music, written about 1800 B.C. on a clay tablet found near Ras Shamra, Syria. Lyrics are above the double line; instructions for playing appear below.

review of the year

man and his world

Rising Population, Rising Hunger. Can the fast-growing population of the world feed itself? Millions of people were starving in six countries in Africa's sub-Saharan region, in the Bangladesh countryside, and in some of India's northern provinces as the United Nations mulled over this question in 1974. The United Nations took some definite steps—long-range rather than immediate—as it sponsored a World Population Conference in Bucharest in August and a World Food Conference in Rome in November.

The population conference drew delegates from 135 countries, and they quickly split into two separate camps on how to deal with problems arising from a 2 per cent annual growth rate—a pace that in 35 years would double the present world population of about 3.9 billion. The poor countries urged the richer ones to consume less food, minerals, and energy, and to be more generous in granting them humanitarian aid. The rich nations, in turn, asked the poor countries to conduct campaigns to reduce their birth rate. For years the birth rate in the less-developed countries has been increasing faster than in the developed countries. Aided by a sharp reduction in childhood deaths, the poor lands have larger percentages of future parents—and thus sharp gains in population are in prospect for them. (In Western Europe, only 24 per cent of the people are under 15 years of age; in the less-developed lands, usually 40 per cent or more are under 15.) Before departing from Bucharest, the conferees adopted a World Population Plan of Action that includes the collecting and disseminating of knowledge needed by countries to operate their own population programs.

The year 1975 has been designated International Women's Year (IWY). Here a photo from a March UN meeting where many women met to discuss the future for both sexes. In June a World Conference met in Mexico City to plan ways to implement IWY aims of equality, development, and peace throughout the world.

When 1,000 delegates from 130 nations gathered in Rome for 10 days for the World Food Conference, they talked about doing what Joseph did in ancient Egypt (as told in Genesis): creating a grain reserve in the years of plenty to feed everybody in the years of famine. However, Earl Butz, U.S. Secretary of Agriculture, pointed out that the world had no excess quantities of grain to put into a reserve. (In October 1974, the United States canceled a grain sale to the Soviet Union because it was not sure it had sufficient supplies to meet the needs of its long-standing overseas customers.) Further, Butz said in Rome, the setting aside of some grain for later use would cause "less consumption this year, higher food prices, and more inflation." The conferees talked about eventually setting up stockpiles with international supervision.

In fact, the conference got considerable adverse publicity because it did not move to meet a request, from an informal "Rome Forum" made up of 25 internationally recognized experts, for an immediate $5 billion outlay to buy grains to stave off starvation. Edward M. Martin of the U.S. delegation summed up the general direction of the Rome meeting by saying, "The conference was not called to get food tomorrow, but to lay out a plan of action to prevent the crisis that we now have from recurring."

As for the principal long-range goal, an assessment report of the conference pinpointed it this way: "The central problem needing attention is how to expand food production more rapidly in the developing countries." Before adjourning the conferees created the World Food Council, to be based in Rome as a United Nations agency closely linked to the Food and Agriculture Organization. Its purpose is to supervise programs dealing with food production, nutrition, and food aid and to try to achieve "a desirable balance between population and food supply."

Dr. Donald C. Johanson with fossils of a woman who walked erect and lived in Ethiopia about 3 million years ago. The Ethiopian finds may prove to be the earliest human fossils yet found.

Earliest Human Fossils. Working in a volcanic deposit near Dessie, Ethiopia, Alemeyu Asfew of the Ethiopian Antiquities Commission found a full upper jaw and parts of two other jaws of human beings in 1974, and announced that they may date back 4 million years. The discoveries therefore would be older than those of Louis S. B. Leakey and his son Richard in Tanzania and Kenya, placed at 2 and 2.6 million years. He is a member of the Afar Research Expedition, which takes its name from a region inhabited by the Afar tribe. In 1973, Donald Carl Johanson of Case Western Reserve University, head of the expedition's U.S. contingent, found the skeleton of a 91-cm (36-in) tall woman who walked erect and lived about 3 million years ago.

Prehistoric Observatory? Dr. John A. Eddy, a solar astronomer at the High Altitude Observatory, National Center for Atmospheric Research, Boulder, Colo., presented a detailed analysis to show that Wyoming's well-known Big Horn Medicine Wheel could have been a prehistoric observatory. Dr. Eddy said that the cairns of the wheel, although just heaps of stones, were aligned so precisely that Indians living on the Great Plains could have determined, for instance, the day of the summer solstice (the extreme northern position of the sun on its apparent annual journey). This astronomical skill would have let the Indians know that the time had arrived for their sun dance.

Oldest Song. The discovery of an Assyro-Babylonian love song from about 1800 B.C. "has revolutionized the whole concept of the origin of Western music," according to Dr. Richard L. Crocker, a professor of music history. Until 1974, musicologists believed that Western music began in Greece about 400 B.C. Then Dr. Anne D. Kilmer, a professor of Assyriology, broke the code of a clay tablet that had been found in the early 1950's near Ras Shamra, a Syrian city on the coast of the Mediterranean. The professors—both on the faculty of the University of California at Berkeley—gave the hymnlike song its 3-minute American premiere as Dr. Crocker played on a replica of an 11-string Sumerian lyre. The lyrics mentioned "beloved of the heart" and "love" in the ancient Hurrian language, but not all the words were decoded. The music, the professors said, was on the seven-tone Western scale, rather than on the Oriental five-tone scale.

2,200-Year-Old Ship. It took about 2,200 years for a Mediterranean merchant ship to travel the last two miles of its journey into the harbor at Kyrenia, Cyprus. The craft spent the centuries in about 30 m (100 ft) of water. Then an archaeological team capped a 7-year excavation and repair effort by getting the ship ready for display in 1974. Michael Katsev, an American who directed the excavation, raised about $350,000 support from the National Geographic Society, the Cyprus Mines Corporation, the Cook Foundation, and the National Endowment for the Humanities. The 14-m (45-ft) hull had been lifted out of 1.5 m (5 ft) of sand in 1969 with about 75 per cent of the wood intact, after which the workers knitted the craft together with stainless steel wire.

Diver aids in preparing a 2,200-year-old ship for raising off Kyrenia, Cyprus. Salvaged by a team of archeologists, the ship is the oldest vessel ever recovered from underwater.

Jury Selection as a Science. A headline in the *Christian Science Monitor* took note of the changing scene in courtrooms: "Social Scientists Win Jury Trials." Psychologists and sociologists have been enlisted by defense lawyers and defendants to help select jurors in several prominent cases recently. The cases involved were so prominent that public attention focused on the question of whether social scientists can do better than defense lawyers in choosing jurors who will give defendants the best possible verdict. In 1974, for instance, Jay Schulman, a former City College of New York psychologist, worked with lawyers defending prisoners in cases stemming from the Attica (N.Y.) prison uprising three years earlier. When, during jury selection, it became possible for the defense to challenge and thus eliminate jurors, Schulman looked for "people low on racism," those who were nonauthoritarian, and those "who don't see crime everywhere." In an earlier trial, five black psychologists helped Angela Davis's lawyers pick the jurors; the verdict was acquittal. Regardless of whether techniques were considered "scientific," criminal lawyers long have tried to use their challenges to create a jury favorable to their clients.

Who Owns the Wealth of the Sea? One hundred and forty-eight countries sent delegates to 1974 and 1975 conferences that were designed to write what they called "the law of the sea." Actually, they worked not on a single law but on six major topics: regulations for exploiting mineral wealth in the seabed, fishing rights, the width of territorial seas (that is, where one country has jurisdiction), environmental problems, freedom of scientific research, and rules for passage through narrow straits. The Fourth United Nations Conference on the Law of the Sea convened in Geneva, Switzerland, in 1975, as a followup to the Third Conference held in Caracas, Venezuela, a year earlier.

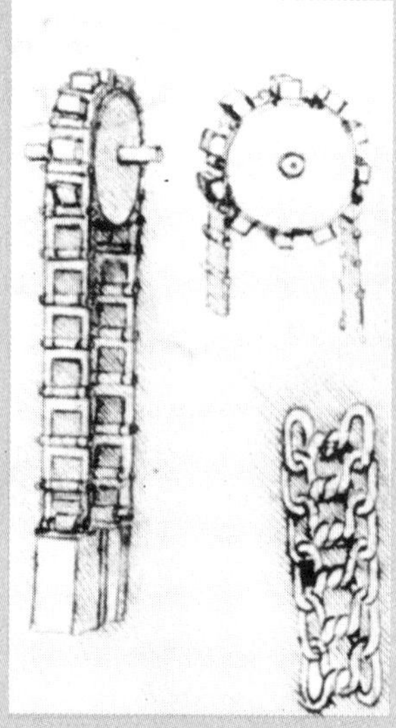

A Leonardo sketch of chain drive. The sketch, long lost in the Spanish National Library, has now been published in facsimile in the *Madrid Codices.*

The stakes are high. The proposed "law of the sea" could control rights to ocean mining, offshore and deep-sea drilling for petroleum, and access to rich fishing areas. In written papers and in debate, it was a case of the developing countries against the developed countries. There was an additional twist: the developing countries sparred with each other over special interests. In particular, land-locked countries wanted to share some of the wealth sought by countries fronting on the oceans.

Much of the talk concerned establishment of a 322-km (200-mi) economic zone. By that was meant an area where a country would control all the wealth in the sea for 322 km from its coastline (even though it didn't claim this as "territory"). The United States and the Soviet Union quickly came out in favor of this idea. Other countries with long coastlines, such as Canada, Australia, and Brazil, also would benefit greatly if the 322-km zone were adopted.

The Fragile *Monitor*. As a result of efforts of the Duke University Marine Laboratory, the U.S. Navy, the National Geographic Society, and the state of North Carolina, the U.S.S. *Monitor* of Civil War fame has been found off Cape Hatteras, N.C. The research vessel *Alcoa Seaprobe* discovered the ironclad in 67 m (220 ft) of water in Diamond Shoals, "the graveyard of the Atlantic." The *Monitor,* which fought the Confederate *Merrimack* (or *Virginia*) to a draw on March 9, 1862, sank while under tow in 1863. Hundreds of photos taken from the *Seaprobe* provided a mosaic that showed the *Monitor* to be upside down, resting partly on its round gun turret.

More About Leonardo. The amazingly broad range of Leonardo da Vinci's scientific foresight is demonstrated in the *Madrid Codices,* 700 pages of drawings and notes long "lost" in the Spanish National Library in Madrid. Found in 1965, the material was published in facsimile and English translation by McGraw-Hill Book Company in 1974. Born in 1452, the Italian artist, engineer, and scientist was centuries ahead of his time with diagrams for a gyroscope, a worm gear, a two-stage rocket, and other mechanical devices.

William E. Kennedy

Science Books of the Year

How To Read the Night Sky *by W. S. Kals. Doubleday, 1974. 155 pp., illus., $4.95.*

Would you believe it? A book about the stars that is so interesting that it takes effort to put it aside.

Any one who takes up astronomy as a hobby knows that trying to figure out star and strip charts is probably the biggest hurdle in studying and locating stars. Kals's explanation of celestial coordinates is one of the clearest to be found. With his book, you need only one simple instrument: your hand.

The author begins by showing the reader how to find the celestial equator in the night sky. Using this reference line, you can locate the 15 brightest stars. These stars are then used to locate the major constellations.

The appendix contains a very useful star calendar that goes through 1980, after which it can be "recycled."

There are only two errors in the book: On page 27 we find a star that rises north of west (stars rise in the east), and on page 98 Kochab is listed as in Ursa Major (it's in Ursa Minor).

This is a very fine book, and should be read by every beginner in astronomy.

Whitney's Star Finder *by Charles A. Whitney. Knopf, 1974. 97 pp., illus., paperback, $4.95.*

Whitney, a professor of astronomy at Harvard, has written an excellent introduction to the heavens. What distinguishes the book is the variety of information not usually found in other astronomy books: how to photograph an eclipse; how to set your watch by the sun; how to use both the sun and your watch to find directions; and how to determine when the sun will be due south.

The book is not really a "star finder," nor a "field guide to the heavens." The use of these terms in the title and subtitle refers to the "locator wheel" that comes with the book. The wheel can be used to find the most important stars at any time of the year. It has other uses—such as determining the time of sunrise and sunset—and these are described in the book.

Whitney's Star Finder is an excellent introductory book for the novice in astronomy.

Nothing Grows For You? *by Frances Tenenbaum. Scribner's, 1974. 118 pp., illus., $6.95.*

So. Your gardenia won't bloom. Your English ivy shriveled up. That hanging Boston fern just up and died one day. If you are one of the millions who want to bring nature indoors, but are worried about your brown thumb, then *Nothing Grows For You?* may be just the book for you.

You would find, for example, that you shouldn't be growing English ivy, gardenias, or Boston ferns in the first place. They are too difficult for the beginner.

What to grow? Ms Tenenbaum tells you. She also tells you how to handle problems of water, light, humidity, fertilizers, and pruning.

There is something in *Nothing Grows For You?* that is rare in such books—the "personality" of the plant comes through. What Ms Tenenbaum has given us is quite possibly the best beginner's book on houseplants that has been written.

God's Dog *by Hope Ryden. Coward, 1975. 288 pp., illus., $12.50.*

Hope Ryden is well known as the author of *America's Last Wild Horses* and for her crusade to save the mustangs. Now she has a new mission: To save the coyote, whom the Navajo Indians value as "God's dog."

The book, illustrated with photographs by Ms Ryden, is a testament to her uncanny ability to study wild animals in their habitat and to an almost unbelievable sensitivity to nature. She writes with love: "A few days after the puppies surfaced, a crisis occurred between Mama Redlegs and Brownie." She writes with anger: "Any animal that cannot be exploited, or any animal that threatens to compete with man's unmitigated exploitation of some other animal, is not long tolerated in America."

Hope Ryden with one of *God's Dogs*

Like the fox and the wolf, the coyote has long been seen only as a wily killer. *God's Dog* reveals it as a beautiful creature in its own right. It took a wonderful person to do this.

The Collector's Encyclopedia of Shells, *edited by S. Peter Dance. McGraw-Hill, 1974. 288 pp., illus., $19.95.*

S. Peter Dance, shell expert

Dance, one of the world's leading experts on shells, has provided not only a comprehensive reference work on more than 2,000 species of shells but also an easy-to-use guide for the amateur who wishes to identify specimens he has collected. An amateur first looks through the 12-page identification key to find a photo and brief description that fits the type of shell he has found. Once he finds this, he is referred to the discussion of the family to which the shell belongs. The family discussions include the description, size, geographic distribution, and frequency of occurrence of shells in the family. Over 1,500 color photographs are closely integrated with the text, with many providing insights into variations within a species.

The only problem for a novice using this book is becoming familiar with the specialized terminology used to describe shells. However, the Introduction to the book provides sketches that show the principal features later referred to. The user of this book might do well to learn these terms first before going on to try to identify particular shells.

The Collector's Encyclopedia of Shells is a handsome book, useful for the amateur collector and as well as for the serious collector and dealer.

The Year of the Butterfly *by George Ordish. Scribner's, 1975. 147 pp., illus., $8.95.*

The action begins on August 8 in a milkweed patch near a service station in Glens Falls, New York, and ends a year later in the same place. Within two days after butterfly eggs are laid, two Monarchs hatch. Ordish names the female "Pliable" and the male "Timorous," and he traces their growth—from caterpillar to chrysalis to adult—and their migration from Glens Falls to Lake Champoyán in Mexico and back to Glens Falls.

In between, Ordish, an economic entomologist, gives us a tremendous wealth of detail not only on butterflies but also on any technical aspect, such as basic navigation vector diagrams, that explains the life cycle of the Monarch. The writing is clear, and the book is beautifully illustrated with drawings by Thomas O'Donahue. Covering the Monarch's entire life cycle, *The Year of the Butterfly* is a wonderful addition to the nature lover's library.

The Jupiter Effect *by John Gribben and Stephen Plagemann, with a foreword by Isaac Asimov. Walker 1974. 136 pp., illus., $7.95.*

People living in earthquake zones—most specifically, the San Andreas fault in California—should be interested readers of this book, especially as the years edge on toward 1982. The authors predict that sometime around that year the world will be subjected to a series of devastating earthquakes. The California quakes, they say, will be at least as violent as any that have struck that region in historical times. The "Jupiter effect" is the trigger that will set things off there. Jupiter and the other planets of the solar system are now slowly swinging into a configuration that occurs only every 179 years. In 1982, all of the planets will be in line with one another. The indirect gravitational effects of this alignment, say the authors, will be the "nudge" needed to set off the series of earthquake disasters.

The idea seems far-fetched on first hearing—and perhaps even on second hearing. But *The Jupiter Effect* is one long chain of interlocking scientific arguments to back up this thesis. The reader may not be convinced by the time the book is done, but the thesis cannot simply be dismissed. Some links in the chain of arguments are clearly true. The San Andreas fault is a very well-known earthquake zone. And the evidence is fairly clear that another major earthquake is likely there before very long, especially near Los Angeles. The authors use theories of plate tectonics to show what is probably happening below the earth's surface in that region, and the news is not good.

They then turn to the ways in which other phenomena may be linked to earthquakes. These include weather changes and slight variations in the earth's rate of rotation, phenomena that are linked to the solar cycle of sunspot activity. The next link in the "Jupiter" argument is more tricky. Making use of statistics, the authors would show that the configuration of the planets as they orbit the sun affects sunspot activity and that when the planets are aligned, as they will be in 1982, the effect should be very strong. The increased sunspot activity would, in turn, affect the earth enough to "trigger" earthquakes.

John R. Gribben is an astrophysicist and an editor of the British scientific journal, *Nature*. Stephen Plagemann is a physicist. Both men know their science. But sometimes their reasoning tends to slip from the "what seems likely" stage to the "since this is so" stage. The relationship between planet configuration and solar activity certainly needs much further proof. The link-up between sunspots and earthquakes is equally unclear. On page 61, the authors note that even the effects of the moon's gravity on earthquake activity are hard to detect, because "the Earth is so large relative to the Moon." If the earth's closest neighbor is this hard to pinpoint as a cause of earthquakes, one wonders just how significant the "Jupiter effect" will be.

There is, of course, good reason for Californians and other dwellers in earthquake zones to be warned about how they build their homes and plan their cities. *The Jupiter Effect* serves this purpose, at least. The text of the book contains numerous typographical errors, and the authors rather annoyingly insist on dignifying astrology by identifying it simply with the study of planetary alignments.

Continents in Motion: The New Earth Debate *by Walter Sullivan. McGraw-Hill, 1974. 398 pp., illus., $17.95.*
Earth's Voyage Through Time *by David Dineley. Knopf, 1974. 328 pp., illus., $8.95.*

Although it sometimes seems as though a "revolution" in science were taking place every day, there is indeed one basic change taking place, in the field of earth sciences: the acceptance of the theory of plate tectonics, and the related concept of continental drift. According to this theory, the earth's crust is divided into giant plates that move around, separating and rejoining, sliding over and under one another. Most geologists now accept the theory, although they are not yet agreed on the forces that move the plates about. The two books listed above are products of this revolution in geological thought.

David Dineley is a geologist. The major portion of this book describes the concepts that make up the theory of plate tectonics, and the last few chapters review the history of the earth in terms of plate movements. Walter Sullivan is a science writer who has taken part in geological expeditions. His book tells the story of the development of plate-tectonics theory and of some alternative theories that have been proposed along the way. The two books therefore do not try to do exactly the same things. But in his review of scientific speculations about the earth, Sullivan gets across the main elements of plate-tectonics theory and geological history, as well.

Dineley has attempted a brief, popular survey of what is known about the earth's geological history, but there are some things wrong with his book. The first chapter, a brief account of past and present thinking about geological processes, is not well organized and is hard to follow. Before getting into plate tectonics, Dineley also reviews the solar system—to little purpose. His writing here is graceless and at times not grammatical. For example: "both the earth and the time it has existed are immensely large" (page 39). There are some errors and confusing statements, also. Dineley says that the "terrestrial" (earthlike) planets increase in density from the sun outward. In fact, Mars—a terrestrial planet—is lesss dense than the earth is (page 101).

When Dineley deals with geological processes and events, he writes more clearly, and his text contains a number of interesting observations. However, he becomes involved in details that are not of use to the general reader, and the main thread of the account tends to get lost. The latter portion of the book moves along well. In general, the book suffers from careless editing and production. The illustrations vary in quality and usefulness and are not always tied in with the text. A production disaster occurred in the chart on page 243, and several of the other charts should have been run larger. It should also be mentioned that Dineley uses British spellings and expressions, so the reader must be prepared to meet "vice" for "vise" and "Cainozoic" for "Cenozoic" and to make sense of such terms as "put paid."

Sullivan's writing is clear and direct. The chapters sometimes read more like journal entries than as parts of a unified account, and the elements of plate tectonics could be presented in a more orderly way. Sometimes the text wanders into secondary areas, such as the chapter on geothermal energy. But Sullivan conveys the excitement involved in this change in geological thinking. We meet such images as that of a gigantic river that once flowed westward across Africa, through the adjoining South American land mass, and into the Pacific Ocean. Or there is the Mediterranean basin, temporarily emptied and then refilled by means of what may have been the largest waterfall ever. The illustrations and diagrams are plentiful, and they aid the text. Ongoing programs of geological research are described, giving the reader a good sense of the current state of plate-tectonics theory. And the final chapter again reviews the difficulties that the theory presents to geologists.

If the Dineley work had been more carefully thought out and prepared, it would have been a useful addition to libraries. As it is, the less geological Sullivan account tells the story of plate tectonics in a more readable way.

Supership *by Noël Mostert. Knopf, 1974. 332 pp., $8.95.*

Noël Mostert, author of *Supership*

So large are the ships that Noël Mostert writes about that one wonders if the use of "super" to describe them may not well be the understatement of the year. These ships do not collide with smaller ships; they simply run over them, much as an auto might run over a small object.

One bleak day in August 1973, for example, the Spanish supership *Mostoles* ran over the South African trawler *Harvest del Mar*, which went down with a big *glug!* The entire *Harvest* crew drowned. "The trawler was trampled into the sea without the crew of the tanker's even being aware. When the master of the *Mostoles* eventually realized that he had struck something, he reported that he had hit a 'submerged object'."

At night a supership must display, as must all ships and boats, lights at the bow and stern. So far apart are these lights—almost a quarter of a mile—that there have been several reported instances of smaller ships trying to sail between the lights. The assumption had been that there were two ships far apart.

Unbelievable as these incidents may be, they are not the reason for this book. What concerns Mr. Mostert is the environmental impact of the floating iron monsters: the destruction of marine life and disabling of large segments of the oceans and their shores by massive oil spills.

For these superships—a consequence of the Arab-Israeli war of 1967 and the closing of the Suez Canal—seem almost jerry-built. Overloaded and in dangerous waters, particularly off South Africa, they pose an ecological peril if they explode, crack up, or sink.

Relentlessly, Mostert documents the disasters. In April 1968 the German tanker *Esso Essen* hit a submerged object near Cape Town and 30,000 barrels of oil poured out.

Shortly thereafter the Greek tanker *Andron* split open at the seams during a storm off the Cape and leaked her cargo into the same area. A third tanker, overloaded, was spotted frantically pumping oil into the ocean. When the oil creeps to nearby islands, the penguin is usually the first to suffer.

"His appearance and behavior when harmed by oil are pitiful," writes Mostert. "Oil affects the balance of the birds when it enters their ears and they stagger drunkenly, or find it impossible to stand at all. Their eyes are infected or blinded. But they are most cruelly maimed by the diesel and other refined oils that are thrown out with the bilge water. These oils burn their skin and stomach lining, and affect their livers. There is usually little that can be done for them when they are in this state."

Already the jackass penguin is on the verge of extinction, the victim of oil. All animals, not just penguins, suffer. The contaminated area contains many species, such as whales, seals, and walruses, that we would like to see preserved.

Superships are built to last 10 years. What bothers Mostert is that the ships are launched without being tested, and that as the ships get older, and weaker—and more dangerous—they may be resold to "flags of convenience" (countries that have very low standards for ships).

Mostert, no armchair conservationist, sailed from Europe on the supership *Ardshiel* around the Cape of Good Hope to the Persian Gulf and back. He found himself with a new breed of sailor: Cut off from the sea, by the very size of the ship, and from the shore—because a supership loads and unloads from offshore riggings—sailors become more like astronauts who have little contact with the planet.

Supership, almost a diary of Mostert's voyage, is a classic among ecology books.

The Medically Based No-Nonsense Beauty Book *by Deborah Chase. Scribner's, 1974. 285 pp., illus., $10.00.*

Another beauty book? Yes, but this time a good one based on medical facts. Deborah Chase, who has herself done medical research and is an accomplished science writer, has given us an excellent beauty manual.

The book is divided into three main sections: The Skin, The Eyes, and The Hair. In each section Ms Chase presents the basic facts of physiology and biochemistry necessary for the interested woman to understand proper beauty care. She tells us, for example, what the skin and hair are made of and how they grow. Then she gives a step-by-step guide to beauty care: what should be done daily, weekly, occasionally.

More than half of the book is devoted to specific beauty problems—some the normal result of aging, some caused by disease, some by drugs, alcohol, the sun —or unsound beauty practices. Ms Chase gives advice for dealing with each problem. All her advice is practical, price-conscious, and specific, citing brand names and at times giving recipes for beauty aids to make at home. In this way the book provides an extra dividend: it will save you time and money.

Ms Chase does not pretend to present an answer for all beauty problems. She frankly says there are some things you can't do much about—some gray hair after 30, some fine facial lines after 25. But she does say what to do to care for them and very importantly, what not to do—such as massage facial skin.

Cosmetics and beauty aids must now be labelled with their ingredients, but a list of complicated chemical terms does not help much. Here again, Ms Chase helps—in providing a "glossary of cosmetic ingredients and terminology."

The Medically Based No-Nonsense Beauty Book is an excellent book, providing a way women can approach beauty care without depending on advertising claims□

An Easter Island statue has its head replaced during the restoration effort begun in 1960. The figure had been purposely broken by the islanders many years ago.

Contemplate the Navel of the World

by William Mulloy

> The battle to feed all of humanity is over. In the 1970's the world will undergo famines—hundreds of millions of people are going to starve to death in spite of any crash programs embarked upon now. Nothing could be more misleading to our children than our present affluent society. They will inherit a totally different world in which the standards, politics, and economics of the 1960's are dead.

MANY have read these grim words from the prologue of the book, *The Population Bomb*, by Paul Ehrlich, professor of biology at Stanford University, and most have forgotten them as too painful to remember. We have required considerably more than a million years to fill our world with over three billion people. Most of us find such time intervals and numbers as well as their frightful implications so vast as to be almost meaningless. It is difficult to evaluate them.

A remote Chilean island, known to its prehistoric inhabitants as *Te Pito o te Henua*, or The Navel of the World, provides an illustration of the essential nature of the problem. That tiny mote of land, better known today as Easter Island, is one of the earth's inhabited places most isolated by the sea. Investigation of its unusually independent arena of human struggle for survival is beginning to reveal on its microcosmic stage some striking parallels to this decisive dilemma of the world at large.

A UNIVERSE IN MINIATURE

The miniature universe is only 22 km (14 mi) long and is the easternmost island of Polynesia. The formerly wooded, but now grass covered, intersecting slopes of three great volcanoes include a triangle of about 117 km^2 (45 mi^2) of good volcanic soil interspersed with lava flows and satellite cones. Pitcairn, of *Mutiny on the Bounty* fame, about 2,250 km (1,400 mi) to the west, is the nearest inhabited island, and one must sail a full 3,700 km (2,300 mi) to the east before reaching the coast of South America. Location near the border of the southern tropical and temperate zones provides the most pleasant of temperate climates. For the most part, the coasts have steep cliffs with few beaches, and good anchorages are lacking. The subsurface peripheries of the island slope too sharply from the shore to permit the formation of a coral reef, and thus there is no lagoon. Fishing, though, is reasonably good.

Neither prehistoric Polynesians nor North American Indians are known to have been capable of precise and systematic navigation over the vast distances that separate this island from the rest of the inhabited world. Thus this remote place was very likely populated by one, or more likely several, small parties of lost seafarers forever unable to return to their original homes.

Single canoeloads of such wanderers may have arrived at widely separated times. Comparative research has suggested the South Pacific islands Marquesas and Mangareva as likely places from which they came. However, some South American Indians also may have been involved, as well as people from other Pacific islands. Such lucky landfalls could only have been rare. Survivors had to develop their life way in a new environment with significantly less of the stimulation of external ideas so vital to communities in most other parts of the world.

COMPLEX CULTURE

Nevertheless, in sharp contrast to the experience of most isolated peoples and for reasons still largely obscure, the people of the island developed a surprisingly complex culture. This culture included such unexpected symbols of advancement as a written language still undeciphered and not known to be related to any other script. Other accomplishments were: a class-organized society with enough coercive power to assemble large crews for spectacular public works projects, an organized priesthood, systematic knowledge of solar movements, an impressive religious architecture utilizing precisely cut and fitted stones weighing many tons, highly stylized stone sculpture productive of about 1,000 statues (some of which weigh hundreds of tons), and the engineering procedures necessary to transport and erect them.

Under such unusual conditions of isolation these achievements reflect an industrious community. Clearer understanding of the forces that encouraged the people would enrich significantly our theoretical knowledge of the mechanism of human cultural advancement.

The Pacific was one of the last parts of the world to be explored by man. So the development of these accomplishments could only have been as rapid as it was independent. The earliest reliable radiocarbon date so far discovered is A.D. 690. It establishes the time of construction of one of the many gigantic outdoor altars—an architectural undertaking certainly not the first activity of new immigrants. A community undoubtedly had been developing for many years before this date—since perhaps 2,000 years ago.

A SCULPTURING OBSESSION

The stockpile of ideas brought from the earliest homelands might have been made ample and diverse by arrivals from a considerable number of other islands and perhaps the South American continent as well. Another important key stimulation to advancement clearly resulted from a curious turn in religious expression developed from ideas widely known in Polynesia. Certainly before the time of our earliest radiocarbon date, these islanders had already embarked upon the most remarkable religious building and sculpturing obsession known anywhere in the Pacific.

This was to establish the orientation of much that followed. The typical architectural product was a variety of Polynesian outdoor altar locally called *ahu*. Similar, though less spectacular, sanctuaries are found on many other Polynesian islands, where they are frequently called *marae*. The Easter Island *ahu* were elongated masonry platforms sometimes approaching 183 m (600 ft) in length and 6 m (20 ft) high. They were usually built along and close to the shores, and frequently included precisely fitted, unmortared stones weighing many tons.

From the inland side of the platforms descended paved, sloping ramps to border spacious plazas on which worshipers assembled. Just inland were rows of houses occupied by the priests. Common people appear to have lived even farther inland. Eventually most shores became dotted with hundreds of such sanctuaries, and they spilled over into the interior. *Ahu* were enlarged and rebuilt as capacities increased. New and increasingly ostentatious features were added in a way reminiscent of the competitive motivations of Western society.

At some point during this architectural development, stone statues began to be carved and erected alone or in rows on the *ahu* platforms. These, we are told by local legends, represented ancestors of special importance in the religious beliefs. In them was thought to reside the impersonal supernatural power called *mana*, which protected the communities that owned them.

The earliest sculpture tended toward crude and naturalistic human forms. Eventually the forms developed gigantic size and an endlessly repeated, highly distinctive local style known to the world today as the special hallmark of Easter Island. The largest of these brooding and disdainful figures ever transported to an altar weighs more than 83 tons and is over 9 m (30 ft) high. Unfinished examples more than twice that height call attention to the ambitious self-confidence of the long-dead engineers in transporting and erecting the colossal monoliths.

Vai Uri, another *ahu*, or outdoor altar, was rebuilt in 1970, using the stones and pieces of statue that remained. The wharf and ramp in the foreground are part of the restoration. They were useful for bringing canoes ashore on the almost beachless island.

STATUES STILL IN QUARRY

Most statues were carved from a buff-colored volcanic tuff. The carving was done in a great quarry located high on the steep interior and exterior slopes of a large satellite volcanic cone called Rano Raraku. Here they were finished almost completely, including fine detail, before being detached from the living rock and lowered to the plain below. Over 200 unfinished examples remain today in the quarry, illustrating every phase of a highly systematic sculpturing process. Others stand at the foot of the slopes, apparently awaiting transportation to their *ahu*.

Statues were transported face down on prepared roads, probably on wooden sledges pulled by many men. The details of the techniques used remain mysterious. Considerable evidence indicates that the hundreds of statues that stood on altar platforms were erected by gradually constructing masonry supports under them as they were elevated by many long levers.

As statues became larger and engineering methods developed, large cylindrical topknots called *pukao* began to be placed on the heads of some of the gigantic figures. They were made of contrasting red scoria (cinder). They were carved in another crater quarry called Punapau, from which they were rolled to their *ahu* destinations. The delicate mechanics of balancing an 11-ton topknot on the head of a high statue may well be the most remarkable engineering achievement performed by these islanders. Today we can only speculate on how they did it.

OTHER CONSTRUCTION

Religious building stimulated other construction. The network of roads with their cuts and fills that permitted statue and topknot transportation was extensive. Paved ramps were built into the sea to bring ashore large canoes, and thus the problem of the scarcity of good beaches was solved. Fantastically shaped volcanic tubes and other kinds of caves were sometimes lined with masonry to form dwellings, refuges, and other structures.

The precisely carved foundation stones of the boat-shaped, thatched houses occupied by the priests are seen everywhere near the *ahu*. Cylindrical towers of unknown purpose are dispersed along the shores, and crematory platforms reflect death customs. Masonry-walled agricultural terraces and enclosures attest to careful conservation of limited soil resources. Thousands of bas-relief carvings, some of heroic proportions, adorn available rock surfaces.

The ceremonial center of Orongo, astride the narrow crest of the nearly mile-wide crater of the volcano called Rano Kau, includes some 47 masonry houses. It was the site of annual religious rites during which specially trained athletes were sent swimming through shark-infested waters to the offshore islet of Motu Nui. Here the one lucky enough to find and bring back the first egg of the sooty tern gained special ceremonial privileges for his sponsor during the following year. This Easter Island egg hunt was a part of spring ceremonies dedicated to the cult of the *Manutara*, as the sooty tern was called. It appears to have been a late feature of the religious practice.

DELICATELY BALANCED SOCIETY

Such spectacular building and ceremonial activities required a society as delicately balanced as were the topknots on the ancestor images. The society had to be capable of diverting large numbers of people to construction, sculpture, religious activities, and other work not productive of food. Still-remembered legends relate details of a class-organized theocracy with specialized groups that included priests, sculptors, masons, fishermen, agricultural workers, and others.

Progressively more of the protective bush was cut down to make available agricultural land for the ever more numerous plantations. These eventually exploited even the most marginal agricultural land. Domination of the natural landscape was intensive and undoubtedly effective in serving the human purpose of the times. Such a people at the climax of development must have felt great confidence in the future and a powerful sense of the impregnability of the accomplishments.

As is 20th century man, the Easter Islanders were technologically successful. They were secure in the protection of the supernatural power of their deified ancestors who lined the shores in an unbreachable bulwark against the mysterious dangers of the empty seas and gazed pridefully inland upon the achievements of their issue. These industrious islanders must have rejoiced in the solid assurance that their success was permanent.

DISASTER FROM WITHIN

But disaster hovered and it was not precipitated by enemies from beyond the seas. The 117 km² (45 mi²) was a finite environment. With ever-increasing labor-consuming emphasis on religious construction, food had to be produced continually more efficiently by those allotted the task. Food-producing potential was probably never completely exhausted, though its limits may have been approached. It was, however, dependent on the uninterrupted maintenance of what must have been a highly coordinated social mechanism. Even slight disruption might have been expected to be sharply felt by many people.

A legend describes dissension erupting from disagreements about the idea of im-

Above: ahu a Kivi's seven ancestral figures gaze inland impassively. Below: the island's culture collapsed so quickly that many statues were left unfinished in the quarries.

proving the productivity of agricultural land by removing surface stones and throwing them into the sea. Animosities, once generated, appear to have produced their usual reactions. Eventually two groups, the Hanau Eepe and Hanau Momoko, fought a great battle along an entrenched line on the slopes of the volcano Poike. The former are said to have been all but exterminated. Radiocarbon dates and genealogical research agree that this decisive conflict took place about 1680.

WAR LEADERS IN CONTROL

A new era appears to have been inaugurated. Very probably because the devastation of war interrupted food production, the established religious aristocracy lost its essentially magical control. The people degenerated into mutually hostile bands controlled by new war leaders called *matatoa*. The hitherto efficient economic equilibrium disintegrated. Crops were burned and farmers were prevented from cultivating in safety. Fishermen were molested. The coordination that had provided food for many nonfood producers could no longer be maintained.

Though ritual cannibalism may have been present in earlier times, this now became a more practical activity, and people were hunted for food. A frequent theme of the legends of this period relates the suffering of fugitives who hid in caves to escape human predators. Horrible atrocities are described.

SIGNS OF CATASTROPHE

The religious building and sculpture that had been considered essential for supernatural aid became difficult and eventually impossible. Because labor parties were no longer safe away from their own territories, work at the great statue quarry ceased. To this day the locality speaks eloquently of catastrophes, hopes unfulfilled, and projects suddenly abandoned. Hundreds of gigantic works of art remain unfinished. Thousands of stone adzes and picks still rest where they were dropped by the artisans. Even the roads mutely reveal sudden work termination, with statue after statue lying abandoned.

The toppling of statues on altars became one of the typical depredations of the time, probably with intent to destroy

The southern slopes of Rano Raraku crater in southeastern Easter Island were the source of the volcanic rock used in making almost all of the yellowish statues.

Near Hangaroa, workers restore the base of Ahu Ko te Riku. The statue bears a *pukao,* or topknot, made of scoria, a reddish volcanic slag quarried from Punapau crater in western Easter Island. Balancing such topknots on a statue was a real feat of engineering.

the supernatural power thought to reside in them. In some cases statues may have been overturned and the masonry of the *ahu* destroyed by owners who had lost faith in their supernatural support, rather than by enemy groups. In many cases the vandalism was carried out with coldly calculated vindictiveness: vertical stone slabs were placed so that statue necks would fall across them and be broken. The beautiful masonry of the altars was pried apart and the great stones were scattered. The destruction continued until no statues were left standing on altars, and the survivors knew only the rubble. Such extreme reactions suggest people forced beyond endurance by intolerable conditions and find a sharp parallel in many familiar events of our own century.

The highly ritualized disposal of the dead by cremation was discontinued, probably because the priesthood charged with its supervision no longer functioned. Vast numbers of burials were made in the ruins of the *ahu*.

In contrast to earlier periods, weapons become the commonest items encountered in archaeological deposits of these times. Land lay fallow, and the unused plantations developed a sparse short grass cover quite different from the original protective bush. Moisture, formerly retained, now sank quickly into the soil and escaped to the sea.

The general cultural level was reduced greatly, and the population had decreased to an estimated 3,000 or 4,000 people by the time the island was discovered by a Dutchman, Jacob Roggeveen, on Easter Sunday of 1722. He and three other 18th century explorers who came after him encountered a remnant people progressively more deprived of the capacity that had produced their earlier achievements. The remnant survived in an impoverished and grass-covered land that retained only slender water supplies.

UNABLE TO RESIST SLAVERS

Local conflicts continued while the disorganized and vulnerable community's ability to resist was further reduced, until it became easy prey for 19th century slavers and whalers. The schooner *Nancy*, out of New London, Connecticut, carried away 22 people as slaves in 1805. This established a pattern that culminated between 1859 and 1862 in systematic raids by Peruvians, who removed about 1,000 people to the mainland for use as agricultural laborers.

The Bishop of Tahiti, with the aid of the French government, was able to enforce the repatriation of the 100 miserable survivors of overwork and unfamiliar living conditions. Of these, only 15 lived through the return voyage to see again the rubble of the Navel of the World. They brought with them the previously unknown disease smallpox. This and other new diseases wreaked havoc among those few who had evaded the slavers. Later a few of the islanders were taken to Mangareva and Tahiti as plantation workers. A population estimate in 1877 recorded only 111 people.

Thus the slave raids and their aftereffects wrote the epilogue of a spectacular culture. The culture appears to have been unable to cope with a population too numerous to maintain the social relationships by which it had adapted to its tiny environment. Once the delicate economic balance was destroyed, the foundation was laid for a sad sequence of later events. With the religious aristocracy dead, the rituals, ceremonies, and values that had made life meaningful were largely forgotten. No one remained who could read the hieroglyphic literature. The wooden tablets on which it was written were used to stretch out the fuel supply in this now nearly treeless land. The architectural ruins remained only as sad mementos of better days and a source of wonder to visitors. The handful of unhappy and demoralized survivors had reached a profound cultural low point.

The stones in the walls of the *ahu* platforms are fitted closely together, without mortar, in a manner very similar to typical Inca stone placement. Some of the stones weigh several tons.

POPULATION RISING AGAIN

More recent events are beginning to suggest that in a typically human fashion few lessons were learned from this devastating past. Several things suggest that this unfortunate history could repeat itself. In 1888 the Navel of the World became part of the Republic of Chile and was used until recently as a sheep ranch. Some of the islanders found work as ranch hands and at other new tasks to supplement their fishing and planting on the again abundant land. The Catholic faith had been introduced, and many of the technological and other ideas of foreign civilization, including its medical techniques, gradually began to be felt more intensively.

With land and the resources of the sea again ample to support the tiny remaining community, the future seemed bright. A will to survive gradually regenerated. In 1886 the population had been 155; by 1900 it had reached 213; by 1934, 456; by 1955, 842; and by 1969, 1,432. There were 1,619 island-dwellers in 1973. Since 1877 there has been an annual increase of nearly 5 per cent. If the trend continues there will be over 2,200 islanders in 10 more years, and in 30 years their numbers will approach 6,000. Immigration from continental Chile, which is already beginning, will augment this increase significantly. With present intensified outside contacts, Ehrlich's predictions would suggest that this time the fate of the Navel of the World may be indistinguishably merged in a worldwide population explosion that is already out of hand.

THE HEYERDAHL EXPEDITION

In 1955–56 an archaeological expedition directed by Thor Heyerdahl spent five months on the island. The best-seller, *Aku-Aku,* which was one of its results, focused worldwide attention in this direction. Gradually it began to be realized that this island held the most remarkable potential open-air museum of Polynesian history to be found anywhere. Even so, it seemed unlikely that many visitors would ever be able to cross the vast distances involved to see this most isolated of islands. The single annual supply ship of that time could carry few passengers beyond those required for special tasks.

Nevertheless, the slice of history illustrated here was of such absorbing interest that in 1960 the University of Chile sent Gonzalo Figueroa, one of their archaeologists, and the writer to experiment with the problem of monument restoration and to determine if such work could be carried out at reasonable cost. During that year the equinox-oriented Ahu a Kivi, with a platform about 82 m (270 ft) long, and bearing seven approximately 16-ton statues, was completely restored. The statues were raised without heavy equipment, by methods similar to those used by the prehistoric islanders. The smaller Ahu Vaiteka was also restored. This experiment produced, from a pile of rubble, the first intact Easter Island *ahu* to be seen in modern times. It impressed the islanders, many of whom were strongly moved by this visual evidence of their former capacities and achievements.

The artistic and architectural merit, especially of Ahu a Kivi, clearly underscored the value of continued work. The president of Chile requested that the Museums and Monuments Division of UNESCO send representatives to draw up plans for conservation and restoration on a larger scale. Plans were prepared for converting the island into an outdoor museum, and about 30 years of survey, investigation, stabilization, and restoration work were projected.

ON SOUTH PACIFIC AIR ROUTE

The very isolation of the island eventually brought its own solution to the problem of visitor access. As the only land in this part of the world, it was recognized as an essential stop on flights across the South Pacific (from South America to Australia and Southeast Asia). This base would forge the final link in the airline girdle of the Southern Hemisphere. In 1966, LAN Chile Airlines inaugurated weekly flights to the island. These flights now go on to Tahiti to make connection with points farther west. There are now two scheduled flights each week. Tourists in considerable numbers have already begun to contemplate the Navel of the World, many as part of trans-Pacific trips. They have carried away enthusiastic stories of what they have seen.

Such contacts, and the prospect of increased future ones, have made imperative an acceleration of conservation and restoration work as well as all the typical measures for reception of visitors. The International Fund for Monuments, Inc., with

The thatched houses were commonly boat-shaped, with boulders in front. The holes in the foundation stones held framework poles.

partial support from the University of Wyoming and the U.S. National Endowment for the Humanities, has been working in cooperation with the National Planning Office and the Bureau of Archives, Libraries and Museums of the Republic of Chile.

A field party, directed by the writer, has worked intermittently on the island from 1968 to the present. An exhaustive archaeological survey is under way that will eventually provide a precise inventory of the locations and conservation needs of the thousands of monuments. Though still only partially complete, the survey has recorded unexpected numbers of hitherto unnoticed villages and isolated domestic establishments among the spectacular monuments. These closely spaced and long-abandoned homesteads wordlessly reveal intensive prehistoric land use and a population desperate for agricultural productivity. Such information will eventually shed clear light on the still-enigmatic question of just what the maximum population of the island was.

Upper: some rocks on the island bear symbols of the former culture's untranslated script. Lower: A stone at Orongo carries petroglyphs of squatting bird-men.

CEREMONIAL CENTER

The party also nearly completely restored the spectacular ceremonial center called Tahai just north of Hangaroa, the island's one modern town, located on the west coast. Here may be seen in restored condition the three great *ahu* called Ko te Riku, Tahai, and Vai Uri, bearing in all seven gigantic statues, of which the largest weighs over 20 tons and wears a *pukao*, or red scoria topknot. Many smaller structures are related to the complex. They include a paved ramp for bringing canoes ashore, masonry-modified caves, house foundations, and more enigmatic structures. More recently Ahu Huri a Urenga, east of Hangaroa, and two other *ahu* near Ahu a Kapu on the west coast have been restored. These and the earlier restorations bring sharply to mind the *mana* relied upon in the old days as inexhaustible supernatural power. Here it continues to live, perhaps as a memorial to an ambitious and vigorous society that tried and came within a hair's breadth of failure.

ENTHUSIASTIC ONCE AGAIN

The failure was not quite complete. Perhaps the *mana* of the statues continues to look after its own. There is no doubt that from the 111 survivors of 1877 has developed a new island community at least as vigorous, ambitious, and intelligent as were their prehistoric ancestors.

Present developments reveal the beginning of a second approach to an optimum

Left: the ceremonial village of Orongo with stone-slab houses. Right: at nearby Ana Kai Tangata—"the cave where men are eaten"—wall paintings can still be found.

period perhaps similar to that before the great battle at Poike. The islanders are more prosperous than they have been for a long time. Everyone is working enthusiastically. Roads have been built over many parts of the island. An airstrip suitable for jet planes has been completed. A hotel with 60 rooms is in operation. Hangaroa now has a new and excellent school, and considerable numbers of young islanders are being sent to continental Chile for higher education. Many of the technical characteristics of civilization unknown only a few years ago, such as piped water, electricity, and tape recorders, are now commonplace. The long isolation of the islanders is at an end. They are now irrevocably part of the 20th century. The problem of their survival has merged with that of the world at large.

ECONOMIC PROBLEMS

Urgent issues emerge clearly as Easter Island enters a money economy and undergoes other effects of outside contacts. The extreme remoteness of the island and the limitations of its tiny environment make it very difficult to produce and market competitively any product capable of maintaining sufficient cash income to secure for the islanders an adequately supplied 20th century life. Sheep raising has been tried and found to be uneconomic, as well as productive of devastating erosion problems. Systematic fishing, especially of tuna, may eventually be a partial solution, though the lack of good anchorages poses a difficulty. Systematic production of coffee or other crops might be helpful. However, the problem as a whole seems to find no easy solutions.

The people of Chile appear to be uniformly proud of and interested in this small segment of Polynesia that rather unexpectedly forms a part of their country. In recent years their government has heavily subsidized its development. However, as in all other parts of the world, if its people are to achieve the dignity of good and full lives the island must eventually become self-supporting.

Clearly, the immediate economic future of Easter Island lies in a new kind of dependence on the monuments—that is, tourism. Happily, the island is as accessible as a major trans-Pacific air route can make it, and it has something valuable and unique to offer.

SPECTACULAR POTENTIAL

The island represents by all odds the most spectacular potential outdoor museum to be found anywhere in Polynesia. It not only illustrates a unique slice of Polynesian prehistory, but for thoughtful visitors, it has the deeper theoretical significance of being perhaps the world's best example of the development of a complex culture in great isolation.

About 70 statues remain upright at Rano Raraku, looking out across the island that they had been erected to guard. Today these massive relics are thought of as part of the world's archaeological treasures.

Beyond its primary archaeological attractions the island has many dividends to offer the tourist. It is, quite simply, a rewarding place to be. Fishing, horseback riding, hiking, and camping can be enjoyed in a unique and satisfying environment. The people, as typical Polynesians, are probably the most unconsciously accomplished hosts and the most outgoing and pleasant companions to be found anywhere.

With these essential advantages in this area it would seem that the economic future of the islanders is secure, and so it probably is. The mechanisms of tourism are already beginning to develop. Groups of islanders have banded together as tour companies to provide vehicle transportation to view the monuments. Beyond the accommodations available at the hotel, many islanders have modified their homes to receive guests.

Others produce carved wooden figurines in the endless traditional motifs—art objects, of which some have real merit by any standard of comparison. These and related occupations have already produced significant new local income, though it would seem that the surface of the possibilities has hardly been scratched.

INSTRUCTIVE RUINS

This orientation will require much future development. Because the prehistoric conflicts have left most of the spectacular monuments so destroyed as to obscure the features of their architecture, many more monuments must be restored. By no means should all or even the majority be so treated, however, for many are both charming and instructive in their present ruined state.

Of equal importance are measures for conservation of monuments in their present state, to stabilize them as ruins and to prevent damage by visitors. The islanders themselves need to form a corps of trained guides of professional quality. They need to be familiar with the monuments and the details of the island's history, and capable of speaking the languages of the visitors. The usual administrative procedures for management of visitors and protection of monuments are needed. The community at large must come to understand the fundamental economic value of the monuments and the necessity of maintaining the island as an unspoiled beauty spot. The Chilean government is highly aware of all these necessities, and they are gradually being met.

For the islanders the future seems as bright as it undoubtedly did in the period before the Poike battle. Yet the specter of overpopulation in this tiny environment is again as powerful as it was then. The old *mana*, or impersonal supernatural power, may have to make a quantum leap of power and understanding to avoid a repetition of that earlier catastrophe□

SELECTED READINGS

Agony at Easter by Thomas Coffee. Penguin Books, 1971.

Aku-Aku by Thor Heyerdahl. Ballantine Books, 1974.

The Ethnology of Easter Island by Alfred Metraux. Reprint of 1940 ed., by Bishop Museum Press, Honolulu, 1971.

The Population Bomb by Paul R. Ehrlich. Sierra Club Books, 1969.

Finding the Ironclad Monitor

by Bob Wilson

ACTING Paymaster William Keeler groped clumsily in the darkness for his watch, found it hanging from a nail, and quickly stuffed the timepiece into a pocket of his uniform. The watch was an ironic reminder that time was running out for his storm-battered ship, and perhaps for his own life as well. Seawater gushing into the U.S.S. *Monitor* through the turret and ventilation holes already chilled him to the waist. There was no way to stop it. The engine fires were dead, and with them the pumps.

On deck, seamen and officers scrambled to make a hazardous transfer by dinghy to the U.S.S. *Rhode Island*, the stricken ironclad's tow ship. A few seasick sailors clung to their bunks, too ill and uncaring to climb out of the *Monitor*'s bowels.

Keeler had stayed below to gather what ship's records he could find, but soon realized that any attempt to save them would be foolhardy. Still, he felt compelled to take with him the *Monitor*'s cache of Union greenbacks, stored in a safe now under water. Keeler's key refused to go into the lock. Frustrated, he turned around and waded toward the turret, struggling through the wardroom as chairs and tables surged "violently from side to side, threatening severe bruises if not broken limbs," as he later wrote his wife.

He expected the *Monitor* to "give the final plunge" at any moment. The paymaster fought to hold back panic gripping some of the crew as he stumbled on deck and "witnessed a scene that was well calculated to appall the boldest heart. . . . Mountains of water were rushing across our decks and foaming along our sides."

LOST FOR 111 YEARS

Keeler was lucky. He made it to the *Rhode Island* and went on to live a full life, eventually settling in Florida. Not so fortunate were 16 other Union sailors, doomed to go down with the *Monitor*. She sank 29 km (18 mi) southeast of Cape Hatteras at 1:30 A.M. on New Year's Eve, 1862 and was to remain lost for 111 years.

The gallant little ironclad was all that had stood between the Confederate Steamship *Virginia*—the reconstructed

This contemporary drawing of the *Monitor*, the famous "cheesebox on a raft," shows the Yankee vessel with a smokestack, a part that was removed before combat. The *Monitor* battled the *Virginia*, or *Merrimack*, to a draw on March 9, 1862.

and renamed *Merrimack*—and certain destruction of the Union fleet nine months earlier at Hampton Roads. So the *Monitor*, though lost, was well remembered. When the *Monitor* slipped beneath the angry Atlantic, she entered the realm of legend. Men came to realize that as a pivotal development in naval history—no longer could nations rely on "wooden walls" for protection—the Yankee "cheesebox on a raft" sailed far ahead of her time.

The 52-m (172-ft)-long gunboat, displacing 960 tons and riding low in the water, was built in 100 working days by John Ericsson, a Swedish-American inventor who also designed her unique revolving turret. The *Monitor* was not the first ironclad—Britain and France already possessed such ships—but she might be properly termed the first modern naval weapons system.

As an example of advanced 19th century technology, the *Monitor* probably stood unchallenged during her brief lifespan of a year. Unfortunately, Ericsson apparently never drafted a comprehensive set of blueprints for her construction, instead dashing off sketches as work progressed. In the more than a century since her loss, romantics and hard-nosed ship buffs alike have yearned to uncover the "inside story" of the vessel.

EASTWARD FITTED FOR SEARCH

Numerous attempts (three in 1973 alone) were made to find the wreck. Scientific talent and sophisticated underwater electronic gear were assembled aboard Duke University's research vessel *Eastward* and two Army Reserve support craft as they steamed out of Beaufort, North Carolina, in mid-August 1974 for the "Graveyard of the Atlantic" off Cape Hatteras.

The 36-m (117-ft)-long *Eastward* carried four co-principal investigators: John Newton, the tall marine superintendent of the oceanographic program at Duke Marine Laboratory in Beaufort; Dr. Harold Edgerton of the Massachusetts Institute of Technology, as actively inventive in his mid-70's as a man half his age; Gordon Watts, a young underwater archaeologist with a soft Carolina drawl; and Dr. Richard Sheridan, a bearded, energetic University of Delaware geologist. The *Eastward* expedition had its beginning a few months earlier in discussions among Newton, Edgerton, and Watts. As plans jelled and ship time became available, the National Science Foundation and the National Geographic Society came forward with financing.

In its final design, the *Eastward* cruise had two objectives. The *Monitor* would be sought during only part of the two weeks allotted for underwater investigations. The other part would be devoted to examination of a geologically interesting feature 20 km (12 mi) off Ocracoke Island, North Carolina.

Three critical factors had to come together if the *Monitor* were to be found: a well-defined search area, precision navigation, and Edgerton's side-scan sonar, able to sweep the ocean floor for a little less than 1 kilometer (a half mile) on each side of the *Eastward*.

Newton, Watts, and Dorothy Nicholson of National Geographic narrowed the search area down to an 8-by-22 km (5-by-14 mi) rectangle by referring to the records of the *Monitor*'s tow ship. The trio plotted the fixes on an 1857 Coast and Geodetic Survey chart of Cape Hatteras, then transferred the data to a current chart by taking into account changes since then, plus time elements from historical records.

ELECTRONICALLY AIDED NAVIGATION

Precision navigation depended on instruments mounted on Hatteras lighthouse and Diamond Shoals light tower. The instruments enabled the *Eastward* to come within about 50 cm (2 ft) of any desired point on the ocean surface, and proved invaluable in finding the *Monitor* site on subsequent visits.

The third critical factor, Edgerton's side-scan sonar, did exactly what it was supposed to do. It recorded the *Monitor* on the bottom of the Atlantic. The sonar's good work almost went unnoticed. On

August 27 a man on watch did not recognize a long, somewhat indistinct echo being traced on the recorder as the *Eastward* followed the sea floor along the northwestern boundary of the search area. Oceanographic Party Chief Fred Kelly, walking past on his way to stow some fishing gear, glanced up at the recorder. The echo spoke volumes to him. He quickly informed watch chief Sheridan and the *Eastward* changed course to investigate what would be named Wreck Site No. 2.

The potential discovery followed profound disappointment aboard the research ship, which only a few days earlier spent three days and nights examining a wreck with many of the features of the *Monitor*. It finally was identified as a trawler with a semi-circular pilot house. Up to that time the *Eastward* had recorded more than 20 sonar and magnetometer contacts in the search area. The trawler lay only 13 km (8 mi) from the position fixed by the *Rhode Island* when the *Monitor* sank, and the search area was being exhausted rapidly.

Now, excitement swelled again among the crew and scientific party. The echo at Wreck Site No. 2 was tantalizing in its final detail. A buoy was splashed over the side to mark the spot, followed by underwater television and photographic cameras. The wreck lay at a depth of about 67 m (220 ft).

"THERE IT IS!"

Anticipation aboard *Eastward* rose to a palpable level as the television camera glided over the wreck: the screen showed iron plates, what appeared to be the flat bottom of a hull, possibly the *Monitor*'s unique waterline "armor belt," and a large circular structure looking very much like the turret. Shouts of excitement—"There it is! That's it!"—suddenly broke the tension.

The crew dropped a dredge to comb the shell-strewn bottom for debris. Back came anthracite coal, clinkers, and wood fragments. It soon became obvious that the wreck was resting upside down at an angle on the turret, which apparently had fallen away as the *Monitor* rolled over on sinking. Most of the stern had either suffered damage or had deteriorated over the years so much that plates had crashed into the interior.

Monitor crewmen in the summer of 1862. Note the cooking gear—food preparation was far more comfortable on deck than below deck.

The fragile condition of *Monitor* was underscored in a costly accident when one of Edgerton's underwater cameras lodged under a fallen plate. The camera remains today within the hull, perhaps laden with photographs of the ironclad's interior.

Marine organisms covered *Monitor*'s remains, in some places forming a crust. Much of the yellow pine used in the ship was gone, and even the rivets holding many of the plates were missing. There was little doubt aboard *Eastward* that *Monitor* had been found, but positive identification was still months away.

The *Eastward* returned to Beaufort—ironically the immediate destination of *Monitor* on her way to Charleston to join the Union blockade—soon after work ended at Wreck Site No. 2. All that could be said about the results of the search was a cryptic "It's only a possibility" when newsmen asked if the vessel had been found.

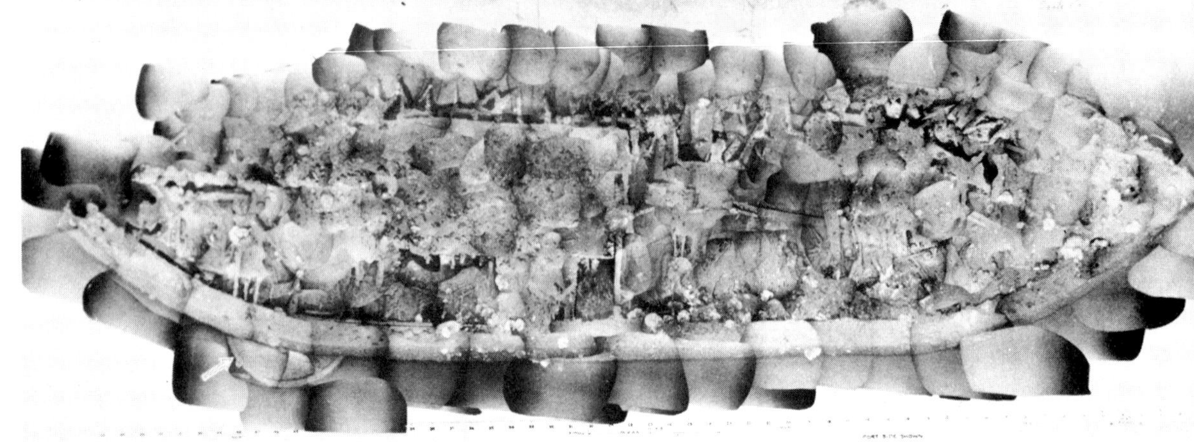

This mosaic of the *Monitor,* bottom-side up, in its 111-year-old grave, was made from hundreds of photos. The arrow points to the turret.

"THE WRECK WAS UNIQUE"

Most of the hard work was just beginning for Watts, the underwater archaeologist. For the next five months, he studied the 15 hours of television tapes and underwater photographs, patiently comparing measurements of what he saw with *Monitor* features described in 1862 records. Like a giant jigsaw puzzle, the pieces slowly came together.

One of the most convincing clues, Newton later said, "was that the wreck was unique—it didn't resemble any other vessel." The *Monitor*'s equipoise rudder was a vital example. It lies beneath the screw, but Watts was able to determine its size. Other telltale characteristics were coal chutes, the armor belt, and the brass ring upon which the turret revolved.

On March 8, 1974, Newton told a packed press conference, "We are prepared to say *Monitor* has been found." He and Watts laid out the evidence, including portions of the videotapes. Not unexpectedly, Newton's announcement raised eyebrows in some sectors of the oceanographic community. The *Monitor* had been "found" several times before. Now, the Duke investigator was saying without benefit of conclusive artifacts that the ironclad lay far off Cape Hatteras on the margin of the Gulf Stream.

RECOVERY SHIP CHARTERED

Even as Newton disclosed the historic discovery, plans were under way for a return visit to Wreck Site No. 2 with the *Alcoa Seaprobe*, a 74-m (243-ft) search and recovery ship that ranks among the world's most advanced of its type. The U.S. Navy had the "seagoing oilrig" under charter for a week to test its capabilities, and the *Monitor* site would be examined to clear up any questions about Newton's claim. Unlike the *Eastward* expedition, which enjoyed excellent weather, the *Seaprobe* voyage did not go smoothly. A gale stopped all work at one point, and rough seas continually hampered recovery and photographic efforts.

The *Seaprobe*, equipped to recover objects down to about 1,800 m (6,000 ft) by stringing a pipestem fitted with a claw, yielded nothing except more videotapes and photographs. But what photographs they were: the *Monitor* was unmistakably the hulk at Wreck Site No. 2. A hastily assembled mosaic showed the turret and armor belt in sharp detail. Other photos revealed the anchor well, unique to the original *Monitor*, that enabled the crew to lower the anchor without exposing themselves on deck.

When the *Seaprobe* returned to Morehead City, North Carolina, disappointment over failure to recover artifacts dampened much of the enthusiasm that bubbled freely at the onset of the voyage. There seemed no possibility for months, perhaps years, to bring up pieces of the *Monitor* for examination and preservation.

ARTIFACTS RECOVERED

Yet, only the next month, Newton and Watts held in their hands artifacts as large as the deck-light covers. Sheridan had taken the *Eastward* on another geological cruise off the East Coast, and he had enough time remaining on the way back to dredge the *Monitor* site. He brought up a rich haul of artifacts.

Sheridan's dredging sparked controversy weeks later when *The Washington Post* published a front-page story headlined, "Geologist Tears Into Wreck of Ironclad." Sheridan told a *Post* reporter who had been following the *Monitor* story that the dredge snagged the wreck at least once. "We may have hooked on to the deck or the turret," he said. "We might have broken off a piece of plate."

Did Sheridan actually hit the wreck, or was he mistaken? Newton and Edgerton fitted a former fishing trawler with navigational and underwater television gear to find out for certain what had happened. Three days and nights of remarkably good weather off Hatteras in August helped yield the answer. Newton said he could find no evidence of damage. Artifacts brought up by Sheridan apparently had fallen off the hulk. Photos showed the dredge scour running alongside *Monitor*, not into it.

PROTECTION NEEDED

Still, the potentially disastrous incident illustrated the vital need for protection. Concern over possible vandalism by souvenir hunters haunted all those who participated in the *Monitor* project. Some way was required to preserve the ironclad for valid research.

That way exists in a portion of the Marine Protection Research, and Sanctuaries Act of 1972. It authorizes the U.S.

Composite photo shows the *Monitor*'s turret, partially obscured by the armor belt, which protected the ship's waterline.

Secretary of Commerce to establish protected marine sanctuary zones for several purposes, among them preservation of historic sites. On Sept. 26, 1974, Gov. James E. Holshouser, Jr., of North Carolina announced that he had nominated the *Monitor* site for marine sanctuary status under control of the National Oceanic and Atmospheric Administration. [In 1975 the site was officially designated as a marine sanctuary.]

The wreck site is expected to be managed by a board of state and federal representatives, which will examine all requests for research and pass on their validity before issuing permits to use the sanctuary.

What Gordon Watts described as "one of the most valuable 19th century archaeological sites" now has been officially put aside in the name of the American people, a fitting memorial for the little ironclad that changed history□

SELECTED READINGS

Aboard the U.S.S. Monitor: 1862 by Robert W. Daly, ed. United States Naval Institute, 1962.

"The Monitor Is Found" by Harold E. Edgerton. *Technology Review*, Massachusetts Institute of Technology, February 1975.

"The Search for the Monitor" by Norman G. Cubberly. *Sea Frontiers*, July–August 1974.

Famine

by Jean Mayer

NEVER throughout history has there been a time when there has not been a devastating famine in some part of the world. In our lifetime, widespread starvation in Asia, Europe, Africa, and Latin America has taken the lives of millions of men, women and children. The present bad—and worsening—state of the total world food supply, particularly the depletion of grain reserves in the United States and the shortage of the fertilizers needed to maintain the "green revolution"—owing to high oil prices—leads one to expect that the extent of any new famine will indeed be catastrophic. (See "After the Green Revolution" by Wallace Cloud, *Science Supplement*, 1974.)

Historically, we have proved ourselves ill-prepared to cope with famines. How well can we hope to deal with them in an even less propitious situation?

A mother from famine-ravaged Bangladesh feeds her baby in a refugee camp in India.

FAMINE IN THE MODERN WORLD

Up to now, individual nations, international voluntary agencies, and especially official international organizations have dealt with the specter of mass starvation as an unexpected crisis—as something to react to when it occurs rather than as a likelihood to be planned for in advance. Prevention has been the exception rather than the rule; the Indian state of Bihar in 1966–67 remains the lone shining example of a large famine averted. Moreover, we act on the occasion of each famine as though mankind had no collective memory. Whoever is faced with the present famine usually acts as though there were no lesson to be derived from the melancholy succession of previous famines and previous efforts to cope with them.

Yet previous famines should have left one beneficial residue: there are individuals and organizations that have acquired first-hand knowledge of successful—and unsuccessful—ways of coping. So little is ordinarily taught of the physiological, psychological, and social problems arising in famines, and of their solutions, however, that each new group of physicians and administrators who are generally called upon to deal with a new catastrophic situation tends to repeat some of the classic errors of omission and commission.

Today, we need, and are technically able to create, an organization that institutionalizes human memory in dealing with starvation. Over time we have made discoveries in compassion as well as in management and technology. For many centuries starvation was essentially inevitable, largely because means of information and means of transportation were not at hand. That there was some food somewhere else on the same or another continent was basically irrelevant: there was no way of delivering it when it was needed or of distributing it to the starving. We now have the technology to keep the whole world under surveillance and transmit early warnings of impending shortages; we can transport the food to the area of famine. Therefore we have obligations that did not exist in past generations.

For action purposes there is a sharp difference between a state of chronic starvation, which is endemic in some sections of certain populations, and a true famine. However precarious their previous state of nutrition may have been, the people involved feel and act differently in a famine. They become acutely conscious that something of a different order of magnitude is happening.

CAUSES OF FAMINE

A true famine is unlike anything else. It can be defined as a severe shortage of food accompanied by a significant increase in the local or regional death rate. In a chronic starvation area people may suffer and be crippled mentally and physically; in a true famine they die in large numbers.

Almost all recorded famines have resulted from widespread crop failures. These, in turn, may be caused by drought, crop diseases or pests, the impact of war or civil disturbance, or a combination of disturbances hitting both crops and farmers, such as floods or earthquakes. All these four sets of causes have been at work in the famines that have occurred since 1950 alone: flood, drought, and civil disorder in India and Pakistan; locusts and earthquakes in the Middle East; floods and dislocation of the agricultural system in China; earthquakes in Latin America; and drought and civil war in Africa (the Sahel, the Congo, and Biafra).

DROUGHT-PRONE AREAS

All of the causes of crop failure and famine are very much alive in the world today. The most threatening, and growing, is now drought. Some scientists are saying that changes in climate have shortened the growing season and reduced the rainfall that we may now expect in key areas such as India and northern Africa. Whether this is true or not, the large areas of the world where rainfall is highly variable and seasonal are inherently drought-prone. In Western Europe or New England a dry year differs from a wet year by less than 20 per cent. In immense land areas elsewhere, the variation may be 80 per cent, and drought years may alternate with years of flood, when gigantic continental rivers, swollen by excessive rains in the mountains, burst their banks and destroy all crops. (See "Ominous Changes in the World's Weather," *Science Supplement*, 1974.)

Apart from their climate and natural characteristics, many nations and areas are particularly vulnerable to famine by reason of lack of communications or social inequality. Chinese famines of the past were due largely to the then-primitive transportation system, and lack of adequate communication is a major aspect of the current Sahel famine. These problems exist in many poor countries. Virtually all such countries are examples of social inequality and of the resulting defects in nutrition for sections of the population.

The United Nations rushed grain to Bangladesh ports after warfare disrupted food output.

RESULTS OF FAMINE

To move from causes to consequences, by the above definition the main and most immediate effect of famine is widespread deaths from starvation. It has been observed repeatedly that in famines old persons and young children die first, and that women and adolescents tend to survive better than men (although adolescents suffering from prolonged undernutrition are particularly susceptible to tuberculosis). For purposes of dealing with a famine, "old age" starts at about 45 years old. From then on, there is a drastic increase in mortality as compared with that among adult men and women below that age.

A second, and dangerous, consequence is the state of social disruption, including large-scale panics, that usually accompanies a famine. Generally people who are starving at home tend to leave it if they can and march toward the area where food is rumored to be available. As a result, families are separated and children are lost. The small children often reach a suicidal state of mind from self-inflicted starvation, refusing to eat because of their grief at the absence of their parents. Adolescents, finding themselves on their own, band together in foraging gangs that create further disruption. (Prolonged and successful practice of banditry also makes members of these gangs difficult to rehabilitate when the famine is over.) This breakdown of the social order makes any relief measure that much harder to put into effect.

TOO FEEBLE TO REVOLT

Contrary to popular belief, however, famines (and, for that matter, prolonged severe undernutrition) are rarely accompanied by revolution. The gravely underfed usually are too feeble and too preoccupied with problems of immediate survival to summon up the energy, single-mindedness, and organization required to initiate and follow through with a revolution. The type of disruption accompanying famine is more likely to entail a large number of unconnected antisocial acts. In turn, revolutions are more likely to take place when food has been again available for some time, but while the memory of the actual or supposed corruption or incompetence shown by the government in dealing with the famine is still fresh. The experience of flood in Pakistan in 1970 contributed directly to the secession of Bangladesh in 1971.

A third common catastrophic result of famines is the spread of epidemics. The combination of physiologically weakened human organisms and a disrupted social organism, with the attendant breakdown of public-health institutions and crowding, lends itself to the explosive spread of infectious diseases. Louse-borne typhus has been the traditional post-famine disease of Europe, cholera and smallpox the post-famine diseases in Asia, although plague, influenza, tuberculosis, relapsing fever, and many other diseases have also followed famine. When famine is due to a drought, malaria is not usually rampant at the same time, but is often deadly on a particularly large scale when the rains finally come.

One last, long-term consequence of many famines is the death of large domestic animals, often on a greater scale than that of humans, and the destruction of seeds for future crops, making it more difficult for farming to return to normal when the famine is over. The Sahel famine is the most recent example of both points. If one is to speak of coping with famine, one must include follow-up measures to restore the food supply and rehabilitate the area—or if this cannot be done, to resettle the population elsewhere.

THE ROLE OF POLITICS

To one degree or another, any famine situation has an element of politics. The nation or nations that contain the famine area must summon large quantities of help, which in an India or a China may come from other parts of the same country but which must usually come from outside. Thus international official organizations, notably UNICEF, the Food and

Agriculture Organization, and the World Health Organization, are almost always involved at an early stage, while international voluntary agencies (such as CARE and church groups) may become substantial sources and channels for relief. Finally, there are the individual outside nations that alone can furnish really large quantities of food, medical supplies, and transportation.

RELIEF EFFORT

Unfortunately even a crisis such as famine does not mean that all these various political bodies necessarily work in harmony either with each other or within themselves. For professional men trying to get on with the job, these political frictions are acutely painful. Some adjustment and cooperative arrangement between the political entities involved is the first essential for coping with a famine—if this is smooth, all else becomes much easier; if not, the drag is immense.

The second obvious requirement is the procurement of food in amounts adequate to stop the developing famine, maintain the population in balance, and eventually rehabilitate the population. Food must be obtained through buying or otherwise acquiring it and moving it to the affected area. In spite of the efforts by some of the leaders of FAO, such as John Boyd Orr and André Mayer in the late 1940's, a World Food Bank or regional food banks for emergency situations have not yet come into existence. There is thus no universal and automatic pathway for famine relief. In the past, the availability of large surpluses of cereals in the United States, Canada, France, and other countries made relief possible. Yet in spite of the creation of such national organizations as Food for Peace in the United States, the actual process of relief was often slow and cumbersome. Now the sharp reduction in North American food surpluses has created a potentially serious situation for famine relief efforts.

The third fundamental element in any famine relief effort is a clear-cut line of command and assignment of responsibility. Even under the most advantageous political conditions, in a country at peace and with a stable government, starvation causes intense political pressures. Typically, the opposition says poor government planning is the cause of the famine, government incompetence and corruption the causes of its continuation. Government sources accuse the opposition of presenting a picture far worse than the reality, of minimizing the effectiveness of relief efforts, and of starting disruptive rumors.

For these political reasons alone, the local authorities are usually in a poor position to run a relief operation properly. Moreover, such an operation, if it is of any significant size, requires able, decisive leadership with high managerial skills. Thus I, for one, am convinced that by far the best method of organization is to have the relevant political entities come to-

Cattle have perished and others roam in search of food in Africa's Sahel region. A severe drought threatens extinction to herds vital to nomads in Mauritania, Mali, Senegal, the upper Volta, the Niger, and Chad.

gether in the appointment of a single "relief dictator." Even fairly ancient history (to younger people) teaches us something here: Herbert Hoover's total control of relief to Belgium and Germany after World War I was by common consent largely responsible for the high degree of success of this pioneer effort in a threatened famine situation.

HOW INDIA MET A CHALLENGE

A fine example of coping with and containing a famine was the national and international effort during the famine in India during 1966–67. What the Indian Ministry of Food and Agriculture feared would be "a natural calamity of a magnitude unknown in recent times" became instead the object of what *The Washington Post* later described as "one of the biggest and most successful relief operations ever undertaken." Of all the subcontinent, the eastern Indian state of Bihar was most affected by the drought and subsequent famine, and it was here that the relief activities were concentrated.

Bihar had at that time the second largest population of the Indian states—roughly equivalent to that of France. Its economy was, and is, almost entirely agricultural. About nine-tenths of its 52 million people were engaged in farming, and of the 27 million acres in crops, less than one fifth were irrigated, and of these only about 7 per cent from sure sources. While Bihar sits on one of the world's largest reservoirs of ground water, digging of wells and irrigation schemes had been postponed or delayed for almost a decade. When the monsoon failed for two years in a row, crop failure was inevitable. Over the two-year period, Bihar fell short of needed grain by almost 30 million tons. Reserves of food grains, including those necessary for seeds, had been mostly consumed. The crop of the fall before was at best one fourth of normal, the spring crop only half. In addition, the Bihar state's administrative apparatus was relatively unsophisticated, and it had no child-feeding program which could have been used as the base of a relief effort.

However, when the famine began, there were some bright spots. During the lesser drought of the previous year, the Indian government had set up fair-price shops and practiced the logistics of importing and transporting large quantities of grain; voluntary agencies had acquired experience in setting up mass feeding programs. Bihar itself had adequate storage and transportation facilities and an administrative structure that lent itself, especially in the Education Department, to relief operations. Moreover, ever since British times the Indian government had placed in the hands of its officials a comprehensive elementary guide to the handling of famines, called a Famine Code.

FOOD AT FIXED PRICES

The basic priority of the Indian government was to obtain and dispense sufficient food. For this, three outlets were used: 20,000 fair-price shops distributed grain at fixed, subsidized prices; 10 ounces of free grain were distributed each day to each aged or infirm person; and a child-feeding program provided one free meal each day to six million children and mothers. Members of the government, vividly aware, some of them for the first time, of the long-term personal and social effects of malnutrition, not only tended to favor the children in relief programs, but also speeded the development of a cereal-based, high-protein food, Bak Ahar, processed and packaged by Indian industry and distributed by the Indian government to the needy.

In the Bihar famine, the need for water was as great as the need for food. Lack of water threatened to cause the mass migration of villagers, thus destroying the food distribution system, in addition to posing health hazards in the hottest months of the year. To meet this need, the government began a program of well-drilling—some of the wells to be permanent, the rest of a more temporary nature, but each providing drinking water and irrigating half an acre of land through the driest period of the summer. Further needs for water were met by establishing an elaborate transport system, comprising modes of travel from railways to bullock carts.

QUICK INOCULATIONS

Remembering the high death toll from cholera and smallpox during the Bengal famine of 1943, the government also disinfected wells and set up an immunization program. The response of the American government to the Indian request for vaccine, incidentally, was a model of promptness and efficiency—vaccine, injectors, and innoculation specialists to train Indians in their use arrived in Delhi five days after the formal request was made.

The government set up an information network that transmitted data by telephone or telegraph to a master control room where they were charted to give day-to-day information on food stocks and prices, water levels, disease rates and deaths, the numbers of people at free kitchens and on work projects, even the rate of local food looting. From this control center, field workers and the population were kept abreast of the changing situation by short-wave and public radio.

In addition, the government undertook to provide millions of dollars in loans to the Bihari farmers for the purchase of seeds, fertilizers, pesticides, and farm animals to rejuvenate the economy and prepare for the next year's crop.

In all these efforts, the local Bihari government and the federal government of India were supported by supplies and cooperation from other nations, the United Nations, and international voluntary organizations. CARE alone set up 27,000 school feeding centers in Bihar to provide free meals to children and nursing mothers; the United States contributed one fifth of its wheat crop.

LIMITED TOLL

In the end, the famine was contained. Instead of the millions of deaths predicted, the highest of the fairly reliable estimates was only a few thousand. It appears that among the poorest segments of society many were better fed during the

Women harvest high-yield wheat crop in India. The UN/FAO World Food Program helped improve the water supply for the region.

famine than before—or perhaps afterward. The success of the emergency feeding program, especially in the health of the Bihari children (they were fed milk, and foods and food supplements high in protein, iron and other minerals, as well as vitamins, under fairly close supervision), led to a long-term commitment by the Indian government to the nutritional needs of the population. Even the work program, which certainly resulted, in some cases, in roads leading to and from nowhere, also sparked projects for more and better irrigation, field leveling, more efficient farming methods with higher yields, and better water conservation.

Despite the resolve of the Indian government to fight this famine with every possible resource, however, the struggle would have been hopeless without the dedicated cooperation of the international community□

The New Alchemy Institute

by Nicholas Wade

THE new alchemists are a small group of people who see modern American agriculture as a mighty edifice built on sand. They expect it to collapse, maybe within 10 to 20 years. Collapse, they believe, could come from intolerable increases in the prices of fuel and fertilizer or from the accumulating biological damage caused by agricultural chemicals.

Others may dispute the analysis, but the new alchemists are acting on it by trying to develop an alternative—and radically different—mode of food production.

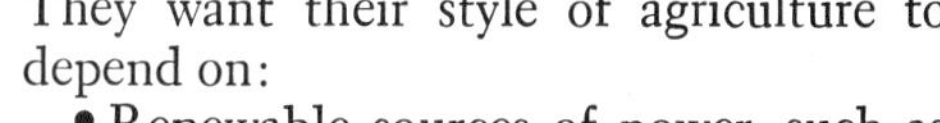

They want their style of agriculture to depend on:

- Renewable sources of power, such as sun and wind, instead of on fossil fuels.
- Natural biological cycles, not on pesticides and chemical fertilizers.
- A diversity of crops and varieties, not on single products cultivated to the exclusion of all others.
- Selection of plants for taste and nutrition, rather than for packaging and trucking qualities.
- Encouragement of people to come back to the land. One way to do this would be to set up forms of agriculture that would require only small amounts of capital investment.

Such an idyll may not be possible, but the new alchemists' effort to attain it will be important even if it fails. In fact, the group has already made quite substantial progress, considering the scantiness of its resources.

UNUSUAL EXPERIMENT

Greenhouse complexes, solar heating devices, and windmills with brightly painted suns on their tails are evidence of an unusual experiment in progress at the New Alchemy Institute's 5-hectare (12-acre) farm near Falmouth, Massachusetts, on Cape Cod. The institute is supported by more than 1,000 associate members, each subscribing at least $25 a year, as well as by grants from the Rockefeller Brothers Fund and other foundations. It is likely that the Canadian government will soon award the institute a contract worth several hundred thousand dollars to set up an "ark"—a new alchemical food producing system—on Prince Edward's Island.

The New Alchemy Institute was founded in 1969 by two marine biologists, John H. Todd and William O. McLarney.

An "ark," or self-contained farming system. Photo was taken from windmill with the windmill's tail, or "rudder," showing at upper right.

The choice of name implied not a rejection of modern science but a harking back to a time when science, art, and philosophy did not have to be practiced as separate, mutually exclusive realms of knowledge. Todd has a broader training than most scientists—a B.Sc. in agriculture, an M.S. in parasitology and tropical medicine, and a Ph.D. in comparative psychology and ethology. Yet he and his associates found that "with all our scientific training, we could not make any little piece of the world work."

The group was concerned about the damage being done to nature by modern agriculture and about the fact that no one seemed to be tackling the problem at its roots. People in universities seemed to be concerned only with patch-up operations. They were trying to make the existing system less harmful instead of replacing it altogether.

The group pooled members' savings to administer the institute and work on a small ranch in southern California, where Todd and McLarney held teaching posts at San Diego State University. The goal of developing ecologically-derived, low-cost, low-energy food production continued at Cape Cod when Todd and McLarney transferred to the Woods Hole Oceanographic Institution in 1970. Since early 1974 they have been working full time at the New Alchemy Institute.

One of the early design goals was to see if it would be possible to raise enough food to support a small group of people on a very limited area. To obtain sufficiently rapid growth of food products, the new alchemists turned their attention to tropical systems. This led them to conduct a number of experiments with the hot environments created by geodesic domes and greenhouses.

Both these structures trap heat during the day, but lose it at night. Water, however, is an effective storer of heat—and that suggested the idea of raising fish.

Commercial aquaculturists nurture their fish with fishmeal, grains, and other foods that could be fed directly to humans. Cattle raisers follow the same practice with feedlot cattle. The new alchemists have tried to devise less wasteful means of production. Their contribution is not so much in terms of uniquely new ideas (though there are some of these) as in the reintegration of existing knowledge and the rediscovery of precepts forgotten since modern agriculture began. For example, they deal with pests by methods other than pesticides.

AN "ARK" FOR PRODUCING FOOD

Several of the new alchemists' concepts are embodied in a food-producing system called an "ark." It is so named in part because of its biological diversity and autonomy and in part because it would serve as a lifeboat if conventional agriculture goes under.

List of tasks is posted for ark workers and visitors. Geodesic dome in background encloses a warm climate for fish and vegetables.

A "new alchemist" adjusts the sails of a windmill. The windmill pumps warmed water for the ark's three ponds.

The ark consists of three greenhouse-covered ponds built one below the other on a slight incline. It is essentially a chain in which the first two ponds grow food for the fish in the third. The bottommost pond holds edible species of fish, chiefly the tropical tilapia. Water from this fishpond is pumped up by a windmill to the top pond. On the way it picks up heat by passing through a solar heater if the sun is shining.

In the top pond the water is shunted through a bed of crushed shells that are permeated with bacteria. That step removes poisons from wastes and degrades certain growth-inhibiting chemicals excreted by the fish. The bacteria convert the ammonia in the fish wastes to nitrites and nitrates, which are then used as nutrients by the algae in an adjacent compartment of the top pond.

Algae-laden water from the top pond flows into the middle pond, which is inhabited by the small, algae-eating crustaceans known as daphnia, or water fleas. The water arrives in the bottom pool completely purified and laden with algae and daphnia, which provide a complete diet for the fish. Tilapia are mostly vegetarian, but the young require animal protein for rapid growth.

The greenhouse space above the pools is used to grow vegetables that are fertilized with fish water and kept free of pests by frogs and spiders.

An early problem with the system was that the oxygen-requiring bacteria in the filter bed tended to die during calm periods when the windmill ceased to maintain water circulation and hence oxygen from the water. The technological way to solve this problem would have been to install a backup electrical pump; the new alchemists' solution was to grow oxygen-releasing water plants next to the filter bed.

UNDENIABLE ELEGANCE

The system is one of undeniable elegance, providing in principle a no-cost method—labor and capital apart—of raising edible fish. A pilot scheme—the "mini-ark"—was constructed in 1974 and was successful in validating the theory. The maximum yield of the system has yet to be determined, but in 1974 the 19,000-liter (5,000-gallon) tank produced two crops each containing about 23 kg (50 lb) of edible fish. According to Todd, this exceeds the yields obtained in the most intense forms of Chinese aquaculture. It

---

We brag of being a nation where food is relatively cheap and agriculture efficient, yet ignore the fact that most measures of food prices and farm efficiency fail to take into account the endangerment to such valuable resources as soil fertility, water, wildlife, public health and a viable rural economy. When we stop to consider the full impact of the agricultural tools that have replaced the people who crowded into the cities, it is clear that "modern" agriculture is causing more problems than it is solving. . . . In recent years, conventional science has come under increasing attack for the moral implications of its basic inquiries and the long term significance of its applied tools. There has been relatively little criticism of the agricultural sciences along these lines since the external costs of farming are just beginning to surface with a broad impact.—Richard Merrill, in *The Journal of the New Alchemy Institute,* No. 2, 1975.

also proves that the various species of plants and animals introduced into the system have already come into productive association.

Construction costs, according to an article in the institute's journal, amounted to some $2,300 for materials alone, even though some components, such as the automobile crankshaft used in the windmill, were obtained from scrap.

Two members of the institute, Todd and Robert Angevine, a former U.S. Army lieutenant colonel who serves as the institute's business manager, have plans to set up a larger version of the ark on Prince Edward's Island in Canada.

Interest in tropical agriculture has led the institute to purchase a small piece of land in Costa Rica. McLarney, coauthor of a textbook on aquaculture, is now searching for Costa Rican species of fish suitable for ark life.

MORE THAN ARKS

In another venture Marcus Sherman of the institute has developed a water-pumping windmill for use in India. A prototype has already been built in the Tamil Nadu state of India. The machine is constructed from materials that are readily available to an Indian farmer, such as a bullock cartwheel, bamboo, and cloth for the sails.

Sherman's Indian windmill has been redesigned with American materials by Earle Barnhart. The redesigned sails have a shape specified by racing yacht sail designer Merrill Hall. Barnhart, a biologist who grew up in a religious farming community in Ohio, chose the institute as a place to do alternative service to the draft. His choice was based on his interest in the combined study of low-energy systems and aquaculture.

Hilde Atema Maingay, another member of the institute, raises vegetables on the farm without the use of pesticides or fertilizers, a method known as organic gardening. Although not trained as a scientist, Maingay last year undertook a careful experiment to test the interaction between the marketability of 20 varieties of

The Green Revolution has not been shaped by an ecological ethic and its keenest enthusiasts are usually manufacturers of chemicals and agricultural implements backed by government officials, rather than farmers and agricultural researchers. . . . A number of biologists and agricultural authorities . . . foresee environmental decimation which will offset the agricultural gains before the turn of the century. Amongst some of them, there is the disquieting feeling that we are witnessing the agricultural equivalent of the launching of the Titanic, only this time there are several billion passengers.
—John Todd, in *The New Alchemy Institute Bulletin*, No. 2, 1971.

Tiny insects called midges are being bred here. They form part of the ponds' food chain, the final members of which are fish.

These flourishing cabbage plants are part of an experiment in plant genetics.

cabbage and their resistance to the small white butterfly (*Pieris rapae*). Earlier studies had measured resistance simply by the number of caterpillars per cabbage. Maingay found that the varieties with the fewest caterpillars also tended to produce the fewest marketable heads. True resistance is the ability of a variety to produce marketable heads in the presence of caterpillars, her study indicates. Maingay says she found the agricultural research literature of little assistance, adding, "Research on the life cycles and other aspects of insect pests came to a halt when DDT was invented."

The use of biocides has triggered a vicious cycle; soils decline in quality, which in turn makes crops more vulnerable to attack by pests or disease organisms. This creates a need for increasingly large amounts of pesticides and fungicides for agricultural production to be sustained. . . . A modern agriculture, racing one step ahead of the apocalypse, is not ecologically sane, no matter how productive, efficient or economically sound it may seem.—John Todd, in *The New Alchemy Institute Bulletin,* No. 2, 1971.

WRONG QUESTIONS

New alchemist Richard Merrill is the co-editor of *Energy Primer,* a do-it-yourself guide to renewable forms of energy such as solar, wind, water, and biofuels such as those produced from recycling organic matter. Proceeds from the sale of the book will help support the California operations of New Alchemy West. These will parallel activities at the Cape Cod institute, but will emphasize raising shrimp instead of tilapia.

Merrill, a biologist, has written *Alternative Agriculture.* Traditional agriculture, he believes, is generating not only the wrong answers but the wrong questions. He explains: "The tools of liberation—chemicals, machinery, monocultures, hybrid crop strains, etc.—while they have alleviated scarcity and one kind of work, at the same time have precipitated mounting economic and ecological problems which . . . threaten the sustaining potential of our farmlands."

ATTRACTING SUPPORT

The New Alchemy Institute has been through some hard times financially but seems now to have proven its ability to attract support. Recently, the institute has been able to attract money from established sources, such as the Rockefeller Brothers Fund. The proposal for the mini-ark was turned down by the National Science Foundation but found favor elsewhere.

The Canadian project aside, the institute has a 1975 budget of about $135,000—enough to make ends meet but less, for example, than Todd received for his lab at Woods Hole. The full-time staff is about 12 during the summer months, but numerous volunteers and visitors give a hand each Saturday.

Public interest in the institute is remarkably keen, considering that its activities have been little publicized. The institute's journal, edited by Nancy Jack Todd, is distributed only to its membership. Sometimes up to 100 letters a day are received. A single article published

Ark workers add grasses and wastes from the gardens to the ark's compost heap. When these materials have decomposed they will be used as natural fertilizer.

in a Canadian newspaper brought in more than 300 subscriptions for associate membership.

SELF-RELIANCE

Part of the attraction may be the institute's emphasis on self-reliance, along with the message implicit in its name that modern science has led the world astray. While the new alchemists deny that they are part of an anti-science movement, they believe that science and technology have created a false confidence in man's ability to solve problems. "We have pretty much made the assumption that the world's problems won't be solved by the kind of technology being developed today," says Todd. "The longer we go after the technological fix, the worse the crash."

According to Merrill, "The purpose of New Alchemy is to bridge the gap between anti-science and the esoteric, inhuman, specialized kind of science which is going on almost everywhere."

There is a tendency in some of the new alchemists' writings to justify their work in terms of "stormy times ahead." In a way, this rationale understates the importance of their experiment. Even if the economy and modern agriculture manage to muddle through, there may still be a viable place for arks and other types of food-producing devices. Maybe of even greater importance is the theoretical significance of the alchemists' attempt to design agricultural systems that are high on biology and low on chemicals. Such systems, if viable, would provide a reference point against which to judge the high-yielding, chemically dependent, people-displacing monocultures that are the essence of the agriculture practiced at the present time.

The new alchemists are not yet in a position to grow enough food for self-sufficiency, let alone a surplus. But if fresh ideas and seriousness of purpose are any guide, they may soon be proving that they have something to teach the world□

 SELECTED READINGS

"Back to the Windmill to Generate Power." *Business Week*, May 11, 1974.

Energy Primer, co-editor Richard Merrill. The Whole Earth Catalog Store, Menlo Park, California.

"Grow 'em Big, Naturally," by M. C. Goldman, *Organic Gardening and Farming*, March 1974.

In Memoriam

by Barbara Tchabovsky

SEVERAL important scientists died in 1974. Among them were Nobel Prize winning physicists Lord Blackett and Sir James Chadwick; Nobel Prize winning physiologist Earl Sutherland; and two Americans closely associated with World War II scientific developments: engineer and administrator Vannevar Bush and physicist Edward Condon.

LORD BLACKETT

Patrick Maynard Stuart Blackett, winner of the 1948 Nobel Prize in Physics, was born in London, England, on November 18, 1897. After studying at the Royal Navy Colleges at Osborne and Dartmouth, he served in the Royal Navy during World War I. In 1919 he entered Magdalene College of Cambridge University. He received his B.A. in 1921 and two years later became a fellow of King's College, Cambridge University.

In 1921 Blackett began working under Lord Rutherford at the Cavendish Laboratory at Cambridge, then the site of many exciting discoveries in nuclear physics. At Rutherford's suggestion, Blackett began working to find better ways to study subatomic particles. In 1912 Charles T. R. Wilson had developed the cloud chamber that allowed physicists to "see" tracks made by atomic particles through space. Photographs taken at random recorded the tracks. Using an improved cloud chamber that took photographs regularly—every 15 seconds—Blackett was able to "see" and photograph the tracks made by the nucleus of an atom as it disintegrates. He photographed the forked tracks produced by the collision of an alpha particle with a nitrogen atom. The photograph showed that two particles emerged from the collision. Analysis revealed that the two particles were a proton, a positively charged subatomic particle and the nucleus of a form of oxygen not previously known. This was the first photographic representation of nuclear disintegration. It was also the first record of the transmutation of one element into another—in this case, the transmutation of nitrogen into oxygen.

In 1933 Blackett became professor of physics at Birbeck College at the University of London and, four years later, professor of physics at the University of Manchester. During World War II he held several important posts, concentrating mainly on operations research. He also took part in studies that led to the development of the atomic bomb. In 1948 he was awarded the Nobel Prize in Physics as "an acknowledgment of his development of the Wilson cloud chamber method of tracing the tracks of swift atomic particles and of his discoveries in nuclear physics."

In 1953 Blackett became head of the department of physics at the Imperial College of Science and Technology, London. He retired in 1963 but continued as professor of physics there. He died in London on July 13, 1974.

SIR JAMES CHADWICK

James Chadwick, winner of the 1935 Nobel Prize in Physics, was born in Manchester, England, on October 20, 1891. He graduated from Manchester University in 1911. After two years of research on radioactivity, he traveled to Berlin to continue his studies. He was interned in a concentration camp in Germany during World War I but received permission to continue some experiments in physics. In 1919, after his return to England, he joined Lord Rutherford at Cavendish Laboratory. In the following years he gradually took over the direction of nuclear physics research at Cavendish Laboratory. In 1921 he received a Ph.D. in physics from Cambridge University.

In 1932 Chadwick discovered the neutron, an uncharged particle of a mass equal to that of a proton. The idea that neutrons existed in the nuclei of atoms had first been put forward by Lord Rutherford in 1920. From then on Chadwick and other physicists devised many ingenious experiments to try to prove the existence of the particle. In 1932 Chadwick started a new series of experiments, the result of which was the general acceptance by most physicists that the neutron did exist. This work provided the basis for the development of nuclear energy.

From 1935 to 1948 Chadwick was professor of physics at the University of Liverpool. During World War II he was involved in research on what later became the atomic bomb. In 1948 he returned to Cambridge University as master of Gonville and Caius College. He resigned in 1958, and he died in London on July 24, 1974.

EARL SUTHERLAND

Earl Sutherland was born in Burlingham, Kansas, on November 19, 1915. He graduated from Washburn College in Topeka, Kansas, and received his M.D. from Washington University Medical School in St. Louis in 1942. After serving as an army doctor in World War II, he did research at Washington University. In 1953 he became director of the department of medicine at Case Western University in Cleveland.

In 1956, while working with Dr. T. W. Rall, Sutherland discovered cyclic adenosine monophosphate, or AMP. This substance is extremely important in directing cell function. Sutherland showed that hormones act as "primary messengers" to the cell. They are sent out from special glands into the bloodstream in response to some stimuli. The chemical AMP responds to stimulation by the hormone and acts as an intermediary, or "second messenger," to trigger specific reactions in the cell. In awarding Sutherland the 1971 Nobel Prize in Physiology or Medicine, the Nobel committee cited him "for his discoveries concerning the mechanisms of the actions of hormones."

In 1963 Sutherland returned to full-time research at Vanderbilt University.

Right: British physicists Lord Blackett and Sir James Chadwick. Below, from left: American scientists Earl Sutherland, Vannevar Bush, and Edward Condon.

In July 1973 he joined the staff of the University of Miami Medical School. He died March 9, 1974, in Miami, Florida.

VANNEVAR BUSH

Vannevar Bush was an American engineer who pioneered in computer technology and led American scientific and technological developments during World War II.

Bush was born in Everett, Massachusetts, on March 11, 1890. He received his B.S. and M.S. degrees from Tufts University and worked for a short time for the General Electric Company. He received his doctor of engineering degree from Harvard University and the Massachusetts Institute of Technology (M.I.T.) in 1916.

After World War I work on submarine detection, Bush became associate professor of electric power transmission at M.I.T. While there, he invented an analytical machine that could predict the performance of electrical circuits. This device saved hundreds of hours of calculations. Bush also invented a differential analyzer that could solve differential equations with as many as 18 variables. This differential analyzer was the forerunner of the modern analog computer. Bush became dean of engineering and vice-president of M.I.T. in 1932.

In 1938 Bush became head of the Carnegie Institution of Washington, a basic research firm. His reputation as an administrator, capable of getting things done, grew. During the early days of World War II, under President Roosevelt's authority, he formed the National Defense Research Committee. To meet the urgent need to update the U.S. war machine, Bush assigned specific government-sponsored research projects to university and independent laboratories across the country. In 1941 he was appointed head of the newly formed Office of Scientific Research and Development. From that position, Bush supervised and coordinated most of the scientific research and technological developments in the United States during World War II. Among the many projects under his overall supervision were the development of radar, antisubmarine devices, and eventually the atomic bomb.

After the war, Bush returned to Carnegie Institution and continued to serve in many advisory posts in the government. In 1957 he was made chairman of the M.I.T. Corporation and then honorary chairman. He died in Belmont, Massachusetts, on June 28, 1974.

EDWARD CONDON

Edward Condon was a leading American physicist of the 20th century. He contributed to the development of several basic concepts in physics, particularly in the field of quantum mechanics. He also served as a scientific leader in the development of radar and the atomic bomb during World War II.

Condon was born in Alamogordo, New Mexico, on March 2, 1902. He received his Ph.D. from the University of California at Berkeley in 1926. After studying in Germany, he returned to the United States and taught at Columbia and Princeton universities.

In the late 1920's Condon and R. W. Gurney developed a model by which the principles of quantum mechanics could be applied to the understanding of the structure of the nucleus. The first atom smashers were later built using this model. Condon also did preliminary work on semiconductors.

During World War II Condon, as associate director of research at Westinghouse Electric Company, led that company's work on the development of radar. Condon also contributed to the development of the magnetic separation equipment that was used to isolate uranium for the first atomic bomb. In 1943 he helped Dr. J. Robert Oppenheimer in organizing the team that developed atomic weapons.

After the war Condon took a series of government, industry, and university posts. From 1963 until his death on March 27, 1974, he was professor of physics at University of Colorado at Boulder□

Leonardo da Vinci

by George Sarton

LEONARDO DA VINCI, one of the immortals of the Renaissance, is as alive today as he ever was.

Since the growth of knowledge is the core of progress, the history of science ought to be the core of general history. Yet the main problems of life cannot be solved by men of science alone, or by artists and humanists; we need the cooperation of them all. Science is always indispensable but never sufficient. We are hungry for beauty, and where charity is lacking nothing else is of any avail. Leonardo typifies the Renaissance man's feeling for both art and science.

[A rich store of new information about Leonardo and his ideas was presented to the scientific world late in 1974. The information came from two leatherbound notebooks containing 700 pages of his drawings and notes. Found in the Spanish National Library in Madrid in 1965, the notebooks were translated by Dr. Ladislao Reti and published as the *Madrid Codices* in 1974. Prepared in a distinctive mirror-writing style, Leonardo's notes—along with the illustrations—added about 20 per cent to what had been known about his scientific work.]

EDUCATED IN AN ART STUDIO

Leonardo was born on April 15, 1452, at Borgo di Vinci, in the foothills above Florence. He belonged on the paternal side to a well-known family but was born out of wedlock. His parents married soon after his birth, but they did not marry each other. His father subsequently founded a new family in which Leonardo was not wanted.

If he had been well born, his father would probably have provided for his education and sent him eventually to the University of Florence, where he would have been crammed with Latin and scholastic learning. Instead, it was thought in the family circle that apprenticeship to a

Leonardo, a self-portrait

skilled craft would be good enough for him, and he was sent to the *bottega* (studio) of Andrea del Verrocchio. This was a blessing, for instead of an academic education that lacked contact with reality, he received the best kind of training for a boy of his temperament and genius. We cannot help being grateful to his father for having entrusted the upbringing of Leonardo to one of the leading artists and craftsmen of Florence at that time.

In Verrocchio's studio Leonardo was given a chance to learn many crafts, to discuss every question of the day, and to solve real and tangible problems such as life and art suggest at every turn. Verrocchio was not only a very great artist; he was a thinker, an ingenious craftsman —Leonardo's prototype. Leonardo was about 12 or 13 years of age when he was

Andrea del Verrocchio, painter, thinker, and craftsman, in whose Florence studio the young Leonardo received a many-sided education.

apprenticed to Verrocchio and he spent about 12 years in the studio on the Via del Agnolo. Leonardo received his whole education from Verrocchio and the many other artists who came to the studio. We may even assume that without Verrocchio the miracle of Leonardo would not have occurred.

AMBIGUOUS GENIUS

The most pathetic document concerning Leonardo is the draft of a letter that he wrote in 1482–83 to the Duke of Milan, Lodovico Sforza, to offer his services. He enumerates all his merits as inventor and military engineer; it is only at the very end that he mentions his artistic abilities. At this time he was 30 years old, and some of his less gifted friends were already famous. All his life he was the victim of his ambiguous genius.

The Duke of Milan accepted his services and, what is better, he seems to have left Leonardo plenty of freedom, for this first Milanese period (1483–99) was fertile in every one of his chosen fields (painting, anatomy, mathematics, technology). After the duke's defeat by French troops and the capture of Milan in 1499, Leonardo's life became that of an exile, a refugee, passing restlessly from one city to another. The best of these errant years (1499–1512) were again spent in Milan, this time under French rule. In this, his second Milanese period, he continued his efforts to canalize streams and studied geometry with Luca Pacioli and anatomy with Marc Antonio della Torre. In 1512, however, Milan was reconquered by the Italians and Leonardo was obliged to move out.

He obtained the patronage of Giuliano de' Medici and went to Rome in 1513, accompanied by his young friend, Francesco Melzi. They spent two years at the Belvedere in the Vatican, but the proximity of Michelangelo, whom he disliked, and of the German Giovanni degli Specchi, who was a deceiver, irritated him and drove him away. He finally accepted the hospitality of François I in Cloux, near Amboise. Leonardo and Francesco traveled to Cloux in 1515. They brought with them three paintings, one of St. Anne with the Holy Virgin and Child, one of St. John the Baptist, and the portrait of a woman (probably *Mona Lisa*, or *La Gioconda*), and also all his notes and anatomical drawings, which he bequeathed to Francesco Melzi. He died in Cloux on May 2, 1519.

PROBLEMS FOR HISTORIANS

Since most of the people who have studied Leonardo's work are men of letters or art critics, it is necessary to explain that the historian of science cannot use their methods without danger. An eloquent sentence, of which there are so many in his manuscripts, may testify to his literary genius. A single incomplete sketch may reveal the great artist. But we cannot draw large conclusions from a single remark on a scientific topic, unless the idea is developed and confirmed. For example, we cannot call Leonardo a predecessor of

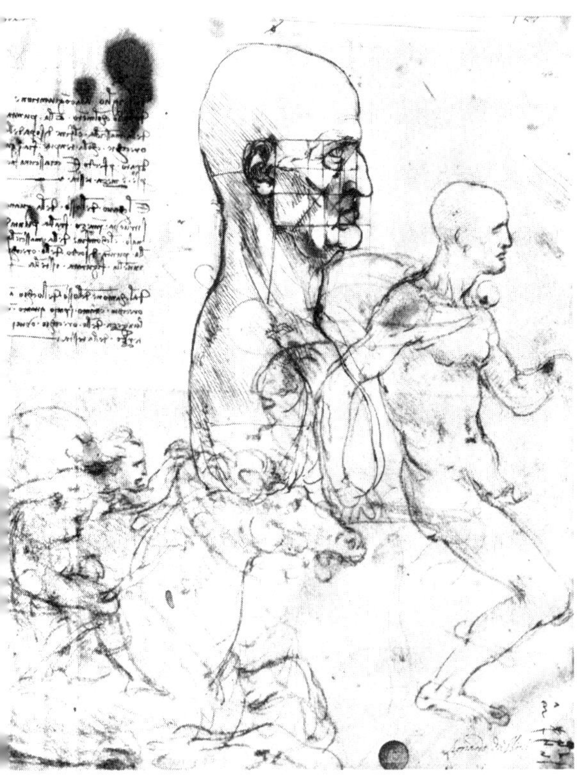

Studies of the human head and of the human body in motion with Leonardo's notes.

Copernicus merely on the ground that he once wrote, "The sun does not move." What exactly did he mean? There is no way of knowing. A man of science must prove, or at least explain clearly, what he has in mind.

Leonardo's literary works consist of an enormous mass of fragments (notes and drawings) that has come to us in the greatest disorder. Some of his thoughts are deep, but the notes and fragments come from many very different books, all mixed together, and to this hodgepodge are added incongruous and capricious notes and dreams.

Another curiosity that has puzzled the critics and will always continue to puzzle them is the fact that the notes are written in mirror writing. In order to read them, one must hold them up to a mirror. Why is this? My guess is that Leonardo was left-handed and that when he began to write without anybody's supervision, he wrote naturally in reverse as left-handed children often do. Then he realized the advantage of such writing for the sake of secrecy and continued to use it. There is no doubt that his mirror writing was fluent and easy; but it is sometimes very hard to decipher it even with the help of a mirror.

THE "SCIENCE OF PAINTING"

Two aspects of Leonardo's scientific work began very early in Verrocchio's *bottega:* the "science of painting" and mechanics. Leonardo's idea that there can

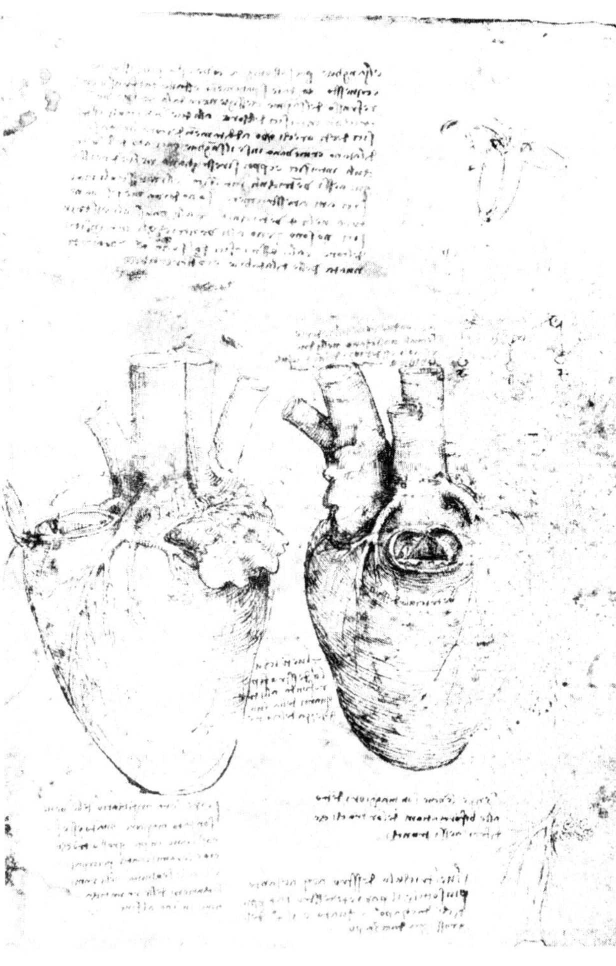

These drawings of the human heart show Leonardo's pioneering work in anatomy. He studied corpses to learn how the body functions.

be a "science of painting" may be an illusion, but after all, why should one not speak of "painting science" just as one does of "medical science"? In both cases scientific facts or theories are applied to an art, the art of painting or of healing. The science of painting included, in the first place, linear perspective, which was exciting Florentine artists, and second, the far subtler matter of aerial perspective, which for centuries had been mixed up with optics, meteorology, the theory of colors and shades, and many other things. The Chinese had made penetrating observations on aerial perspective at least as early as the sixth century, and Leonardo was the first to make some of the same observations in the West.

Leonardo was a born mechanician as well as a painter; his mechanical tendencies were fostered in Verrocchio's studio. Verrocchio was a sculptor, a painter, and a goldsmith. His best-known work is the equestrian statue of Bartolommeo Colleoni in Venice, perhaps the greatest monument of its kind in the world. The erection of such a monument involved the solution of many mechanical problems. During the years of his adolescence Leonardo was constantly speculating about various machines that would make it easier to satisfy the needs of peace and of war. The only available source of continuous power was hydraulic; it was necessary to dig canals, which were the best means of moving heavy materials, and to build watermills on running rivers.

Soldiers destroyed the plaster model of this horse before Leonardo could cast it in bronze.

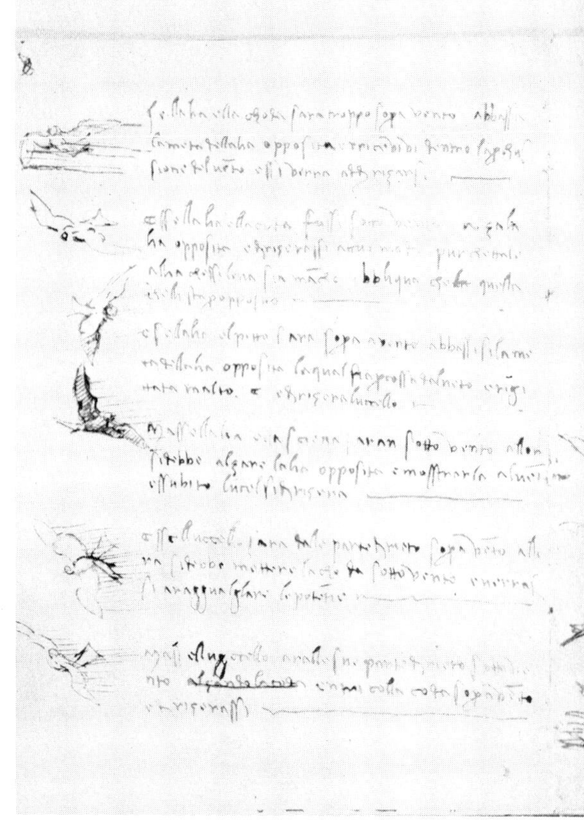

Leonardo's notes and drawings are full of mechanical projects, drawn in such complete and precise detail that they sometimes look like blueprints. In fact, it has been possible to reconstruct some of the machines that he invented. But had he invented them? That is not certain. There were many inventors in the 15th century, and even in the 14th. Most of them were illiterate, and in many cases secrecy was their only protection.

AVIATION PIONEER

From hydraulics Leonardo passed to aerodynamics, and he made a good many observations, detailed and accurate, concerning the flight of birds. Leonardo

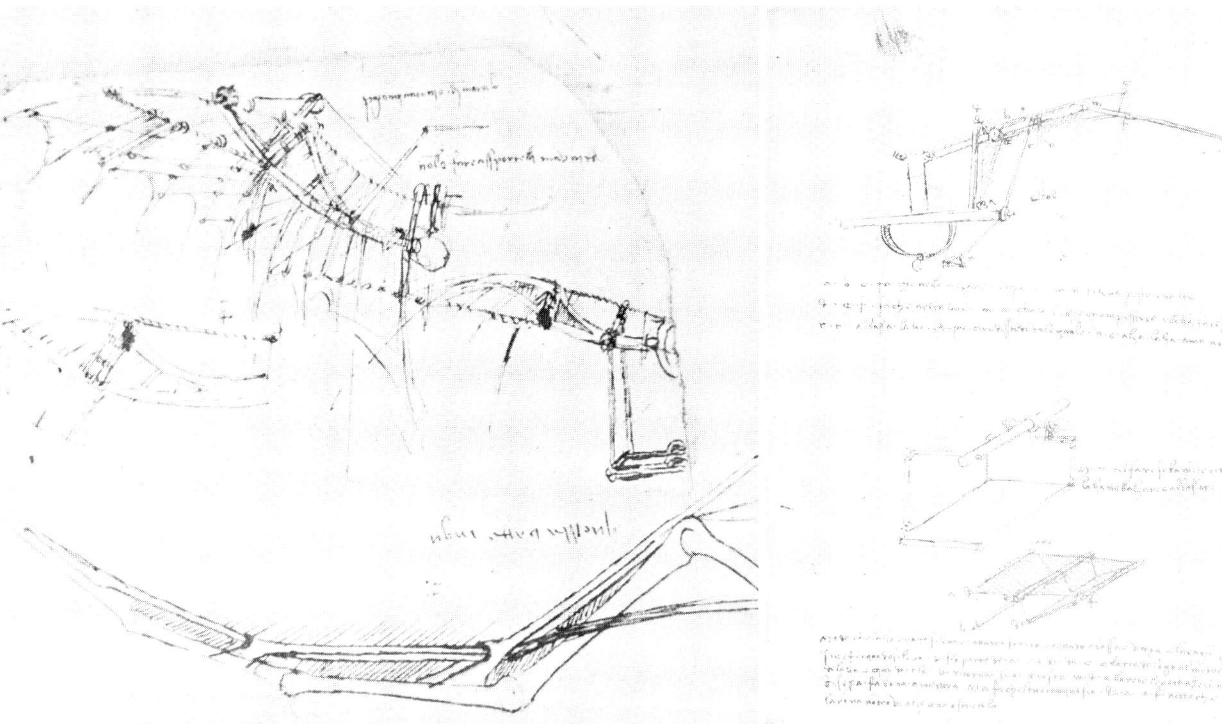

Studies of the mechanics of flight: Opposite page, a leaf from Leonardo's *Manuscript on the Flight of Birds.* Center, an artificial wing closely based on the bird's wing. At right, a purely mechanical wing for a flying machine.

asked himself very reasonably, "Why should man not be able to do what the birds do?" and reasoned that to imitate them we should, first of all, find out exactly how they do it. The observations he made on that subject were not equaled until the 19th century.

How do birds soar, how do they fly with or against the wind, how do they direct their flight and reach their goal? He observed the adjustment of wings and their flexing, the various kinds of feathers, the movement of the tails, and how these means are used for going up and down, gliding, soaring, balancing, and alighting without breaking their legs. In short, Leonardo did everything that could be done in his time. It would be wrong to call him a forerunner of Copernicus, but he fully deserves to be considered one of the pioneers of aviation.

It would be very misleading to imagine that Leonardo resembled a present-day inventor, whose aim is more often than not to make money. He was a practical man, but he was also a philosopher, so much in love with his ideas that he lost interest in their realization. When an inventor suddenly has a great idea, that is not the end of the matter but the beginning; the most difficult task is still to come. He has to work out innumerable details, ascertain industrial and commercial possibilities, and adjust his plans to reality. Leonardo, having no patience and no talent for that sort of thing, could not be a successful inventor. He was a philosopher rather than an engineer, and so he was more interested in principles than in their application.

NO MATHEMATICIAN

In spite of what has been claimed to the contrary, he was not a mathematician. He loved mathematics in the Platonic style but knew only the elements. And it might even be said that he did not understand these very well. He was a mechanician by instinct and tried all of his life to understand the phenomena of statics and dynamics. He even tried to understand the rules of hydraulics and aerodynamics, but in vain.

He could write: "Mechanics is the paradise of mathematics because it gives us the fruits of that science." That was a poetic saying, an admirable intuition, but the fruits were still very far from maturity. It was impossible for Leonardo to solve the fundamental problems that claimed his attention, because they could not yet be formulated.

Leonardo continued bravely as part of the medieval gestation period. The birth could not take place until the time of Simon Stevin and Galileo, and mechanics began to mature only toward the end of the 17th century with Christian Huygens and Sir Isaac Newton.

Warfare, like everything else, interested Leonardo. These studies of weapons were made when Milan was threatened with attack.

VALUABLE RESULTS IN ANATOMY

In the field of mechanics Leonardo, genius though he was, could only grope his way like a blind man. In another field, however, it was possible to obtain valuable results at once. This was anatomy. Here again he was continuing medieval traditions, for it is wrong to believe that dissections were forbidden throughout the Middle Ages. There were distinguished anatomists such as Mondino de' Luzzi and Guido da Vigevano. Human dissections, however, were rare and badly organized. The obstacles came from scholasticism rather than from religion. The experimental spirit was hardly awakened, and what is worse, the art of observing with precision and without prejudices was almost unknown. Physicians were dominated by Galen and Avicenna to such an unbelievable extent that they were unable to see with their own eyes. It was here that Leonardo's genius revealed itself, though even in this case the revelation was incomplete and miscarried.

One can say that modern anatomy was founded by two men, Italian and Flemish: Leonardo and, a little later, Andreas Vesalius of Brussels. There is an essential difference between them. Leonardo dissected some 30 bodies and left an abundance of notes and drawings, but he never composed an anatomical treatise. Vesalius, however, published in 1543 a great work, *De humani corporis fabrica,* which is truly the basis of modern anatomy. Leonardo's notes and drawings remained almost unknown until our century; Vesalius' book deeply influenced all the anatomists who followed him. So, because Leonardo's work had virtually no influence on the development of the science, one must conclude that Vesalius alone is the founder.

ASTOUNDING WORK

Nevertheless, although Leonardo's immediate influence was negligible, his anatomical work was astounding. Vesalius was a physician and a professor of anatomy, who might have been expected to perform dissections. Yet Leonardo, an

Leonardo's drawings of flowers show the blossoming process—from closed bud to full bloom to wilting blossom. He was interested in the way the flower passed from one stage to another.

artist and a mechanician, performed many and did them as well as Vesalius, though not as methodically.

The dissections that students perform today in the antomical laboratories of our medical schools are very easy; running water, refrigeration, and antiseptics have greatly lessened the unpleasantness of such work. None of these conveniences was available to Leonardo, and the fulfillment of his self-imposed task required tremendous will power. Moreover, while Vesalius was assisted by a professional artist, John Stephen of Calcar, Leonardo was obliged at various stages of his arduous task to interrupt it and begin immediately another kind of work of extreme delicacy, drawing as accurately as possible what he saw. Some of his anatomical drawings have never been equaled.

Leonardo's curiosity went far beyond that of other painters and sculptors, who were obliged to have some knowledge of artistic anatomy, that is to say, the layout of superficial muscles. The Florentine artists, who were draftsmen rather than colorists, studied that kind of anatomy with enthusiasm. That tradition, begun by Donatello, was carried to extremes by Antonio Pollaiuolo and brought back to moderation by Verrocchio and Leonardo. The sculptor's model or the painter's sketch must be sufficiently precise and sensitive to indicate the presence of mus-

A device used in a clock to compensate for the change in tension as the spring unwinds.

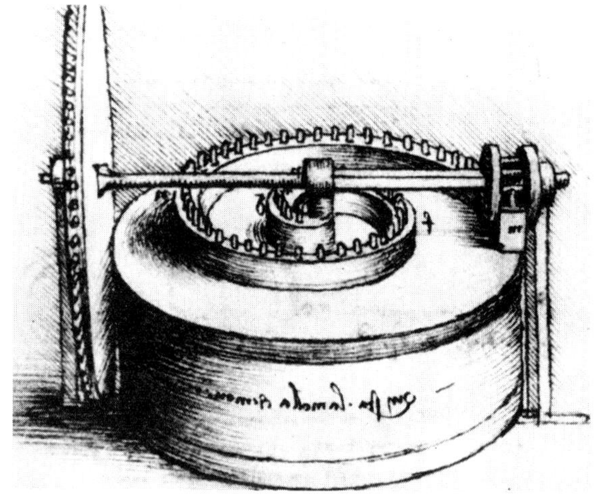

cles. The spectator must be able to divine their presence without being too conscious of them.

Artistic anatomy has been dominated from the beginnings of art by mathematical and mystical considerations. The love of symmetry and of numbers has led artists of all times to discover arithmetical relations between the sizes of different parts of the body and to establish a canon of human beauty. Such preoccupations existed in ancient Egypt, India, and Greece. And Leonardo was no stranger to them.

BEAUTY IN NATURE

Leonardo was interested not only in the beauty of the human body; he was searching for beauty in all of nature. He left behind many sketches of animals, plants, shells, and rocks. Some of his investigations would be classified today in the fields of physical geography, mineralogy, and geology. His drawings make us think of those of John Ruskin, whose curiosity in both art and science was equally keen and complex. He was one of the first to give a rational explanation of fossils: the shells found imbedded in mountain rocks were the remains of creatures that had lived in the seas or on beaches. The remains had been trapped in sedimentary rocks which were lifted up later on to form mountains. He was one of the first men in the West to explore the high Alps not only as an artist but also as a man of science. The peoples of Europe were generally afraid of mountains, which they fancied were inhabited by goblins, gnomes, and devils.

PURSUING HIS OWN MISSION

Leonardo was one of the greatest men of science in history, but the world which admired him as an artist did not discover the man of science until many centuries after his death. He remained unknown by his own fault, for he did nothing to publish his discoveries; in most cases, indeed, he did not even bother to complete them. Leonardo was a pure artist, a disinterested inventor, a man of science, a cogitator, a Bohemian; he was decidedly not a businessman or an administrator. He was anxious to obtain not money, or power, or comfort, but beauty and truth. He wanted to understand God, nature, art, himself, and other men.

Few people are able to understand this, because their ideals are confused and upside down. They like to speak of spiritual values but they always give top priority to material values. They speak of beauty and art but comfort comes first. They speak of peace but make war almost unavoidable. They pray on the Sabbath but their motto is: Business first, business and power, conformity to social conventions. Most men are social hypocrites. Leonardo was not.

Leonardo was a rebel, one of the worst or the best kind, one who does not even bother to state his disagreement and disapproval but pursues his own mission.

Leonardo's self-portrait, made by him toward the end of his life, shows a tired face. Leonardo was then less than 67 years old, but he had suffered much because of the world's cruelties and his own anxieties. His outstanding merit is to have shown by his own example that the pursuit of beauty and the pursuit of truth are not incompatible. He is the patron of all those men, few in number, who love art and science with equal fervor.

Leonardo was a defender of reason and an enemy of superstition, but an idealist. There was in him an original and deep conviction that the only things that really matter are spiritual. The supreme discipline is that of love. As he puts it, "The love of anything is the fruit of our knowledge of it, and grows as our knowledge becomes more certain."

One might add, and no doubt he did so, that without love there can be no real knowledge□

"A New Light on the Legendary Leonardo." *Popular Mechanics*, January 1975.

The Unknown Leonardo by Ladislao Reti. McGraw-Hill Book Co., 1974.

The World of Leonardo by Robert Wallace. Time-Life Books, 1966.

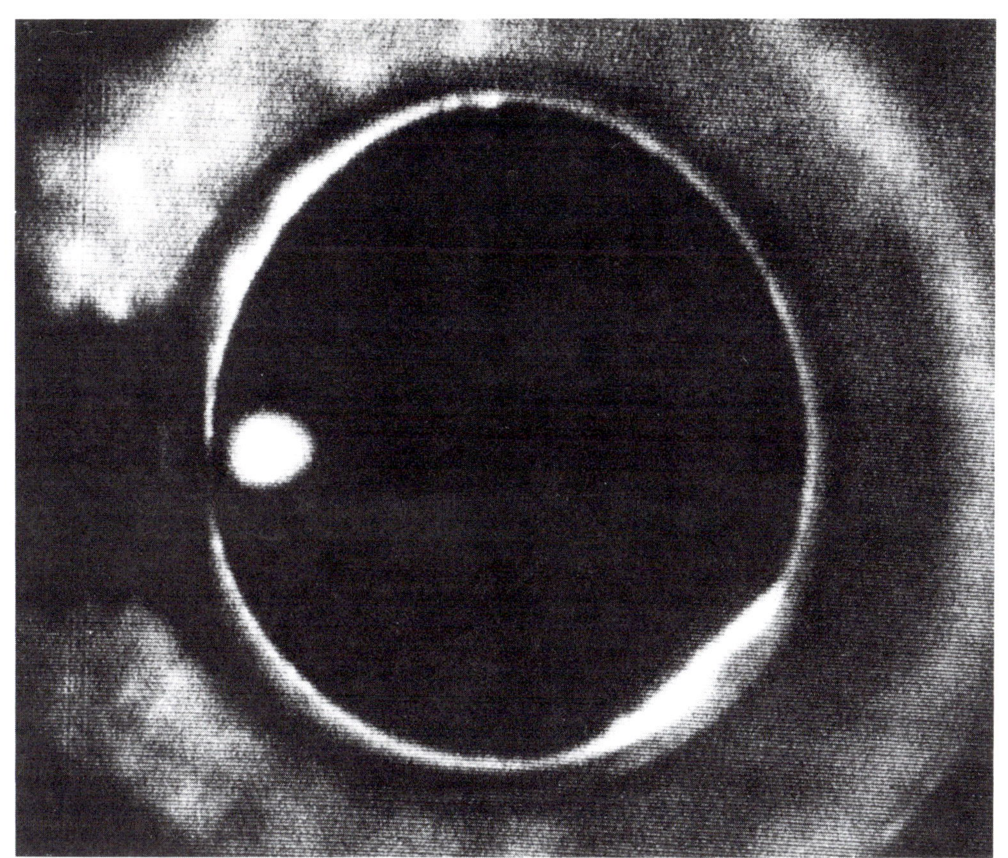

physical sciences

First photograph of pure electricity in liquid droplet form. A mass of electric charges is revealed as a single sphere glowing with infrared radiation. This is the first visual evidence of another state of matter—low-energy plasma.

review of the year

physical sciences

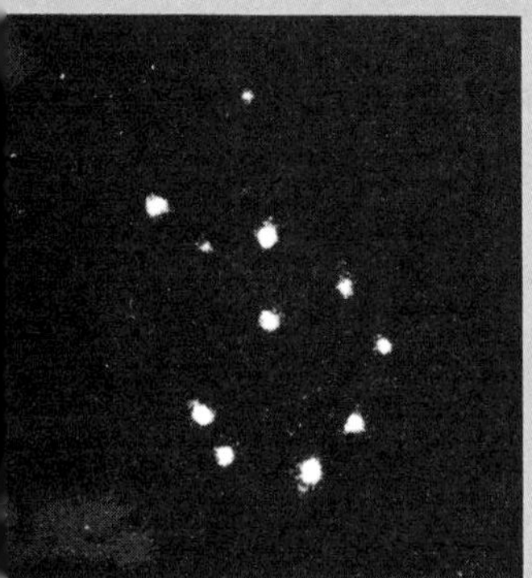

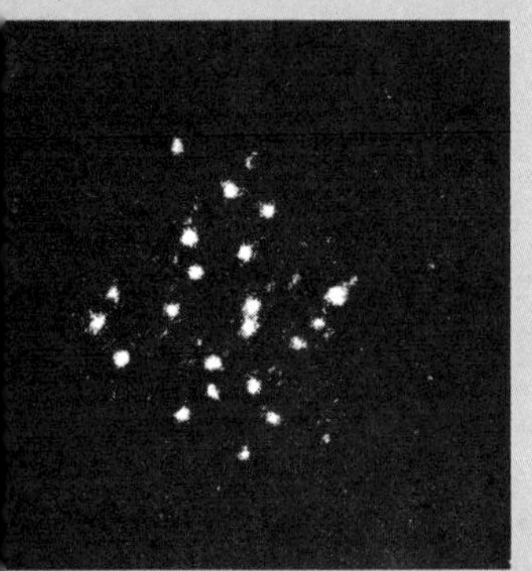

When superfluid helium is spun, the vortex lines are produced in steps—or, in other words, the fluid exhibits quantization.

Physics. Particle physics came up with another surprise in 1974. Experimental studies at two separate facilities—Brookhaven National Laboratory in New York, and the Stanford Linear Accelerator Center in California—indicated the existence of two new, very massive particles. See "Discovery of Two New Particles," beginning on page 326.

Among other discoveries in particle physics, the Fermi National Accelerator Laboratory near Batavia, Illinois, has found that the sizes, or cross sections, of neutrons and other particles apparently increase with increasing energy. This was previously thought to be true only of protons. ■ Particles such as electrons and muons have now been produced by direct collisions between particles, rather than by radioactive emission from other particles following such collisions. For various reasons, these results can be viewed as evidence against the reality of quarks and partons. These two kinds of theoretical particles are very useful in some current models of atomic structure, but their existence has not been justified experimentally. The results also support the possibility that there is a principle unifying the four forces that hold matter together: the strong and weak nuclear forces, the electromagnetic force, and gravitation. ■ Cosmic ray observations in Australia have given the first experimental indication that tachyons may be a reality. The tachyon, another theoretical "particle," may be thought of as the antiparticle to the photon.

Physicists may have created another very heavy element in 1974. The new transuranium element would become number 106 in the periodic table. The achievement was reported separately by researchers in the United States and the Soviet Union. The Americans produced the new element by bombarding nuclei of californium-249 with oxygen-18 nuclei, whereas the Russians produced it by bombarding lead isotopes with chromium-54. Perhaps ironically, 1974 also saw the establishment of an international committee to determine the validity of claims made for the discovery of elements 104 and 105.

Quantum mechanics is based on the concept that steplike changes take place in the behavior of subatomic particles, rather than smooth, continuous changes. The concept is fundamental to present theories of atomic structure and behavior. However, except in one instance, this quantization, or steplike change, of behavior has not been directly observable on a large scale. Now physicists have found another large-scale display of quantization. The phenomenon involves helium II, the form of liquid helium that exhibits the property known as superfluidity. Physicists discovered that when helium II is rotated in a cylinder, the vortex lines produced in the liquid by this spinning motion display quantization. They are quantized in units, or steps, that are proportional to Planck's constant, the fundamental ratio in quantum physics.

American scientists disclosed a new laser process that can separate one isotope of an element from another. A similar technique was described by the Soviet Union in 1975. It is of special importance in the isolation of uranium-235, the isotope used in nuclear weapons and commercial reactors.

The technique is based on the fact that the energy (or light frequency) needed to excite one isotope of an element—that is, raise it to a higher energy level—is slightly different from that needed to excite another isotope of that element. A laser beam "tuned" to a specific frequency will therefore excite only the atoms of one particular isotope. These "excited" atoms of the isotope are then ionized by ultraviolet light and thereafter can be separated from the other, nonionized atoms of other isotopes. The technique has been successful with a number of elements besides uranium.

Hugh F. Henry

Chemistry. The study of the functions of metallic elements in living tissues was emphasized in 1974. This relatively new field is called bioinorganic chemistry, because it combines the inorganic chemistry of metals with the science of biology. One example of an organometallic compound is hemoglobin, a complex protein that contains iron. In bioinorganic studies, hemoglobin-like but much simpler molecules have been synthesized in order to learn more about how hemoglobin functions in the body. Current work has centered on two questions. What happens when heme, the iron-containing portion of hemoglobin, combines with oxygen? How does the surrounding protein portion of the molecule affect the oxygen-binding properties of the iron?

Pollution continues to be a worldwide problem. In studying this problem, it is difficult to make reliable estimates of the kinds and amounts of pollution to which a given individual has been exposed. Now chemists have found that chemical analysis of the individual's hair reveals the presence of pollutants such as metals. This procedure is less hazardous and expensive than the surgical removal of body tissues for analysis. Hair-sample analyses of large numbers of people in a given population group can reveal wide-scale nutritional deficiencies as well.

The ongoing energy crisis is also of worldwide concern. One serious candidate as a future resource is solar energy, but the methods thus far developed for tapping this great resource are relatively inefficient and expensive. Heating and cooling units for homes and factories have been devised, one of the most promising of which involves a lithium bromide system for absorbing the sun's energy directly. Other systems use silicon cells to convert solar energy to electrical energy, which is then stored in sulfur-lithium batteries. However, only in the past year have the costs of fossil fuels risen high enough to make these systems economically feasible.

The storage and transport of captured solar energy, in particular, is a very hard problem. In one proposed system, "sun farms" would be constructed in the relatively cloudfree southwestern United States. The sun's energy would be used to break down a chemical called sulfur trioxide into oxygen and sulfur dioxide. These two chemicals would be moved to an energy-transfer system and recombined. The energy given off by the reaction would ultimately be transformed into electrical energy and set on to the consumer. The recombined sulfur trioxide would be recycled through the process. ■ Another proposed system would use focused solar energy to break water down into oxygen and hydrogen. The hydrogen would be burned, and the heat energy thus released would be converted into electrical energy. A variant on this system would derive the hydrogen by a process resembling photosynthesis. Special enzymes would break down water into its components. In the future, an electrical cell based on this process might make it possible to convert the sun's heat directly into electrical energy.

Jay A. Young

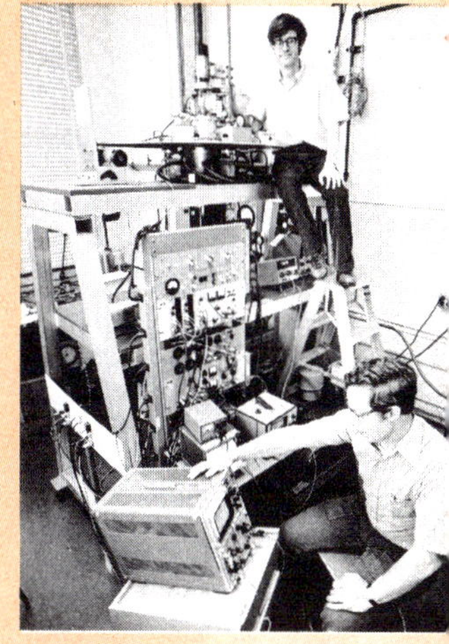

University of California physicists Richard E. Packard and Gary A. Williams who developed the apparatus for verifying quantization in superfluid helium.

The production of silicon solar cells has been advanced by the successful growth of a continuous ribbon of crystalline silicon in experiments by Tyco Laboratories and Harvard University.

Discovery of Two New Particles

by William D. Metz

PHYSICISTS around the world have been frantically pursuing the meaning of an extraordinary set of new discoveries. On November 11, 1974, two teams of researchers working at the Brookhaven National Laboratory, Upton, New York, and the Stanford Linear Accelerator Center (SLAC), Palo Alto, California, discovered a new subnuclear particle. The properties of this particle were so peculiar that it did not fit into any of the familiar particle groupings. It was named "J" in the East, and "psi" in the West. Within days, researchers at the ADONE facility in Frascati, Italy, confirmed the new particle discovery. Thereupon practically every physicist in the field rushed to try to explain the new phenomenon.

But only 10 days after the original discovery, before the ink was dry on the first explanation, the team at Stanford found a second peculiar particle. They renamed the original particle "psi(3105)" for its mass of 3.105 giga electron volts, or Gev (1 Gev equals 1,000,000,000 electron volts). The second particle was then named "psi(3695)," according to the same notation.

The suddenness of the discoveries left almost everyone baffled about what it all means. Many physicists think that the discoveries may have opened a whole new territory in the world of subnuclear particles. They have compared it to the finding of the first of many so-called strange particles in 1947. Apparently not just an isolated phenomenon but a whole new family of particles has been found.

The most distinguishing characteristics of the new particles is that they are very massive and relatively long-lived—that is, in terms of events in the world of particle physics. As a rule, massive particles are short-lived. The two new particles, however, live at least 80 times longer than the most similar particle known before, even though the new ones are at least three times heavier. The new particles have not been seen directly. Their lifetime of 10^{-19} second is too brief for them to leave a visible track. But the ordinary considerations of particle physics suggest that their lifetime should be at least 1,000 times shorter.

The Brookhaven team that discovered the very massive new particle, psi(3105), was led by physicist Samuel C. Ting (foreground).

Within days after the first new particle was discovered by Brookhaven scientists, a team at the Stanford Linear Accelerator Center came up with an even heavier entry, psi(3695).

CHARMED QUARKS?

Many more experiments are needed to pinpoint other properties of the new particles. The biggest question is whether they are weak or strong. That is, do they exert the strong force that binds together the particles in an atomic nucleus? Or do they exert the weak force involved in the process known as radioactive decay? No one knows the answer yet. All that is known for certain is that, since neither particle is charged, they do not exert the electromagnetic force—the third basic force in nature. (The fourth is gravity.)

If the particles can exert the strong force, which is responsible for nuclear energy, they would be called hadrons. But they would be peculiar types of hadrons. If they are, they may never have been seen before because they are set apart by a quality called "charm," which was predicted in 1963. Charm is a complex combination of mathematical properties involving the way a particle is produced and the means by which it splits up into other particles. One physicist has called the possible classification of the new particles as hadrons the most conservative explanation. That is, many different families of hadrons have already been found, so one more family wouldn't be such a drastic change. In contrast, there is really only one family of weak particles. So a new family of such particles —if the two discoveries lead to that— could be much more revolutionary.

In a way, the idea that the first new particle might be charmed led the Stanford researchers to the right place to find the second one. Charmed elementary particles were postulated to exist if they were composed of charmed quarks. Quarks are hypothetical basic units of matter, proposed a decade ago by American physicist Murray Gell-Mann as a useful concept in explaining particle behavior. Charmed quarks are a further extension of this concept. Thus, when the first new particle was discovered in 1974, a popular explanation was that it was made of a charmed quark and a charmed antiquark bound together. The appeal of this suggestion to particle physicists was that it would explain to them why the new particle did not decay quickly into ordinary hadrons, which are thought to be composed of uncharmed quarks.

By making a rough analogy between the constituents of the new particle and the constituents of the hydrogen atom, the Stanford physicists were led to look for a particle with a mass of about 3.7 Gev. The predicted mass indeed turned out to be the mass of the second particle. But the analogy didn't work when they looked for a third particle that the analogy would have indicated. The search continues, however, and there were some indications that such a particle exists.

OR ARE THEY WEAK?

A completely different explanation is that the new particles may be weak. For many years physicists have known that the particle called the photon transmits the electromagnetic force. But they have searched in vain for the particle that is the carrier of the weak force. Some of them now think the new particles could be versions of the neutral carrier of the weak force. However, various experiments suggest that the charged carriers of the weak force would actually be much heavier—at least 10 Gev. The two new particles are each less than 4 Gev so this theory seems unlikely.

Another possibility is that the new particles may be responsible for the phenomenon called a neutral current that was discovered in 1973 at CERN, the European nuclear research center outside Geneva. The term "currents" refers to the transformations that occur when hadrons collided with light particles, or leptons. When the lepton involved is the chargeless, massless neutrino, its interaction with a hadron is controlled only by the weak force. According to theory, this reaction should always be through a charged current. But new efforts at developing a "unified field theory"—a theory linking all four basic forces in nature—led to the prediction that in the above interaction, the current would sometimes be neutral. This was confirmed in the 1973 discovery at CERN. And this is the phenomenon that some physicists would now link to the two newly found particles. According to J. D. Bjorken at SLAC, it is natural to relate the new particles to neutral currents. But whether they are related to the rest of the weak interactions is a matter of speculation.

These two suggestions—for strong and weak particles—only define the extremes of the spectrum of possible explanations. Every possibility in between may be viable too. So many theorists are busy preparing explanations that one of them predicted that the journal *Physical Review Letters* "had better be braced for an avalanche." None of the explanations advanced so far may be correct. Many physicists are nevertheless optimistic that the new discoveries will help with an assortment of problems that have accumulated in recent years—problems seeming to hint that something "funny" was happening in the mass range between 3 and 4 Gev.

TWO ROUTES TO ONE DISCOVERY

The first new particle was discovered by scientists working separately at the Alternating Gradient Synchrotron (AGS) at Brookhaven and the SPEAR storage ring at SLAC. At Brookhaven, a proton beam hitting a target generated pairs of electrons. At SLAC, colliding beams of electrons and positrons generated various hadrons. The two experiments were almost exactly inverses of each other. In both cases, the number of particles produced in the experiment peaked sharply at an energy of 3.1 Gev. The results indicated that a new type of particle had been produced with a mass of 3.1 Gev. This is more than three times heavier than the proton. The decisions to publish the two experiments were made within hours of each other.

The experiment at Brookhaven seems to have been motivated by a sequence of curious results dating back several years. Generally the same phenomena studied with electrons can be studied with muons—leptons with the same electric charge as electrons but with a much greater mass. In 1970, Leon Lederman of Columbia University saw anomalies in the production of muon pairs. After that, interest in muon pair experiments grew to the point that by late 1974, the Fermi National Accelerator Laboratory in Batavia, Illinois, had to hold a separate program meeting on the subject. But the brainstorm behind the Brookhaven experiment was the idea of looking for electron pairs instead of muon pairs. This procedure was chosen because at a proton accelerator such as the Brookhaven machine, the background of spurious electrons is much less than the muon background. Nevertheless, the experiment at Brookhaven

Mass Class	Particle	Mass (Million Electron Volts)	Electric Charge	Average Life-Time (Seconds)
Zero-Mass Boson	Photon	0	neutral	stable
	Graviton	0	neutral	stable
Lepton	Neutrino, electronic	0	neutral	stable
	Neutrino, muonic	0 ?	neutral	stable
	Electron	0.5	negative	stable
	Muon	105.6	negative	2.2×10^{-6}
Meson	Pion	139.6	positive	2.6×10^{-8}
	Pion	139.6	negative	2.6×10^{-8}
	Pion	135	neutral	0.9×10^{-16}
	Kaon	493.8	positive	1.2×10^{-8}
	Eta	548.8	neutral	$+1 \times 10^{-22}$
Baryon	Proton	938.3	positive	stable
	Neutron	939.5	neutral	1,010
	Lambda hyperon	1,115.4	neutral	2.5×10^{-10}
	Sigma hyperon	1,189.4	positive	8.1×10^{-11}
	Xi hyperon	1,320.8	negative	1.7×10^{-10}
	Omega hyperon	1,675	negative	1.5×10^{-10}
?	Psi (3105)	3,105	neutral	1×10^{-19}
?	Psi (3695)	3,695	neutral	1×10^{-19}

Chart of Some Subatomic particles

In this selective listing of subatomic particles, the positions of the two newly discovered particles, if confirmed, are indicated. Both particles are far more massive than any previously detected particles.

was a difficult undertaking. Approximately 10^9 particles had to be rejected for every two that were found.

Unlike proton accelerators, storage rings for electrons and positrons produce very little particle debris. Therefore, in the data taken at the Stanford storage ring, the peaks that indicated the new particles stood out sharply above the background. After the team working at Stanford began tracking down the causes of certain inconsistencies in earlier experiments, they were quickly able to find the first new particle. For similar reasons, the discovery of the second particle was rapid. This type of experiment was also well suited to determine how long the new particles live. Thus it was the team at Stanford that was able to establish this information about the particles, as well.

The new discoveries were not made with the world's most powerful accelerators. In fact, the Brookhaven AGS is the oldest accelerator in operation in the United States, though not the one with the lowest energy. The new particles are right in the middle of the mass range that can be studied with the AGS. If sufficient motivation had been available in the past, the new particle might have been found sooner. At the Italian facility in Frascati, where the first electron–positron storage ring was built, the new particle could have conceivably been found five years ago.

Ironically, the Brookhaven AGS is running short of money just now, and the SLAC budget is also restricted. "We'll bend every effort to follow up the new discovery," says Ronald Rau of Brookhaven, "but we will run out of money in the not too distant future and have to quit. That's a shame because this is an exciting time"□

"Physics in a Ferment of Theories Over Discovery of Two Particles" by Walter Sullivan, *The New York Times*, Dec. 16, 1974.

"New Particles Excite Experimenters and Puzzle Theorists" by B. G. Levi. *Physics Today*, January 1975.

"New Particles: Subtleties Mount." *Science News*, Feb. 8, 1975.

Benjamin Franklin: Scientist

by Thomas Fleming

FROM bright June sunshine, the sky above hot, muggy Philadelphia began changing to a gloomy gray. Soon there came glowering down upon the neat red-brick colonial metropolis a succession of huge black clouds. Windows slammed, tradesmen shut doors left open to relieve the stifling heat, mothers hastily called children indoors, and idlers vanished from street corners into the nearest tavern. The city was about to endure that natural phenomenon known as a thunderstorm. People hoped it would bring some relief from the humid heat, which often made June in Philadelphia as unpleasant as equatorial regions. But they also shivered with apprehension as the first rumble of thunder surged over the city. Those clouds carried in them deadly bolts of lightning.

Only one man in Philadelphia greeted the oncoming storm with delight. Benjamin Franklin had been waiting impatiently for weather like this for days. In his comfortable house, he called excitedly to his 21-year-old son William. In a moment, Billy, as he was known in the family, appeared, his face all aglow with excitement.

Franklin asked if everything was ready. William nodded. Quickly they slipped into loose cloth coats and hurried into the next room, where on a long table stood a variety of strange machines and apparatus. There were glass tubes and jars bound with strips of tin, glass globes on spindles, silk strings dangling from the ceiling. To anyone acquainted with 18th-century science, this apparatus, especially the tubes, and the peculiar tin-encased jars with corks in their tops, through which a wire protruded, meant that this was the laboratory of a man interested in exploring the mysteries of electricity. For the last four years, this exploration had occupied almost all of Benjamin Franklin's days and nights. To find extra hours he had even resigned from his printing business, sacrificing half his income, and moved to this house on the outskirts of Philadelphia where he was less accessible to the numerous friends who made a habit of dropping in to visit him whenever possible.

MAKING GOLD GLOW

When Franklin began his experiments electricity was a curiosity in the world of science. Experimenters created "electrical fire" by rubbing glass tubes with silk. They then stored the accumulated charges in the tin-lined bottles, called Leyden jars, in honor of the university where they were first invented. But beyond the fact that electricity created magical effects—it could, for instance, animate a piece of twisted wire so that it looked like a living spider, or in a darkened room cause the gold border on an expensive book to glow—no one knew very much about it. In a series of classic experiments, Franklin had transformed electricity from a curiosity to a full-fledged branch of science. He was the first scientist to describe plus and minus charges; he invented such terms as battery, conductor, and resistor. Now he was about to test his most daring hypothesis: that electricity and lightning were identical.

As the first pattering of rain pelted the windows, William Franklin took from a dark corner of the laboratory a strange looking kite. It was made of a large thin silk kerchief. To the top of the vertical stick was fastened a pointed wire about 38 to 41 cm (15 to 16 in) long. Benjamin Franklin took a Leyden jar and concealed it under his loose-fitting coat. Down the stairs and out the door went father and son. They hurried through the scattering raindrops to an open field not far from their house, part of the "common," or grazing grounds, of Philadelphia. On one side of the field was a shed, where citizens who grazed their cattle could take shelter from the rain or hot sun. While Franklin stood unobtrusively—he hoped—inside the shed, William raced across the empty pasture, and got the kite aloft in the tricky, gusty wind of the gathering storm. Then he too retreated under the shed.

AVOIDING RIDICULE

William Franklin must have felt a little foolish, flying a kite in the rain. But he did not look nearly as ridiculous as his father would have looked if someone had seen one of the leading citizens of Pennsylvania prancing across the common on the same errand. There was the very large possibility that the hypothesis was wrong. If so, Benjamin Franklin did not want people guffawing at him in the streets, and asking him where he got his ridiculous idea about lightning. If his experiment failed, only William would know.

There was another reason why William was along. The experiment was dangerous. Franklin knew electricity could kill. He had killed animals with it, in his laboratory. Twice, by accident, he had knocked himself unconscious with it and, in another experiment, had prostrated six grown men with a single charge. He also knew that lightning was far more powerful electricity than anything he had created in his laboratory. He had seen it reduce the metallic part of a roof, such as a drainspout, to molten jelly. This was not an experiment you could ask a friend to share. Only a son, who had already shared

Above: Franklin (right) and son lure an electric charge down a kite string and capture it in a jar. Below: Franklin shows onlookers how a lightning rod protects a house.

many lesser risks in the laboratory, could join Benjamin Franklin at this climactic moment.

SILK AS AN INSULATOR

In a few minutes, the kite was only a small dancing dot in the gloomy sky. William handed the kite string to his father. To the end of the twine was tied a strip of silk ribbon. Silk did not conduct electricity; it was an insulator. This was the only safeguard Franklin used against the deadly amount of electricity in the clouds above him. Contrary to the traditional Currier and Ives print, which shows Franklin and his son (pictured as a small boy) gleefully rejoicing when a bolt of lightning hit the kite, this was the last thing Franklin wanted to happen. The pointed wire at the top of his kite was designed to silently draw off some of the cloud's electric charge, just as a pointed conductor attracted electricity from a charged body in the laboratory. There was no need, much less a desire, for the massive and dangerous discharge of a lightning bolt.

Two versions of Franklin's "electrical machine." With these devices, also called "frictional machines," Franklin produced static electricity.

Where the twine and the silk joined, a small house key was fastened. This was where Franklin hoped the electricity would appear. Again and again, he touched the key with his knuckle. Nothing happened.

Over the city, the storm increased in fury. Thunder rumbled and lightning glinted. Then, William pointed excitedly toward a massive cloud moving downwind toward them. On it came, booming thunder while it passed right over their heads. The little kite danced and dived in the gusts of turbulence. Again, Benjamin Franklin touched the key with his knuckle. Surely now—

His face fell. The key was as cold and inert as it had been the day it was made.

CLOSE TO DESPAIR

Now the sky was so black it was impossible to tell one cloud from another. More rain began to fall. The kite whirled and twisted and dived. Close to despair, Franklin gave up touching the key and stared disconsolately up at the murky sky. His mind raced back across the hundreds of experiments he had conducted, the studies he had made of the effects of lightning on houses and trees, trying to see where he had gone wrong. Then his eyes drifted toward the string in his hand. With an exclamation of triumph, he clapped his son on the back and pointed excitedly at the twine.

The loose threads were standing erect, separate from each other, just as if they had been electrified when suspended on a laboratory conductor. Cautiously Benjamin Franklin moved his knuckle toward the key. Through his hand and up his arm rushed that familiar tingling, shocking sensation which experimenters called an electric spark. Again and again he touched it and then let William touch it.

DANGER—AND SUCCESS

Now the rain began in earnest. As sheets of it swept across the field and thoroughly wet the string, Benjamin Franklin picked up the Leyden jar and touched its wire to the key. Electricity from the charged air within the cloud poured into it.

This was the moment of maximum danger. If the kite had been struck by a lightning bolt at this point, most scientists agree that the charge would have leaped the strip of silk and both Franklins would have become charred corpses there on the Philadelphia common. But father and son were too enraptured by their discovery to worry about danger now. It was true! Electricity and lightning were one and the same. It meant that if men could control this no-longer-so-mysterious fire in the laboratory, they could also tame its brother from the heavens.

FOLLOW-UP TESTS IN EUROPE

In the 18th century scientists were celebrities whose writings were read by every educated man. When Franklin made his historic experiment with the kite in June of 1752, he had already written his masterwork, *Experiments and Observations on Electricity, Made at Philadelphia in America.* It was soon translated into Latin, French, German, and Italian. Scientists all over Europe attempted to prove or disprove his discoveries.

In Franklin's report of his laboratory experiments, he had suggested another way to prove the identity of lightning and electricity. Erect a sentry box on a mountaintop or inside a church steeple, he said. The box should have a pointed iron rod in the roof, which would be connected to a Leyden jar inside.

Because there was neither a church steeple nor a high mountain in the vicinity of Philadelphia, Franklin had not tried the experiment himself, and only later had the idea of a kite occurred to him. Now, before he had time to make his report to the world, letters from Europe informed him that a half dozen French and English scientists had successfully performed the "Philadelphia experiment," as it was soon called, using sentry boxes. Later, from Russia, came news that emphasized the danger of Franklin's experimental approach. A scientist in St. Petersburg had tried a variation on Franklin's sentry box idea, and put a rod on top of his house. He had failed to ground it properly and had been killed by a direct hit from a lightning bolt.

Franklin's Pennsylvania fireplace, later called the Franklin stove, sent its heat out across the room instead of up the chimney.

ELECTED TO ROYAL SOCIETY

But the risk only made Franklin's triumph greater in the eyes of an admiring world. The King of France sent his personal congratulations across the ocean. The Royal Society, the elite of the English scientific world, elected Franklin a member by unanimous vote and bestowed upon him its highest accolade, the Copley Medal. Yale, then Harvard, gave him honorary degrees of Master of Arts, and Immanuel Kant, the greatest philosopher of his time, called him the modern Prometheus, who had brought down the fire from Heaven.

Kant's words underscore the emotional explanation of Franklin's fame. In 1752, most men still believed that there was something divine about lightning. Emanating from the heavens, striking with such arbitrary yet devastating force, it was easily associated with the vengeance of an angry God. The man who tamed it readily acquired an awesome, almost superhuman image.

PREVENTING MISCHIEF FROM LIGHTNING

But instead of capitalizing on such a potentiality, Franklin avoided it. He announced the practical application of his discovery in an offhand, matter-of-fact way in a publication that had already gained him some modest fame in America —*Poor Richard's Almanack*.

> *It has pleased God in his goodness to mankind at length to discover to them the means of securing their habitations and other buildings from mischief from thunder and lightning. The method is this: provide a small iron rod (it may be made of the rod-iron used by the nailers) but of such a length that one end being three or four feet in the moist ground, the other may be six or eight feet above the highest part of the building. To the upper end of the rod fasten about a foot of brass wire the size of a common knitting needle, sharpened to a fine point; the rod may be secured to the house by a few small staples. If the house or barn be long, there may be a rod and point at each end, and a middling wire along the ridge from one to the other. A house thus furnished will not be damaged by lightning, it being attracted by the points and passing through the metal into the ground without hurting anything. Vessels, also, having a sharp pointed rod fixed on the top of their masts, with a wire from the foot of the rod reaching down, round one of the shrouds, to the water, will not be hurt by lightning.*

OTHER INVENTIONS

Although it would be difficult to patent an invention as simple as a lightning rod, it was typical of Franklin to give his idea away. When he invented a stove in 1742 which heated a room instead of allowing most of the warm air to go up the chimney, the governor of Pennsylvania proposed to give him a monopoly patent. Franklin not only refused the favor, he published a pamphlet in which he completely described the construction and operation of the stove, so that any good blacksmith could make one.

He redesigned the street lights of his time, discarding the globe shape and substituting "four flat panes with a funnel above to draw up the smoke." This meant that the lamp did not grow dark in a few hours, but remained bright until morning. When one of his older brothers became afflicted with a bladder disorder, Franklin invented the rubber catheter which is still in use today. When his eyes began troubling him, he invented bifocals, which enabled him to get along with only a single set of glasses. All of these ideas he donated to the world, free of charge. "As we enjoy great advantages from the inventions of others," he said, "we should be glad of an opportunity to serve others by any inventions of ours."

Gradually, cities began to sprout these small sharp pointed spires, called lightning rods. When an earthquake struck Boston in 1755, one preacher assured his congregation that it was a warning from on high, because so many in the city were defying the divine will by resorting to those works of the devil, lightning rods.

In Europe, what made Franklin's name even more famous was the last part of the title of his historic essay on electricity. That such discoveries could be made by a man from "Philadelphia in America" was doubly amazing to Europeans who had become accustomed to thinking of the New World as a region inhabited largely by savages and frontiersmen with little more brains than it took to swing an ax, plow a furrow, and fire a gun.

ELECTRICAL SHOWMANSHIP

At home, Franklin delighted in entertaining his friends and acquaintances with electrical showmanship. He placed a lightning rod on his chimney and connected it to two bells on his staircase. Between the bells was a little brass ball suspended by a silk thread. When the wire was charged, the ball would dance back and forth, striking the bells and announcing that the house was electrified. Often the bells rang when there was neither lightning nor thunder, making visiting ladies squeal with alarm. One night so much electricity rushed down the rod that Franklin was able to see it "in a continued dense white stream seemingly as large as my finger" between the bells. Suddenly the whole staircase was "inlightened as with sunshine," he said, "so that one might see to pick up a pen."

In his laboratory, Franklin let the ladies feel the tingle of gentle shocks, he created miniature bolts of lightning, he made metals glow and wires dance. Once, on the banks of the Schuylkill, he ignited some rum by sending an electric charge from one side of the river to the other. It was during one of these laboratory demonstrations that Franklin almost killed himself. He was showing how electricity could kill a turkey, using a charge from two specially constructed Leyden jars which contained as much power as 40 of the ordinary size. The spectators were talking to Franklin and to one another. The conversation distracted him, and he accidentally touched the top wires of the jars while his other hand held the chain which was connected to the outside of both jars. There was an enormous flash and a crack as loud as a pistol. Franklin's body vibrated like a man in an epileptic convulsion. He described the impact as "an universal blow from head to foot throughout the body." Although he did not fall, for a few moments he blacked out completely. Lucky as usual, he escaped with nothing more serious than a soreness in his chest, "as if it had been bruised."

A JOLT FOR THE GAWKERS

One day a crowd of gawkers gathered in front of Franklin's house, hoping to catch a glimpse of an electrical miracle, or of the electrician himself. Franklin got rid of them with a humorous demonstration of his powers. He sent a healthy charge surging through the iron fence around the front of his house. The galvanized curiosity seekers vanished in a cloud of dust.

The printing press operated by the young Franklin when he worked in London.

This was the Franklin that Philadelphia loved—a man who somehow managed to combine laughter with everything, even the pursuit of scientific truth. Already his close friends in Philadelphia treasured gems of his wry humor. Once a neighbor came to him and asked how he could stop thieves from tapping a keg of beer he had in his backyard.

"Put a cask of Madeira beside it," was Franklin's answer□

 SELECTED READINGS

Benjamin Franklin by Carl C. Van Doren. Greenwood, reprinted 1973.

Benjamin Franklin: As Others Saw Him by George Sanderlin. Coward, 1972.

The Man Who Dared the Lightning: A New Look at Benjamin Franklin by Thomas Fleming. Morrow, 1971.

The Most Dangerous Man in America: Scenes from the Life of Benjamin Franklin by Catherine Drinker Bowen. Little, Brown, 1974.

Laser Fusion: Tomorrow's Energy?

by Lawrence Lessing

THE process of thermonuclear fusion is widely regarded as the ultimate solution to the world's energy problems. Thermonuclear fusion is the awesome process in which hydrogen fuses to form helium at extremely high temperatures. It is the source of the energy of the sun and other stars.

Ever since the first hydrogen bomb was exploded in 1952, scientists have been striving to find ways to tame this energy-producing process for peaceful use on earth. All attempts so far have proved unsuccessful. The difficulties have appeared so great that the common view is that they cannot be conquered before the next century. Several recent and generally overlooked developments, however, offer the hope that man can put controlled fusion to practical use well before the end of this century. The most notable one appeared in the late 1960's, when researchers hit upon the idea of using intense laser beams to blast pellets of frozen hydrogen to thermonuclear temperatures. The result would be a potentially vast release of use-

A laser beam splitter in operation at Lawrence Livermore Laboratory. A single laser beam is directed against a reflector (right corner), which splits it into two beams.

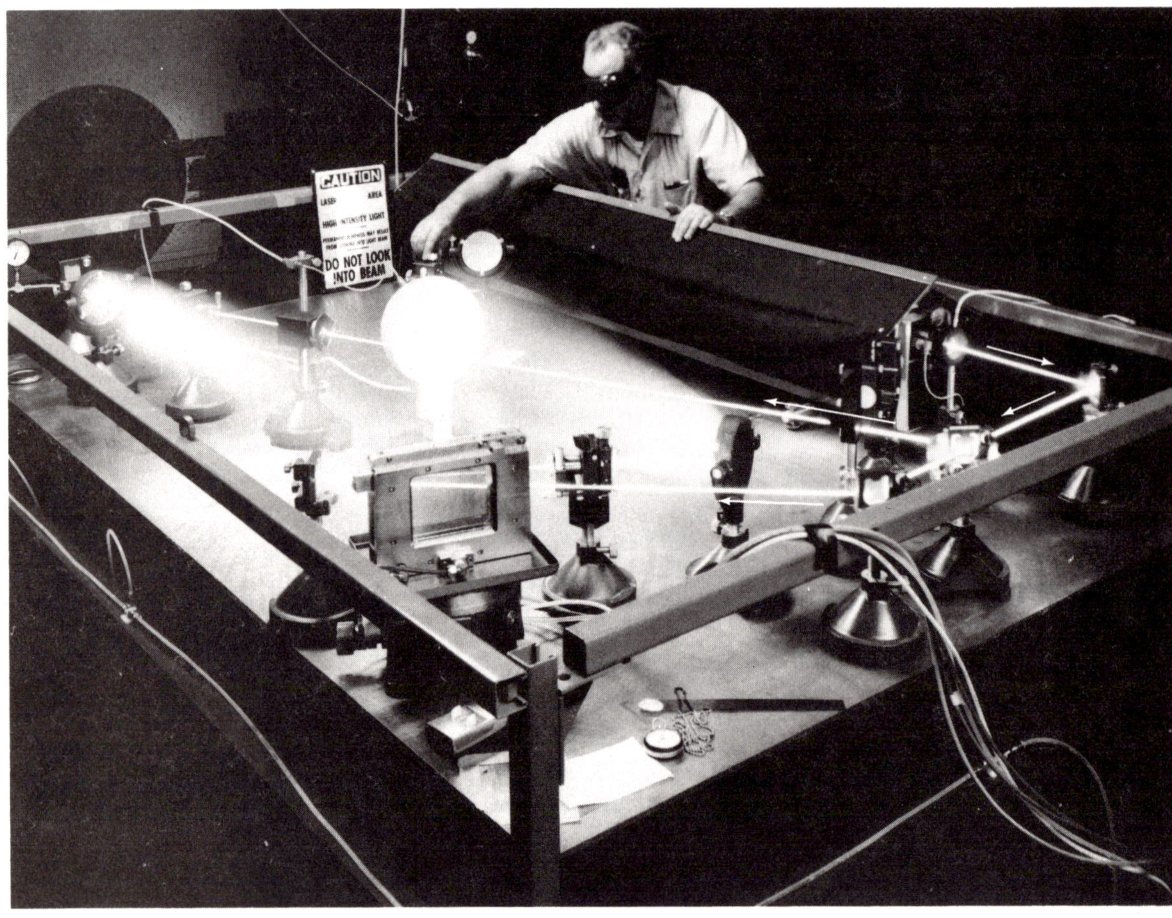

ful energy. A laser is a device that produces pure and precisely focused beams or pulses of light. A growing number of scientists have now come to believe that this "Buck Rogers" approach may well leapfrog over techniques under development for several years. They believe that it will yield the first major breakthrough to harnessing fusion for the benefit of mankind. Indeed, there is a good chance that laser fusion could even overtake the fast-breeder fission reactor—scheduled to go into operation by 1985—as a prime source of atomic power. But this presumes there will be enough money for research—and also an end to the secretiveness that has held back the useful exchange of ideas.

The Soviet-developed Tokamak magnetic containment machine has held plasmas longer and at higher temperatures than any other device.

TRYING TO HOLD THE SUN

For some two decades, researchers in at least half a dozen countries have attempted to solve the formidable problem of creating and then containing a sunlike fire on earth. The central problem is to raise the temperature of the hydrogen fuel to somewhere near 100,000,000° C (225,000,000° F) and hold it there long enough for fusion to take place. This temperature is almost seven times hotter than the interior of the sun. At such a temperature hydrogen, the lightest of the elements, is stripped of electrons down to its naked nuclei. It becomes an exceedingly hot, dense, and active gas called a *plasma*. To allow this process to take place, scientists found that they had to confine the plasma by magnetic force to the center of a container. If it expanded enough to touch the container's walls, the plasma quickly lost fusion heat or even burned through the container.

A variety of such containing devices—heavy apparatuses surrounded by massive electromagnets—were built. But for years no way could be found to prevent these so-called "magnetic bottles" from leaking and thus yielding only a very tiny amount of fusion. Only since 1970 has a glimmer of hope appeared that a leakproof magnetic bottle may be devised. A new type of containment machine called a Tokamak was developed by Soviet scientists in the late 1960's. With later U.S. improvements, it has held plasmas longer and at higher temperatures than ever before. The results are very promising, even though the temperatures are still short of the levels required for continuous fusion. Therefore magnetic containment is still a leading contender for achieving large-scale fusion power. But much bigger and more costly machines and superconducting magnets must be developed to prove, if possible, that this approach will really be practical.

The laser fusion concept, on the other hand, eliminates the whole problem of magnetic containment. A pellet of frozen hydrogen is dropped into a relatively simple round vessel made of metal alloys. This vessel, as first designed, is filled with molten lithium to absorb heat. Midway in its descent the pellet is hit by a short, powerful pulse of laser light through a porthole in the sphere. The burst of energy instantly sets off a small thermonuclear reaction. When pellets are injected at a rate of about two or three per second, a steady series of microexplosions takes place, like a string of miniature flaring suns. Thus a continuous flow of high heat energy is transmitted to the surrounding liquid lithium. This energy, in turn, can be used to create steam to run an electric power plant.

The process resembles the series of explosions in the cylinders of an internal combustion engine that provide continuous power to run an automobile. No expensive magnets are needed. Only a spherical shell thick and strong enough to withstand the shock waves and the flux of neutrons created by the reactions is required.

Numerous problems must be overcome before it can be demonstrated that the laser technique is a practical source of energy. But these problems are not as great as those confronting the development of magnetic containment. The use of lasers is a simpler concept, and the physical equipment required is smaller. Development of the laser concept is now progressing faster—thanks in part to the understanding of plasmas gained in the research on magnetic containment.

CHEAPER, CLEANER, AND SAFER

There are compelling reasons for pressing on with research on ways of controlling and using thermonuclear power—including both laser fusion and magnetic containment—as fast as possible. Nuclear power plants today rely on fission—the splitting of heavy atoms of uranium or plutonium. But fusion produces much more energy per unit of fuel than fission, because it transforms more mass into energy. And the cost of building a fusion plant is likely to be lower. Fusion is a much cleaner process than fission. It creates no radioactive cesium or strontium, the notably dangerous wastes of fission. Fusion is also inherently safer than fission, because there is no danger that a fusion plant will surge out of control and melt or explode. If the fusion process goes awry, the reaction would instantly halt.

Finally, the basic fuel for fusion is a slightly heavier form of hydrogen called deuterium. And deuterium is practically inexhaustible. It is contained in all the waters of the world. The deuterium in the seas alone could supply all the world's energy needs for hundreds of millions of years. It may be obtained at a current fuel cost of .003 mill (1 mill equals 0.1 cent) per kilowatt-hour, a fraction of the price we now pay for fossil fuels.

A growing awareness of the great prizes to be won is beginning to animate fusion research. Since the early 1970s, outlays—mainly governmental—for development work on laser fusion have almost doubled annually. Even more significant is the fact that laser fusion research is the only thermonuclear process to have attracted any substantial amount of private capital. General Electric, Esso Research & Engineering Co., and a consortium of northeastern utilities got together in 1972 to support a three-year, $3 million program at the University of Rochester's new Laboratory for Laser Energetics, a pioneer in the study of laser fusion. And a small but substantial electronics and laser company in Ann Arbor, Michigan, KMS Fusion, Inc., has undertaken a $50 million joint project with Burmah Oil Co. Ltd. to develop a laser system of its own.

But it is Soviet scientists who have led the way. The race to harness laser fusion began in 1968 after a progress report from researchers at the P. N. Lebedev Institute in Moscow, led by academician Nikolai Basov. They stated that they had succeeded in getting a laser to start a slight and fleeting fusion reaction. This announcement was at first greeted with some skepticism, even though Basov was one of the inventors of the laser itself. But Western scientists soon confirmed the Soviet finding by repeating the experiment. On a small scale, the U.S. Atomic Energy Commission (AEC) then began research on laser fusion in its laboratories. At the same time, government and private laboratories in France, West Germany, Britain, and later Japan started laser fusion research of their own.

SEARCHING FOR A LASER

At first, scientists calculated that setting off an appreciable fusion reaction with lasers would require such a strong bolt of power that it might be beyond man's

Target chamber at the University of Rochester's Laboratory for Laser Energetics. This target chamber (above) has 18 ports through which laser beams hit the fuel pellet, starting a fusion reaction. Inside the chamber (right) a copper-coated cryostat, or refrigerated target "factory," produces some of the pellets.

ability. They figured that in one billionth of a second a laser would have to deliver 1,600,000,000 joules of energy—about 1,000,000,000 times the output of Grand Coulee Dam—to a target pellet a few millimeters in diameter. This was about ten million times more power than the most energetic pulsed laser had yet produced. The great speed was needed because, if the pellet were heated more slowly, the resulting plasma would have time to expand, lose density, and fall apart before much fusion could take place. No pulsed lasers with such speed and a rapid rate of repetition were yet available. But researchers pressed on with the instruments at hand.

The chief experimental implement selected was the neodymium-glass laser—a glass tinted violet by the rare earth element neodymium. This was one of the earliest solid lasers created after the original single-crystal ruby rod. The neodymium laser fell far short of the energy needed. However, it could deliver short, sharply focused light pulses and, unlike the ruby laser, it could be larger and more powerful. In 1970 a group led by Moshe J. Lubin, professor of physics at the University of Rochester and founder of its new laboratory for laser fusion, built a large laser system. The new system employed a series of big neodymium-glass plates as amplifiers. The arrangement raised the energy of a single laser pulse to some 1,000 joules, the most powerful then known in the United States. At the focal point, that pulse proved to be intense enough to heat a dense target to some 25,000,000° C (45,000,000° F)—one quarter of the way to the temperature goal.

THE MULTIBEAM APPROACH

Early in 1972, word leaked out from a number of laboratories about a new idea for bringing laser fusion closer to reality. Essentially it consisted of hitting the target pellet simultaneously from all sides

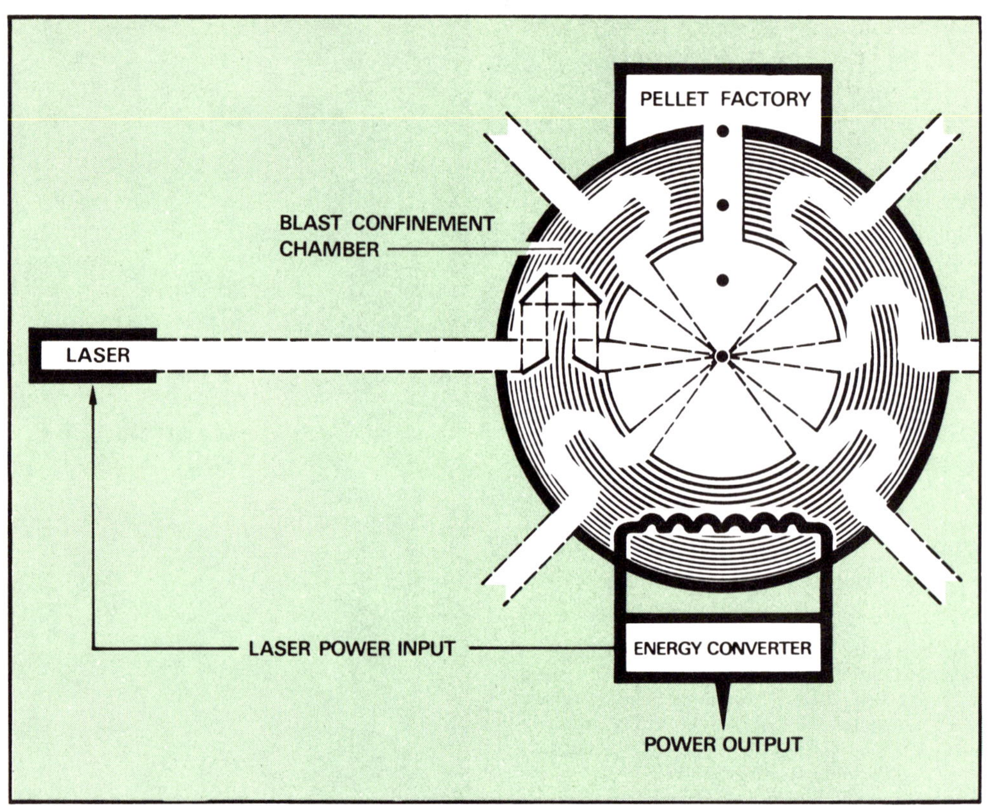

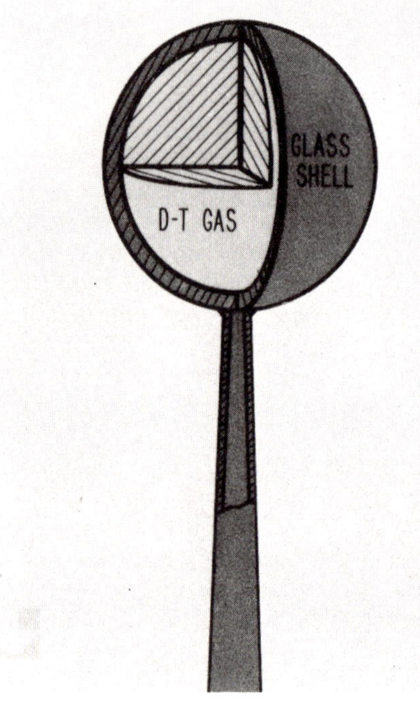

How Lawrence Livermore Laboratory envisions a laser-fusion reactor. Reflected laser beams hit a heavy-hydrogen pellet, which implodes. A micro-thermonuclear reaction occurs. This heats liquid lithium (concentric circles), which, in turn, boils water to run a conventional generator. Left: Fuel pellet—glass shell filled with mixture of deuterium and tritium—schematically and actually, as ready for irradiation.

with multiple laser beams rather than with a single beam. In the fall issue of the British journal, *Nature,* John Nuckolls and a group of associates at the AEC's Livermore Laboratory in California reported their computer studies showing how such a multibeam technique could work to great advantage. Hit equally on all sides by the beams, the entire surface of the pellet would immediately vaporize and explode with immense force. Since every action produces an equal and opposite reaction, the vaporizing of the pellet's surface would instantly set off an implosion in the interior of the pellet. Its inner core would be compressed to an enormous density. And this state would be conducive to maximum fusion.

The big advantage of the multibeam technique lay in the fact that fusion is dependent on the density as well as the temperature of the plasma. The higher the density achieved, the lower the amount of heat needed to start fusion. Calculations by Nuckolls's group showed that compressive implosion could permit fusion with 100,000 times less laser energy than previously estimated. The new level —around 10,000 joules—was closer to the reach of existing laser technology. By this means, earthly fusion could begin to approach the efficiency of nuclear processes deep inside the sun.

The Russians, it soon became clear, had carried the same idea beyond mere theory. At an international conference in France late in 1972, Soviet scientists reported on the successful operation of a nine-beam neodymium-laser apparatus and on plans to build a twenty-seven-beam machine. In the Soviet device, a primary laser beam, delivering a 600-joule pulse in two billionths of a second, was split into three separate beams by prisms and mirrors. Next each split beam was raised to the original intensity by laser amplifiers. Then each of the three beams was again split three ways and reamplified. The total of nine pulses struck a target pellet with a total impact of some 2,000 joules. The Soviet device only had enough power to test the multibeam principle experimentally. But it was successful enough to justify moving on to larger designs.

Now the race to achieve laser fusion quickened. In Rochester, Lubin's group launched its joint effort to build a still larger neodymium-laser system. The group uses new, very powerful laser amplifiers to boost the laser output to 2,000 joules with only four beams. At least three other multibeam machines are now being developed. The most elaborate is a system that will use as few as twelve or as many as twenty laser beams. The Livermore Laboratory expects to complete it by 1977.

But the 27-beam Soviet system now under construction is moving toward a total output of 10,000 joules. This power level will be on the edge of the breakeven point—that is, where the fusion energy produced just equals the energy required to run the lasers. Doing this would show that laser fusion can be put to actual work. Thus in barely five years of development, laser fusion is reaching a point that took 20 years to approach with the magnetic containment system.

DIVIDENDS FROM DEATH RAYS

Whether or not any of these laser systems breaches the breakeven barrier, the next big step is already under way: to find a much more powerful laser. Neodymium glass has too many drawbacks for practical power production. Its peak energy is limited to about 1,000 joules. Beyond that the glass heats up and is apt to crack, so that the laser no longer works. Its efficiency is also low. Only three tenths of 1 per cent of the electric energy that goes into operating it is emitted as light.

However, some 20 to 30 other types of lasers may fit the exacting requirements of controlled fusion. In the last few years, laboratory experiments have yielded a dramatic rise in laser power. Most of the advances have come from military research. From the start, the U.S. Defense Department heavily supported laser development. They saw the possibility of creating a devastating "death-ray" weapon from high-intensity beams of light. The department first sponsored work on the neodymium-glass laser, but its bulk and fragility at higher powers made it appear unsuitable. Defense researchers then turned to a newer, more powerful gas laser developed by Bell Telephone Laboratories in 1964. This laser used a mixture of carbon dioxide and nitrogen in a sealed tube and was operated by an electric discharge down the length of tube. But it proved even more unwieldy. One installation required 15 tubes, each 12 m (40 ft) long, coupled together and backed by heavy electric-discharge equipment.

In 1968 and 1969, however, defense research led to the development of three higher-powered and more compact lasers. The first and most powerful appears to be the "gas-dynamic" laser, developed by Arthur R. Kantrowitz at Avco Everett Research Laboratory near Boston. A heated carbon dioxide mixture is spewed through a rocketlike nozzle and down a tube at supersonic speed to achieve very high-powered laser action.

The second newcomer, the so-called "TEA" (for Transverse-Excited-Atmospheric-pressure) laser, also involves carbon dioxide gas flowing down a tube, but at atmospheric pressure. The third is a chemical laser that employs a complex chemical reaction to supply not only the medium but also the energy to activate it. The most useful one so far uses hydrogen fluoride. All three new lasers have achieved power output in the hundreds of kilowatts, higher than any other lasers so far.

The aim in "death-ray" research has been long-range, long-pulse lasers. Laser fusion, on the other hand, requires short-range and very short-pulse lasers. But every increase in laser power improves the hopes for practical laser fusion.

One major drawback to military involvement in laser research, however, has been the matter of "secrecy." Despite a 1958 international agreement on the sharing of information on controlled fusion, the U.S. military has often put a tight lid on work in this field. For example, the development of the TEA laser system was not made known for a full five years. A common reaction among scientists is that such an attitude hampers basic research and is largely pointless. Time and again the military has classified as "secret" a laser development that eventually turned out to be known already by other nations such as the Soviet Union.

Laser fusion research has also had to deal, off and on, with another serious problem: a lack of adequate funds. Part of the reason for this lies in the changing evaluations of such research by the U.S. Congress and the Office of Management and Budget. But in addition there is by now a large vested interest, in the United States, in fission-based systems. Therefore, funds tend to remain channeled in that direction. Many scientists have expressed concern over this slighting of laser fusion research. They feel that from almost every standpoint—economics, safety, or environmental hazards—fusion looks like a better bet for the future than the fission breeder reactor.

THE QUESTION OF POLLUTION

The first fusion reactors, scientists agree, should be fueled by a mixture of deuterium and a still heavier form of hydrogen known as tritium. Less energy is required to start a reaction using both hydrogen forms than if only deuterium is used. Found only in minute amounts in nature, tritium is made synthetically by nuclear bombardment of lithium. But the process is much more costly than that for separating deuterium from water. In fusion reactors using lithium as a moderating liquid, some tritium is naturally created by the fusion reaction itself. This enables the unit to "breed" part of its own fuel.

The use of tritium is laser fusion's only big pollution problem, at least through the first generation of reactor development. Tritium is radioactive. At temperatures above those approaching absolute zero, which is approximately −273° C (−460° F), tritium is a gas that could escape into the atmosphere. There it could combine with moisture in clouds and fall to earth in rainwater. In debates about nuclear energy, proponents of the fast-breeder fission reactor have seized upon the latent hazards of tritium in an effort to discredit fusion. One industry spokesman even charged that the potential environmental contamination caused by tritium from fusion would be far greater than any potential pollution from fission reactors.

In fact, however, the liquid-metal fast-breeder reactor—now operating in the first prototype plants in the Soviet Union, England, and France—poses the largest long-range safety and pollution problems of any nuclear power source yet conceived.

Indeed, the hazards are so great that the U.S. program to build a large test reactor by 1975 and a demonstration plant by 1980 is already running two years behind schedule and causing huge cost overruns.

But the biggest problem is that the fission reactor, initially fueled by uranium and plutonium, breeds more plutonium. This is a solid, heavily toxic, long-lived radioactive element and one of the most potent causes of cancer known. If breeder plants were to proliferate, tons of radioactive wastes would have to be buried. The output of plutonium could easily reach 1,000,000 kg (2,200,000 lb) a year by the end of the century. To prevent accidents or theft, that plutonium would have to be stored, transported, and processed into fuel under a security system far tighter than any now in existence. For it is comparatively easy to make plutonium into bombs.

On the other hand, gaseous tritium, fusion's only potential pollutant, would be extremely difficult to steal for clandestine bomb making. Biological studies show that its potential hazards are only about 3 per cent those of plutonium from a breeder reactor, and about a million times less than those from fission's major radioactive waste. Gaseous tritium is more easily trapped and contained than are solid wastes. Moreover, since tritium can be directly cycled back into fusion's fuel chain, there will be a lot of incentive to catch all of it. Sometime in the future, tritium may be eliminated entirely by going to a straight deuterium–deuterium reaction. However, that will require a laser of far greater power than any yet in prospect.

In a gas-dynamic laser (GDL) system developed by Avco Everett mirrors facing inward at opposite ends of a channel direct heated gas back and forth at supersonic speed until the full power of the gas is extracted.

FUSION-POWERED TRAINS?

The flexibility and comparatively low cost of laser fusion also enhance its prospects for opening the path to an age of nuclear power. Fission reactors and even the possible magnetic fusion devices must be scaled up to giant size to yield more energy than they consume. The laser reactor, in comparison, may well be economical in smaller units, because it involves a series of small implosions. Thanks to the relative safety of fusion, these units might be placed in small communities, individual industrial plants, and large apartment or office complexes. This would eliminate both the high construction cost and power losses of long transmission lines. Laser reactors might even be built small enough to run ships and trains. And a number of reactors could be linked together to form large central power stations.

All in all, the potentials are enormous. To a growing number of people it seems reasonable to make every effort to develop fusion power as fast as possible□

SELECTED READINGS

Energy in the World of the Future by Hal Hellman. Evans, 1973.

"Fusion Power by Laser Implosion" by John L. Emmett, John Nuckolls, and Lowell Wood. *Scientific American*, June 1974.

"Power from Laser-Initiated Nuclear Fusion" by Keith Boyer. *Astronautics and Aeronautics*, August 1973.

The Race for Electric Power by Jerry Grey. Westminster, 1972.

The 1974 Nobel Prizes in Physics and Chemistry

by Steven Moll

ASTRONOMERS entered the ranks of Nobel Prize winners for the first time when the Swedish Royal Academy awarded two of them the 1974 prize in physics. The prize in chemistry honored a noted chemist for his lifetime of research on polymers, which are very large complex molecules.

The physics prize was given to two English astronomers—Sir Martin Ryle and Antony Hewish, both professors at Cambridge University—for their work in radio astronomy. Radio astronomy is the study of radio emissions from outer space. Ryle was cited for his contributions to radio-telescope technology. Hewish was honored for his discovery of the radio objects called pulsars.

The chemistry prize was given to Paul J. Flory, a professor of chemistry at Stanford University. The Academy cited his research, "both theoretical and experimental, in the physical chemistry of macromolecules"—that is, polymers.

THE PRIZE IN PHYSICS

Radio astronomy did not really get started until after World War II. Through the efforts of such scientists as Martin Ryle, it has become one of the most active branches of astronomy. It has also required the development of a whole new family of instruments.

The simplest radio telescope is the paraboloid antenna, shaped like a large bowl. It is comparable to the mirror of a reflecting telescope, which collects and focuses light waves. Radio waves are much longer than light waves, however, and the resolving power of a simple paraboloid antenna is very low. The telescope merely records the strength of a radio signal coming from a given direction. It can be rotated to map different regions of the sky, but this process becomes more and more unwieldy with increasing antenna size.

Ryle was a leader in the development of the more powerful telescopes needed if radio astronomy were to advance. The technique he perfected is known as "aperture synthesis." In it several smaller paraboloid antennas are combined in a system that functions like a single giant telescope —one so large that, technologically and financially, it would not be feasible. "Aperture" refers to the receiving surfaces of

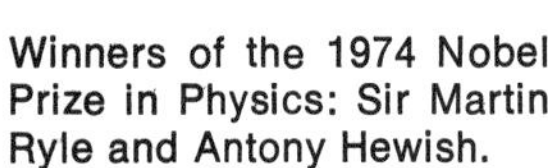

Winners of the 1974 Nobel Prize in Physics: Sir Martin Ryle and Antony Hewish.

Portion of the Cambridge University radio telescope used by Sir Martin Ryle in some of his early work. Two of the dishes, or antennas, are shown.

the antennas, and "synthesis" refers to the mathematical handling of the signals being received. Many multiple-antenna systems, known as interferometers, have been built. Aperture synthesis is an extension of this work, involving complex computer analyses of radio data.

One of radio astronomy's most exciting and significant achievements has been the discovery of pulsars—radio sources that emit short, regular radio pulses. In the 1960's, using the facilities at Cambridge's Mullard Radio Astronomy Observatory, Antony Hewish and a group of students were engaged in observing short-term radio phenomena. In 1967 one of the students, Jocelyn S. Bell, detected a source that was emitting signals at very regular intervals. In a short time a few other such sources were found as well.

At first Hewish and Ryle, director of the Mullard Observatory, speculated that the signals could be a sign of intelligent life elsewhere in the universe. The radio sources were accordingly named "LGM's" —for "Little Green Men." The Mullard team kept their discovery secret for a few months while they investigated further. Eventually it was agreed that the sources were natural phenomena. The radio sources were named pulsars, and the discovery was announced to the world. Today it is widely accepted that pulsars are rapidly spinning neutron stars. Neutron stars are dead or dying stars. They have collapsed gravitationally to the degree that their atomic particles have condensed into uncharged neutrons.

Martin Ryle was born on September 27, 1918, and was educated at Bradfield College and Oxford University. He is the nephew of the philosopher Gilbert Ryle.

Ryle worked on radar devices in World War II. Afterward he joined Cambridge University's Cavendish Laboratory. Seeking ways to apply radar technology to astronomical research, he invented a device for measuring the angular sizes of stars. From 1948 on, he and his colleagues observed and charted radio sources in the sky. In 1958 he was appointed director of the Mullard Observatory, and in 1959 he became the first professor of radio astronomy at Cambridge.

In the 1960's Ryle supervised the development of a powerful aperture-synthesis device, using Cambridge's computer EDSAC. It pushed back the "edge" of the observable universe to a distance of 7,000,000,000 light-years. An even more powerful system was completed in 1972.

Ryle was knighted in 1966 and is a fellow of the Royal Society. In 1972 he was named Astronomer Royal, an honorary post that traditionally has gone to the director of the Greenwich Observatory.

Antony Hewish was born in the Cornish town of Fowey on May 11, 1924. After military service at the Royal Aircraft Establishment in Farnborough, he joined Martin Ryle's research group at Cambridge. He received his Ph.D. in physics at that university in 1952.

Hewish became a lecturer in physics at Cambridge in 1962. The next year he was a visiting professor of astronomy at Yale University. In 1969 he became a reader in radio astronomy at Cambridge and in 1972 gained the title of professor. He is a fellow of the Royal Society.

THE PRIZE IN CHEMISTRY

All chemical and biochemical researches that deal with the giant molecules known as polymers have benefited from the work of Paul J. Flory. A polymer is a long-chain molecule made up of many smaller units that may be of one or more kinds. Natural and synthetic rubber, plastics, synthetic fibers, and many other materials of the modern world are polymers. Living things also contain such molecules—for example, muscle fibers, connective tissues, and the nucleic acids that carry the genetic code. Thus it is evident that polymers are of great importance. The chemical and physical properties of polymers vary greatly, depending on their size and structure and the nature of their basic units. In the 1930's Flory developed a statistical approach to polymer research. Before that there had been no consistent method for investigating the properties of such substances.

Paul J. Flory, 1974 Nobelist in Chemistry.

Flory elucidated the processes of polymerization reactions. He was the first to describe how one molecule can transfer its "growing" power to another molecule and how certain polymers develop branches on their molecular chains. He also found that any polymer can be heated to a certain temperature at which it is in an ideal state for being studied. He called this the "theta" temperature of the polymer. It is now called the "Flory" temperature.

The work of Flory and other polymer chemists enabled the plastics industry to develop rapidly. As knowledge of polymers increases, it may become possible to build giant molecules to order. Flory has also pointed out the potential that polymer research has for helping us understand living things.

Paul John Flory was born in Sterling, Illinois, on June 19, 1910. Educated at Manchester College and Ohio State University, he received his Ph.D. in physical chemistry in 1934. Until 1948 he was an industrial chemist, his first post being with the DuPont Experimental Station in Delaware, where he worked under Wallace Carothers, the developer of nylon.

From 1948 to 1956, Flory was a professor of chemistry at Cornell University. He then directed research at Pittsburgh's Mellon Institute until 1962, when he was named Jackson-Wood Professor of Chemistry at Stanford University. He also became chairman of the university's research department. Since retiring in 1975, he has had an active schedule of visiting professorships. Flory has received many scientific honors, including the 1973 Gibbs Medal and the 1974 Priestley Award of the American Chemical Society. One of his books, *Principles of Polymer Chemistry*, is a classic in its field□

Is Gravity Getting Weaker?

by Jane Samz

IMAGINE the planets soaring away from the sun, trees and houses flying off into space, and the earth blowing up like a balloon. Could these things ever happen? They might—if gravity disappeared.

Although the first scientific explanation for the basic force of gravitation was discovered over 300 years ago, it is still hard for a scientist to say what gravity is. It is easier to say what gravity *does*. Gravity is the force that pulls you to the earth. It makes water flow downhill. It keeps the planets revolving about the sun. It holds the galaxies together.

If someone suddenly turned gravity off, everything would be weightless. We would float around like astronauts in orbit around the earth. Gravity, however, doesn't suddenly turn on and off.

We depend on gravity to stay the same. We know that the pull of gravity on the moon is weaker than the pull of gravity on the earth. This is because bodies with more mass (matter) have stronger gravity.

The force of gravity between two bodies decreases as the distance between them increases. It decreases as the distance *squared*—distance multiplied by itself. But the force of gravity of the whole universe stays the same. Or does it?

Scientists are not sure anymore. Recently, Thomas Van Flandern, of the U.S. Naval Observatory in Washington, D.C., discovered that gravity may be getting weaker. Van Flandern studied the motion of the moon in its orbit. He found that the moon is slowing down; its orbit is getting larger. This is nothing new. Scientists already knew that the moon is slowly moving away from earth—about 4/5 cm (1/3 in) each month. Van Flandern, however, reported that the moon's orbit is expanding faster than expected. Why? He believes the force of gravity throughout the universe may be getting weaker.

If gravity is getting weaker, then the whole universe must be expanding. All the planets and stars must be slowly drifting apart. Even the stars and planets themselves may be getting larger.

The moon is slowly moving away from the earth.

WHAT IS GRAVITY?

Gravity is the most important force in the universe. Yet, it is the weakest force we know. Imagine two astronauts floating one meter (about a yard) apart in space. It would take the force of gravity about five hours to pull them together.

Electrical forces are billions of times stronger than gravity. So are the forces that hold together the nucleus of the atom. Nuclear forces "work" only over very short distances—inside the nucleus of the atom. Electrical forces only work on bodies with a positive or negative charge. Most of the universe is electrically neutral. So, most of the time, electrical forces are not working.

The force of gravity is everywhere. It acts over both large and small distances. Gravity is an attractive force; it tends to pull bodies together. Every particle in the universe attracts every other particle.

But wait! Smoke rises. Leaves float to the ground. Rocks fall. And planets orbit the sun. Does gravity control all this?

For hundreds of years, people thought gravity acted differently for different things. They thought that heavy bodies "wanted" to fall. Very light bodies

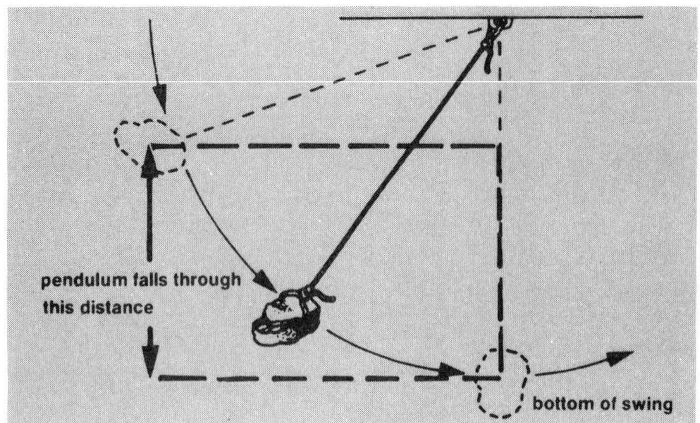

Light bodies fall just as fast as heavy bodies. Galileo hung weights on different lengths of string, watched the weights swing back and forth, and timed the swing of each pendulum. He found that the weight at the end of the pendulum did not affect the timing. Light and heavy pendulums of the same length fall through the same distance in the same time.

"wanted" to rise. A heavy rock would "naturally" fall faster than a light one.

Then, in the late 16th century, Galileo surprised everyone. He showed that what seemed natural was not true. Galileo experimented with falling bodies. He discovered that light bodies fall just as fast as heavy bodies.

Is gravity only an earthly force? What force, if any, controls the motions of the moon and planets? People once believed the motion of the heavens was "naturally" circular. Circular motion, however, did not seem to be natural on earth. Tie a weight to a rope, and swing it around in a circle. If you suddenly let go, it will fly off in a straight line.

Isaac Newton believed straight-line motion was natural. Any change in speed or direction would have to be caused by some outside force. An object moving in a circle is constantly changing direction. So, Newton reasoned, some force must be keeping the planets in their circular orbits. This force was pulling the planets toward the sun. This force, he said, was gravity.

So gravity was not just an earthly force. Newton had "found" it in the heavens as well. But how can one object pull on another without being connected to it? How can the sun pull on planets millions of miles away?

Newton did not believe that the force of gravity could mysteriously "act at a distance" through a vacuum. He did not believe that gravity was a part of bodies themselves.

He suggested that the force of gravity might be caused by something acting in the space between bodies. Yet, he never explained what this could be. For Newton, gravitational "attraction" did not have a definite physical meaning. Newton's force was a mathematical concept. He explained how it worked—not what it was.

EINSTEIN'S GRAVITY

Gravity did have a physical meaning for Albert Einstein. His gravity was not a mysterious force. His gravity was geometry —the geometry of space itself.

Think of space as a kind of stretched rubber sheet. Place something heavy in the center of the sheet—a baseball, a small rock. Notice that the sheet is no longer flat. It dips down into a "valley" with the ball at the center. The ball has changed the geometry of the sheet. We can say that the flat sheet was "warped" or "curved" by the ball.

The same sort of thing happens in space, Einstein said. Place a body in space, and the geometry of space changes. Space—like the rubber sheet—becomes "curved" near a body. Heavier bodies cause space to curve even more.

The "force" of gravity can easily be explained by this "rubber-sheet" geometry. Again, place a heavy ball in the center of the sheet. Let a marble spin around the ball. Suppose the marble goes too fast. It will curve around and swing off in another direction—just as a comet swings around the sun. If the marble spins too slowly, it will spiral in toward the ball. We can say the "gravity" of the ball "pulls" the marble toward it. But when the marble has just the right speed, it will keep spinning around the ball. It will be "in orbit," like the planets around the sun.

But how did Einstein decide that gravity is geometry? Imagine a man inside a spaceship, far from any star or planet. If the spaceship is not accelerating (changing its velocity), the man will be "weightless." Everything not attached to the spaceship's walls will float around the ship. Now start the engines. Make the spaceship go faster and faster. Make it accelerate. Suddenly, the man is no longer weightless. He is pushed against the wall next to the engines. This wall he calls the "floor." He feels a force—like gravity.

Now, suppose the man has brought along two marbles—one heavy, one light. While he holds on to these marbles, they move along with him and the spaceship. When he lets go of the marbles, they continue to move. But the marbles only move as fast as they were moving when he "dropped" them. Meanwhile, the spaceship keeps moving faster and faster. Soon the "floor" catches up to the marbles. The floor hits both marbles at the same time. The man inside sees the marbles fall and hit the floor together. He knows that gravity makes all objects fall at the same rate. And he feels a force pulling him to the floor. (See drawing on this page.) It seems as though someone must have turned on gravity.

But how can anyone turn gravity on or off? *We* see that the man is accelerating. *He* thinks he is in a *gravitational field* (a region in space where the force of gravity is felt). Who is right?

Einstein tells us that both descriptions are right. The man in the spaceship cannot know whether he is accelerating, or whether he is in a gravitational field. The laws of physics are the same in an accelerating spaceship as they are in a gravitational field.

BEND A BEAM OF LIGHT

Now let's give some orders to the man in the accelerating spaceship. Tell him to send a beam of light from one wall of the ship to the other. (Suppose the spaceship's cabin is dusty, so that we can see the path the light takes.) We watch the light beam from outside the ship. We see that the light travels in a straight line through space. The spaceship, however, is not standing still. It is moving faster and faster all the time. We see the floor of the ship rushing up toward the light beam. The man inside the ship sees that the light beam has "bent" toward the floor. (See drawing on next page.) Again, the man does not know he is being accelerated. He thinks he is in a gravitational

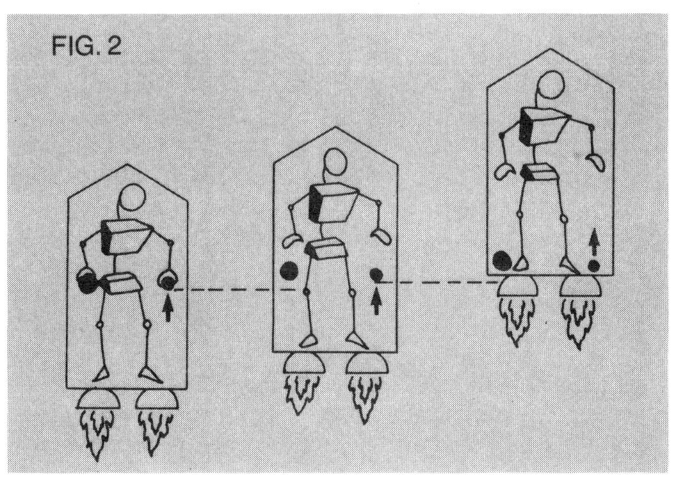

Experiments carried out in an accelerated field have the same results as experiments performed in a gravitational field. If a man inside an accelerating spaceship drops two marbles—one light and one heavy—at the same time, he observes that they hit the floor of the spaceship at the same time —just as they would if gravity were operating within the spaceship.

field; and he observes that light bends in a gravitational field.

This discovery gave Einstein problems. Physicists had defined a straight line as "the path light follows in a vacuum." Einstein had found that gravity bends light. Light paths are curved, not straight lines.

Then what is a straight line? What would space be like without straight lines? Einstein did not want to change the definition of "straight line." This meant he had to change the shape of space. If light beams are not curved, space itself must be curved. And light travels the straightest path possible (*geodesic*) in that curved space.

Einstein's curved space now looked like our rubber sheet. Just placing a body into space changes the shape (geometry) of that space. A falling body is not "pulled" to earth. It falls because the space around the earth slopes "down" toward the earth. (Remember the rubber sheet.) Heavy and light bodies dropped together land together because they follow the same path in space. Curved space had replaced fields of force. Gravity was no longer a mysterious force that made one body pull on another. Gravity was simply the geometry of space.

WHO IS RIGHT?

What did this do to our ideas about the universe? Once people thought the universe was infinite—spreading out in space forever in all directions. Einstein found that his theory of gravity (general relativity) led to a closed (finite) universe. This universe would alternately expand and contract—like blowing up and deflating a balloon.

Other scientists developed other theories on the "birth" and "death" of the universe. Almost all these theories depended on Einstein's general relativity theory. General relativity says the "force" of gravity does not change. However, some theories of the universe (not based on general relativity) say gravity is getting weaker all the time. Who is right?

Thomas Van Flandern has studied the motions of the moon. He has found that the moon is orbiting more slowly than it should. Van Flandern thinks this may show that gravity is getting weaker. But he has not proved it.

What if gravity is decreasing?

The outer stars in our galaxy would fly away into space. The orbits of the planets would get bigger. Even the earth itself would grow larger. (This could explain why continents drift apart and the sea floor spreads.) If gravity is decreasing, the whole universe—and everything in it—will probably slowly expand, forever□

SELECTED READINGS

"Gravitation Theory" by C. M. Will. *Scientific American*, November 1974.

The New Gravitation by H. Arthur Klein (grades 7 to 9). Lippincott 1971.

The Riddle of Gravitation by Peter G. Bergmann. Scribner's 1969.

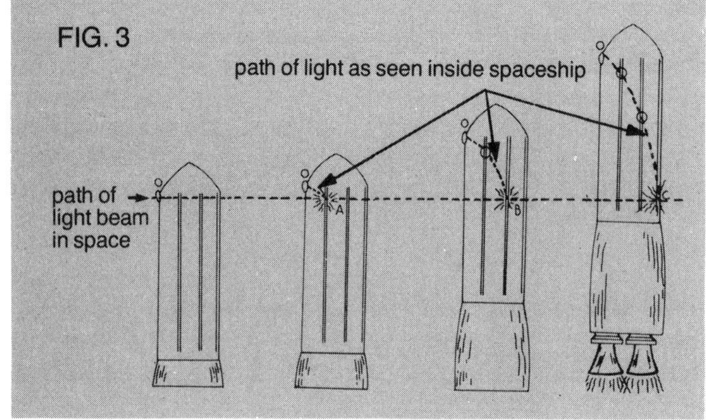

Light travels in a straight line through space. But a man in an accelerating spaceship sees a beam of light as "bent" toward the floor of the spaceship. Light bends in an accelerated field—and in a gravitational field.

The Proton Scanning Microscope

ANOTHER window is being opened on the world. The window is a new kind of microscope called a proton scanning microscope. When it is fully developed, the instrument will provide valuable new information on the structure of matter.

FROM LIGHT BEAMS TO PROTON BEAMS

The microscope was invented in the early 17th century. Until fairly recently, all microscopes have been optical instruments, using beams of visible light. The light beam passes through or is reflected from the specimen being observed in a microscope. The changes that this produces in the beam provide an image of the specimen that is then magnified by a series of lenses. The magnified image finally reaches the eye of the observer.

There is a limit to what optical microscopes can do, no matter how well they are designed. Light travels in waves, and specimen details that are smaller than the shortest of these waves cannot be revealed by the use of light. That is why scientists have tried to develop new kinds of microscopes that do not use light.

The first such instrument appeared in the 1930's. It is known as an electron microscope because it is based on the use of a beam of electrons—tiny particles of matter that carry a negative electrical charge. When a beam of electrons is transmitted through or reflected from a specimen in this kind of microscope, the paths of the electrons are changed. These changes provide an electronic image of the specimen. The image is magnified by passing the beam through magnetic "lenses." It is then focused on a display screen that translates the electronic information into a visual image.

A number of kinds of electron microscopes have been developed. For example, in a scanning electron microscope a very finely focused electron beam scans the specimen, sweeping back and forth across it. Some of these electron microscopes can reveal details as small as about two angstroms in width. One angstrom is 1/100,000,000 meter, or 1/4,000,000 inch, very small indeed. Smaller details cannot be seen, because the effective wavelength of the beam is about two angstrom units.

Now scientists are working on yet another kind of microscope—one based on the use of a beam of protons, rather than electrons. Protons are tiny particles that have a positive electrical charge. Like electrons, protons can be transmitted through a specimen or reflected off its surface, pro-

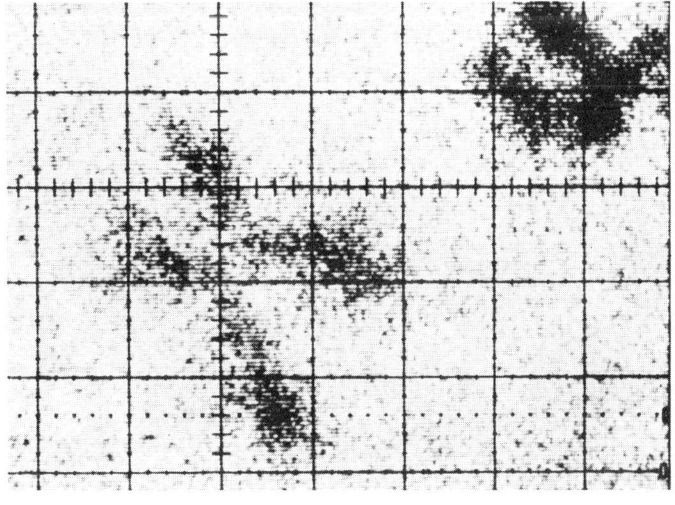

A photomicrograph of two human chromosomes, taken with the proton scanning microscope at the Enrico Fermi Institute of the University of Chicago. Each dot upon the screen is accounted for by a single proton. There are 200 scan lines in this image, but improved microscopes should yield sharper pictures in the future.

viding an image that can be magnified by means of magnetic "lenses." The proton-based microscope being developed is of the scanning type, so it is called a proton scanning microscope.

It is also known as a scanning transmission ion microscope (STIM). The term "ion" means a charged particle. The proton is a positively charged ion. In the simplest case, an ordinary hydrogen atom is made up of a single electron revolving around a nucleus consisting of a single proton. When the electron is stripped away, the nucleus becomes a positively charged particle, or positive ion.

WHY A PROTON MICROSCOPE?

There are several reasons why physicists are interested in developing a proton microscope. The fact that protons are much more massive than electrons is itself one reason. Protons are so massive that they will be stopped—that is, absorbed—by the specimen if it is thick enough. Depending on its thickness, some protons will be stopped and others will pass through. The depth limit for proton penetration is very sharply defined. Thus, variations in the density of a specimen can be observed by using a proton beam, providing information on the specimen's internal structure.

Some scientists have feared that, because protons are so massive, they will cause too much damage in biological specimens. But this is not so. Any particles will, in fact, do some damage. It cannot be avoided. And in an electron microscope, the production of a single "bit" of information about a specimen—that is, a single "dot" in the image—requires about 10,000 electrons. Of these, however, only 100 actually contribute to the signal that produces the image. In comparison, each massive proton contributes to the final image. Thus it takes only 100 protons to do what it takes 10,000 electrons to do. The effects of a proton beam on a specimen are not much different from those of an electron beam.

There are also some other ways in which proton microscopes can provide additional kinds of information. Of the protons that enter and pass through a specimen, about 40 per cent are single protons. The other 60 per cent are paired protons. When the paired protons strike the specimen, they tend to break apart. Each single proton that results then has only half the energy of the original two-proton ion that traveled through the specimen. This difference provides a contrast when the image is magnified by the magnetic "lenses." This contrast is a source of useful information about the specimen.

Proton-beam microscopes provide yet another source of information. As some of the protons in the beam move through the microscope, they acquire, or pick up, electrons. This then makes them hydrogen atoms once again. These newly formed hydrogen atoms, in a sense, form a separate beam that provides further contrasting information about the specimen. In particular, the hydrogen atoms are expected to reveal the presence of hydrogen that is bound in the specimen's organic molecules. Such bound hydrogen is practically "transparent"—that is, undetectable—in an electron microscope.

Finally, interactions of the proton beam with the specimen produce many electrons. The electrons then also provide information about the specimen.

THE CHICAGO TEAM

The proton scanning microscope is not really new. An early form of a proton microscope was built in the 1950's in France. The problems that its designers faced were not all worked out, however, before the rapid development of the electron microscope caused the proton microscope to be set aside for several years.

Now a team of scientists at the University of Chicago has taken up this work, under the direction of physicist Riccardo Levi Setti. By early 1974 Setti and assistants were producing their first crude proton photographs. Today, the scanning beam in the proton instrument cannot yet provide very fine details. But there is no reason to think that the technical problems will not be solved. Scientists should soon have another valuable tool□

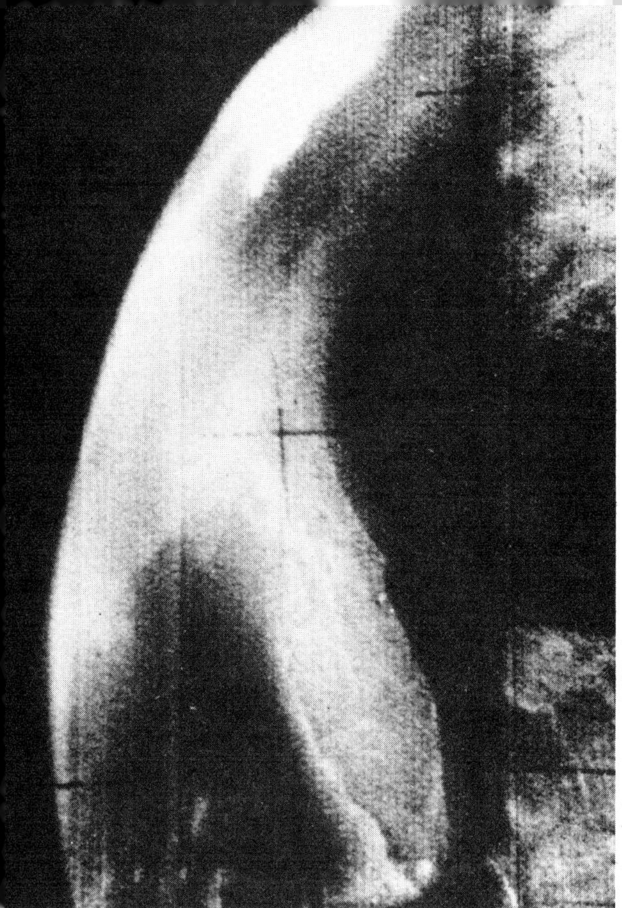

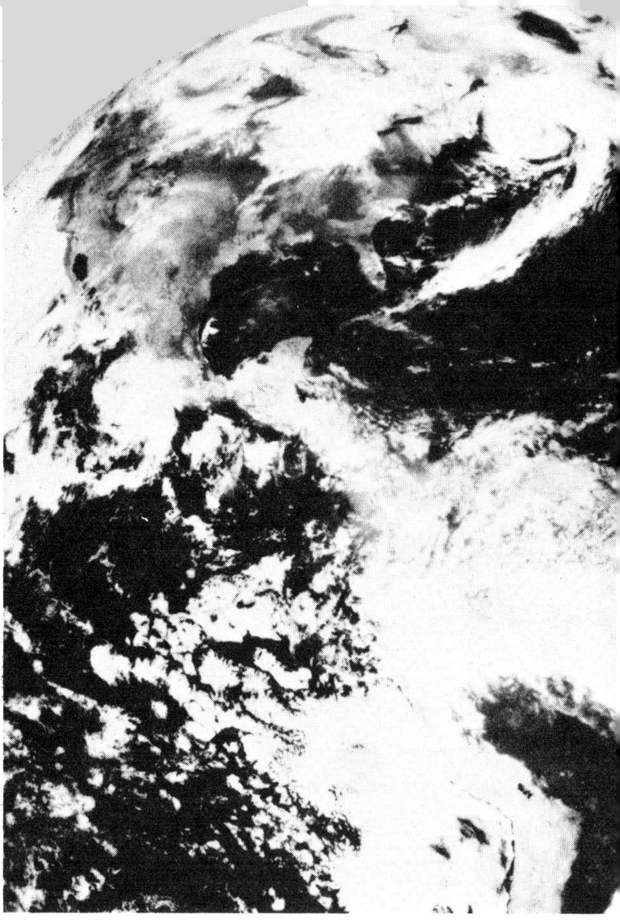

space exploration

contents

Cloudy skies or not, the weather picture itself is growing clearer with time. The improvement in space photography is evident when an early Tiros and a recent satellite photo are compared.

review of the year
space exploration

The United States concentrated much of its space effort in 1974 on the application of spacecraft to more down-to-earth activities, on the further exploration of the solar system, and on preparations for a joint manned mission with the Soviet Union in 1975.

ERTS-1 looks down at the U.S. coast from Florida to South Carolina. Water appears dark in this infrared view, so that the Everglades area is more shaded than the rest of the Florida peninsula.

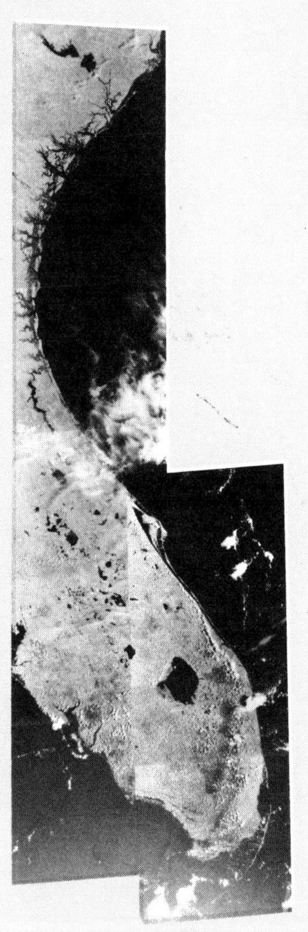

Earth Satellites. On July 2, 1974, the first educational course ever taught via space satellite television began with the transmission of a lesson from the University of Kentucky to elementary school teachers scattered throughout eight Appalachian states. The course was transmitted through the U.S. National Aeronautics and Space Administration (NASA) Applications Technology Satellite-6. The satellite was later used for similar education communications in the Rocky Mountains and Alaska and for long-distance medical diagnosis. Late in 1975, the satellite will be shifted to provide similar educational services in India.

On Nov. 13, the fourth of the Improved Tiros Operational Satellite (ITOS) series of weather satellites was launched into polar orbit by the U.S. National Oceanic and Atmospheric Administration (NOAA). It provides weather coverage of each local area every 12 hours. Riding with it into space were two other satellites, a scientific spacecraft built by Spain, and a small communications relay satellite, OSCAR-7, that will be used by amateur radio operators.

NASA launched two spacecraft in the Synchronous Meteorological Satellite series, one on May 17, 1974, and the other on Feb. 6, 1975. These spacecraft are designed to keep continuous watch on fast-changing storms, sending back high-resolution pictures every 30 minutes, day and night. The results were a vast improvement over the fuzzy pictures from the first weather satellites, launched 15 years ago.

One of the most productive of U.S. satellites, Earth Resources Technology Satellite-1 (ERTS-1), is approaching the end of its useful, nearly three-year lifetime. A companion vehicle with a new name, Landsat-2, was launched Jan. 22, 1975. It has begun where ERTS-1 left off, transmitting a stream of data on the earth's resources—identifying crops, locating pollution, updating maps, locating potentially rich geologic formations, monitoring the advance of glaciers, and searching out underground water supplies.

On April 9, 1975, Geodynamics Experimental Ocean Satellite-C (GEOS-C) was launched to map the topography of the ocean surfaces with precision radar altimeters. The altimeter data are expected to contribute to the refinement of present knowledge of the level that would be assumed by the ocean surface in the absence of winds, currents, and tides.

The Planets. Unmanned missions to three planets—Venus, Mercury, and Jupiter—were conducted during 1974. Mariner 10, a camera-carrying spacecraft launched Nov. 3, 1973, returned the first close-up photographs of Venus and other important data that provided new clues to the origin and evolution of that cloud-shrouded planet. After flying by Venus at a distance of 5,800 km (3,600 mi) on Feb. 5, 1974, Mariner 10 proceeded to Mercury for the first flyby of the planet nearest the sun. On its first pass, on March 29, the spacecraft radioed back photographs of nearly half of the planet's cratered surface, hitherto unseen by man. Then, with a boost provided by Mercury's gravity, Mariner 10 started two loops around the sun. This enabled it to make two bonus encounters with Mercury—on Sept. 21, 1974, and March 16, 1975. (See "A Look at Mercury" on page 363.)

Pioneer 11, meanwhile, explored the outer reaches of the solar system. Following up on the successful operations of its predecessor, Pioneer 10, the spacecraft swept past Jupiter on Dec. 3, 1974. Pioneer 11 came within 43,000 km (27,000 mi) of the sun's largest planet, three times closer than Pioneer 10 did a year earlier. The spacecraft returned images of Jupiter and new information on its atmosphere and radiation belts. After its flyby of Jupiter, Pioneer 11 was aimed to reach the vicinity of Saturn in 1979.

On Dec. 10, 1974, a West German spacecraft, Helios 1, was launched to gather data on interplanetary space in the region close to the sun. On March 15, 1975, it flew within 45 million km (28 million mi) of the sun—the closest any man-made object has yet come to the sun. The Helios launching also proved the reliability of the new Titan-Centaur rocket that the United States plans to use to send automated life-detection laboratories to Mars in 1976.

Helios 1, a West German satellite (below), began its long sunward journey from Cape Kennedy aboard a Titan-Centaur booster (above). Three months later it passed close to the blistering sun.

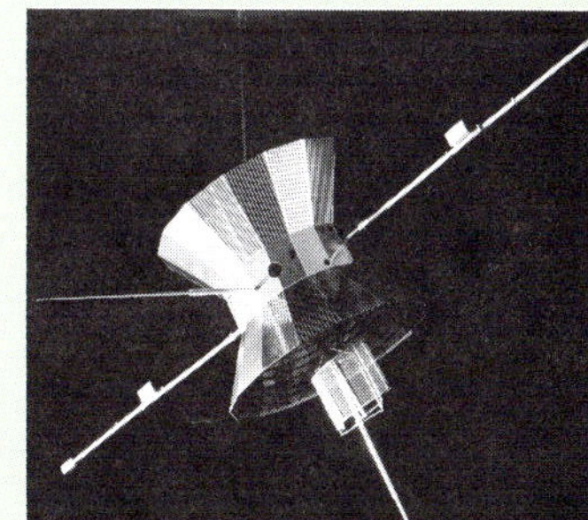

Apollo-Soyuz. The only American manned operation in space during 1974 was the concluding flight of the Skylab Project. The third crew to man the earth-orbiting space station returned to earth safely on Feb. 8, ending a record 84-day mission.

Then all attention turned to the Apollo-Soyuz Test Project. The mission will involve the link-up in earth orbit of an Apollo spacecraft, carrying three Americans, with a Soyuz spacecraft, operated by two Soviet cosmonauts. For at least two days the crews are to move back and forth between their joined vehicles, conducting some scientific experiments and exhibiting Soviet-American goodwill. (See "Apollo-Soyuz Test Project" on page 359.)

Several 1974 Soviet manned space flights were at least partly devoted to testing a modified Soyuz spacecraft and new navigation systems for the joint mission. Soyuz 14, launched July 3, saw two cosmonauts link their spacecraft with the U.S.S.R.'s Salyut 3 space station. The flight—with Soviet cosmonauts Pavel Popovich and Yuri Artyukhin on board—ended 15 days later and was hailed as a successful test of systems for the joint mission. But in August Soyuz 15 failed to accomplish a docking with the Salyut, raising some doubts about the reliability of the Soviet systems.

Additional docking tests were conducted by Soyuz 16, launched on Dec. 2, 1974. Cosmonauts Anatoly V. Filipchenko and Nikolai Rukavishnikov returned Dec. 8. Soyuz 17 set a Soviet endurance record of 30 days. Launched Jan. 11, 1975, cosmonauts Aleksei Gubarev and Georgi Grechko successfully steered their spacecraft to a link-up with the Salyut 4 space station and returned to earth Feb. 9, 1975. Failure struck again, however, in April 1975. Soyuz 18, with two men aboard, had to be aborted shortly after lift-off when an upper stage of the Vostok rocket began veering off course. The rocket shut down automatically and the spacecraft was set free to return to earth, out in Siberia. The two cosmonauts, Vasily Lazarev and Oleg Makarov, escaped unharmed.

John Noble Wilford

"Hanging In" at L-5

by Michael Cusack

SOMEDAY, you may live in space. Of course, that has been said before. Perhaps you have wondered what life would be like on Mars, on Venus, on earth's moon, or on a moon of Jupiter.

The first space colonists from earth, however, may not settle in any of these places. The first human colonies in space may be formed at what are known as libration points between the earth and the moon.

A libration point is a place in space where the pull of gravity is not felt. A space station at a libration point would not be pulled to the earth. It would not be pulled to the moon or to the sun. It would just hang in there.

How can that be? How can any place be beyond the grip of gravity? Isn't gravity the force that holds the universe together?

Yes. Gravity is the force of attraction that all objects have for each other. It's a mysterious force, and scientists still do not know why objects attract each other.

Objects do attract each other, though. All things in the universe—from stars to atoms—pull on each other. An apple falls because the earth pulls it. The apple also pulls the earth, but the earth is millions of times larger than the apple. So earth's pull is millions of times stronger than that of the apple. It is the apple, therefore, that is forced to move.

THE INVISIBLE STRING

The strength of gravity depends on the mass (amount of matter) of the objects and on the distance between the objects. The greater the mass, the greater the pull. The greater the distance, the less the pull. Actually, the force of gravity decreases as the square of the distance (distance multiplied by itself) between the objects increases, and vice versa.

Gravity is the "invisible string" that "ties" the earth to its orbit around the sun. It is also the "string" that "ties" our moon to its path around the earth. Without the pull of earth's gravity, the moving moon would travel off into space.

That brings up a question: Since the earth and moon are pulling on each other, why doesn't the moon come crashing down on us?

The moon doesn't fall because it has enough momentum (mass times velocity) to resist earth's pull. Let's see what that means.

Earth's gravity is pulling the moon inward. But the moon is moving, and, like any other object in motion, it tends to travel in a straight line. If there were no gravity, the moon would travel off in a straight-line path. This means that there is an outward reaction to the inward pull of gravity.

This outward reaction and inward pull are so balanced that the moon does not fall to earth. Neither does it escape into space. It circles the earth in a certain orbit.

Of course, if the moon's momentum were changed, the moon's orbit would change. If some outside force were to slow the moon down, the moon might crash down on us. If some force were to speed the moon up, the moon might shoot off through the solar system.

Neither of those things is likely to happen. Such things do happen, though, to man-made satellites—space vehicles.

We can send a vehicle into orbit by making it go fast enough. At a speed of 27,000 kph (around 17,000 mph), the vehicle's momentum will counter-balance earth's pull. Then, the vehicle will go into an orbit around the earth. Slow the orbiting vehicle's motion, and it will drop back to earth. Speed up the vehicle, and it will swing out toward the moon, or to some other part of the solar system.

INTO THE MOON'S GRIP

As the vehicle travels toward the moon, the earth's gravitational pull gets weaker and weaker. Finally, a point is reached

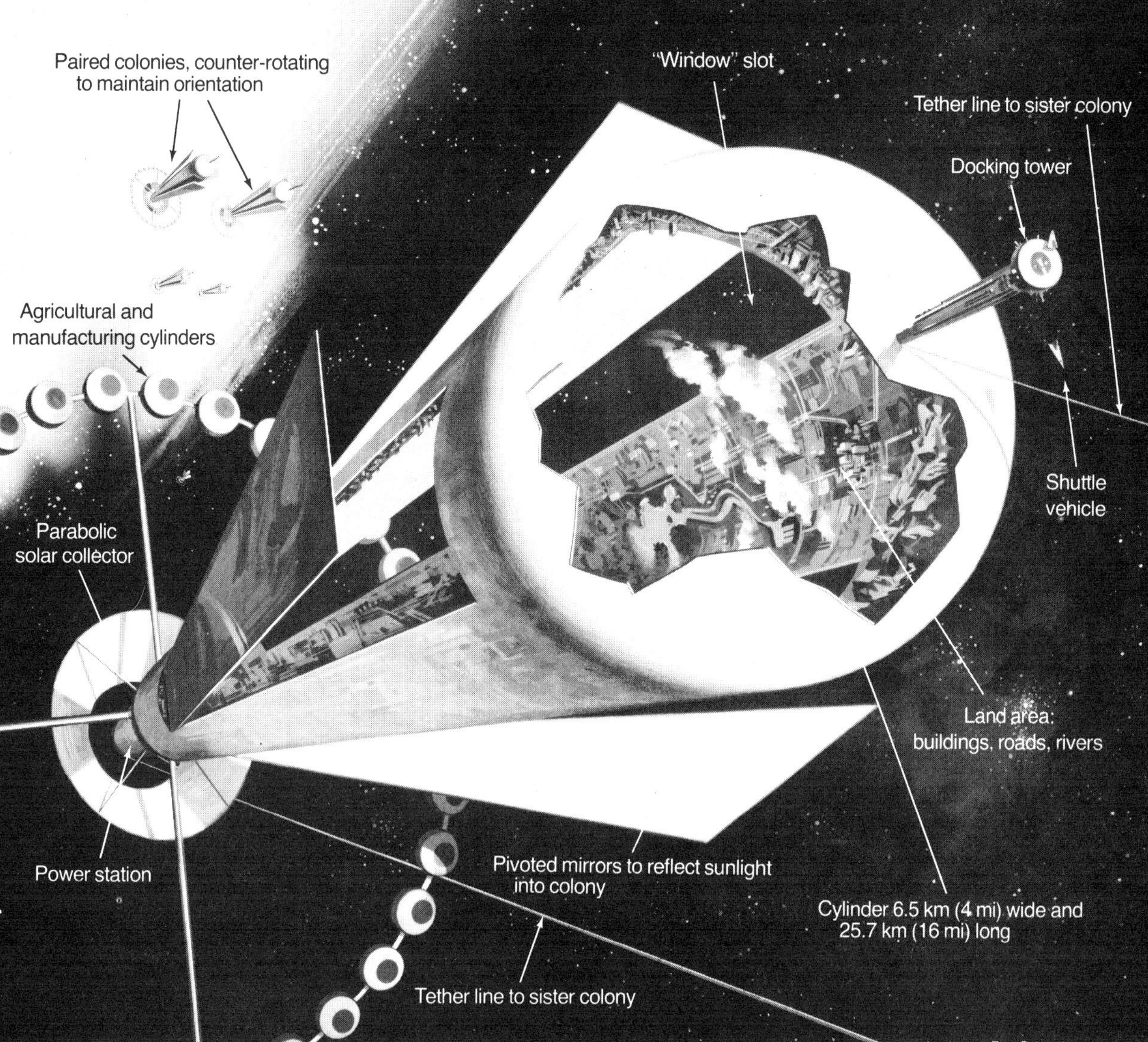

where the moon's pull on the vehicle is stronger than earth's pull. The vehicle then slips out of earth's "grip" into the moon's "grip."

Usually, the passage from earth's "grip" to the moon's "grip" is smooth and easy. That is because the gravitational fields of the earth and moon overlap. On most paths to the moon, the vehicle would at all times be pulled either by the earth or by the moon.

That does not apply to all paths to the moon. There are five points in earth-moon space where a vehicle would not be pulled by the earth or by the moon. A vehicle would tend to stay put at one of those points.

How do we know that such points exist? A famous Frenchman discovered them nearly 200 years ago. Count Joseph Louis Lagrange (1736–1813) figured out that there are five points in space where the gravitational fields of the earth and moon balance one another. The effects of the two fields are canceled out at those points. As a result, an object at one of those points would not fall to earth or to the moon.

These points are known by many names: Lagrangian points, critical points, or equilibrium (balance) points. However, many space scientists prefer to call them libration points. A vehicle at one of those points is likely to *librate*—wiggle back and forth across the point. Why should that happen? Are not the gravitational fields of the earth and moon in balance at those points?

Yes. In theory, an object put at one of those points should stay there. In reality, the earth and moon are not alone in the universe. Gravitational pulls of the sun and planets other than earth would tend to disturb an object at a libration point. As a result, the object might bounce around.

All libration points, however, are not alike. Look at the drawing on this page. Points L-1, L-2, and L-3 are fairly unstable. The other two points—L-4 and L-5—seem to be fairly stable. Space scientists are now very interested in those "stable" points.

LIFE AT L-5

Just think of what could be done with a stay-put point in space. Millions of tons of construction material could be parked there over the years. The material would not drift away. It would not fall to earth or to the moon. It would just stay there. Then, at some future time, the material could be assembled into a huge space station.

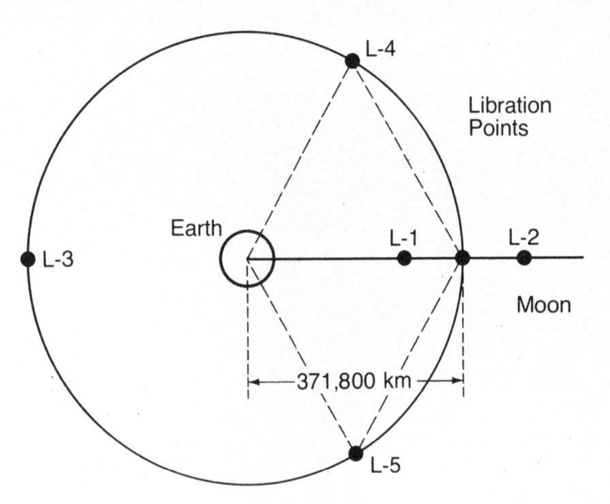

Dr. Gerard K. O'Neill, of Princeton University, says that we could build a colony station for about 2,000 people at the L-5 point. (See illustration, page 357)

Less than five years from now, he says, manned and unmanned spacecraft could start hauling space-station parts to L-5. About 20 years later, the first space settlers could move in. Once a space colony has been started, it would surely grow.

Dr. O'Neill says that there are no shortages of energy or raw materials in space. Sunlight would be a continuous source of cheap energy for a space colony. There would be no night-time interruptions to that energy flow.

Metals are almost as plentiful as sunlight in space. Many of the asteroids traveling around the sun are almost pure chunks of nickel-iron. Some of those asteroids could be easily "captured" and towed to L-5. Rarer metals—such as titanium—could be mined on the moon and shipped to L-5.

With unlimited energy available, a large space colony could meet all its own needs. It could produce all its own food, air, and water. It could ship manufactured goods to earth.

Some scientists say that 100 years from now, most "dirty" industries may be located at the libration points. In fact, more people may live outside the earth than on the earth. Earth itself might become an enormous park—a huge vacation area for visiting space-dwellers.

Eventually, when the libration points near the earth and moon are filled, people would seek out other libration points in the solar system. Scientists know that there are libration points at places where the gravitational fields of the sun and Jupiter meet. And beyond that. . . .□

SELECTED READINGS

We Reach the Moon, rev. ed. by John N. Wilford. Norton 1971.

I Want to Know About Flight to the Moon (grades 3 to 6) by Alfred M. Worden. Doubleday 1974.

"Space to Grow" by Paul T. Libassi. *The Sciences*, July/August 1974.

The Apollo spacecraft (left) has linked up with the docking module, in this drawing, and is approaching the Soyuz craft (right) for the final docking maneuver.

The Apollo-Soyuz Test Project

by Raymond N. Watts, Jr.

FOR a decade or more, national space programs have been heavily criticized for duplication of effort. Both the Soviet Union and the United States developed and flew spacecraft designed to study the earth, near-earth space, the solar system, and deep space. Both countries mounted planetary probes and lunar explorations, as well as manned satellites of the earth. However, throughout these parallel efforts, there was relatively little exchange of scientific and technical information.

In October 1970, the National Aeronautics and Space Administration (NASA) and the U.S.S.R. Academy of Sciences took steps that led to a series of six meetings of space scientists alternately in Moscow and Houston. Finally, on May 24, 1972, President Richard M. Nixon and Chairman Aleksei N. Kosygin established the guidelines for cooperation between the two countries. Their agreement called for shared activities in space meteorology, the natural environment, exploration of near-earth space, exploration of the moon and planets, and space biology and space medicine.

As a specific starting point, they agreed on a joint effort toward an American-Soviet space rendezvous in 1975. This pact triggered a series of meetings in the two countries that continues today.

Which spacecraft would be used and where would they meet? A suggestion that the Russians visit a Skylab was scrapped when that program was reduced to a single three-part mission. However, Apollo, Soyuz, and Salyut vehicles could be used in several combinations, and finally it was decided that a Soviet Soyuz should rendezvous with an American Apollo some 240 km (150 mi) above the ground.

Because each country had developed its own hardware and docking procedures for space rendezvous, a compromise had to be reached. Being the larger and more powerful craft, the Apollo carries aloft a special docking module, one end connected to the Apollo by standard American techniques, the other a special adapter for the Soyuz. As the spacecraft move toward each other, large guide plates ensure proper alignment, and three capture latches complete the initial contact. Eight structural latches then make a firm con-

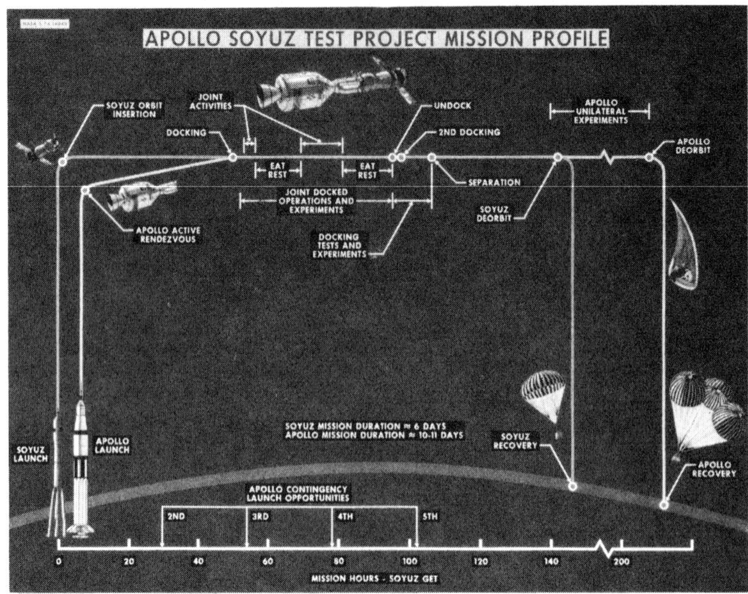

The schedule and timetable of events in the Apollo-Soyuz mission are shown above.

nection, with rubber seals for a vacuum-tight fit of the two craft.

SOYUZ AND ITS CREW

The Soyuz crew, Aleksei A. Leonov and Valeri N. Kubasov, will leave the Baikonur launch complex in Kazakhstan, U.S.S.R. at 12:20 Universal Time (UT) on a July day in 1975. Their big 6,680-kg (14,726 lb) spacecraft will be launched northeasterly into an orbit with an inclination of 51.8 degrees to the earth's equator. The low and high points will be 188 and 228 km (117 and 142 mi). After the fourth revolution, a ground-controlled maneuver will begin to raise the perigee, or point nearest the earth. A second maneuver, during the 17th circuit of the earth, will effect a nearly circular orbit at 225 km (140 mi) altitude.

The Soyuz spacecraft has three major sections. At the forward end, the 1,224-kg (2,700-lb) orbital module is 2.35 m in diameter and 2.65 m long (about 7.7 by 8.7 ft). The crew uses it for work and rest while in orbit.

Behind this, the descent module houses the main controls and crew couches. To be occupied during launch, descent, and landing, it weighs 2,802 kg (6,177 lb) and is 2.2 m (7.2 ft) long.

The instrument module is at the rear, with systems for power, communications, propulsion, and life support. Its weight is 2,654 kg (5,850 lb), and its 2.3-m (7.5-ft) extent brings the spacecraft's overall length to 7.15 m (23.5 ft).

APOLLO AND ITS CREW

Meanwhile, 7½ hours into the mission, at 19:50 UT a Saturn 1B launch vehicle will carry the Apollo crew into orbit from Kennedy Space Center in Florida. The astronauts are to be Thomas P. Stafford, Vance D. Brand, and Donald K. Slayton.

The Apollo also has three major sections, two of them being the command and service modules, which stay together until the return to ground. Out in front is the newly designed docking module, a cylinder 1.5 m (4.9 ft) in diameter and 3 m (9.8 ft) long, with an air-lock hatch at each end. It is housed in the launch adapter, where the lunar excursion module was carried for moon missions. It contains radio and TV communications equipment, antennas, heaters, and the displays and controls needed for transferring the crew. Excluding the docking module and the service engine's expansion nozzle, the modified Apollo spacecraft is slightly more than 7 m (23 ft) long.

The docking module had to be designed for compatibility with the two ships' very different atmospheres—the result of a traditional difference between

American and Soviet space technology. In orbit, Apollo astronauts breathe pure oxygen at a reduced pressure, while Soyuz cosmonauts have a mixture of nitrogen and oxygen at sea-level pressure.

The docking module can hold two crewmen simultaneously. Hatches with controls on both sides are installed at each end of the module. While the spacecraft are docked, the Soyuz pressure is reduced to 700 g per cm^2 (10 lb per in^2), making it possible for Russian crewmen to transfer from Soyuz to Apollo without taking time in the air lock to breathe pure oxygen and force nitrogen from their blood. The Apollo pressure remains at 350 g per cm^2 (5 lb per in^2).

DOCKING AND CREW EXCHANGE

After being launched, the Apollo will have an orbital inclination of 51.8 degrees and initial perigee and apogee heights of 150 and 167 km (93 and 104 mi). In little more than an hour it will begin a series of maneuvers familiar to observers of American manned moon missions.

The Apollo command and service module will separate from the last-stage booster, make a U-turn, then connect with the docking module. By 9 hours 14 minutes GET (Ground Elapsed Time measured from the Soyuz launch), command-module thrusters will be fired to speed up the spacecraft by about one meter (over three feet) per second to avoid its bumping into the launch vehicle.

Next, by a series of maneuvers, the Apollo crewmen must match their orbit to that of the Russians. Then, if all goes well, at 49:55 GET the two craft will be ready for final approach and docking. The operation is scheduled for completion at 51:55 GET, during the Soyuz's 36th revolution and Apollo's 29th.

Although the joint maneuvers and docking are a main purpose of the project, the two ships will spend only about two days locked together. Before final separation, they will practice redocking, but at about 99:15 GET the Apollo will change its velocity by one meter per second to avoid further contact. After this, each crew will conduct its own experiments. Remaining in orbit for about 43 hours more, the Soyuz will land in Kazakhstan at about 142:00 GET. The Apollo will stay aloft for approximately six days. Then it will splash down in the Pacific Ocean in the manner usual for American manned flights.

RADIATION STUDIES

The most important benefits anticipated from the Apollo-Soyuz Test Project are long range. It is a first step toward other international missions on a larger

Standing are (left) Thomas Stafford, the U.S. crew commander, and Aleksei Leonov, the Soviet crew commander. Seated (left to right) are Donald Slayton, Vance Brand, and Valeri Kubasov. Stafford and the Soviet men are veteran space pilots. Slayton was one of the original team of astronaut trainees but had made no flights.

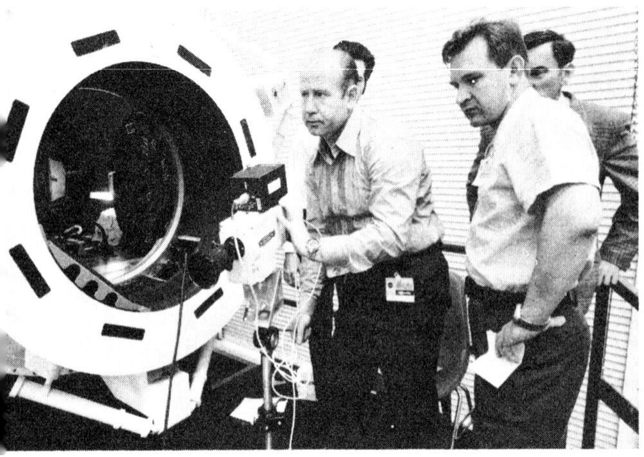

In training at the Johnson Space Center, Leonov tries out a television camera as Kubasov watches. A docking module mock-up is at left.

scale. Also, with a compatible technique of rendezvous and docking, either the United States or the Soviet Union will be able, in the future, to rescue the other nation's spacecraft if either of the vehicles is in distress.

The project also provides a valuable opportunity to conduct scientific experiments in space. An ultraviolet absorption experiment aimed at measuring the concentrations of the various parts of the atmosphere at the 250-km (155-mi) orbital altitude has been designed by T. M. Donahue at the University of Pittsburgh. Light signals from the docking adapter will be returned by a retroreflector on the Soyuz. Measurement of the intensity of the reflected light will indicate the amount of ultraviolet absorption that is taking place.

C. S. Bowyer of the University of California at Berkeley is the principal investigator in a search for sources of extreme ultraviolet radiation in the night sky. No systematic hunt has yet been made for such sources. They may include stellar coronas, defunct pulsars, and stars that are accumulating matter. The main instrument will be a special-purpose telescope, mounted outside the Apollo spacecraft, with an ultraviolet detector at its focal point.

In another experiment provided by Dr. Bowyer, a photometer will measure the helium glow of the night sky. The data could give the distribution of helium in interplanetary space and indicate the penetration of interstellar helium into the solar system.

To measure soft X rays from both the earth and the sky, Herbert Friedman of the U.S. Naval Research Laboratory built a detector to be mounted in a bay of the Apollo service module. Rocket observations have detected a diffuse celestial background of soft X rays, but a systematic sky survey has not previously been made in the 100- to 1,000-electron-volt energy range. The satellite observations should provide the finer angular resolution needed to determine the various X ray sources.

OTHER USES OF SPACE

Apollo is to carry a small multipurpose electric furnace with which a number of metallurgical tests will be made. In one such experiment, magnetic materials will be melted and resolidified at controlled rates to see whether cast materials with improved properties can be made under the weightless conditions that are available to manufacturers who decide to make use of outer space.

A number of biomedical experiments are scheduled, including one on the white blood cells that are important in protection against bacterial infection. In a study of possible effects of weightlessness on the functioning of these cells, blood samples taken from the astronauts before and after the mission will be subjected to laboratory tests with bacteria. More information should be secured on how resistance to infection may change during a prolonged space mission□

SELECTED READINGS

A Young Person's Guide to Space by Arthur C. Clarke and Robert Silverberg. Harper-Row Publications, Inc., 1971.

"Soviet-American Rendezvous in Orbit," by G. Reznichenko. *Space World*, March 1975.

A Look at Mercury

by J. Kelly Beatty

ON Sept. 21, 1974, Mariner 10 swept past Mercury at a distance of 47,981 km (29,814 mi). The flyby was the spacecraft's second visit to the planet's vicinity. Within a 49-hour interval, the pair of television cameras aboard Mariner 10 obtained about 500 high-quality images of the surface of Mercury.

Unlike the situation during the first encounter, the point of closest approach was on Mercury's sunlit side on this second pass. Therefore some areas unobserved in March 1974 could be photographed, including the neighborhood of the south pole. The September flyby was specially designed for picture-taking. In fact, only the television and extreme-ultraviolet experiments were operated this time.

Transmitted over a distance of 169 million km (105 million mi) to earth, the images were received by huge antennas at Goldstone, California, at Canberra, Australia, and at Madrid, Spain. These comprise the Jet Propulsion Laboratory's Deep Space Network. Since the onboard tape recorder was not working during the flyby, the high-resolution pictures had to be transmitted instantly, as they were made, one frame every 42 seconds. Upon reception, the signals were taped so that the photographs could later be computer processed to clarify and enhance their details.

The rate of picture transmission was 117,600 bits of information per second, not the 22,050 bits for which the 64-m (210-ft) Canberra and Madrid antennas were prepared. Hence those stations could accept only every fourth data bit. But Goldstone received 117,600 bits per second with one 64-m (210-ft) and two 26-m (85-ft) dishes, which are set in a line about 16 km (10 mi) long. The receivers

On its third Mercury flyby, Mariner 10 looked closely at the plains of Caloris Basin. The largest crater seen is 11 km (7 mi) wide.

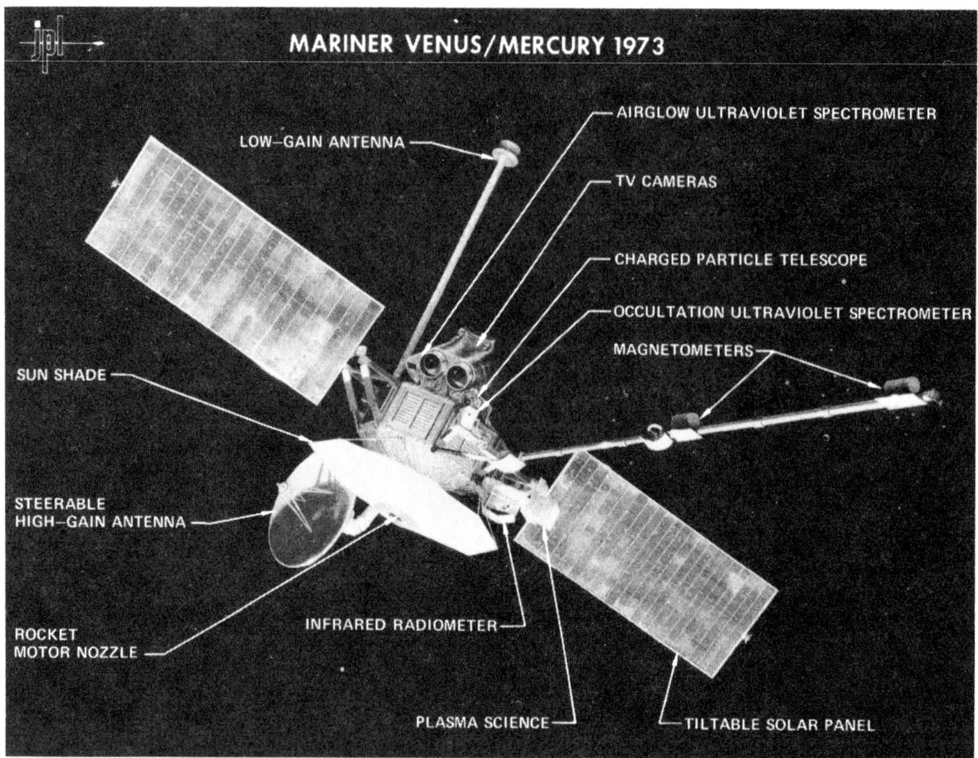

Mariner 10, a 500-kg (1,100-lb) spacecraft launched in 1973 and fitted with many scientific instruments, was one of the most successful of all planetary probes.

were adjusted to bring the three signals into phase, providing a greatly improved signal-to-noise ratio.

To relay an image to earth, each of its 582,400 picture elements (pixels) was assigned a brightness value from 0 (black) to 255. Converted digitally to an eight-bit "word" for transmission, this information was reassembled into a photograph by computers at the Jet Propulsion Laboratory (JPL) in Pasadena, California.

BACKGROUND NOISE

Such "raw" photographs have some background noise and data losses that lower the resolution. To bring out the rich detail contained in the pictures, special computer kinds of programs were run by technicians at JPL's Image Processing Laboratory. In these programs, the gray tones in areas of low contrast were revised so as to increase contrast. (This same technique was of great value in processing Mariner photographs of Mars.)

The new pictures confirm many of the striking characteristics observed during the first encounter. They extend Mariner 10's useful photographic coverage from about 25 per cent of the planet's surface in March 1974 to about 37 per cent, most of the gain being in the southern hemisphere. In the 176 days between the two flybys, Mercury had completed almost exactly three rotations, so substantially the same half of the planet's globe was sunlit on the two occasions.

The remarkable similarity of Mercury's surface to the moon's indicates that the two bodies have similar histories. For example, Mercury shows some large plains containing relatively few craters, analogous to the lunar "seas." Indeed, the Mariner 10 television experiment team, headed by Bruce Murray of the California

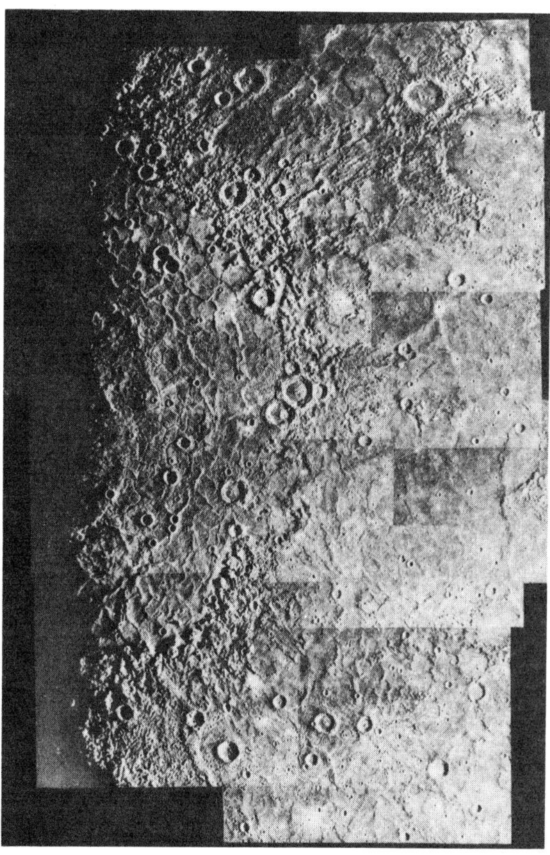

Half of Caloris Basin is seen in the photo mosaic at left. On Mercury's opposite side, shown above, is a region of craters, hills, and ridges that may have resulted from shock waves set up when Caloris was formed.

Institute of Technology, has reported, "Extensive flooding by rock materials at least grossly similar to those of the lunar maria has occurred on Mercury."

If the material covering the plains is indeed moonlike and therefore of low density, some important further inferences may be drawn. Because Mercury's average density is as great as 5.44 grams per cm³ (3.40 lb per ft³), this means that the planet's core must be more dense than the lighter materials of the surface. It is quite possible that Mercury has an earthlike iron core extending outward for as much as 80 per cent of the planet's radius, with a silicate crust some 500 to 600 km (310 to 375 mi) thick.

IMPORTANT DIFFERENCES

Nevertheless, there are several important differences between the surfaces of Mercury and the moon. Some differences are directly the outcome of the planet's larger surface gravity. Mercury's craters are shallower than lunar ones of the same size, and their ejected matter covers only a fifth as much area. Terraces along the inner walls and central peaks are commoner in Mercury's craters. Preliminary studies indicate that such features occur in virtually all Mercurian craters larger than 14 km (9 mi), but on the moon this is generally the case only for those over 50 km (31 mi).

Perhaps the most significant features of the photographs are the huge scarps, or cliffs, that run for hundreds of kilometers across the planet's face. Possibly as high as 3 km (1.9 mi), these cliffs generally have wavy, snakelike outlines and cut across both craters and intercrater areas. Their lobed form suggests they may be thrust or reverse faults, possibly caused by compressive stresses induced while the surface was cooling during the planet's early history.

Another perplexing problem is posed by the complex patterns of ridges inside several large, flat-floored craters. Early studies have not indicated whether these ridges originated from faulting or from flows of plains material. Perhaps some ridge systems may have resulted from both processes.

One area of the planet has a "weird terrain" characterized by a rough, scabby surface and greatly degraded crater rims. Often there are formations like landslides. This kind of terrain is found on the moon in the areas antipodal (directly opposite) to the large impact basins Mare Imbrium and Mare Orientale. And it happens that Mercury's "weird terrain" lies opposite the 1,300-km (808-mi) impact area known as Caloris Basin. There is a possible connection between the two features. It has been suggested that the Caloris impact produced a shock wave intense enough to travel all the way through the planet. The wave, being concentrated at the antipodal point, caused a violent upheaval that produced the area.

SYSTEM OF FRACTURES

Caloris Basin itself contains many features not found elsewhere on Mercury. The floor is laced with a complex system of fractures, both concentric and radial. Robert Strom, a TV experiment team member from the University of Arizona, notes that there seems to be less fracturing in a ring-shaped area extending inward some 200 km (124 mi) from the Caloris Mountains. These mountains form the rim of the basin and tower on the average 2 km (1.25 mi) above its floor.

Sometime after marelike material flooded the impact area, the central part of the basin gradually subsided until it was about 2 km (1.2 mi) lower than the rest. This subsidence was responsible for the pattern of tensional fractures and ridges identified in Mariner 10 photographs of Caloris Basin. Such features have been observed nowhere else on the planet.

INTERPRETATIONS

How do all these observations affect theories of the planet's history? Here are some tentative interpretations by the TV experiment team:

- "The Mariner 10 picture data suggest to us that Mercury underwent a period of early heavy bombardment, including formation of huge basins, followed by the widespread volcanism represented by the plains material.
- "A striking feature of Mercury (and of the moon as well) is that an ancient heavily cratered terrain has been preserved in extensive regions without major modification by either internal processes like volcanism or surface processes such as atmospheric erosion.
- "The planetary-scale scarps and ridges are suggestive of a major episode of compression. . . . An obvious speculation is that an iron-rich core underwent shrinkage, resulting in compression of the outer layers. . . . Such an episode of surface compression apparently prevailed during the terminal phase of heavy bombardment but not throughout much of the rest of the history of the planet."

Mariner 10 made its third and last useful flyby of Mercury on March 16, 1975, skimming to within about 320 km (200 mi) of its surface. The fruits of this encounter include more than 300 additional high-resolution photographs of the cratered surface and new information on Mercury's magnetic field. Because the flyby occurred much closer to the surface than the previous two passes, the TV cameras gave increased resolution. Some photographs were expected to reveal details as small as about 45 m (148 ft) in diameter. The improved resolution will tell us that much more about Mercury□

SELECTED READINGS

"Mariner Photos Reveal Mercury Scarps." *Aviation Week*, July 1974.

"Mercury Revisited by Mariner 10." *Sky and Telescope*, May 1975.

"Never-Before-Seen Face of Mercury" by Wernher von Braun. *Popular Science*, July 1974.

Very long cliffs, or scarps, are an unusual kind of surface feature on the planet. They may be formed by compressive forces in the planet's crust. The scarp that extends from upper left to lower right across the picture is more than 300 km (185 mi) long.

Right: rays of light-colored material extend out from a relatively new crater lying to the right of the photo, near Mercury's south pole.

Below: the dark-rimmed crater at left, surrounded by ejected material, resembles the crater Tycho on the moon. It is 67 km (42 mi) in diameter.

Space Stations

by Wernher von Braun and Frederick I. Ordway

SPACE station—the words bring an image of a huge wheel-shaped structure like that often found on the covers of science fiction magazines. Such a structure was stunningly depicted as "Space Station 5" in the film *2001: A Space Odyssey*.

But space stations are not just in the imaginations of science fiction writers. The success of the United States Skylab program in 1973–74 brought space stations a step closer to reality. In mid-1975 the United States and the Soviet Union plan a joint space effort in which a U.S. Apollo and a U.S.S.R. Soyuz spacecraft will dock in space. A successful docking will be another important step toward the development of a practical space station and the ability to maintain it.

WHAT IS A SPACE STATION?

First and foremost, a space station is an orbital spacecraft. It must be placed in orbit around the earth or some other body, such as the moon. This, of course, makes a space station a kind of artificial satellite.

Second, a space station is designed, built and maintained to accommodate an astronaut crew as well as non-astronaut passengers—scientists, engineers, communications specialists and others. This makes it a large manned artificial satellite.

But a space station is still more. Space stations are larger than the manned artificial satellites we know today. They can remain in orbit for a longer time, they can carry more passengers, and they are more complex.

We normally think of a space station as capable of receiving at least five or ten persons and of supplying them with what they need in order to live and work for months at a time. Ferry flights from earth

Rendezvous with a space station—a striking moment in the film *2001*. The space stations of the future may very well look like this.

would resupply the space station at intervals. These differences already indicate that a space station is larger than the familiar Mercury, Gemini, and Apollo spacecraft that orbited the earth and also larger than the Skylab "laboratory in the sky." Skylab was, incidentally, called an embryonic space station.

In discussing semipermanent stations in space, the terms space laboratory, space platform, space base and space station are all used. Generally a space laboratory is the smallest, a space station the largest.

The complexity of a space station depends on the number of persons who will live in it, on the experiments it is to perform and on the other work it is to do. A highly complex space station may be expected to perform many different kinds of astronomical and astrophysical investigations. It might also be expected to serve as a facility where medical research, particularly research on the effects of space travel on man, can be conducted. It can also be used as a space hospital to care for the health needs of space travelers.

The space station might also serve as a space factory, manufacturing certain products on board. Some products can be made more easily under the conditions of weightlessness and the near-vacuum that exist in space. The behavior of certain materials in the unique space environment could also be studied.

A section of the same space station could be given over to biological studies. Another part of the station could house special cameras and other equipment to examine and monitor the land and oceans below, studying the earth's agricultural, mineral and other resources. Still other sensors could observe worldwide weather patterns and improve our knowledge of the atmosphere.

Someday space stations may be able to assemble, refuel and maintain spaceships traveling between planets. Truly, the potential of space stations is almost limitless.

THE BRICK MOON, AN UNUSUAL STORY

As modern and futuristic as the term space station sounds, it is an idea that has been around for a long time. More than one hundred years ago, the magazine *Atlantic Monthly* published an unusual short novel, titled *The Brick Moon.* The story appeared in four parts—in the November and December 1869 issues of the magazine and in the January and February 1870 issues. It was not until the end of 1870, however, that the author of *The Brick Moon* was revealed. It was Edward Everett Hale, the American clergyman today known to all schoolchildren as the author of the famous short story "The Man Without a Country."

The Brick Moon tells the story of a space station named the Brick Moon. The station was spherical, with a diameter of 60 meters (200 ft). It was built to orbit the earth at a distance of 6,400 kilometers (4,000 mi). It was intended to serve as a navigational or directional guidepost for oceangoing vessels. Today we would call it a navigational satellite.

As things turned out, the Brick Moon was launched accidentally while its construction workers and their visiting families were on board. It thus became, quite

Skylab, an adapted Apollo craft operated successfully by three U.S. crews in 1973–74, was a prototype of space stations to come.

NASA's Space Shuttle is being readied for 1980. The reuseable craft will carry cargo to and from space at greatly reduced costs. Left: the Shuttle is launched by two solid-propellant boosters. Right: the external fuel tank is jettisoned.

unexpectedly, the world's first space station. Food and other supplies, including books, were quickly sent up to the surprised and stranded colony of 37 persons. The colonists soon became used to their new way of life. They lived in a tropical climate and were able to grow all sorts of crops that they harvested ten times a year.

Hale, meanwhile, said of his "little world":

> Now let it fall. . . . Let it fall. . . . The curve it is now on will forever clear the world . . . will forever revolve, in its obedient orbit, the Brick Moon, the blessing of all seamen—as constant in all change as its older sister [the Moon] has been fickle, and the second cynosure of all lovers upon the waves, and of all girls left behind them.

So much for the Brick Moon.

EARLY 20TH CENTURY IDEAS

Many pioneering spaceflight scientists of the early 20th century showed how space stations might be placed in orbit. They also explained the purposes that such space stations might serve. Hermann Oberth, in books published in Germany in the 1920's, suggested that space stations would be useful for communications, for refueling spaceships, and for observing the earth and its atmosphere below. If rockets were to be placed "around the Earth in a circle," he wrote,

> they will behave like a small moon. Such rockets no longer need to be designed for landing. Contact between them and the Earth can be maintained by means of smaller rockets.

At about the same time, an Austrian Imperial Army captain, Hermann Potochik, under the pen name Hermann Noordung, presented a plan for a space station. He proposed a space station consisting of three main parts: a *Wohnrad*, or "living wheel," where the crew would live; a power-generating module; and an observatory module.

The *Wohnrad* was shaped like a doughnut. It had a 15-meter (50-ft) radius and was designed to rotate, or turn, around a central hub. The rotation served to provide artificial gravity along the perimeter, or outer rim, of the doughnut.

Noordung's space station was to be placed 35,900 kilometers (22,300 mi) high and was to have a 24-hour orbit. Thus the space station would have the same period

In space, the Shuttle can perform many different tasks. It can retrieve satellites for repair (upper left) or deploy them for use (lower left). Returning to earth (right), the craft can carry a load of up to 14,400 kg (32,000 lb).

of rotation—24 hours—as the earth, which rotates on its axis once every 24 hours. Such an orbit is called a stationary, or geosynchronous, orbit. A space station placed in such an orbit appears stationary in the sky. Noordung thought that such an orbit would make earth-observation easier.

An even more ambitious idea was presented by the Englishman J. D. Bernal in his book *The World, the Flesh, and the Devil,* published in 1929. Bernal looked to the day when man would build permanent homes in space. He predicted:

> At first space navigators, and then scientists whose observations would be best conducted outside the earth, and then finally those who for any reason were dissatisfied with earthly conditions would come to inhabit [extraterrestrial] bases. Even with our present primitive knowledge we can plan out such a celestial station in considerable detail.

Bernal's space station was spherical and extremely large—16 kilometers (10 mi) or so in diameter. He did not plan on creating artificial gravity in his station. Rather, he felt that "there is no reason to suppose that we would not ultimately adjust ourselves to weightlessness."

IDEAS AFTER WORLD WAR II

During most of the 1930's and 1940's, few original space station ideas appeared. Attention was focused on developing rocket engines and on military missiles. But, after the war, H. E. Ross of Great Britain published an article on a large rotating space station that would be used for research in meteorology, astronomy, zero-gravity conditions, high-vacuum physics, radiation, and communications.

In 1951, Wernher von Braun designed a 60-meter (200-ft), inflatable, wheel-shaped station to be placed in a 1,730-km (1,075-mi) high orbit. He wrote that

> a person observing the earth from up there would have a unique view of cloud formation on earth, particularly above the oceans. This offers novel possibilities for weather forecasting. By using high-powered telescopes, you may observe ships crossing the oceans and you may flash iceberg warnings to endangered ships. And, believe it or not, magnification factors could be used that would enable you to see people moving around on the earth's surface. This is because the atmospheric disturbances,

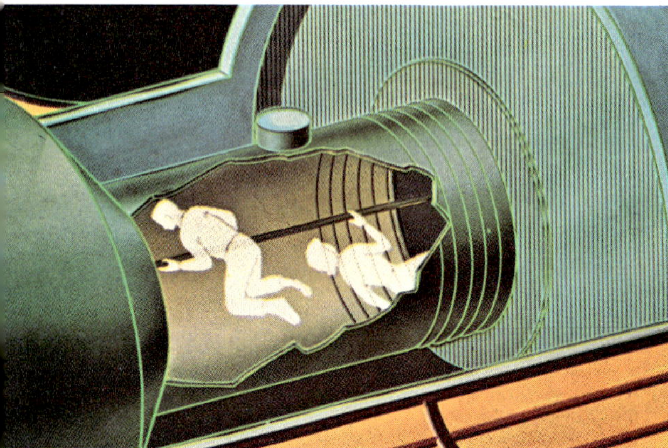

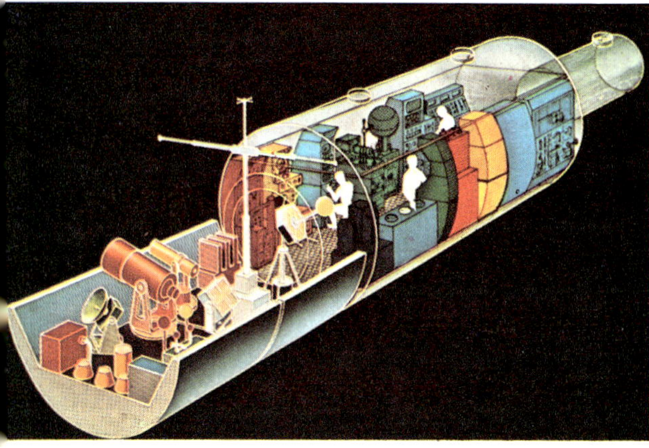

when looking from outer space through the earth's atmosphere, are much less serious than those affecting astronomical observations from telescopes mounted on the bottom of the atmospheric shell. If we turn such a satellite telescope to the outer reaches of the universe, the planets and the stars, we shall find observation conditions which no terrestrial observatory could equal.

In 1953, Heinz Hermann Kölle presented his *Aussenstation* concept. It was a station that consisted of a ring made up of 36 spheres, each one nearly 5 meters (16 ft) wide. The ring was connected to a central hub by 8 supporting tubes, 4 of which had elevator shafts. This station could accommodate up to 65 persons and would weigh 150 metric tons. Kölle planned his elaborate space station to serve many purposes: weather observation, forecasting and control; research on the behavior of solids, liquids, and gases in space; biological studies of plants under zero- and low-gravity conditions; navigational aids; earth-resources observation; communications relay; and intermediate assembly, refueling and navigational as-

Spacelab, a project of the European Space Research Organization, will be put in orbit by the Space Shuttle. Left, from top: Spacelab ready to be placed in Shuttle; a cutaway view of the laboratory module; crew moving from living quarters to lab; and view of external instrument platform adjacent to pressurized lab. Above: data being transmitted to earth.

sistance for lunar and planetary exploration spaceships.

By the late 1940's and into the mid-1950's, engineers were thinking in terms of still larger manned space stations and, at the same time, in terms of minimal-size unmanned satellites. At this point it became clear that long before huge space stations could be built, much highly valuable research could be carried out by small unmanned satellites. The results would be radioed down to earth. Moreover, large launch vehicles needed to orbit space stations were still many years away. Therefore attention was concentrated on unmanned earth satellites. Once, however, the Sputniks, Explorers, Vanguards, and other satellites of the late 1950's and early 1960's had been successfully orbited, interest in space stations revived.

MSOL'S, MOSS'S, MORL'S, LORL'S, MSS'S

By the mid-1960's, smaller and more realistic space-station designs began to appear. These new designs were for crews numbering no more than half a dozen to a few dozen men. Typical of the names given to them were MSOL for manned scientific orbital laboratory, MOSS for manned orbital space station, and MORL for manned orbital research laboratory.

As designed, the MORL had a useful lifetime in space of at least five years. It had two independently pressurized compartments connected by an air lock. The air lock is an airtight chamber in which air pressure can be regulated to permit transfer of people and material from an environment with one air pressure to an environment with a different pressure. The larger of the compartments was to contain a control deck from which most of the experiments would be conducted, an internal centrifuge that would create short periods of artificial gravity, and living quarters. The smaller compartment was designed as a hangar where cargo from ferry vehicles would be transferred, and for use in other support activities.

Somewhat larger space-station designs inevitably appeared—but not too much larger. One was the 24- to 36-man LORL, or large orbital research laboratory, and another was the MSS, a 36-man multipurpose space station. MSS consisted of three experiment and crew modules, a hangar for arriving and departing ferry craft, and a zero-gravity laboratory.

INTEGRAL AND MODULAR DESIGNS

Beginning in the spring of 1969, the U.S. National Aeronautics and Space Ad-

The cargo bay doors of the Shuttle swing open when orbit is achieved, to expose the Spacelab—whose pressurized laboratory section is shown in cutaway form. Up to four scientists will make up the Spacelab crew, and each crew will spend up to 30 days in space, working around the clock on 12-hour shifts. The huge cargo bay is 18 m (60 ft) long and 4.5 m (15 ft) wide.

ministration (NASA) and its industrial contractors concentrated their efforts on two basic types of space station. One design calls for a large, "all-in-one" *integral* station that could be placed in orbit by large launch vehicles of the Saturn 5 class. The other design is based on the *assembly-in-orbit* modular approach. Many small modules are carried aloft by space shuttles and are then assembled, or brought together, into a single unit. The core module, or main part, of an integral station, incidentally, could also receive separately orbited small modules, so, clearly, a combination of the two designs is possible.

The core module, the basic element of a 12-man integral station, would typically be a cylinder, 10 meters (33 ft) in diameter and 15 meters (50 ft) long. The cylinder would include six or seven docking ports for ferry craft, four internal decks, and a main pressurized area at each end. A central tunnel would connect the decks as well as air-lock facilities placed between the two main pressurized compartments. A tunnel would also lead to the emergency room where the astronauts would seek protection during periods of strong solar flare activity. During such periods tremendous explosions on the sun release massive electrical discharges.

The advantage of having the station divided into two pressurized compartments is that a mission could continue even if one of the compartments became damaged and had to be evacuated. Each pressure compartment would have two escape routes. All hatches would be large enough for space-suited crewmen to pass through without difficulty.

The other design—the modular, or assembly-in-orbit, design—became attractive to NASA planners once they realized that reusable space shuttles would be available by the early 1980's. Shuttles will be able to carry individual passenger, cargo and experiment modules into orbit. Once in orbit these modules may be assembled into the space station proper, or be prepared for detached "free-flying" service, or simply be unloaded and made ready for return to earth. Thus, at any one time, a modular space station might consist of its permanent living and experiment modules, a recently docked cargo or passenger module, and one or more temporarily docked free-flying modules. When attached, these modules would use the main station's electrical and other subsystems, but otherwise would be on their own.

Free-flying modules would house experiments that require extremely precise "pointing" control. The experiments must be isolated from contaminating gases and radiations produced by the station proper and by arriving and departing shuttles. All modules would be protected against

Manned observations of the earth from the vantage point of space will provide much-needed information on resources and the environment. Here a composite photo of the Middle Atlantic states.

micrometeoroids by "bumpers" placed over the pressurized compartments. Micrometeoroids are small solid particles traveling through space.

One advantage of a modular space station is that its individual modules can be returned to earth by shuttle for repair, maintenance and modification. The shuttle can also be used to carry new supplies to the station in cargo modules. These cargo modules can return to earth with exposed film, instruments needing repairs, and the like.

Rotating crews can travel in passenger modules. Should an emergency occur, a shuttle can be readied, launched and be on hand at the space station in orbit within 48 hours. For even more rapid service, a special Apollo rocket could be stored in a docking port at all times, ready to carry back to earth at least part of the crew—for example, an astronaut requiring immediate medical attention on earth.

SELECTION OF ORBIT

The orbit of a space station will have to be above the earth's atmosphere, yet below the Van Allen radiation belts, a band of intense radiation surrounding the earth. Circular orbits between 250 and 275 nautical miles at an angle of 50° to 55° to the equator turn out to be the best for space stations and allow the best observation of the earth.

ON BOARD THE SPACE STATION

Whether integral or modular, the space station includes a number of specialized areas. Among the areas are:

Living quarters that include sleeping rooms, toilet and washing facilities, individual study areas, clothing storage space, and medical facilities.

Wardroom and galley, where food is stored and prepared and the crew eats, relaxes, and exercises.

General-purpose area, where "everyday" types of experiments are conducted and equipment is checked over.

Command, control and data-management center to handle all communications to and from the space station. Computer systems, automatic checkout systems, and various on-board consoles and displays related to routine operations of space stations, free-flying modules and ferry craft are also used.

Storage for spare parts and miscellaneous supplies.

Provision for artificial gravity, if it is required.

SPACE-STATION SUBSYSTEMS

In addition to the main areas described a space station may have many subordinate systems that make it possible for the crew to carry out its many activities over long periods of time. The principal subsystems of a space station are:

Attitude, pointing and position control. These subsystems maintain the station precisely in the desired orbit and angle. They point cameras, telescopes and other sensors at a particular subject. The main elements of these subsystems are momentum wheels and an array of small rocket engines placed outside the station.

Electric power. These subsystems provide, control and distribute electric power to the space station proper and to any free-flying modules that may be temporarily docked to the space station. The source of electric power can be either a solar-cell array or an internal nuclear reactor. Solar-cell arrays convert the rays of the sun into electric power. This system must, however, be complemented with electrochemical batteries. These batteries will provide electric power when the orbiting space station is passing through the shadow of the earth and its solar cells are not receiving any direct sunlight.

Environmental control and life support. These subsystems furnish the astronauts with an appropriate environment. They will provide for oxygen and nitrogen gas storage and supply, for temperature and humidity control, for carbon-dioxide control, for water and waste management, for food management, and for hygiene.

Information handling. These subsystems display and communicate information on overall space-station operations, flight control, experiments, scheduling and many other activities. To ensure full-time contact with earth-based mission-control centers, communications from an orbiting space station will be routed through communications satellites.

USES OF SPACE STATIONS

In a 12-man space-station crew, three or four members will be needed to operate a typical integral or modular space station. The other eight or nine persons will thus be able to perform research and to conduct studies. Non-astronaut scientists and engineers are the "users" of the space station, and are supported by the crew.

Work in future space stations will build on research completed in February 1974 aboard the three-man Skylab orbital laboratory. Astronomers, for example, plan to conduct experiments to study X rays and other energy sources, as well as the sun and other stars. Earth-observation work will include a careful study of many of the earth's surface features; special mapping assignments; inventory of the earth's nonrenewable and renewable resources; and global environment studies. The goals of the communications and navigation research facility are to serve international requirements for worldwide communications between ground, ocean, airborne, and spaceborne terminals. Such research should also improve ground, ocean, air, and space navigation and traffic control.

Space stations will be ideal for making advanced studies in materials science and for making studies of manufacturing in the zero-gravity space environment. Scientists will try to work out on-board processing methods for new materials and products. This, in turn, may someday lead to commercial manufacturing operations in orbit.

The life sciences will by no means be neglected. A large number of space facilities and activities have been proposed to permit basic biological research to be carried out. For example, biologists are eager to study how changes in gravity affect living organisms, how differences in day-night cycles can change the functioning of an organism, how organisms age in space, and many other questions. Space biologists will also try to determine how to use the space environment to help advance medicine, agriculture, and health.

Education will also greatly benefit from space stations. In the future, scientists and other specialists will be able to broadcast and televise summaries of their findings directly into the world's schoolrooms.

FUTURE SPACE STATIONS

After the establishment of a modular space station, it will be possible to move individual modules into higher orbits—including the 35,680-kilometer (22,300-mi) geosynchronous orbit—by auxiliary spacecraft called *space tugs.* Tugs contain a special propulsion system that allows them to move from one orbit to another. They can carry space-station modules all the way to orbits around the moon. Such modules, stacked up to form a two- or three-stage rocket, may also propel unmanned spacecraft from earth orbit to an orbit around the planet Mars.

In due time, 12-man stations will almost certainly be expanded, and eventually 50- to 100-man stations may be established in orbit around the earth. Since crews and researchers will most likely spend many months at a time in the space stations, the living and dining areas of the station may be provided with artificial gravity for convenience. Still further in the future may come orbital hospitals, hotels and recreational facilities. Who knows—perhaps zero-gravity gymnasts will follow up where the Skylab astronauts left off and someday perform acrobatic stunts in orbit for television audiences all over the world. Whatever can be done in space stations probably will be done□

SELECTED READINGS

Into the Unknown: The Story of Space Shuttles and Space Stations by Don Dwiggins. Golden Gate, 1971.

"Orbital Stations: Aims and Tasks" by B. Petrov. *Space World,* February 1973.

"Space to Grow: There's Plenty of Room Beyond the Exosphere" by Paul T. Libassi. *The Sciences,* July/August 1974.

A safety check precedes launchings in model-rocket meets. The range safety officer, left, has finished his inspection, and he hands the rocket to a contestant, who will place it on a launchpad. The scale, foreground, is used to make sure that rockets do not exceed weight limits.

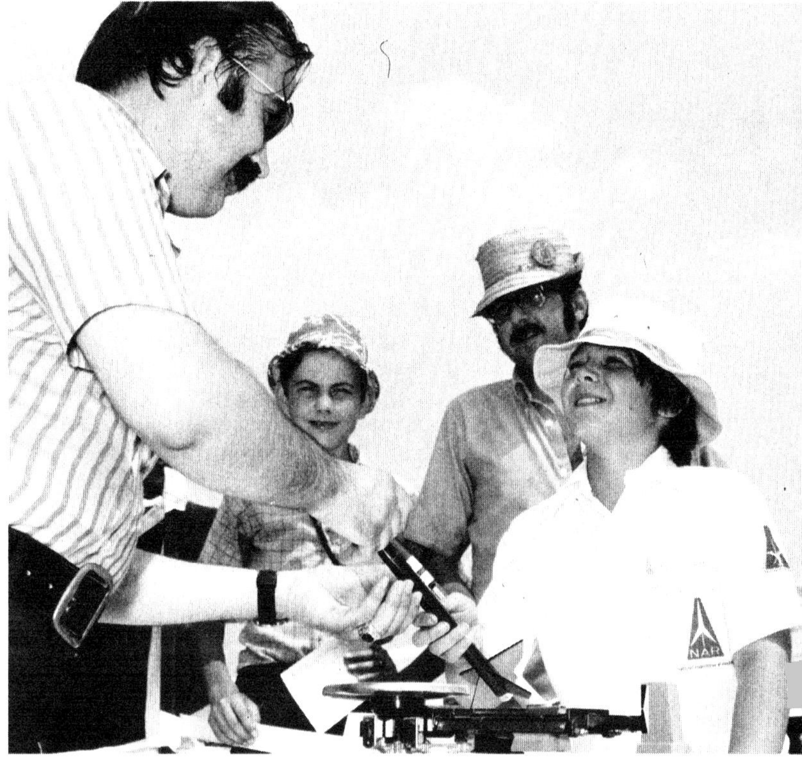

Rockets as a Hobby

By Norman J. Ward

"FIVE . . . four . . . three . . . two . . . one . . . Ignition!" Liftoff! Another safe and successful launch! At Cape Canaveral, Florida? At Wallops Island, Virginia? At Point Mugu, California? No, at none of these famous rocket-launching sites. This launch took place in the small playground of a local school. Here, in miniature, the excitement of the liftoff of a full-scale rocket has been duplicated by model rocketeers.

The little rocket shoots skyward, at speeds of up to 500 km (300 mi) an hour, until it reaches the peak of its flight. Suddenly a large, colorful parachute is ejected and spreads out. The spent rocket begins its slow, graceful descent to earth, the parachute billowing in the breeze.

This is a scene from model rocketry, a safe, enjoyable, and educational hobby for young and old alike, for the beginner and for the aerospace engineer. It is also a hobby that is growing in popularity. There are rocketry clubs to join, and national and international competitions to take part in. These clubs emphasize safety. Gone are the amateur rocketry experiments of earlier years, which were often hazardous. With the regulations in force today, modern model rocketry is both fun and safe.

MANY KINDS OF MODEL ROCKETS

Model rockets differ as much among themselves in design and purpose as their full-scale counterparts do. They can have one stage (single-stage) or more than one stage. They can be made to carry payloads.

They can be designed as aerodynamic lifting vehicles—vehicles that use their surfaces for support in the air, as airplanes do, as they descend through the atmosphere.

Single-stage rockets. The simplest rocket to build and fly is the single-stage rocket. A beginner who buys such a model in kit form can learn the basic principles of construction, launch, flight and recovery. After this introduction to rocketry, the rocketeer can then begin to design his own models and experiment with them, learning how to make them fly higher and longer and more efficiently.

Multistage rockets. Models with more than one stage present new challenges to the rocketeer. For example, a two-stage rocket is launched by the first stage. After this stage "burns out" (runs out of fuel), the second-stage engine ignites and boosts the rocket to even higher altitude. Meanwhile, the first stage drops off. Unlike the ignition of the first stage, the ignition of the second stage takes place automatically while the rocket is in flight.

Rockets with payloads. Any instrument or object placed on board a rocket, other than its basic components, is called a payload. In model rocketry, payloads can be designed to offer the rocketeer the same kinds of problems that aerospace engineers meet when they design rockets to carry men or complex instrument packages into space. For example, a rocketeer can send a chicken egg aloft on his model to see if it can be returned gently to earth without breaking. Or he can test his model with payloads of differing weights, to see how high they can be lifted with one particular kind of rocket engine.

In advanced model rocketry, payloads may consist of instruments to collect environmental information and radio transmitters to send it back, still or motion-picture cameras to take pictures during flight, and so forth. In fact, there are as many payload possibilities as there are ideas in the rocketeer's head.

Booster-gliders and rocket-gliders. Some model rockets are designed so that they lift off from the launchpad in the usual way, but return to earth using aerodynamic lift, as airplanes and gliders do. In the case of the booster-glider, the booster portion of the launch vehicle launches the rocket portion, releases it, and then glides back to earth. In the case of the rocket-glider, the entire launch vehicle is returned to earth by means of aerodynamic lift. Such systems combine both rocketry and aeronautics, and provide the rocketeer with challenging problems in design.

Scale models. As a rocketeer practices his hobby he may want to construct working scale models of actual rockets such as the Nike-Tomahawk, Saturn V, or Aerobee. The craftsmanship that this requires is another of the challenges of model rocketry.

CONSTRUCTING A MODEL ROCKET

Model rockets are made of lightweight materials such as balsa wood, cardboard and plastic. They contain no substantial metal parts. These materials provide maximum strength with minimum weight—a desirable goal in rockets large or small—and greatly increase safety.

Basic rocket parts. Rocket parts are available at most hobby shops, either individually or in kits; or they may be purchased directly from the manufacturers by mail. Except for the engines, rocket parts can also be made from scratch by the modeler. Although they may differ greatly in appearance and purpose, most models have the following main components (see Figure 1).

(1) Nose cone: the front end of the rocket, shaped so as to lower air resistance when the rocket is in flight.

(2) Body tube: the frame to which all the other components are attached.

(3) Launch lug: the device on the body tube that helps to guide the rocket as it leaves the launchpad.

(4) Fins: the rudderlike surfaces that stabilize the rocket's flight.

(5) Recovery device: the system used to slow the rocket's descent so that it can land softly and be used again. Parachutes, streamers, and airfoils (gliders) are the most common recovery devices.

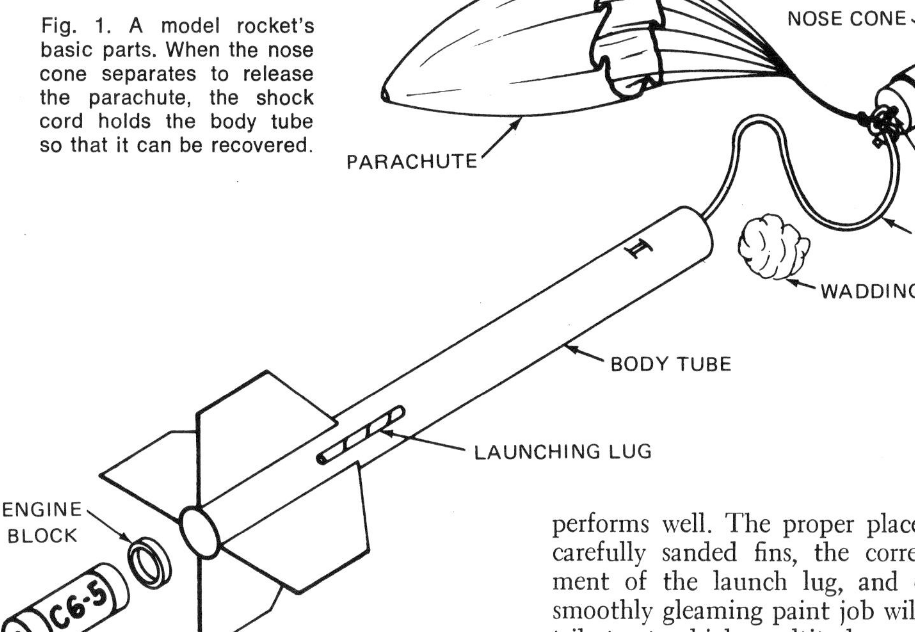

Fig. 1. A model rocket's basic parts. When the nose cone separates to release the parachute, the shock cord holds the body tube so that it can be recovered.

(6) Engine block: the device used to hold the engine securely in position while the rocket is in flight.

(7) Engine: the rocket's source of power. The engines most often used in simple rocketry burn a solid fuel and are made of nonmetallic parts. They are commercially manufactured and are not reusable.

Putting the parts together. For the rocketeer's first "bird"—as rockets are often called—a simple, single-stage kit from any model-rocket manufacturer is recommended. All of the parts except the engine are furnished in the kit, and the instructions are simple and detailed.

Whether building from a kit or from scratch, only the simplest tools and equipment are needed in addition to the construction material: sandpaper, glue, a modeling knife, scissors, a pencil, a ruler, and paint for finishing.

The building of a rocket should always be a careful, deliberate process, done without hurry. The final result will be a display model to be proud of, and one that performs well. The proper placement of carefully sanded fins, the correct alignment of the launch lug, and even the smoothly gleaming paint job will all contribute to higher altitudes and faster speeds.

MORE FACTS ABOUT ROCKET ENGINES

Engines for a model rocket, whether it is built from a kit or constructed from components, must be purchased separately. The hobby shop where the kit or components are bought normally will have a large selection of engines. If not, engines can be ordered by mail directly from the manufacturer. Each kit will list the recommended engine, or engines, for that particular rocket. For the modeler who wants to design his own rocket, using the components of his choice, engine selection is more difficult. This modeler must rely on the experience gained through building many rockets from kits in which the proper engine is identified. He may also seek guidance in engine selection from an experienced rocketeer, rely on the advice of a hobby dealer, or obtain a chart of recommended engines from one of the manufacturers.

There are only two acceptable kinds of engines for model rocketry: solid propellant and cold propellant. Both kinds are commercially manufactured. Approved engines are tested for safety and certified by the National Association of Rocketry (NAR), a nonprofit organization affiliated with the National Aeronautic Association (NAA). In cold-propellant engines, a pressurized liquid is used that is noncombustible, nontoxic and noncorrosive.

Performance characteristics. The operation of all rocket engines is based on Newton's third law of motion: for every action there is an equal and opposite reaction. Like the balloon that zooms wildly around as air rushes out when it is released, the rocket engine is propelled forward by the force of escaping gases. The rocket engine provides a stronger force, however, and the rocket's body tube is streamlined for flight through the air.

A rocketeer wants to know the average force, or *thrust,* provided by the engine he uses. He also wants to know the engine's total power, or *impulse,* and how long the rocket will coast before it ejects its recovery device. This information appears on all commercially available rocket engines. When solid-propellant engines—the type most widely used in model rocketry—are tested and certified to conform to exact NAR specifications, each engine is given a code that describes its performance capabilities.

The rocket engine in Figure 2 is an example. The first symbol represents the total impulse range of the engine, given in a metric unit of force called a *newton.* (One newton is equal to 4.448 pounds.) The following chart lists the impulse

Fig. 2. A solid-propellant rocket engine, manufactured to exact specifications, is coded with a letter and numbers to show its capabilities.

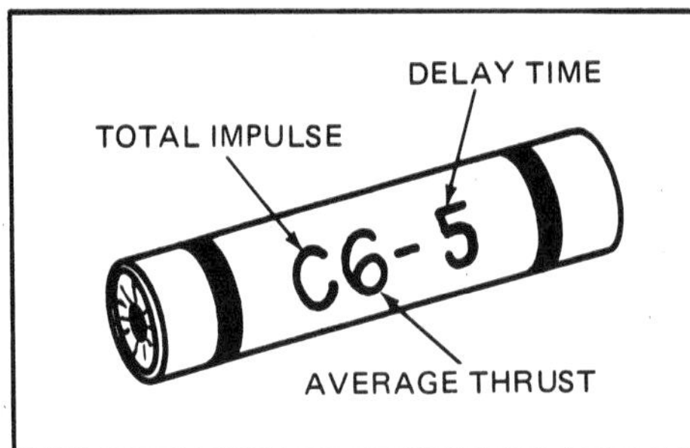

ratings of various solid-propellant engines, together with their symbols. Thus the engine in Figure 2 has a total impulse of C, or 5.01 to 10.00 newton seconds. (Newton seconds represent the average thrust force in newtons, multiplied by the number of seconds that the thrust lasts.)

SYMBOL ON ENGINE	RANGE OF TOTAL IMPULSE IN NEWTON SECONDS
½A	0.626 to 1.25
A	1.26 to 2.50
B	2.51 to 5.00
C	5.01 to 10.00
D	10.01 to 20.00
E	20.01 to 40.00
F	40.01 to 80.00

The second symbol gives the average thrust of the engine, rounded off to the nearest newton. The third symbol is the length of time, in seconds, that the delay charge burns. The main purpose of the delay charge is to act as a fuse between the propellant and the ejection charge, and so allow the rocket to continue coasting upward before the recovery device is ejected.

Engine safety. Rocket engines can be used with complete safety, but proper care should be observed in handling and storing these devices. On the other hand, the "basement bomber"—the experimenter who thinks that mixing his own propellant is more fun—is not only endangering his life, he is also missing the challenge and excitement of designing a "bird" that will fly higher and stay up longer than the rocket of a competitor who is using the same kind of engine.

GETTING READY FOR THE LAUNCH

Once the "bird" has been built and the engine selected, the next step is to get the rocket into the air.

Safety rules. Just as there are safety considerations in the choice of construction materials and the use of engines approved by the NAR, so are there safety precautions to be observed in the launch

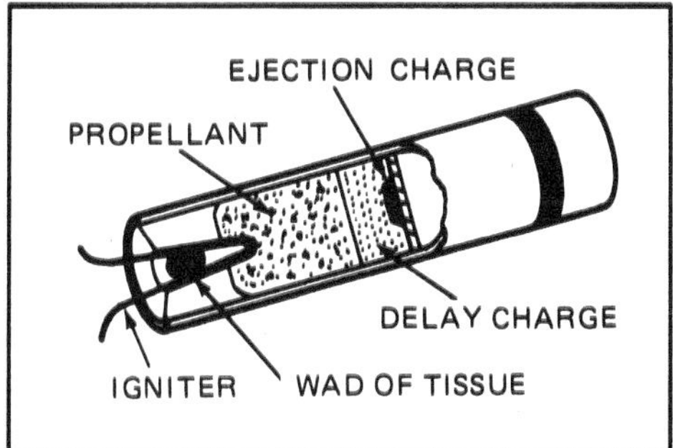

Fig. 3. Just before launching, an igniter made of Nichrome wire is inserted into the engine until it touches the propellant.

operation. These precautions are simple and are based on common sense.

(1) Solid-propellant engines must be ignited by remote control and electrical means. The rocketeer should be at least 5 m (16 ft) away from the launch point. Cold-propellant engines can be ignited by either mechanical or electrical means.

(2) The launch area must be cleared of people and be free of any materials that burn easily. Generally speaking, the length of the shortest side of the launch area should be no less than one fourth the maximum height that the rocket is expected to reach.

(3) The wind should be less than 30 km (20 mi) per hour. This can also save a lot of running after a gently descending rocket that is being swiftly carried away by a high wind.

(4) Some means must be used to direct the rocket so that it rises vertically after takeoff, until stabilized flight is attained. The usual and easiest method is to use a rod that guides the rocket by means of a launch lug.

(5) Beginning five seconds before liftoff, a loud, clear countdown should be conducted to alert spectators that a rocket is about to be launched.

There may also be local safety conditions that apply in a given launch area. For example, a local limit may be placed on a rocket's maximum altitude.

Launch facilities. Since solid-propellant engines are to be ignited by electrical means only, each engine is furnished by the manufacturer with an igniter made of Nichrome wire. When the rocket is ready to be placed on the launchpad, the igniter is inserted into the engine until it touches the propellant. It is then held in place with a piece of wadded tissue or tape, and the engine is inserted into the rocket. The rocket is now "prepped" and ready for the launchpad (Figure 3 shows igniter).

The launchpad consists of a launcher base; a launch rod to direct the rocket vertically on liftoff; a metal exhaust deflector to direct the hot exhaust gases away from the launcher base; and an electrical ignition system. The rod should be made of steel, 3 mm (⅛ in) in diameter and at least 1 m (3 ft) long, and mounted firmly on a wooden base. The rod is always positioned more or less upright and never more than 30 degrees from the vertical. The exhaust deflector can be a coffee-can top with a small hole cut in the center. It is set at the bottom of the launch rod, and a small rock can hold it in place (as in Figure 4).

Ignition. The electrical ignition system can be either a 6- or a 12-volt portable battery, or a car battery (which can remain in the car). When the igniter re-

Fig. 4. Launchpad assembly for a model rocket. The rocketeer at the firing switch stands at least 5 m (16 ft) from the launch point.

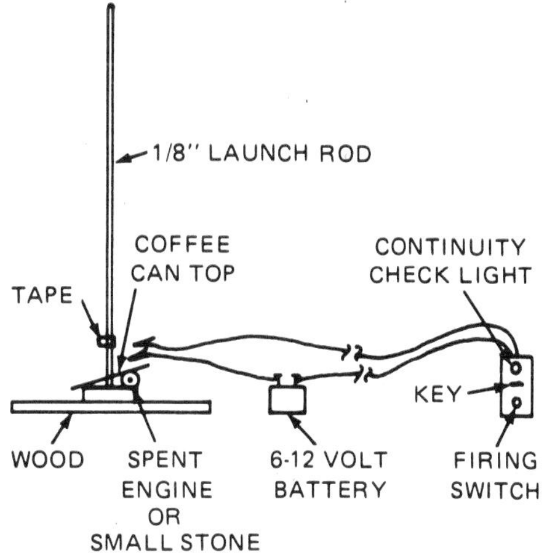

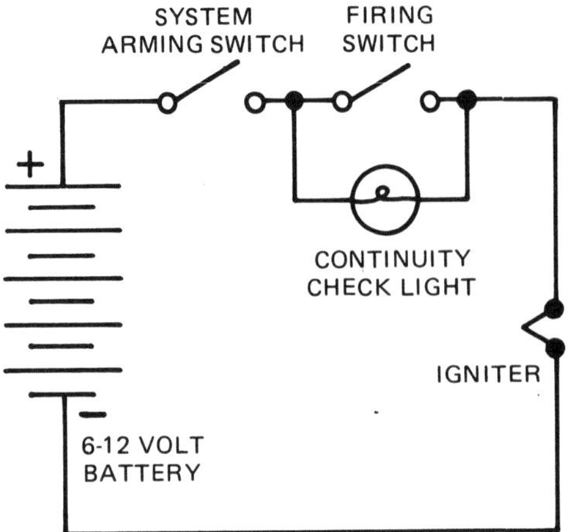

Fig. 5. A typical electrical ignition system has one switch that arms the system and another that launches the model rocket.

ceives an electric current from the battery it becomes red-hot, which causes the propellant to ignite.

Figure 5 illustrates a typical ignition system. It has two switches, one to arm the system and the other to launch the rocket. The two switches are another safety consideration, to ensure that the rocket is not launched accidentally. The arming switch is usually a removable plug or key that can be carried to the pad by the rocketeer. When the plug is inserted, a check light will glow to indicate that the igniter is properly hooked up. The push-button switch is then depressed to launch the rocket.

THE MOMENT OF LIFTOFF

The launchpad has been installed, launch control has been located at the correct distance from the launchpad, and the arming plug has been removed. The rocketeer now places the "prepped" bird on the pad, sliding the launch lug over the launch rod and firmly attaching micro clips (small, spring-loaded clips) to the exposed ends of the igniter (Figure 6).

The rocketeer moves back to launch control, and the launch area is checked to see that no low-flying aircraft are overhead. All persons in the area, having been advised that a launch is imminent, stand back of the firing position. The arming plug is inserted, the check light is checked, and the countdown begins.

"Five . . . four . . . three . . . two . . . one . . . ignition!" The thrill of a beautiful launch is ample reward for the time spent in making the rocket and ensuring that all safety considerations have been met. The ohs and ahs of admiring observers are only a well-deserved bonus.

SAFETY CODES

The word "safety" has been emphasized thus far. This is not to scare the reader off or make him think that model rocketry is unsafe. Rather, it is to reassure him that the hobby—when conducted according to commonsense safety rules—is as safe as stamp collecting and safer than any contact sport. Millions of rockets are launched each year without any serious accidents. The NAR provides a total liability protection of $1 million to its members at no charge, yet in its more than 16

Fig. 6. When a rocket is ready for launch, it is placed upon its launchpad by sliding the launch lug over the launch rod.

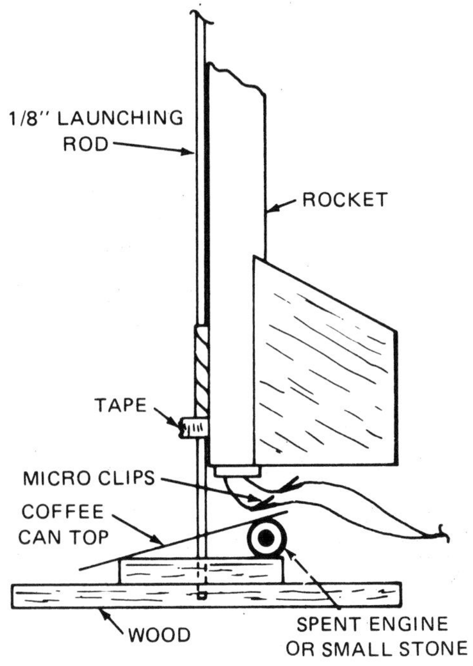

years, of existence there has never been a major claim against this policy.

Close attention has been paid to setting up safety standards for model rocketry. The codes given below were developed by the NAR and have been endorsed by the Hobby Industry Association of America and makers of supplies and equipment.

SOLID–PROPELLANT SAFETY CODE

(1) My model rockets will be made of lightweight materials such as paper, wood, plastic and rubber, without any metal structural parts.

(2) I will use only preloaded, factory-made model rocket engines, in the manner recommended by the manufacturer. I will not change in any way or attempt to reload these engines.

(3) I will always use a recovery system in my model rockets, which will return them safely to the ground so that they may be flown again.

(4) My model rockets will weigh no more than 454 g (16 oz) at liftoff, and the engines will contain no more than 113 g (4 oz) of propellant.

(5) I will check the stability of my model rockets before their first flights, except when launching models of already proven stability.

(6) The system I use to launch my model rockets will be remote-controlled and electrically operated, and will contain a switch that will return to "off" when released. I will remain at least 3 m (10 ft) from any rocket that is being launched.

(7) I will not let anyone approach a model rocket on a launcher until I have made sure that either the safety interlock key has been removed or the battery has been disconnected from the launcher.

(8) I will not launch my model rocket in high winds; near buildings, power lines, tall trees or low-flying aircraft; or under any conditions that might be dangerous to people or property.

(9) My model rockets will always be launched from a cleared area, free of any materials that burn easily, and I will use only nonflammable recovery wadding in my rockets.

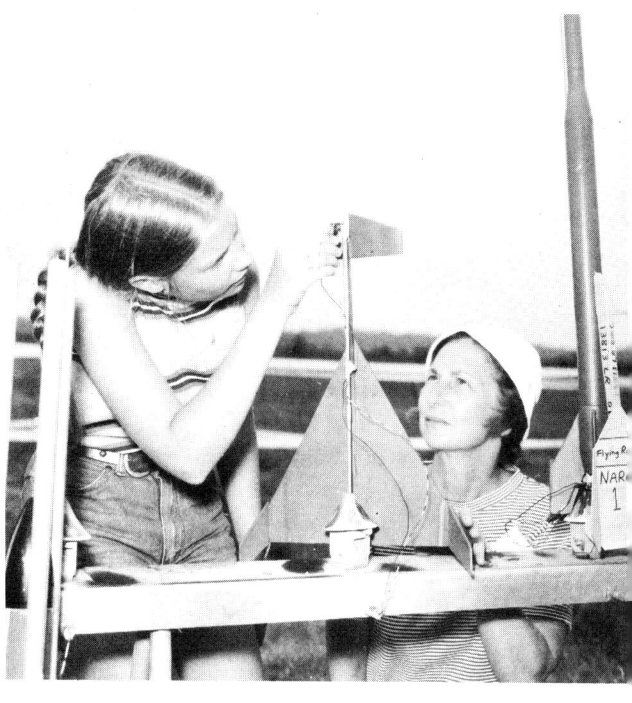

A rocketeer attaches micro clips to the igniter of her booster-glider. The pad is a multiple unit used in competitions.

(10) My launcher will have a jet deflector device to prevent the engine exhaust from hitting the ground directly.

(11) To prevent accidental eye injury, I will always place the launcher so the end of the rod is above eye level, or cap the end of the rod with my hand when approaching it. I will never place my head or body over the launching rod. When my launcher is not in use, I will always store it so that the launch rod is not in an upright position.

(12) I will never attempt to recover my rocket from a power line or from other dangerous places.

(13) I will not launch rockets so that their flight paths will carry them against targets on the ground, and will never use an explosive warhead or a payload that is intended to be flammable. My launching device will always be pointed within 30 degrees of the vertical.

(14) When conducting research activities with unproven designs or methods, I

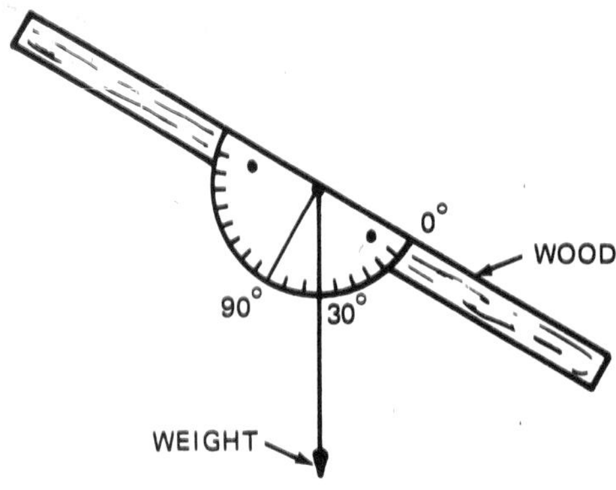

Fig. 7. A sighting instrument for an altitude-measuring experiment is made out of a protractor, a piece of wood, and string.

will, when possible, determine their reliability through prelaunch tests. I will conduct launchings of unproven designs in complete isolation from persons who are not participating in the actual launching.

COLD-PROPELLANT SAFETY CODE

(1) I will use only factory-made model rocket engines, in the manner recommended by the manufacturer. I will reload cold-propellant rocket engines only with the propellant that is recommended by the manufacturer of the engine.

(2) I will always use a recovery system in my model rockets, which will safely return them so that they may be used again. I will conduct preflight tests to ensure that the recovery system functions properly before launching the rocket.

(3) My model rockets will weigh no more than 454 g (16 oz) at liftoff.

(4) I will check the stability of my model rockets before their first flights, except when I am launching models of proven design.

(5) I will not launch my model rocket in high winds; near buildings, power lines, tall trees or low-flying aircraft; or under any conditions that might be dangerous to people or property. I will never attempt to recover a model rocket from a power line or other dangerous places.

(6) To prevent accidental eye injury I will always place the launcher so that the end of the rod is above eye level, or cap the end of the rod with my hand when approaching it. I will never place my head or body over the launch rod. When my launcher is not in use, I will always store it so that the launch rod is not in an upright position.

(7) I will not launch rockets so that their flight paths will carry them against targets on the ground, and will never use an explosive warhead or a payload that is intended to be flammable. My launching device will always be pointed within 30 degrees of the vertical.

(8) I will never store or leave a loaded rocket untended. I will always keep a loaded rocket on a launcher or firmly restrained. I will never point a loaded rocket or its rocket nozzle at anyone, nor allow anyone to be in the flight path of a rocket during launch preparations.

(9) I will never use metal nose cones or metal fins.

EXPERIMENTS FOR BEGINNERS

It is a thrilling, unforgettable experience to build your own rocket and to savor the excitement of liftoff, a beautiful flight and a successful recovery. However, there is much more to model rocketry than this. There is the challenge of conducting real experiments with the rockets. The following simple experiments will add new excitement to activities at the launchpad. With growing experience in rocketry, the experiments can become more and more sophisticated in design and purpose.

Experiment 1. Find out how high your rocket actually flies. Using readily available equipment, you can learn the answer quite easily and with a fair degree of accuracy.

You will need a straight piece of wood, a protractor, a piece of string, a small weight such as a stone, and graph paper. You will also need the help of a friend.

Construct a sighting instrument by gluing the protractor to the side of the piece of wood as accurately as possible, so that the straight side of the protractor runs parallel to the length of the stick.

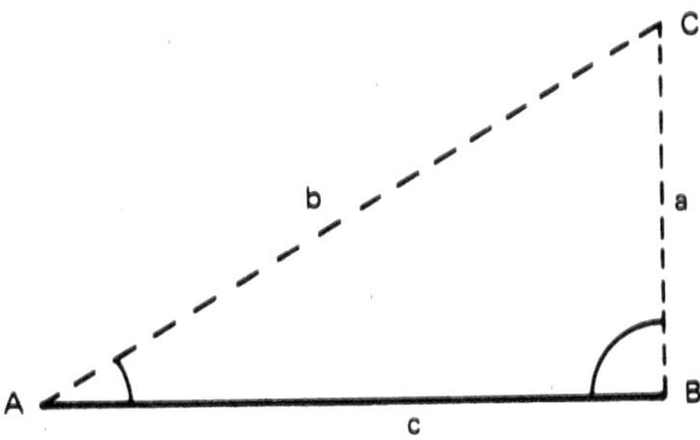

Fig. 8. In the graph of the altitude-measurement experiment, length *c* and angles *A* and *B* are known. Height *a* is easily determined.

Tie the weight on the string, and affix the other end of the string to the midpoint on the straight side of the protractor. (This can be done with glue, or by drilling a small hole through the protractor and wood and then passing the string through it.) The finished instrument should look like Figure 7.

Hand the instrument to your friend and have him position himself 150 m (500 ft) from the launch site, making certain that he is within hearing distance of the countdown. As the rocket is launched, he must follow its flight by looking along the straight side of the sighting instrument. As the rocket attains its peak and starts to descend, he must immediately take note of the reading on the protractor where the string intersects it.

On the graph paper, draw what has happened. A good scale would be 1 centimeter = 100 meters or 1 inch = 100 feet. Your drawing should look like Figure 8, with A the point where your friend stood, B the point of launch, angle A the angle read from the protractor, and angle *B* a 90 degree angle (assume that the rocket went straight up). You know the length of line *c*, and you can now draw lines *a* and *b*. The point where they intersect, C, is the highest point reached by the rocket, and the length of *a* on the graph will give you this height.

Experiment 2. Find out how fast the rocket flies. This is easily determined once you have done the first experiment. The same equipment is used, with the addition of a stopwatch (or a watch with a sweep-second hand) held by another friend.

Follow the same procedure as in the first experiment, but have the friend with the watch time the rocket from the moment of liftoff to the moment when it reaches its peak altitude. The rest is simple arithmetic. The peak altitude divided by the time in seconds gives you the rocket's average speed in feet or meters per second. From this you can figure out the speed in miles or kilometers per hour.

This result is the rocket's average speed. Actually the rocket goes faster during the thrust stage and slows down during the coasting stage of its journey.

Experiment 3. Find out how fast and how high your rocket can be made to go.

There are many ways to increase the efficiency of a model rocket. Construction techniques can be improved, nose cones redesigned, fins made more aerodynamically efficient, and so forth. In this experiment, you will test the effect that engines of differing powers have on your rocket's performance. You will need a well-built, simple single-stage rocket, three engines (a ½A, an A, and a B impulse engine of the same size and from the same company) and the equipment and friends you used before.

Using the same techniques as before, launch the same rocket three times, each time with a different engine. As expected, the larger the engine, the greater the altitude and the higher the speed attained. But when you study the results—perhaps plotting them on a graph—see whether the increase in power produces a comparable increase in altitude and speed. For example, did approximately twice as much power loft the rocket approximately twice as high and at twice the speed? Or were the effects somewhat less? See whether you can tell at what point it appears that the rocket would have to be redesigned to take full advantage of the greater power of the larger engine.

This experiment can form the basis for many fascinating future experiments in model rocketry. As you learn more about designing rockets, you can change nose cones, fins and tails, individually and in combination, to see what effects these changes have. Later, you can begin to install payloads for experiments in photography, radio signaling and so forth. Such experiments, even when done with model rockets, could lead to new discoveries in the aerospace field.

INTERNATIONAL COMPETITIONS

Model rocketry, like any other activity, is enjoyed most when shared with others of like interests. Rocketeering with an informal group of friends or classmates who have also discovered the fun of building and launching rockets can increase the enjoyment of all. The friendly spirit of competition at the launch site adds to the interest and challenge of the hobby.

If you have enjoyed this kind of relationship, why not form the group into a club, complete with bylaws and dedicated to the enjoyment of model rocketry in your area? Throw down the gauntlet! Challenge other individuals and groups to meet at your launch area or theirs. Gain the experience of competing individually and then as a group or club.

And, finally, become a member of the NAR. Enroll your club as a Chartered Section of the association, and compete as an individual or as a club on the national and international level.

The NAR, as an affiliate of the NAA, is the official body for the conduct of all model rocketry activities in the United States. Many local and regional contests are held each year throughout the country, and only NAR members are eligible to compete. The contest year culminates in the National Association of Rocketry Annual Meet, in which the national champions for each age group.

Competition at the international level is conducted under the sanction of the Federation Aeronautique Internationale (FAI). Every other year a world championship meet is held among the nations accredited to the FAI.

From individual rocketeering to being a member of a team on the international level may seem a long step. But each member of each year's U.S. rocket team started as an individual rocketeer, joined a club, competed on local, regional and national levels, and finally was selected to be a member of the U.S. International Model Rocketry Team. So from the time of your first rocket launch, your horizons in this fascinating hobby can be truly international□

Model Rocketry Manual by G. Harry Stine. Follett Publishing Co., 1970.

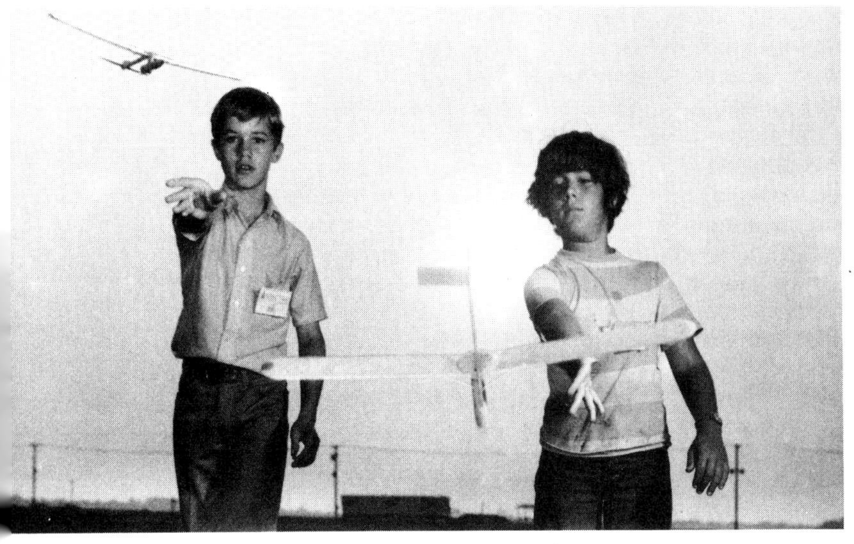

Rocket-gliders are tested for their gliding qualities with gentle hand tosses before they are submitted to the rigors of rocket launches at high speeds. These models are designed to return to earth by using their surfaces for support in the air as airplanes do.

Drawing by Richter

technology

contents

Probably signs like the ones in the above cartoon will never be seen in supermarket windows. But canned goods may indeed all be line-coded someday, for rapid computerized checkout service.

review of the year

technology

Even though 1974 was a year of widening inflation, some kinds of products actually became cheaper. The lower prices were made possible by rapid advances in technology in certain areas. Perhaps the most striking advances of all were made in the radically changing world of solid-state microelectronics.

Inexpensive Calculators and Computers. In recent years, manufacturers have been learning how to compress electronic circuitry into smaller and smaller areas. Thousands of transistors can now be combined into a single, tiny integrated circuit. As a result, a transistor that cost $15 in 1959 now costs a fraction of a cent, and the price of products such as pocket calculators, minicomputers, and digital watches actually declined during the past year. For example, the most simple pocket calculators—ones that only add, subtract, multiply, and divide—dropped from about $40 to as low as $15. Devices as inexpensive as this can be used in elementary school arithmetic classes and carried about for such purposes as shopping trips. More elaborate calculators are selling for as little as $100. As for small computers that have recently been developed, the Review of the Year in Computers and Mathematics describes one desk-sized system that is now on the market. A similar computer unit that has been designed for employment in schools is priced at less than $8,000.

Chrysler announced a computerized engine, called the electronic lean burn system, that eliminates the need for a catalytic converter. Two circuit boards operate two minicomputers that are sealed in a container on the outer rim of the air cleaner.

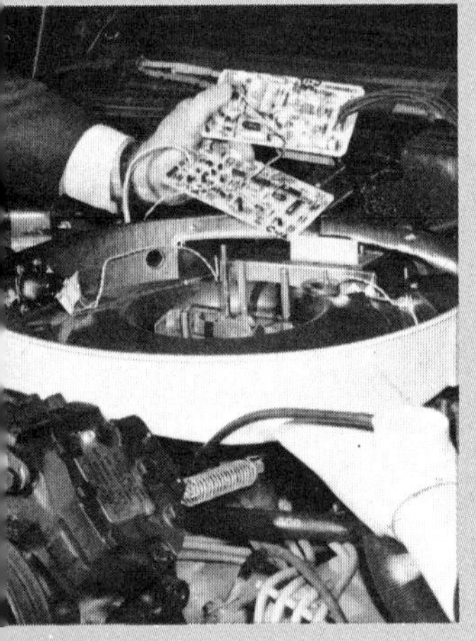

Microcomputer systems are cropping up everywhere. Electronic scales in post offices automatically compute the cost of mailing a package to any address. Computerized cash registers in stores can calculate the local sales tax, add up and print the bill, and record the information of the sale in their memory systems. A modified and computerized automobile engine has been ordered into production by Chrysler Corporation. An automobile fitted with this system will have a pair of very small computers mounted under its hood. The minicomputers will control the mixing of air and fuel in the engine and will instruct the spark plugs when to ignite the mixture. The aim is to combine maximum efficiency of performance with the lowest emission of pollutants into the environment. With this system the manufacturers claim to be able to avoid the use of catalytic converters, to which they have objected in the past. Another computerized device relating to automobiles is a computer-controlled automobile battery charger that was invented by workers at General Electric. When it is fully developed, the device will be able to bring a car battery to full charge within only an hour or two.

Finally, advances in microelectronics technology have greatly reduced the cost of solid-state digital watches. These watches, which use electronic number displays rather than the conventional dial face, were primarily a luxury item until 1974. Now some models are selling for less than $100, and factories are preparing to turn out the watches in large numbers. A digital watch is reliable and accurate, and it does not need to be taken in to a jeweler for periodic cleaning and adjustment. Electronic number displays are turning up with increasing frequency in other applications as well.

Energy Problems. Because of the energy crisis that flared up dramatically in 1973, there has been greatly increased interest in the development of technologies that can tap new sources of energy. But 1974 was a disappointing year in this respect. Many of the mammoth projects that had been proposed either fell behind schedule or were postponed indefinitely. In several instances the real stumbling block—besides the matter of soaring costs—was not any technological difficulty but the matter of environmental damage. For example, the oil-shale program under way in Colorado suffered from second thoughts, for reasons indicated in the Review of the Year in Energy. Similar problems of possible environmental damage are apparently plaguing the huge coal gasification plants that are also being planned for the western United States.

Solid-state digital wristwatches began appearing in larger volume in 1974. Seiko Time Corp. introduced this liquid crystal quartz model that displays hour, minute, and second.

It was not a good year for nuclear power, either. Nuclear plants ran into a variety of safety and equipment problems, while the nation's top energy project—the liquid-metal, fast-breeder reactor—sank deeply into trouble. The breeder reactor creates more nuclear fuel than it burns, a big advantage over existing reactors. It was to have become the primary source of new electrical power by the mid-1980's. However, the breeder program has long been under attack by environmentalists, for reasons described in the Review of the Year in Environmental Sciences. Technologically, as well, the breeder reactor has proved to be a tough nut to crack. Unexpected development costs have sent costs up to about $10 billion, more than four times higher than the government had estimated only one year earlier. It now looks as though the breeder reactor will not be generating commercial power until the 1990's, even if the environmental problems that the reactor presents are overcome in one way or another.

Transportation. Japan is moving ahead in the development of new forms of urban mass transportation. The Japanese government has invested money in a number of rapid transit projects in recent years. Now it is proceeding with one particular project, the CVS, or Computer-controlled Vehicle System. A city using this system is covered with a network of elevated ramps. Electronically propelled vehicles move along these ramps, guided by a track at the center of the ramp. The vehicles are controlled by a central computer. The small cars seat up to four persons and travel at about 40 km (25 mi) an hour. CVS is being installed in Tokyo. By 1985, the network may extend a total of 225 km (140 mi).

This computer-controlled vehicle system is now being tested in Tokyo.

In the meantime, the U.S. government's showcase "people-mover" system that was built in Morgantown, West Virginia, is still not operational. And it is still embroiled in controversies over rising costs and other matters. The model transit system was begun five years ago at a projected cost of $13.5 million. Thus far more than $57 million has been spent on it, and officials anticipate that $61 million more will be needed. So far the model project has not yet been completely abandoned. ■ In St. Louis, Missouri, plans for a computer-operated rapid transit system collapsed in 1974, because of cost considerations and a general lack of enthusiasm for the project. ■ In California, the Bay Area Rapid Transit System (BART) continues to function in the San Francisco-Oakland metropolitan area as an example of the type of computerized mass transit system that may be needed to save our cities from their ever-increasing traffic and pollution problems. However, BART itself is having some problems of its own. There have been several operating failures, and the cars break down more frequently than would be desired. Furthermore, people do not seem to be using the system in the numbers that had originally been hoped. Nevertheless, BART remains the most modern rapid transit system in the United States.

The popularity of cycling has increased dramatically in the last few years. There are now more than 70 million bikes in the United States.

Bicycles: Care and Maintenance

by Irene Cumming Kleeberg

UNTIL just a few years ago, most people who had a bicycle thought of it as being "just for fun," though they might have also reflected that it was a useful way of getting around town. Now, with our realization of the dangers of pollution, we know that bicycles are a means of transportation that doesn't interfere with the environment, that bike riding can indeed make the world a less-polluted place.

Bikes themselves have become better and more complicated in recent years. And, at the same time, more and more people have stopped depending on repairmen to fix things that go wrong with their bikes and are doing their own repairs. Using a book, you should be able to make these simple repairs yourself.

TO MINIMIZE PROBLEMS

Here, to begin with, are a few suggestions that will minimize repair problems on any bicycle.

First, make sure the bicycle you get is the right size for you—whatever its cost.

If you haven't reached your full growth yet, you'd probably be wise to wait until you do to get a fine racing bike. Why spend a lot of money on a bicycle you'll soon outgrow? Get a touring bike instead. If it's a boy's bike, make sure that you can straddle the bar on it with your toes on the ground. On a girl's bike, make sure you can reach the seat easily.

If you do have your full growth, you still have to be sure the frame size is right for you. A general rule is to divide your height by three to find out your correct frame size.

Frame sizes range from about 48 to 64 cm, or exactly 19 to 25 in in U.S. customary measures. Be sure to try the bike, though, before purchasing it. The formula may not apply if your legs are longer or shorter than average for your height. Girl's model racing bikes generally are not as good as those for boys and there is a much smaller selection of them.

Once you have a bike, don't let someone walk off with it. Buy a chain and lock for it when you buy the bike—or don't leave it without someone watching it.

If your town requires bicycle licenses, be sure to get one before you ride.

Car drivers, generally speaking, still aren't used to people riding bikes. This means you'll have to look out for them rather than counting on their looking out for you.

Regular maintenance of any bike will cut down on the need for repairs. Taking good care of your bike from the start will save you many headaches in the long run and will increase the pleasure you get out of bicycling.

PREVENTIVE MAINTENANCE

Oiling. There are a number of points on a bicycle that should regularly be given a small squirt of bicycle oil. You can buy the oil at a bicycle shop. Try to get the kind that comes in a can with its own spout. Don't use oil that you have around the house unless you are positive it is the right kind. The wrong kind of oil can interfere seriously with the operation of your bicycle.

Oil should be put in the oil holes on your bicycle. They are small holes at various points such as the hub of your wheels.

Bicycles with coaster brakes and three-speed bikes usually have an oil hole in the rear wheel hub. Put a few drops of oil into this hole about once a month.

On caliper brakes, oil the pivot bolt, which is between the brake arms, lightly about once a month. Remember to keep oil away from the wheels and the brake shoes.

The derailleur (for gear shifting when there are five or more speeds) is a complicated mechanism, but it can benefit from a little simple, regular care. Keep it clean. Put a drop of oil on the pivot bolts about once a month (3-in-1 oil will suffice).

Your bicycle—especially if it's one of the 10-speed or more derailleur types—should have a complete overhaul and be completely lubricated twice a year. Have this done at your bicycle shop.

Cleaning and Waxing. Keep your bicycle clean by wiping it off after it has been ridden in mud or rain. Wax the chromium and painted parts, using a good automobile wax. Put the wax on in thin light coats. Let it dry until it looks

Bicycle racing has become an important sport throughout the world. And amateurs now often have sophisticated racing bikes like the one used here by a professional track racer.

dull and then buff it until it shines. Regular waxing will keep your bicycle from being damaged by moisture and will also keep it looking handsome. Keep wax away from the wheels and brake shoes, of course, to avoid brake trouble.

REPAIR CHECKLIST

- Check the chain for damaged links. Be sure the fit of the chain is right—snug but not too tight. Keep the chain clean and lubricated.
- Check the brakes regularly. Be sure they brake evenly every time you use them. Keep the wheel and brake shoes free from grease or anything else that would interfere with quick stops. Replace the brakes when worn.
- Make sure the seat is adjusted correctly for your height. Check the nut that holds the seat to the bicycle regularly to be sure it has not come loose.
- Adjust handlebars to the right height for you. Check the nut that holds the handlebars on to be sure it has not come loose.
- Be sure you have a reflector on your bicycle. Check to be sure that it is securely fastened to the bike. If you lose the reflector, replace it at once.
- Check the spokes on the wheels of your bike regularly to ensure that the wheels will stay in alignment. If you have any broken spokes do not ride the bike until they have been replaced.
- Examine your wheels to be sure that they are in proper alignment. If they are not, correct the problem.
- Check the air valve to be sure it is straight and without leaks.
- Keep grips on your handlebars. If they become worn, get new ones. If you lose a grip, replace it at once.
- Be sure you have a warning device—either a bell or a horn—required by your state laws. Be sure whichever you have is fastened securely to the bike.
- Check the nuts on the hubs of your wheels regularly to be sure they are tight.
- Keep your tires inflated and check regularly for glass and other objects that may work through and cause a puncture. If the treads are worn, get new tires.
- Replace worn-out pedals.
- Replace any lights that do not work properly. Check them frequently so that the batteries do not oxidize. Even if you do not plan to ride at night, it is best to have lights.

TIRE CARE

Tires are probably the one part of your bicycle that will give you the most trouble —or require the most careful maintenance, depending on your point of view.

First, you must remember that any tire will be damaged if you abuse it. Don't ride up and down curbs, even on the balloon type of tire. These tires will stand up to this kind of riding fairly well, but not indefinitely, and better tires won't take it at all.

Second, keep in mind that it is important to maintain the right air pressure in bicycle tires. If you are heavier than the average person of your height, be sure the tire doesn't bulge when you get on the bike. If it does bulge, it means that it needs more air.

If the weather is cool, fill the tire to the maximum. On hot days, fill it slightly under the maximum. Heat makes the air expand, so filling a tire to the maximum pressure in hot weather can result in a blowout.

The first step in filling tires is, of course, to know the pressure required. You can use a gas station air pump, but only if it has a gauge that you can set to the right pressure. Otherwise you risk blowing out the tire. The safest way to use a gas station pump is with very short bursts of air. If you don't know what pressure your tires take, raise it a little and put more air in. You can determine if the tire is filled if you can barely put a dent in it when you squeeze the sides of it very hard.

The safest way to fill a bicycle tire is to use a bicycle pump. If you have a very expensive bike with tubular tires, you'll be wise to use a hand pump with a gauge to tell you when you've reached the right pressure.

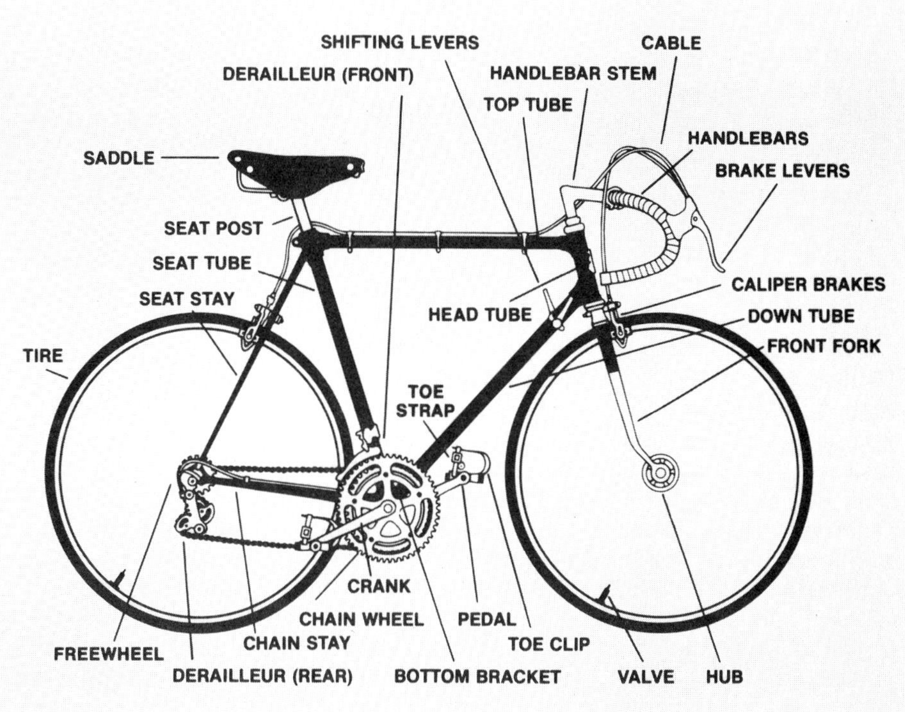

Freewheel
The five sprocket assembly on the rear wheel of a five or ten speed bicycle. Freewheels may have only one sprocket, or as many as six. They are also known as clusters or cogs.

Gear Inches
Determined by the number of teeth on the front chainwheel divided by the number of rear teeth multiplied by the wheel diameter. An average ratio for most situations is a mechanism with a 52 x 40 chainwheel and a 14, 17, 20, 24, 28 rear cluster.

Head tube
The front frame member holding front fork and connecting top and down tubes.

Hub
The center of the wheel to which the spokes are attached and which houses the axle and bearings. Better multi-geared bicycles have lightweight alloy hubs.

Huret
A French company that makes derailleurs and other parts.

Maes handlebars
Most common design for turned down handlebars. It is the most flexible and comfortable for most riding conditions.

Mattress Saddle
A wide, padded seat designed to support the full weight of the rider. Used only on straight handlebar bikes, where the rider sits up straight.

Panniers
Lightweight bags usually with several compartments that fit over the rear carrier of a bicycle.

Quick-release brakes
A button or lever allowing the caliper to open wide enough to allow the tire to pass through for easier removal. Usually found in conjunction with quick release hubs.

Quick-release hubs
Allows rapid wheel removal by merely flipping a lever rather than having to loosen the axle nuts.

Racing saddle
A narrow seat designed for leg freedom used on racing and touring bicycles.

Seat post
The part that holds the saddle to the frame.

Seat stays
Frame members that run from the seat tube to the chain stays.

Seat tube
The central frame member that holds seat post.

Toe straps
Used to secure foot in toe clip on pedals.

Tubular tire
Having a round cross section, the tire is sewn together around the tube, then glued or taped to the rim. Lighter and more delicate than clinchers, they are impractical for city riding.

KINDS OF TIRES

There are two kinds of bicycle tires and, confusingly, they have names that are similar.

Tubular tires are just that—tubular. They are completely round, look as if they're made of the thinnest material possible (they are), and puncture easily.

Tube tires, also called "wired on" or "clincher" tires, are the kind that are on most bicycles.

Tubular tires are the best for speed and distance. They are usually used for special road riding and for racing. They are more expensive than tube tires and are vulnerable to puncture when used for street riding. Tube tires are better for riding around town when it isn't always possible to avoid things that may puncture your tires.

If your bike has tubular tires, you may want to get another set of wheels with tube tires so you can switch quickly.

Tube tires usually come with Schraeder valves. This is the kind of valve that car tires usually have, too, so gas station pumps will fit this valve. A few tube tires, though, and all tubular ones have Presta valves instead. These will need an inexpensive adapter if you want to pump them up at the gas station, and you can get one at a bicycle shop.

A cyclist adjusting the brake cable on his bicycle. The brake should be checked regularly.

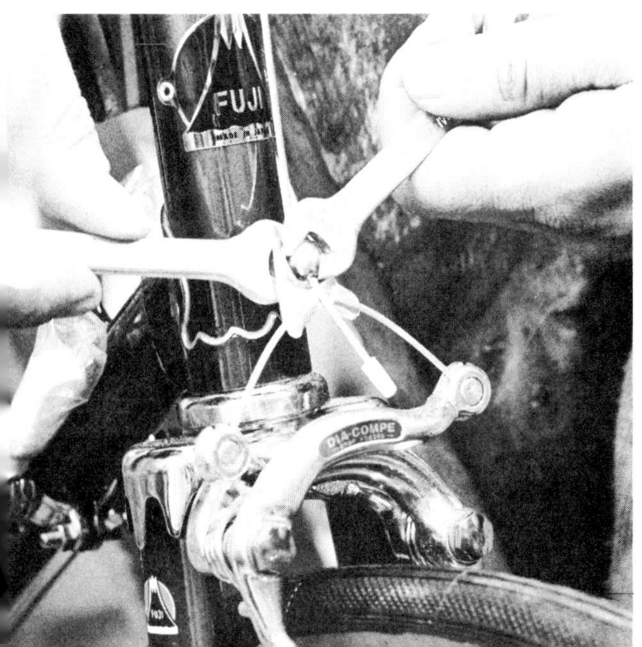

FIXING FLATS IN TUBULAR TIRES

Fixing a flat in a tubular tire is more complicated than repairing a tube tire (the latter is a procedure dating back to the early days of the automobile). But because you will be fixing a tubular tire more often, eventually you will learn to do it with great speed.

You'll need thin tube patches, a three-pointed needle, linen thread, rubber cement, sandpaper, chalk, a screwdriver, a knife or razor blade, and talcum powder.

You can get a repair kit for tubular tires that contains most of these things at many bike shops. Don't make do with a kit for tube tires—the patch will be much too thick.

Here is how to fix a tubular tire:

1. Let all the air out of the tire.
2. Take the tire off the rim.
3. Put air in the tire again and put it in a large basin or pail to find the leak. Don't stop if you see bubbles coming out at the valve—it's the point of least resistance. Keep looking for the puncture that caused the trouble.
4. When you find the puncture, mark it with the chalk, first drying off the tire.
5. There's tape glued to the bottom of the tire. Pry that up (you'll probably need to use a screwdriver, but be careful not to make more holes) over a small area around the puncture.
6. With a sharp knife or razor blade, cut the stitching around the puncture.
7. Take out the tube and find the exact spot where the leak is. You can use saliva or soapy water to find it. Where it bubbles is where you have a leak.
8. Roughen up the tube around the leak with the sandpaper. Take the paper off the back of the patch—keep your hands away from the sticky part when the paper is off or it won't stick—and put the patch over the hole.
9. Dust the tube with talcum. This will prevent it from sticking to the casing (the outside part of the tire).
10. Feel around inside the casing to be sure that whatever made the hole isn't still there. If it is, take it out.

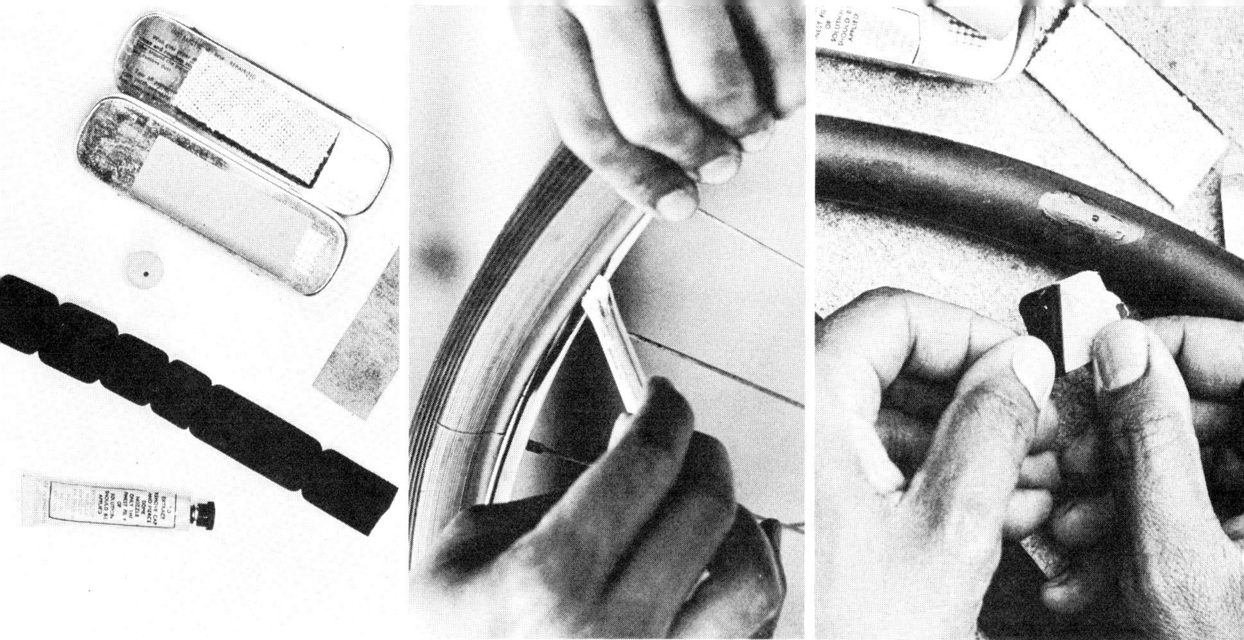

Fixing a flat in a tube, or clincher, tire. Left: A repair kit generally contains all you will need for fixing flats. Center: Once you have found the puncture, chalk it. Right: preparing to place patch over the leak.

11. Put the tube in the casing, thread your needle, and sew up the spot where you cut the old stitching, using the old holes and being careful not to stick the needle into the tube by mistake. The stitches should overlap about 12½ to 25 mm (½ to 1 in) into the original stitching.

12. Put rubber cement on the inside of the tape you peeled away and on the tire where you peeled it away. Then wait until the rubber cement is completely dry. Then, being sure you are putting the tape down at exactly the right point, stick it on the tire.

Now you are ready to put the tubular tire back on the rim of the wheel. There are three ways to do this. The slow way is the best way. The middle way is for when you are just about to go somewhere (not too far) and you cannot take much time. The really fast way is when you are on the road and have to catch up with everyone else.

The slow way is first to let all the air out of the tire. Then put the valve in and with the rim resting on something soft, put the tire on over the rim, starting at the top and working down. The last part will be hard to do. Turn the tire so the last part is toward you and pull it on the rim with both hands.

Next, roll back a little of the tire and put tire cement on the rim and on the casing. Go all the way around the tire doing this on both sides of the tire. Now, blow up the tire. Let it dry for about six hours to make sure the glue sets well.

The middle way of putting your tire back on is to put the tire cement on the rim and the tire first. Let the cement dry until it's just tacky, then put the tire on the rim in the same way.

The quickest way is to trust the tire cement that's already on the rim. But this is dangerous because the tire may come off as you go around corners.

Finally, you may want to try using double-sided rim tape (you can get it at most bicycle stores). It's much quicker and easier than cement□

 SELECTED READINGS

Anybody's Bike Book: An Original Manual of Bicycle Repairs by Tom Cuthbertson. Ten Speed Press, 1971.

"Best Bicycles and Gear for Commuting, Shopping, and Touring" by Eugene A. Sloane, *Popular Mechanics*, June 1974.

Bicycle Repair by Irene Cumming Kleeberg. Franklin Watts, Inc., 1973.

Bicycling: The Bicycle in Recreation, Competition, Transportation by Nancy Neiman Baranet. A. S. Barnes and Company, 1973.

The Complete Book of Bicycling by Eugene A. Soane. Trident Press, 1970.

How to Read a Can

by Tom Mahoney

IF you live in one of a few scattered areas of the United States or Canada, you may already have experienced something new in your grocery supermarket—a novel change on the shelves and packages, and at the checkout counter, which marks a revolution in electronic retail marketing and accounting systems.

On the self-service shelves, prices may not appear on each package, but simply be posted on the shelf. Each package has a weird set of symbols printed on it by the packager—a bunch of vertical lines of varying thickness with numbers under them, all crowded together in a little patch, typically about 38 mm long and 25 mm high (1½ by 1 inches). There is another number off to the left. Each packaged item has a distinct set of these lines which identifies it for what it is, by maker, product, size, and weight. The size of the symbol can vary. Wrigley's chewing gum will use a miniature version. The little patch can separately identify 100 billion different items.

Millions of people have already seen these symbols on packages in stores and some have seen them in use. They are known as the Universal Product Code. By the end of 1975, about 70 per cent of all prepackaged food store items will bear the code.

NO FRANTIC TURNING

When you take your purchases to the checkout counter in a store that uses the system, the checker exposes the symbol on each package to an electronic scanner, instead of turning it every which way to see what price is marked on it. The scanner is hooked to a computerized cash register. The checker doesn't punch keys to register each item. Instead, the scanner-computer identifies the package on sight from the symbol, reads a program of its own to find the price, and flashes the information for each package in turn on a lighted read-out screen, visible to you. The checker can bag most of your items in the time she formerly used to punch keys.

Was it a 39¢ can of dog food? The screen may flash .39 DOG FOOD, with or without the brand name. No more just GR for groceries or MT for meat. As fast as the checker can expose each package to the scanner, the price and item flash on the screen. At the end of the sale the computer spits out your sales slip, with a printed record for every item, the name and address of the store, the checkout lane, the checker, the date (and possibly the hour and minute), the sales tax, and the amount of change due you.

INSTANT RECORDS

Internally, the computer records the sales—and the changes in store inventory and cash supply—in the accounting system of the store and perhaps of the central office of the chain of stores, as fast as the symbols on the packages can be viewed.

A pilot model of this type of checkout was run for 15 months, a while back, in a Kroger store in Kenwood, Ohio, outside of Cincinnati. A later version went into brief use in early 1974 at the Finast Big Buy store on Route 30 in Framingham, Mass. A Marsh supermarket in Troy, Ohio, put six checkout lanes on a scanner-computer system. Steinberg's, Ltd., Canada's second largest supermarket chain, started using such a scanner system in a Montreal store, printing the sales-slip information in both French and English. A big Pathmark store in South Plainfield, N.J., put one in service, and nine checkstands went on scanners in a Brockton Public Market at Stoughton, Mass. Many more major food chains later tested scanner checkouts in some of their stores. By 1980 or so virtually every food store that is big enough to afford the expensive equipment may be pushing its customers through electronic scanner checkout lines.

Checking Out by Computer. The can shown above has no price marked on it—not even in the symbol. A computer reads the symbol on the can by scanning the vertical lines to "see" the numbers beneath. The longer lines at the extreme ends and in the center position the scanner, telling it that when it sees them as vertical it sees the symbol correctly. Then the computer reads:

- the second pair of lines from the left for the zero at left. In this case, the zero says that the item is one regularly sold in grocery stores.
- the lines above 11132, which tell the name of the company packaging the product—in this case, Allen Products Co., Allentown, Pa.
- the lines above 00012, which tell the name of the product and the quantity packaged—in this case, a 14½-oz can of Alpo Chicken & Liver Dinner "for dogs and puppies."

All of the lines must be read at the same time if the computer is to interpret them correctly.

The computer is programmed to read an entire symbol as a specifically priced item—in the case illustrated, as a 39¢ sales-taxable item. If the price is changed, the computer can be reprogrammed to assign a new price when it "sees" the symbol.

LESS CHANCE OF ERROR

There is more in this for the stores, perhaps, than for the customers, but there's something in it for everyone. You will see more clearly what you are being charged for and get a better record of it. Once the computers are working smoothly, there should be less chance of error in charging you for your purchases, or of ringing up items you didn't buy. The big stores are counting on running you through the checkout counters almost twice as fast as you go through them today.

The food merchants expect large operating cost reductions. This should help hold back food prices, as merchants compete for your trade with reduced overhead for themselves. The scanner system may be bad news for small merchants who can't afford it, if the savings are as great as the big merchants expect.

An obvious saving may come from eliminating labor now used to mark prices on every package on the self-service shelves. Some stores carry 8,000 price-marked items at any time. If dog food is 39¢ today, the computer is programmed to charge 39¢ for it on reading its symbol on the package. If the price goes to 42¢, each item needn't be marked with the new price. The price posted on the shelf is changed, and the computer is reprogrammed to charge 42¢ when it reads the symbol.

SCANNABLE STICKERS

The scanners will be able to handle every prepackaged item except for those of unusually large size. The system does not provide a universal way of scanning things like bunches of bananas, heads of lettuce, or cuts of meat that vary in weight from package to package. But it has a built-in method for allowing the stores to affix scannable stickers of their own to such things.

The stores expect enormous advantages from the record-keeping aspects of the computer-scanner-registers. It should be possible for the transactions of every checkout counter to be instantly available to the store itself, to its chain's district office and its central office, on a minute-to-minute basis—to show what's selling where and to keep instant inventories of every store and the whole chain. In effect, the moment you buy your dog food, the computer system tells the store and the whole chain to "scratch one can" of that particular item.

From this it is a simple jump to the computer telling the chain how much of what to buy and which stores to send how much of it—or even placing the orders itself. The information will also give rapid data to indicate the sales results of advertising and special pricing.

Consumer opposition may present some problems to checking out groceries with the computer. The National Consumers Congress has gone on record as in favor of keeping the price on every can, and legislation to this effect has been introduced in several states. Some are fearful that the costs of the systems may increase rather than cut food prices. Supermarkets believe they can meet these objections by educating the public and by placing more readable prices on the shelves.

IDEA PROPOSED IN 1932

If you think that pushbutton electronic shopping has been an obvious possibility for some time, in view of the advances in electronics, you are right. It was obvious long before it was possible. Wallace N. Flint, the son of a Brockton, Mass., wholesaler of soft drinks and confectionery products, wrote his master's thesis at Harvard University on automating checkout counters in 1932, when checkout counters themselves were a novelty.

This was before electronic computers, and Flint's system proposed the use of IBM punch cards. It included another novelty, too. If you wanted a can of Heinz beans you'd pick up an IBM punch card for it in the store and insert it in a device. Not only would it register the sale, but it would cause the item to be picked up by a traveling belt and brought to you.

Flint's 1932 proposal was impractical for many reasons—but the basic idea was not. Flint stayed with it, and he has been one of the leaders in urging and helping the food industry to develop the new scanner system, some 40-odd years later.

He recently retired to Hilton Head, S.C., but he remains a consultant to the industry in its complex problem of devising and maintaining a uniform code of symbols to identify packages of innumerable products turned out by any number of manufacturers and packagers, to be read by any of many brands of computer-scanner-registers.

That, of course, has been the real problem in the years since electronics became so advanced: how to get everyone who is selling, making, packaging or distributing foodstuffs and other grocery store items to agree on a uniform code and symbol, and how to integrate the operation with various electronics manufacturers. The real revolution coming to the checkout counters is one of successfully coordinating people and firms who compete with one another.

Wallace Flint did a lot of the pushing to bring it about, as did some of the chain stores and innovators in the electronics and cash register industries. The Singer Company, National Cash Register, Sperry Rand, International Business Machines, and more than a dozen other companies are competing intensely in the business of supplying the basic technology for pushbutton shopping□

SELECTED READINGS

"Automated Supermarket." *Nation,* November 1974.

"Bringing Home the 33900–10020." *Time,* Dec. 30, 1974.

"Grocery Checkout by Computer—What It Means to Shoppers." *U.S. News and World Report,* Dec. 30, 1974.

"How You'll Zip Through the Zap-out Counter" by Tom Mahoney. *Popular Mechanics,* February 1975.

Blimps, still in commercial use, are the current survivors of the airship era.

The Helium Horse

by Kurt R. Stehling
and J. Gordon Vaeth

GIANT dirigibles may be taking to the skies again. Longer than three city blocks, these gas-filled airships are cousins to the blimp but have a rigid framework.

Lighter-than-air craft of this type haven't flown since 1939, when Germany's *Graf Zeppelin II*, sister ship of the *Hindenburg*, cruised off England to sample British radar transmissions days before the outbreak of World War II. Placed in a hangar thereafter, this last of the great dirigibles was later dynamited and its aluminum used by the Nazis for airplane production. Airships of such size and type have been a dead issue ever since.

But no longer.

Increasingly there is talk of bringing them back. More and more they are being proposed for the next major U.S. aerospace initiative. Some people are even calling them the dream vehicle of tomorrow's airways.

American interest in these flying cigars supposedly ended forever when a hydrogen fire destroyed the *Hindenburg* on May 6, 1937, while it was completing its 37th commercial ocean crossing. What has now changed the picture so drastically, after nearly four whole decades?

GROWING ENTHUSIASM

Engineers have begun to look at the rigid airship in a different light, for one thing—no longer just in historical terms of what it could do in the 1930's but, instead, of what it can accomplish in the future if given modern capabilities. Technological progress has not been applied to the design and building of a large dirigible in almost 40 years. Give to it, these engineers say, the level of technical achievement found in the jumbo jets, in Skylab, or in the space shuttle. There is then no reason why it cannot be made just as safe, reliable, and useful as the airplane.

The growing enthusiasm for airships is also explainable on environmental grounds: land usage, particularly for airports, has become a nationally sensitive issue. Opposition to the transformation of ever more countryside into large areas

The first great age of airships ended on May 6, 1937, when the *Hindenburg* burned up.

of concrete and to the introduction of aircraft exhaust pollution and engine noise must now be taken into careful account in planning the nation's aeronautical growth. It explains much of the aerospace industry's interest in quiet V/STOL (Vertical/Short Take Off and Landing) aircraft. It is the basis for the concept of building offshore airports.

The dirigible is actually a VTOL vehicle, with a potential payload as great as 500 tons. It makes no take-off and no landing run. It needs no costly heavy-duty runways. It simply floats up or settles down. It has to have a clear approach and departure path, of course, but on the ground all it requires is a flat clearing—a grassy field will do—a little more than twice its length to permit it to be blown around a mast like a weathervane.

Operational concepts being developed even include airship "arrivals" and "departures" without landing. Cargo and passengers would be taken on and off by airplane shuttle. Or, in the case of freight, shipments would be hoisted up and down as the dirigible hovered overhead. If airships operate this way, land usage can be kept to an absolute minimum.

CLEAN AND QUIET

The dirigible is inherently clean and can be propelled by steam. Powered by large, slow-turning, counter-rotating, stern-mounted propellers, it can also be made exceptionally quiet. Thus it holds promise of being permitted to operate exempt from airport curfew hours or other flight restrictions imposed by environmental considerations.

The airship is attractive, also, in light of the need to conserve energy and energy

Airships went into battle in World War I. Pilots in the gondola of a C-class dirigible of the U.S. Navy prepare to take off. A small bomb is attached to the gondola.

The most famous commercial airship, the German-built *Graf Zeppelin,* flew successfully from 1928 to 1937, carrying more than 21,000 passengers in all.

resources. For an aircraft, it makes efficient use of energy because its lifting gas is what enables it to fly. Since it needs propulsive power only to move through the air, its energy needs are remarkably low.

A dirigible of the 1970's would not simply be an improved larger version of the *Hindenburg* or other pre-1940 rigid airships, such as America's *Akron* and *Macon* or Britain's *R–100*. (That would be rather like building a modernized version of the Ford Trimotor.) Rather, designers would use the many recent advances in propulsion, materials, guidance and control, navigation, aerodynamic theory, and electronic data management. The modern ship would likely be a very large craft with a pre-stressed metallic or plastic skin and with a minimum of internal girderwork. The skin might even serve as a combination gas container and structure.

Such a vehicle would be capable of 160–240 kph (100–150 mph) and measure something like 300 m (1,000 ft) long and 90 m (300 ft) in diameter. It would have a gross lift of about 700 tons and a useful lift of 400–500 tons. It could be powered by a single lightweight, nonpolluting, quiet, liquid-fueled steam turbine driving counter-rotating tail propellers. That would be a distinct contrast to the numerous diesel and gasoline-burning engines (as many as eight at a time) carried by airships in earlier days.

To avoid the danger of fire, the ship would be filled with helium. Lightweight, high-strength alloys would be used. Key structural elements would be made of fiber-reinforced composites. Helium might be cycled—alternately vaporized or liquefied—to help control buoyancy, something done in the past by dropping water ballast and valving off gas. Excess heat from the turbine could perhaps be conducted by the helium to the metal skin. The skin could then be used as the world's largest airborne radiator.

THE BENEFITS OF BIGNESS

A threefold increase over the 200,000 m³ (7,000,000 ft³) of the *Hindenburg* may seem extreme, but designers are no longer afraid of bigness (witness the development of the supertanker). Airship efficiency, like that of the tanker, increases dramatically with size. Helium capacities could go as high as 1,415,000 m^3 (50,000,000 ft^3). Volumes, however, as well as speeds, ranges, payloads, and altitude performance, will vary according to the particular design and its intended role or application. It would be a mistake to think of dirigibles as limited to low altitudes, incidentally. The early Zeppelins, for example, had operational ceilings approaching 7,600 m (25,000 ft).

Whatever its size or abilities are, the dirigible, in being reborn, will necessitate also the rebirth of a lighter-than-air technology long abandoned. Designers and builders will have to start again almost from scratch. Theirs will be the task of applying to the rigid airship the modern technology developed out of the National Aeronautics and Space Administration, the Defense Department, and industry programs. The opportunities offered them for creative engineering and technical innovation—including the application of nuclear propulsion—will be virtually without limit.

Engineering challenge and appeal, however, will not by themselves revive the airship. It must meet the needs of the times and meet them better than can other vehicles. It must have capabilities that are both advantageous and unique.

AN AIRBORNE HOTEL

Various uses are foreseen for the dirigible that fulfill these requirements. They range from recreational vehicles to scientific laboratories, to humanitarian ships of international goodwill, and transporters of cargo. Let's look at some of these applications, starting with the "flying cruise ship."

The *Hindenburg* was an airborne hotel. Inside its cavernous hull, it provided the 50 passengers—who paid $400 for a North Atlantic trip between Frankfurt, Germany, and Lakehurst, New Jersey—with staterooms, lounges, promenade decks, and even a bar and smoking room. The latter was slightly pressurized to discourage the entry of any free hydrogen that might be about. The noise level was in the range of a loud whisper. Vibration was virtually nonexistent, the water or wine in the goblets on its dining room tables showing hardly a ripple. It was so steady and stable that cut flowers could be placed in tall vases with little risk of tipping over. The meals, selected from the ship's larder and cooked on board in an electric kitchen, were first-rate. And, no one was ever airsick. The crossing was so restful and appealing that passengers had a saying: "You fly in an airplane, but you voyage in a Zeppelin."

That same appeal could be re-created today. Now, however, 200 to 500 could be carried. They would dine and dance in a glass-covered "ballroom beneath the stars," located atop the ship. Their bedrooms and public rooms would rival those of a luxury resort. They would glide quietly over some of the most spectacular sights and scenery the world has to offer, stopping in mid-air for a closer look through the ship's draft-proof open windows before moving on. Those wanting to "go ashore" could do so, geography permitting, by helicopter or airplane carried on board and used as a shuttle back and forth to the ground.

A trip up the Amazon . . . a photographic safari to observe the plants and animals of distant rain forests, jungles, and plains . . . an airborne sightseeing tour of the ruins of ancient civilizations in Latin America . . . a history-laden cruise along the perimeter of the Mediterranean (with particular attention to the fabled islands of Greece and the site of Carthage) . . . an aerial exploration of the Spanish Main . . . and, in summer, a flight above the permanent ice pack to the North Pole . . . these are some of the unusual sightseeing experiences a dirigible could offer the public.

AN ALTERNATIVE CRUISE SHIP

Nor is the appeal of the airship for this purpose solely recreational. The cruise trade now belongs almost entirely to non-U.S. vessels. As an alternative form of cruise ship, offering something excitingly different, the dirigible should prove a popular drawing card to U.S. and other travelers alike.

As for transporting passengers point to point, the dirigible is not a likely contender with the jet airliner for moving people who have places to go. Admittedly there is probably a segment of the nonflying American public that would be attracted more to the airship than to the airplane. And admittedly airships (the first *Graf Zeppelin* and the *Hindenburg*) provided a transoceanic service at a time (1928–1937) when it was beyond the capability of the airplane to do so. Even so, dirigibles should not today be considered an economic competitor to the airplane for routine passenger carrying. Their role is more properly glamour trips and luxury travel.

A PLATFORM FOR SCIENTISTS

The airship's on-board roominess and steadiness in flight, so useful in making passengers comfortable, could be put to good use in the service of science as well. These characteristics, plus the ready availability of its structure for the mounting of equipment, would make it specially suitable as an environmental sensing and work platform, one with very long range and very long staying power. Its hull could mount antennas larger than any ever carried by an aircraft. With increase in size would come, also, an increase in data-gathering ability. New frequencies might become practicable for use in radiometric work.

For underwater studies, very large sonar arrays could be towed without the disturbing interference of surface-ship hull and propeller noises.

Very high resolution cameras—airships have always made superb photographic platforms—would be carried, as would gravitometers, magnetometers (trailed, perhaps, to keep them at a distance), and various atmospheric and oceanic sensing devices.

Not to be overlooked is the substantial data-processing capability that the dirigible would carry with it wherever it went. Observational results could be obtained, at least roughly, on the spot. An experimenter could thus sort out quickly the data that seemed questionable and repeat the test or observation, using the same or different techniques, instruments, frequencies, or special intervals. In making his original or repeat observations, he would appreciate, in many cases, the ability given him by the airship to do so while standing still in the air.

As a remote-sensing vehicle, the dirigible could play a major role in environmental and earth resources work. It also

The mini-blimp, shown being launched, may become a standard tool for cities. It can be used for monitoring traffic and so on.

could serve as a measurer of "ground truth," obtaining temperature and other data used to evaluate the accuracy of such values as reported by earth satellites or by other aircraft.

ADVANTAGES OVER SURFACE SHIPS

But it is for oceanographic work that the revived and modernized rigid airship holds promise of being particularly useful. Unlike surface craft, it would not be sensitive to ocean conditions. Its time to, from, and between stations would be very much shorter. Its range—about 16,000 km (10,000 mi) if nonatomically powered, unlimited if atomically powered—could be extended by in-flight refueling from ships at sea. Endurance could be further prolonged by anchoring or engaging in protracted hovering flight.

Ice-blocked regions, normally out of bounds to surface ships, could be flown over and reached. The very surface of the ocean could be sampled from above, using a sensor string, providing a minimum of disturbing influences such as propeller slipstream or rotor downwash (as would be the case if an airplane or helicopter were used). As for aircraft, several of them would be based on the dirigible to be deployed, like launches from a survey ship, to extend its radius of observations greatly.

Buoys could be lowered from its belly without the danger, so common with a surface vessel, of damaging them by striking the hull while they are being put over the side in heavy seas. Repeating the process in reverse, it could also retrieve and bring buoys back on board for servicing and maintenance.

With a surfeit of power provided by nuclear propulsion, this airborne tender might even recharge a buoy's power supply in midocean by maneuvering into position close overhead and aiming microwave energy at it. As mother ship to one or more research submersibles, to sound-

Another standard use for lighter-than-air craft in the future may be the transportation of cargo. Here, a balloon carries a load from shipboard to the shore.

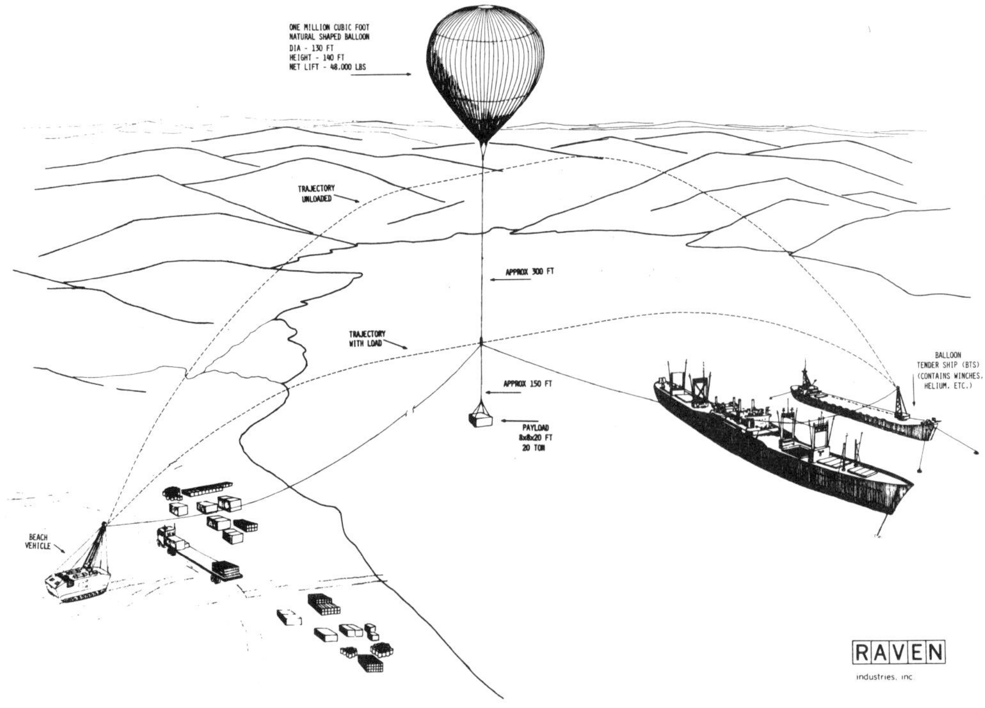

Aerocrane, a cross between a helicopter and a balloon, is designed to carry heavy cargos across the countryside. About 60 per cent of the odd vehicle's lifting capacity comes from the aerodynamic lift provided by the vanes as the balloon rotates. The helicopter-type lift also gives the craft greater maneuverability and does away with the need for ballast.

ing and survey boats, and also to an underwater habitat, it would keep its winches busy indeed.

The oceanographic studies made possible by the dirigible, its aircraft, buoys, submersibles, and workboats, are considerable. With its speed, range, and sonar, it should be able to keep up with and successfully track the migration of whales. Given the advantages of a slow-moving airborne platform, who knows what it might do in the way of marine surveys, the location of good fishing areas, and the cleanup of marine pollution? Able to operate above and well clear of an oil spill or a large accumulation of tar, plastic, or other particles, the airship should be in an ideal position to deal with such events. Crisscrossing the area, it could lay down chemicals or physically mop up the spill by towing booms, sweeps, or other devices to clean the surface. Not out of the question would be scooping or vacuuming up the surface water and straining out the gunk before dumping it back. One of its more important environmental roles in years to come may be that of an airborne scavenger of marine pollution.

AN AID IN TIME OF DISASTER

For natural disaster relief, too, a dirigible seems ready-made. Delivery of food, water, medical supplies, shelter, clothing, and other urgently needed items to survivors is the inevitable aftermath of every such calamity, be it storm surge, flood, earthquake, landslide, or whatever. Often the runways and airports to which such help would be flown in have been crumpled or washed away. And if helicopters are used, the loads they can carry over the distances required may be pitifully small compared with the need.

In this kind of situation, a large airship, fitted out as a flying first-aid center or hospital and carrying perhaps 225,000 kg (500,000 lb) of emergency provisions and equipment—including heavy pieces such as power generators and bulldozers—could reach the scene, take up a hovering position overhead, and lower its cargo of help to those on the ground. The seriously injured would be hoisted on board for medical treatment.

While performing these roles, the ship would be relatively unimpeded in its operations by the extent or severity of the destruction on the ground. Conditions accompanying a major natural disaster may be so chaotic that provisions airlifted in cannot be moved or distributed—but not so if they are brought in by airship. Not only could an airship deliver its supplies and equipment, it could also illuminate the stricken area with powerful searchlights and serve as a vantage point for overseeing rescue, firefighting, and demolition activities below.

To be sure, the dirigible is no match for the airplane in reaching a disaster site as fast as possible. (Even so, at 240 km per hr (150 mph), it would cover 5,800 km (3,600 mi) in 24 hours.) But once it arrived there, such would be its capability for giving help that local officials, after boarding it by hoist, helicopter, or airplane shuttle, would be sure to press it into service as their command post for the salvage and rehabilitation work remaining.

Such a vehicle, always kept equipped and on call for its emergency mission, might be appropriately funded for, sponsored, and operated under international auspices. When not on such a mission, it would be available to spray locust breeding areas, carry out agricultural seeding, dust crops, stock inland waters with fish or supply them with nutrients, transport scientific and engineering teams to inaccessible areas and deliver them there (by hoist) for exploration and construction, take wildlife censuses, and do a variety of other tasks important to countries throughout the world.

Besides disaster relief, another major humanitarian role awaits the dirigible as an airborne version of a hospital ship. An airship, equipped with a 100-bed hospital, clinics, laboratories, and education facilities, could extend international friendship and goodwill deep into continental interiors. It would moor and be based there in clearings, using a stick mast (brought in aboard the airship itself).

NEW VISTAS IN CARGO HANDLING

Undoubtedly the most economically important of the dirigible's future applications is that of moving cargo. Its aptitude for vertical take-offs and landings while carrying hundreds of thousands of pounds of payload, and also its ability to load and unload while hovering, open up new vistas for transporting things by air. More than ever before, factories, assembly plants, warehouses, and distribution centers with a need to ship or receive directly by air would be able to do so. Of course, there will be places where, because of obstructions or unsuitable terrain, on-the-scene airship pickup or delivery may not be practicable. But there will be so many situations where it is possible that the implications for the future pattern of air transportation, in the United States and overseas, could be very great indeed.

So, too, are prospects for carrying cargo that, for reasons of weight or size, is economically not feasible to carry by airplane or is even physically impossible to be transported by the largest airfreighters. Fresh produce is a case in point. Hauling it by dirigible has been independently proposed by one of the major growers.

Lettuce, for example, being highly perishable, must now be shipped from its Arizona growing area to the East by refrigerated railroad cars. The destinations this lettuce can be shipped to are limited by where the tracks go. It takes about six days to move a shipment from Phoenix to one of 16 distribution centers east of the Mississippi. One large airship could carry a load of lettuce equivalent to that handled by 10 or 12 refrigerated cars and deliver it to the Eastern states in 24 to 30 hours, fast enough so that refrigeration would not be required. And deliveries, of course, would not be limited to the destinations now dictated by the availability of rail lines and service.

Even more promising is the use of airships for moving produce overseas and opening up foreign markets, notably in Western Europe and Japan. What has hindered the development of these overseas markets has been the difficulty in transporting strawberries, lettuce, and other fresh fruits and vegetables from the growing areas to the seacoast and then by surface ship to transoceanic destinations. The immense cargo bays of rigid airships, with or without refrigeration, could well change this picture by offering point-to-point delivery without transshipment.

SELLING THE DIRIGIBLE

And, lest it be lost sight of, the dirigible is itself an exportable item—worth perhaps $30 million apiece in production.

This raises the question of costs.

What would be the price tag of an airship three times as large as the *Hindenburg*, built as a cruise ship or as a trans-

The "helium horse" (above) may look ungainly, but such airships of the future may be able to carry much heavier payloads than any airplanes in existence today. Shown being loaded, such a ship could take on 450,000 kg (1,000,000 lb) of cargo. At right is a proposed design for a commercial airship of the future.

oceanic transporter of small or compact cars? (Two hundred cars might be carried at a time, at four or five times the usual speed, and at considerably less cost, if one takes into account transshipment and storage requirements.)

The first large rigid airship of modern design would weigh in at between $200 and $400 million, depending on its mission and upon how it must be equipped. Follow-ons would decrease in price until, in quantities of a dozen or so, they would approximate the cost of a Boeing 747, which is between $25 million and $30 million. Before any large-scale operational prototype could be begun, however, a training airship, of perhaps one seventh the volume eventually desired, should be constructed to develop the critical piloting and ground handling skills required.

This scaled-down craft, which would serve also as a test facility for developmental items, might be put into the air in two years and at a cost of about $50 million. It, and the larger ships that would follow, could be built in the 13 airship hangars still standing and potentially available for such use in the United States.

How well the amortized costs of large dirigibles—plus their operating costs—would permit them to become competitive with other forms of transportation remains to be seen. The answer depends on many factors, not the least of which is the means by which their technical development happens to be funded. If industry or a commercial user pays the price, that's one thing. If a government agency foots the bill, it's quite another. An agency, for example, might build one to move a space shuttle about or quickly recover the shuttle's expended reusable boosters from the ocean before saltwater corrosion can set in. Once resurrected and brought to a state of operational usefulness, however, the large airship, it would appear, can be extremely competitive: operating costs may be approximately those of merchant ships.

DREAM VEHICLE OF TOMORROW?

Taking all these things into account, will the dirigible be returned to the skies? No one can say as of now. But the more that its quiet operation, environmental cleanliness, energy conservation, long range, large payload, stable and vibration-free flight, onboard roominess, and ability to "land" without landing are recognized, the greater are its chances.

Is it possible, as some people think, that the dream vehicle of tomorrow, instead of being the supersonic transport, the rocket, or the surface effect ship, will be the dirigible?

There's increasing reason to believe that it may□

SELECTED READINGS

"A New Outbreak of Zeppelin Fever" by Tom Alexander. *Fortune*, December 1973.

The Age of the Airship by Edward Horton. Henry Regnery Co., 1973.

Airship: A Popular History by Robert Jackson, Doubleday & Co., Inc., 1973.

"Don't Sell the Airship Short" by John F. Pearson. *Popular Mechanics*, September 1974.

The Great Dirigibles: Their Triumphs and Disasters by John Toland. Dover Publications, rev. ed., 1972.

Another kind of cargo balloon is tested for logging use in rugged terrain. The craft is 32 m (105 ft) wide and can carry more than 9,000 kg (20,000 lb).

A fish-eye view of a fairly typical maze of intersecting highways in a U.S. city. Some people believe that the design of the roads contributes to highway deaths.

Roads That Kill

WHO could believe

- That millions of dollars worth of guardrail has been incorrectly installed along U.S. highways, some of it actually endangering rather than protecting life?
- That clearance distances marked on overpasses are so unreliable that some trucking firms make their own measurements and publish their own guides for drivers?
- That a maintenance crew assigned to remove a hazardous roadside tree would cut it off so high as to leave an equally hazardous stump?
- That a commonly used minimum standard for lettering on road signs is so small that 20 per cent of the driving population can't read the message?
- That studded tires are causing millions of dollars of damage to U.S. highways while making a questionable contribution to safety?
- That signs frequently are so poorly placed that a motorist traveling at the legal speed limit cannot assimilate the information needed to choose his route?
- That a rigid pole in the "gore" area, or wedge, where an exit leaves a freeway, can be knocked down time after time, causing death and injury, and yet always be replaced in the same spot?
- That signs mounted on the same support can give the driver contradictory messages?

The answer, of course, is that anyone who drives can believe all of these things. The average motorist, particularly when he travels an unfamiliar road, constantly finds signs, signals, road configurations and roadside clutter that create confusion and indecision. Even familiar streets and highways contain features that can become booby traps for the unwary.

Over a six-year period, the U.S. House of Representatives' Committee on Public Works (Subcommittee on Investigations and Review) held hearings on the role played by the road environment in the annual toll of death and injury in auto-

Exits from a freeway are a frequent trouble spot. Here is a well designed gore area, or wedge, that helps provide for safe exit from the freeway.

mobiles. This article is an edited version of the Subcommittee's Report.

The transcript of the hearings, published in four volumes, contains 2,616 pages of testimony and exhibits, and more than 2,800 photographs. For the federal, state, and local official, as well as the serious teacher and scholar, the volumes represent perhaps the most complete record available in any place as to how we have misdirected so much effort involving the highway environment.

This road environment must accommodate the needs of the vacationing motorist driving cross-country, the truck driver making a delivery, the rush-hour commuter, the child trying to cross his neighborhood street, the housewife maneuvering her loaded station wagon, and many, many others.

"Projection" so often has been the missing element—failure of the designer and others in the highway professions to project themselves into the role of the various users whom they have intended to serve. As a result, all too often their handiwork has contributed unintentionally to tragedy.

Every government agency that has a part of the "action" must see that the basic message is communicated, in understandable fashion, to the next level. Through this series of hearings the Congress seeks to direct the Department of Transportation and particularly its two component agencies, the Federal Highway Administration and the National Highway Traffic Safety Administration. Those agencies have the responsibility to give direction to the state highway departments and state highway safety agencies, and to insist upon compliance.

The same chain-of-command responsibility applies to the state agencies in their relationships with county, city, and other local jurisdictions. State, county, and city officials must concentrate on indoctrinating the supervisory personnel who manage the activities of designers, planners, and even construction and maintenance crews. Everyone must be trained to look at his job in the context of achieving the safest and most efficient road attainable.

The basic concept is disarmingly simple. In a complex world, perhaps the utter simplicity of it all has confounded minds overwhelmed with complicated jargon and sophisticated equipment. What is the message, the fundamental truth that emanates not from an impersonal computer or even a wizened guru, but from a pragmatic Subcommittee that spent six years looking at the broad panorama of the nation's road system?

The message is simple: Think people!

ROADSIDE HAZARDS

If the admonition is to "think people," who could be more appropriate as lead-off witness than a representative of the

The materials used for highway signs, poles, and fences can contribute to the safety or dangerousness of the road. Here a light-weight aluminum light pole is designed to break clean on impact. The pole breaks at its base and flips into the air.

people? On May 23, 1967, 49-year-old Joseph Linko, a New York television repairman, settled into the witness chair opposite the Subcommittee Chairman, the Honorable John A. Blatnik, and a down-to-earth, real-world atmosphere was established that prevailed throughout the hearings.

Joe Linko had become fed up as he traveled the streets and freeways around New York in connection with his business. Later, as his sense of outrage mounted, in a kind of one-man crusade that consumed even his free time, he concluded that either (1) highway and traffic engineers didn't know what they were doing, or (2) if they did know, no one was paying any attention to them. Everywhere that Joe Linko drove it seemed his thesis gained new credibility. He was astounded by the numbers and kinds of serious hazards that littered the roadsides of some of the busiest and newest highways in the New York area. And every day those hazards were claiming their toll of victims.

Linko's testimony was replete with photographic evidence, straightforward comment, and, all too frequently, the chronicling of disaster. At times, he reported, he had made personal interventions with authorities to get hazardous conditions corrected.

Showing the Subcommittee a slide of a guardrail that was pointed like an arrow toward the approach end of a concrete bridge, Linko declared that he had taken the photograph because motorists were "chipping away on this thing" and he knew it was going to cause trouble. Eight months later, a mother and two of her children were killed when the guardrail deflected their car into the bridge abut-

Left: base of light pole with an effective breakaway insert. Right: a hazardous light pole base: concrete footing canceling out breakable base.

Top: dangerous butterfly gore sign. Bottom: Safe type of signing. Signs are attached to an overhead structure and overhead arrows clearly indicate lanes.

ment. Four days later, another person was killed at the same spot. Only when Linko wrote a personal letter to the governor of the state was belated remedial action taken.

In this, as in other instances, Linko pointed out specifically what was wrong: "If this guardrail were installed properly and secured to the bridge abutment, a car would slide by and continue on its way. But when you touch this guardrail, the way it is, it just moves back and you hit the abutment head on. . . ."

Dramatizing the insensitive, unconsciously "anti-people" character of some of the work that had been done was this exchange between Chairman Blatnik, Linko, and Charles W. Prisk, deputy director of the Office of Traffic Operations in the Bureau of Public Roads and subsequently special assistant to the Federal Highway Administrator:

> MR. LINKO. This is the particular installation. All it says is "Exit 52," and it is an easy-knockdown sign and they have 48 feet of guardrail which cost a fortune of money. It is not serving any real purpose, and it kills the driver if he happens to run into the guardrail.
>
> MR. BLATNIK. This is the guardrail that was struck in the preceding picture?
>
> MR. LINKO. This man died because they were protecting this easy-knockdown sign.
>
> MR. BLATNIK. The only function this guardrail serves, Mr. Prisk, is to protect the sign, which is a breakaway sign?
>
> MR. PRISK. I would say that is correct. There is a very curious reverse of emphasis about this word "protection." You talk about putting the guardrail in to protect the sign, where actually the guardrail should be put in to protect people that might possibly run against it.

Another witness succeeded in succinctly stating the need to be aware of human behavioral frailties in design and maintenance when he called for engineering "a forgiving quality" into the roadside. This is a suggestion that perhaps has relevance in other parts of our sometimes harsh, adversary society. A "forgiving quality."

FREEWAY SIGNS

A second phase of the Subcommittee's investigation explored a subject close to the heart of every motorist who, at one time or another, has found the information on road signs, or the road configuration itself, to be perplexing. Again, this probably describes all who use the nation's freeways and highways.

Indecision and confusion contributed by elements of the environment can lead to serious accidents. And contribute they do, enticing the driver from the road to impact roadside obstacles or triggering roadway collisions with other vehicles or with pedestrians. Freeway signs are a special case in point, and deficiencies illustrated before the Subcommittee included:

—Signs that are placed so close to the point of decision, or contain lettering so small, that once a driver can read

them, he cannot safely react to them.
—Signs that mark the way to tiny, distant towns or geographical areas "where nobody seems to be going" and overlook major nearby points.
—Signs that fail to mention commonly used route names such as the New York Thruway, the Massachusetts Turnpike, or the Long Island Expressway.
—No signs at all in places where the driver is confronted with alternative routes.
—Signs hung in such big clusters that a motorist traveling at a normal speed is befuddled.
—Signs that have confusing symbols, incorrect shape or color.
—Signs that may be dirty, concealed, lost in roadside clutter, poorly reflectorized, or unlighted where they should be lighted.
—Signs that contain abstract technical advice, such as "Advance Green When Flashing."

A behavioral psychologist testified that the popular rule of thumb among traffic engineers to determine the size of lettering on highway signs is to require 1 inch in size for every 50 feet of distance at which the sign must be read. And yet tests among the driving population show that 20 per cent of all motorists do not have vision to read such a sign.

A driver going at even moderate speed would find it difficult to see this STOP sign amidst the jungle of advertising signs. When he does, he will likely make a dangerous sudden stop.

The motoring public is often unaware of subtle but important pieces of information that can be useful in understanding the highway system. How many drivers realize that even-numbered Interstate highways run east and west, odd-numbered ones north and south? Drivers should have this knowledge.

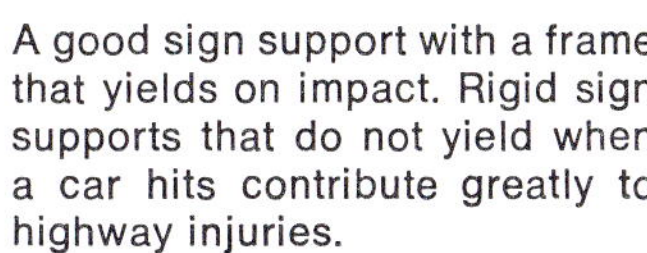
A good sign support with a frame that yields on impact. Rigid sign supports that do not yield when a car hits contribute greatly to highway injuries.

An example of a well-marked safe exit lane off a multi-lane highway.

GOOD SIGN PRACTICES

The basic principles of good signing have remained unchanged over the years, although the techniques of implementing these principles necessarily have had to be altered as the nation's highway system has undergone its transformation. The essentials of good signing include:

Stating messages in a way that avoids misinterpretation.

Giving advance notice and repeating that notice.

Maintaining an accurate relationship between sign messages and other sources of information, such as maps.

Requiring that signs be of sufficient size for traffic volume and speed.

Giving special emphasis to signs wherever the road design requires unusual maneuvers.

Modern freeway driving has created additional demands for effective signs, including the need to provide adequate information for freeway connections and better information for the disoriented driver once he leaves the freeway. Clear street name information is essential, and on this point the Subcommittee is perturbed. How delighted the motorist would be to learn the name of the next cross street before he got there—in time to position himself correctly! Mid-block, advance street name signs would do it nicely. Why don't we see them more often?

Failure to take into account actual human capability was illustrated time and time again in slides and motion pictures of signs and other elements of the highway environment. The Subcommittee, and the motorist, would have had to have a course in speed reading, for instance, to read and assimilate the information communicated by one display which included 10 "shields" with route numbers and two city destinations, all on one sign.

Movies taken of entrances and exits to I-495, the Capital Beltway encircling Washington, D.C., documented how drivers of passenger cars and commercial vehicles often make sudden, dangerous maneuvers because of inadequate advance route information. The films showed vehicles stopping in highly vulnerable gore areas, backing up exit ramps against the flow of traffic, and swerving over grassed areas. The cameras of staff personnel recorded several "near misses," and, in one subsequent phase, actual accidents that dramatized the various deficiencies revealed during the months of hearings.

OFF THE FREEWAY

During the course of the hearings the Subcommittee periodically examined traffic control operations on some of the nation's non-freeway roads, both on and off the Federal-aid system. The situation can be characterized in a single word: worse.

Signs and control devices are inadequate on a large scale, with traffic management typically a montage of old and new technology, low cost expedients, nonuniformity, and a "make do" inventiveness that produces many bizarre conditions for the unsuspecting motorist. The Subcommittee found:

—Signs that carry the wrong message for the shape and color of the sign. Glance recognition of an octagon sign suggests "stop," but octagon signs are also used incorrectly to convey such messages as "slow" or "crosswalk" or, in one unique case, to warn the motorist about flying golf balls.

—Signs that are the wrong color, for example, green, yellow or white instead of red for a stop sign; blue or green instead of yellow for warning signs; and red signs that convey an essential message of "go."

—Advance warning signs located at intersections, instead of upstream from the intersection.

—Signs that require the motorist to know the exact time of day to pursue a certain course of action, or require him to know if it is an "odd" or "even" day.

—Markings that end abruptly because one community marks center or edge lines and an adjoining one does not.

—Large intersections with only one inconspicuous traffic control signal; there should be at least two indications facing every approach.

—Pedestrian "walk" signals placed overhead or in some other place than directly opposite the pedestrian as he faces the street he wishes to cross.

—Stop signs and traffic signals used in tandem for the same direction of traffic, inviting rear-end collisions.

—Signs and control devices that confuse motorists because they are visible for more than one direction of traffic.

—Traffic signals that may have such easily misunderstood features as flashing green, the simultaneous display of yellow and red, and varied positions for the red, yellow and green indications (particularly hazardous for color-blind drivers).

—Lights in front of or surrounding signs so that they obscure them or create adverse nighttime glare.

—Signs that require unnecessary stops at railroad crossings and consequently breed disrespect among drivers that cross them frequently.

—Disparities in posting speed limits, locating speed limit signs in inconspicuous places, or failing to take into consideration the total road environment and traffic characteristics in fixing the actual limit.

WET WEATHER PERFORMANCE

The Subcommittee was disturbed to learn of the large number of highway crashes that take place on wet pavements —more than 3 million each year—including some 7,500 fatal and 250,000 injury-producing accidents.

To determine the nature of the wet weather skidding hazard in particular, the Subcommittee directed Associate Counsel John P. O'Hara to photograph some locations in the Washington, D.C., area and to show his films to the Subcommittee in public hearing. O'Hara earlier had taken a great deal of film showing the erratic and bewildered behavior of motorists when confronted by confusing signs.

The same technique of monitoring sections of Interstate highways in nearby Maryland provided some dramatic, even frightening, evidence of why motorists may, at the very least, "get the blues when it rains." O'Hara's camera systematically recorded skidding accidents as they actually happened. Films showed car after car "fish-tailing," spinning, bumping into guardrails, and even hurtling from the road. Some slid down a steep slope onto a busy highway below. One car turned upside down and O'Hara had to abandon his camera to extricate the driver.

The testimony demonstrated convincingly how wet weather trouble spots can be improved. When the curve filmed by O'Hara was banked properly and given a skid-resistant surface, at a total cost of $30,362, wet weather skidding accidents at the location dropped from an average of 18 a year to approximately one a year.

Confirmation that this experience was not unusual was provided by an official of the Federal Highway Administration, who declared that efforts to upgrade the frictional characteristics of pavements by surface overlays, grooving, and other means have produced reductions in wet weather accidents ranging from 50 to 100 per cent. Grooving alone reduced the annual total of wet weather accidents at seven California locations from 253 to 9, truly a spectacular safety achievement.

Many factors influence skidding and the ameliorative action that can be taken by state and local officials. One of the most common problems is poor surface drainage which results in water accumulating on the pavement. This has an adverse effect on friction between the tire and the pavement and the control of a vehicle becomes more difficult, particularly at higher speeds. The phenomenon of "hydroplaning" may occur, in which the vehicle tires actually ride up on a cushion of water. In such cases, steering or braking is almost impossible. Where adequate surface drainage cannot be provided through conventional techniques, pavement grooving or other corrective techniques should be employed.

STUDDED TIRES

Closely related to driving on wet pavements is the problem of driving on ice and snow. To provide better traction under these conditions, tire manufacturers in the early 1960's began marketing the so-called "studded tire," which has achieved considerable popularity in the intervening years, particularly in northern states.

The testimony about studded tires was, to say the least, ambivalent. There is no denying that studded tires serve the purpose of providing additional traction and stopping ability on certain glare ice conditions. But testimony by officials from Minnesota and New York showed driving on glare ice accounts for a maximum of five per cent, and perhaps nearer one or two per cent, of all driving, even in those northern states. In return for this benefit, a continuing price is being exacted, as summarized by Christian K. Preus, research coordinating engineer, Minnesota Department of Highways, in the following exchange with Chairman Wright:

> MR. PREUS. There is no question, no argument about the studded tires being beneficial on icy surfaces. We do not dispute that and do not disclaim it, but the benefits with respect to behavior of vehicles under other circumstances are very small. I am speaking now particularly of the winter period of time.
>
> We also have to take into consideration the effects of the pavement damage upon the year round travel and this is where we find that we get into some problem because of the damage to the pavement in the form of ruts, causing problems for the drivers.
>
> MR. WRIGHT. What kind of troubles?
>
> MR. PREUS. These ruts that are developing in the pavements may result in vehicle drivers becoming more erratic in their control of the vehicle.
>
> You have, in effect, almost a guided path, but this is not always good under these circumstances. The ruts which we are thus far measuring reached a maximum depth of about ⅖ of an inch [1 cm].
>
> Now, this is not enough that the average driver can observe it, but you can feel the effect of it as you drive along and it does provide a means of accumulation of water in these paths which, in turn, is objectionable in that it causes an excessive amount of splash. It may help hydroplaning under certain conditions and the vehicles tend to veer out of their normal channel in the lane, tend to crowd over toward the other lane in order to get off these rutted areas.
>
> The surface on these worn paths becomes quite rough, very often, with certain aggregates so that the people tend to try to avoid them. They move over and shift laterally in driving down the roadway.

Added to the question of safety is the very real consideration of additional maintenance costs being incurred in states where such tires are widely used.

George W. McAlpin, deputy chief engineer, research, New York Department of Transportation, estimated studs were wearing away $20 million worth of pave-

By no means can all highway injuries be blamed on poor road design. The fast driver causes much death and injury. This fact was well documented in late 1973 when because of the gasoline shortage the speed limit on all U.S. roads was reduced to 55 miles per hour. The effect: a dramatic decrease in highway deaths.

ment annually in New York state. Preus said unrestricted use of studded tires would cost Minnesota an estimated $55 million in added maintenance by 1980.

It is for this and other reasons that the Minnesota Legislature, acting upon a recommendation from the Minnesota Highway Department, in 1971 refused to extend the authority under which studded tires were permitted. The action had the effect of prohibiting the use of studded tires by Minnesota residents, under penalty of $300 fine, 90 days in jail, or both. Thus, the State of Minnesota resolved, at least to its own satisfaction, the issue of how studded tires fit into what sometimes appears to be a product- rather than a people-oriented world.

OPERATIONAL DEFICIENCIES

For hearing purposes an operational deficiency was considered to be a feature, or a combination of features, of street or highway design, or of traffic control measures, which causes undue delay, hazard or confusion.

"In this series of hearings we shall ask the critical question," Chairman Wright declared at the outset. "How well does the system serve the individual . . . the person caught up—wittingly or unwittingly—in the complex intermix of vehicles, roadways, signs and signals, noise and light, the down-to-earth world of traffic operations?"

Again, the testimony of witnesses dramatized an apparent overriding inability on the part of officials at all levels adequately to project themselves into the role of various types of highway users and to make the system compatible with their needs. Color slides illustrated specific deficiencies:

Complicated freeway signing in Dallas and Cincinnati . . . failure to provide continuity in signing around the Baltimore Beltway . . . an abrupt lane drop on a Louisville freeway . . . rural roads without center lines in Tate County, Mississippi . . . a mind-boggling array of signs to "guide" the motorist around Hartford, Conn. . . . an eye-catching billboard in Milwaukee that misdirects motorists seeking a major hotel . . . the problems facing the out-of-town visitor arriving at Boston's Logan Airport and driving his rented car "downtown" . . . indeed, even the definition of "downtown," which can be designated "city center," "civic center," "Capitol area," "business district," or in any number of ways.

A special in-depth look at Mansfield, Ohio, and the surrounding area painted the picture in tragic human terms:

A woman and her granddaughter killed at a railroad crossing located next to a road intersection, where the proximity of the two invited attention to one or the other but not to both.

A high school senior killed at another crossing that lacked adequate warning devices and pavement markings.

An 85-year-old man killed at an intersection where the sharpest kind of visual acuity would have been required to read a sign warning him that he was turning the wrong way onto a one-way road.

A woman killed at an intersection controlled by an illegal stoplight.

VALUE CONFLICTS

A broad range of environmental issues must be resolved in connection with highway construction and maintenance.

At the same time that highway safety advocates urge the removal of roadside trees to improve sight distances and to eliminate roadside hazards, environmentalists may advocate not only their retention, but the planting of additional trees as well.

Where traffic engineers may recognize the need for additional signs, or larger signs, to regulate and inform motorists, the quest for a more esthetically attractive environment causes some citizens to urge that signs be eliminated or reduced in size.

Some major design deficiencies can be overcome only by widening pavements, rebuilding intersections, and claiming more land for the highway right-of-way. In the minds of some this raises the specter of "paving over the countryside."

GETTING THE MESSAGE

The overriding message of the hearings is a distressing one to the members of the Subcommittee. We must conclude, with regret, that hundreds of thousands of Americans have died on and along the highways of the nation not because we have lacked the wisdom or the technology to save them, but because we have lacked the will to apply it.

A highway is more than a pavement. It is, at once, part of a local community and part of the national panorama. It is judged by various criteria and from different viewpoints. From the very beginning, it must serve all kinds of users, drawn from all walks of life, possessing the widest range of individual competence and skills.

A passive and stationary thoroughfare, it will pulsate with the people and goods of a society in motion. It must be designed and constructed to withstand the ice and snow of winter, the heat of summer, and the relentless wheels of commerce. It must be built in the right place, relating intelligently to land use and population patterns. It must create a reasonable feeling of confidence in those who venture onto its surface in the quest of safe and efficient passage to their various destinations.

But looked at in the context of the hearing, there is no way that it can fulfill its intended purpose of safe and efficient transportation unless it goes beyond its obvious characteristics to incorporate such features as:

—Appropriate traffic control devices that provide clear, understandable guidance and information.

—A roadside that is "forgiving" of the motorist when he errs, as inevitably he will.

—Configuration and operational aids that are realistic given the wide range of user capabilities.

When proper attention has been given to these, plus esthetic, social, and natural environmental factors, then and only then do you have a highway□

The Catalytic Converter

AMERICANS have a love–hate relationship with the automobile. Nearly every aspect of American life is organized around the automobile in one way or another. And yet many people think of the automobile as the greatest offender in the nation's air pollution problem.

It is certainly true that the internal combustion engine of the automobile has been the major producer of some atmospheric pollutants. In 1970, for example, it accounted for over two thirds of the nation's carbon monoxide pollution and, possibly, for half of the hydrocarbons in the air. Both carbon monoxide and hydrocarbons result from incomplete combustion of the fuel. Carbon monoxide is dangerous in dense traffic in enclosed spaces such as tunnels, when the gas cannot be dissipated quickly enough. The hydrocarbons are toxic as well, but the main objection to them is that they contribute to smog by combining with the nitrogen oxides also emitted by cars. One of these oxides, nitrogen dioxide, is itself a poison.

The U.S. National Academy of Sciences has stated that as many as 4,000 people die each year from auto pollution, and that damage to health and property runs between $2.5 billion and $10 billion each year. The U.S. Congress faced up to this growing health hazard in 1970, when it passed the Clean Air Act. The auto exhaust emission standards called for by this act have grown tougher from year to year.

To meet these standards, auto makers were forced to put control devices under the hoods of their cars. The added hardware made the engines more complex and harder to service and caused them to burn gasoline less efficiently. But even these steps were not enough to meet the emission control standards set for car models brought out in 1975. Something else was required: a controversial device called a catalytic converter.

WHAT A CATALYTIC CONVERTER DOES

Ever since it was first proposed in 1970 as a way to reduce auto exhaust emissions, the catalytic converter has been under attack by various groups. Manufacturers complained that the converter would not work well, and that it would cost too much even if it did. Oil men balked at the cost of producing the lead-free gaso-

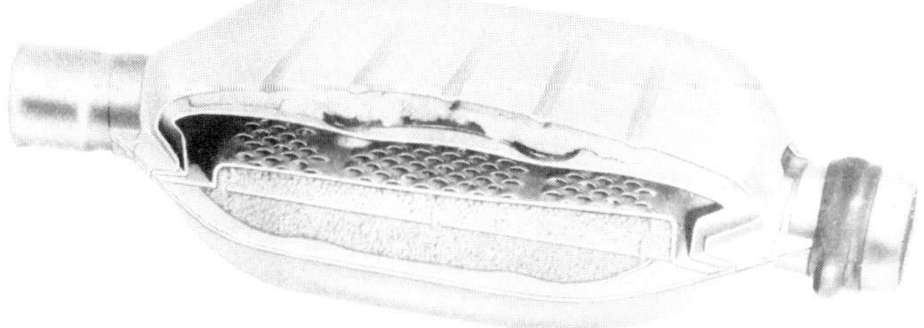

One common form of catalytic converter consists of a container filled with ceramic pellets coated with platinum and palladium. When exhaust gases move through the converter, toxic constituents are changed into harmless ones (detail below).

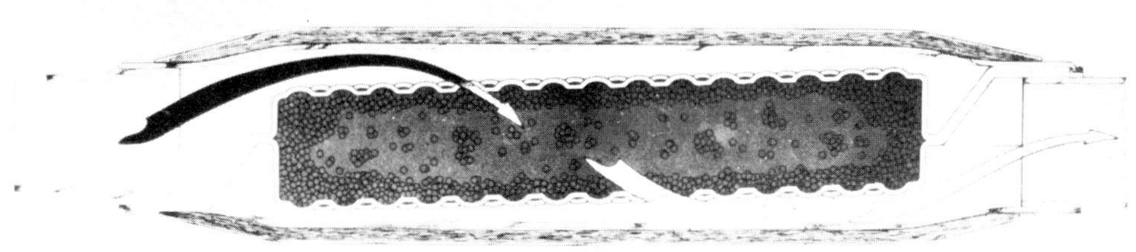

line that the converter would require. The U.S. Environmental Protection Agency (EPA) favored the device. But even among EPA scientists, there were some who suspected the converter—for reasons that will unfold below. Nevertheless, nearly 90 per cent of the 1975 models rolling off Detroit's assembly lines are now equipped with the device.

What is a catalytic converter, and what does it do? It is a mufflerlike device that is mounted under the body of a car, midway between the engine and the muffler. The converter's design is simple, even though the job it does is complex. It is nothing more than a stainless steel container that is filled with ceramic pellets or with a single, honeycomblike ceramic structure. In either case, the ceramic material is coated with a thin layer of platinum and palladium, two of the rarest and most expensive of metals.

As the exhaust gases flow through the converter on their way out of the tail pipe, the thin metal layer acts as a catalyst. It transforms the carbon monoxide and the hydrocarbons into harmless carbon dioxide and water vapor.

A catalytic converter adds about $110 to the price of a car. However, by switching to converters, auto companies were able to get rid of much of the hardware they had squeezed under the hood to meet earlier emission requirements. And thus far the converters have been doing their job well. They have cut back about 50 per cent on the carbon monoxide and unburned fuel spewing out of the tailpipes of 1974-model cars.

One surprising result of the switch to converters has been an improved efficiency in the burning of gasoline. This is a major benefit at a time of potential fuel shortages and rising fuel prices. Indeed, some cars are getting as much as 30 per cent more distance out of a given amount of gasoline. This is not a direct result of the converter. The converter does not improve engine performance in any way, but it does take care of the pollutants. Thus engineers can design engines for maximum efficiency without regard to emissions.

THE SULFURIC ACID THREAT

It is ironic, then, that the catalytic converter itself may be creating a new air pollution problem, even as it goes about cleaning up old ones. There is a great deal of controversy today over just how serious this new problem is.

The first warning came from the EPA. They found that the catalytic converter produces a fine mist of sulfuric acid when it is in use. All gasolines today contain some traces of sulfur. In automobiles not equipped with a converter, the sulfur leaves the car in a form that is not an immediate problem to the environment. But a car with a converter is another matter. The converter oxidizes about one half of the sulfur into a more troublesome form that combines with water vapor in the exhaust to form a sulfuric acid mist.

Just how serious a problem this new kind of pollution is, no one knows. The main concern of the EPA is that the poisonous sulfuric acid mist can build up to dangerous levels along heavily traveled highways. In early 1975 EPA scientists concluded that sulfuric acid mist "represented a very real health hazard that would come about over a period of time." Further studies of the rate of sulfuric acid emissions and the effects of this pollutant are underway. Some of them appear more favorable again to the converter.

If the EPA decides that new regulations are needed, this will create new problems. Auto makers would then say that the cheapest solution would be to remove the sulfur from the gasoline at the refinery, rather than trying to trap it as it leaves the catalytic converter. But gasoline refiners argue against this. They estimate that it would cost them about $3.7 billion extra to do so.

OTHER PROBLEMS, POSSIBLE SOLUTIONS

Even without this problem, the auto makers face other difficulties. Under the Clean Air Act they are obliged to reduce auto emissions—particularly nitrogen oxides—still further. The manufacturers have received a two-year extension on

The converter in place on car. Other emission control devices are also shown.

their deadline, but they say that this is still not long enough. They insist that they cannot meet the 1977 and 1978 standards without giving up the gains made in efficiency of performance. For example, they maintain that the price of a new car will climb by $260 and fuel economy will drop 12 to 15 per cent, if 1977 standards are enforced. President Ford has proposed to Congress that it delay the imposition of these standards for yet another three years. In return, the auto industry would promise a 40 per cent improvement in fuel economy by the time the three years were up.

The issues continue to be argued. Whatever the outcome, it is not likely to mean the end of the catalytic converter—at least not right away. The auto industry and its suppliers have invested too much money in the device, and in developing the mines needed to ensure a steady supply of platinum and palladium.

It is true, however, that auto makers are searching for other solutions to the emission problem. For example, to improve the converter itself, they are looking for catalysts other than the two precious metals now being used. Other catalysts could permit the return to standard, leaded gasoline. And some auto makers are moving in bolder directions. For example, Honda Motor Company has developed a "stratified charge" engine that produces an exhaust so clean that no catalytic converter is needed. Honda's engine uses a new kind of cylinder head and carburetor system. It has passed the EPA emission standards and is now being sold commercially in Honda vehicles. Another step is being taken by Chrysler Corporation. It has begun production on a computer-monitored engine that Chrysler officials claim does away with the need for a converter. But other companies appear not to be ready to move this rapidly into the production of new kinds of systems for monitoring their car engines.

At any rate, it takes several years to convert completely from one production design to another. Whether we like it or not, the catalytic converter will most probably be with us for a while□

SELECTED READINGS

"All About the New Catalytic Converters." *Changing Times*, October 1974.

"Catalytic Converters in the '75 Cars—Do We Really Need Them?" by J. P. Norbye and J. Dunne. *Popular Science*, October 1974.

Economics and Public Policy: The Automobile Pollution Case by Donald N. Dewees. MIT Press 1974.

index

a

b

d

e

f

g

h

i

j

k

l

m

n

o

p

q

r

s

t

u

v

z

ACKNOWLEDGMENTS

The following articles were reprinted with the kind permission of the publications and organizations indicated:

NEW JOVIAN VISTAS, Page 6: © 1974 by Astro-Media Corp. Reprinted from *Astronomy* magazine.

THE LOST PLANET, Page 15: © 1974 by Astro-Media Corp. Reprinted from *Astronomy* magazine.

TITAN, Page 12: Reprinted with permission from *Natural History* magazine, April 1974. © The American Museum of Natural History, 1974.

BEHAVIOR MODIFICATION, Page 30: Reprinted with permission from *The National Observer,* © Dow Jones and Company, Inc., 1974.

SHOPLIFTING, Page 43: Reprinted with permission from Menninger *Perspective,* Fall 1974.

GARDENS UNDER GLASS, Page 60: © 1975 by the National Wildlife Federation. Reprinted from the December–January 1975 issue of *National Wildlife* magazine.

WHALES, Page 72: Courtesy of *Oceans,* a publication of the Oceanic Society. Published originally as "What is Leviathan's Future?" May–June 1974 *Oceans.*

A NEW FORM OF MATHEMATICS, Page 92: © 1975 by The New York Times Company. Reprinted by permission.

THE COMPUTER RIP-OFF, Page 95: Reprinted from the July 1974 issue of *Fortune* magazine by special permission. © 1974, Time Inc.

THE BAND-AID PRINCIPLE, Page 105: From *3.1416 and All That,* © 1969 by Philip J. Davis and William G. Chinn. Reprinted by permission of Simon and Schuster.

THE REPORTER'S NEW TOOL: THE COMPUTER, Page 110: © 1975 by The New York Times Company. Reprinted by permission.

PROJECT GATE, Page 117: Adapted with permission from NCAR press release. Permission from National Center for Atmospheric Research, Boulder, Colorado.

INSTANT ISLANDS, Page 119: Reprinted with permission from *Sea Frontiers,* © 1974 by the International Oceanographic Foundation, Rickenbacker Causeway, Virginia Key, Miami, Florida 33149.

MINING THE SEAS, Page 125: Reprinted by permission from *GEOS* magazine, Summer 1974 issue, published by the Department of Energy, Mines, and Resources, Ottawa, Ontario, Canada.

THE EVER-CHANGING SEA LEVEL, Page 132: Reprinted by permission from *Sea Frontiers,* © 1974 by the International Oceanographic Foundation, Rickenbacker Causeway, Virginia Key, Miami, Florida 33149.

WINDOW ON EARTH'S CORE, Page 140: © 1974 by Saturday Review/World, Inc. First appeared in *Saturday Review/World,* Nov. 30, 1974. Used by permission.

ACID RAIN, Page 146: Reprinted from February 1974 issue of *Technology Review.* © 1974 by the Alumni Association of the Massachusetts Institute of Technology.

HURRICANES, Page 150: Reprinted by permission from *Sea Frontiers,* © 1974 by the International Oceanographic Foundation, Rickenbacker Causeway, Virginia Key, Miami, Florida 33149. (Original title: "Planet's Powerhouse.")

SOLAR HEATING, Page 158: Condensed from November/December 1974 issue of *Architecture Plus.* © 1974 by Informat Publishing Corporation.

OFFSHORE OIL, Page 166: Reprinted with permission of *The Wall Street Journal.* © 1974, Dow Jones and Company, Inc. All rights reserved.

PEAT—THE FORGOTTEN FUEL, Page 171: Adapted and reprinted by permission from *Science World.* © 1974 by Scholastic Magazines, Inc.

OIL AND GAS: HOW MUCH IS THERE? Page 175: An adaptation of two articles from *Science,* Vol. 187, pp. 723 and 725–727, Feb. 28, 1975; and Vol. 185, pp. 127–130, July 12, 1974. © 1975 and 1974 by the American Association for the Advancement of Science.

ATHABASCA TAR SANDS, Page 185: Reprinted by permission from *GEOS* magazine, Summer 1974 issue, published by the Department of Energy, Mines, and Resources, Ottawa, Ontario, Canada.

CUTTING YOUR HOME ENERGY BUDGET, Page 190: © Smithsonian Institution 1974, from *Smithsonian* magazine, March 1974.

ALTERNATIVE AUTOMOTIVE FUELS, Page 198: adapted from article "Some Fuel for Thought" by Jerry E. Berger, in Winter 1974 issue of *Ecolibrium,* a publication of Shell Oil Company.

THE RACE IS ON FOR ANTARCTICA, Page 204: © 1974 by the National Wildlife Federation. Reprinted from the November–December 1974 issue of *International Wildlife* magazine.

EUROPE'S CESSPOOL, Page 212: © 1974 by the National Wildlife Federation. Reprinted from the March–April 1974 issue of *International Wildlife.*

HERE COMES THE TRANSAFRICAN HIGHWAY, Page 218: © 1974 by the National Wildlife Federation. Reprinted from the May–June issue of *International Wildlife.*

AEROSOLS AND THE OZONE LAYER, Page 223: Reprinted by permission from *The Sciences,* vol. 14, No. 10, December 1974. © 1974 The New York Academy of Sciences.

HOW SAFE IS OUR DRINKING WATER? Page 227: Reprinted from *Chemistry* with permission. © 1975 by the American Chemical Society.

HERPES VD, Page 236: Reprinted with permission of *The Wall Street Journal.* © 1974, Dow Jones and Company, Inc. All rights reserved.

A PRIMER ON VITAMINS, Page 241: Reprinted from the May 1974 issue of *FDA Consumer,* the official magazine of the U.S. Food and Drug Administration.

INSOMNIA, Page 246: Reprinted with permission from *The National Observer,* © Dow Jones and Company, Inc. 1974.

VEGETARIANISM, Page 251: Reprinted from the October issue of *Today's Health,* published by the American Medical Association. © 1974 by AMA.

FALSE TEETH, Page 257: Reprinted from the August issue of *Today's Health,* published by the

American Medical Association. © 1974 by AMA.

VINYL CHLORIDE, Page 264: Reprinted with permission of *The Wall Street Journal.* © 1974, Dow Jones and Company, Inc. All rights reserved.

CONTEMPLATE THE NAVEL OF THE WORLD, Page 285: Reprinted from *Américas,* monthly magazine published by the General Secretariat of the Organization of American States.

FINDING THE IRONCLAD MONITOR, Page 295: Taken from the December 1974 issue of Marine Technology Society *Journal,* Vol. 8, No. 10.

FAMINE, Page 300: Condensed, with permission, from "Coping With Famine," *Foreign Affairs,* October 1974 by the Council on Foreign Relations.

THE NEW ALCHEMY INSTITUTE, Page 306: Reprinted with permission from *Science,* Vol. 187, pp. 727–729, Feb. 28, 1975. © 1975 by the American Association for the Advancement of Science.

LEONARDO DA VINCI, Page 315: From *Six Wings: Men of Science in the Renaissance* by George Sarton. © 1957 by Indiana University Press, Bloomington, Indiana. Reprinted by permission of the publisher.

DISCOVERY OF TWO NEW PARTICLES, Page 326: Reprinted with permission from *Science,* Vol. 186, pp. 909–911, Dec. 6, 1974. © 1974 by the American Association for the Advancement of Science.

BENJAMIN FRANKLIN: SCIENTIST, Page 330: Adapted by permission of William Morrow & Co., Inc., from *The Man Who Dared the Lightning* by Thomas Fleming. © 1970, 1971 by Thomas Fleming.

LASER FUSION: TOMORROW'S ENERGY? Page 336: Reprinted from the May 1974 issue of *Fortune* magazine by special permission. © 1974, Time Inc. (Original title: "Lasers Blast a Shortcut to the Ultimate Energy Solution.")

IS GRAVITY GETTING WEAKER? Page 347: Adapted and reprinted by permission from *Science World,* © 1974 by Scholastic Magazines, Inc.

THE PROTON SCANNING MICROSCOPE, Page 351: Adapted with permission from the *University of Chicago Magazine,* Autumn 1974. © 1974, the University of Chicago.

"HANGING IN" AT L-5, Page 360: Adapted and reprinted by permission from *Science World.* © 1974 by Scholastic Magazines, Inc.

APOLLO-SOYUZ TEST PROJECT, Page 356: Reprinted with permission from *Sky and Telescope,* October 1974. © 1974 Sky Publishing Corporation.

A LOOK AT MERCURY, Page 363: Reprinted with permission from *Sky and Telescope,* November 1974, © 1974 Sky Publishing Corporation. (Original title: "Mariner 10 Looks at Mercury.")

BICYCLES: CARE AND MAINTENANCE, Page 390: Adapted from *Bicycle Repair* by Irene Cumming Kleeberg. © 1973 by Irene Cumming Kleeberg. Adapted by permission of Franklin Watts, Inc.

HOW TO READ A CAN, Page 396: © 1974, *The American Legion Magazine.* Used by permission.

THE HELIUM HORSE, Page 399: Reprinted from the October 1973 issue of *NOAA,* published by the National Oceanic and Atmospheric Administration.

ROADS THAT KILL, Page 409: Condensed from "Highway Safety, Design, and Operations," Report of the Subcommittee on Investigations and Review, to the Committee on Public Works, U.S. House of Representatives, July 1973.

ILLUSTRATION CREDITS

Sources for the illustrations appear below. If more than one illustration appears on a page, the credits are separated by semicolons. Illustrations are credited as they appear on a page, left to right, top to bottom.

COVER: Merck & Co., Inc.

ASTRONOMY: 3 U.S. Forest Service. Photograph by Roger M. Williams. 4 top—NASA; bot—Cerro-Tololo Inter-American Observatory. 5 top—Hale Observatories; bot—Westerbork Observatory, the Netherlands. 7 NASA. 8 *Astronomy,* November, 1974. 9 NASA. 10 NASA. 11 NASA diagram. 12 NASA. 13 *Astronomy,* November, 1974. 14 NASA. 15 Harvard College Observatory. 16 New York Public Library Picture Collection. 19 Paul Roques, Griffith Observatory. 20 Griffith Observatory. Photo by James E. Klein. 21 From the collection of Ronald A. Oriti, Griffith Observatory. Photo by James E. Klein. 22 Painting by Chesley Bonestell, Griffith Observatory. 23 Lowell Observatory. 24 Lowell Observatory. 25 NASA.

BEHAVIORAL SCIENCES: 27 Wide World. 28 Wide World. 29 top—Courtesy of Dr. Robert Buckhout, Brooklyn College. 30 The New York *Times*/Don Hogan Charles. 31 Robert W. Kelley—*Time* Magazine, © Time Incorporated. 33 all—Achievement Place Research Project, Lawrence, Kansas. Photos by Rob Lubert. 35 both—Smokenders, Inc. 36 Pictorial Parade. 37 Stanford Research Institute. 38 Stanford Research Institute. 39 Thelma Moss/UCLA Neuropsychiatric Institute. 41 Institute for Parapsychology, Durham, North Carolina. 42 Institute for Parapsychology, Durham, North Carolina. 43-45 all—John Dunigan. 47 both—George Holton/Photo Researchers. 48 Russ Kinne/Photo Researchers. 49 James H. Charmichael/Photo Researchers. 50 Photo Researchers. 51 left—Russ Kinne/Photo Researchers; top right—Tom McHugh/Photo Researchers; bot. right—Twomey/Photo Researchers. 52 Karl H. Maslowski/Photo Researchers. 53 Harry F. Harlow, University of Wisconsin Primate Laboratory. 54 Tom McHugh/Photo Researchers.

BIOLOGY: 55 New York Zoological Society. 56 all—Courtesy, Dr. J. W. Shay, University of Colorado. 57 top—Public Broadcasting System; bot—USDA. 58 Université Catholique de Louvain. 59 left—Yale University; right—Rockefeller University. 61-63 all—George A. Elbert. 64 New York Horticultural Society. 65 left—New York Horticultural Society; top right—Burpee Seed Co.; bot. right—Derek Fell. 66 left—New York Horticultural Society (NYHS); top center—NYHS; bot. center—Derek Fell; right—Derek Fell. 67 top left—Derek Fell; top right—NYHS; bot. left—NYHS; bot. center—NYHS; Derek Fell. 68 Derek Fell. 69 top left—NYHS; top right—NYHS; bot. left—NYHS; bot. right—Jenny Tesar. 70 all—NYHS. 71 all—Derek Fell. 72-73 Kendall Whaling Museum, Sharon, Mass. 75 Eastman Kodak Co., photo by J. Douglas Heyland, Quebec Wildlife Service. 76 Gianni Tortoli/Photo Researchers. 77 all—Thomas D. W. Friedman/Photo Researchers. 78 top—Dan Guravich/Photo Researchers; bot—Thomas D. W. Friedman/Photo Researchers. 81 New York Public Library. 83 USDA-Soil Conservation Service. 85 USDA. 86 General Mills. 87 USDA. 88 General Mills.

COMPUTERS AND MATH: 89 Intel Corp. 90 IBM. 91 top—IBM; bot—Stanford Research Institute, Menlo Park, Calif. 93 © 1975 by The New York Times Company. Reprinted by permission. 95 Stanford Research Institute, Menlo Park, Calif. 96-97 reprinted with permission from *Fortune* Magazine. 99 IBM. 100 IBM. 101 IBM. 102 Lawrence Livermore Laboratory. 103 Wide World Photos. 105 Universitaetsbibliothek, Basel, Switzerland. 105-109 from *3.1416 and All That,* © 1969 by Philip J. Davis and William G. Chinn. Reprinted by permission of Simon and Schuster. 110 both—The Detroit *News*. 111 Wide World Photos.

EARTH SCIENCES: 113 © by The New York Times Company. Reprinted by permission. 115 top—Woods Hole Oceanographic Institution; bot—Jet Propulsion Laboratory. 116 top—Cornell University. 117 GATE photo. 119-122 © Solarfilma, Iceland. 123 S. Thorarinsson. 124 © Solarfilma, Iceland. 125 The International Nickel Co., Inc. 126-130 Courtesy of Deepsea Ventures, Inc., a subsidiary of Tenneco Inc. Photos by B. J. Nixon. 131 The International Nickel Co., Inc. 132 French Government Tourist Office. 133 top—C. Swithinbank; bot—A. Carr. 134 top—Varig Brazilian Airlines; bot—A. Carr. 135 both—U.S. Coast Guard. 136 Spence Air Photo Collection, Geography Dept., UCLA. 139 NOAA. 140 Woods Hole Oceanographic Institution. 141 U.S. Naval Research Laboratory. 142 top—Woods Hole Oceanographic Institution; bot—U.S. Naval Research Laboratory. 143 NOAA. 144 CNEXO photo. 146 EPA-DOCUMERICA-Marc St. Gil. 147 U.S. Forest Service. 148 UPI. 149 Special permission granted by *Current Science,* published by Xerox Education Publications, © Xerox Corp. 1974. 150 U.S. Navy. 151 Courtesy of *Sea Frontiers*. 152 top—U.S. Air Force; bot—NOAA. 153 Australian Information Service. 154 both—Australian Information Service.

ENERGY: 155 Wheelabrator-Frye Inc., Energy Systems Division. 156 top—EXXON; bot—Bell Laboratories. 157 both—General Electric. 159 EPA-DOCUMERICA-Charles O'Rear. 160-163 Chart adapted with permission from *Horizon* Magazine (vol. 10, no. 1, 1974), Grumman Aerospace Corporation. 164 Grumman Aerospace Corp. 165 New York Botanical Garden, photo by Bill Swan. 166 EXXON. 168 American Petroleum Institute. 169 both—EXXON. 170 EXXON. 171-172 all—Irish Tourist Board. 173 Battelle Memorial Institute, Columbus Laboratories, Ohio. 174 Novosti from Sovfoto. 175 American Gas Association. 176 Eric Poggenpohl. 177 Alyeska Pipeline Co. 178 Alyeska Pipeline Co. 179 Alyeska Pipeline Co. 180 EPA-DOCUMERICA. 181-182 El Paso Natural Gas Company. 183 Tass from Sovfoto. 185 EXXON. 186 Sun Oil Company. 187 EXXON. 188 both—Sun Oil Company. 189 Sun Oil Company. 190 National Bureau of Standards. 191 UPI. 193 Grant Heilman. 195 both—National Bureau of Standards. 197 Grant Heilman. 198 UPI.

ENVIRONMENTAL SCIENCES: 201 Fritz Goro. 202 UPI. 203 top—French Embassy; bot—Union Electric Co. 204-208 all—U.S. Navy. 209-211 all—U.S. Forest Service. 212 United Nations. 213 United Nations. 214 top—EPA-DOCUMERICA-Yoichi Okamoto; bot—United Nations/Tsagris. 215 UNESCO/Dominique Roger. 216 top—FAO photo/F. Botts; bot—United Nations. 217 UNESCO/Dominique Roger. 218-222 Clement Merowit/ Friends of Africa. 223 *The National Observer,* photo by Edward Earnshaw. 227 American Water Works Association. 228 Perkin-Elmer Corp., Norwalk, Conn. 229 Wide World Photos.

HEALTH AND DISEASE: 231 Wide World. 232 Lee Lockwood/Black Star. 233 bot—*Medical World News*. 234 Bell Laboratories. 235 top—March of Dimes; bot—Grumman Corp. 237 both—Photos courtesy of Dr. John M. Knox. Joe Baker, photographer. 238-240 Merck Sharp & Dohme. 241-245 all—FDA. 247 Collection, The Museum of Modern Art, New York. Gift of Mrs. Simon Guggenheim. 248-249 all—*Hospital Practice* Magazine. Photos by Dennis Galloway. 251 Grant Heilman. 253 both—Culver Pictures. 255 Schocken Books, photo by Richard Garrett. 256 both—Grant Heilman. 257 Universal/Lactona, a division of Warner-Lambert Company. 258 New York Historical Society. 259-261 all—Universal/Lactona, a division of Warner-Lambert Company. 263 The New York *Times*/William Sauro. 264 both—EPA-DOCUMERICA. 265 UPI. 266 National Cancer Institute. 267 all—Courtesy of Dr. Irving J. Selikoff/Environmental Medicine, Mount Sinai School of Medicine, New York. 268 American Cancer Society. 269-271 The Arthritis Foundation.

MAN AND HIS WORLD: 273 From the book Ugaritica, Vol. V (equals *Mission de Ras Shamra,* Tome XVI), edited by C. F. A. Schaeffer. 274 United Nations/T. Chen. 275 top—The Cleveland Museum of Natural History; bot—The New York *Times*/John Veltri. 276 From the *Madrid Codices* © 1974 by McGraw-Hill Book Company (UK) Ltd. 277 Doubleday & Co. 278 top—Charles Scribner's Sons; center—Alfred A. Knopf; bot—Coward, McCann & Geoghegan. 283 Dr. William Mulloy. 285 Dr. William Mulloy. 287 top—George Holton/Photo Researchers; bot—Bjorn Bolstad/Photo Researchers. 288 Jim Woodman. 289 George Holton/Photo Researchers. 290 George Holton/Photo Researchers. 291 George Holton/Photo Researchers. 292 both—Jim Woodman. 293 left—Jim Woodman; right—George Dineen/Photo Researchers. 294 Jim Woodman. 295-299 all—Duke University Marine Laboratory. 300 WFP/FAO photo by T. Page. 301 United Nations 303 United Nations/AID. 305 WFP/FAO photo by Peyton Johnson. 306-311 all—The New Alchemy Institute. 313 top left—The Royal Society, London; top right—Wide World; bot. left—Vanderbilt University; bot. center—M.I.T. Historical Collections; bot. right—University of Colorado. 315 Alinari-Scala. 316 Alinari-Scala. 317 left—Alinari-Scala; right—Royal Windsor Library. "Reproduced by Gracious Permission of Her Majesty the Queen." 318 top—Scala New York/ Florence; bot—Royal Windsor Library. 319 both—Scala New York/Florence. 320 Alinari-Scala. 321 top—Alinari-Scala; bot—From the *Madrid Codices* © 1974 by McGraw-Hill Book Co. (UK) Ltd.

PHYSICAL SCIENCES: 323 *Physical Review Letters*. 324 University of California, Berkeley. 325 top—University of California, Berkeley; bot—Tyco Laboratories, Waltham, Mass. 326 Brookhaven National Laboratory. 327 Stanford Linear Accelerator Center/Stanford University. 331 both—New York Public Library. 332 New York Public Library. 333 Culver Pictures. 335 Smithsonian Institution, Washington, D.C. 336 Lawrence Livermore Laboratory. 337 Sovfoto. 339 both—University of Rochester Laboratory for Laser Energetics. 340 Lawrence Livermore Laboratory. 343 Avco Everett Research Laboratory. 344 The Nobel Foundation. 345 John T. Scott, *Physics Today*. 347 NASA. 348-350 all—*Science World* graphics. 351 University of Chicago.

SPACE EXPLORATION: 353-355 NASA. 357 Reprinted by Permission of *Popular Mechanics* © 1975 by The Hearst Corporation. 358 *Science World* graphics. 359-362 NASA. 363 Jet Propulsion Laboratory. 364 Jet Propulsion Laboratory (JPL). 365-367 JPL. 368 "From the MGM release '2001: A Space Odyssey,' " © 1968 Metro-Goldwyn-Mayer Inc. 369 Rockwell International. 370 Rockwell International. 371 Rockwell International. 372 ESRO (European Space Research Organization). 373: ESRO. 374 Goddard Space Flight Center. 377-386 The National Association of Rocketry.

TECHNOLOGY: 387 Drawing by Richter, © 1975 *The New Yorker* Magazine. 388 Chrysler Corp. 389 top—Seiko Time Corp.; bot—Japanese Consulate. 390 Schwinn Bicycle Co. 391 Raleigh Industries of America, Inc. 393 Raleigh Industries of America, Inc. 394-395 The *Christian Science Monitor*. 397 E. A. Egret photo. 399 Goodyear Aircraft. 400 top—U.S. Air Force; bot—U.S. Navy. 401 Goodyear Aircraft. 403 Raven Industries, Inc. 404 Raven Industries. 405 All American Engineering Co. 407 both—J. Gorden Vaeth/ NOAA. 408 Raven Industries, Inc. 409 EPA-DOCUMERICA. 410 Highway Users Federation. 411 top—Aluminum Company of America (Alcoa); bot—Federal Highway Administration. 412 both—Federal Highway Administration. 413 top—Highway Users Federation; bot—Federal Highway Administration. 414 Highway Users Federation. 417 Wide World Photos. 419 both—General Motors. 421 General Motors.